The AGE of PILGRIMAGE

THE MEDIEVAL JOURNEY
TO GOD

Jonathan Sumption

HiddenSpring

Cover image by Charlie Waite / Getty Images
Cover design by John Gall
Text design by Jennifer Daddio

First published as *Pilgrimage* in 1975 by Faber and Faber.

Library of Congress Cataloging-in-Publication Data

Sumption, Jonathan.
[Pilgrimage]
The age of pilgrimage : the medieval journey to God / Jonathan Sumption.
p. cm.
Originally published: Pilgrimage. London : Faber & Faber, 1975.
Includes bibliographical references and index.
ISBN 1-58768-025-4 (alk. paper)
1. Church history—Middle Ages, 600–1500. 2. Christian pilgrims and pilgrimages—History—To 1500. 3. Travel, Medieval. I. Title.
BR252 .S9 2003
263.041′09′02—dc21

2003001682

Published by
HiddenSpring
an imprint of Paulist Press
997 Macarthur Boulevard
Mahwah, New Jersey 07430

www.paulistpress.com

Printed and bound in the United States of America

Contents

To My Friends

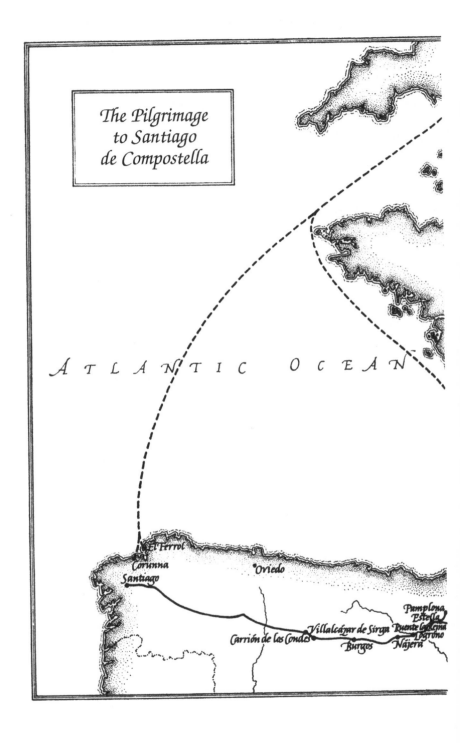

The Pilgrimage
to Santiago
de Compostella

ATLANTIC OCEAN

El Ferrol
Corunna
Santiago
°Oviedo
Pamplona
Estella
Villalcázar de Sirga   Puente la Reina
Logroño
Carrión de los Condes
Burgos   Nájera

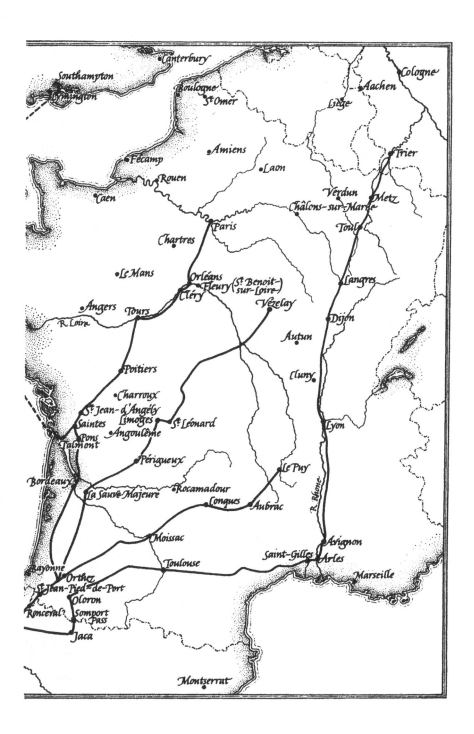

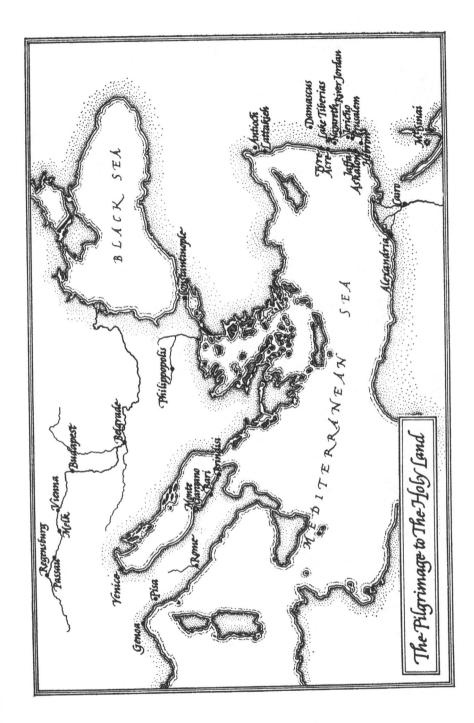

The Pilgrimage to The Holy Land

Preface

I began by imagining (perhaps all historians do) that the subject of this book could be neatly confined between two convenient dates, like a row of disintegrating French paperbacks between two bookends. 1050 to 1250 was the period I had in mind. In fact, religious history cannot be divided into digestible slabs in this convenient fashion. Mediaeval Christianity inherited certain ideas from the classical past and bequeathed others to the modern world. The spiritual ideals of St. Bernard's day are incomprehensible when divorced from their origins, and misleading without some account of the process of distortion and decay which ultimately overcame them. Even the Reformation is not as decisive a break as one would suppose.

So, as it stands, the book is an attempt to draw a thin line through a very long period of history. In an age of academic specialization this approach has advantages and disadvantages. It does make it possible to present a reasonably coherent picture of mediaeval spiritual life as a whole, through the medium of an important and, I believe, representative part of it. So much for the advantages; now the disadvantages, of which the chief is that I may often have indulged in broad generalizations which lack of space has prevented me from justifying at length. I wish it were possible to write about the Middle Ages as Keith Thomas has done about the sixteenth and seventeenth centuries. But the evidence does not exist. The search for origins and consequences in mediaeval history is bound to be fruitless. Finality is an illusion. The conclusions drawn here must be regarded as my own impressions buttressed by examples which I consider representative. For every example, a counter-example could easily be cited. I have tried to avoid a tone of bold confidence, but there are no doubt places where the reader should insert a mental 'probably' at the beginning of a sentence.

One major omission should be mentioned. I have concentrated heavily on France and on the cultural world of which France was the centre—England, northern Spain, central and southern Italy. Germany has not been entirely ignored, but major sanctuaries like Cologne and Aachen have not received the attention they deserve. There are a number of reasons for this, amongst them the extreme sparseness of the evidence before the fifteenth century. There is a homogeneity about the French cultural world which makes it possible to speak of it as a whole. Germany and central Europe are in some respects exceptional and ought to be considered separately. This is already a long book. I had no desire to make it longer.

I owe a very considerable debt to the President and fellows of Magdalen College, Oxford, for the leisure and agreeable surroundings which I have enjoyed there both as an undergraduate and as a fellow. I have benefited enormously from conversations with my old tutor, Karl Leyser, more, perhaps, than he realizes. Dr. Hugh Sinclair and Dr. David Robson have helped me out with some medical matters in chapter five. The staff of at least a dozen libraries in this country and in France and Italy have been unfailingly helpful, none more so than the staff of the Bodleian Library, who staggered daily to seat U.219 bowed down beneath the weight of ancient folios. My greatest debt is to my wife, and the fact that this is a common experience among authors will not prevent me from saying so.

Jonathan Sumption

1

Introduction

The world which the mediaeval pilgrim left behind was a small and exclusive community. The geographic and social facts of life made it oppressive and isolated and, except in the vicinity of major towns and main roads, the chief qualities of human life were its monotonous regularity and the rule of overpowering conventions. Existence, for the great majority, meant rural existence. Towns were few and small, and separated themselves from the country by moats of legal privilege. Villages asserted their independence and marked out their territory with rows of stakes and crosses. Even where migration occurred, it was not allowed to disturb the placid conventions of rural life. English villages of the thirteenth century were forbidden to receive strangers, and were held collectively responsible for crimes committed in their midst. Townsmen were enjoined to watch for strangers and lock their gates at sunset.

Nowhere was the closeness of these communities more apparent than in their religious life. 'What is a parish?', asked the thirteenth-century canonist Henry of Susa; 'it is a place with well-defined frontiers whose inhabitants belong to a single church.' The parishioner 'belonged' in a very real sense to his church, and lived his whole life under its shadow. There, and there alone, he was baptized and married, attended Sunday

Mass, paid his tithe and offerings, and there he was buried when he died. The statutes of the church constantly reminded him of the fact. No one may receive the sacraments in any church but his own. 'On no account admit to confession any person from another parish.' 'No stranger is to be allowed burial or marriage in the parish church.' A thirteenth-century archbishop of Bordeaux excommunicated 'all strangers who have abandoned their own parish churches which they ought to be attending,...for the parish priest should be able to see the face of every member of his flock.' Pierre de Collemieu, archbishop of Rouen, required parish priests to keep a list of their parishioners, and to eject any strangers whom they found in their churches on Sundays except for noblemen and beggars. It was not unknown for those who died outside their own parishes to be exhumed and brought back to their own churchyards.

The Lateran council of 1215 reinforced this dependence on the parish by making every layman confess his sins at least once a year to his parish priest, and to no one else. Only bona fide travellers and those in danger of death were permitted to confess to a strange priest, while those clergy who had no parishes were forbidden to hear confessions at all. The right of the mendicant orders to hear them was hotly resisted by the secular clergy as an intrusion upon their prerogatives, and was only tardily recognized by the papacy. Confession, the most personal act of piety which the ordinary man performed, was far from being the anonymous ceremony found in the modern Roman Catholic Church. It is true that the actual words spoken were inaudible, but the sacrament itself was held in public, 'openly, and not in some private place, especially in the case of women', as the synod of Nîmes ordained in 1284. Moreover the parish priest was expected to probe for further, undeclared sins, and to inflict a lengthy cross-examination on the penitent. Several handbooks for priests were available in which useful and pertinent questions were set out for this purpose.

Dignity and privacy were not concepts dear to the hearts of mediaeval men and women, who conducted their communal lives on the unspoken assumption that the sins of one were the business of all. This was particularly true of breaches of sexual morality. In a small village near Bonneval in the Loire valley, the repentance of a prostitute at the end of the twelfth century was an event of public importance. Most of the inhabitants gathered in the street to debate whether she should go immediately to the nearest priest in Bonneval, or await his arrival for Mass on the following day. They decided to wait. In the morning they accompanied the sinner in a body to the church and, all speaking at once, recited her history to the priest. After a short homily, the priest confessed her in the presence of the villagers and sentenced her to an annual pilgrimage to Chartres. Then he absolved her amid scenes of emotion and jubilation. In the records of episcopal visitations it is clear that the majority of witnesses regarded eavesdropping and peeping through windows as a duty. When bishop Trefnant of Hereford visited his diocese in 1397, most of the laymen who appeared before him were accused by their neighbours of adultery, bigamy, quarrelling with their wives, denying conjugal rights to their husbands, and other matters which would now be regarded as private. A similar picture emerges from the records of a provincial society in France. When a Poitevin peasant-woman, Clémente Gaboreau, failed to appear in church one Sunday in 1387, her fellow parishioners recalled that she had often been seen entering and leaving the house of one Guillaume Achale and immediately suspected the worst. It was common knowledge in the village of Asnois

(Poitou) that the wife of Pierre Vigoureux was the mistress of the parish priest. Jean Bourdeau, carpenter of Courlay (Poitou), was completely unaware that his wife was unfaithful to him, until several peeping-Toms told him so, whereupon he killed her with a sickle. The fifteenth-century author of a manual for parish priests no doubt had such incidents in mind when he warned his readers against 'all that standeth or hearkeneth by nights under walls, doors, or windows, for to spy touching evil.'

The popularity of the mendicant friars and of local holy hermits was undoubtedly due in part to the fact that they offered an escape from the stifling framework of parish life. Pilgrimage offered another escape. A surprisingly large number of pilgrims seem to have left their homes solely in order to deny their parish priest his monopoly over their spiritual welfare. Contemporary churchmen frequently accused them of seeking to confess to a strange priest or to avoid the moral censure which they deserved. In one extreme case a lady of London, on learning that she was dying, had herself carried in a litter to Canterbury in order to avoid the payment of a five shilling burial fee to her parish priest. At the end of the fifteenth century a writer castigating the excessive devotion of the populace to pilgrimages reflected that their principal motives were 'curiosity to see new places and experience new things, impatience of the servant with his master, of children with their parents, or wives with their husbands.'

The twelfth-century chronicler Orderic Vitalis describes the dreadful fate of a priest who went with his mistress on a pilgrimage to St.-Gilles, in order to avoid the opprobrium of his family and friends. But many of the penitential pilgrims who filled the great shrines no doubt honestly felt that they would never live down their obsessions of guilt so long as they remained at home. St. Hugh of Lincoln once met a man in Rochester who admitted that he had led an evil life in his youth, 'until, unable to endure my shame and hating the scene of my destruction, I secretly left my mother's house and the city where I had been born,…and wandered I knew not whither.' Paul Walther, a German Franciscan who visited the Holy Land in 1481, confessed before his departure that he had not lived up to the requirements of the Franciscan rule 'and therefore I have resolved to go away to a place where the German language is unknown, and there I shall exorcize my sins from my wretched body.'

The Reality of Evil

The peculiar intensity of mediaeval piety had as many causes as it had symptoms. But pre-eminent among them was a view of the natural world as a chaos in which the perpetual intervention of God was the only guiding law. God appeared to control the entire natural world from moment to moment. He was the direct and immediate cause of everything that happened, from the most trivial to the most vital incidents of human life. Indeed it was not until the eighteenth century that people were prepared to concede to nature any power of her own, or to attribute the workings of the natural world to anything other than divine intervention. In these circumstances, people were inclined to feel that their lives were directed by irresistible forces. Since they could not control them, the only remedies available were supplication, and the performance of pious acts considered likely to propitiate them.

The reactions of men and women when faced with what they conceived to be overpowering supernatural forces, changed remarkably little in a thousand years of Christian history. At the end of the sixth century Gregory of Tours collected eight books of the miracles of the saints, every page of which demonstrates that the most normal incidents of daily life were interpreted as signs of divine favour or disfavour, provoking displays of general jubilation or incalculable terror. Simple men were terrified of the dark, sometimes to the point of insanity. Thunderstorms brought panic to whole communities and drove them to take refuge round the altars of the saints. A flash of lightning created havoc in a small village, 'the people all fearing that the punishment of God was about to descend on them wherever they might try to escape.' Terrible cries were heard during an eclipse of the moon. Since all such phenomena sprang not from natural causes but from the direct action of God, it followed that the will of God could be discerned in them if only people knew how. To the inhabitants of Paris, a red sky at night three times in succession was a certain presage of war. A partial eclipse of the sun foretold disaster in the Auvergne. The heavens themselves blazed forth the death of princes.

These attitudes are not peculiar to the sixth century. They are found throughout the mediaeval period, and indeed afterwards. Unreasonable fear of the dark was one of the popular superstitions condemned by the eleventh-century canonist Burchard of Worms; 'many men dare not leave their houses before dawn, saying that…evil spirits have more power to harm them before cock-crow than afterwards.' Guibert of Nogent used to keep the lamp as close to his bed as possible in order to ward off demons. Shortly after the death of Robert the Pious, king of France, in 1031, it was recorded that the event had been presaged by three years of epidemics, famines, and 'prodigies'. In the fourteenth century it was still generally accepted that natural calamities were the just punishments inflicted by God on sinners. This was, for example, the moral drawn from the hurricane which struck southern England in January 1362, uprooting the fruit trees and destroying the harvest. In *Piers Plowman* Reason preached before the King and

> *...proved that this pestilence were for pure sin,*
> *And the south west wind on Saturday at even*
> *Was pertlich for pure pride and for no point else.*

The same notion that a conflict of irresistible forces governed individual lives gave a desperate, almost frenzied quality to the religious life of the later Middle Ages. Jean de Meung, one of the authors of the *Roman de la Rose,* attributed this belief to most of his contemporaries, though he does not seem to have subscribed to it himself. Because of it, he observed, men attached excessive importance to trivial events. Of this attitude was born the conviction that they had been set upon by demons. Sick men were driven to panic, sometimes to hysteria. Sorcery, necromancy, conjuring of spirits, visions of Heaven and Hell, were all, in the poet's view, products of the same aberration.

Ordinary people could not regard evil as an abstract force; to them it was real, visible, and tangible, capable of inflicting actual physical damage. A crude pantheistic view of nature suggested to them that the physical world harboured malignant powers hostile to men. A gust of wind might be the breath of Satan. Gregory of Tours once met a woman of the Limousin who believed that her child had been struck blind because she failed to make the sign of the cross when the wind blew up. Even at the end of the fifteenth century a gust of wind which blew open the doors of an abbey near Dunkirk was enough to strike panic in the hearts of the inmates. The friars of one Dominican convent of northern Germany habitually went about in pairs for fear of the Devil, who had broken all the windows of their church. According to St. Bruno, the founder of the Carthusian order, devils, the incarnation of all evil, moved in the air and in the dust that floated in every stream of light; 'a breath of wind, a turbulence in the air, the gust that blows men to the ground and harms their crops, these are the whistlings of the Devil.' The whole atmosphere, thought Ivo of Chartres, was filled with the spirit of evil, ubiquitous, all-knowing, powerful, spying out the inner thoughts and weaknesses of men. Anything which inspired fear might be evil, and thus the daily accidents of life suddenly took on a sinister import.

In some of the oldest writings of the Church the Devil takes the form of wild animals. He appears to St. Martin, for example, as a bull. According to Sulpicius Severus, St. Martin 'could see the Devil with his own eyes however cleverly he might disguise himself'. Peter the Venerable, the scholarly twelfth-century abbot of Cluny, collected a large number of stories illustrating the various forms in which the Devil assaulted sinners—a spider, a vulture in the sky, a bear seen in the forest near Cluny, a black pig found in the chapter house at Norwich, and a thousand other frightening creatures. Savage dogs occupied a sinister place in the mediaeval imagination. Walter, a monk of Durham in the twelfth century, was attacked by the Devil in the form of a huge black hound, while Guibert of Nogent's mother believed that lesser devils appeared as packs of small dogs to terrify children.

The Devil's most sinister form was that of a deformed, distorted human being, the horrifying figure so familiar from the sculptures of the Romanesque churches of France, or from Flemish paintings of the fifteenth century. This vision of the Devil makes its first appearance in the writings of the desert

monks of the third and fourth centuries and particularly in one
of the most influential saints' lives ever written, the *Life of St.
Anthony* by Athanasius. During his twenty years in the desert,
St. Anthony was said to have suffered temptations which are
clearly modelled on those of Christ. He was perpetually conscious that 'the air around him was full of evil spirits'. The Devil
frightened him at night, aroused carnal desires in him, tempted
him to return to the comforts of civilization, and even struck
him blows. The Devil commonly appeared to St. Anthony as a
'little black boy, his appearance matching his mind, with flash-
ing eyes and fiery breath, and horns on his head, half-man, half-
ass'. This is probably why the Devil is so often described by
mediaeval writers as a 'negro' or 'Ethiopian'. It is also the origin
of the idea that the Devil was a being, almost human, possessed
of human cunning and human malice. In his biography of St.
Benedict, Gregory the Great describes the temptations of his
hero in terms borrowed from the *Life of St. Anthony* while the
same conventions are observed more than five centuries later
by Peter the Venerable. When the Devil visited the sick-bed of
a monk of Cluny who had experienced fleeting doubts about
the doctrine of the real presence, he was 'like a small black
Ethiopian, horribly deformed, with horns coming out of his
ears and fire from his mouth as if he was about to eat the very
flesh of the sick monk'.

It was very widely believed that dreams were a direct revelation of the supernatural world. A deepening sense of guilt
about real or imaginary sins frequently resulted in nightmares
in which all the sinister fantasies found in the writings of Peter
the Venerable seemed to become reality. In the 1170s the
daughter of a knight called Sewal had a recurrent nightmare in
which she was attacked by devils in the form of vicious black

dogs; she was convinced that her dream had actually happened, and was taken by her parents to St.-Léonard de Noblat, near Limoges, and then to Canterbury in the hope of a cure. A boy aged fifteen from the Cluniac priory of Pontefract dreamed that demons were trying to strangle him, and he too was taken to Canterbury. Nor did such nightmares afflict only the sensitive and the simple. Stephen of Hoyland, a knight and a man of some substance, suffered from the same nocturnal terrors for thirty years before a visit to Canterbury brought him peace of mind. In a window of the south-west transept of the cathedral, he is shown lying awake at night with a devil at the foot of his bed and another at the head.

In popular thinking, the Devil's organization and methods were a reflection of God's. He too had his twelve apostles of evil, his rites, and his Church. Just as God lived in the righteous, so the Devil 'possessed' the sinful. Sin physically delivered the sinner into the Devil's hands. 'In sign', explains a fifteenth-century preacher, 'that of them that are like hogs in gluttony, the fiends have power to dwell in them and to drench them in the sea of Hell.' 'Possession' of this sort was physical as well as spiritual. Hysteria, however caused, was a symptom of possession, and doubtless it was often in practice caused by intense guilt. Romanus, a monk of St.-Evroul in the eleventh century, was an incorrigible kleptomaniac who frequently had to be rebuked by the abbot for petty thefts in the monastery.

'One night as he lay in bed, a demon set upon him and horribly tormented him. Hearing his hideous shrieks the monks rushed to his aid and by shaking him and sprinkling him with holy water, they finally succeeded in freeing him from the devil who possessed him. When he came to himself he recognized that the devil had gained this power over him through the thefts that he had committed.'

The idea of devils 'possessing' the sexually unchaste is particularly common in monastic writing, and the sculpted figure of 'Luxuria' abetted by a demon is found in many monastic churches of the eleventh and twelfth centuries. In the nave of the abbey of Vézelay there is a terrifying capital showing Woman the seductress leading a young man to despair and ultimately to suicide, while a similar capital in Autun cathedral shows a young man tempted by a naked woman and thereupon being grasped from behind by a devil.

The Approach of Death

The sense of constant menace which these malignant forces aroused was heightened by a preoccupation with death verging on the obsessional. The brevity of human life and the imminence of death were commonplaces of mediaeval preaching for, as Chaucer's parson observed, the majority of conversions to the pious life were probably due to the fear of damnation: 'the...cause that oghte moeve a man to contrition is drede of the daye of dome and of the horrible peynes of hell.'

The celebrated thirteenth-century preacher Jacques de Vitry one day encountered a man who asserted that a single word had turned him to God. He had asked himself whether the souls of the damned could be freed from torment after a thousand years. He answered in his mind: 'no.' If after a hundred thousand years: 'no.' If after a thousand thousand: 'no.' 'And pondering these things he saw how transitory life was, and thus a single word, "no", converted him to God.' The sermons of mediaeval preachers are full of such 'conversions'. A loose-living student of Bologna was reformed when a Dominican told him how hard would be the beds in Hell. Caesarius of Heisterbach knew of several who were converted by hearing great preachers. Another was reformed by the sight of a funeral service, while sudden illness and imminent death were responsible for countless conversions. 'Indeed', Caesarius concluded, 'the occasions of conversion are innumerable.' But not all such conversions are edifying tales in sermons. Many people undoubtedly experienced genuine transformations during which they regarded themselves as beginning a new life, as entering an elite order for whose members the chances of salvation were infinitely greater. In the early Church, Christians were frequently not baptized until they had resolved to live the most perfect possible life. St. Augustine was not baptized until the age of thirty-three, and he spoke of it then as his 'conversion'. Bede and Gregory the Great both used the word 'conversion' to mean entry into the monastic life. Indeed the 'conversion' of saints was the classic stock-in-trade of mediaeval hagiographers from the time of St. Athanasius onwards. The same pattern— worldliness, conversion, sanctity—is repeated in biographies of St. Martin, St. Benedict, St. Dunstan, Odo of Cluny, Bernard of Clairvaux and countless others who attracted the admiration of their contemporaries.

From the notion of the converted elite was born the belief that the overwhelming majority of people were damned. This tradition was strong in the early Church and, indeed, it was natural in a minority religion suffering abuse and persecution. But it survived to become a corner-stone of the moral teaching of the mediaeval Church, a recurring feature of the sermons of revivalist preachers and the visions of mystics. St. Bernard had little doubt that there were 'few, very few who will be saved', while Berthold of Regensburg, the great German preacher of the thirteenth century, assured his audiences that less than one in a thousand of them would ascend to Paradise. 'If we believed', wrote the fifteenth-century Dominican John Herolt, 'that one man only out of the entire human race, was doomed to perdition, would not every man be afraid lest he himself should be that one?...How much more then does he have cause to fear, when God himself has said that "many are called but few are chosen." '

In 1091 a parish priest of Normandy reported an extraordinary vision to the bishop of Lisieux. As he was returning from his rounds one winter's night he seemed to hear the tramp of a great army in the distance. At first he assumed that it was the army of the notorious Robert de Bellême, engaged in some private war. But then a great ghostly defile appeared in the moonlight and marched past him, well-known murderers, noble ladies on horse-back, thieves, prelates, judges, and knights. All were being escorted to Hell by squads of negroid demons. Amongst them were men of great repute in their lifetimes, some of whom had seemed to be holy men. Hugh, bishop of Lisieux, was amongst them, as were the abbots of St.-Evroul and St.-Wandrille 'and many others whose names I forget, for man's eye is frequently deceived but God sees them to the very marrow.'

It is difficult to decide how far this uninviting philosophy commanded general acceptance, for the denunciations of preachers are not always a true reflection of mediaeval religious life. As the preachers themselves readily admitted, their words often fell on deaf ears, and there is no doubt that the later mediaeval period, for which surviving sermon material is richest, was also a period of notable popular worldliness. The prior of Holy Trinity, London, reported in 1200 that 'many believe neither in good nor in bad angels, nor in life or death or any other spiritual things which they cannot see with their own eyes.' There were scoffers, complained Vincent of Beauvais, who openly laughed at graphic representations of Hell. Berthold of Regensburg devoted a whole sermon to the refutation of those sceptics who argued that the soul must become insensitive to the pains of Hell if they are indeed of infinite duration. Belief in a merciful God was even, occasionally, regarded as evidence of heresy. An Albigensian who appeared before the Inquisition of Languedoc declared that if he could lay his hands on that God who saved but one out of a thousand of the creatures he created, he would tear him to pieces and spit in his face. Most people, however, were not inclined to criticize official doctrines, and they continued to provide audiences for mendicant preachers. Margery Kempe, the visionary of King's Lynn at the beginning of the fifteenth century, had originally refused to believe that most people were damned 'and when Our Lord showed her any that should be damned she had great pain; she would not hear of it...and put it out of her mind as much as she might.' But the Lord was displeased at this aberration and punished her until she came to accept the orthodox doctrine.

Mediaeval men and women were familiar with a number of detailed descriptions of Hell. The picture of Hell was repeatedly presented to them by imaginative preachers like master Richard Alkerton, who declared in 1406, in a sermon delivered in London, that the damned would be

'boiled in fire and brimstone without end. Venomous worms...shall gnaw all their members unceasingly, and the worm of conscience shall gnaw the soul....Now ye shall have everlasting bitterness....This fire that tormenteth you shall never be quenched, and they that tormenteth you shall never be weary neither die.'

The scenes carved on the west fronts at Conques or Bourges find their counterpart in the hand-books of preachers. The *Pricke of Conscience,* one of the most popular of these manuals, draws a picture of Hell with intense dramatic power: the hideous din, the shrieks of the tortured, the 'raumping of devils, the dyngyng and dysching' of their glowing hammers, and the closely packed mass of humanity swaying this way and that in the infernal oven, each fighting and scratching at his neighbour's face like a grinning madman, or ripping off his own flesh with indescribable passion. A good many of these descriptions originated in visions, or in the accounts of those who claimed to have descended bodily into Hell. In the time of Bede, a Northumbrian who claimed to have returned to life described it as an ever-deepening pit where sinners suffered extremes of cold and heat, their cries drowned by the harsh laughter of demons. 'Do you know who all these souls are?' asked his guide: 'they are the souls who failed to confess and atone for their sins until they were dying.' Amongst seventh-century writers it seems to have been agreed that the torments of Hell consisted of alternating extremes of heat and cold. The hermit Guthlac saw it as 'sulphurous eddies of flames mixed with freezing hail', a mental image which remained common throughout the Middle Ages. Even Shakespeare's Claudio feared

To bathe in fiery floods or to reside
In thrilling region of thick ribbed ice
(*Measure for Measure* III. i)

Educated men may not always have believed these tales of bodily descents into Hell, though Bede and Gregory the Great certainly did. But the descriptions of Hell which were based on them reflected notions held more or less consistently by every generation. Guibert of Nogent's mother, after the death of her husband, 'saw by a wonderful dispensation of God in frequent visions the clearest possible images of the pains he was enduring in Purgatory.' A servant of Ludwig, landgrave of Thuringia, claimed that he had been permitted a glimpse into Hell, where he had been able to watch the torments of his former master. Such accounts were received everywhere with considerable interest. When, for example, a monk of Eynsham experienced an unusually vivid dream of Purgatory in 1196, the bishop of Lincoln instructed a detailed record to be made of it for the edification of his diocesans.

Profound pessimism was one of the principal characteristics of mediaeval religion. At a popular level it bred a fatalism in which the resort to rituals with the object of expiating sin, becomes somewhat easier to understand. The salvation of an individual person was nothing less than a miracle, to be sought of God through the intercession of the saints. In a powerful sermon on damnation, Berthold of Regensburg asserted that the salvation of a sinner was 'one of the greatest miracles that ever God does. That is why we sing in the Mass *"Mirabilis Deus in sanctis suis"*, God is wonderful in his saints.' The relics of the saints, repeated a theologian of the twelfth century, were the means whereby the faithful might resist the power of evil in the world. They gave health to the bodies of men and absolution to their souls: 'the body of Elijah give life to the dead and remove death's sting from the living.'

2

The Cult of Relics

The cult of the saints was the counterpoint of the fear of evil. Just as people tended to associate evil with objects familiar to them, so they attempted to give a human quality to the forces of good. This habit of mind was already common in the west at the beginning of the fifth century, when the Frankish collector Victricius of Rouen portrayed the saints as an army of auxiliaries in the cosmic battle against evil: 'see, a great host of saints comes to us....Victory is certain when we fight along side such allies with Christ for our general.'

The veneration of the relics of the saints is attested by unimpeachable evidence as early as the second century, and it is probably even older than that. In a letter written in about A.D. 156 to the church of Philomelium, the Christians of Smyrna described the martyrdom of bishop Polycarp, who had been burned to death shortly before. From this it appears that the Christians 'took up his bones which are more valuable than refined gold and laid them in a suitable place where, the Lord willing,...we may gather together in gladness and celebrate the anniversary of his martyrdom.' During the most violent of all the persecutions, that of Diocletian (303–11), relics of the martyrs were eagerly collected by their followers. After the death of St. Vincent the onlookers dipped their clothes in his blood, and when seven brothers were martyred at Samosata in 308, a number of noble ladies bribed the guards to let them wash the bodies with sponges and collect drops of the blood.

The cult of relics was criticized from its inception by purists who regarded it as pagan. Amongst the earliest critics was the Gallic priest Vigilantius whose opinions are known to us from the denunciations hurled at him by St. Jerome. Vigilantius condemned the veneration of all inanimate objects such as the bodies of the saints, and especially the bodies of St. Peter and St. Paul in Rome. In reply, Jerome stated the classic Christian justification of such cults, that the relics were not worshipped in themselves, but were an aid to the veneration of martyrs of undoubted holiness whose lives were a model to later generations.

> 'We do not worship their relics any more than we do the sun or the moon, the angels, archangels, or seraphims. We honour them in honour of He whose faith they witnessed. We honour the Master by means of the servants.'

Ideas not unlike those of Vigilantius were advanced in the fifth century by the Pelagian heretics and by a number of individuals of varying orthodoxy. Many of the greatest thinkers of the patristic period concerned themselves with elaborating the theoretical basis of the cult of relics. In the first place, they argued, relics were the earthly reminders of holy men, who deserved at least as much respect as the inhabitants of the later Roman Empire commonly accorded to their own ancestors. Moreover they were, in the words of St. Augustine, 'temples of the faith' whom Christians should venerate in order to 'associate themselves with the merits of the martyrs that they may secure their intercession by prayer'. In Augustine's view the cult of the martyrs was no different from the cult of holy men still alive—both were a proper model for other Christians. Following Augustine, a later writer asserted that 'we revere the relics of the martyrs with the same respect as we accord to holy men now living; but perhaps we honour them more because we can be confident of their efficacy, for they have already fought the battle and won it.'

Popular piety went far beyond this modest account of the cult of relics, and certain theologians, particularly in the east, were inclined to accord intrinsic powers to the relics of the saints. Cyprian of Carthage defended the veneration of relics in themselves and even of objects touched by the martyrs. The chains they wore, for example, should be honoured for they have honoured the feet of the martyrs and led them to a glorious death. St. Cyril of Jerusalem also went further than Augustine in allowing the bodies of the saints some intrinsic power to work miracles. Even though the soul had left the body, the body was still venerable 'on account of the virtuous soul that once inhabited it. For it is well known that such external objects as handkerchiefs and aprons have cured the sick after touching the martyr's body; how much more then will the body itself heal them.

The early Church then produced a weak and a strong defence of the cult of relics, and elements of both appear in every major apologist of the Middle Ages. In the middle of the thirteenth century, Thomas Aquinas summarized all the various opinions canvassed in his own day and concluded that relics should be venerated for three reasons. First, they are the physical reminders of the saints and 'he who loves some one reveres the things that they leave behind them.' By means of their relics we retain a personal friendship with the saints. Secondly, adds the *doctor angelicus,* bodily relics enjoy a certain intrinsic merit, not as mere objects but on account of their connections with the soul of the saint. The Holy Spirit worked mainly through their souls (which are in Heaven), but also through their bodies, which may be venerated on earth. Thus these bodies are sanctified by God—a fact which distinguishes them from the holy images venerated in the Greek Church. Thirdly, by working miracles at their tombs God has plainly demonstrated that He wishes them to be venerated. 'We ought therefore to hold them in the deepest possible veneration as limbs of God, as children and friends of God, and as intercessors on our behalf.'

The Objects of Veneration

Most of the relics venerated by the early Christians were not bodily relics but simple mementoes, objects that had been in contact with the saint or his shrine. Pilgrims brought pieces of cloth or paper to the shrine, which they retained as private relics of the saint. Cyril of Jerusalem had remarked that handkerchiefs and aprons worked miracles after touching the bodies of the martyrs. The shrouds of popes were customarily divided amongst the people of Rome, until the practice was abolished by Gregory I. In the eyes of ordinary men and women these *brandea,* as they were called, enjoyed as much esteem as the body itself and occasionally even more. Indeed, a remarkable account of the tomb of St. Peter by Gregory of Tours suggests that quite literal notions prevailed as to the manner in which such *brandea* became impregnated with holiness.

'He who wishes to pray before the tomb', writes Gregory, 'opens the barrier that surrounds it and puts his head through a small opening in the shrine. There he prays for all his needs and, so long as his requests are just, his prayers will be granted. Should he wish to bring back a relic from the tomb, he carefully weighs a piece of cloth which he then hangs inside the tomb. Then he prays ardently and, if his faith is sufficient, the cloth, once removed from the tomb, will be found to be so full of divine grace that it will be much heavier than before. Thus will he know that his prayers have been granted.'

It is difficult to imagine that these recommendations were ever put to any practical test, but they tell us much about the frame of mind of an intelligent man who could accept such stories without question.

Pieces of tombs, oil from the lamps that burned before them, dust from the ground around them, found their way into the most distinguished relic collections of the west. While on a pilgrimage to the shrine of St. Julian of Brioude, Gregory of Tours broke off a piece of the tomb and placed it in the basilica at Tours, where it shortly worked miracles. Dust from tombs, particularly from the Holy Sepulchre, was venerated from the earliest times. A funerary table of the fourth century, now in the Louvre, bears an inscription which declares that it once contained 'dust from the land of our redemption', and Augustine observes that miracles were commonly worked by such dust. Worshippers at the tomb of St. Theodore 'believed that merely to touch the body was a blessing of indescribable holiness, and if anyone can carry off any of the dust that has settled on the martyr's tomb he counts himself fortunate indeed.' Relics of this sort were often enclosed in little reliquaries that hung from a chain around the owner's neck. Gregory the

Great, for example, used to wear a small crucifix containing fil-
ings from the chains of St. Peter and the gridiron of St.
Lawrence. St. Jerome compared such charms to the phylacter-
ies carried in their robes by the scribes and pharisees, and the
practice attracted disapproval in certain quarters throughout
the succeeding centuries. The acts of the council of Braca in
675 reveal that the Spanish bishops of that period were in the
habit of wearing the relics of their churches around their necks,
which the council characterized as a 'detestable presumption'.
Similar observations were made six centuries later by Thomas
Aquinas, but the practice showed no signs of abating. St. Hugh
of Lincoln, an insatiable collector, carried about with him
'innumerable relics of saints of both sexes' in a small silver casket which he later presented to the Grande Chartreuse; a tooth
of St. Benedict, presented to him by the monks of Fleury, was
set into his ring.

Although *brandea* could not compete with the bodily relics
of the saints which increasingly became available after the seventh century, their popularity never altogether waned and the
practice of collecting them survived into relatively modern
times. An acquaintance of Guibert of Nogent, who accidentally
swallowed a toad, was saved from death by the application of
dust from the tomb of St. Marcel. Similar miracles are attributed to many other saints. Rocks from the seashore at
Mont-St.-Michel were collected by pilgrims in the eleventh
century and even used to consecrate churches. As late as the fifteenth century the Dominican Felix Faber took with him to
the Holy Land a bag of jewels belonging to friends who had
asked him to press them against any relics which he might
inspect en route. His well-travelled contemporary, Joos van
Ghistele, brought various gems which had been in contact

with the relics of the Magi at Cologne in the belief that, should he discover the land of the legendary Prester John, they would make an acceptable gift to that potentate.

Most of the saints whose relics were venerated in the fourth century were martyrs of the last and most terrible of the persecutions. But a succession of spectacular discoveries (or 'inventions') at the end of the fourth century and the beginning of the fifth dramatically increased the number of distinguished relics available. The floodgates were opened by the discovery of two quite unknown saints called Gervase and Protasius in the basilica of Milan by St. Ambrose in 386. As he was dedicating the basilica in the presence of a large crowd, Ambrose dug in the ground beneath him and uncovered two unidentified bodies which were spontaneously gathered up by the crowd and venerated as the relics of saints and martyrs. The timing of this event was particularly opportune, for the Arian empress Justina was even then attempting to expel Ambrose from his bishopric. We cannot rule out the possibility that the invention was elaborately contrived for immediate political ends. There can, however, be no doubt of the enormous impact which the discovery made on contemporaries. St. Augustine, who was in Milan at the time, constantly refers to it, and the cult of the two saints enjoyed immediate popularity throughout the Christian world. The result seems to have been to make Christians more credulous in accepting the fabrications of visionaries or charlatans. Two unknown saints, Vitalis and Agricola, were unearthed in rather similar circumstances in Florence in 390. In the same year two monks claimed to have found the head of John the Baptist in the ruins of Herod's palace in Jerusalem. Even more celebrated than the invention of St. Gervase and St. Protasius was the discovery of the body of St. Stephen, the first Christian martyr, in 415. A certain Lucian, priest of Caphargamala in Palestine, experienced a revelation in which Gamaliel, the enlightened pharisee mentioned in the Acts of the Apostles, informed him that he had translated Stephen's body to Caphargamala. The relics were immediately located and portions of them distributed to churches in north Africa and the eastern Mediterranean. Some of them remained at Caphargamala, while the bulk of them were translated to Jerusalem. But fragments found their way to Uzalis, Calama, Minorca and Ancona amongst other places. St. Augustine acquired some for his church at Hippo, which became the object of an important north African pilgrimage.

The common feature of most of these discoveries was that they were alleged to have been inspired by visions or dreams. The belief in dreams as a revelation of the supernatural world is one of the commonest features of primitive religions. St. Augustine, for example, had no doubt that God spoke to men in visions, and his critical powers appear to have been suspended whenever other men's dreams were reported to him. Throughout the Middle Ages, dreams were cited to authenticate more or less bogus relics. Thus, for example, Moses' rod, whose discovery at Sens created a sensation at the beginning of the eleventh century. When the Provencal hermit Peter Bartholomew discovered the Holy Lance at Antioch during the first crusade his story was doubted by Adhémar, bishop of Le Puy, but it was enthusiastically accepted by the rank and file of the army. In some hagiographical works it is even suggested that it was sinful to ignore instructions conveyed in dreams, and indeed in the fourteenth century, Jean de Meung found that an exaggerated respect for them was almost universal amongst his contemporaries.

In doubting the authenticity of the Holy Lance of Antioch, Adhémar was probably fairly typical of educated churchmen of his day. He may perhaps have remembered another Holy Lance at Constantinople whose claims were rather more ancient. The absence of rational criteria for assessing the authenticity of relics bred a dangerous anarchy in which several churches might lay claim to the same relic, each discovered by revelation and each equally believed. Thus at least two heads of John the Baptist were venerated in the fifth century, and in the eleventh century they were both to be found in Constantinople, while a third head had made its appearance at St.-Jean d'Angely in central France. For such reasons the Church endeavoured at an early stage to stem the tide of dreams and visions. A north African council as early as 401 had occasion to denounce 'inane revelations which men suppose themselves to have received in their sleep'. Even Augustine, usually credulous in such matters, advised caution. Although the multiplicity of relics does not seem to have disturbed the populace, intelligent churchmen were aware that it discredited the cult of certain saints. For as Guibert of Nogent pointed out:

> 'Some say they have such and such a relic and others loudly assert that they have it. The citizens of Constantinople claim the head of John the Baptist while the monks of St.-Jean d'Angely confidently believe that they have it. Now what could be more absurd than to suppose that this great saint had two heads. Let us therefore take this matter seriously and admit that one of them is wrong.

It was Guibert's opinion that all doubts about the authenticity of relics were due to the partition and translation of bodies.

'All the evils of contention over relics would be avoided if we permitted the saints to enjoy the repose of a proper and immutable burial place.' In fact, the early Church had originally refused to countenance either the partition or the translation of bodies. The burial of the dead was governed by strict rules of Roman municipal law. In the Theodosian code, it was absolutely forbidden to disturb the dead even if it was only by moving the coffin a few feet. But at the time the code was published these precepts had already been abandoned, notably by the emperors themselves. The co-emperor Gallus translated the relics of St. Babylas to a disreputable suburb of Antioch shortly after 351, while the reign of Constantius (351–61) saw a series of spectacular translations to the great church of the Apostles in Constantinople. Magnificent displays signalled the arrival in the city of St. Phocas, St. Paul the confessor, John the Baptist, the prophet Samuel and a host of minor martyrs. Thus it was that the capital of the Byzantine empire, which had begun its life with no relics at all, possessed by the end of the fifth century the world's finest collection. These developments attracted unfavourable comment in the west where the dead remained inviolable until the seventh century. The popes repeatedly refused to allow the emperors to translate relics from Rome to Constantinople. A request for the bodies of St. Peter, St. Paul and St. Lawrence, was rejected by pope Hormisdas in 519 on the ground that Roman custom would not allow it. Gregory the Great refused a request for the head of St. Lawrence in 594, pointing out that 'it was not the custom in Rome to permit any one so much as to touch the relics of the saints'; those who had recently opened the tomb of St. Lawrence by mistake had all died within ten days.

Similar considerations applied *a fortiori* to the dismemberment of bodies. But this too was ultimately permitted in both east and west. This development, the source of most of the abuses of the mediaeval period, was readily justified by eastern theologians. Theodoret of Cyrus proclaimed that 'in the divided body the grace survives undivided and the fragments, however small, have the same efficacy as the whole body.' Victricius, bishop of Rouen, himself an enthusiastic collector of relics, uttered the same opinion at the beginning of the fifth century. In the Latin Church, however, dismemberment continued to be regarded with distaste. Gregory of Tours once met a Syrian merchant who was offering a detached finger bone for sale, 'though not, I think, with the approval of the martyr'. When bodies were dismembered, efforts were sometimes made to secure the saint's approval; the priest whom St. Radegonde sent to collect some relics of St. Mammas reported that on his approach a finger had detached itself from the body of its own accord.

The practice of fasting and praying before removing a relic was a survival of these ancient prejudices. Gregory of Tours reported that three bishops fasted for three days before opening a casket containing the blood of John the Baptist. Similar austerities were considered advisable in much later periods. When the Bohemians captured Gnesen in 1039 they were prevented by divine intervention from removing the body of St. Adalbert until they had fasted for three days, renounced polygamy, and promulgated effective laws against murder and rape. The elaborate precautions taken by abbot Samson of Bury before opening the tomb of St. Edmund are recorded by his biographer Jocelyn of Brakeland. The rebuilding of the abbey church had made it necessary to move the coffin and Samson, accompanied by a chosen few, flagellated himself and dressed in white robes before proceeding to lift the lid of the coffin. Even then Samson did not dare unwrap the saint's winding sheet but cradled his head in his arms and said: 'Glorious martyr St. Edmund,…condemn me not to perdition for this my boldness that I, a miserable sinner, now touch thee. Thou knowest my devotion and my good intent.'

Two factors combined to create an unprecedented demand for relics, however dubious the source. The first was the growing feeling that relics were necessary for the consecration of churches. Relics must have been used for the consecration of Roman churches as early as the fourth century, for on the famous occasion of the invention of the relics of St. Gervase and St. Protasius, the crowd shouted 'consecrate it in the Roman manner', to which Ambrose answered 'I will if I find relics.' Similarly Gregory the Great sent to Augustine and his fellow-missionaries in England 'all things needed for the worship of the church, namely sacred vessels, altar linen, ornaments, priestly vestments, and relics of the holy apostles and martyrs.' In 787 the second council of Nicaea insisted on the use of relics in the consecration of new churches and decreed that any churches which had been consecrated without them should acquire some as soon as possible. The conversion of northern France, England, and Germany brought into the Christian fold nations with few indigenous martyrs, who were obliged to acquire their relics abroad. In practice they usually acquired them in Rome, and the eighth and ninth centuries saw an unprecedented series of translations and partitions of the relics of Rome for the benefit of her newly converted daughters.

The second factor, which was of far greater long term importance, was the accumulation of enormous private collections of relics by connoisseurs at least as avid as the wealthy art collectors of post-Renaissance Europe. The earliest and most

successful of these were the emperors of Byzantium whose collection, built up over five centuries, was dramatically dispersed
across the face of western Europe when the fourth Crusade
took Constantinople in 1204. This extraordinarily large and varied collection was lodged partly in the churches of the city, and
partly in the various royal palaces. It was a constant source of
wonder to Latins who passed through on their way to the Holy
Land. When Amaury, king of Jerusalem, visited the emperor
Manuel Conmenus in 1171 he was taken aback by the rich display of silks, jewels, and reliquaries in the imperial chapels.
Surviving lists demonstrate that most princes of western Europe
at all times expended a great deal of money and energy in
enlarging their collections. Charlemagne and the German
emperors accumulated an astonishing collection of relics at
Aachen, many of which had come by more or less devious
routes from Constantinople. Henry I of England sent emissaries
to acquire relics in Constantinople, and he appears to have
given much of his substantial collection to Reading abbey.
Louis IX of France endowed the Sainte Chapelle with the
crown of thorns, a portion of the true Cross, a piece of the
Holy Lance, and fragments of the purple cloak of Christ, all of
which had been sold or given to him by the bankrupt Latin
emperor of Constantinople.

The unrestrained popular enthusiasm which greeted each
new accession of the Byzantine collection demonstrates that
relics were regarded as a proper object of national pride. On
occasions the emperors were prepared to forgo significant
political advantages in order to acquire an important relic. In
944, for example, the army of the emperor Romanus
Lecapenus, at the climax of its triumphal campaign in Asia
Minor, spared Edessa and released two hundred captives in

return for the celebrated portrait of Christ which was preserved there. This attitude to relics explains much of the frenzied acquisitiveness of Latin rulers and their subjects
throughout our period. Relics were the guarantors of political
prestige and spiritual authority. William of Malmesbury
described Cologne as 'the metropolitan city of Germany...
with the patronage of the saints'. France, declared a French
monk of the eleventh century, was 'like the treasure-house of
the Lord' on account of the priceless relics that were to be
found there. A sermon of Walter Suffield, bishop of Norwich,
was largely devoted to the proposition that England was
exalted above other nations by its collections of relics. The
occasion was the translation in 1244 of a vase of the blood of
Christ to Westminster abbey together with 'numerous sealed
documents attesting its authenticity'. In the course of his
speech, the bishop recalled that Louis IX of France had
recently acquired a fragment of the True Cross.

> 'But we must consider not the nature of matter but the
> causes thereof. Now it is true that the Cross is a very
> holy relic but it is holy only because it came into con-
> tact with the precious blood of Christ. The holiness of
> the Cross derives from the blood whereas the holiness
> of the blood in no way derives from the Cross. It there-
> fore follows that England, which possesses the blood of
> Christ, rejoices in a greater treasure than France, which
> has no more than the Cross.'

Not only a nation but a region, a city, or an individual an
acquired new status when it obtained a valuable relic. To a
powerful collector, the body of a saint might quite literally be
worth more than gold or silver. So much was admitted by

Fernando count of Carrion who, when collecting his debts from the emir of Cordova in 1047, rejected all the bullion that he was offered: 'of gold and silver I have enough already; give me the body of St. Zoyl.'

The Sale and Theft of Relics

So long as even an august churchman like Gregory of Tours was satisfied with *brandea*, few problems arose. But as soon as they began to insist on bodily relics the demand rapidly outstripped the supply and a nefarious trade in relics sprang up which provided a constant source of indignation among satirists and reformers from the fourth century to the sixteenth. When the eastern Church abandoned its objections to the translation of relics, the itinerant salesman came into his own. St. Augustine complains of wandering relic-hawkers dressed as monks at the beginning of the fifth century, while Gregory of Tours mentions with distaste the activities of Syrian merchants in France.

By the ninth century there was a large market for relics in the newly founded abbeys of northern Europe, which was supplied by highly professional relic merchants. In the 820s a Roman deacon called Deusdona is known to have travelled to Aix in order to sell relics looted from the Roman catacombs to churchmen at the court of Louis the Pious. Hilduin, abbot of St.-Medard of Soissons, and Einhard, the biographer of Charlemagne, were among his clients, 'and by this means', we are told, 'he succeeded in supplementing his low income.' In the eleventh and twelfth centuries the sale of relics was practised on an alarming scale and active measures were taken to discourage it. Emma, Canute's queen, bought several relics of doubtful authenticity. The bishop of Benevento sold her the arm of St. Bartholomew in 1017, having come to England for the express purpose of finding a buyer. During her exile in Rouen after 1016 she bought several bones of St. Ouen, at the thought of which William of Malmesbury blanched when describing it a century later, even though his own monastery proved to be the ultimate beneficiary. The trade in relics reached epidemic proportions after the sack of Constantinople in 1204, when the market was inundated with objects whose authenticity was impossible to prove. The fourth Lateran council condemned the traffic as sacrilege and simony but this did not prevent Jean d'Alluye, for example, from selling a piece of the True Cross to the abbey of La Boissière for 533 *livres tournois*. Nor did it deter Baldwin, the impecunious Latin emperor of Constantinople, from pawning the crown of thorns to the Venetians for 13,075 *livres* in order to mount a campaign against the Bulgars.

Few relic merchants had satisfactory credentials and fewer still could explain the origin of their wares. For this reason, the more important collectors preferred to steal relics than to buy them. Many of the greatest pilgrimage churches in Europe, including St. Benedict at Fleury, St. Foy at Conques, St. Nicholas of Bari and St. Mark in Venice, owed their prosperity to some pious theft. Einhard, friend of Charlemagne and founder of the abbey of Seligenstadt, had no compunction about stealing the bodies of Marcellinus and Peter from the Roman catacombs; his servant prised open the tomb with his own hands. Pilgrims were constantly attempting to steal relics, and as early as 385 armed deacons surrounded the True Cross at Jerusalem in order to prevent pilgrims from kissing it and taking a splinter away in their teeth. Fulk Nerra count of Anjou was alleged to have obtained a splinter in this way when he visited Jerusalem at the beginning of the eleventh century, and at

Bury St. Edmunds, pilgrims to the shrine of the martyr king had to be prevented from biting off pieces of the gilt.

It is clear that contemporaries did not consider it possible to have any property in the body of a saint, and accordingly the customary canons of ethical behaviour did not apply to relics. This attitude is found in Greek hagiography very early but it does not make its appearance in the west until the seventh century or later. One of the earliest attempts to give moral justification to an audacious theft is found in the official account of the translation of the bodies of St. Benedict and St. Scholastica from Monte Cassino to Fleury. This event occurred at the end of the seventh century after the devastation of the abbey of Monte Cassino by the Lombards. According to the oldest account a French priest visited the ruins and, finding the tomb of the two saints in the midst of the desolation, placed them in a casket and carried them off to France. The body of St. Benedict was laid in the recently founded abbey of Fleury on the Loire, while his sister was taken to Le Mans. The official account by Adrevald, a monk of Fleury, was not composed until two centuries later, and it is full of apocryphal details designed to prove that God and St. Benedict had brought the translation about. Here we learn that abbot Mummolus was advised in a vision of the desolate state of Monte Cassino, while a similar vision was vouchsafed to the clergy of Le Mans. Two parties of clergy made their way to Monte Cassino, where a divine revelation led them to the tomb. Further miracles saved them from pursuit by the Romans and Lombards by causing night suddenly to descend. As soon as they had reached the Loire valley a man blind from birth was healed and a constant succession of miracles began which had not ceased in the writer's own day. In this account we have all the elements of the classic mediaeval justification for the theft of relics, which remained for several centuries the stock-in-trade of hagiographical writers: neglect of the saint in his or her former resting-place; revelation of the saint's whereabouts to the thieves; divine assistance in accomplishing the theft; constant miracles on their return.

One of the more remarkable thefts justified according to this formula was the translation of St. Nicholas to Bari in 1087. St. Nicholas was a bishop of Myra on the Lycian coast of Asia Minor, who was believed (on no very sound basis) to have been martyred during the persecution of Diocletian. His body had been preserved at Myra for several centuries, but recurrent raids by Arab pirates had depopulated the region, and after the collapse of Byzantine power at Manzikert in 1071 the city was almost entirely deserted by its inhabitants. In the spring of 1087, several merchants of Bari met on a trading mission to Antioch and resolved to remove the saint to their native city. They completed their business as quickly as possible, purchased some crowbars and sailed to Myra. Forty-seven men, heavily armed and carrying the crowbars, knocked at the door of the monastery of St. Nicholas and asked to be admitted to pray at the shrine. Their prayer completed, they turned on the monks and demanded to know where the martyr lay, declaring that the pope himself had ordered them to remove the body 'on the express instructions of St. Nicholas who had appeared to him in a dream.' After threatening the monks with a naked sword, they located the body, disinterred it, and removed it to Bari where spectacular miracles immediately occurred.

The author of this account plainly believed that the theft was a pious act and that the end justified the means 'for as it is written in scripture, *bona est fraus quae nemini nocet*'—there is no harm in deceit if no one is injured. The fundamental argument of the author, an Italian Greek called Nicephorus, is that St. Nicholas demanded proper veneration and this the partially depopulated city of Myra was no longer able to give him. Bari on the other hand was at the height of its prosperity in the eleventh century, and its citizens were particularly devoted to St. Nicholas. According to Nicephorus the thieves replied to the protests of the citizens of Myra with the argument: 'We too are worshippers of Almighty God, so why distress yourselves? You have had the precious body of St. Nicholas for 775 years and St. Nicholas has now decided to bestow his favours on another place....The city of Bari deserves him.' Thus it was that the distribution of relics could be changed in accordance with a new balance of power and prosperity among nations. The thieves further argued that if St. Nicholas had desired to remain in Myra he would have intervened miraculously to prevent his removal. 'Do you suppose', asked the monks of Myra, 'that St. Nicholas will permit you to take him away?' And Nicephorus reports that when St. Nicholas offered no resistance the monks cried out 'with lamentable wails', realizing that it was their punishment for deserting the shrine when the Turks had attacked the city some years before. 'We left him alone in the town and now he is leaving us to the mercy of the Turks....It is clear that we are unworthy of so great a saint.' Then, when the thieves picked up the relics, they exuded a miraculous odour 'and everyone rejoiced for thus they knew that St. Nicholas consented to his translation.'

The view that the saint had a mind of his own to decide where he wished to be venerated amounted to a real conviction which was no doubt sincerely held by the thieves who translated St. Nicholas to Bari. According to Adrevald of Fleury (the story is certainly apocryphal), St. Benedict intervened to prevent Pippin from restoring his relics to the monks of Monte Cassino: 'The holy saint will only permit himself to be moved of his own free will', the abbot of Fleury is supposed to have said, '...and if it is indeed his wish, on account of our sins, to leave France and return to his native country, then there is nothing we can do to prevent him.' One of the commonest stories found in mediaeval miracle collections relates that a body remained rooted to the spot as soon as impious hands tried to move it without the saint's consent. A single example will stand in lieu of many. In 1053 Garcia, king of Navarre, resolved to move the body of St. Millan, an obscure Spanish saint of the sixth century, from Cogolla to Nájera where he had recently built a church in honour of the Blessed Virgin. A powerful deputation led by several bishops was sent to Cogolla for this purpose. The monks were unable to resist and the sequel might have been like the story of St. Nicholas of Myra. 'But God, the consoler of the troubled, had otherwise disposed. As soon as the party set out on the road with the coffin and entered the valley, the coffin suddenly refused to move an inch further and became so heavy that the bearers had to lay it down.' Garcia resigned himself to respecting the wishes of the saint and built an oratory on the spot where the miracle had occurred. The author of the twelfth-century *Guide for Pilgrims to Santiago* believed that such incidents were regular occurrences, and repeated a legend to the effect that four saints, St. James himself, St. Martin of Tours, St. Leonard, and St. Gilles had resisted all attempts to move them, even by the king of France.

August churchmen of saintly reputation are known to have shared the view that the sanctity of property did not extend to relics, that one was entitled to whatever one could get by fair means or foul. St. Hugh of Lincoln, then staying as a guest at the abbey of Fécamp, was permitted to see the arm of St. Mary Magdalene, which was tightly wrapped in cloth bandages that the monks had never dared to open. In spite of the furious protests of the surrounding monks he took out a knife, cut open the wrapping, and tried to break a piece off. On finding it too hard he bit at a finger with his teeth, 'first with his incisors and finally with his molars', and by this means broke off two fragments which he handed to his biographer for safe-keeping. Turning to the abbot, Hugh remarked: 'If a little while ago I handled the sacred body of the Lord with my fingers in spite of my unworthiness, and partook of it with my lips and my teeth, why should I not treat the bones of the saints in the same way…and without profanity acquire them whenever I can.' So long as St. Hugh's attitude prevailed it is no surprise to learn that churches with valuable relics took elaborate precautions against theft. The Lateran Council of 1215 instructed that relics were not to be exposed except in a reliquary, and a provincial synod in Bordeaux in 1255 forbade the removal of relics from their reliquaries in any circumstances whatever. Whenever the relics of St. Cuthbert were exposed at Durham, a group of monks was appointed to stand guard over them all night. Four armed men stood guard day and night in Chartres cathedral in the fourteenth century. When the Spanish traveller Pero Tafur visited the Lateran basilica in Rome in 1437, he found the portrait of Christ by St. Luke perpetually guarded by four men with iron maces.

False Relics

Acquisitiveness on this scale created a demand which could only be satisfied by fraud. It was acknowledged by most contemporaries that wicked men did sometimes fabricate relics, and some quite celebrated relics were regarded with intense suspicion. When Henry III of England solemnly received a vase of Christ's blood from the representatives of the crusading orders in 1247, 'certain hesitant and incredulous persons' in the crowd ventured to express doubts about its authenticity. The prior of the Hospitallers of Clerkenwell demanded to know whether these scoffers were accusing the military orders of fraud, but the objections still continued unabated. 'How can any of the Lord's blood exist on earth', insisted the doubters, 'when the Saviour was bodily resurrected on the third day?' Nor were they silenced until Robert Grosseteste delivered an angry oration proving its authenticity with arguments drawn from Scripture and natural reason.

Guibert of Nogent observed that in many cases the pressures of popular belief prevented any non-conformist from voicing his doubts. He vividly recalled attending a harangue in which a relic monger was advertising his wares in Laon. He was holding up before the appreciative crowd a little box which, he said, contained a piece of the very bread which Our Lord chewed at the Last Supper. Then, seeing Guibert in the audience, he pointed him out and exclaimed: 'there is a distinguished man, famous for his learning. He will confirm that I am telling the truth.' To his eternal shame, Guibert was frightened and simply blushed and held his peace. Contemporaries do not seem to have been greatly disturbed by such incidents. It was generally agreed that it was no sin to honour the relics of one saint under the honest impression that it was another, and even Guibert of Nogent was of the opinion that a man who in good faith revered as a holy relic something which was not, might nevertheless enjoy some merit in God's eyes. A story told by the German Cistercian Caesarius of Heisterbach suggests that God even worked miracles through false relics venerated in ignorance.

The problem caused embarrassment only when two churches claimed to possess the same relic. This commonly occurred when a church had lost its relics by theft, fraud, or force; it would then claim that the wrong relics had been taken in error. The confusion which followed was, in a sense, the penalty which the thief had to pay for his success. In some cases the thief does appear to have taken the wrong relic. Odo of Bayeux, for example, who bought the relics of St. Exupéry from a venal sacristan of Corbeil, was given the body of a peasant of the same name. Fulbert, bishop of Cambrai, practised a similar fraud in the tenth century when the emperor Otto I demanded the relics of two canonized bishops of Cambrai in order to enrich the city of Magdeburg. Fulbert gave him the bodies of two ordinary priests together with a few trappings from the graves of the saints. At the end of the eleventh century the monks of Monte Cassino claimed to have discovered the body of St. Benedict beneath the rubble during the rebuilding of their church, and the controversy which then erupted was still raging fiercely in the nineteenth century. The achievement of the Barians in acquiring the relics of St. Nicholas was so spectacular that others inevitably tried to deflect some of the glory to themselves. In every part of Europe churches announced that they had obtained part of the body of St Nicholas. A monk of Angers made off with the arm of the saint, which had been detached from the rest of the body and sheathed with silver for use in blessing crowds. But he was unable to escape to France and the relic ultimately came into the possession of the abbey of the Trinity at Venosa. Within a few months the abbot of Angers nevertheless announced that the attempt had in fact succeeded and the arm was in his church. The sailors who had brought the body from Myra gave it out that they had retained the saint's teeth and fragments of his tomb; a Norman pilgrim bought some of them in 1092 and gave them to the church of St. Peter at Noron. The Venetians claimed that the Barians had left half of the body behind at Myra, which they solemnly translated to Venice in 1099. Almost every successful pilgrimage provoked competition from imposters. The much-visited shrines on the routes to Santiago all had determined rivals who provoked the indignation of the author of the *Guide for Pilgrims to Santiago.* The church of St.-Léonard de Noblat was afflicted with a rival body set up by the monks of Corbigny, who attributed all St. Leonard's miracles to their own relics. St. Gilles was claimed by at least four churches in addition to the celebrated Provençal monastery which bore his name: 'Shame upon the Hungarians for claiming part of his body. Curses upon the monks of Chamalières who imagine that they have the whole body. The same to the people of St.-Seine who boast of his head, and to the Normans who actually display a body purporting to be his. For it is quite impossible that a single particle of the holy body could ever have left its hallowed tomb.'

Such impostures usually made little or no impression on the flow of pilgrims to old-established shrines. But there were exceptions, of which the most interesting is perhaps the pilgrimage to the shrine of St. Mary Magdalene. During the eleventh century the belief arose that Mary Magdalene was buried in the abbey church of Vézelay, which consequently grew from an impoverished religious backwater in an isolated corner of Burgundy into a powerful and wealthy monastery. The monks encouraged this improbable belief and put about a legend designed to explain how the body came to be there. According to this story Mary expiated her sins after Christ's death by taking ship for France and exiling herself in the Provençal desert. When she died she was buried in what is now the town of St.-Maximin la Sainte-Baume, until in the middle of the eighth century the place was deserted by its inhabitants and the saint's remains transferred to Vézelay. Such was the legend which was commonly received in the eleventh and twelfth centuries. But the great age of Vézelay ended at the beginning of the thirteenth century. The days when Vézelay had seen the launching of the second crusade and the departure of the third were no more. Disputes within the monastery, constant warfare with the counts of Nevers and the citizens of the *bourg,* and heavy papal taxes had eroded the abbey's wealth. In 1279 the monks of St.-Maximin took advantage of the troubles of Vézelay and turned the Burgundian legend to their own use. On December 9 they announced that they had discovered the body of the Magdalene in their crypt. A 'suave odour' emitting from the sarcophagus and an authoritative inscription permitted no doubt as to its authenticity and it was immediately put about that the monks of Vézelay had taken the wrong body in the eighth century. Charles of Salerno, count of Provence, was only too pleased to promote a major pilgrimage within his dominions and five months later he presided over a splendid ceremony at which the newly found relics were displayed to a gathering of princes and ecclesiastical dignitaries. St.-Maximin seems to have been accepted immediately as the true resting place of the Magdalene, and Vézelay entirely forgotten. Boniface VIII proclaimed several indulgences in favour of the Provençal shrine, and large numbers of pilgrims hastened to take advantage of them. So matters rested until the cult of Mary

Magdalene sank into obscurity during the later Middle Ages, and pilgrims ceased to care where the penitent of Judaea was buried.

Disputes such as these have a somewhat unreal appearance, for in almost every case neither relic would survive modern critical scrutiny. Procedures for verifying the authenticity of relics consisted rather in a dramatic assertion of belief than a scientific examination of the evidence. When, in the mid-eleventh century, the monks of St. Emmeran at Regensburg raised pretentions to possess the body of St. Denis the Areopagite, the reaction of the abbot of St.-Denis near Paris was to open the shrine of the abbey church in the presence of a crowd of bishops, abbots, and noblemen, including several members of the royal family, and to declare with great solemnity that its contents were authentic. The claim of St.-Denis to the body of the martyr was constantly disputed by other churches, and the monks invariably replied with imposing ceremonies at which their own relics were publicly displayed. In 1186 the canons of the church of St. Stephen in Paris 'discovered' the head of St.-Denis in their own church. The monks of the royal abbey were outraged, and when their complaints fell on deaf ears they separated the head from the body and exposed it in a separate reliquary for a whole year. It may be assumed that before the relics were publicly displayed they were surreptitiously examined to ensure that all was well. Indeed, when abbot Suger failed to take this elementary precaution before the ceremonial opening of a reliquary, he was rebuked by his monks, who declared that 'it would have been better for the reputation of the abbey if we had secretly ascertained in advance whether the description on the labels was true.'

Despite the elaborate stage management of these proceedings the populace took a passionate interest in them, and seems to have been readily convinced. Any suggestion that a relic of note was false or had been stolen provoked intense public concern. The object of the ceremonies was therefore to create an atmosphere of popular enthusiasm in which the doubts of individuals would be silenced. In 1162, for example, a rumour spread in Paris that the head of St. Genevieve, the city's patron saint, was missing from its reliquary in the church dedicated to her. Within hours riotous mobs had gathered at the church. Louis VII threatened to have the canons of St. Genevieve flogged and expelled from their posts, while the archbishop of Sens announced his intention of holding a solemn examination of the relics. On the appointed day the king and the royal family, together with civil and ecclesiastical dignitaries, watched from a specially erected stand as the archbishop and his suffragans opened the reliquary and pulled out the head intact. This was immediately accepted by the crowd as proof, and the prior of St. Genevieve led them in a spontaneous rendering of the *Te Deum*. Some of the officiating bishops were, however, disturbed at this unexpected change in the protocol of the ceremony, and remained unconvinced of the relic's authenticity. Manasses, bishop of Orléans, demanded to know who had given them permission to sing, and pointed out that the head in the reliquary might not be that of St. Genevieve, but a substitute placed there by the monks. The prior offered to prove the authenticity of the head by carrying it over a bed of burning coals, but his faith was not put to the test. The bishop's objections were drowned by the singing and the archbishop of Sens peremptorily ordered him to be silent. The prior's biographer remarks with satisfaction that Manasses was shortly afterwards ejected from his diocese and struck down by the Lord in condign punishment for his presumption. But the truth is less dramatic. The bishop survived for twenty-five years in his see and died peacefully in his bed at an advanced age.

A miracle constituted certain proof of the authenticity of a relic and a common method of testing relics was to provoke one. In the 830s Erchanbert, bishop of Friesing, ordered the clergy of his diocese to fast for three days when doubts had arisen about a relic of St. Felix; 'and by this means we hope that we will become worthy of a sign from Almighty God indicating whether the Devil has been deceiving us.' According to a Canterbury legend, four Norman monks once offered some bones of St. Ouen to King Edgar, promising to prove them genuine by provoking miracles. 'We can prove it in any manner you suggest by casting them in the fire, for example, and withdrawing them unharmed. And if no such miracle occurs then we will admit that the relics are false and that we are outrageous liars deserving of all the penalties of the law.' Ultimately it was agreed that a leper should be brought in and touched with one of the bones, and when the leper was immediately healed 'the whole company fell on their knees in thanksgiving for the merits of St. Ouen.' The story has no historical basis, but it is eloquent of the frame of mind of its twelfth-century author.

Casting relics in the fire was the simplest method of provoking a miracle and was widely practised, particularly in the early mediaeval period. In 979 Egbert, bishop of Trier, doubting the authenticity of the body of St. Celsus, broke off a finger joint and threw it into a brazier of burning coals, where it remained unharmed throughout the canon of the Mass. The monks of Monte Cassino, who possessed a piece of the cloth with which Christ washed the feet of the disciples, placed it in a red hot crucible where 'it changed to the colour of fire but as soon as it was removed from the coals it reverted to its original appearance.' A great crowd gathered to watch Meinwerk, bishop of Paderborn, putting St. Felix to the ordeal of fire. Again, when the townsmen of Clermont-en-Beauvaisis entertained doubts about the arm of St. Arnoul they cast it in the fire and it immediately jumped out again. Crude tests of this sort were generally applied when large numbers of relics were suspected. In the sixth century, for example, numerous churches were recovered from the Arian heretics and converted to Catholic use. They were usually found to contain relics of unknown provenance, and the second council of Saragossa in 592 officially sanctioned the use of fire to test them. A variety of methods were employed after the Norman conquest of England to test relics of the unknown saints venerated by the Anglo-Saxons. Indeed, the constant attempt to provoke miracles was by no means peculiar to the Middle Ages. Anna Gonzaga, dowager countess palatine of the Rhine, who died in 1685, left to the abbey of St. Germain a piece of the True Cross 'que j'atteste avoir veue clans les flammes sans bruler.'

3

The Saints and Their Relics

Heretics and Cynics

Individual relics might be discredited, minor abuses exposed, but opposition to the cult of relics as such was extremely rare. The same pressures of mass belief which enabled spurious relics to be venerated as genuine without exciting protest, applied *a fortiori* to stifle objections to a practice which was so basic to mediaeval religious life.

Levity and popular irreverence in the face of the saints there sometimes was. But even this was limited by the over-powering conventions of religious life of which the most powerful was that the saints, being possessed of a will of their own, mercilessly chastised those who mocked them. Gerald of Wales, in pointing out the extreme devotion of the Welsh to relics, explained that 'owing to a certain occult power granted to all relics by God, and owing to the special vindictiveness of Welsh saints, those who despise them are usually punished.' Cautionary tales describing these punishments can be found in almost every surviving collection of miracle stories. Out of the 139 stories by five different authors in the *Miracles of St. Benedict*, approximately half deal with the fate of those who scoffed at the saint, ignored his feast day, invaded the lands of his abbey, and so on. William of Malmesbury remembered from his childhood how a boy who laughed at a cortège of monks bearing the relics of St. Aldhelm was thereupon tortured by demons. Some courtiers who scoffed at the body of St. Evroul were forthwith struck dead by a thunderbolt. The man who spoke slightingly of St. Emmeram found that his tongue adhered to his palate, while the woman who 'raising her clothing displayed her posterior to the saint, behaviour which God on no account allows to pass unpunished' was afflicted with hideous ulcers. Contempt for the relics of the saints was regularly visited with dumbness, bodily distortion, disease, madness, and death.

If educated men ever expressed criticisms of the cult of relics, their opinions have rarely survived. The mediaeval Church vigorously suppressed heterodox writings and until the later Middle Ages the views of non-conformists are generally known only through the writings of their opponents. From this source we know that there existed in the fourth and fifth centuries a substantial body of opinion which totally rejected the cult of relics. It is also clear that opposition to the veneration of relics was characteristic of many heresies. The iconoclastic disputes which engulfed the Greek Church in the eighth century affected relics as well as icons. Constantine V, the second of the iconoclastic emperors, conducted a vigorous campaign against relics held by the monasteries of the capital. The iconoclastic position on images and relics was condemned by the council of Nicaea in 787, but it found several sympathizers in the west, particularly among the Franks. Claudius, bishop of Turin, denounced all pilgrimages to the relics of the saints and broke or burnt crosses venerated in his diocese; he was regarded by his contemporaries as a heretic and vigorously condemned by a synod at Paris in 825. In Spain, objections to the cult of relics emanated from the numerous groups of monophysites and manichaeans who had fled from their persecutors in the east. The council of Cordova in 839 was greatly concerned with the activities of a group called 'acephalites' whose errors included the rejection of the veneration of relics. But until the fourteenth century these opinions never attained any importance in the west. Such disputes as did occur were usually pale reflections of controversies in the eastern Church, and these had themselves been silenced by the end of the ninth century. With a single exception, orthodox writers rarely considered the spiritual basis of the cult of relics and never criticized it.

The single exception is Guibert of Nogent, whose writings constitute a remarkable corpus of evidence for almost every aspect of the religious life of his day. Guibert, who died in about 1125, was the abbot of Nogent-sous-Coucy near Laon. He was a prolific writer whose works included an autobiography with unusually introspective details, a treatise in honour of the Virgin, a number of Biblical commentaries, and a history of the first Crusade. He also wrote a treatise *On the Relics of the Saints* in which he examined some of the relics venerated in his own day in the most acid and critical tone. Guibert applied to relics the critical standards developed by Christian scholarship in connection with Biblical exegesis, and he concluded that many of them were wholly unreasonable and based on insecure historical foundations. This, together with his passionate nationalism and fascinating prejudices, has procured for him the unanimous acclaim of historians, one of whom has indeed compared him to Calvin, Rabelais, and Voltaire.

The historian of popular religion owes much to Guibert's book, but to contemporaries it passed entirely unnoticed. It survives in only one manuscript which, moreover, came from Guibert's own abbey of Nogent, and it is never referred to by other mediaeval writers. Although it surveys the whole field of popular religion, its purpose was limited to exposing a particular relic, a milk-tooth of Christ preserved at the abbey of St. Médard at Soissons. The monks of St. Médard had, it seems, issued a pamphlet advertising the miracles of the tooth. Guibert had no difficulty in demolishing this booklet without straying from the line of strict theological orthodoxy. The Christian's hopes of salvation depended on the doctrine of the resurrection, which could not be completely true if a single particle of Christ's earthly body remained on earth. The only true relic of Christ was therefore the Eucharist which contained Him altogether and was incompatible with the existence of any other relics. To these conventional theological arguments, Guibert added historical ones. Since Christ would not have appeared particularly remarkable to his contemporaries until the beginning of his ministry, no one would have troubled to collect relics of his childhood. Guibert was not impressed by the miracles claimed for the tooth. There was no evidence to connect them with this relic rather than another. Indeed, God might work miracles through the relics of notorious sinners as easily as through the bodies of the saints. In the course of his argument Guibert warms to his subject and mentions other relics of doubtful authenticity. The two heads of John the Baptist and the two bodies of St. Firmin are the object of some scathing comments. The milk of the Virgin preserved in a crystal vase at Laon is condemned as an imposture. The absurdities of several contemporary collections are exposed.

Guibert had no objection to the cult of relics as such. His own abbey of Nogent claimed to possess pieces of the rope which bound Christ to the whipping post and of the scourges that struck his body, together with fragments of the crown of thorns, a portion of the True Cross, and a few shreds of the tunic of the Virgin. In his autobiography, Guibert defends the authenticity of these objects with the most improbable of stories. Guibert was in fact very selective in the relics which he attacked, and we cannot rule out the possibility that he was motivated by some unknown quarrel with those who possessed them. He defended, for example, the authenticity of the Holy Lance of Antioch which his contemporary, Fulcher of Chartres, had questioned. Indeed, in the treatise on relics Guibert asserted that the veneration of genuine relics was wholly justifiable: 'that which is connected with the divine is itself divine, and nothing can be more closely connected with the divine than God's saints who are of one body with him.' Guibert's quarrel was against the lax standards which his contemporaries applied when assessing the authenticity of relics. In the first place many popular saints did not exist, and of others nothing whatever was known. The Church was beginning to apply stringent tests before recognizing a saint. It had, for example, refused to proclaim the bodily assumption of the Virgin on account of the lack of evidence, a commendable reserve, abandoned in the twentieth century. The populace, however, was satisfied with miracles reported by ignorant men or visions vouchsafed to hermits. The Church might refuse to sanction doubtful cults, but it was in no position to resist them, for by permitting the translation and dismemberment of bodies it had allowed the destruction of the only conclusive evidence.

The basis of Guibert's views on relics was his devotion to the inner and spiritual life. In his other works he stresses the value of preaching and confession and of all spiritual exercises which held up a mirror to the faithful in which they might see their inward souls. He sought to create an 'inward world where nothing is either high or low or localized, where there is neither time nor place.' By contrast, in the world which he actually saw around him, popular piety was based on the wholly accidental location of the relics of the saints.

The Body of Christ

The excesses of which Guibert complained were largely a popular phenomenon. The official doctrines of the Church, created in the earliest centuries of its existence and formalized by the thirteenth-century schoolmen, never made any direct impact on popular piety. Orthodox theology was purveyed to ordinary people by a lengthy and indirect route and was considerably distorted in the process. Such religious education as the populace received was based on the teaching of ritual formulae and above all on stories, or *exempla*, from the lives and miracles of the saints. All these had the effect of greatly simplifying doctrinal issues and often unintentionally encouraged heterodox notions. In particular they encouraged the uneducated to look on the mysteries of the faith in a somewhat literal and pictorial fashion. Religious thought, in Johann Huizinga's brilliant phrase, 'crystallized into images'.

The transformation of the bread and wine at the consecration into the body and blood of Christ was constantly misunderstood, and as early as the fifth century stories were current in which the host literally turned to flesh and the wine to blood. A tenth-century writer related that Gregory the Great once settled the doubts of a woman who had confessed to him that she was unable to understand how God could be really present in the Eucharist. He told her that she would see the mystery with her own eyes and thereupon transformed the host into flesh on the altar before her, 'and all who saw it were overcome with the love of God and faith in the orthodox doctrine.' Guibert of Nogent reported that the figure of a small boy had been seen in the host in a small town near Soissons, and a similar miracle is described by Peter the Venerable. Jacques de Vitry tells of a woman who kept the host in her mouth for later use and found that it turned to flesh and adhered to her palate so that she could not speak. In the fourteenth and fifteenth centuries such stories multiplied prodigiously, and at a popular level they appear to have been accepted as a normal incident of daily life. The *Pupilla Oculi,* an English manual for ordinary parish priests, warns its readers of the possibility of such occurrences, as also does the *Summa Angelica,* an Italian production of the fifteenth century. In the Netherlands it was considered inadvisable to cut the host lest the body of Christ be damaged. George Carter, a servant of the abbey of Sawtrey who was examined for heresy in 1525, asserted that the host had a special band around it to prevent the blood from dripping out and that this notion was universally received amongst his acquaintances. The bishop's chancellor 'moved him otherwise to believe'.

In the later Middle Ages the doctrine of the immaculate conception and the mystery of the Trinity were literally portrayed in statues and popular devotional pictures. These were not usually works of art and few of them have survived, but several contemporaries have left descriptions of them. The dukes of Burgundy, for example, possessed a small gold statuette of the Virgin, whose body could be opened to reveal the Trinity inside. Jean Gerson saw another in the Carmelite convent in Paris and was horrified, not, it seems, because of the crudeness of this literal image of the miracle, but because of the heresy of representing all three persons of the Trinity as the fruit of the Blessed Virgin. Many churches in southern France and Spain had scenes of the Visitation carved in wood, in which the abdomen of both the Virgin and St. Elizabeth were open, revealing Christ and John the Baptist within. Some had little mechanisms whereby the stomachs might be opened and closed at will.

The relics of Christ's body afford the clearest example of the distortion of orthodox theology by popular imagination. The official position on such relics was that the doctrine of the resurrection was incompatible with the existence on earth of any bodily relics of the Saviour. On this ground Guibert of Nogent denounced the tooth of Christ at Soissons as a fabrication, and Thomas Aquinas expressed doubts about the blood of Christ venerated at Bruges. The relics of Christ preserved at Rome caused some embarrassment to Innocent III: 'What shall we say', he asked, 'of the foreskin or umbilical cord which were severed from His body at birth? Were they too resurrected?... Perhaps it is better to leave the resolution of such problems to God.' In the course of the late mediaeval period these theological scruples were slowly overcome in response to the strong popular demand for relics of the Lord. The earliest class of relics to achieve theological respectability included those which were separated from the Lord's body during his lifetime. Such, for example, were his foreskin, umbilical cord, and conceivably the milk-tooth conserved at Soissons. The umbilical cord and foreskin were already preserved in the Lateran basilica in the eleventh century, and the official explanation of their origin was that they had been spirited from Jerusalem by an angel and presented to Charlemagne at

Aachen, whence they had been brought to Rome by Charles the Bald. These relics were seen in the Lateran by generations of pilgrims but were clearly regarded with some misgivings by the Popes. At the end of the fourteenth century the Swedish visionary St. Bridget enjoyed a revelation in which the Virgin assured her of their authenticity and this seems to have carried some weight. The foreskin was removed by a German *lanzknecht* during the sack of Rome in 1527 and subsequently lost. The Lateran basilica contained by far the most celebrated relics of Christ's body venerated during the Middle Ages. But it had several rivals. At the very end of the eleventh century the monastery of Charroux in Poitou claimed to possess a foreskin, and based its claim on a legend which is clearly modelled on the Roman one. This relic enjoyed an uneven popularity for four centuries until the destruction of the church by the Huguenots in the 1560s, and there was even a brief attempt to revive the cult in the nineteenth century. Another foreskin was venerated in the Benedictine abbey of Coulombs: it was sent to England in 1421 in the baggage of Henry V's bride, Catherine of France, in the hope that it would bring good fortune on her marriage bed. Pope Martin V proclaimed an indulgence for a foreskin at Boulogne, while at Antwerp another had made its appearance by the beginning of the fifteenth century.

The blood of Christ was venerated in a growing number of churches after the eleventh century. A phial of Christ's blood was discovered in Mantua as early as 804, and created a profound sensation. Charlemagne asked the pope to investigate its authenticity but the outcome of this inquiry and the subsequent fate of the relic are not known. However, the memory of the event was revived when a second phial of blood was unearthed in the garden of the hospice of St. Andrew in Mantua in 1048. On this occasion, the cult took root, and Mantua became an important stage on the pilgrim's route to Rome. We do not know how the clergy of Mantua explained the existence of their relic or reconciled it with the doctrine of the resurrection. But when relics of the blood of Christ began to multiply in the thirteenth century, the commonest explanation given was that the blood had been miraculously exuded by a eucharistic host or an image of the Lord struck by heretics or Jews. This legend, which has an ancient lineage, served to account for the relics of the Divine Blood exhibited in many western churches in the late Middle Ages, especially in the Low Countries. A typical variation on the theme was given out by the clergy of Aasche in the fourteenth century. A woman had been inveigled by the Jews into stealing a consecrated host one Easter Sunday, but on the way home she took fright and hastily buried the incriminating host in a tree trunk at the side of the road. There it bled profusely until the inhabitants of the area alerted the local clergy, who took the bloodstained wood away and preserved it in the church at Aasche. Stories of this kind were already commonplace in the time of Thomas Aquinas who declares them to be theologically sound, though he does not speak of them with any enthusiasm. A number of churches traced the origin of their phials of blood to the celebrated wooden statue of Christ at Beirut which had begun to bleed when pierced with nails by Jews. A small quantity of it kept by the Franciscans of La Rochelle aroused 'certain dissentions' in the diocese, which were referred in 1448 to the arbitration of the University of Paris. The faculty of theology declared that the veneration of the blood was in no way repugnant to the faith, and their opinion was confirmed by pope Nicholas V.

More controversial was the blood which was alleged to come from the very wounds of Christ. This Thomas Aquinas declared to be impossible. But several churches, notably the Norman abbey of the Trinity at Fécamp, claimed to possess it, and when a vase of blood was presented to Henry III of England by the military orders in 1247, Robert Grosseteste applied his considerable scholarship to its defence. Nothing was more probable, he argued than that when Christ was taken down from the cross, His blood had splashed over Nicodemus and Joseph of Arimathea. Grosseteste listed five occasions when His blood had been shed and suggested that the disciples would naturally have gathered it up and preserved it.

In the fourteenth and fifteenth centuries churches which displayed the divine blood found powerful defenders in the Franciscan order, which had espoused the cult of the Passion of Our Lord since its inception. In 1351 the Franciscan prior of Barcelona stated in a public sermon that the blood shed at the crucifixion thereupon lost its divinity and so remained on earth after the resurrection. He was immediately prosecuted by the Inquisitor of Aragon and obliged to make a humiliating retraction. But more than a century later another Franciscan, Giacomo della Marca, revived the forbidden doctrine in a sermon at Brescia and was accused by the Dominicans of heresy. In December 1463 a formal debate between representatives of the two orders was held in the presence of Pius V, at which the matter was argued with such vehemence that although it was December the protagonists were shortly bathed in sweat. As the Franciscans pointed out, the relics venerated at Rome, Mantua, Bruges, and countless lesser shrines depended on the outcome. Perhaps it was for this reason that the jury of cardinals adjourned the debate, and no decision was ever made public.

This softening of the official attitude was the result of continuous popular pressure. The great processions in honour of the Holy Blood at Bruges were spectacular displays of popular devotion, and the plebeian nature of such cults was increasingly recognized by the growing band of critics. John Hus observed that there were now 'innumerable places where the Devil has moved the people through the wickedness of greedy priests to worship the body and blood of the Lord as a relic'. It was in the fourteenth century that the practice began of displaying the host from the altar in a monstrance. Tabernacles made their appearance at the same time, where the Eucharist would be placed for the adoration of the faithful instead of being left in the sacristy between services.

The extensive devotional literature surrounding the pilgrimage to the Holy Blood at Fécamp demonstrates beyond doubt that belief in the bodily relics of Christ was a form of eucharistic piety. The blood of Fécamp was already venerated in 1120 when Baudri of Deuil visited the abbey of the Trinity and remarked on 'the blood of Christ, buried by Nicodemus,...and now solemnly revered by large crowds of pilgrims'. In a twelfth-century poem composed for the abbey, pilgrims are urged to come to win their redemption at Fécamp by beholding the precious blood of Christ 'not as you do in the sacrament but just as it flowed from the Saviour's side when be died for us':

Non pas comment au sacrement
Mes en sa fourme proprement
Vermel comment il le sengna
Quant pour nous mort soufrir degna.

The same passionate desire to translate the mysteries of the faith into realities is reflected in every aspect of the cult of relics. Ordinary people looked on the saints as individuals no less immediate, no less visible and tangible in death than they had been in life. It was essential to this view of things that a saint should be considered to inhabit the place where his or her relics were preserved, and in that place should above all be venerated. Hence the fact, observed in the fifteenth century by Reynold Pecock, that many of those who went on pilgrimages to Mont-St.-Michel expected to find there the bones of the archangel. From this Pecock drew the perceptive conclusion that 'without rememorative signs of a thing,...the rememoration or remembrance of that thing...must needs be feebler, as experience sufficiently witnesseth. And therefore, since the body, or the bones, or other relics of any person is a full rememorative sign of the same person, it is full reasonable and full worthy that where the body or bones or any relic of a saint may be had, it be set up in a common place to which people may have their devout...access.'

The process by which the veneration of the saints became associated with particular places is especially striking in the case of the Virgin Mary. The earliest collections of miracles of the Virgin, which date from the early twelfth century, were not associated with any particular sanctuary. The stories are set as far apart as Germany and Spain, Pisa and Mont-St.-Michel, and in none of them is there any question of relics. Pilgrimages to shrines of the Virgin were common in the east, but there is no mention of them in the west until the tenth century, when a monk of Bobbio observed that the Blessed Virgin frequently worked miracles for the benefit of those who came to the abbey of St. Columban with their troubles. Bodily relics of the Virgin were almost unknown, and thus when Geoffrey de Montbray, bishop of Coutances (d. 1110) discovered some of her hair in his cathedral, accompanied by imposing certificates of authenticity, some of the canons objected on the ground that 'hitherto no relic of the Virgin was known to exist on earth.' The popularity of the cult of the Virgin spread rapidly in the twelfth century, and as it did so countless relics came into existence. Laon cathedral had a 'splendid little reliquary' containing some hair of the Virgin at the beginning of the twelfth century, when it was carried about England and northern France to raise money for the rebuilding of the cathedral. More hair existed at Astorga in northern Spain; this caused some astonishment to Ida, countess of Boulogne, who arranged for eleven of the hairs to be sent to Boulogne and subjected them to the ordeal of fire. Most early relics of the Virgin consisted of parts of her clothing. The most celebrated of these was undoubtedly the tunic preserved in Chartres cathedral, which had a mass following in northern France, and was believed to ease the pains of pregnancy. But others, sometimes older than that of Chartres, were claimed by churches in Germany and eastern France. The bishops of Verdun possessed a tunic, 'somewhat battered and torn', in the tenth century, while another is found at Munchsmunster in a list of relics compiled in 1092. Other tunics were venerated at Regensburg and Trier at the same time. The church of S. Maria Maggiore in Rome was alleged to have a large number of relics of the Nativity, including the original crib, together with parts of the Virgin's hair, milk, and clothing. Milk of the Virgin made its appearance in the same period, though the days of its greatest popularity were yet to come. The famous *arca santa* of Oviedo Cathedral was believed to contain a phial of milk of the Virgin; it is one of the items listed on the inscription which Alfonso VI caused to be engraved on the outside in 1075. The relic list of

Munchsmunster includes 'milk of the Virgin which flowed from her breast', presumably labelled thus in order to distinguish it from 'miraculous' milk which was already appearing at Chartres and elsewhere.

Thus the first result of the popularization of the cult of the Virgin during the eleventh and twelfth centuries was that the cult became 'localized' in a number of relatively new shrines. Pilgrimages did not, of course, supersede other forms of devotion to the Virgin, but they were the principal means by which that devotion was expressed by uneducated people. These people did not see the Virgin as the ubiquitous power, uncramped by time or place, who was venerated by St. Anselm or St. Bernard. To them she was Our Lady of Chartres or Our Lady of Soissons, and the distinction between them loomed large in the eyes of contemporaries. The author of the *Miracles of Our Lady of Chartres* tells of a lady of Audignecourt who was cured of a skin disease by praying to the Virgin. As she was about to set out for Notre-Dame de Soissons to give thanks, the Virgin appeared to inform her that it was by Notre-Dame de Chartres that she had been healed. The purpose of the miracle collection of Rocamadour was declared to be to demonstrate that 'the Blessed Virgin Mary has chosen Rocamadour in Quercy above all other churches'. The enemies of Coutances cathedral attempted to dissuade a pilgrim from going there by asking her, 'why go to a strange church to seek the help of the Blessed Virgin whose power is universal and could just as easily cure you in your own home?' But they were confounded when the woman returned, fully cured, from Coutances. Indeed, the author of the Coutances miracle collection devoted much of his work to refuting opinions of this sort. He pointed, for example, to the fate of Vitalis, a Norman who came to the 'insipid conclusion' that 'the Blessed Mary of Bayeux and the Blessed Mary of Coutances were one and the same person, that is, the mother of God; and that consequently the Virgin of Coutances could not possibly be more merciful or more powerful than the Virgin of Bayeux.' Vitalis accordingly refused to accompany his fellow villagers on a mass pilgrimage to Coutances, for which the Virgin severely chastised him. Already pilgrims had accepted a plurality of Virgins inhabiting defined places, the view caricatured in the pleasant conversation once overheard by Sir Thomas More: '"of all Our Ladies, I love best Our Lady of Walsingham"; "and I", saith the other, "Our Lady of Ipswich."'

The Image of the Saint

Saints were physically present in the altars of their churches. When a saint's relics moved, he moved with them. He was the protector of the sanctuary, and offerings were made to him personally. The saint was quite capable of defending his property from the shrine. Thus, when, shortly after 946, the monks of Fleury quarrelled with the bishop of Orléans over the possession of a vineyard, they came to harvest the grapes bringing with them the remains of St. Benedict, whereupon the soldiers posted there by the bishop made way and departed. The monks of Bobbio brought the body of St. Columban to the royal court of Pavia in order to complain about the invasion of their lands by powerful noblemen. The notion of the saint residing in his reliquary is literally portrayed in the stained glass of Canterbury cathedral, where St. Thomas is seen climbing out of his shrine in order to appear to a sleeping monk.

The very atmosphere of a pilgrimage church encouraged the impression of the saint's physical presence. From the eighth century onwards relics were placed on the altar in the east end of the church, or else in a crypt designed for that purpose. At Santiago, Conques, St. Sernin of Toulouse, and St. Martin of Tours there were vast double aisles through which, on feast days, superb processions made their way towards the gilded shrine. The sense of the saint's latent power was often fostered by the fact that his or her relics were contained in a statue. These statue-reliquaries originated in southern France in the tenth century. Stephen, bishop of Clermont, ordered a statue of the Blessed Virgin in 946 to house some of her relics. Stephen was also the abbot of Conques in the Rouergue, whose monks had recently stolen the relics of St. Foy from Agen, and it seems likely that he commissioned the celebrated statue-reliquary which is still preserved there. The Conques statue, which is of gold encrusted with precious stones, shows St. Foy seated on a throne stretching out hands which once held a model of the grid on which she had supposedly been martyred. It survives as a solitary reminder of the enormous number of such statues which were once venerated in southern France. At the synod of Rodez in 1013, Bernard of Angers, a stranger to the south, described how each church was represented by its clergy carrying the statue-reliquary of its patron saint beneath a splendid canopy: St. Armand of Rodez, St. Marius of Vabres, St. Sernin of Toulouse, a golden statue of the Virgin, and St. Foy herself were all carried processionally round the walls of the city before the opening of the council. "Hitherto', Bernard wrote, 'I have always believed that the veneration of images and paintings of the saints was improper, and to raise statues to them would have struck me as absurd. But this is not the belief of the inhabitants of these parts, where every church contains a statue of its patron made of gold, silver, or base metal, depending on the wealth of the church. And inside it they place the head or some other important relic of the saint...Jupiter or Mars might well have been venerated like this.'The statue of St. Foy was a potent means of impressing the saint's presence not only on pilgrims but on the population of the remotest valleys of the Auvergne. Whenever the possessions of the abbey were threatened or an epidemic ravaged the area, the statue was drawn through the valleys mounted on a horse and surrounded by young monks clashing cymbals and blowing ivory horns. The inhabitants of the villages would gather at the side of the road on these occasions, and in an atmosphere of extreme religious excitement repeated cries would signal the occurrence of new miraculous cures.

These reliquaries, which so faithfully reflected the popular piety of the tenth and eleventh centuries, passed out of fashion in the twelfth. Few of them have survived. But at one time they were venerated not only in the Midi but throughout northern France and even in England. A gold statue-reliquary with one hand outstretched in blessing was made for the abbey of St. Martial of Limoges in 952. The famous black wooden statue of the Virgin at Chartres (the existing one is a copy of it) may have been modelled on that of Conques. A statue-reliquary was venerated at St. Bertin in the late eleventh century, and in England bishop Brithnod of Ely had four of them made for his cathedral out of gilded wood. Even after the pilgrimage churches had ceased to commission new statue-reliquaries, artistic representations of the saints continued to exercise a potent influence on the popular imagination. When Guibert of Nogent's mother dreamed of the Blessed Virgin she dreamed of the Virgin of Chartres cathedral. Witbert, the blind peasant whose sight was restored by St. Foy, had a vision of her corresponding exactly to the statue-reliquary which can be seen today at Conques. Similarly when a young monk of Monte Cassino saw St. Michael taking away the soul of a dead brother, he saw him 'exactly as he is usually depicted by painters'. Indeed, it seems possible that the special reputation which St. Foy acquired for healing the blind was due in part to the staring jewelled eyes of her statue at Conques.

The cult of relics brings into sharp relief the classic problem of the mediaeval Church. It has often been accused by enlightened historians of fostering popular superstition and resisting the intellectual development of the laity. Usually this has been attributed to the avarice of the clergy and indeed there are many mediaeval writers who could be found to support such a view. Nevertheless it overlooks the fact that the mediaeval Church not only did not but could not control and direct popular religion. In the broadest sense of the word, it did not have the educational resources to convey anything but the most elementary formulae to the people en masse. For the most part the parish clergy must be regarded as splinters from the same wood as their parishioners, sharing their misconceptions and their simplified view of life. In fact, insofar as one can trace the movement of ideas in the history of mediaeval piety it is often in the reverse direction. Popular religious practices continually influence the behaviour of the establishment. With a few eminent exceptions such as Guibert of Nogent, few churchmen were found who appreciated this fact, still less made a conscious effort to resist it. The following chapter will show how popular influences of the same sort determined the attitude of the Church to miracles.

4

The Pursuit of the Miraculous

Until relatively recent times the overwhelming majority of people have believed in miracles. Mediaeval men and women in particular had no doubt that miraculous events occurred not occasionally but with such continuous regularity as to be almost part of the natural operation of the universe. Some of them indeed, intelligent and experienced individuals, not only described miracles of which they had heard but claimed to have witnessed them with their own eyes. Moreover the belief in the miraculous, although predominantly a characteristic of the mediaeval Church, is found in the ancient world as it is in the modern. Few mediaeval saints had as many miracles attributed to them as the Quaker leader George Fox who died at the end of the seventeenth century, leaving behind him a *Book of Miracles* recounting more than a hundred and fifty marvellous feats for the edification of his followers.

The phenomenon poses serious evidential problems which have, on the whole, exercised the minds of philosophers more than historians. More than two centuries ago David Hume disturbed the fat slumbers of the eighteenth-century Church by declaring in his *Essay on Miracles*—

'A miracle is a violation of the laws of nature; and as a firm and unalterable experience has established these laws, the proof against a miracle, from the very nature of the fact, is as entire as any argument from experience can possibly be imagined....The plain consequence is...that no testimony is sufficient to establish a miracle unless the testimony be of such a kind that its falsehood would be more miraculous than the fact which it endeavours to establish.'

Hume's argument turned on his definition of a miracle as a 'violation of the law of nature', a question-begging phrase which is open to legitimate theological objections. But the historian, limited by the evidence at his disposal, can only work on the basis that miracles have never happened, though the descriptions of them which contemporaries have left may provide valuable evidence of the attitudes of those who wrote them.

Hume was inclined to believe that the evidence for miracles was fabricated, either for missionary purposes or else for reasons of self-interest and greed. Self-interest and greed were, indeed, the principal explanations offered by the Protestant tradition for the phenomenon of mediaeval miracles. The view propagated by the Reformers was that miracles were concocted by a conspiracy of clergymen in order to induce simple men, who knew no better, to part with their money. This was the opinion of Thomas Cromwell, whose injunctions to the English clergy in 1536 require them to desist from such activities in future.

On the eve of the Reformation there was considerable evidence to support such a view, and the Church's critics made

full use of it. In his diatribe against the pilgrimage to Wilsnack,
John Hus alleged that the clergy paid handsome sums to beggars to wander from town to town announcing that they had
been cured or exorcized at Wilsnack. Hus had himself sat on a
tribunal convened by the archbishop of Prague to examine
those citizens of Prague who asserted that they had been cured
there. These included a boy whose deformed foot was found to
be worse than ever, and two women who were said to have
recovered their sight 'but who, on clear investigation, were
found never to have been blind.' One witness testified that after
three days and nights of fruitless vigils at Wilsnack he was suddenly seized by a priest who cried out 'A miracle! A miracle!
Come and see this citizen of Prague whose withered hand has
been healed.' 'O priest, why do you lie thus', the man exclaimed
with unusual presence of mind, 'see my hand is as withered as
ever.' On the eve of the Reformation many orthodox Catholics
were found who made similar allegations. Thomas More's
imaginary heretic gave it as his opinion that all miracles were
based on fraud, and More himself was constrained to admit that
this was sometimes true:

> 'Some priest, to bring up a pilgrimage in his parish, may
> devise some false fellow feigning himself to come and
> seek a saint in his church and there suddenly say that he
> hath gotten his sight. Then ye shall have bells rung for a
> miracle, and the fond folk of the country soon made
> fools. Then women coming thither with their candles.
> And the parson buying of some lame beggars three or
> four pair of their old crutches, with twelve pence spent
> in men and women of wax thrust through divers places
> some with arrows and some with rusty knives, will

make his offerings for one seven year worth twice his tithes.'

The commissioners for the dissolution of the English monasteries found some evidence that miracles were simulated by various histrionic contraptions. Such was the notorious rood of grace at Boxley, a life-size figure of Christ which rolled its eyes, shed tears, and foamed at the mouth and which was found to have 'certain engines and old wires with old rotten sticks in the back of the same'. John Hoker wrote to the Swiss reformer Bullinger exulting over the public destruction of a similar device from Kent which nodded its head, winked its eyes, and bowed at the waist to receive the prayers of pilgrims.

The rapid expansion of popular pilgrimages in the fifteenth century undoubtedly encouraged frauds, particularly in the smaller and less well-established shrines. The disappearance of all restraints on popular religious enthusiasm in the later Middle Ages deserves a chapter of its own. But to make an assessment of mediaeval religion solely on the basis of the last hundred and fifty years of its history is a seriously misleading procedure which, moreover, avoids the principal historical problem. For most of the period under consideration miracles were proclaimed without the assistance of elaborate mechanical devices and without obvious fraud. Moreover, the evidence for them was accepted by intelligent men who made some attempt to ascertain the truth. Evidently they were deluded, but the basis of their delusion is worth examining.

The Missionary Church

The missionaries who converted northern Europe were dealing with people whose religion was fundamentally pantheistic.

To them it seemed that the entire natural world was inhabited and controlled by unseen powers; every tree had its own spirit, every pool its devil, every mountain its god. This being so, there was no distinction drawn between the laws of nature and those of God, and the suspension of the one by the other did not arise. Insofar as pagans embraced Christianity they did so because they believed Christ to be a more powerful God than their own, and missionaries would endeavour to prove this, for example by felling the holy oak of Thor at Geismar and remaining unscathed. The converts expected the new God to intervene as often and as powerfully in nature as the old, and if He failed to do so they would frequently revert to their old beliefs. Thus, when plague attacked the region of Melrose in the time of St. Cuthbert the people 'forgot the sacrament of the Gospel which they had received and returned to the delusive cures of idolatory'. It was quite common for new converts to Christianity to continue to worship pagan gods, like Redwald king of the East Saxons, who used the same temple to worship Christ and offer sacrifices to devils. Such people insisted on miracles, and the Church was not willing to endanger the success of the missions by denying them. Gregory the Great recommended to Augustine that the cult of the saints and martyrs be presented to the English as the equivalent of pagan pantheism, 'for one cannot efface everything at once from their obstinate hearts. He who would climb the highest peaks must ascend by steps and not by leaps.'

Thus the first thing that was required of missionaries was the performance of miracles, and we are told that Augustine proved the truth of Christianity to king Ethelbert of Kent by working miracles daily, on which pope Gregory congratulated him: 'Rejoice that the souls of the English are drawn by outward miracles to inward grace.' No less decisive was the role of miracles in the conversion of Gaul. The only resurrection from the dead performed by St. Martin in his lifetime had the effect of converting a large body of pagans, and even the posthumous miracles of St. Martin were believed to have convinced heretics as well as pagans of the truth of the Catholic religion. According to St. Nizier, Clovis was brought nearer to the faith by an early visit to St, Martin's basilica at Tours, and it was after seeing evidence of the miracles performed there that he promised to be baptized. In a letter of about 565, addressed to Clovis' granddaughter, St. Nizier observed that 'such miracles never occur in Asian churches thus proving that God and his saints do not reside in them.' In this context the numerous exorcizings of demons were particularly important for 'no demon can survive in the habitation of the saints whence it follows that God resides in places where demons are exorcized.'

It was broadly recognized that miracles were necessary to assist the propagation of the faith, and that when the faith was established they would cease. Consequently each new missionary enterprise, every threat to the orthodox faith, convinced the Church that the age of miracles was not yet past, a process which can be clearly seen, for example, in the mind of Augustine of Hippo. In his treatise *On the True Faith* written in 390, Augustine asserted that the apostles had enjoyed power to work miracles in order to assist the foundation and expansion of the Church in the most vulnerable period of its history. 'But now that the Church is established across the whole world, miracles no longer occur.' However, in the face of powerful assaults on the orthodox creed by the Donatists and Pelagians, Augustine changed his mind, and in the last two decades of his life he made good use of the miracles of St. Stephen at Uzalis and Hippo, in support of Catholicism. Moreover, in describing these miracles Augustine was avowedly bidding for the support of precisely those popular elements in the Church which he had once despised. The problem of the cessation of miracles continued to perplex later generations. Gregory the Great compared miracles to the watering of plants. We water plants when we plant them but as soon as they have taken root we stop watering them. Similarly, now that Christianity has taken root in men's minds, we no longer have need of miracles. Yet Gregory's *Dialogues* are largely devoted to miracle stories, often of the most improbable kind. It is clear that in Gregory's mind there were two divergent tendencies, the theological (that there are no modern miracles) and the hagiographical (that for didactic purposes miracles continue). This dichotomy was very common amongst Gregory's contemporaries and while it survived no actual theory of miracles was possible.

In later generations the received view was that miracles would continue for as long as there were holy men alive. The age of miracles, thought Bede, had ended, but some men, by their extraordinary holiness, had recovered the power of working miracles which others had lost. In an unspeakably wicked age miracles would cease altogether. Orderic Vitalis, writing in the twelfth century, took this proposition for granted. In his view his own age was one of unparalleled wickedness, and he asserted that miracles had indeed ceased.

The true explanation of the continuance of miracles is that the plant of Christianity never took root as firmly as Gregory had hoped. At a popular level pantheistic notions survived throughout the mediaeval period, and constant efforts utterly failed to eradicate them. It is perhaps true, in the broadest possible sense, to speak of the Middle Ages as an 'age of faith', but it was an age of extremely varied and heterodox faith, in which the missionary aspect of the Church's work was kept alive by ignorance and heresy. With it survived those missionary attitudes which are so characteristic of the Church's teaching on miracles. Gregory of Tours once described a dispute on some doctrinal issue between an Arian preacher and a Catholic priest. When all argument had failed the priest ordered a cauldron of boiling water to be brought forward and said: 'enough of these futile arguments. Let works speak louder than words. Let us heat up a cauldron of boiling water and throw this ring into it. Whoever first takes the ring out with his bare hands will be proved right.' A theological argument in these circumstances took on the character of a trial by ordeal, and orthodoxy is said to have triumphed in such ordeals not only against Arians but later against Albigensians, Hussites, Protestants and even Muslims. Conflicts between rival magicians are frequently recorded in connection with the Albigensian heresy at the end of the twelfth century. Two heretics at Besançon, for example, attempted to impress their doctrines on the inhabitants by walking on flour without leaving footprints, jumping on burning coals, and standing on the surface of water all of which, we are told, they achieved by means of elaborate stunts. The officials of the bishop of Besançon were obliged to work their own miracles in order to expose these frauds. St. Dominic, in very similar circumstances, claimed to have demonstrated the truth of the orthodox doctrine by a process akin to the testing of relics by fire. At a formal disputation, so he told the historian Pierre des Vaux-de-Cernay, he had cast a written statement of his beliefs into the fire and watched it jump out unconsumed. A hundred and fifty Albigensians are said to have been converted on this occasion, and the memory of the miracle was

potent enough, two centuries later, to inspire a painting by Fra
Angelico.

The serious threat posed to the Church in the twelfth century by heresy and by Islam undoubtedly contributed to striking
expansion of the cult of the miraculous. The miracles of St.
Thomas Becket, for example, by frequently transmuting water
into milk, are alleged to have confirmed in the minds of the
onlookers the doctrine of the real presence. Frequent revivals of
the dead provided graphic confirmation of the doctrine of the
resurrection amongst the ignorant and faithless. The bishop of
Evreux knew of a rich Muslim merchant of Palermo who was
converted to Christianity by the stories of St. Thomas's miracles.

It was axiomatic that no heretic or unbeliever could perform a miracle, and reports that any such had done so invariably provoked the authorities to displays of indignation and
alarm. In the case of the Albigensians of Besançon the bishop
had retorted that it was 'impossible that God should work miracles through men of impure doctrine'. Nevertheless a community of heretics at Moncoul in southern France claimed to
have a miraculous statue of the Virgin, and orthodox writers
such as Lucas of Tuy were most anxious to discredit it. In 1440,
miracles were alleged to have occurred at the grave of Richard
Wyche, a Lollard executed in London some weeks earlier; a
royal writ complained that certain of the King's subjects openly
averred that Wyche had been a holy man and that miracles had
been performed by him which they had not. Such claims, irri-
tating enough when made by heretics, posed a serious intellectual problem when uttered by Muslims. In the late Middle Ages
scholars became aware of the fact that the Qur'an attributes
many miracles to Muhammad, and that in parts of the Islamic
world holy men still claimed to have performed them. Ricoldo

of Monte Croce, a thirteenth-century Italian Dominican who lived for many years in Baghdad studying Islamic religion, indignantly denied the Arab assertion that God worked miracles amongst them just as he did amongst Christians. Miracle-workers in Baghdad, 'sons of perdition every one of them', were constantly deceiving large audiences in this way. The occurrence of miracles in the Latin west remained, to Christian minds, a conclusive argument against Islamic theology. Thus in the fifteenth century Denis the Carthusian not only denied that Muhammad or his latter-day followers had worked miracles, but cited the miracles of Christian saints as proof of the Christian faith. In his imaginary dialogue with a Muslim he argued that 'no one who denies the divinity of Christ can work miracles.' Christians on the other hand have always worked miracles. The dead have been raised, the deaf, the dumb, the blind and the lame have been healed. No one who has read the miracles of St. Martin, St. Nicholas, St. Servatius, St. Germanus, St. Bernard, or St. Francis can possibly doubt the reality of the God they worshipped.

That the need for miracles was as strong on the eve of the Reformation as it had ever been, is clear from the career of John of Capistrano, vicar-general of the Observant Franciscans and a preacher of remarkable powers. During his mission to the Hussites (1452–6) he drew audiences which contemporaries reckoned at 120,000 and which, even allowing for exaggeration, must have been unusually large. In his sermons he would condemn heresy with fierce fanaticism and would perform astonishing miracles, all of which were immediately recorded at his direction, together with the names and depositions of witnesses. One of these stories is typical enough. At Breslau some Hussites advanced through a crowd during a sermon, bearing

a coffin in which there was a Hussite feigning death. They
demanded that John resuscitate him and he refused. Thereupon
one of the heretics announced that he would bring him back
to life, but there was no response, for the unfortunate youth was
found to be really dead. A contemporary who followed John of
Capistrano through central Europe recalled that he sometimes
performed thirty miracles or more in the course of a sermon,
most of them miraculous cures, and that these exhibitions were
usually followed by large scale conversions from among the
audience.

The mediaeval Church never formally abandoned the
notion that miracles were the milk-teeth of the Church, superfluous after the earliest years of its life. But during the bitter
schisms of the fourth and fifth centuries miracles became
bound up with the moral teaching of the Church, and thus the
ambivalent attitudes of Augustine of Hippo and Gregory the
Great survived as long as the belief in the supernatural itself.
Not only were miracles presented to the faithful as evidence of
the truth of the Church's teaching at times when that teaching
was questioned, but they were constantly used as *exempla* or
illustrations of the spiritual life. This is plainly true of preachers
like Jacques de Vitry or teachers like Caesarius of Heisterbach,
whose collections were avowedly made for this purpose. But it
is no less true of historians such as Bede or Gregory of Tours,
addressing a limited audience and not professing to preach a
sermon. For they, like all mediaeval historians, wrote in accordance with the prevailing belief that history should be written
for the edification of its readers by showing them the perpetual action of God in the physical world. Their purpose was not
to inform posterity but to teach their contemporaries. It was
essentially didactic, though that is not to say that they did not

believe everything that they wrote to the letter. 'For all chroniclers', as a twelfth-century author thought, 'have a single purpose: to relate noteworthy matters so that the invisible power
of God may clearly be seen in the march of events, and men
may, by stories of reward and punishment, be made more zeal-
ous in the fear of God and the pursuit of justice.'

Miraculous Tales and Their Audience

The authors of mediaeval miracle stories were not completely
unconcerned with truth, nor were their readers invariably sim-
pletons who believed all that they were told. It is clear from the
terms in which some of the miracles were couched that there
was a considerable body of opinion which looked on miracles
with a jaundiced eye and which may even have rejected the
possibility of modern miracles altogether. Gregory of Tours
found it 'impossible to pass over in silence the tale of what hap-
pens to those heretics and unbelievers who doubt the miracles
which God has wrought on earth to reinforce the faith of his
people.' The author of *The Miracles of St. John of Beverley* knew
that some men regarded his work as the delusion of a simple
mind and so many old wives' tales, but he confidently antici-
pated that they would suffer the fate of all blasphemers.
Nicholas of Clun laughed aloud when it was suggested that he
should go and witness the miracles of St. Wulfstan at Worcester.
At least one parish priest of Worcestershire did not believe in
St. Wulfstan's miracles, and used to recommend herbs and
blood-lettings when his parishioners were sick. The chronicler
who described this aberration remarked that the man was 'of a
frivolous turn of mind...and quite unlike other men', but in
fact we have no evidence on which to decide what proportion
of mediaeval men did not believe in modern miracles. Those

who appear in the sources are almost invariably those who repented or suffered punishment for their scepticism, but there must have been many who did neither.

Exalted and educated persons were probably more inclined to doubt marvellous stories than their inferiors. Robert II, count of Namur (d. 1031), protested against the miracles of St. Gengulph of Florennes on the grounds that that saint had been a pagan. The courtiers of William Rufus declined to believe that the body of St. Edmund had been found incorrupt by the monks of Bury in 1094. The revelation that St. Cuthbert had been found incorrupt at Durham at the beginning of the twelfth century provoked similar suspicions and amongst those who demanded to see the body were Ranulf Flambard, bishop of Durham, Ralph, abbot of Seez, and Alexander, brother of the king of Scotland. Two bishops (they are not named) refused to believe the miracles attributed to Ailred of Rievaulx in Walter Daniel's *Life*. Wise men would not believe in miracles until they had seen the evidence. When king William of Scotland heard that a knight had been miraculously saved from drowning in the Tweed, he sent the bishop and archdeacon of Glasgow to question the man. A ducal official in Périgord in the time of Henry II would never believe tales of miraculous cures until he had seen the sufferer with his own eyes.

At the opposite extreme a surfeit of miracles might be accepted at the expense of its significance. So many miracles were performed by St. Swithin of Winchester on the occasion of his translation at the end of the tenth century, that the monks began to find them wearisome. William of Canterbury complained that so many exaggerated stories were told in the twelfth century that interest in them was waning at the very time that he was composing his massive collection of the miracles of St. Thomas. 'It is well-known', Thomas of Monmouth declared, 'that the occasional reading of miracle stories is a valuable stimulus to devotion. But as each miracle follows the last and the astonishing is succeeded by the spectacular, I must take care to restrain my enthusiasm, or else the piety of my readers will be dampened by the tedium of reading so many marvels.'

The churches which suffered most from public scepticism were those which used their relics for the purposes of self-aggrandisement. Churches with the patronage of a great saint were always enriched by offerings, many of which consisted of land, and vigorous efforts were made by the monks to acquire intervening holdings which would consolidate their estates. The miracles of the saint and the acquisitions of his or her monastery were intimately connected. A lady of Brabant, for example, presented the title deeds of her estates at the altar of the abbey of Lierre near Malines, in gratitude for a miraculous cure. But the document adhered to her fingers for it was improperly made out; she had kept some of her possessions to herself. 'And St. Gummarus delivered her from her physical bonds once he had acquired full legal rights over her. As for her, she was reinforced in faith and her worldly goods multiplied exceedingly.' Many miracle collections, notably the *Miracles of St. Benedict,* are largely concerned with showing how the saint had miraculously intervened to defend the estates of his or her abbey. The acquisitiveness of houses such as St.-Denis or Fleury made them many local enemies, who regarded the miracle stories as so many fabrications designed to justify the encroachments of the abbey. Thus we learn that many ill-disposed persons doubted the miracles of St.-Denis in the ninth century and the same complaint is made in the eleventh. Some of them went as far as to reject 'all such modern miracles'. The growing wealth of the abbey of Conques can be traced in the four books of the miracles of St. Foy. We have already seen how the statue-reliquary was carried through the valleys of the Auvergne when the abbey's lands were threatened. It is clear that the relics of St. Foy were the means by which the monastery acquired enormous landed wealth in the Rouergue as well as psychological control over the minds of the inhabitants. Consequently, as Bernard of Angers, the author of the miracle stories, admits, the saint had many detractors and it was a source of quiet satisfaction to the monks that many of them met untimely ends. A group of scholars from Angers once encountered a man of the Rouergue on the road to Le Puy. 'You must know that man Bernard who left Conques this year', he said; 'how many lies has he written about St. Foy this time? Does he expect me to believe all that nonsense about eyes gouged out and then restored, dead animals brought back to life, and other absurdities'? 'Truly', Bernard observes in relating these words, 'this man was a son of Satan, an enemy of truth, and a minister of Antichrist.'

When the consequences of a miracle were of more than local importance, the temptation to doubt it was correspondingly greater. The miracles of Thomas Becket, for example, were an important political phenomenon. Not only were they regarded as vindicating Becket's case against Henry II, but they were also believed to have justified the claims of Alexander III against the anti-pope. Many interested parties, including Richard de Lucy and Joscelyn, bishop of Salisbury, publicly proclaimed their disbelief, and some asserted that the monks had brought about the miracles by dabbling in the black arts with the assistance of the Devil.

Faced with an increasingly astute public, the clergy of the pilgrimage churches began to examine miracles more carefully before publicizing them. There is no doubt that the miracles reported in the eleventh and twelfth centuries are less fantastically improbable than those of earlier periods, while some writers show an interest in names, dates, places, and witnesses which is altogether absent in their predecessors. At the beginning of the eleventh century the monks of Fleury held an investigation before accepting that miracles had occurred in one of their Burgundian cells; two women who claimed to have been healed there were interrogated at length and the findings were given the greatest possible publicity. When miracles occurred at St. Frideswide's, Oxford, in the twelfth century, a formal enquiry was always held, followed by a solemn announcement of the details. Correspondents who wrote to the monks of Christ Church Canterbury, describing the more distant miracles of St. Thomas, were careful to enclose the depositions of witnesses and testimonials as to their good character. When pilgrims came to Canterbury and told of marvellous happenings in their home villages, the monks would normally write to the local bishop or civic authorities asking them to investigate it. How detailed these investigations were is not usually revealed, and no doubt some churches made more strenuous efforts than others to discover the truth. At Worcester in the thirteenth century witnesses seem to have been required before any miracle was inscribed in the record. When a boy of Droitwich was miraculously saved from drowning he was brought to Worcester by his mother, together with several local worthies who attested the absolute truth of his story. Another boy was shortly afterwards revived from the dead at Petton in Shropshire but the bishop refused to allow premature exhibitions of jubilation until the villagers had been summoned to give evidence in the cathedral and the boy's parents had solemnly sworn an affidavit on the tomb of St. Wulfstan.

In the course of time these enquiries became more thorough and a higher proportion of alleged miracles were rejected as spurious. This was chiefly due to the stricter rules imposed by Rome before permitting the canonization of a saint. After the twelfth century, miracles were usually collected with a view to canonization, and in many cases they were no longer recorded after the process of canonization had been brought to a successful conclusion. In the cases of Thomas Becket and Gilbert of Sempringham, whose miracles were recorded for some years after their canonizations, it is noticeable that those which occurred after canonization are much more fantastic than the earlier ones, and the intrusion of hearsay evidence becomes more common. The commissioners who investigated miracles during a process of canonization performed their work with rigour. The instructions issued to the commissioners in the process of Gilbert of Sempringham, who was canonized in 1202, required them to interrogate all those who claimed to have been miraculously healed. How long had they been ill? What was the nature of their illness? Had their cure been complete? Were there any trustworthy witnesses? In reputable pilgrimage churches the same questions were asked even when no process of canonization was pending. At Mont-St.-Michel, those who alleged that they had been healed by the Almighty were sometimes interrogated for three days. Humble people who indiscriminately boasted of the miracles from which they had benefited frequently found themselves facing an imposing judicial tribunal. Thus ten inquisitors with a staff of clerks and notaries were appointed to examine one

Moriset de Ranton who asserted that St. Louis had healed his wounded leg.

The Evidence

If the majority of educated men of the twelfth and thirteenth centuries accepted the evidence for miracles, it was not because they were unduly credulous or irrational, still less because they cared nothing for the truth. It was rather because in assessing the evidence they applied criteria very different from those of David Hume. They may often have been misled by lying witnesses, but the fundamental cause of their error was that they considered a miracle to be a normal, though nonetheless remarkable, incident of life. It was the natural consequence of that combination of humanity and omnipotence which they ascribed to the saints. Thus they did not require the same high standard of proof as the eighteenth-century philosopher, and indeed they were inclined to attribute events to the intervention of the Almighty which could quite easily have been explained without. People accepted the evidence for particular miracles because they passionately desired to believe in miracles in general. Their beliefs on this subject become intelligible when we consider them in relation to their other beliefs, as part of a system of thought which, although quite unlike our own, is nevertheless based on perfectly rational deductions from a number of faulty premises.

'We speak of a miracle', thought Caesarius of Heisterbach, 'whenever anything is done contrary to the normal course of nature, at which we marvel.' Few mediaeval men and women would have quarrelled with that definition, but their understanding of the 'normal course of nature' was limited. Their ignorance of the causes of the simplest natural processes evidently made them more inclined to proclaim a miracle. The doubts of intelligent men and women when considering the physical world were reflected in the sensitive mind of St. Augustine. Augustine was fascinated by the sight of the two halves of a centipede wriggling across a writing desk, and the behaviour of a magnet seemed to him to be little less than miraculous. In his attack on the 'rationalism' of Julian of Eclanum, he listed several observable natural phenomena, such as the grafting of olive branches, which appeared to have no natural explanation. Augustine was profoundly aware of the limits of human knowledge, and he argued that in the existing state of man's knowledge, rational criticism of the evidence for miracles was misguided. 'Where in all the variety of created things is there anything that is not wonderful, even if our familiarity with them has reduced our amazement. How many common things are trodden underfoot when, if we stopped to pick them up, we might be astonished. Take, for example, the seeds that grow into plants: does anyone really understand…the secret power which makes them evolve from such small beginnings into such great things?' Why then, he concludes, should we look for rational explanations of the resurrection or the miracles of the saints and martyrs?

Underlying Augustine's arguments was the belief in a 'higher law of nature' which was synonymous with God. 'God does nothing against nature.…When we say that he does so, we mean that he does something against nature as we know it.… But he no more acts against the highest laws of nature than he acts against himself.' Looked at in this way the 'laws of nature' became mere conventions of God. God controlled the entire natural world from moment to moment. Everything that happened was his doing, from the most sublime to the most

insignificant. Although human beings might, in their ignorance, accustom themselves to the fact that God normally
worked in a particular way, there was no reason why He should
not behave quite differently if the circumstances of the
moment seemed to call for it. Thus the true significance of a
miracle was not its rarity but its usefulness as a means of discerning the will of God. 'These things are indeed marvellous',
wrote abbot Samson after describing the miracles of St.
Edmund, 'but only to those who consider the ordinary laws of
matter instead of the nature of the Creator. For if He created
the laws of matter in accordance with His whim, why should
He not alter them whenever he chooses?'

This characteristically mediaeval view of causation suggests
why it was that perfectly natural explanations of events were
constantly discarded in favour of supernatural ones. Amongst
the 'miracles' collected by Gregory of Tours are included the
author's recovery from headaches, eyesores, pimples, and even
indigestion; 'truly, I cannot count how often the miraculous
power of God has healed my headaches, fevers, blocked ears,
tiredness in the eyes and pains in my limbs,' the bishop confessed. The monk of Fécamp did not hesitate to proclaim as a
miracle the story of a child whose throat was blocked by a large
piece of meat until he drank a glass of water in the abbey of
Fécamp. William of Canterbury saw the hand of God in the
tale of a knight who lost his horse while riding in the forest of
Ponthieu. After invoking the aid of St. Thomas and walking
through the forest for the rest of the day, he found his horse in
a clearing and hurried away to announce the miracle to the
local clergy. These events prompted in William some rare
reflections on the problem of causation:

'Some would say that the finding of the horse was due
to chance, that it had no cause at all. Others would
argue that if it had a cause then that cause was directed
towards some other end, and the recovery of the horse
was merely an incidental consequence. There are others
who would hold that it was a combination of causes....
But the truth is that not a leaf falls from a branch without cause, for to admit the power of chance in the physical world is to detract from the power of the Creator.
The Creator has ordained the laws of matter such that
nothing can happen in His creation save in accordance
with His just ordinance whether good or bad. If we are
to seek the cause of things, we must look for the original cause, which is not itself caused by something else.
And the original cause (that is, God) is the true cause of
the miracle I have just described.'

This argument is, of course, a licence to find miraculous
explanations in everything that occurs, however trivial. It was
readily accepted because it was more flattering for a man who
had recovered his horse to believe that God had intervened on
his behalf, than to admit that a chance encounter in a forest
clearing had brought the beast back into his possession. Indeed a
very high proportion of surviving miracle stories, especially after
the eleventh century, can be explained without recourse to the
supernatural. A particularly striking example is the story of the
prisoner whose escape was assisted by a miracle. Such tales were
legion, especially in the twelfth century, when most of the beneficiaries were crusaders in the hands of the infidel, either in
Spain or in the Middle East. St. Foy seems to have been the first
saint to specialize in the release of prisoners, and at the beginning

of the eleventh century she was already 'famous above all others for releasing prisoners who invoke her, casting aside their chains and ordering them to hurry thankfully to Conques'. Crusaders were frequently released by St. Gilles, St. James, or St. Leonard. Similarly, during the Hundred Years' War, St. Martial acquired a reputation for releasing prisoners of war on both sides. These miracles followed no discernible pattern, for although most of the captives were deserving prisoners of war, some were less deserving criminals, such as the various cattle thieves released by St. Gilles and the convicted murderer who owed his freedom to St. Mary Magdalene. In almost every case the escape was entirely due to the cleverness of the escaper or the carelessness of his jailors, but the escaper preferred to attribute it to the intervention of the Almighty. The release of Bohemond prince of Antioch from a Turkish prison in 1103 was universally attributed to St. Leonard, notwithstanding the fact that his friends had paid a ransom of 100,000 besants to the Danishmend emir. Bohemond himself certainly encouraged the legend, for he swore to make a pilgrimage to the shrine of St. Leonard and actually did so some years afterwards. There seems to have been a presumption, at any rate amongst the authors of miracle stories, that any release from captivity was miraculous. Hence the twelfth-century legend of Gregory bishop of Tarsus who, on being released from the custody of a middle eastern slave-owner, travelled to all the principal shrines of Europe in an attempt to discover which saint was responsible. Stories of this sort were still popular in the fifteenth century when John Hus acidly pointed out their illogicality:

> 'Peter Layman is a thief and a murderer, justly imprisoned for life. He vows to go to the Holy Blood of

Wilsnack if he is freed. He breaks his chains and escapes by brute force, and everyone exclaims that the blood of Wilsnack has freed him. Henry, out of sinful pride, challenges Frederick to a duel and promises to go to Wilsnack if he wins. He slays Frederick in armed combat and then invites us to believe that this was the work of the Holy Blood of Christ.'

Yet the explanation was not, as Hus thought, the lies spread about by the clergy, but the desire of Peter Layman and Henry to be considered the beneficiaries of a miracle. As Guibert of Nogent judiciously observed, 'many miracles owe more to the vanity of men than to the power of the saints.' Those who visited distant shrines not only desired but expected that their prayers would be answered. When, for example, a Welsh girl failed to recover her sight at the shrine of St. Wulfstan, her mother went away vowing angrily that she would never pray to St. Wulfstan again, 'for such', commented the chronicler, 'is the nature of that simple-minded and bad-tempered race.' At Montserrat, the celebrated Marial shrine in Catalonia, pilgrims were exhorted 'not to lose their tempers if they failed to obtain a miraculous answer to their prayers...for God, from whom all benefits proceed, knows better than we do what is right and fitting for our souls.' Indeed some unsuccessful pilgrims became objects of derision at home, especially if they lived far from the shrine in places where the achievements of the saint had been exaggerated by much repeating. Two blind women returning from Canterbury were openly laughed at as they passed through the streets of Leicester. On the other hand those who returned with visible proof of a miraculous cure were treated as heroes and were flattered by the obvious implication that God had thought it worth intervening on their behalf. Pilgrims who believed that they had witnessed or experienced a miracle were usually most anxious that the fact should be recorded. The monks of Christ Church Canterbury received a constant stream of letters informing them of astonishing occurrences, not all of which were believed. When Samson of Bury was writing his book on the miracles of St. Edmund, he was visited by three Londoners who demanded to be mentioned in it on the ground that St. Edmund had once sent them a fair wind when sailing to St.-Gilles.

Evidently the wish was frequently father of the thought. The combination of a pilgrim who had convinced himself that he had experienced a miracle, and a public which was over-whelmingly anxious to believe him, was impossible for the clergy to resist, even if they wished to. Many miracles were proclaimed, without any supporting evidence, in circumstances which ruled out the possibility of a cool and judicious examination of the facts. Thus, a knight who had come to believe that St. Gilles had released him from the Moors, repaired to the saint's Provençal shrine and there 'before the altar of the saint, and in the presence of a great crowd of people, publicly recited the facts, praising God and St. Gilles.' Another knight died in battle and was raised from the dead by St. Mary Magdalene; a friend of his, who had witnessed the miracle, rushed to Vézelay where he announced it to a jubilant crowd of pilgrims. Every major shrine was perpetually besieged by a motley crowd of pilgrims, hawkers, musicians, beggars and idlers whose appetite for new wonders was insatiable. Amid the scenes of collective euphoria that followed each announcement, no churchman could publicly voice his doubts without doing serious damage to the prestige of his church. An increase in demand could, in this way, stimulate a corresponding increase in supply. A striking instance of this economic law at work occurred at Fleury in the late eleventh century. A mason working on the roof of the new basilica fell from the scaffolding and was gravely injured. The monks took him into the monastery and attended to him, praying fervently for his recovery because, they averred,

> 'we were afraid that if he died the whole building programme would be interrupted as a result of a sudden fall in contributions to the building fund. For the vulgar mob is very fickle and bends like a reed whatever way the wind blows it. If the mason had died they might have murmured that St. Benedict did not care about his own monastery or the troubles that befell it.'

It must be admitted that this is an unusually blatant example of the invention of miracles for self-interested purposes, but the same dilemma must have presented itself whenever the clergy at a shrine were informed of a miracle and asked to take note of it.

Their position was particularly delicate because the mediaeval notion of sanctity was inextricably linked with the performance of miracles, not only in the popular mind but also in canon law. In the bull of canonization of St. Cunegonde, Innocent III stated that 'merit without miracles and miracles without merit are both equally insufficient if a saint is to be venerated by the Church Militant.' But long before the Church had made them a prerequisite for canonization, the populace had shown that it would not venerate a saint who performed no miracles. Their attitude was grounded in the proposition that since God's will was expounded to humans by means of miracles, the only certain proof that He had designated a particular saint for their veneration was the occurrence of miracles at the saint's shrine. To deny these miracles was therefore tantamount to denying the sanctity of the person venerated. Similarly, if miracles were reliably attributed to an individual after his death, then he was to be venerated, be his reputation in life never so black. Thomas Becket, for example, was a man who aroused bitter controversy both before and after his death. The parish priest of Nantes spoke for many of his contemporaries when he declared that Becket was a 'traitor against his lord the king, and the King of Kings will no more glorify him than he will that dog over there'. This situation was, however, transformed by the frequent miracles, skilfully publicized, which made the hysterical and somewhat unattractive archbishop into the 'holy blissful martyr' of later days. Joscelyn, bishop of Salisbury, Gilbert Foliot, and Richard de Lucy, all of them prominent opponents of Becket in his lifetime, all confessed themselves converted to his merits by the news of his miracles, though Richard tartly expressed his astonishment that a man who, as chancellor, had been so harsh on the Church, should become its foremost miracle-worker. Two obstinate canons of St. Frideswide's, Oxford, would not be convinced of Becket's sanctity till one of their colleagues was miraculously relieved of his constipation. 'I shall never believe that St. Thomas is a saint', declared the sacristan of St. Remy at Rheims, 'until he returns my lost service-book.' Indeed in a debate in the University of Paris the miracles were held to be conclusive evidence that his life was pleasing to God, notwithstanding all arguments to the contrary. Master Roger, we are told,

> 'swore that he had deserved to die (though not to die in such a manner), and judged the constancy of the

blessed saint to be mere obstinacy. Master Peter on the other hand asserted that he was a worthy martyr of Christ, since he had died for the liberty of the Church. But the Saviour himself resolved their debate when he glorified him with many wonderful miracles.'

This definition of sanctity gave rise to the most perverse conclusions, on account of the popular tendency to proclaim miracles in unpredictable circumstances. Abbot Odo of Cluny protested against the universal prejudice of his contemporaries who, like doubting Thomas, refused to believe anything which they could not see with their own eyes. The cult of a saint ceased with his or her miracles. Guibert of Nogent argued that it encouraged the populace to proclaim bogus saints and firmly declared that God had been known to work miracles through evil men as well as good. Indeed Guibert had himself seen Louis VI, no saint he, touching for the king's evil. This feeling gained in force in the fourteenth and fifteenth centuries as the consequences of unrestrained popular enthusiasm manifested themselves. Wyclif's comments on miracles are substantially the same as Guibert's. Jean Gerson, chancellor of the University of Paris and an indefatigable critic of popular religion, pointed out that St. Jerome and Gregory the Great performed no miracles though no one had ventured to doubt their sanctity. But these were the parting shots of a brilliant, though ineffective, rear-guard. The miracle remained the decisive test of sanctity as far as ordinary people were concerned, and no pilgrimages succeeded without them. As the Lollard William Thorpe complained, 'both men and women delight now more for to hear and know miracles than they do to know God's word.'

Every pilgrimage church faced, on a smaller scale, the same missionary problem as the Church as a whole. They could not convey their message, in this case the virtues of their patron saint, without adducing supernatural arguments. They took an indulgent view of the aberrations of the faithful, partly because they were powerless to do otherwise, and partly, no doubt, because they felt that even misdirected faith was better than no faith at all. As Chaucer's parson remarked of charm-healing, 'it may be peradventure that God suffereth it for (that) folk sholden geve the more faith and reverence to His name.'

The initiative for the proclamation of miracles almost invariably came from the laity, and those who fabricated the evidence for miracles were more often the pilgrims themselves than the clergy of the shrine. Every popular cult drew its share of charlatans. The growing reputation of St. Thomas of Canterbury attracted so many that the authors of his miracles had difficulty in distinguishing true miracles from false. Geoffrey Musard, a knight of Gloucestershire, pretended to be blind and asked for miracle-working water to be smeared over his eyelids. A woman of Lichfield asserted that her son had been crushed to death beneath a mill-stone and then revived by St. Thomas, but she was unable to find witnesses to corroborate her story. A noble lady who claimed to have been raised from the dead did indeed produce witnesses, but they were found to be 'mendacious sluts'. Many pilgrims were evasive and obstructive when questioned about the miraculous cures that they had experienced, and one of them, a pauper from Woodstock, lost her temper when Benedict refused to inscribe her name in the book of miracles. The miracles of St. Thomas were probably more closely scrutinized than any other miracles of the twelfth century. Even so the authors could do no more than eliminate the more obvious liars, while those who had convinced themselves that they were speaking the truth went undetected. At other, less scrupulous shrines, both classes were indiscriminately recorded and thus achieved a brief moment of celebrity before the crowd passed on to more recent wonders and consigned them once again to oblivion.

5

The Medicine of the Sick

Mediaeval Afflictions and Their Treatment

Mediaeval men and women were pathetically vulnerable to the hazards which contemporary life held for their health. Their sense of impotence before the forces of nature was at no time stronger than during the great famines and epidemics. 'Neither by bleeding nor by clysters nor by any precautions could anyone who had once caught this plague escape it, except by death,' recorded a Parisian diarist during an epidemic in 1433. 'In Florence', Boccaccio wrote at the time of the Black Death, 'all human wisdom was unable to avert the onset of the terrible disease. The city had been cleansed and sick folk kept outside the walls....But nonetheless, towards the beginning of spring, the first appalling symptoms of the plague began to appear.... Which plague set at naught the skill of the physicians and the virtues of their science.' The incidence of disease, unpredictable, irresistible, bred a kind of fatalism which inclined men to look to the supernatural for their only hope of relief.

Bread was the chief source of the B vitamins and almost the only source of carbohydrates. Its supply depended on an agricultural system whose productivity was low at the best of times. A yield of ten bushels an acre was considered exceptional, and in most regions a normal harvest did little more than feed the immediate locality. Grain was difficult to transport and expensive to store, with the result that a bad harvest might threaten a whole region with starvation. It was thus possible for a traveller to pass in the space of a single day from an area of plenty to one where fodder was unobtainable and men were dying of starvation at the side of the road; such was the experience of John, bishop of Norwich, when travelling through central France in 1176. After the end of the thirteenth century, certain climatic changes occurred in western Europe, and famines followed each other with increasing frequency, with the consequent weakening of people's resistance to petty illnesses and major epidemics alike.

Even in times of plenty, the diet of both rich and poor was far from healthy. A shortage of green vegetables and fresh fruit in winter was responsible for a serious deficiency of vitamin C which manifested itself in muscular pains and mild scurvy. People in the Middle Ages depended chiefly on milk, eggs, and fish for vitamin A. Fish was often scarce in inland areas, and in winter the low quality of the feed given to cows and hens must have caused a progressive fall in the intake of vitamin A by all classes. In the towns, where milk was almost impossible to keep, this problem presented itself throughout the year. Thus arose the most characteristic of mediaeval maladies. Stone in the bladder and urinary tract was probably due to a deficiency of vitamin A combined with a very high intake of calcium, while the same dietary deficiencies weakened resistance to infections and caused the appearance of skin lesions. The widespread complaints of sore eyes and fading sight (xeropthalmia) have the same ultimate origin.

The result was that people suffered from an interminable succession of minor afflictions as well as the occasional major one. Indeed a sense of complete physical well-being was probably extremely rare. Gregory of Tours tells us that he constantly suffered from headaches, inflammations of the ears and throat, sore eyes, and muscular pains. The letters of Peter the Venerable perpetually refer to his ill-health and physical discomfort; he was often constipated and afflicted throughout his life by what appears to have been a mild form of malaria. Digestive problems were common complaints. In 1171 Robert, count of Leicester, was reported to have suffered from chronic indigestion ever since a tour of duty in Ireland, while Geoffrey of Binbrooke, a pilgrim to Canterbury in the same year, had never recovered from the effects of eating unwashed fish. Benedict of Peterborough, who took some pride in his medical knowledge, warned against the evil effects of excessive eating and drinking, and reported that female pilgrims at St. Thomas's shrine were occasionally suffering from an incautious choice of diet during pregnancy or lactation.

It was in part because so many mediaeval ailments had dietary origins that contemporary medicine was unable to offer a cure or even a good diagnosis. It is true that special diets were prescribed for the sick. They were an essential adjunct to Hippocratic medicine. But their object was not to restore nutritional deficiencies; it was to correct supposed imbalances between the four 'humours' in the patient's body, and when this failed to cure the patient's afflictions, he or she tended to look elsewhere for relief. The malady often disappeared quite suddenly when the dietary deficiency had been made good, for example by a journey to another province or a change of season. In these circumstances it seemed plausible to attribute both the original affliction and its ultimate disappearance to divine intervention. The frequent outbreaks of ergotism in northern Europe afford a classic instance of this. Ergotism, which was known to contemporaries as '*Ignis Sacer*', or 'Holy-Fire', was caused by eating rye infected by a specific kind of mould or fungus. Outbreaks of it commonly occurred after a wet summer. Large numbers of people were afflicted simultaneously by its alarming symptoms, severe gangrene accompanied by a sharp burning sensation in some cases, convulsions and nervous disorders in others. The most serious epidemics occurred in England and France in the first half of the twelfth century, and the result in almost every case was a mass pilgrimage to one or other of the sanctuaries of the Blessed Virgin.

'This horrible disease', wrote Hughes Farsit of the epidemic of 1128, 'spreads beneath the stretched blue skin, separating it from the bones and slowly consuming it. The pain and heat steadily increase until the victims long for death as their only hope of release. As the fever wastes the limbs, a raging fire burns the internal organs, yet it produces no heat and it never abates, however much the wretched victims pour cold liquids over themselves....It was horrible to behold the sick and the recently cured, the sign of death still visible on their bodies and in their faces. Yet the mercy of God is even greater than the afflictions of men. When no human remedy could be found,...the sick, even as the fire raged inside them, took refuge in the benevolence and healing power of the ever-virgin Mother of God, and she did not disappoint them in their hopes.'

Sufferers crowded into Coutances cathedral in the closing years of the eleventh century. In the autumn of 1128 they came from every part of northern France to the church of Notre-Dame at

Soissons. In 1132, after another wet summer, several hundred citizens of Beauvais suffering from ergotism trekked in a body to Chartres. Notre-Dame in Paris was the object of a similar mass pilgrimage during the outbreak of 1206. In each case the disease passed away in the course of time and the Virgin acquired a growing reputation as a healer of the sick. 'She is the sovereign remedy for the sick', proclaimed the prior of Sauxillanges, 'for she can obtain from her son all that she desires. She is merciful on our sins and relieves us in all our troubles.'

There were physicians available throughout the Middle Ages, and in parts of Europe, such as southern France, they were organized in powerful corporations. But the medicine which they practised was of a somewhat rudimentary and unscientific nature. It was based on the distant influence of Arab science, and on the works of Hippocrates and Galen, manuscripts of which were conserved at Salerno and in many monasteries during the 'dark ages'. It consisted in examining the patient, particularly the urine, and in diagnosing an imbalance of the four humours, namely blood, phlegm, green bile and black bile. The imbalance could then be corrected by means of purges, blood-letting, special diets, and so forth. Peter the Venerable's doctor diagnosed in his patient an excess of phlegm, the qualities of which were cold and moist; he therefore prescribed myrrh which was hot and 'actively wet yet potentially dry'. Even formal medicine of this sort was usually available only to a small number of wealthy and important persons. The medical attention which these persons received was certainly no more effective than the folk medicine of the villages, and it may in some cases have been positively harmful. Peter the Venerable's health was not improved by the 'baths and stoves, fumigations and poultices, pills under the tongue, pills for catarrh, balsam potions, gargles and similar things' which were recommended to him. William, dean of Coutances, was brought to death's door by the potions which his doctor prescribed. One John Chadleton made a pilgrimage to St. Frideswide's, Oxford, in order to recover from the effects of a near-fatal blood-letting, while pilgrims at Rocamadour complained that the hot baths recommended by the celebrated physicians of Montpellier had done grave injury to their health.

Many of the pilgrims who were cured at the shrine of St. Thomas had already received the best attention that the medical profession could offer. The son of a knight of Surrey was taken to London to see the foremost consultants of the day, but they were unable to cure his liver disease. A 'copious supply' of surgeons laboured in vain to remove an arrow-head from Tancard de Carew's right eye. Robert of Bromton's physician inspected his urine with great diligence, diagnosed an imbalance of the humours, prescribed pills and potions and laxatives, and finally gave the case up as hopeless. William of Dene was close to death after unwisely entrusting his health to 'mere human physicians, with whom there is no hope of recovery'. Some doctors, indeed, are alleged to have admitted their shortcomings and advised their patients to go forthwith to Canterbury.

Consequently the practice of medicine was not held in high esteem, and writers from Sidonius Apollinaris onwards spent their harshest invectives on the ignorance and incompetence of the medical profession. One of them, a canon of St. Frideswide's, Oxford, stoutly declared that any surgeon who operated for the stone was guilty of murder. Ordinary people preferred to rely on herb doctors, charm-healers and 'wise women' of the locality. Although these were normally found in rural areas, their services were much in demand even in the towns. In Langland's day, Londoners used to resort to witches at Southwark and Shoreditch. These unorthodox physicians probably did more for their clients than most doctors, and what we know of their methods suggests that they were sometimes soundly based on common sense and traditional herbal medicine. A twelfth-century witch at Palinges in the Loire valley used to prescribe 'herbs and potions, beet or the juice of local plants, or even the fat of various animals', a mixture which may well have been effective in restoring certain dietary deficiencies. But Raoul Tortaire, who tells us of this lady, had nothing but contempt for her remedies which, he averred, served only to raise false hopes in ignorant people.

Such sentiments were common enough among the clergy of pilgrimage churches who constantly upheld the invocation of the saints as the only sure remedy for sickness. 'Why waste your breath in calling for a mere human doctor', a Merovingian bishop asked a dying nobleman, 'when a celestial doctor is at hand,…the body of St. Andrew?' By the time of Gregory of Tours the denigration of 'human medicine' had become a commonplace of hagiography. 'Physicians', explained a twelfth-century churchman, 'are out to enrich themselves in any way they can; their promises are mere verbiage designed to augment your hope and their fees'; only by a pilgrimage to the shrine of St. Donatian could one be certain of good health. The *Liber Sancti Jacobi* echoes these feelings. It is better to study the divine medicine by which Christ brought salvation to men than the pseudo-medicine of Hippocrates, Dioscorides, and their ilk. Whether the medical profession resented the success of its celestial rivals is not recorded. The doctors of Montpellier apparently regarded a miraculous statue of the Virgin there with some envy. The physicians of the prior of Chaalis, according to Guillaume de St.-Pathus, were dismayed to learn that their patient had been cured by the miraculous intervention of St. Louis, 'for if this is indeed the case, we shall all be out of a job.' As for the patients, there must have been many like Raoul le Cavetier of Fourmont, who made three pilgrimages to Noyon and paid a fortune to his doctors before concluding that 'neither doctors nor pilgrimages were any use at all to his wounded leg.'

Medicine and Religion

In all the great miracle collections of the Middle Ages, miraculous cures account for an overwhelming majority of the stories, and it is clear that the desire to witness or experience a miracle was the principal motive for many pilgrimages. Pilgrims to St. Thomas were 'not merely attracted by the miracles but, as it were, compelled by them'. The association of pilgrimage with the healing of the sick was so close that a youth of Warbleton is reported to have refused to go to Canterbury 'for I am neither dumb nor lame, and my health is perfectly sound.' 'I am in excellent health', protested another, 'what need have I of St. Thomas?' His father gave him a sound beating, but his was nevertheless the prevailing attitude among those unruly pilgrims who in Chaucer's day still trekked to Canterbury.

> *The holy blisful martir for to seke*
> *That them hath holpen whan that they were sick.*

This was not only a reflection of the inadequacy of medical science. At the root of it was a powerful conviction that physical diseases had spiritual causes. Illness was brought on by sin, from which it followed that penitence at the shrine of a saint effaced not only the sin but the illness as well. Frequently enough, the malady had been deliberately inflicted by the saint as a punishment for sacrilege or for some other offensive behaviour. In the Latin west, the healing function of the saints was originally regarded as the natural corollary of their spiritual function. As early as the sixth century, diseases are inflicted in punishment for sin, and no sooner is the sin absolved but the symptoms pass away. Thus the sixth-century biographer of St. Hilary of Poitiers informs us that a woman who worked on the Lord's Day received a withered hand which was healed at the moment of her absolution on the following Sunday. Similarly, a blind woman recovered her sight as soon as a bishop laid hands on her in blessing. King Clothaire, whose sins caused him great physical suffering, visited the tomb of St. Germain and applied the pallium of the saint to his bleeding wounds; as soon as he had confessed his sins aloud, the pain disappeared. This notion was already well-established when Gregory of Tours was writing at the end of the sixth century. In his works we discover that a man who violated the sanctuary of St. Julian's basilica at Brioude was struck blind until the moment of his confession. A woman who had baked bread on the Lord's Day went every month to beg forgiveness at the shrine of St. Martin, but her withered arm was not healed until after she had received absolution.

The basic form of these punitive miracles did not greatly change through the centuries. It did, however, become broader in scope with the growing conviction that not only 'punitive' sickness but all sickness was caused by sin, After the fall of man, it was said, original sin had given Satan power over the bodies of men as well as their souls. Baptism might afford some protection against sickness, but only by remaining in a state of grace could a man preserve his health; as soon as he sinned the Devil was able to reclaim his body. 'There is no doubt', John Chrysostom had thought, 'that sin is the first cause of bodily disease.' The author of that most popular of hagiographical collections, the *Golden Legend,* believed that illness in unbaptized infants was due to original sin, and that children generally recovered after baptism.

Gregory of Tours had spoken of illness as an *'incursio diaboli'*, an invasion of the body by the Devil, and it is clear that many people entertained the most literal notions as to how this came about. Gregory himself had described how the Devil could be vomited up with one's bile. Peter the Deacon, the historian of the abbey of Monte Cassino, claimed to have seen a devil fleeing from the mouth of an epileptic recently cured by St. Benedict. When Guibert of Nogent's cousin was gravely ill, the arm of St. Arnoul was brought to his sick-bed, with results which Guibert described in the following terms:

'When the arm of the blessed martyr was laid upon him, the sickness shifted its ground and settled in another part of the body. Then the virulence was put to flight again and the holy arm pressed hard against it. The whole force of the disease ran up and down his face and limbs and finally flowed into the region of his throat and shoulders, the skin being a little raised like a mouse. Then gathering into a ball it vanished without pain.'

Similarly, infection could be explained as the physical transfer of a devil out of one body and into another.

The diabolic theory of sickness seemed particularly plausible to contemporaries in the case of mental illness. 'Possession by the Devil' was the usual synonym for any kind of delirium. The expression seemed natural to Bede, who tells us, for example, that at Bardney abbey in the late seventh century

> 'there came a guest who used very often to be troubled in the night without any warning by an unclean spirit....When he lay down on his bed he was suddenly possessed by the Devil and began to gnash his teeth and foam at the mouth, while his limbs were twisted by convulsive writhings....A great crowd tried vainly to hold the man down while the priest pronounced an exorcism and did all that he could to sooth the wretched creature. Then the abbess suddenly remembered the soil from the shrine of St. Cuthbert and ordered a servant to go and fetch the casket in which it was kept. No sooner was it brought...but the demoniac was suddenly silent and laid his head down as if in relaxed sleep, while his limbs became quiet and composed.'

The thirteenth-century *Miracles of St. Wulfstan* contains a remarkable account of the methods used to exorcize demons from delirious pilgrims at Worcester. From this it appears that a madwoman, dragged screaming to Worcester, was repeatedly struck blows, and a potter who suddenly lost his mind was bound to the altar and passers-by invited to scourge him with sticks. The basis of this treatment was that the patient's body became uncomfortable for the Devil who was presumed to be inhabiting it. One boy who recovered his sanity at Worcester actually saw the Devil departing, shaking his fist at the shrine as he did so. Other shrines are known to have been more gentle in their methods, but their attitude was broadly similar. An

Italian madwoman at St.-Gilles was taken into the crypt, where passages were read from the Gospels and the names of Jesus, Mary, and St. Gilles solemnly invoked; no devil, it was alleged in defence of this procedure, could survive in the house of God or bear to hear such holy names pronounced.

The conviction that sin was the origin of sickness does much to account for the confidence with which people relied on healing saints. It explains also the unconcealed hostility with which the Church at various times regarded the medical profession, which attempted to cure the bodily symptoms while ignoring the spiritual origins of the patient's complaint. For this reason the Lateran council of 1215 forbade physicians to visit a patient for the second time unless a priest had seen him beforehand. 'Since bodily ailments usually spring from sin', the fathers of the council added, 'we decree hereby, and strictly enjoin, that all doctors…shall warn their patients that they stand in need of a spiritual physician, not a physical one.' This injunction was frequently repeated by diocesan synods. Indeed, a synod meeting in Paris in 1429 went so far as to forbid physicians to give any treatment at all to patients who were in a state of mortal sin. Public preachers constantly returned to this theme. Jacques de Vitry urged his audiences that their only hope of good health was to look to the salvation of their souls, to which the instructions of doctors were positively deleterious. 'God says keep vigils; the doctors say go to sleep. God says fast; the doctors say eat. God says mortify your flesh; the doctors say be comfortable.' The fifteenth-century preacher Olivier Maillard could think of no words harsh enough to describe those physicians who would not call the priest until it was clear that the patient was dying: 'of what use is such treatment; take care in future that you recommend spiritual remedies to your patient before applying physical ones.' For the same reasons the Church made several attempts to prevent Jews from practising medicine for, the root cause of sickness being sin, the ministrations of a heathen could not possibly be effective. The council of Béziers (1246) excommunicated all Christians who allowed themselves to be treated by a Jew, and similar prohibitions were uttered wherever Jews practised medicine. In Spain, where the tradition of Jewish medicine was strong, decrees to this effect were issued at regular intervals, but equally regularly ignored.

Some afflictions were particularly liable to be regarded as divine punishments. Leprosy, for example, was often regarded as the punishment for fornication. Gonorrhoea was invariably diagnosed as 'leprosy', and the fact that it is usually acquired through sexual intercourse could only reinforce in contemporary minds the connection between sin and disease. Odo of Beaumont, whose symptoms are described in some detail in the *Miracles of St. Thomas,* had contracted gonorrhoea by frequenting brothels, as a result of which he was segregated as a leper. The same fate had befallen a debauched Norman knight whom abbot Samson once met at Bury St. Edmunds.

Female fertility was taken to be the gift of God, from which it followed that barrenness was a sign of God's displeasure. Particularly common were cases in which women who married within the prohibited degrees of affinity, or committed adultery, were unable to conceive. In 1063 we hear of a Norman couple who travelled to Rome 'on account of their sterility'. At the end of the eleventh century a landowner presented two estates to the abbey of Conques, in the hope of an heir. Thereafter, such donations became fairly common, and in some cases, the connection between sin and barrenness was heavily underlined. A Frenchman who visited Santiago in 1108 to pray for the birth of a son, 'as is customary', found his request refused on account of the gravity of his sins; not until he 'wept, cried out, and prayed with all his heart' did he have his way. No class was immune from the curse of barrenness and its occurrence, especially among princes, tended to provoke dramatic displays of penitence. When Wladislaw Hermann, king of Poland, was unable to beget an heir in 1085, he underwent a rigorous programme of fasts, vigils, and prayers, and lavishly distributed alms to the poor. Finally, on the advice of a French missionary bishop, he sent an embassy to the shrine of St. Gilles in Provence, bearing numerous gifts, including a small golden model of a baby boy. His son, the future Boleslaw III, was born shortly afterwards.

Miraculous Medicine

On the feast day of the saints the crowds of the sick and the dying filled the great basilicas. Around the shrine they lay in makeshift beds or wrapped themselves in blankets, surrounded by a host of relatives and well-wishers, the wealthier among them attended by their own physicians and servants. Many of them waited for weeks and even months as the clergy of the basilica fulfilled their daily rounds of offices and ceremonies. Some dramatically recovered and the miracle was proclaimed amid scenes of hysterical rejoicing; others died within sight of the shrine.

The rituals for the treatment of the sick differed from century to century and from church to church. Pilgrims were not normally permitted to touch the relics themselves. Public exhibitions of relics were rare and imposing ceremonies, while private views were enjoyed only by the great or the exceptionally persuasive. In 1088 a woman with withered hands asked to be allowed to touch the body of St. Gilles 'asserting that if this was done she would undoubtedly be cured, for so much had been revealed to her in a dream the night before'. Her request was granted, but in terms which show that this was an unusual favour, to be explained only by the possibility that her dream was of divine origin. Most pilgrims never saw the relics of the saint who had healed them.

Instead they applied to their bodies objects such as dust, stones, or scraps of paper which had been in contact with the saint or the saint's shrine. Eating or drinking such substances was believed to be particularly effective, perhaps because it underlined the similarities between human and celestial medicine. In the time of Gregory of Tours sick men ate wax from the candles which burned before the shrine and some even ate the charred wicks. During an epidemic of dysentery in the Loire valley at the end of the sixth century, many of the sick drank water containing dust from the tomb of St. Martin, while others drank the water used to wash down the sarcophagus before Easter. Both methods, according to Gregory, were equally effective. Sick men drank water in which a splinter of the True Cross had been immersed or chewed the length of silk in which it had been wrapped. Gregory himself had been cured of an inflammation of the eyes by drinking wine poured into a footstep of St. Benigne preserved in the ground at Dijon.

The dipping of relics in water or wine remained the commonest method of healing practised in the pilgrimage churches of the eleventh and twelfth centuries. It was a convenient way of parcelling out the miraculous power of the relics among large numbers of people. At the end of the eleventh century a crowd estimated at several thousand gathered at Chateau-Gordon during an epidemic to receive jars of the wine that had been used to wash down the tomb of St. Benedict. 'Experience has repeatedly proved', explained Raoul Tortaire, 'that whenever a sick person washes any part of the shrine with wine or water and then drinks it with faith, he will immediately recover.' At Norwich cathedral, pilgrims drank water mixed with scrapings of cement from the tomb of St. William. At Reading abbey the hand of St. James was dipped in water, phials of which were sent off to cure the sick in their own homes. After swallowing it, they would usually vomit violently, suffer a high fever for several hours, and then suddenly recover. Much the same effects are recorded at Canterbury, where 'water of St. Thomas' was one of the most celebrated medicines of the twelfth century. This consisted of the blood of St. Thomas, wiped up from the floor of Canterbury cathedral after his murder and diluted in a large cistern of water, thus ensuring, says Becket's biographer, both that there was plenty available and that it would not be too repulsive to drink. The water was continually diluted as demand for it rose, and one of the monks of Christ Church priory was charged with the task of preparing it and pouring it into little ampullae for the use of the sick. A London priest was cured by this concoction within a week of Becket's death. Not only was it drunk by the sick and smeared on the eyelids of the blind, but cases were reported in which it was used for the magical detection of thieves and even for extinguishing fires. A small ampulla worn around the neck became the badge of a Canterbury pilgrim. Parallels with eucharistic piety obviously suggest themselves and Benedict of Peterborough did not hesitate to draw them: 'just as St. Thomas in his lifetime sought to achieve the same perfection as the Son of Man, so, after his death, he was honoured in the same fashion, by the partaking of his blood.'

There are some indications that sensitive persons found this practice repellent. This was one reason why the blood of St. Thomas was so heavily diluted. A sick monk of Mont-St.-Michel refused a draught of the wine which had washed the skull of St. Aubert, 'preferring to die than drink wine swilled in the head of a corpse'. It may be that growing sensitivity on this point explains the fact that these macabre beverages passed out of fashion after the twelfth century.

Any genuine cures which occurred at the shrines of the saints evidently occurred in spite of such methods rather than because of them. In most cases the sick no doubt owed their recovery to the strength of their constitutions, and the symptoms disappeared in the natural way. Since they frequently remained at the shrine until they recovered or died, sometimes indeed for several months at a time, it would be surprising if there were not many 'cures' of this kind. Such factors as a change of diet or climate may well have assisted the natural recovery of these pertinacious pilgrims. Moreover, it must not be forgotten that the clergy, although relying principally on the celestial medicine of their patron saints, were not above practising terrestrial medicine as well. Many pilgrimage centres had excellent medical libraries which included parts of the Hippocratic corpus and the works of Galen. Canterbury cathedral priory had an enormous library of medical books, with which William, one of the authors of the *Miracles of St. Thomas,* seems to have been familiar. Bury St. Edmunds too had a substantial collection. Among the French abbeys where book-medicine thrived were Cluny and St. Martial of Limoges, both of them major pilgrimage churches. The practice of medicine by monks was quite common, though the Church made periodic attempts to discourage it. Thus, the celebrated

Baldwin, physician to Edward the Confessor and William the Conqueror, was first a monk of St.-Denis and then abbot of Bury St. Edmunds. William of Malmesbury tells us that one of the monks of his abbey, a certain Gregory, was a very famous physician in his day, and would occasionally give consultations to pilgrims at the shrine of St. Aldhelm.

At these churches it seems likely that the cult of the saints was superimposed upon a pre-existing body of medical lore, some of which may conceivably have been sound. Some of the miraculous streams visited by the sick probably had a genuine therapeutic value. Pilgrims came from as far away as Burgundy and Aquitaine to the one which flowed past the Norman monastery of St. Evroul, thus causing great distress to local farmers whose crops were trampled down by the crowds. St. Thomas is said to have recommended a variety of homely medicines to his devotees. One woman was healed after he had instructed her in a vision to drink the juice of certain herbs in her garden and then to have a long sleep. A physician of Bergerac was told to cure his dropsy by making an incision in his stomach in accordance with contemporary surgical practice. The daughter of Ralph Raison, who for two years had suffered from boils on her feet, was recommended by a vision of St. Gilbert to go to his shrine at Sempringham and there apply a poultice to them. If the treatment was successful it was, of course, attributed to the saint on the ground that no medicine could be effective without God's merciful intervention. Baldwin of Bury himself hesitated before claiming the credit for healing a patient. When he successfully healed the bishop of Thetford's eye, the feat was acclaimed as a miracle of St. Edmund for, as the bishop's amanuensis pointed out to him, 'not even Hippocrates or Galen themselves could have cured you unless you had been found deserving of God's mercy.'

The less spectacular miracles can often be explained in psychological terms. In addition to the physical ailments suffered by pilgrims, a very high proportion of them suffered from mental illnesses signified by dumbness, delirium, epilepsy, and the like. This is particularly true of the Merovingian and Carolingian periods; approximately half the miraculous cures recorded by Gregory of Tours involved some form of insanity or mental abnormality. Moreover, contemporaries were only too ready to diagnose insanity in persons who were suffering from nothing more than temporary depression or nervous tension. The English peasantry, according to William of Canterbury, looked upon melancholy or broodiness as a symptom of insanity. Even purely physical afflictions may have been cured, at least temporarily, by psychosomatic means, for physical discomfort, even severe physical discomfort, can be induced by hypochondria, a fact which was not realized by orthodox medical practitioners until the nineteenth century.

The powerful belief that sin was the cause of sickness may itself have been responsible for a number of maladies of psychological origin. 'Punitive' miracles in particular are well attested in primitive societies today, where those who have broken a universally accepted taboo go into a state of excitement and panic which can have serious effects culminating often in paralysis, occasionally in death. The victim's expectation of death is a powerful factor in bringing on his or her illness. Research into Voodoo and battle shock has suggested that this can be explained by prolonged adrenal overexcitement and a sharp fall in blood pressure, leading to a state analogous to surgical shock. Such seems to have been the fate of Waldo, a youth of Matrignac at the close of the eleventh century, who had a spell laid on him by a witch whom he had slighted; as a result, he lost his memory and became dazed, aimless, and finally delirious. Similarly fourteen-year-old Luciana Torel of Austrey (Worcestershire) lost her speech and was partially paralysed when her father cursed her for sewing on St. Cecilia's day. The closeness of mediaeval society greatly intensified the feelings of guilt experienced by those who had flouted the more formidable moral canons. Helen of Luttershall arrived at St. Frideswide's, Oxford, in the 1180s suffering from chronic insomnia and nervous exhaustion, the result of having allowed herself to become the concubine of a priest for three months. After confessing her sin and praying at the shrine, her anguished feelings of guilt appear to have been relieved and she made a complete recovery. Such conditions as hysterical loss of appetite can almost invariably be traced to psychological causes and were consequently amenable to psychological treatment. In this category falls the case of Nicholas of Dover, who refused all food and drink for eighteen days and was saved from death only by being carried to the shrine of St. Thomas.

Sickness, even when it is not caused by stress, is easily aggravated by it. Illnesses tended to be long lasting for lack of the simplest curative measures, and in the absence of a comprehensive system of 'social security' they posed a serious threat to the economic survival of a family. They were therefore accompanied by very considerable emotional stress. William of Malmesbury gives us the case history of a woman of Malmesbury 'of moderate means' who was suddenly paralysed. For five years she was bedridden and paid out the bulk of her wealth in medical fees. Her family were gradually reduced to poverty until at length they were unable even to buy bread. The husband at this stage deserted her, leaving her dependent on charity. It is clear from the sequel that her paralysis was not permanent but had been prolonged by the distressing social consequences which it produced. The woman was ultimately cured at the shrine of St. Aldhelm in Malmesbury.

In circumstances such as these, 'miraculous' cures contained two essential ingredients which had the effect of relieving psychological stress. First came the diagnosis (i.e. sin) accompanied by the confident assurance of the possibility of a cure. Then followed the ceremonies at the shrine or the making of a vow, accomplished with formality and pomp, marking the moment of dramatic recovery. The patient, given his desire to be cured and his conviction that he would be, usually persuaded himself that he had recovered and may actually have done so. 'Hope invited her; faith instructed her,' Thomas of Monmouth percipiently remarked of a woman healed in Norwich cathedral. Persuasion was the most important element of miraculous healing in the Middle Ages. Modern research has suggested that persuasion, or 'faith-healing', can have marked physiological effects, which can be observed by injecting saline into a hypochondriac who believes it is morphine; the patient's symptoms are relieved by the strength of his or her own belief. Caesarius of Heisterbach admitted that a man might be cured by a false relic, provided that he believed that it was genuine. Benedict of Peterborough told an unusually candid story of a young man who lay on his death-bed and begged his friends to bring him some 'water of St. Thomas'.

> 'But unfortunately none of them had any, so one of the friends ran to a nearby fountain and filled a glass with fresh water. "Here", he said, "here is the saint's water for

which you asked." The sick man believed it and drained the glass. Happily deceived, he immediately felt himself much improved; and thus, he who had lately been staring death in the face, got out of bed feeling nothing worse than a slight stiffness.'

If the sickness was a serious one, a psychosomatic cure would normally have been short-lived. But any relapse would have occurred after the pilgrim had left the shrine and returned to his former environment. The authors of the miracle stories either did not know of them, or chose to ignore them. The *Miracles of St. Thomas* are unique in that they not only describe the symptoms and case histories of each patient, but sometimes they record what became of him. From this it appears that relapses were remarkably common. A madwoman of Rouen recovered her sanity at Canterbury but lost it when she returned home. A monk of Poitiers found that his leprosy returned once he had left Canterbury. A Fleming called Gerard was only temporarily relieved of his ulcer. The authors found it hard to explain such occurrences. In one case the relapse is attributed to the patient's immediately engaging in hard agricultural labour. Very common are cases in which the patient relapsed because he omitted to express proper gratitude to the saint, or did not fulfil a vow of pilgrimage, or did fulfil it but failed to make a sufficiently generous offering. But there are others where the authors are frankly mystified and are driven to the conclusion that the patient had committed some obscure and horrible sin. Ralph of Langton was cured of leprosy in May and relapsed in December 'owing to some hidden judgement of God,...for the cause of this relapse only He can know.' Defective cures at one shrine were commonly recorded by the clergy of another, and from this it is plain that relapses were by no means confined to Canterbury pilgrims. Thus Ralph Attenborough, a mental defective, was cured as soon as he accepted from a priest the staff of a pilgrim of St. James; but his afflictions returned three months later, after he had come back from Santiago, and he was finally cured at Sempringham in September 1201. Hubald, archdeacon of Salisbury, was relieved of pains in his neck by touching the shrine of St. Aldhelm, but on his return home the pains began once more and continued until he made a second pilgrimage to Malmesbury.

Some of those who visited the great sanctuaries of the Middle Ages did undoubtedly enjoy a genuine recovery, for reasons which can quite easily be explained in the light of modern medical and anthropological knowledge. It is possible to accept most of the facts as contemporaries stated them while maintaining scepticism as to their miraculous causation. The British Medical Association has suggested six factors which account for most miraculous cures reported in modern times: 1. mistaken diagnosis; 2. mistaken prognosis; 3. apparent alleviation of symptoms; 4. periodic remission of the symptoms; 5. spontaneous cure; 6. simultaneous use of physical remedies. All these factors can be found in the exceptionally well-documented miracles of St. Thomas of Canterbury, and some of them are present in almost every miracle collection. Such consideration will not, of course, explain every miraculous cure. Many stories must be regarded as fabrications or pious legends. But it should be remembered that a very small number of genuine cures will suffice to excite general belief in a large number of fictitious ones. To cite a modern parallel, in the nineteenth century less than a hundred cures at Lourdes were officially certified by the Roman Catholic Church as being of miraculous origin; but this tiny proportion has been enough to draw many millions to St. Bernadette's grotto in the Pyrenees. In an earlier age, ill-equipped to understand the mysteries of sickness and health, it would be surprising if people did not put their faith in unorthodox medicine and magic rituals.

6

Origins and Ideals

The Steps of the Master

It is a striking paradox that the most celebrated tomb visited by pilgrims in the Middle Ages was empty, the tomb, once prepared for Joseph of Arimathea, in which the dead Christ had lain for three days and then risen from the dead. The pilgrimage to Jerusalem had a longer history than any other, and it remained throughout in a class of its own. Time brought to the Holy Places most of the abuses which popular enthusiasm had already created in the west, but the Jerusalem pilgrimage was nonetheless consistently the most spiritual pilgrimage of the Middle Ages.

For the first three centuries after the death of Christ there was very little to see in Jerusalem. Most of the city which Christ had known was utterly destroyed by Titus in A.D. 70. Christian travellers were chiefly interested in its remarkable library which made it, by the end of the second century, a meeting place for the foremost scholars of the first age of Christian philosophy. Melito, bishop of Sardis (d. c. 190), visited Palestine in order to copy out extracts from the Old Testament. At the beginning of the third century, bishop Alexander greatly expanded the library, which was visited by Origen and

Fermillian of Caesarea. It was in this library that Eusebius gathered the materials for his great *History*.

Few mediaeval pilgrims to the Holy Land were scholars, and yet they shared with these early travellers a desire to recreate in their imagination the scenes of Christ's ministry and passion. Origen declared that he had come to 'walk in the footsteps of the Master'. At the close of the fourth century Paulinus of Nola wrote:

> 'No other sentiment draws men to Jerusalem than the desire to see and touch the places where Christ was physically present, and to be able to say from our very own experience "we have gone into his tabernacle and adored in the very places where his feet have stood" (Ps. CXXXII. 7)....Theirs is a truly spiritual desire to see the places where Christ suffered, rose from the dead, and ascended into heaven....The manger of His birth, the river of His baptism, the garden of His betrayal, the palace of His condemnation, the column of His scourging, the thorns of His crowning, the wood of His crucifixion, the stone of His burial: all these things recall God's former presence on earth and demonstrate the ancient basis of our modern beliefs.'

The deeds of the Old Testament prophets and the events of Christ's life, so remote from the medieval minds, took on a thrilling immediacy when they were recited on the very soil which they had trodden. It was a common practice amongst the early pilgrims to read aloud passages from the Scriptures in the places to which they related. 'Etheria', the remarkable Spanish lady whose travels at the end of the fourth century took her as far afield as Sinai and Edessa, had read not only the

Scriptures but the *Ecclesiastical History* of Eusebius and the Acts of the more important Christian martyrs. Coming to the cave of Moses in the side of Mount Sinai she and her party paused to read out the passage of Exodus (33:22): '...and it shall come to pass...that I will put thee in a cleft of the rock and cover thee with my hand while I pass by.' With the Old Testament in her hand she was able to follow, as she thought, the exact route of the Israelites in their flight out of Egypt. At the shrine of St. Thecla near Seleucia she had the *acta* of the saint read to her. It was a feeling for the Holy Places compounded of imagination and romanticism, an attempt not merely to read the Scriptures but to relive them in her own actions.

The services held at Jerusalem during Holy Week were designed to reinforce this feeling. On each clay of the week the congregation met at the site of the events which had occurred on that day in the first Holy Week. Most of these sites were now covered by churches and the crowds moved from one to the other while the relevant passages of the Gospels were recited to them. Thus on the Wednesday they met in the Garden of Gethsemane, where a deacon read from the Gospel of St. Matthew the account of the betrayal. On Good Friday, the climax of the pilgrim's journey, the relics of the Passion were displayed and the account of the crucifixion read to the crowd, together with passages from the Old Testament foretelling it. When Etheria was there in c. 382 'every one present was overwhelmed by emotion and the strongest men there could not contain their tears.'

St. Jerome, who lived at Bethlehem for the last thirty-five years of his life, was the foremost exponent of this scholarly attitude to the Holy Places. He could not conceal his contempt for those pilgrims who supposed that their souls would benefit by the mere fact that their bodies were in Jerusalem. In a famous and often quoted letter Jerome observed that a pilgrim should 'not merely live in Jerusalem but live a holy life there'. It was at Bethlehem that Jerome made his great translation of the Bible, and in pungent letters to admirers in the west he asserted that only in Palestine was a true understanding of the Scriptures to be had. To study the Bible anywhere else was like learning Greek at Lilibaeum or Latin in Sicily. 'One may only truly understand the Holy Scriptures after looking upon Judaea with one's own eyes.' Jerome himself lyrically described the emotions of his protégée Paula when she visited the Holy Places for the first time:

> 'She threw herself down in adoration before the cross as if she could see the Lord himself hanging from it. And when she entered the tomb, she kissed the stone which the angel had rolled away....What tears she shed there, what sighs of grief, all Jerusalem knows....After this she came to Bethlehem and entered the cave where the Saviour was born; and when she looked upon the inn, the stall, and the crib...she cried out in my hearing that with the eyes of her soul she could see the infant Christ wrapped in swaddling clothes and crying in the manger.'

Paula's pilgrimage was a constant effort of imagination, a mystical experience as intense in its own way as that of St. Francis at La Verna. But before long this mystical adoration of the Holy Places had crystallized into a naive and literal view which attached the greatest importance to the physical survival of relics of the Passion. The practice of collecting soil from the Holy Land, already common in the time of St. Augustine, was a popular echo of the words of the psalmist, 'we have adored in the places where his feet have stood.' Augustine's contemporary, Paulinus of Nola, commended it on the ground that 'we must not ignore the simple and literal sense of this passage, even though it may contain a deeper one as well.' Indeed, Paulinus believed that the footprints of Christ were physically preserved in the ground at the point whence He had ascended into Heaven 'so that we may adore the imprint of the divine feet in the very dust trodden by the Lord, and then we may truly say that "we have adored in the place where his feet have stood." ' At the end of the seventh century the Gallic traveller Arculf observed these footprints exactly as Paulinus had described them, and reported that pilgrims took pinches of dust from them as souvenirs of their visit.

The veneration of the Holy Places as a living and visible commentary on the Bible did not, of course, die with the generation of St. Jerome, any more than did the tradition of meditation on the Passion which these early pilgrims had inaugurated. Arculf, for example, was described by a contemporary as 'learned in scripture'. At Bethany he was able to follow in the synoptic Gospels the very path of Christ and the apostles. In later times, the mendicant orders, who ultimately acquired control of the Holy Places, encouraged meditation on the Scriptures, and on the Passion in particular. A Franciscan novice who visited the Holy Land in the middle of the thirteenth century remembered how, reading his Bible in the Holy Places, he had felt as if he was witnessing with his own eyes the tortures inflicted on Christ. At the end of the fifteenth century the Dominican Felix Faber remarked that experienced Biblical exegetes were regularly confounded by the arguments of those who had been to the Holy Land.

The growing emphasis on the humanity of Christ in the spiritual literature of the eleventh and twelfth centuries found its reflection in the behaviour of pilgrims in the Holy Land. The pilgrimage of Richard of St.-Vanne to the Holy Land in 1026–7 followed a prolonged period of meditation on the Passion and death of Christ. What the Holy Places meant to this man is indicated by his actions in Jerusalem in Holy Week:

> 'It is not for me', his biographer wrote, 'to describe the anguished tears which he shed when at last he reached those venerable places. When he saw the pillar of Pilate in the Praetorium he witnessed in his mind's eye the binding and scourging of the Saviour. He thought of the spitting, the smiting, the mocking, and the crown of thorns. Then, on the place of Calvary, he passed through his mind an image of the Saviour crucified, pierced with a lance, reviled and mocked by all around him, crying out with a loud voice, and yielding up his spirit. And meditating on these scenes, he could no longer hold back his tears, and surrendered to the agony which he felt.'

Richard's experience was not uncommon. St. Silvinus, according to his ninth-century biographer, stood on the mount of Calvary and 'although he could not see God with his bodily eyes he could nevertheless see Him with his spiritual eyes, standing in the very place where He had saved humanity from the power of Satan by the shedding of His precious blood.' The twelfth-century ascetic Rayner Pisani used to pray so fervently on Mount Tabor that he would actually see Christ with Moses and Elias, exactly as Peter, James and John had once seen Him.

These ascetics and visionaries saw themselves as reliving the life of Christ. They often referred to their pilgrimage as an *imitatio Christi*. By re-enacting in their own lives the sufferings of Christ they felt that they were performing an act of personal redemption just as Christ, by His death, had made possible the salvation of all people. On Maundy Thursday 1027, Richard of St.-Vannes knelt down in the square in front of the Holy Sepulchre, and washed the feet of the poor. Rayner of Pisa fasted for forty days on Mount Tabor in remembrance of Christ's forty days in the desert. All pilgrims who could baptized themselves in the Jordan at the point where John the Baptist was believed to have baptized Christ. Some, like St. Bona of Pisa (d. 1207), spent several months following the exact path of Christ's ministry, beginning at the Jordan and ending at the place of Calvary. Others, like Fulk Nerra, count of Anjou, flagellated themselves before the basilica of the Holy Sepulchre, and in the latter half of the twelfth century it was common for pilgrims to have themselves flagellated at the very pillar preserved in the church of Mount Sion. One contemporary went so far as to describe Henry II's visit to Canterbury in July 1174 as an *imitatio Christi* for, like Christ, he allowed himself to be beaten with scourges; 'save that Christ did this for the remission of our sins whereas Henry did it for the remission of his own.'

At its highest level, a pilgrim's life in Jerusalem was conceived as a continuously repeated drama of the life of Christ. The rituals which he performed, more than a mere passion play, had something of the regenerative qualities of the celebration of the Eucharist. In this idea lies the distant origin of the modern liturgical practice of the Roman Catholic Church known as the 'stations of the Cross'. Already in 1231 the exact route which Christ was believed to have followed from Pilate's prison to Calvary was marked out in the streets of Jerusalem. Some seventy years later Ricoldo of Monte Croce 'followed the path which Christ ascended when he carried the Cross', which took him past the house of Pilate, the place where Simon of Cyrene was made to help him, and thence to the Golgotha chapel in the basilica of the Holy Sepulchre. The sire d'Anglure followed the same route in 1395 with a few stations added, 'a thing which every pilgrim who makes this journey can and ought to do.' The journey of the ideal pilgrim could be presented, as Franco Sacchetti presented it at the beginning of the fourteenth century, as an elaborate allegory of the life of Christ from the Nativity to the Resurrection. The pilgrim's entry into a roadside hospice was likened to the incarnation in the womb of the Blessed Virgin. The dangers of the route found their counterpart in the Passion of the Lord. The pilgrim may be betrayed and killed by his companions as Christ was betrayed by Judas and killed by the Jews. He may be betrayed and killed by his host, as Christ was welcomed into Jerusalem by those same Jews who later killed him. Robbers may waylay and despoil him just as the soldiers divided Christ's belongings amongst themselves. It is a naïve, anti-Semitic picture which must have been offered to countless groups of pilgrims departing to the Holy Land. Yet it conceals one of the profoundest sentiments of an age which reduced all spiritual ideas to images. At a popular level people sought to associate themselves with the life of the Saviour, to express literally their conviction that he had saved them by his death. They wished to tear down the barrier of remoteness that separated a person of the thirteenth century from the events of the first. At the highest levels of Christian mysticism they sought, like St. Francis, to 'enter into the mind and body of the crucified Christ and take on Christ's sufferings in their own persons'.

The Rejection of the World

Contempt for the society which they left behind was at least as important to the followers of St. Jerome as their longing for the promised land. His entourage at Bethlehem saw in their pilgrimage an act of self-denial, of voluntary exile whose object was to take them away from Rome and thus from the 'damnation to which the rest of the world is destined'. Equally negative were the motives of the younger Melania, who left Rome in 410 allowing the wind to take her ship where it would; it took her not to Palestine but to north Africa, where she passed seven years before setting eyes on the Holy Places. 'Depart from the midst of Babylon', Jerome urged a friend who had stayed behind in Rome, 'for it is the house of Satan, the stronghold of iniquity and sin.'

The desire to renounce civilization as contemporaries knew it was a powerful spiritual impulse of the late classical period. Born in the deserts of Egypt in the third century, it remained until the twelfth a strong element of Christian piety. Its inspiration in Jerome's day was the *Life of St. Anthony* by Athanasius. The decisive moment of Augustine's 'conversion' had come when he had heard of two ordinary soldiers who had abandoned the world to live as hermits after reading the *Life of St. Anthony*. Jerome's friend Marcella had had a similar experience in Rome. During his three years in Rome between 382 and 385 Jerome gathered round him a self-conscious group of ascetics, most of them women, who felt that the Christian society of the city had compromised with paganism, come to terms with the world and the flesh. They saw them-

selves as an elite corps, besieged on every side by flabby worldliness, forced by the ordinary necessities of life to descend to
the level of those around them. The true spirit of Christianity
they saw in the communities of hermits in the Egyptian desert,
and it was these communities, as much as the Holy Places, that
drew western pilgrims to the east. Paula, who visited Egypt in
Jerome's company in 386, 'threw herself at the feet of these holy
men and seemed to see the Lord himself in every one of them.'
The elder Melania spent five years in Egypt in the 370s before
proceeding to Jerusalem. Etheria would not return home until
she had visited the Egyptian monasteries, and the younger
Melania returned to Egypt after only a few weeks in the Holy
Land 'in order to learn about the perfect life from her spiritual
superiors, the desert hermits.'

Pilgrimage in the early Church was very often motivated by
a purely negative rejection of urban values. Jerome spoke of himself as 'forsaking the bustling cities of Antioch and Constantinople
so as to draw down upon myself the mercy of Christ in the soli-
tude of the country.' It was a process of self-exile, of social and
physical isolation. To Jerome, a pilgrim was not a vulgar tourist, an
audience for the lying guides who plied their trade in the Holy
City. He was a monk. His place of exile did not matter; how he
lived was more important than where, and even the sites of the
Crucifixion and Resurrection were of no intrinsic spiritual value
unless the pilgrim was ready to carry the cross of the Lord and be
resurrected with him. St. Anthony, whom Jerome intensely
admired, had never seen Jerusalem.

Jerome was well aware that his austere views were visibly
rejected by most pilgrims of his own day. But they are worth
dwelling on, because Jerome bequeathed a tradition to mediaeval Christianity, and his works were on the book-lists of serious

pilgrims for ten centuries after his death. The monastic ideal remained for many years inseparable from contemporary notions of pilgrimage, though Egypt lost its fascination for western pilgrims after the fifth century. During the monastic revival of the eighth century, pilgrims regarded Rome in much the same light as they had once seen Egypt and Palestine. Four Anglo-Saxon kings retired to die there in the space of fifty years. The Lombard king Ratchis walked to Rome with his wife and children in 749 and accepted the monastic habit at the pope's hands. Just as in the fifth century the empress Eudoxia, estranged wife of Theodosius II, had exiled herself to Jerusalem to escape her enemies, so in the eighth century Pippin's brother Karloman left the Frankish court and settled in a Roman monastery on Monte Soracte.

Jerome's attitude to pilgrimage as an escape from civilization was unconsciously revived by the Irish. Their distinctive contribution to the spiritual life of the 'dark ages' was the idea of the aimless wanderer whose renunciation of the world was the most complete of which man could conceive, far more austere than the principles of Benedictine monasticism. In the wandering Irish hermits of the sixth and seventh centuries, western Europe came as near as it would ever do to those 'athletes of Christ', the desert fathers of Egypt and Syria in late antiquity. By wandering freely without destination, the Irish hermit felt that he had cut himself off from every material accessory to life. In his eighth sermon St. Columban dwells on the transitory nature of life, and declares: 'I know that if this earthly tent of mine is taken down, I shall get a new home from God made by no human hands. It makes me sigh, this longing for the shelter of my heavenly habitation...for I know that while I am in my body I am travelling away from God.' The notion of a specific destination did not enter into Columban's thinking; his only destination was the heavenly Jerusalem. The spirit of Columban's teaching was precisely expressed by an Irish pilgrim of the twelfth century, who quoted with approval Jerome's strictures against 'Babylon' (i.e. Rome) and urged his hearers to 'be exiles for God's sake, and go not only to Jerusalem but everywhere, for God himself is everywhere.' The same conviction brought three Irishmen to the court of king Alfred in 891 'in a boat without any oars, because they wished for the love of God to be in foreign lands, they cared not where.' Only in the ninth century did some Irish begin to regard Rome as a place of special spiritual merit, and even then a marginal annotation in an Irish hymn-book informs us that 'going to Rome involves great effort and little reward, for the King whom you seek there you will not find unless you bring him with you.'

Bede has left us the spiritual portrait of an Englishman of his own day, the Northumbrian monk Egbert, who passed much of his early life in Ireland and became deeply imbued with Irish spiritual values. According to Bede's informant, Egbert had once suffered from a serious illness during which he became terrifyingly conscious of his own sinfulness. He persuaded himself that even the slender material ties which kept him in an Irish monastery were dragging him to perdition. He determined to become an aimless wanderer fulfilling in exile the daily rituals of the monastic life. 'He would live in exile and never return to his native Britain. In addition to the solemn psalmody of the canonical offices, he would recite the entire psalter in praise of God, unless prevented by illness. Every week he would fast for a day and a night.'

Religious wandering was recognized by contemporaries as

a peculiarly Irish practice. 'Why is it', asked the hagiographer Heiric in a letter to Charles the Bald, 'that almost the entire population of Ireland, contemptuous of the perils of the sea, has migrated to our shores with a great crowd of teachers? The more learned they are the more distant their chosen place of exile.' 'Wandering is an ineradicable habit of the Irish race,' observed a ninth-century monk of St.-Gall. The popularity of aimless pilgrimage in the seventh and eighth centuries on the continent can usually be traced to Celtic influence. Irish missionaries spread their ideas amongst the Anglo-Saxons, many of whom exiled themselves to monasteries in Ireland. St. Colman built a monastery in Mayo in 667 exclusively for their use, and Englishmen were still living there more than a century later. St. Cyran (d. 697), founder of the abbey of Lonrey, was converted to the wandering life by an Irish hermit whom he encountered. When the Norman monk Wandrille was commanded in a vision to abandon his home and friends, he made straight for the Irish monastery at Bobbio in northern Italy. Some Irish wanderers, like St. Cadroe at the beginning of the eleventh century, were joined by ever-growing bands of disciples as they trod their erratic paths across western Europe.

Isolated examples of this eccentric behaviour can be found in Germany well into the twelfth century, but as a way of life it had died more than two hundred years earlier. As the missions conquered paganism in central and northern Europe, formal Churches were established with the hierarchical organization familiar to older Christian lands. The wandering of priests across diocesan boundaries and the departure of monks from their monasteries were discouraged by St. Boniface after the 740s, and strenuously condemned by his successors. The reorganization of the monastic life in the ninth century, which is associated with the name of Benedict of Aniane, reinforced the hostility of the authorities to wandering monks. A Frankish synod forbade them to go without permission to Rome 'or anywhere else' as early as 751. The same prohibition was embodied in the capitularies of Charlemagne, which rehearsed that these unauthorized wanderings were destructive of ecclesiastical discipline and instrumental in spreading 'unnecessary doubts' among the people. The spiritual ideals of the Irish thus found themselves in conflict with the tendency of the Carolingians to make use of Benedictine monasticism as a stabilizing force, a propagator of what one might call the 'cultural colonialism' of the ninth century. Henceforth renunciation of the world was to mean entering a monastery or a fixed hermitage. Itinerant clerics were to find themselves condemned even by such fierce ascetics as Peter Damian. When Everard de Breteuil, *vicomte* of Chartres, suddenly renounced the world in 1073, he became a hermit living a 'life of freedom', and earned his living by burning charcoal; he was persuaded, however, that the irregularity of his life was unpleasing to God, and so entered the monastery of Marmoutiers.

7

The Penitential Pilgrimage

Penance and Pilgrimage

An age which loved definition and codified religious observances also divided pilgrims into categories. The lawyers and theologians of the thirteenth century distinguished between voluntary pilgrimages undertaken as an act of personal piety, and compulsory ones imposed by confessors or courts of law. Yet the distinction was unreal, for the need to expiate their sins was common to both classes. In the first centuries of Christianity sinners occasionally exiled themselves voluntarily to Jerusalem as an act of penitence. One of Jerome's correspondents, a notorious adulterer called Sabinianus, retired to expiate his sins at Bethlehem, though he shortly returned to his old ways. In Constantinople, St. Marcian persuaded several ladies of loose morals to withdraw to the Holy Land at the end of the fifth century. The monasteries of Palestine, like those of Egypt and Syria, drew a large number of penitents.

Yet the early Church knew neither judicial nor penitential pilgrimage. Rituals and panaceas had little place in a penitential system as strict as that which was known to St. Augustine. The notorious sinner was excluded from the life of the Church, and the conditions on which he was readmitted amounted to a promise to live an almost monastic existence for the rest of his days. Public penance was a 'second baptism'. Like baptism it could be performed only once in a lifetime, and in practice it was nearly always postponed to the eve of death. Pilgrimages were not imposed on penitents until the sixth century, when the whole notion of penance was transformed by the Irish missionaries. The Irish confessor imposed penances, which varied with the gravity of the sin, in accordance with a penitential 'tariff', of which several were already in circulation by the end of the sixth century. Here were found comprehensive lists of sins together with the appropriate penances ranging from short fasts to perpetual exile. Pilgrimage was much favoured by the Irish as a spiritual exercise. As a penance for the more enormous transgressions it was thought especially appropriate. Pilgrimages of varying duration are specified for murder (particularly by clerics), incest, bestiality, and sacrilege. The sins of monks and those of the higher clergy were visited more often with penitential pilgrimages than those of any other class.

In the Irish penitentials we have the origin of the distinction between 'public' and 'private' penance, which was defined and elaborated by the thirteenth-century schoolmen. Public penance, which usually meant pilgrimage, was imposed for public sins with overtones of scandal, notably the sexual offences of the clergy. It was a useful penance, wrote the canonist Raymond of Peñaforte, for 'those scandalous and notorious sins which set the whole town talking'; when they were committed by laymen the penance was described as 'solemn', when by clergymen as 'public'. This idea was still very much alive at the end of the Middle Ages when Chaucer's parson explained the distinction to his fellow-travellers: 'commune penaunce', the *penitentia publica non sollemnis* of the schoolmen, was used 'when a man hath sinned openly, of which sin the fame is openly spoken in the country....Common penance is that (which) priests enjoin men commonly in certain cases, as for to go, peradventure, naked in pilgrimages or barefoot.'

The scandalous overtones were obviously stronger in cases involving clerics or noblemen, and it was above all these classes who were wont to be sent on long pilgrimages. The emperor Otto III was advised by St. Romuald to walk barefoot to Monte Gargano after murdering a Roman senator in breach of his safe-conduct. Romuald's biographer Peter Damian imposed pilgrimages to Rome, Tours, and Santiago on the corrupt and rebellious clergy of Milan; a marquis called Renier he sent to Jerusalem 'on account of the grave sins which you have confessed to me.' A pilgrimage was thought the appropriate sentence for count Thierry who murdered the archbishop-elect of Trier in 1066, as it was, more than a century later, for Henry II after the murder of Becket, and for Raymond VI of Toulouse after the death of the papal legate on the steps of the abbey of St.-Gilles. These penances were in no sense voluntary. Even in the cases of kings the pressure of public opinion could be overpowering, and to ignore it would have been politically most unwise, as both Raymond of Toulouse and Henry II discovered to their cost.

For such notorious crimes the penitential pilgrimage remained in use throughout the later Middle Ages. During his regular visitations of the province of Rouen, archbishop Odo Rigaud constantly imposed pilgrimages on both clerics and laymen for their sexual indiscretions. Other offences which were punished thus included forgery, breaking sanctuary, and public irreverence towards the services of the Church. For seizing and imprisoning a cleric, Robert de Frechesne, *bailli* of

Rouen was sent to St. Michael's church in Rouen, there to recite fifty *Pater Nosters* and fifty *Ave Marias,* to fast for three days, and to distribute five shillings to the poor. In the province of Cologne a synod of 1279 recommended pilgrimages in cases involving self-indulgence of any sort. The publicity which long-distance pilgrims drew to themselves made it the obvious penalty for spectacular crimes. Roger da Bonito was sent to Rome, Santiago, and Jerusalem in 1319 for murdering the bishop of Fricento. For his attack on Boniface VIII at Anagni Guillaume de Nogaret, chancellor of the king of France, was ordered to visit Notre-Dame de Vauvert, Rocamadour, Boulogne, Chartres, St.-Gilles, Montmajour, and Santiago, and finally to exile himself to the Holy Land, though none of this did he actually do.

For those whose sins were venial or well-concealed, the penitential pilgrimage remained an act of personal piety, voluntarily undertaken. After the end of the tenth century growing numbers of the humble as well as the mighty performed distant pilgrimages to expiate crimes that weighed on their consciences. The reasons for this sudden upsurge are far from clear. Introspection and guilt were not inventions of the eleventh century, and the condition of western Europe at the millennium is not, on its own, enough to account for the phenomenon. There was, however, one aspect of contemporary religious life by which it could hardly fail to have been coloured. The period witnessed radical changes in the role of the sacrament of penance. Two centuries earlier the Carolingian reformers had taken exception to the penitential practices of the Irish which, to their thinking, failed to bring the penitent back to the straight and narrow path. Rabanus Maurus had insisted that penances should be performed under the direct supervision of the confessor who had imposed them, and that the penitent should not be absolved until it had been completed. This had always been the practice of the early Church. It gave a certain finality to the ritual of absolution which marked the sinner's readmission to the body of the Church. From the end of the tenth century, however, penitents were usually absolved and reconciled with the Church immediately after confession. Thus arose the distinction between sin and punishment: the former was expunged by confession; the latter remained to be suffered in Purgatory. The penitent was reconciled to the Church, but he still had to do satisfaction for his sins, and the view ultimately prevailed that by performing good works in this life he could reduce the punishment that awaited him in the next. Against this background the unprecedented number of monastic foundations and the extraordinary popularity of pilgrimages and the crusades which mark out the eleventh century, become intelligible.

This obsession with the remission of sins can be discerned in all the more notable pilgrimages of the period. Robert the Pious, king of France, did a tour of nine shrines including some as far away as Toulouse and St.-Gilles shortly before his death in 1031. His biographer tells us that he hoped in this way to 'evade the awful sentence of the day of judgement'. Robert, duke of Normandy, who was under strong suspicion of having murdered his brother, travelled barefoot to Jerusalem in 1035 'driven by the fear of God'. A contemporary who saw king Canute at St.-Omer on his way to Rome reported that he shed bitter tears and implored the pardon of the saints, beating his breast and heaving heavy sighs. The three (or perhaps four) pilgrimages of Fulk Nerra, count of Anjou, to Jerusalem were accompanied by exhibitions of repentance as spectacular as the crimes they were intended to efface. According to Radulph Glaber 'the fear of Gehenna' entered into him in the year 1000 on account of his slaughter of the Bretons at the battle of Conquereuil, and the murder of his wife can only have added to his feelings of guilt. His first journey to the Holy Land occurred about three years after this. On his last, which was accomplished at a great age in 1038–40, Fulk had himself dragged on his knees by a halter to the church of the Holy Sepulchre, while two servants followed behind flogging him with birches. 'Accept, O Lord, the wretched Fulk', he cried from the steps of the basilica; 'I have perjured myself before thee and fled from thy presence. Receive, O Christ, this my unworthy soul.'

These pilgrims were as different as they could possibly have been from the Celtic wanderers of an earlier age. They had a particular destination in mind and, having spent a short time there, they returned home to resume their normal lives. Fulk Nerra and his contemporaries took it for granted that certain places were intrinsically holier than others and this, as we have seen, was very far from being the view of the Irish. The penitential pilgrim, according to an Anglo-Saxon writer of the tenth century, underwent 'the most profound of penances': 'he throws away his weapons and wanders far and wide across the land, barefoot and never staying more than a night in one place....He fasts and wakes and prays by day and by night. He cares not for his body and lets his hair and nails grow freely.' A pilgrimage of this sort is in fact a development of the penalty of judicial exile which is so common in primitive legal systems. The offender became an outcast. In the words of the *Penitential of St. Columban* he was to be 'like Cain a wanderer and a fugitive on the face of the earth, never to return to his native land.'

The destination of this penitent was immaterial. Indeed it was often laid down that in the case of particularly heinous offences the pilgrimage was to be perpetual. In 585 the council of Mâcon decreed that a bishop guilty of murder should pass the rest of his life in pilgrimage. In the Irish penitentials perpetual exile is ordained for incest, bestiality, the murder of clerics or close relatives, and various kinds of sacrilege. As late as c. 1000 some Irish canons collected at Worcester require that the murderer of a bishop's servant be condemned to perpetual exile, while lesser offences are visited with pilgrimages of up to twenty years. Indeed it was still possible for a preacher in the middle of the twelfth century to speak of pilgrims at Santiago as being 'sent into exile by their parish priests'.

In no other period was it so much better to travel hopefully than to arrive. But these wanderings were not devoid of religious significance, and penitents were often reported to have been pardoned by the intercession of the saints. Gregory of Tours had observed in the sixth century that 'by praying to the saints sinners can often obtain the remission of their sins and thus be saved from the torments of Hell....Those who have fallen into grave sin should therefore pay special reverence to God's saints.' In some miracle stories of the period the saint signified that the penitent was pardoned by causing his chains to break asunder in front of the shrine. Typical of such stories is the tale of the priest Willichar, whose enemies were unable to imprison him because the fetters fell from his feet every time he invoked the name of St. Martin. Two criminals are reported to have been released from their chains by St. Nizier in the sixth century, and at the church of St. Victor in Marseilles a traveller saw with his own eyes the rows of broken fetters hanging before the altar. But no one shrine was the special destination of these pilgrims, and when the chains broke the place was usually fortuitous. They wandered from shrine to shrine as aimlessly as any Irish exile. The wanderings of one such outcast are described in a Norman text of the ninth century. He was a nobleman called Frotmund who, in 850, had murdered his father, a chaplain of the emperor Lothair. Together with a large company of others in a similar predicament, he first made his way to Rome and then proceeded to Jerusalem, then to the shrine of St. Cyprian at Carthage, and back to Rome. Divine pardon was not forthcoming in Rome, so he returned to Jerusalem by way of Mount Sinai, then back to Rome and across northern Italy and France, until his fetters broke in the church of St. Marcellin at Rédon.

The notion that a pilgrim had only to go to a particular shrine to be pardoned is scarcely found before the ninth century and did not command universal acceptance until the eleventh. At the very beginning of the ninth century we are told that St. Mestrille went to Tours in order to be pardoned for his sins. In the same period we find pilgrims commanded in visions to go to particular shrines. A ninth-century editor included in the works of Gregory of Tours the story of a penitent who was directed by a vision of Christ to the shrine of Moutiers-St.-Jean near Lyon. Another story in the same vein told of St. Peter and St. Paul appearing to a criminal on the road to Rome and directing him to the shrine of St. Bavo at Ghent.

Bishops and confessors only now begin to impose specific pilgrimages on penitents. Rome was the usual destination. An Irish penitential written at the end of the ninth century suggests that parricides should be sent there to receive their penance from the pope in person. A certain Ratbert, who battered his mother to death in c. 870, was sent by the archbishop of Sens on two pilgrimages to Mont-St.-Michel and one to Rome. Such penances were still fairly uncommon a century later when the renowned confessor Abbo of Fleury sent Bernard, abbot of Beaulieu, to Jerusalem, and on learning that the roads east were blocked, to Rome and Monte Gargano instead. Bernard had confessed to having obtained his abbacy by simony, and Abbo's biographer believed that the penance was 'almost the first of its kind in France'.

Thus arose the characteristic mediaeval belief in the automatic remission of sins by formal visits to particular shrines. The story of the criminal whose fetters burst asunder was gradually replaced by still more dramatic indications of divine forgiveness. Charlemagne, for instance, was stated in a legend of the eleventh century to have written out his sins on a sheet of paper, which was then wiped clean by the miraculous power of St. Gilles. This story, with its simple, literal approach, plainly struck a sympathetic chord in contemporary minds, for other pilgrims are alleged to have had similar experiences. A woman who visited Vézelay in the early twelfth century laid on the altar a *scedula* of her sins, which were immediately erased. The same happened to an Italian, whose sins were so vile that his bishop refused to absolve him, and sent him instead to Santiago with a written list of his enormities. 'From this', writes the author of the *Miracles of St. James,* 'it is plain that whoever goes truly penitent to St. James and asks for his help with all his heart, will certainly have all his sins expunged.' Writing at the beginning of the twelfth century, Hughes de Sainte-Marie saw this as the principal function of the saints. The Merovingian saints had healed the sick and punished iniquity; those of the twelfth century did so too, but they were also pastors, concerned above all with the moral welfare and eventual salvation of their flock. 'Who can say how many souls have won God's mercy by the merits of St. Benedict; how many men have been reformed, turned away from the vain prattle of the world, and subjected to the light yoke of Christ. For in so doing, St. Benedict revives the dead and heals the open wounds of sin.'

Pilgrimages Imposed by the Law

The responsibility for introducing the judicial pilgrimage into the civil law of Europe probably belongs to the Inquisition. The systematic juridical persecution of heresy, which began in southern France in the early years of the thirteenth century, left its mark on several aspects of mediaeval law. An organized system of tribunals, possessed of established rules and procedures, the Inquisition was active at one time or another in every country of Europe except England. For those who confessed to minor offences against the faith, pilgrimages were amongst the commonest penances which it imposed.

The Inquisition of Languedoc classified pilgrimages as 'major', 'minor', or 'overseas' (i.e. to the Holy Land). The nineteen minor pilgrimages were all in France, while the four major ones were Canterbury, Santiago, Cologne, and Rome. Depending on the gravity of the offence, the penitent might be sent to any number of these shrines or even to all of them. It was nevertheless regarded as one of the lighter penances and was commonly used when large numbers of people were suspected of heresy without there being any definite evidence against any of them. When the inquisitors visited the small towns of Gourdon and Montcuq in 1241, most of those brought before them were sentenced to one major pilgrimage and a host of minor ones. Ninety-eight people were sent to Santiago via Le Puy and St.-Gilles; thirty-eight citizens of

Gourdon were obliged to visit Canterbury by way of St.-Léonard de Noblat, St. Martial of Limoges, and St.-Denis. By comparison, Bernard Gui, inquisitor of Toulouse, who dealt with more serious cases and was in any case reckoned a hard judge, made much more severe use of pilgrimage as a penance. In his surviving book of sentences, which covers the years 1308–22, only sixteen out of 636 offences were considered so venal as to merit a mere pilgrimage. Even these sixteen had to undergo long journeys on foot. These offenders who had unwittingly attended a Waldensian meeting in their childhood were directed to visit seventeen 'minor' sanctuaries as far apart as Vienne and Bordeaux.

Civil courts had occasionally ordered malefactors to make distant pilgrimages in the twelfth century. Not very often, however. It was not until the middle of the thirteenth century that they came into general use. Most early examples are found in the ecclesiastical principalities of the Low Countries where, at first, they were reserved for offence against the Church. They were rapidly adopted by criminal lawyers as a convenient, easily enforced penalty which brought about the temporary disappearance of the offender without the expense of imprisonment. In Liège the *Paix aux Clercs,* a code of ecclesiastical law issued in 1207, ordains that assaults inside churches shall be punished with pilgrimages. Two months later, a code of civil law was published which specified pilgrimage as the penalty for all assaults resulting in mutilation. By 1328, when the next major legal code of Liège appeared, pilgrimage had become an all-purpose penalty for violent crimes. A similar process can be traced in almost every city of the Low Countries, and by the fourteenth century it was firmly established in France and Italy as well. Only in England did the secular courts ignore it.

Pilgrimages of this sort were little more than the traditional penalty of banishment renamed. City-states have almost invariably banished serious disturbers of the peace, and in Flanders, for example, this tradition had an uninterrupted history going back well beyond the eleventh century. Pilgrimage and banishment were almost interchangeable terms. Hence the practice of the kings of France of periodically commuting short banishments to even shorter pilgrimages; thus did Philip VI allow the town of Douai in 1346 to commute all banishments of less than five years. The religious element in these journeys was usually small, a fact which became apparent in the later Middle Ages when Arab hostility sometimes made it impossible to visit Jerusalem. On settling his quarrel with the count of Namur in 1402, Robert de Roux promised to go to the Holy Land or, if that proved impossible, to Cyprus. Indeed it was to Cyprus, a place of little spiritual importance, that the most heinous offenders were sent. There they were required to stay for a specified number of years. It was very rare for the judges to require from the offender any display of religious enthusiasm. Perhaps it was a reflection of the ecclesiastical character of the government of Liège that criminals sent from thence to Rome were required to mount the steps of the Lateran basilica on their knees and to remain kneeling for the duration of five masses. Other cities did not think it worth including such details in their statutes.

Pilgrimage, like banishment, was a particularly suitable punishment for those enormities which threatened the tight-knit urban communities of the late Middle Ages. Thomas Aquinas regarded it as the obvious penalty for a grave breach of public order. Murder and wounding, riot and affray, conspiracies of various sorts all carried the penalty of exile. At Liège in the fourteenth century any person who committed an assault that caused bleeding but broke no bones, who sheltered someone involved in a vendetta, or who obstructed the course of justice, was liable to be despatched to Rocamadour, a distance of some six hundred miles. Arson, the most terrifying crime that a mediaeval townsperson could commit, was punished by a pilgrimage to Jerusalem or Santiago as early as 1186, when Frederick Barbarossa issued a constitution to this effect. Arson was punished at Namur in the late Middle Ages with a visit to Cyprus, and it is probable that the same practice prevailed in other cities of the Low Countries. Cyprus too was the destination of twenty-five citizens of Nieuport who had been amongst the crowd which in 1235 lynched the ambassadors of the neighbouring town of Furnes. In 1483 insulting a town councillor of Namur was added to the list of offences which were held to merit a pilgrimage to Rocamadour. Indeed by this time pilgrimage had become a convenient and flexible penalty for all those whose continued presence in a small community was felt to be a nuisance. Henri le Kien, a painter of Tournai who was sent to Rocamadour in 1428, was accused of no crime at all except that he 'made a habit of insulting and criticizing other people…and thus caused great dissensions and troubles'; it was resolved that the unfortunate artist was 'never to return to the city unless the citizens gather together in their guilds and districts to re-admit him.'

Mediaeval lawyers did not make the same rigid distinction between civil and criminal law as their modern counterparts. The victim of a violent crime, or the victim's heir, was held to be the prosecutor and the sentence inflicted on the malefactor was at least partly for the victim's satisfaction. The honour of the injured party was satisfied by the banishment of the assailant. This is an attitude as old as the penitential pilgrimage itself. One of the oldest Irish penitentials, the *Penitential of Finnian,* prescribes that a cleric found guilty of murder shall pass ten years in exile, after which 'he shall be received into his own country and make satisfaction to the friends of him whom he slew and compensate his father and mother, if they are still alive.... But if he does not fulfil this obligation he shall never be allowed back.' This outlook did not disappear, even in the more formal circumstances of thirteenth-century law. Thus in Frederick Barbarossa's constitutions of 1186, men banished for crimes of violence are not to return until they have compensated the victim or his family. Grave crimes might be settled by private agreement, the courts intervening only to ensure that the agreement was kept. In 1434, for instance, a certain Gerard de Rostimont of Namur was obliged to make peace with the relatives of a man whom he had killed in a brawl, the condition being that he should go immediately to Cyprus. A document of 1333 in the town archives of St.-Omer records the return of a clerk called William Bondulf from a pilgrimage to St. Andrew's in Scotland. He showed his testimonials to the judge to prove that he had been, and paid twelve *livres* for the repose of his victim's soul. Then the victim's heir, who was present in court, publicly acquitted him of all further responsibility. Indeed at Liège the victim's claim was considered quite separately from that of the state, and in cases of assault in churches the evil-doer might be required to go twice to Santiago, once to the profit of the Church and once to that of the victim.

From the state's point of view these arrangements had the advantage of settling a potential vendetta. Indeed, most of the

earliest judicial pilgrimages are the result of timely agreements
designed to avoid family feuds. In 1264 the four murderers of
Godfrey and Jaquemon de Clermont, two brothers of a
wealthy Flemish family, agreed to depart to the Holy Land
until the victims' relatives allowed them to return. Pilgrimages
were often imposed by arbitrators in private quarrels.
Beaumanoir records the case of a villager who killed another's
horse under him, and repenting of his rashness, promised to
submit his quarrel to the arbitration of three other villagers.
These decided that he should go barefoot to Boulogne,
Santiago, and St.-Gilles, before finally exiling himself to the
Holy Land for three years. According to Beaumanoir the sentence was considered excessive and it was never executed. But
when two families of Dieppe submitted a blood-feud to the
archbishop of Rouen in 1264, he sent the head of one of them
to St.-Gilles and Santiago, observing that in this way 'the honour and peace of mind of the aggrieved parties will be saved.'

The judicial pilgrimage was more fearsome in theory than
it was in practice, for a sinner could usually be released from his
penance by paying a fee to the state or damages to the injured
party. The Inquisition scarcely ever allowed its victims to escape
their penances in this way. According to the inquisitor Bernard
Gui, only the old and the infirm were permitted to make a
money payment in lieu of a pilgrimage, and even then the cost
was high—fifty *livres* for the old, a hundred for the infirm. By
contrast, the civil courts allowed criminals to buy their way out
of the journey for quite small sums. Nothing more clearly illus-
trates the slender spiritual basis of these pilgrimages than the
lists of tariffs in which the price of evading each pilgrimage was
advertised. Here is one such list, which was in use at
Oudenarde in the fourteenth century:

To Santiago	*livres* 12-0-0
To Rome	*livres* 12-0-0
To St. Julian of Brioude	*livres* 4-0-0
To St. Simeon of Paris	*livres* 0-40-0
To St. Martin of Tours etc.	*livres* 3-10-0

The sum required varied considerably from place to place. A pilgrimage to Rocamadour could be bought off for five *livres* at Alost, while at Ypres it cost seven; Oudenarde charged eight *livres* and Limburg ten gold florins. Occasionally a court would refuse to allow commutation at all in serious cases. At Maestricht, for instance, murderers were allowed to buy their way out of a pilgrimage if it was imposed to the profit of the victim's family, but if it was imposed on behalf of the town it had to be performed. In general it was assumed that the malefactor would pay if he could afford to. After the sentence had been announced there was usually a pause of several weeks during which he would try to raise the money from friends or moneylenders. If the money was not paid, the victim or the victim's family would then apply for a court order enforcing the sentence. Many French towns enjoyed royal privileges which entitled citizens to buy off pilgrimages as of right. In confirming the privileges of Corvins and Epinoy in 1371, Charles V found it necessary to warn them that the pilgrimage must be enforced if the offender could or would not pay. Similar privileges were granted to Bergues, Furnes, and several other towns of Flanders, Artois, and Brabant.

Pilgrimages were imposed not only by law courts and arbitrators, but by any corporation which exercised a quasi-judicial authority over its members. Universities, guilds, and similar corporations were all entitled to send recalcitrant members to distant parts and often did so. For breaking a minor rule, the armourers' guild at Malines sent one of its members, barefoot, bareheaded, and fasting on bread and water to the shrine of Battel. The drapers' guild at Malines had been known to send rebellious members as far as Rocamadour. Contemporaries appreciated the humiliation which was thus inflicted on the victim. For this reason pilgrimages were commonly inflicted on whole towns after an unsuccessful war or rebellion. At the treaty of Arques (1326), which marked the defeat of the Flemish towns in their revolt against Charles of France, Bruges and Courtrai were required to send a hundred prominent citizens to Santiago, a hundred to St.-Gilles, and a hundred to Rocamadour. On this occasion the offending towns commuted the penalty to a payment of 10,000 *livres*, but they were not always let off so lightly. Robert de Cassel paid for his part in the same rebellion by visiting Santiago, Rocamadour, Le Puy, and St.-Gilles, and bringing back testimonials to prove it. Sixty citizens of Bruges performed a civic pilgrimage to Avignon in 1309, and in 1393 dignitaries of the town were sent to Rome and Jerusalem after an unsuccessful quarrel with the Hanseatic League. In 1468 a hundred inhabitants of Haut-Pont presented themselves at Notre-Dame de Boulogne bearing wax candles weighing three pounds each in penance for their seditious designs against Charles the Bold, duke of Burgundy.

Enforcement

The solemn and exemplary character of a judicial pilgrimage was emphasized by the way in which it was performed. The practice of sending the convict on his way loaded with chains belongs to the Merovingian and Carolingian periods, but it did not altogether die out until the end of the twelfth century. Even in 1319 the murderer of the bishop of Fricento was despatched to Rome and Santiago with an iron collar round his neck. Fetters were attached to the convict's arms and sometimes to his legs, neck, and waist as well. In the case of murderers it was usual to hang the murder weapon from one of the fetters as a permanent advertisement of the crime. In the early mediaeval period these awful wanderers were a familiar sight in every part of Europe, but in the eleventh and twelfth centuries most of them came from southern France, Germany, or Scotland. When chained convicts are reported at English shrines they are almost invariably foreigners. A pilgrim who came to Norwich n the 1150s 'clothed in a coat of mail on his bare flesh, fettered with his own sword' was a nobleman of Lorraine. Scottish convicts were constantly arriving at the shrine of St. Cuthbert at Durham. In 1164, great interest was aroused by the appearance of a murderer wearing an iron girdle made of the sword with which he had killed his victim. Another Scotsman had been fettered by the arm, waist, and neck, and had already been to the Holy Land and St. Martial of Limoges before coming to Durham. At each place part of his load had broken away, 'and thus', explained Reginald of Durham, 'St. Cuthbert can free the body from its chains just as he frees the soul from the bonds of sin.'

It is difficult to know what to make of these stories of the spontaneous bursting of iron chains, especially when they are reported by those who claim to have been present. Thomas of Monmouth complained that some of his contemporaries were inclined to doubt them, ascribing them to fraud or rust, but Thomas asserted that he had watched with his own eyes as the fetters of Philip of Lorraine fell to the ground. A high proportion of these stories must have been pure fiction, Thomas's own tales among them. But many of the pilgrims who clanked their chains along the roads of Europe in the eleventh and twelfth centuries had probably put them on voluntarily and may have removed them themselves as soon as they felt that God had pardoned them. In such cases the 'miracle' consisted of the sudden relief of their feelings of guilt, a circumstance which it is rather easier to visualize. A penitent who arrived at Fleury at the end of the eleventh century is stated to have confessed his crimes out of fear of God's vengeance and then placed the fetters on his own arms 'in the firm conviction that as soon as God deigned to remit his sins the chains would fall away of their own accord.' A pilgrim released at the shrine of St. Egwin of Evesham had loaded himself with chains. So had a fratricide of Cologne who confessed his sin to the archbishop and then wandered for seven years from shrine to shrine. It was an extreme form of mortification of the flesh, following an ancient and still powerful tradition. A twelfth-century penitent called Bernard, who ended his days in the abbey of St. Bertin at St.-Omer, had committed the most trivial of crimes. His biographer does not reveal what it was, but observes that 'no one would think ill of him even if the stories were true. He had done nothing particularly vile or bestial, nothing we would consider sinful nowadays. But it is the mark of a saint to look upon everything worldly as loathsome.' Accordingly Bernard had condemned himself to wander for seven years with seven tight irons around his limbs and neck. It seems likely that by this time the majority of fettered pilgrims seen at the great shrines had chosen to add thus to the discomforts of their penance.

Those who had been sentenced by the Inquisition were not chained and fettered, but they were required to wear on their back and front two large crosses made of saffron-coloured cloth, and there were severe penalties for tearing them off. It is quite probable that these crosses subjected the wearer to scourging at each of the shrines visited. Certainly the crosses were regarded as the most humiliating part of the penance. Those who wore them were ostracized by their fellow-travellers and excluded from inns and hospices, in spite of the orders of the inquisitors that they should be sheltered like any other pilgrim. Some complained that they found it hard to marry off their daughters, others that the stigma attached to wearing crosses lasted for many years after the pilgrimage had been completed. Even those convicted by civil courts found that the worst part of the sentence was the public humiliation which accompanied it. In the fifteenth century a rich man like Joos Pieterseune, who was ordered to Rocamadour for involuntary manslaughter, could do the journey in six months; but his conviction was quashed on appeal on the ground that judicial pilgrims were known as amadours and generally regarded as men of evil repute, a stigma which, it was felt, the unfortunate Pieterseune did not deserve.

The problems of enforcing compulsory pilgrimages were considerable. Successful evasions must have been frequent though it is, on the whole, the unsuccessful ones which are recorded. Convicts who pleaded illness were required to prove it. Bodechon de Bourges, who was convicted by the magistrates of Namur in 1413, produced a posse of witnesses to testify that he could scarcely lift himself from his bed. He was allowed to put off his departure for forty days, but six months later he was still in Namur trying to borrow the money to buy his release. Victims of the Inquisition were constantly being reminded of their unperformed pilgrimages, and in 1251 the inquisitors of Carcassonne issued a general warning of the awful consequences of leaving a pilgrimage unperformed. Corporations which punished their members by despatching them to distant shrines often had some difficulty in enforcing their sentences. Much of the *acta* of the University of Louvain for the year 1448 are taken up with the transgressions of one Jan Vogel van der Elst, a servant of the mayor of Louvain who had conceived a virulent hatred of the university, and had repeatedly assaulted its students and dignitaries. For this he was ordered by the rector of the university to go on a pilgrimage to Milan cathedral. Vogel's reaction was to insult the rector loudly, and declare that he would not go to Milan unless he was tied to a cart and driven there by force. He then stood outside the university hall as the officers of the university passed by, and shouted 'Where is the cart? Is it not ready yet?' Vogel was ultimately arrested for his contumacy and was only released on the understanding that future assaults on students would result in his execution or perpetual banishment. He did not, however, go to Milan.

Many offences for which pilgrimages were imposed were capital offences, and this brief period of exile was often a merciful alternative to execution. When Lambert de Soif was sent to Rome in May 1515 for seizing his cousin by the hair and threatening his wife with a razor, the sentence was described as a 'merciful one, preferable in the circumstances to the full rigour of the law'. If the malefactor failed to perform the pilgrimages the full rigour of the law might be enforced. Pierot the Porter, who left Namur for Santiago after murdering a lawyer in 1405, turned back a few miles outside the town and settled in a quiet suburb. When he was discovered there a few weeks afterwards, he was immediately beheaded. In France, many of the letters of pardon which the crown habitually granted to convicted felons were made conditional on the performance of a pilgrimage. In 1393, for example, two cut-throats of Azay le Brulay (Poitou) escaped death by carrying a candle to Le Puy and buying a hundred masses for the soul of their victim. In urban communities, where evading a sentence was easier to detect, the simplest method of enforcing it was to refuse to let the evil-doer return unless he could prove that he had performed his pilgrimage. At Liège, failure to perform the relatively mild pilgrimage to Walcourt meant banishment for a year; to Vendôme, for two years; to Rocamadour, for four, and to Santiago, for five. When he returned, the convict sent his certificates ahead of him and waited outside the boundaries of the city until the magistrates signified that they were content to readmit him.

These certificates or 'testimonials' were first devised by the inquisitors of Languedoc, who required their penitents to collect signed documents from the clergy of the shrines they visited, proving that they had been there. Like other inquisitorial practices, they were quickly adopted by secular judges. Those of Namur, for example, ordered criminals to bring back a certificate 'showing that they had visited the said places in person without any kind of dishonesty or deceit, and without evading any of the obligations traditionally fulfilled by pilgrims.' On his return, the penitent showed his testimonials in court, and collected a certificate of acquittal for which he might have to pay a small fee.

The judicial pilgrimage had always had its opponents. Even in the heyday of the chained pilgrim, there was a substantial body of opinion which doubted how effective it was in reforming the sinner. This view is rehearsed in a capitulary of Charlemagne in 789 and it became in the following century part of the orthodoxy of reforming churchmen such as Rabanus Maurus. Not only did compulsory pilgrimages endanger the salvation of the sinner, but they also set loose upon the roads large numbers of dangerous criminals who terrorized peaceful travellers. This was the reason for Charlemagne's complaint against them in 789, and it remained a serious problem in later periods. In the thirteenth century Jacques de Vitry had occasion to complain of the hordes of 'wicked, impious, sacrilegious, thieves, robbers, murderers, parricides, perjurers, adulterers, traitors, corsairs, pirates, whoremongers, drunkards, minstrels, jugglers, and actors', who were unleashed on the Holy Land by the courts of Europe. A growing appreciation of the force of these arguments is found in writers of the later Middle Ages. Thomas Aquinas reflected the views of most of his contemporaries when he protested against the imposition of pilgrimages on women or by ordinary parish priests. At the beginning of the fourteenth century Durand de Saint-Pourçain held that their moral effects were disastrous and that they were too often imposed by ignorant parish priests. He proposed to restrict the power of inflicting them to bishops and confessors appointed by them, but in practice pilgrimages were rarely imposed by any spiritual authority after the middle of the fourteenth century. After the gradual decay of the Inquisition of Languedoc the secular courts of northern Europe were the only tribunals which still had recourse to them. This they continued to do until some decades after the

Reformation. It was a source of some surprise to count Mansfeld, Philip II's lieutenant in the Low Countries, to discover in 1592 that convicts were still being sent to Rocamadour and Santiago, in spite of the bitter civil war raging in France. But penances of this kind were not spiritual exercises. For most sinners of the later Middle Ages the decision as to whether to undertake a pilgrimage was one which the Church was content to leave to their own consciences.

8

The Great Age of Pilgrimage

'Some three years after the year 1000', wrote the Burgundian chronicler Radulph Glaber, 'there was a sudden rush to rebuild churches all over the world, and above all in Italy and France. Although most of these churches were in perfectly sound condition, Christians everywhere vied with each other to improve them. It was as if the world itself had thrown aside its old rags and put on a shining white robe of churches.' In southern France, broad strips of Glaber's 'white robe' still stand as evidence of the extraordinary spiritual intensity of the eleventh century, of a mood which manifested itself in the climax of monastic history, in the crusades in Spain and the middle east, and in the transformation of Christianity by a world of emotion and sentiment. In an age of religious sensitivity, pilgrimage fulfilled a real spiritual need. By inflicting severe physical hardship on pilgrims, it satisfied a desire for the remission of their sins and opened up to them the prospect of a 'second baptism'. By showing them the places associated with Christ and the saints, it gave pilgrims a more personal, more literal understanding of their faith.

Profound changes in the spiritual life of Europe coincided with political developments which made it possible, for the first time, for large numbers of people to travel long distances overland. The barbarian invasions of the ninth and tenth centuries had had a particularly destructive effect on the shrines of western Europe. These wealthy churches, protecting tombs of precious metal encrusted with jewels, proved an irresistible prey to raiding parties of Arabs, Vikings, and Magyars. Many of the more famous relics led a peripatetic existence as their owners carried them from church to church, fleeing before the invaders. When the Normans invaded the Loire valley in 853 the body of St. Martin was carried to Corméry and thence to Chablis, Orléans, and Auxerre. It was more than a hundred years before it returned to its home at Tours. After suffering a succession of Viking raids at the end of the ninth century, the monks of Lindisfarne took the body of St. Cuthbert and 'wandered across the whole of Northumbria, having no settled home, like sheep fleeing before wolves'. The body was venerated at Chester-le-Street for more than a century before the monks fled once again from the Vikings and found a permanent home at Durham. In such conditions regular pilgrimages were impossible. The exact location of the relics might be changed or it might be forgotten altogether. Libraries were dispersed or burned, collections of saints' lives lost. No one knew, in Orderic Vitalis's time, the exact location of the fifteen hermitages founded by St. Evroul. Recurrent raids, and the political disintegration which accompanied them, made it unsafe to travel long distances on the roads. The monk Bernard, returning from the Holy Land in the 860s, observed that it was safer for a Christian to travel in the dominions of the Caliph than on the highways of southern Italy. In the tenth century, Arab raids in the Alps made a pilgrimage to Rome an extremely hazardous undertaking. Even if a pilgrim escaped ambush and death, he was unlikely to find a monastery or hospice to receive him. Successive edicts emanating from the chancery of the Frankish Emperors failed to halt the decay of the Irish hospices, and a document of 841 shows that by then all the hostels maintained by the abbey of Monte Cassino were in ruins.

By mediaeval standards the period which followed the millennium was a peaceful one. All over Europe the barriers to travel were lifted. Most dramatic of all was the opening of the overland route to Jerusalem at the end of the tenth century. The victories of the Byzantine emperor Nicephorus Phocas placed Antioch once more in Christian hands and secured the route through Asia Minor. Basil II (976–1025) overthrew the Bulgarian empire and extended his dominions to the Danube. When duke Geysa of Hungary announced his conversion to Christianity in 985 the whole land route from western Europe to northern Syria was brought under nominal Christian rule. Geysa's son Stephen accommodated pilgrims at court and founded hospices for their use. The great monastery of Melk on the Danube was founded at this time by 'wealthy Christians from neighbouring provinces for the accommodation of pilgrims and the poor'. The overland route to Palestine was cheaper and safer than the sea voyage. The chance of a pilgrimage to the Holy Land was now embraced by an 'enormous multitude, both noble and common' whose grandfathers could never have afforded it.

At the opposite end of Europe developments of the same kind marked the rise of the great sanctuary of Santiago de Compostella. The decline of the Ummayad caliphate of Cordova left northern Spain in peace and freed the route from France to Santiago. The reign of Sancho the Great of Navarre (970–1035) marks an epoch as significant for the Spanish pilgrimage as the reign of Stephen of Hungary was for the

Palestinian one. Hospices were constructed along the *camino de Santiago* by kings, bishops, and noblemen, and by a horde of immigrants from France. In the middle years of the century, Alfonso VI rebuilt every bridge between Logroño and Santiago. Diego Gelmirez, the great archbishop of Santiago, who completed the existing cathedral, made it his chief concern to keep open the 'Frenchmen's road'. To this end he rebuilt one ruinous town on the route, bought up another, and sprinkled northern Spain with churches and *mansiones* for the use of pilgrims. In his time the *camino* was probably the busiest trunk road in Christendom. When, in 1121, the ambassadors of the Almoravid Caliph of Cordova traversed the route on their way to León, they were taken aback by the crowds of travellers using it, and confessed that 'they had not thought so many people could be found in all Spain.'

Yet Santiago is scarcely heard of before the end of the ninth century, and no pilgrim is known by name until Gottschalk bishop of Le Puy visited it in 950. It was lifted to the front rank of mediaeval shrines by a combination of shrewd promotion and excellent communications. Other towns attempted, though less successfully, to do the same, and the eleventh century was probably the last in which totally specious 'discoveries' of relics could command universal acceptance. In France, England, and Italy, new shrines sprung up like mushrooms after rain, sometimes taking firm root, sometimes provoking a brief spurt of enthusiasm before falling back into oblivion. At Sens, archbishop Leoteric 'discovered' part of Moses' rod in the foundations of his cathedral, 'at the news of which the faithful converged on Sens not only from every province of France but even from Italy and overseas.' This, according to Radulph Glaber, was the first of an unprecedented spate of discoveries. In Italy the citizens of

Salerno rediscovered their lost relics of St. Matthew the apostle in 1080, while the monks of Monte Cassino rediscovered in the rubble beneath their church the body of St. Benedict. Reading abbey was not founded until 1121, yet by the 1190s its list of relics contained 242 items, including twenty-nine relics of Our Lord, six of the Virgin, nineteen of the patriarchs and prophets, fourteen of apostles, seventy-three of martyrs, fifty-one of confessors, and forty-nine of virgins.

Several saints were more or less invented under the stimulus of the pilgrimage to Santiago. St. Leonard, who was venerated in a small town near Limoges on one of the busiest roads to Spain, was completely unknown to any writer before the eleventh century. He began to corruscate in miracles around 1017, and the first biography of the saint (a tissue of falsehoods) was written in about 1030. Almost as fraudulent as the cult of St. Leonard were those of St. Eutrope at Saintes and St. Gilles near Arles, both of which owed their considerable prosperity to the fact that they lay on one or other of the roads to the great Galician sanctuary.

Lay Piety and the Monasteries

The strongly local character of eleventh-century piety is one of its most remarkable features. Glaber's boast that 'men of every nation' filled the roads to Jerusalem was the truth, but it was far from being the whole truth, for a very high proportion of them came from a few provinces of France and the Rhineland. Burgundy and Lorraine, Gascony, and above all Normandy and Aquitaine, were the homes of these long-distance pilgrims.

South-western France in particular was struck with great force by the spiritual movements of the eleventh century. The delicate civilization of Languedoc and Aquitaine thrived in an atmosphere of harsh religious extremes. In Limoges, Périgueux, and Angoulême, the proclamation of the millennium and the forcible baptism of the Jews were greeted with enthusiasm several decades before the same distressing symptoms appeared in the Rhineland. It was here that the movement for the moral reform of the Church took its most violent form. In 1031 the councils of Limoges and Bourges published canons of draconian severity against clerical immorality, pronouncing the bastards of priests to be slaves of the Church on whom no one could confer property and whom no judge could set at liberty.

Shortly after the millennium, Guy, count of Limoges, and his brother bishop Hilduin led a large party of pilgrims to the Holy Land ranging from the great seigneurs of his court to the most obscure citizens of Limoges. Another unwieldy band departed in 1010 under the leadership of the bishop of Périgueux and the count of Malemart. The army of pilgrims who accompanied William, count of Angoulême, to Jerusalem in 1026 was believed to be the largest mass pilgrimage which had left France since the opening of the overland route. Nor was it only to Jerusalem that these Aquitainian pilgrims went. Among local shrines, St.-Jean d'Angély, St. Eutrope at Saintes, and St. Léonard de Noblat all leapt to prosperity in the wake of the pilgrimage to St. James. William V, duke of Aquitaine, apparently visited Santiago or Rome every year. Gerald of Corbie, founder and first abbot of La Sauve-Majeure had been to both Rome and Jerusalem in his time,

The Christian faith of the dukes of Normandy dated only from the middle of the tenth century, but few princes were more assiduous in sending alms to the Holy Places. Their subjects were notoriously the most energetic pilgrims of the eleventh century and became the leaders of the early crusades.

The considerable cost of the pilgrimage of the abbot of St.-Vannes to Jerusalem was met by duke Richard, and the army of hangers-on who accompanied the abbot across central Europe included a substantial Norman contingent. Robert, duke of Normandy, went to Jerusalem in person in 1034. His grandson, Robert Curthose, was a prominent figure in the first crusade. In spiritual matters, as Orderic Vitalis remarked, the Normans tended to follow the example of their rulers. Normans were among the leaders of the Spanish crusades, and many of them visited Santiago. In Rome there were hostels which specialized in the business of accommodating them, and the horde of coins discovered beneath the walls of the basilica of St. Paul in 1843 includes a large number of eleventh-century coins minted in Rouen.

The aggressive habits of Norman travellers, pilgrims, and soldiers of fortune alike, earned them an unsavoury reputation which made it wise for them to make their pilgrimages in large, well-armed bands. In Italy, Norman pilgrims met with intense local hostility after a group of their compatriots, gathered at the shrine of Monte Gargano, had embarked with astonishing success on the conquest of Apulia. John, abbot of Fécamp, complained to pope Leo IX that Norman pilgrims were being robbed, imprisoned, or murdered 'every day' by enraged Italian peasants. The Norman conquest of southern Italy also earned them the undying hatred of the Greeks. For three years in the 1020s, every Norman who passed through Constantinople on his way to Jerusalem was cast into prison. Few Normans needed to travel far to find an enemy. Roger I de Tosny had made so many in his violent lifetime that he was afraid to make a pilgrimage to Conques lest he should meet one of them on the road. Instead he founded a church at Conches in Normandy and dedicated it to St. Foy.

In both Normandy and Aquitaine there were powerful movements of monastic revival. From the abbey of St. Martial at Limoges the influence of Cluny radiated through south-western France, while in the Bordelais a succession of monastic foundations enjoyed the patronage of the counts of Aquitaine. At La Sauve-Majeure Gerald of Corbie created a strange mixture of the monastic and eremitical lives which, by the time of his death in 1095, had been implanted in twenty priories throughout Gascony and Aquitaine. The same pattern can be discerned in Normandy, where the ancient foundations of Mont-St.-Michel and Jumièges combined with the new ones at Bec and Caen to produce a spiritual revival with a strong local character. The third area which sent pilgrims and crusaders in large numbers to Spain and Palestine was Burgundy, and here the influence of Cluny was overpowering. The Cluniac monk Radulph Glaber recorded a steady stream of departures for the Holy Land including several of those strange mass-pilgrimages which are so characteristic of the eleventh century. The enthusiasm for these distant shrines seems to have been strongest at Autun whence, in 1024–5, an immense leaderless mob of pilgrims left for the Holy Places. The news of their doings created a considerable stir in the surrounding provinces. Radulph Glaber's friends came to tell him in his priory at Bèze. Two years afterwards Richard of St.-Vannes confessed that their example had prompted him to make his own pilgrimage to the Holy Land. Aganon, bishop of Autun, visited the Holy Places at an advanced age in 1083, and lived to see the synod, held at Autun in 1094, which first proposed the launching of the crusade.

The enthusiasm which the fate of the Holy Places aroused in these three provinces of France had much to do with the monastic revival. The interest of the monks in the Holy Land was reflected in their libraries. The library of St. Martial at Limoges was a mine of topographical information on the Holy Land. It included a manuscript of the pilgrimage of Etheria which, had it survived, might have contained the part missing in our text. The library of Moissac contained several itineraries, including a manuscript of the fourth-century 'Bordeaux pilgrim' and another written in the vernacular *('simplice sermona scripta')*. The books which they read, the hymns which they sang, the sculptures which they passed on their way through the cloister to the chapter house, all betray the same passionate interest in the Holy City. Several monasteries of southern France administered estates on behalf of the basilica of the Holy Sepulchre, which had by now acquired extensive endowments in the west.

The abbey of Cluny is often credited with having organized the pilgrimage to the Holy Land. Certainly the abbots looked on it with favour, and had done much to produce the spiritual environment which nurtured it. But of active direction there is no evidence at all. Much more significant is their role in promoting the pilgrimage to Santiago. The Spanish crusades were followed with great interest at Cluny, and the Burgundian knights who took part spent much of their spoil on the enrichment of the abbey. In the reign of Alfonso VI of Léon and Castile (1065–1109), Cluny obtained a firm grip on the Church in north-western Spain. In 1094 a Cluniac monk became bishop of Santiago. By the close of the eleventh century many of the shrines and monasteries on the pilgrims' roads to Santiago had become dependencies of Cluny, including Vézelay, St. Martial of Limoges, St.-Gilles, Moissac, and St. Eutrope at Saintes.

Particularly interesting is the hand of Cluny in composing the elaborate promotional literature put out by the church of Santiago. Most of it is contained in the *Liber Sancti Jacobi,* an exquisitely produced manuscript in the cathedral library. The *Liber* consists of five quite separate books bearing on the pilgrimage to St. James, proclaiming at the beginning and end that it was written for the benefit of the abbot of Cluny by pope Calixtus II. The attribution is fictitious, for there are parts which could not have been written by any Cluniac. But the second book, which consists of the *Miracles of St. James,* bears strongly the imprint of Cluny. Most of the miracles occurred to inhabitants of Burgundy, the Viennois, or the Lyonnais, and some happened within a few miles of the abbey. A few are attributed to a canon of Besançon, while another was related by an abbot of Vézelay. Three miraculous stories which St. Anselm told to abbot Hugh during a prolonged visit to Cluny in 1104 all appear with minor alterations in the *Miracles of St. James.* These miracles were Cluny's greatest contribution to the pilgrimage of St. James. They were plagiarized by every collector of marvellous stories, copied out in a great number of manuscripts from the twelfth century to the sixteenth, set forth in sculpture and stained glass throughout Europe. Arnaldo de Monte, a monk of Ripoll who saw the *Liber Sancti Jacobi* at Santiago in 1173, justly remarked that it was these miracles which had made the apostle 'shine forth as bright as the stars in every part of the world'.

Cluny's message faithfully reflected the spiritual values of the age. It insisted on the overriding importance of the remission of sins, and although men like St. Hugh had no doubt that the best possible chance of remission lay in taking the monastic habit, they appreciated the value of pilgrimage for those whose responsibilities prevented them from abandoning the worldly life. Abbot Mayeul, according to his twelfth-century biographer, 'knew that life itself was but a pilgrimage and that man lived as a fleeting guest upon the earth. He would often undertake the hardships of a pilgrim's life, expending all his bodily strength…on travelling across the Alps to Rome.' One of Mayeul's contemporaries, who knew him well, recorded that tears would come to his eyes as he approached the city 'for he knew that he would shortly behold the glorious apostles as if he were standing face to face with them.'

The message was addressed with special urgency to the nobility, whose social responsibilities forced on them a worldly existence and exposed them to the temptations of power. The abbots of Cluny, like so many reforming churchmen of their day, believed in knighthood as an order of the Church, upholding the values of the Church not only in war but also in peace. So, in his treatise *On the Christian Life,* Bonizo of Sutri devoted a whole chapter to the duties of knights—the keeping of the peace, the protection of the poor, the defence of the Church, the persecution of heresy. The aristocratic poetry of the period shows that the nobility itself was acutely aware of its special spiritual needs. The *troubadour* William IX, duke of Aquitaine (d. 1127), sang of the dissipation of his youth and the imminence of death and judgement. A new age of religious sensitivity made William's contemporaries deeply uncomfortable about the inevitable sinfulness of their way of life. A century later the seigneur de Berzé was induced to join the fourth crusade by his overpowering feelings of guilt for the sins which his social status had forced on him:

Li un de nous sont usurier
Li autre larron et murdrier
Li autre son plain de luxure
E li autre de desmesure;
Li autre sont plain d'envie
E d'orgueill e de tricherie,
E tantes manières pechommes
Nous qui en ce vill siècle sommes
Que molt grant merveille sera
Se ja Diex de nul en ara
Misericorde ne merci.

Some of us are usurers, others thieves and murderers. We sin by self-indulgence, by excess, pride, and deceit. We who live the worldly life are drawn so deeply into sin that it will be a miracle indeed if God has mercy on us.

But by almsgiving, pilgrimage, or taking the Cross, such men were offered an immediate opportunity of bringing that miracle about. 'Every day we see with our own eyes the death of men', wrote Roger count of Foix when presenting a church to Cluny; 'we know that we too must shortly die, and mindful of these things we have given much thought to the salvation of our souls and the remission of our most terrible sins.' It was a pity, as the seigneur de Berzé naively remarked, that one could not be warned of one's approaching death a year or two in advance, so as to prepare one's soul for the great tribunal 'where I shall have no essoins to delay the awful verdict.'

In the early tenth century, abbot Odo of Cluny presented to his contemporaries an idealized portrait of the model knight in his *Life of Gerald, Count of Aurillac.* Gerald, who died in 909, is shown as a man who renounced the brutal and worldly side of knightly life, its hunting, revelry, and violence. He did not, like many aristocratic hermits, renounce his knightly status, but used it to keep the peace and protect his vassals and tenants. He remained in the world and yet above it, and he chose devotional exercises which were in keeping with his noble status. Pilgrimage was the foremost of these. Gerald first visited Rome in the 880s, accompanied by several knights of his household, and on his return he founded a monastery at Aurillac dedicated to St. Peter. Thereafter he went every other year to Rome, and in the intervening years visited other shrines, including those of St. Hilary at Poitiers, St. Martial at Limoges, and St. Martin at Tours. Odo believed that these pilgrimages were the outcome of his feelings of guilt, born of the conflict between his semi-monastic way of life and his knightly status.

> 'When he prayed to God from his innermost heart…he was afraid that God would not listen to him as long as evil thoughts remained in his mind….For his sins, which might perhaps seem trivial to us, weighed heavily on his conscience and he was always thinking of ways to atone for them and secure the remission of them from a merciful God. And so God, in his mercy, showed him the way, that is, the way of prayer…and he developed the habit of going regularly to Rome.'

Idealized as it was, Odo's description did much to mould contemporary notions of lay piety. According to Adémar de Chabannes, William V, duke of Aquitaine, was 'amiable to all, of good counsel, generous with his wealth, a defender of the poor, the father of monks, and a builder and lover of churches, particularly the Church of Rome'. Like Gerald, he found pilgrimage a congenial method of expiating his sins, compatible with his almost royal status as the principal feudatory of the French Crown. From his earliest youth, 'he was accustomed to go every year to the tombs of the apostles in Rome, and if he could not get there, to St. James of Compostella....Such was the splendour of his retinue and the nobility of his bearing on these occasions, that onlookers took him for a king rather than a duke.' The annual or biennial pilgrimage became a recognized mark of aristocratic piety. An Aquitainian knight whom St. Mary Magdalene raised from the dead in the mid-twelfth century used to go annually to Vézelay, as did Adalard, another knight who benefited from the Magdalene's miraculous powers there.

No materials exist to make a statistical analysis of the clientele of a great mediaeval shrine, but the pilgrimage to Canterbury in the decade after Becket's death is probably typical of other major sanctuaries of the twelfth century. The two massive collections of miracles identify a total of 665 pilgrims who visited Canterbury between 1171 and 1177. The authors describe the social status of nearly two-thirds of these pilgrims, from which it appears that more than eight per cent of them were of the higher nobility (i.e. earls, great magnates, *potentes*, etc.), and no less than twenty-six per cent were knights. Some allowance should be made for the fact that the arrival of a nobleman was more likely to be recorded than that of a peasant, but these figures are out of all proportion to the numerical importance of the nobility in the population at large. Moreover the scraps of evidence which survive from continental shrines suggest that they are no means untypical. It was very different in the fourteenth century, when the Florentine diplomat Paolo Vergerio was told by his guide in Rome that bishops and princes had long abandoned the Lenten 'stations" which were now given over to the scum of the earth. Very different too from the situation in England on the eve of the Reformation, when the commissioners for the dissolution of the monasteries could dismiss the pilgrims they found at Bury St. Edmunds as poor fools and old women.

The Mortification of the Flesh

One of the less admirable characteristics of aristocratic pilgrimages was the comfortable, sometimes luxurious manner in which they were often performed. William V of Aquitaine was not the only nobleman whose manner of travelling led onlookers to believe that he was a king. The official historian of the dukes of Normandy recorded that such was the magnificence of duke Robert when passing through Constantinople in 1035, and such the largesse which he dispensed to the inhabitants, that they concluded that he was the king of France. Ealdred, bishop of Worcester, travelled through eastern Europe in 1059 'in such state as none had displayed before him'. Gunther, bishop of Bamberg, who led several thousand Germans on a mass pilgrimage to the Holy Land in 1064, informed the canons of his cathedral that the citizens of Constantinople, seeing his splendid array, had assumed him to be a king disguised as a bishop in order to avoid capture by the Arabs. Gunther had every reason to fear capture by the Arabs, for he and the other leaders of the host of pilgrims travelled in litters carried by liveried retainers; their tents were hung with silk and they ate splendid repasts nightly off gold and silver plate which was carried behind them on long trains of pack-horses. As a result they found themselves attacked at every stage by the covetous inhabitants of eastern Europe and Palestine, losing much of their treasure and suffering heavy casualties. At least one contemporary, the annalist Lambert of Hersfeld, regarded this as a proper punishment for their sinful pride.

Others were inclined to agree with him, and for this reason there is a certain ambivalence amongst churchmen of the twelfth century towards the pilgrimage to the Holy Land. When a knight called Hugh Catula decided to go to Jerusalem instead of entering the monastery of Cluny, Peter the Venerable wrote to him protesting that although pilgrimage might be a valuable spiritual exercise if properly performed, it could not offer the same prospect of salvation as the monastic habit: 'it is better to serve God in humility and poverty for ever than to set out in grandeur and luxury for Jerusalem. Whence it follows that if it is good to visit the Holy Land and survey the places where Our Lord trod, then it is even better to enter Heaven where you will see Our Lord face to face.' Salvation, he remarked on another occasion, was 'achieved by holy lives, not holy places'. Yet Peter's attitude is not as straightforward as it appears. Writing to an abbot of his acquaintance, Peter commended his decision to go to Palestine, observing that a pilgrimage to the Holy Sepulchre over such a distance would be as pleasing to God as that first pilgrimage of the holy women to the tomb on Easter Sunday. In Peter's opinion, the ideal pilgrim was one whose pilgrimage was a monastic exercise as exacting as that which St. Jerome had required of his followers in the fourth century. Jerome's ideal was thus reasserted in all its rigour at a time when the coming of the penitential pilgrimage had made it very largely meaningless.

In the first book of the *Liber Sancti Jacobi* there is a remarkable sermon, known from its opening words as the sermon *Veneranda Dies*. It was attributed (wrongly) to pope Calixtus II, and intended to be read to pilgrims on the vigil of December

30th, one of the two feasts of St. James. 'The way of St. James', it
begins, 'is fine but narrow, as narrow as the path of salvation itself.
That path is the shunning of vice, the mortification of the flesh,
and the increasing of virtue.' The preacher's purpose was to deny
that pilgrims to St. James would automatically be saved as if the
apostle had waved a magic wand over them, 'for a wand', he told
them, 'is an external, material thing, whereas sin is an internal,
spiritual evil.' Having thus dismissed the spiritual ideas of most of
his audience, the preacher urged them to make their pilgrimage
a monastic exercise of the most austere sort:

> 'The pilgrim may bring with him no money at all,
> except perhaps to distribute it to the poor on the road.
> Those who sell their property before leaving must give
> every penny of it to the poor, for if they spend it on
> their own journey they are departing from the path of
> the Lord. In times past the faithful had but one heart
> and one soul, and they held all property in common,
> owning nothing of their own; just so, the pilgrims of
> today must hold everything in common and travel
> together with one heart and one soul. To do otherwise
> would be disgraceful and outrageous....Goods shared in
> common are worth much more than goods owned by
> individuals. Thus it is that the pilgrim who dies on the
> road with money in his pocket is permanently excluded
> from the kingdom of heaven. For what benefit can a
> man possibly derive from a pilgrimage undertaken in a
> spirit of sin?'

The preacher then turned his attention to those comfortable
persons who ate and drank their way across the roads of
Europe in the hope of salvation.

'Truly, these are not real pilgrims at all, but thieves and robbers who have abandoned the way of apostolic poverty and chosen instead the path of damnation....If the Lord chose to enter Jerusalem on a mule rather than a horse, then what are we to think of those who parade up and down before us on horseback?...If St. Peter entered Rome with nothing but a crucifix, why do so many pilgrims come here with bulging purses and trunks of spare clothes, eating succulent food and drinking heady wine?...St. James was a wanderer without money or shoes and yet ascended to heaven as soon as he died; what, then, will happen to those who make opulent progresses to his shrine surrounded by all the evidence of their wealth?'

Turning from the general to the particular, the preacher directed his invective against those who entered Santiago fattened on the profits of usury, lying and swearing, joking, and singing bawdy, drunken songs. In fact, a pilgrimage was worthless unless it was accompanied by a total moral reformation in the pilgrim. Not only must he go to Santiago in the right spirit, but he must persevere in that spirit for the rest of his days. 'If he was previously a spoliator, he must become an almsgiver; if he was boastful he must be forever modest; if greedy, generous; if a fornicator or adulterer, chaste; if drunk, sober. That is to say that from every sin which he committed before his pilgrimage, he must afterwards abstain completely.'

These opinions were not simply mouthed in vain by a few idealistic churchmen. A small minority of pilgrims attempted to put them into practice, not, perhaps, on the roads to Santiago, but certainly in Palestine during the century of Christian rule.

Some of them, like St. Godric, the hermit of Finchale who visited Jerusalem in the early twelfth century, tended the sick in the Hospital of St. John. Others chose the traditional eremetical life and retired to an isolated cabin in the desert wastes of Palestine. The Greek monk John Phocas, who visited the Holy Land in about 1175, met several of these lonely 'men of God'. In a hut by the Jordan, he encountered an aged Spaniard, 'a very pleasing and admirable person from whose conversation we derived great benefit.' Another hermit, this time an Italian from Calabria, was found with twelve brethren inhabiting a shed by the ruins of Mount Carmel. Even after the disaster which engulfed the Christian kingdom of Jerusalem in 1187, communities of Christian hermits survived in Syria, at the Quarantana, in the valley of the Jordan and the district of Galilee. Jacques de Vitry, writing in the 1220s, regarded the preservation of their way of life as a legitimate reason for launching another crusade. Those pilgrims who became hermits and recluses were drawn chiefly from the noble and well-to-do. Rayner Pisani, who suddenly went to live alone on Mount Tabor in the middle of the twelfth century, was a wealthy merchant of Pisa whose 'conversion' occurred when he listened to a sermon on the humanity of Christ, during a business visit to Tyre. 'Because the life of the world was onerous', wrote his biographer and disciple, 'he prayed to God day and night to help him put aside all his wealth, to put on the pilgrim's habit and be worthy of it.' Many of these hermits came from northern Italy, the birthplace of the eremitical movement of the eleventh and twelfth centuries. William of Mallavalle, who ended his days as a recluse in the wilderness north of Pisa, was a knight who had marked his 'conversion' to the spiritual life by 'throwing aside his breastplate' and making a pilgrimage to the Holy Places. Such figures were the spiritual heroes of the twelfth century, and their example was frequently highly infectious. In June 1200, when Berthold von Neuenburg sold all his belongings and retired to a hermitage in Palestine, he found many followers in the Breisgau region; 'a large number of noblemen, together with their wives and children, sold all their goods and vowed to become serfs of the Holy Sepulchre.' The ideal of renouncing the world was adopted by some crusaders. Jacques de Vitry knew a crusader who had his family brought before him as he left in order to make his departure the more bitter and meritorious. Indeed, the preacher complained that some crusaders were worthless as fighting men on account of the austerities which they inflicted on themselves. Nevertheless it was generally agreed that a crusading army was bound by spiritual conventions which would not have applied to any other army. Hence when Saladin offered to accommodate Hubert Walter at his expense in Jerusalem, the archbishop refused on the ground that 'we are pilgrims and can never accept such comforts.'

For pilgrims and crusaders alike the normal method of renouncing the world was to enter a monastery on their return. Peter the Venerable heartily approved of those knights whose pilgrimages were merely the prelude to taking the monastic habit. Cluny received many of them. Peter tells us of a knight who gave his horses, fine clothes, and money to Cluny and proceeded 'as a pauper' to Jerusalem before ending his days in the abbey. Another spent forty days in Rome and then took the habit at Cluny.

Even those who made no attempt to live up to this ideal, usually made some conventional gestures towards the mortification of the flesh. Pilgrimages on foot were very common, and

among sincere penitents almost obligatory. A long tradition of
the Church held that walking was the most virtuous method
of travelling. According to Sulpicius Severus, St. Martin had
expressed his contempt for priests who went mounted about
their duties. St. Hilary of Arles (d. 449) is stated to have walked
to Rome at the end of his life 'because he so much admired the
ideal of poverty that he insisted on doing without horse or
mule.' As so often happened, the hagiographic tradition of the
early Church moulded the behaviour of later generations. Thus
the idealized 'holy man' of the eleventh century, in this case St.
Aibert, travelled on foot:

> 'Walking completely barefoot, clothed in a simple
> tunic, and with scarcely a penny on them, he and his
> companions set out for Rome rich in the abundance of
> their poverty. They rode on horseback rarely or never,
> and used their mule only to help weak and infirm pil-
> grims whom they met on the road.'

Matilda of Thornbury walked to Canterbury on her crutches
at the end of the twelfth century, and even so august a pilgrim
as the countess of Clare threw away her shoes as she began her
pilgrimage. Barefoot pilgrims were particularly esteemed, and
at Limoges in the fourteenth century there is even a reference
to pilgrims arriving completely naked. The author of the *Life
of St. Godric of Finchale* gloried in the austerities of the saint
during his journeys to Jerusalem. Not only did he go barefoot
till his feet were covered in hideous sores, but he ate nothing
but dry barley bread; if only fresh bread could be obtained he
would keep it in his bag until it was hard and almost unbreak-
able. Pilgrims rode on horseback at their peril, risking not only
the imprecations of idealistic churchmen, but also the possibil-

ity of divine chastisement. A canon of Dol, riding to Chartres at the close of the eleventh century, began to feel ill as he approached Orléans, and so thought it prudent to do the rest of the journey on foot. John King found his horse unusually restless on the road to Canterbury and took it as a divine warning to dismount. A woman who suffered from deformed feet was obliged to go to Reading abbey in a carriage and pair, but she was healed during the journey, and thereupon dismounted and proceeded on foot. Thus, although the austere warnings of the Santiago preacher fell on deaf ears, a distant echo of his voice was sometimes heard on the pilgrimage roads.

Renewal and Death

One of the stories which Jacques de Vitry collected for use in his sermons told of two brothers, the one an assiduous visitor of shrines, the other not. When they died, the pilgrim was escorted to heaven by flights of angels, while the other made his way alone. At the tribunal of St. Peter both brothers were found wanting, but only the pilgrim was admitted: 'open to him', the Lord commanded, 'for he was a pilgrim.' The story, like so many of Jacques de Vitry's, expresses in the simplest pictorial fashion the aspirations of his audiences. The overwhelming majority of mediaeval pilgrims expected to have their sins expunged from their souls as if by a magic wand, and the austere warnings of the preacher of *Veneranda Dies* fell on deaf ears. The moral theology of the Church laid an overpowering emphasis on the sinfulness of men. The material world they lived in, everything they touched and saw, all that they enjoyed, drew them towards sin, and the few introspective writings which survive are all characterized by a morbid obsession with the accumulated burden of guilt. The penitential system of the eleventh and twelfth centuries offered only a partial solution, for by preserving an elaborate distinction between guilt and punishment, it left the sinner with most of his or her burden. The prospect of a second baptism, of starting the spiritual life anew, stood before the sinner like a mirage, irresistibly attractive.

This was what the great shrines offered, with increasing openness, to the sinner. Baptismal imagery constantly recurs in the devotional literature which they put out. At the shrine of Thomas Becket criminals were reformed, sinners amended, debauchers returned to the path of holiness: 'the moment they approach the shrine...they promise to mend their ways as if rebaptized in the font of their own tears.' Sentiments of this sort became a commonplace of the later Middle Ages. Christ informed the Swedish mystic St. Bridget in a vision that she was cleansed of her sins at the moment of entering the basilica of the Holy Sepulchre 'as if she had just arisen from the baptismal font'. When a noble woman of Bologna entered the Franciscan church of the Portiuncula in 1336, a voice declared to her: 'just as you were freed of all sin in the baptismal font, so you are now, by the act of entering this church, relieved of the entire burden of your sins.'

One of the most popular legends of the Middle Ages was the story of St. Mary the Egyptian, a prostitute who was purified by a visit to the Holy Land. On the feast of the Invention of the Cross she attempted to enter the basilica of the Holy Sepulchre together with the crowds of other pilgrims, but a miraculous force prevented her from passing through the door. Then Mary realized that she alone was unworthy to enter that place. Guided by the Blessed Virgin she walked to the point in the Jordan where Christ had been baptized, and swam across, to live a hermit's life on the other side. In the eleventh and twelfth centuries the story enjoyed an undying popularity. Honorius of Autun preached on St. Mary the Egyptian, and Hildebert of Tours wrote her life in verse. Her story was sculpted on the capitals of the church of St. Etienne in Toulouse. Within a decade of the Christian conquest of Jerusalem, the door which she had been unable to enter and the place where she had immersed herself in the Jordan were marked out for the benefit of pilgrims.

St. Mary the Egyptian had purified herself by reliving the baptism of Christ. The sins of her past had been obliterated and her spiritual life begun afresh. It was this process of regeneration which mediaeval pilgrims to the Holy Land tried to repeat by bathing in huge numbers in the Jordan. The biographer of St. Silvin, writing at the beginning of the ninth century, recorded that the saint walked to the Jordan 'to the very place where Christ, the son of God, was baptized...and immersed himself totally in the holy waters. Overcome with elation, he emerged from the river as if reborn, his spiritual ills cured, and his life's desire fulfilled.' This symbolic act eloquently explains what it was that brought pilgrims to the Holy Land in such numbers. It became, in the eleventh century, an almost obligatory part of any pilgrimage to Jerusalem to trek the twenty miles to the Jordan and baptize oneself in its waters. After the capture of Jerusalem by the crusaders a large detachment of the victorious army, led by Raymond of St. Gilles and the visionary Peter Bartholomew, marched to the Jordan and swam, fully clothed, across the river. On emerging from the water Raymond was presented by the hermit with a palm of Jericho and, having fulfilled thus the object of his pilgrimage, he began his homeward journey. The ritual was not peculiar to western

Europeans. The Danish hero Thorstein Ricardson baptized himself in the Jordan in about 1025. The Russian princess Euphrosine, as she lay dying in Jerusalem, was unable to go to the Jordan, but one of her companions brought her some of the precious water in a bottle, 'which she received with joy and gratitude, drinking it and spreading it over her body to wash away the sins of the past'. When Dietrich of Wurzburg visited the Holy Land in c. 1172, he counted 60,000 pilgrims (an exaggeration, no doubt) standing with candles in their hands on the banks of the Jordan. So popular had the ritual become that it was adopted at Santiago. Two miles before the city there was a stream where French pilgrims were in the habit of totally immersing themselves 'for love of the apostle'.

According to Jacques de Vitry there were three reasons for the pilgrim to immerse himself in the Jordan. First, the waters of the Jordan were a relic which Christ had sanctified by the touch of His flesh. Secondly, every pilgrim should seek to imitate, however inadequately, the perfection of Christ; by bathing in the Jordan, Christ had bestowed upon it regenerative powers through which the pilgrim could enjoy a second baptism. Finally, Naaman the Syrian had been cleansed of his leprosy in the Jordan 'which was the model of purification for future generations'.

The tendency of the later Middle Ages was to venerate the Jordan exclusively as a relic. In a guide-book written at the end of the thirteenth century, the three reasons given by Jacques de Vitry are reduced to one, namely that 'these are the very waters which came into contact with the body of Christ, our Redeemer.' In 1483 Felix Faber reported that several knights of his party dived into the Jordan fully clothed, in the belief that their clothes would become impenetrable to the weapons of their enemies. Others brought small bells with them which they dipped in the water in the hope that, if they were rung thereafter, no thunder or lightning would threaten any area within earshot. 'However whether these vulgar opinions are true or false', the Dominican discreetly added, 'I leave for the sensible reader to decide for himself.' Certainly it was by now common for pilgrims to bring bottles of Jordan water home with them, for in 1480, as a pilgrim ship lay becalmed in the bay of Jaffa, its passengers vigorously debated the question whether the boat was capable of movement so long as part of the Jordan remained on board. One of them stood on the rail and announced that he had himself seen a papal bull at St. Peter's in Rome excommunicating those who removed water from the Jordan. This statement was evidently found convincing, for most of the pilgrims hastily threw their phials of water overboard, and the wind rose immediately.

When princess Euphrosine came to Jerusalem in 1173, it was with the fixed intention of dying there. A desire to die in Jerusalem was in fact expressed by several of those pilgrims of the eleventh century who believed that the end of the world was imminent. It is closely allied with the notion that the Holy Places offered to sinners the means of wiping clean the slate of their past sins. Pilgrims who felt that they had just experienced a process of spiritual renewal hoped to die while they were still in their perfect state. The notorious sinner Eskill Sveinsson prayed: 'I am afraid, O Lord, that when I return to my native country, I shall be seduced by Fortune and tempted into sin, and then I shall return to my old ways. I pray you therefore that for the good of my soul, you will deliver me now from the bonds of this earthly life and from the weight of my sins, and lead me to everlasting rest.' 'Lord Jesus Christ, who knowest all things', another begged, 'if I cannot purge myself of my former vices, then permit me not to return to my country but grant that I may die here…and be saved.' According to Caesarius of Heisterbach his prayer was answered, 'and thus, a few days later, he was united with the citizens of the heavenly Jerusalem.' The field of Aceldama' where pilgrims who died in Jerusalem were buried, bore eloquent witness to the vast number of pilgrims who died far from their homes, happy in the conviction that the stains of sin had been washed away.

The place of a man's burial was a matter of some importance to him, for the mediaeval Church firmly believed in the bodily resurrection of the dead. Those who were buried near the shrine of a great saint would rise in that very place on the Last Day, in the company of the saint. He would throw a mantle of protection over them at the tribunal of Christ, and they would ascend to Heaven in his wake. In Rogier van der Weyden's great altarpiece of the *Last Judgement,* in the hospital at Beaune, the blessed and the damned can be seen emerging from the ground and reaching out to grasp the robes of the saints above them. In the early Church this was a very powerful idea which shaped the attitudes of churchmen to the burial of the dead. Paulinus of Nola had his son buried near the martyrs' tombs at Alcala, in Spain, 'so that the proximity of their blood might purify his'. When the early Christian cemetery at Arles was excavated, it was found that all the sarcophagi were piled, one on top of the other, over the tomb of a local martyr. In the Middle Ages this notion was held with the same immovable conviction. When abbot Suger closed his biography of Louis VI with an account of the obsequies of the dead king at St.-Denis, he concluded with these words: 'in that place he awaits the resurrection of the dead at the last day. At St.-Denis he is closer in spirit to the army of the saints because his body is buried close to the holy martyrs Denis, Eleutheria, and Rusticus. And so at the Last Day he will benefit by their advocacy.'

At the Last Day Christ too would be found in the place where he had been buried, and would dispense judgement to men from his sepulchre. The author of a guide to the Holy Land, written at the beginning of the twelfth century, states as a fact that the Last Judgement would be held in the valley of Jehosaphet on the eastern side of Jerusalem, not far, in fact, from the pilgrims' cemetery of Aceldama. Some seventy years later a German pilgrim reported that the tribunal would be set up in a field in the valley of Ennon and that simple-minded pilgrims were in the habit of reserving stones for themselves to sit on and enjoy a good view. This belief still prevailed at the end of the fifteenth century, when several of Felix Faber's companions set about claiming seats not only for themselves but also for their friends at home. The pilgrim who was buried within yards of the site of the Last Judgement would be resurrected in the holiest place on the earth. Just as Louis VI would enjoy the patronage of St. Denis at the awful tribunal, so the pilgrim who died in Jerusalem would have the favour of the divine judge himself. This is what the Autun pilgrim Lethbald meant when, in 1025, he entered the basilica of the Anastasis in Jerusalem, and prayed to be allowed to die there, 'for I believe that thus...my soul shall follow in the track of yours and enter Paradise.'

In the eleventh century, millenarian fears, always a strong undercurrent of mediaeval thought, gave a peculiar urgency to the quest for the remission of sins. No period had such a strong belief in the imminence of divine judgement. To mediaeval men and women history was not an ever-continuing process. It

had a formal, dramatic unity, for the events of which the chroniclers wrote were the direct consequences of the fall of Man and
they led directly to the end of the world. The chronicle of Otto
of Friesing, who died in 1158, begins at the Creation and ends
with the Last Judgement. 'Manifest signs portend the destruction
of the world, and ruin builds up around us', began a charter of
the seventh century. These fears were strangely linked with political events, for chaos and disorder in the affairs of humans were
certain portents of the Last Day. In the middle of the tenth century the notion was embodied in a little book, the *Libellus de
Antichristo* of Adso of Montiérender, which held the field
amongst millenarian writings until it was replaced in the later
Middle Ages by the even stranger works of Joachim of Fiore.
Adso borrowed from the Book of Daniel the prophecy that
there would be four empires in the history of the world, asserting that the fourth and last of these empires was the Roman
empire. Like all his contemporaries, Adso recognized in the
Christian German empire of his own day a continuation of the
Roman empire, and it followed that when the Christian
German empire ended, so too would the history of the world.

Adso himself had every confidence in the resilience of the
empire. But he wrote at the end of a century of political chaos
during which western Europe had been continuously raided
and pillaged by Arabs, Norsemen, and Magyars, and its political fabric had come close to total dissolution. His contemporaries had no reason to be confident of the future, and the
imminence of divine retribution was their constant preoccupation. They not only knew that the world was drawing near to
its end, but they had clear ideas as to how and where the Last
Judgement would occur, and what signs would precede it.
There would be famine, earthquakes, and other natural disas-

ters, followed by the dissolution of all political power, as the Apocalypse had foretold. Then Antichrist would be born in Babylon of the tribe of Dan and would rule the world until the descent of Christ and his saints. When the time came for the dissolution of all political power the emperor would march to Jerusalem and surrender the insignia of office in the church of the Holy Sepulchre. There he would witness with his own eyes the Last Judgement. The polemicist Benzo of Alba saw his contemporary, the emperor Henry IV, in this role. He would be the last emperor, and would lead his army to Jerusalem 'where he will visit the Holy Sepulchre and be crowned by He who lives for ever and ever, and whose tomb shall shine forth in glory.' At that moment the earthly and the celestial Jerusalem would be one.

In his youth, Abbo of Fleury had heard a popular preacher in Paris promise his audience that the world would end in the year 1000. A profound fear of imminent destruction undoubtedly existed in the tenth century, but the millennium itself was an uneventful year. It required some portentous event to liberate these suppressed feelings, and this event occurred in 1009 with the total destruction of the Holy Sepulchre in Jerusalem by caliph Hakim. The destruction, which was the result of a short-lived outburst of hysteria in an unbalanced caliph, had profound effects in the west. Suddenly it was clear that Hakim was the Antichrist of whom the Apocalypse had spoken. In parts of France the prevailing view was that Hakim's act had been suggested to him by the Jews of Orléans, and the mob reacted by invading the ghettos and murdering or forcibly baptizing the inhabitants. In some towns, particularly in Aquitaine, they were actively encouraged by the clergy. From western France, Normandy, and Burgundy departed the first of a series of mass pilgrimages to the Holy Land. The bulk of these pilgrims were obscure, frightened men, but amongst them were several distinguished churchmen and a few lay princes to testify to the striking homogeneity of eleventh-century piety. Gauzlin, abbot of Fleury and later archbishop of Bourges, a bishop of Périgord, Raymond, count of the Rouergue, and Fulk Nerra were amongst the pilgrims of that year.

An even larger exodus followed the thousandth anniversary of the death of Christ in 1033. The year was ushered in by famine and torrential rainstorms, which lasted throughout the spring and flattened the crop in many parts of France. 'Men thought', wrote Radulph Glaber, 'that the very laws of nature and the order of the seasons were reversed, that those rules which governed the world were replaced by chaos. They knew then that the end of the world had arrived.' Glaber was born in Burgundy and lived there all his life. His work gives us an insight into the religious imagination of the eleventh century, for he shared the moods and enthusiasms of those whom he described. A superstitious and emotional man, he was several times possessed by the Devil and was plainly an embarrassment to his superiors, who moved him from one monastery to another at frequent intervals. In 1033 Glaber was living at Cluny, and from behind its sheltered walls observed the growing panic of his fellow-countrymen. Beginning in Aquitaine, the terror had reached Burgundy by summer. Large assemblies of men joined in public displays of repentance and swore to keep the 'peace of God'. 'The entire people, great and small, willingly attended, each one ready to obey the instructions of his pastor as if he had heard a voice from the sky speaking to all men on earth.' The wealthier pilgrims who returned from Jerusalem at that time, expressed their relief and gratitude for the survival of mankind by founding churches. 'I Hictor', wrote one of them, 'mindful of the compassionate kindness of God the supreme judge, do hereby found this church on the occasion of my return from Jerusalem. For I know that the fleeting life of the world is brittle and yet harsh; I know too how great is the reward of the virtuous, and how dreadful the torments of the damned.' Hervé, archdeacon of the church of Ste.-Croix d'Orléans, had been convinced in 1033 of the approaching dissolution of the earth:

> 'The life of the world is uncertain and fragile. No one knows when his passage on earth will end, for does not the whole world rush rapidly to its destruction?…I pondered many nights on the frailty of life and so came to live in fear of sudden death. I went to Jerusalem to atone for my sins and to beg for mercy on my knees…. Now, God having permitted me to return safely….I have endowed this church….not only for the remission of my own most grievous sins but for the salvation of the souls of my family; for my parents Havranus and Adela and my brother Peter, all dead, as well as for the rest of my family who are still, thank God, alive.'

The mass pilgrimage of 1033, though probably the most dramatic, was not the last occasion on which eschatological fears were to send frightened hordes to the Holy Land. The turn of Germany came in 1064. The army of pilgrims which left Passau in that year seem to have been persuaded that the world would end when Easter Sunday fell on the 26th of March, the date given in some mediaeval calendars for the original resurrection. This coincidence occurred in 1065 for the first time in seventy-three years. Again, on the 15th of July

1099, when the crusading army entered Jerusalem, some of them saw in their achievement the prelude to the end of the world, and the dazed remnants of the Provençal contingent waited, silent and inactive, for the descent of Christ and his saints.

Two images of God drew the attention of people to the Holy Places. The religion of the eleventh and twelfth centuries was characterized by a new devotion to the humanity of Christ, to his nativity and childhood as much as to his death and resurrection. The formal, stylized, infinitely distant God of the Moissac tympanum gave way to the human God of Chartres cathedral, and thus to the suffering God of Cimabue and Giotto. But the same Christ who took on the weakness and vulnerability of manhood was also the terrible judge portrayed with frightening realism on the west fronts of Conques or Autun. Here indeed, carved in stone, was the *rex tremenda majestatis* whom the pilgrims sought to appease with their prayers. In contemporary eyes these two notions offered no contradiction: the one led on naturally to the other.

> 'Tell me then', wrote Peter Damian in his treatise on flagellation, 'you who proudly mock the Passion of Christ, you who disdain to be stripped and scourged with him, you who laugh at his nakedness and sufferings and dismiss them as the triflings of pious old fools, tell me what you will do when he who hung naked on the Cross appears in glorious majesty, surrounded by angels and the incomparable splendour of all creation. What will you do when he who took on the ignominy of humanity and death, comes to judge the living and the dead?'

Only by imitating Christ the man could one placate Christ the judge. In this way the romantic desire to relive in one's imagination the life of Christ, was combined with a very real fear of His anger, and a firm conviction that by renouncing one's ordinary life and following His footsteps in the Holy Land, the force of that anger could be deflected. Thus it was to a stern and vengeful God that the author of the *Dies Irae* addressed his impassioned plea for mercy:

> *Iuste iudex ultionis*
> *Donum fac remissionis*
> *Ante diem rationis.*

The minority of pilgrims who lived according to the precepts of the sermon *Veneranda Dies* felt that they had fully earned this mercy. They had, at least temporarily, renounced the world and entered an order of the Church, an elite body whose chances of salvation were infinitely greater than those of the mass of humanity. This feeling of belonging to an initiated caste of holy men, as formal in its own way as the monastic order itself, the pilgrim expressed by wearing a distinctive 'uniform', and by receiving at his departure the blessing of the Church. The great monastic reformer William of Hirsau, who always had the 'mot juste' for everything, distinguished five orders of the Church in Germany, for each of which he had a separate spiritual message. To the order of bishops and priests, he would teach theology and ecclesiastical law; to the order of monks, humility and piety; to the order of laymen, faith and submission; to the order of virgins, chastity; and the order of pilgrims and hermits he would teach to be content with their lot 'for their faith has made them glorious in the sight of God and the world is at their feet'.

9

The Legacy
of the Crusades

The first crusade is the central event in the history of mediaeval Christianity. In proclaiming the holy war at the council of Clermont in 1095, Urban II promised salvation to a world obsessed with its own sinfulness. 'God has invented the crusade', Guibert reflected, 'as a new way for the knightly order and the vulgar masses to atone for their sins.' In the two centuries which followed, the crusade offered a route to salvation which eclipsed every other spiritual exercise. In the celebrated phrase of Gibbon, the pope had unwittingly 'touched upon a nerve of exquisite feeling'. Yet, although it was born in the mood of intense spiritual feeling which hung over the eleventh century, the crusading movement was ultimately to destroy the spiritual values of Christian Europe. Those who fought on the crusades or contributed to their cost, received a 'quantum of salvation' which was precisely defined and measured. In the course of time their rights and duties were embodied in the codes of canon and civil law. This uncompromising precision greatly simplified the moral values of Christendom, and it was without doubt the root cause of the astonishing success of crusading preachers from Peter the Hermit to Jacques de Vitry. The crusades brought a new formality to the notion of pilgrimage, a formality which radically altered its character. Thus the doctrine of indulgences, whose development was greatly assisted by the crusades, transformed the pilgrim's journey into a ritual, devoid of the intensely personal and spiritual quality of the pilgrimages of the eleventh century. The enforcement of the crusading vow became the principal method of recruiting crusaders, and in its wake came an apparatus of dispensations and financial commutations with far-reaching consequences for the spiritual life of the west.

These symptoms affected every aspect of spiritual life in varying degrees. Pilgrimages were, perhaps, affected more than any other because the crusaders regarded themselves as pilgrims, and in contemporary eyes, so they were. They shared the same hopes of spiritual rebirth, performed the same rites, enjoyed the same legal privileges and expected the same esteem from their fellow men. They were surprised and angry when the inhabitants of Asia Minor refused to sell them food 'taking us to be no pilgrims but mere bandits and plunderers'. Moreover, the early crusades were joined not only by 'armed pilgrims' of this sort but by crowds of unarmed hangers-on who travelled in the unshakeable conviction that God would reward their piety by delivering Jerusalem into their hands without a battle. The expeditions of 1096 and 1146 were both accompanied by a lunatic fringe which castigated in violent terms the bearing of any arms at all. This fifth column was brutally excluded from the later crusades, but their ideal of conquest by holiness alone lived on. Even the sober Jacques de Vitry believed that the crusaders had lost Jerusalem on account of their degenerate and sinful ways. The notion of the true crusader remained inseparable from that of the pilgrim.

The Pilgrim's Vow

'Is there anything that a man can do to atone for a vow unful-filled?' asked Dante of Beatrice in Paradise; 'nothing', she replied, 'for when you consent, God consents, and nothing can stand in place of God's consent.'

Though the vow of pilgrimage was as old as pilgrimage itself, the age of its greatest impact began with Urban II's momentous pronouncement at Clermont. Towards the end of his speech, the pope required every crusader to swear a solemn oath to fulfill his pilgrimage and, when he had raised his hear-ers to a high pitch of emotion, the pope had crosses quickly distributed among the crowd 'for whoever accepted this sign...could never go back on his decision.' Fifty years later St. Bernard too had crosses sewn to the tunics of his audience when he was preaching the second crusade at Vézelay. In 'tak-ing the cross' the pilgrim, often unwittingly, passed a point of no return. So much so that a thirteenth-century satirist warned his readers against attending revivalist meetings lest they should suddenly find themselves 'imprisoned by crosses'.

Canon law prescribed that no one could break a vow of pilgrimage and be saved. Whether the culprit was a peaceful pilgrim or an armed crusader was immaterial. The vow was enforced by excommunication and in parts of Europe failure to fulfil it was punished by both secular and ecclesiastical courts. Such sanctions were rarely necessary in the twelfth century, but as enthusiasm for the crusade began to wane, so the authorities became more vigorous in their attempts to enforce vows. The fourth crusade, which developed into a war against the Christian empire of Byzantium, was the first to encounter really serious recruiting problems. Innocent III sternly reminded the Hungarian king of his crusading vow. The doge of Venice was informed that his salvation should be regarded as unlikely 'if, ignoring the wrath of God, you fail to do as you are told.' The fifth crusade drew a similar series of testy letters from Honorius III. The tardiness of the emperor Frederick II in fulfilling his vow involved him in a prolonged dispute with the papacy which culminated in his excommunication.

In some circumstances a pilgrim might even be bound by the vow of another. In a letter to duke Andrew of Hungary, Innocent III declared in general terms that if a pilgrim died before fulfilling his vow, his heir might be made to do it for him. This ambitious idea cannot have been enforced in practice, but it had a certain moral authority even when the pilgrim was not a crusader. In the 1170s a parish priest in Lincolnshire was cured of a fatal illness after two women had vowed in his name to visit the shrine of St. Thomas of Canterbury. A vision of St. Thomas made it quite clear that he was bound by the vow: 'others promised for you; the fulfilment of their promise is your duty.'

Until the thirteenth century, these stern rules admitted few exceptions. It was agreed that vows made in childhood were not binding, and Alexander III formally declared this to be a principle of the canon law. Would-be crusaders who were prevented by illness or some other impediment had always been allowed to send a substitute, as Thierry, duke of Lorraine, did in 1096. Such dispensations were common enough in the twelfth century, and in 1200 Innocent III laid down a procedure for granting them. The procedure applied to crusaders and non-crusaders alike, but in the course of the thirteenth century a distinction was gradually recognized. The canonist Henry of Susa appreciated that there was a difference between 'pilgrims who fight and pilgrims who pray'. In practice an ordinary pilgrim obtained his dispensation without much difficulty.

As dispensations became increasingly common, the crusading vow imperceptibly ceased to be a spiritual act. The growing difficulty of recruiting volunteers made the thirteenth-century crusades dependent to some extent on expensive mercenaries. In 1240 Gregory IX made an important pronouncement to the effect that all crusading vows could be commuted for money whether or not the would-be crusader was capable of fighting in person. According to the jaundiced English chronicler Matthew Paris, large numbers of women, children, and old men took the cross in order that they could buy a dispensation and still gain the crusading indulgence. Thereafter, an excuse was sometimes required, sometimes not. The friars who preached the crusade in 1290 were empowered to commute vows for two hundred *livres* of Tours, and the same authority was given to them in 1308.

Until the end of the fourteenth century the Church did not concern itself much with vows of pilgrimage, other than those involving the Holy Land. Such vows were, however, enforced by strong spiritual pressures especially if they had been made in public. Countless popular stories related the fate of those foolhardy persons who broke a promise to their saint. One was struck blind, another afflicted with paralysis or leprosy. Infirmities cured by a saint returned if patients failed to show their gratitude by praying at the shrine. An English knight whose broken arm was healed by St. James forgot to visit the hand of St. James at Reading, and the apostle therefore broke his other arm. 'And by this example', the author of the tale concluded, 'one may see how powerful is faith and how dreadful it is to break an oath.' By promising to visit a shrine,

the pilgrim conceived that he was uniting himself to the saint
by a bond of mutual self-interest: the saint wished to be venerated and desired offerings for his clergy; the pilgrim wanted to
be protected against sin, disease, and natural disasters. Failure to
fulfil a vow was both sinful and imprudent. This notion was
implicit in the prayer of a Polish nobleman who visited St.
Gilles-de-Provence towards the end of the eleventh century,
after narrowly escaping death in a hunting accident: 'Holy St.
Gilles, on condition that you offer me your good offices with
the Lord and preserve me from human perils, I solemnly agree
that I shall mend my ways and forthwith make a pilgrimage to
your shrine.'

Bargains of this sort were particularly common in the fourteenth and fifteenth centuries, when fewer miracles were
reported at the shrines themselves. In large miracle collections
of this period, the great majority of stories tell of marvellous
happenings near the pilgrim's own home. He has come to the
shrine, not to beg for a miracle, but to give thanks for one
which has already occurred. When, in 1388, St. Martial of
Limoges suddenly began to corruscate in wonders, in almost
every case the miracle occurred before the pilgrimage; the one
was, in fact, conditional upon the other. A citizen of Limoges
declared that 'if the ever-glorious St. Martial were to heal my
sick son, I would offer a candle at his shrine'; the son recovered
and the father presented his candle in the saint's basilica. A
cowherd swore to visit St. Martial if he protected his cows from
English bandits. Another would do so if ever he found his lost
gold pennies. Thus the subtle idea that human troubles were
caused by sin and removed by penitence slowly lost its force,
and was replaced by the simpler notion of a contract, freely
entered into, between a saint and his or her votary.

Indulgences

When a Christian confessed his sins and sought absolution, a penance was imposed on him. An indulgence was a formal act of the Church by which that penance was remitted. An indulgence did not pretend to release the sinner from his guilt (only confession and absolution could do that), but in the words of a thirteenth-century schoolman it 'excused him from suffering the temporal punishment due for his sins'.

The indulgence grew from modest beginnings. In the tenth century the Frankish Church allowed penitents to redeem their penances by payment if they were physically incapable of performing them, and remissions of this sort were pronounced to be legitimate by the council which met at Rheims in 923–4. Such indulgences were only granted if the circumstances of the individual case warranted it. The earliest general indulgences, offered to anyone who was prepared to fulfil the conditions, did not make their appearance until the eleventh century, when Christendom was becoming morbidly preoccupied with the problems of *remissio peccatorum*. The rapid development of indulgences, like that of the vow of pilgrimage, owed everything to the crusades. At the council of Clermont, Urban II declared in unequivocal terms that 'every man who sets out for Jerusalem with the army to liberate the Church of God shall have the entire penance for his sins remitted.' Urban was offering them a 'plenary' indulgence, that is, an indulgence which erased all the penance due for the sins of a lifetime. It was, in the words of the Lateran council of 1215, a guarantee of salvation.

The crusading indulgence was the first plenary indulgence, and for two centuries it remained the only one. But partial indulgences, which remitted a stated proportion of the sinner's outstanding penance, made their appearance at about the same time. The earliest papal indulgence which can be accepted as authentic dates from 1091, when Urban II promised that all who assisted the restoration and repair of the Norman monastery of St. Austreberthe at Pavilly would enjoy the remission of 'a fourth part of the penance enjoined by a bishop or priest'. During Urban's tour of France in 1095 several pilgrimages were favoured with indulgences of this kind. 'It is right to consent to pious requests', one of them begins, 'in order to help the sinner to achieve his salvation.... We recommend therefore that the church of St. Nicholas of Angers be honoured, protected, and visited by the faithful..., and we accordingly remit a seventh part of the penance imposed for any sins, for all those who visit the church in a devout frame of mind on the anniversary of its dedication.'

During the twelfth century the papacy granted indulgences sparingly, and made only modest claims for them. Others, however, were less restrained. The churches which received indulgences grossly exaggerated their efficacy, while those that did not, forged them. Moreover, bishops also claimed the right to issue indulgences and showed themselves much more generous to local shrines than the papacy. Their indulgences were far more numerous than those issued by the papacy, and their impact on contemporary religious life correspondingly greater. In 1215 the Lateran council addressed itself to the problem. Bishops were forbidden to issue indulgences of more than forty days for the feast of a patron saint or one year for the anniversary of a dedication. Within a few years, however, the excessive indulgences granted by some bishops to insignificant shrines had attracted the hostile attention of the University of Paris. The decree of 1215 was reissued with a frequency which suggests that it was widely ignored. In 1339 the council of Aquilea complained that bishops not only exceeded the limits laid down by the Lateran fathers, but even granted indulgences outside their own dioceses.

Towards the end of the thirteenth century the issue became less important as the papacy itself started to issue indulgences more generously. The charity of the popes began, naturally enough, at home. In the reign of Alexander III (d. 1181), the basilicas of the apostles already offered indulgences which were extremely large by the standards of other pilgrimage churches. A century later, at the death of Nicholas IV (1292), indulgences of astounding generosity were available in every church of Rome, and at every altar of the basilicas of the apostles. But no pilgrimage offered a plenary indulgence until 1294, when Celestine V 'opened the treasury of mercy confided to him by Christ and bestowed it upon those who were truly confessed and penitent.' In fact, he issued a plenary indulgence to the church of Collemaggio, near Aquila, for the feast of John the Baptist. After Celestine's abdication in the following year, this act was quashed by his robust successor Boniface VIII together with all his other indulgences issued 'in ignorance of the canon law and of all his pastoral responsibilities'. But only five years later Boniface issued a plenary indulgence of his own, to the basilicas of the apostles on the occasion of the first Roman Jubilee.

The indulgence which finally opened the floodgates was the indulgence of the Portiuncula. St. Mary of the Portiuncula was the small chapel near Assisi which had been made over to the use of St. Francis and his earliest followers. It was here, in 1226, that Francis had died. By the middle years of the thirteenth century the Franciscans were claiming that the founder had secretly obtained from Honorius III a plenary indulgence for the chapel which would, if genuine, have been the only plenary indulgence in existence other than the crusading indulgence. Its authenticity was disputed from the outset on several grounds. It was said to be prejudicial to the reconquest of the Holy Land. The Portiuncula chapel was said to be too obscure to enjoy an indulgence which was denied to the greatest churches of Rome. It was an incitement to sin, others alleged; it brought other indulgences into contempt. These arguments, which could never have been advanced a hundred years later, are alone sufficient to show how novel and unfamiliar the idea of a plenary indulgence for pilgrims was in the thirteenth century. A commission of enquiry met in 1277 to examine the authenticity of the indulgence, and much scholarly ink has been spilt over the matter ever since. It is, on the whole, unlikely to be genuine, and even if Honorius III did grant an indulgence to the Portiuncula, it was certainly not a plenary one. None of these considerations, however, weighed very heavily with contemporaries. By 1295 the number of pilgrims was already greater than the friars serving the chapel could deal with, and in the early years of the fourteenth century the brothers were stated to be dealing daily with cardinals, archbishops, bishops, abbots, priors, kings, dukes, counts, and barons. However dubious its origins, the pilgrimage of the Portiuncula was among the most prosperous in Europe. It was the first pilgrimage which owed its success entirely to the skilful advertisement of an indulgence. Other shrines were quick to learn the lesson of the Portiuncula, and Celestine V undoubtedly had the Franciscan indulgence in mind when he declared a plenary remission of sins for pilgrims to Collemaggio.

No indulgence ever purported to release pilgrims from guilt as well as penance. Confession was therefore an essential preliminary to every pilgrimage. The preacher of the sermon *Veneranda Dies* inveighed fiercely against those who imagined that a pilgrimage to Santiago would erase their sins without it. However, there is no doubt that many, perhaps most, pilgrims did not appreciate this point. Many of those who flocked to Assisi to claim the Portiuncula indulgence, or to Rome to claim the Jubilee indulgence of 1300, had dispensed with the formality of confession, and in strict canon law their journey was wasted. Their error is scarcely surprising in view of the extravagant claims made for some indulgences by preachers and writers of miracle stories. In the fourteenth and fifteenth centuries these claims were regularly made notwithstanding repeated declarations that priests responsible for them were automatically excommunicated. In unlettered minds the confusion was exacerbated by the use of the misleading term '*a pena et culpa*' ('free from guilt and penance') to describe plenary indulgences. This phrase did not in fact mean what it said. Almost every papal document which used it, even the notorious Jubilee indulgence of 1510, insisted in the next breath that those claiming it must be 'truly confessed and penitent'. But few pilgrims would have seen these documents and fewer still would have read the learned commentaries of the canon lawyers. Their mistake would be discovered, if at all, only when they reached the shrine. By then it was often too late, for until the fourteenth century the Church insisted that confession be made to one's own parish priest before departing and, outside Rome, very few pilgrimage churches enjoyed the privilege of confessing visitors on the spot. At Rocamadour in the twelfth century, pilgrims were asked whether they had confessed and were sent home if they had not. A favourite anecdote of mediaeval preachers told how unconfessed pilgrims had suffered every kind of disaster, or how a mysterious force had physically prevented them from entering the church. A Burgundian pilgrim was physically unable to climb the steps of Mont-St.-Michel until she had confessed her sins. Ten strong men were unable to push a French nobleman through the entrance to the church of Our Lady at Villalcazar de Sirga on the road to Santiago, for his mortal sins had not yet been absolved. 'And the moral of this is that no man may enter the church of God who has not first confessed his mortal sins.' These considerations applied just as strongly in the later Middle Ages, when the doctrine of indulgences had provided a measuring-stick with which to assess the merit of a pilgrimage. The fourteenth-century *Miracles of St. Martial* tell of a pilgrim who was struck to the ground when he tried to kiss the sarcophagus of the saint, and this, says the author, was because he tried to claim an indulgence recently granted by pope Gregory XI without first going to confession.

The canonists and theologians of the later Middle Ages fought hard against the more extreme versions of the doctrine of indulgences. But even if the orthodox view had been universally understood, which it was not, the widespread use of indulgences would still have had the inevitable consequence of transforming the spiritual life of many laymen into a sequence of elaborate rituals. The indulgences of the twelfth and thirteenth centuries almost certainly did make pilgrimages more popular. On the other hand, they invited the pilgrim to measure the worth of his pilgrimage by standards which were mathematical, not spiritual. At the end of the twelfth century we find Gerald of Wales in Rome attending 395 masses in the shortest possible time, in order to obtain a total of ninety-two years of indulgences; finding that he was only eight years short of a century, he enrolled himself in the confraternity of the Holy Spirit which offered an indulgence of one-seventh of the penance due for his sins. Yet Gerald of Wales was an intelligent man, though not perhaps a very spiritual one. How many simpler souls must have raced from church to church, guide-book in hand, in the hope of collecting even more than a century of remission.

10

The Growth of a Cult

Canonization

The first stage in the rise of a great pilgrimage was the recognition of a saint. In the modern Roman Catholic Church this is a formal process, conducted with deliberation and ceremony. But it was not always so. In the earliest years of the cult of the saints, during the persecutions of the later Roman empire, veneration was accorded only to martyrs. The fact of their martyrdom being fairly easily ascertainable, no formal process of 'canonization' was necessary. It was only in the course of the fourth century, after the last of the great persecutions, that the veneration began to extend to 'confessors,' i.e. those who had witnessed the true faith in their lives but not in their deaths. The *Life of St. Anthony* by Athanasius was a landmark in this respect, for it showed how a holy man might achieve sanctity by the spiritual quality of his life. In time, however, the broader definition of sanctity created problems of its own, notably the problem of deciding whether the sanctity of the holy man was such as to warrant his public veneration by believers. What was needed was some kind of official procedure by which sanctity could be recognized.

No such procedure existed until the eleventh century, and even after that it was imperfectly respected. In its place, saints were usually recognized by spontaneous popular acclaim, assisted by the enthusiasm of the local clergy. It was an unreliable method at the best of times. Guibert of Nogent tells us at the beginning of the twelfth century that he had known many bogus popular 'canonizations' in his time, and mentions a striking example which had occurred in a small village near Beauvais in recent memory.

> 'A young man of low birth, the squire of some knight I believe, died on Good Friday and was spontaneously venerated as a saint, simply because of the holy day on which be died. The peasants, looking for something novel, brought offerings and candles to his grave from the entire surrounding area. Then a tomb was erected on the site, and after that a chapel, while troops of pilgrims, all of them peasants with not a nobleman among them, arrived from the furthest confines of Brittany. The learned abbot and his holy monks observed all this and, won over by the gratifying flow of offerings, allowed themselves to be convinced by all manner of spurious miracles.'

Guibert is at pains to point out the popular character of this pilgrimage. The dead squire was of low birth and so were those who came to venerate him; men of good birth were conspicuously absent. The resistance of the monks was weakened by greed, and the reserves of the authorities swept away by popular enthusiasm.

When the Normans conquered England they encountered spiritual traditions very different from their own, and they viewed with considerable suspicion some of the most popular saints of the Anglo-Saxon Church. Lanfranc was astonished and displeased to learn, on becoming archbishop of Canterbury, that Elphege, one of his predecessors, who had been killed by the Danes in 1012, had been solemnly translated to the cathedral and was revered there as a martyr. 'These English amongst whom we live', he complained to the abbot of Bec, 'have set up certain persons whom they revere as saints. At times, when I reflect upon the lives of these persons,....I entertain serious doubts as to their sanctity.' Abbot Paul of St. Albans, who also found his predecessors venerated as saints, dismissed them as 'boors and half-wits', thus giving deep offence to his monks. When Warin, the second Norman abbot of Malmesbury, arrived at the abbey, his first act was to throw out the remains of St. Meindulf and other saints of doubtful worth.

Nominally, the power of authorizing a cult rested with the bishop. Laymen and local clergymen had been forbidden since the fifth century to set up shrines without his approval, but in the west it was several centuries before the bishops achieved even a limited measure of control. Before the eleventh century, the normal method of inaugurating the cult of a saint was by 'elevation', which involved disinterring his or her relics and placing them on an altar. In 688, eleven years after the death of St. Cuthbert, the monks of Lindisfarne opened his tomb and, finding the body uncorrupt, they resolved to 'replace them in a new coffin in the same place but above the floor, where they could be more worthily venerated.' Before doing this they consulted their bishop, and this seems to have been the usual practice. In the Frankish territories the bishop's consent was made mandatory by the ecclesiastical legislators of the Carolingian period. How much care the bishop took to investigate the candidate's claims to sanctity varied from place to place. When the bishop of Cambrai authorized the 'elevation' of St. Hadulph at

Arras in the ninth century, he was satisfied with an assurance from the sacristan that miracles had occurred. Salomon, bishop of Constance, on the other hand, asked for a copy of the life of St. Otmar before proceeding to his 'elevation' and, having duly found the life edifying, he summoned a synod to consider the matter.

When vested interests were involved, obtaining approval for a new cult might be a prolonged and complex business. In 918 St. Gerard founded the monastery of Brogne near Liège, and translated to it the relics of an obscure Spanish saint called Eugenius, which he had been given by the abbey of St.-Denis. On his way back to Brogne with the relics he stopped to ask the bishop of Liège for permission to perform a translation. This was readily granted. But when the relics were enshrined at Brogne the popularity of the new cult spread so rapidly that other churches of the locality became jealous. A number of priests complained to the bishop that it was wrong for an unknown saint to be venerated in this way. The bishop decided to intervene. At this point, the contemporary historian of Brogne alleges, the Lord struck him down with a fatal disease. The bishop, who had correctly divined the cause of his illness, summoned a diocesan synod at which a life of the saint was read and the cult approved.

Papal consent was rarely sought before the tenth century and was not considered to be essential until the end of the eleventh. The first papal canonization known to history was that of St. Udalric of Augsburg, whose cult was officially approved by John XV in 993 at an imposing ceremony in the Lateran palace. Even so, John's consent was more or less a formality, no attempt being made to investigate the saint's life in any detail. Popes and synods were usually satisfied with the *acta* of the saint, hastily compiled by the local bishop. The first sign of any significant papal enquiry is found in 1099 when Urban II was invited by the clergy of southern Italy to authorize the cult of St. Nicholas of Trani. Urban commissioned the archbishop of Trani to investigate the case and, after hearing the *acta* and miracles of St. Nicholas recited in council, the pope duly performed the canonization. When, shortly afterwards the abbot of Quimperlé asked Urban to canonize his predecessor as abbot, the pope replied that this would not be possible 'unless witnesses can be found who will attest that they have seen his miracles with their own eyes.' We should probably regard Urban II as the father of the modern process of canonization.

One consequence of the new state of affairs was that canonizations no longer occurred on the spur of the moment. The canonization of Thomas Becket within three years of his death was regarded by some observers as excessively hasty, and so indeed it was by comparison with other processes of canonization. Lengthy judicial formalities were already the rule at the end of the twelfth century. The cardinals appointed to examine the miracles of St. Edmund of Abingdon in 1247 pointedly remarked that few of the fathers of the Church would have been canonized if this procedure had always been applied. Indeed, after about 1300 relatively few canonizations were performed although the flow of applications to Rome continued unabated. The canonization of St. Louis of Toulouse (d. 1297) was applied for in 1300 by his father, Charles of Anjou. Seven years elapsed before the investigation even began, and the business then proceeded slowly with five proctors, twenty witnesses, and a crowd of clerks, notaries, and dignitaries. A favourable verdict was announced in May 1313, but the canonization did not finally occur until April 1317. No wonder that it was necessary for John XXII to explain patiently to the earl of Lancaster that the canonization of archbishop Winchelsea was not as simple a matter as he imagined. It had to be 'debated in consistory by experienced persons from amongst the prelates, clergy, and people of England, attesting the archbishop's saintly life and miracles'. Winchelsea was never canonized.

For all the care with which the popes considered canonizations it is unlikely that their deliberations were of great interest to ordinary pilgrims. Except, perhaps, insofar as canonizations and translations were the occasion for splendid ceremonies at the shrine. Becket and Louis IX, for example, were both canonized by the populace long before their veneration was officially authorized by the Church. Louis IX, indeed, was almost venerated in his lifetime. One of the pilgrims who visited the tomb at St.-Denis shortly after the king's death, had this to say to the commissioners investigating his miracles: 'It is my belief that Louis is a saint because of all the miracles that I have heard about and because of his worthy life. But most of all I believe it because everybody round here says that he is a saint and calls him St. Louis.'

Publicity

What considerations dictated a pilgrim's choice of shrine is as much a mystery to us as it must have been to contemporaries. Sometimes the choice was determined by such factors as the pilgrim's name or trade. Sometimes it was determined by lot. Reginald of Durham knew of several pilgrims who had decided on a visit to the shrine of St. Cuthbert after drawing lots between the various alternatives. One had named three candles after different saints and decided on the shrine whose candle burned out first; another had drawn twigs. According to William of Canterbury, this was a common practice in Wales and the west of England.

The ebb and flow of fashion was undoubtedly the most important factor. Notable events such as inventions of relics, canonizations, or translations served to draw attention in dramatic fashion to the existence of a saint and to provoke an outburst of popular enthusiasm which rarely lasted more than half a century. A minor cult might be forgotten within a few weeks. The tendency of the laity was always to visit the saint whose cult was the most recently established. St. Wulfstan of Worcester, who was canonized in 1203, is referred to shortly afterwards as 'the new saint'. St. Thomas of Canterbury was the 'new saint' *par excellence* of the late twelfth century. His cult was established within a fortnight of his death and was propagated with exceptional skill by the monks of Christ Church, Canterbury. William of Canterbury, who was the author of a great deal of this propaganda, reflects that all saints have their period of miracle-working; then they command the veneration of Christians; then they withdraw gracefully and leave miracle-working to saints of more recent creation, such as St. Thomas. The French pilgrim Hugh Brustins, who had been possessed by the Devil, visited St.-Denis only to discover that that saint had 'left to his colleague St. Thomas the business of curing the sick...in order that a new and relatively unknown martyr might make his name.' It is often forgotten how sporadic was the cult even of a great saint like St. Thomas. Canterbury was a shrine of European importance, probably the most prosperous in Christendom, for about ten years after Becket's brutal death. But only a few years later a canon of St. Frideswide's is found expressing the opinion that Canterbury is now old hat, and Caesarius of Heisterbach felt that St. Thomas was not as potent as most older martyrs. In the early thirteenth century pilgrims who used to go regularly to Canterbury are reported to be abandoning it in favour of the holy rood recently acquired by Bromholm priory. A renewed outburst of popular devotion to St. Thomas marked the translation of the relics to the choir of the new cathedral in 1220, but by the middle of the thirteenth century the great days of the pilgrimage were past. In the fourteenth century a miracle at the shrine was so unusual as to be the subject of a special letter of congratulation from the king. A Jubilee indulgence of 1370 served to bring large crowds to Canterbury, including the poet Chaucer, and other Jubilees were held in 1420 and 1470. But except on these famous occasions the cult of St. Thomas scarcely deserved the hostile attention which it received from the sixteenth-century reformers. The history of the Canterbury pilgrimage was in this respect very typical. Amongst its rivals only Rome, Jerusalem, and Santiago were able to attract pilgrims throughout the mediaeval period.

By far the most effective advertisements for a saint were his or her miracles. Contemporaries followed the posthumous doings of the saints with extreme interest and the news of miraculous happenings could be relied upon to spread without any active assistance from the clergy of the sanctuary. When, for example, a blind man was healed by St. Eutrope as he sat by the side of the road outside Saintes, 'a deafening clamour arose and all the nearby villages resounded with the news. People rushed to the spot and young men clapped their hands in delight. The whole city of Saintes throbbed with excitement and everyone was increased in love of Christ and of his holy saint, Eutrope.' On another occasion a pilgrim who had visited the shrine of

St. Eutrope is described as going back home and inviting in all his neighbours to persuade them to go too. How far the news carried by word of mouth depended on the importance of the saint and the quality of the miracle. The canons of Laon who toured England in 1113 in search of funds for the rebuilding of their cathedral, returned with stories of the miracles of St. Swithin at Winchester and St. Edmund at Bury. News of the miracles at St. Gilles-de-Provence is known to have penetrated as far as Denmark and Poland.

Although the most spectacular miracles needed no advertisement, the clergy of the greater sanctuaries did go to considerable lengths to publicize them by compiling collections of miracle stories known as *libelli miraculorum*. The habit of recording every marvellous event as it occurred dates back at least to the time of St. Augustine, who collected depositions from the pilgrims healed by St. Stephen at Hippo. These accounts were then included in Augustine's sermons and circulated in neighbouring dioceses. In the west the classic miracle collection of the early Middle Ages was the celebrated account of the miracles of St. Martin by Sulpicius Severus, which was written at the beginning of the fifth century. The extraordinary repetitiveness and lack of originality which characterize almost every mediaeval miracle collection, is in a large measure due to the fact that their authors were modelling themselves on Sulpicius Severus. The clergy of every major shrine conceived that they owed a duty to their patron saint to increase his or her glory by writing down all miracles. Geoffrey, prior of Canterbury, believed that God had brought misfortunes upon his head to punish him for his failure to record a miracle he had witnessed. The monk who wrote up the miracles of St. James at Reading pointed out that the servant who increased his talents found more favour with God than the one who buried them in the ground; 'and in just the same way, we who by God's gracious favour have seen the miracles worked by St. James...have a solemn duty to pass the knowledge of them on to posterity, that their faith may be strengthened and that God may be glorified.'

Most collections of miracles were pure propaganda and few of them had the slightest literary merit. The rivalry between competing shrines found expression in aggressive assertions that this or that saint was more consistently effective than any other. The authors never fail to point out how many other celebrated shrines a pilgrim has visited in vain before he is restored to health at the shrine of St. Benedict, St. Foy, or St. Thomas as the case may be. 'Why are you wasting your time here?' a mysterious voice is alleged to have declared to a sick Englishman in St. Peter's at Rome; 'go back home to England and make your offering at the monastery of St. Egwin at Evesham, for there alone will you be healed.' A lady of Luton apparently went blind after visiting St.-Gilles-de-Provence when she ought to have gone to St. Thomas of Canterbury. But it was above all the rivals of St. Thomas who excelled at this kind of competitive propaganda. The sudden rise of Canterbury as a major shrine eclipsed every other English pilgrimage. The literature put out by the older English shrines in the late twelfth century is therefore full of slighting references to the inability of St. Thomas to cure a pilgrim who later found his health at Durham, Bury St. Edmund's, St. Frideswide's, or Reading. The Reading author, who was much the most aggressive of this group, reports the following conversion between an apparition of St. James and a pilgrim in the choir of Canterbury cathedral:

'What are you doing hanging about here?'

'I am waiting to be healed by the merits of the blessed apostle Thomas.'

'You will wait in vain. What you ought to do is go back to my abbey at Reading. There, and there alone, will you be healed.'

'I know nothing of Reading and I have never heard of your abbey. How do you think I can get there in my state of health?'

This pilgrim was punished for her contumely but she was ultimately cured by the hand of St. James at Reading.

The twelfth century saw the first attempts to influence the decisions of pilgrims by advertising techniques which strike a surprisingly familiar note in modern ears. Much of the fame of Canterbury in the 1170s was due to skilful promotion by its monks, who sent abstracts of St. Thomas's miracles to numerous prelates and religious houses in England and France. Other churches proclaimed the benefits of their pilgrimage in pamphlets, rhymes and jingles. The monks of the abbey of the Trinity at Fécamp composed a poem in French entitled 'Why everyone ought to love and visit the holy church of Fécamp and hear the story of the Precious Blood.' Jerusalem, it pointed out, was far away 'so remember that you are never far from Fécamp where the Lord has sent his Precious Blood for your benefit'. In the early years of the twelfth century when both St. Adalbert's abbey in Rome and the church of Benevento claimed to possess the body of St. Bartholomew, the pamphlets issued by St. Adalbert's abbey sang this untranslatable jingle:

Roma tenet corpus, tu famam, tu modo tumbam;
Roma tenet corpus, tu non nisi corporis umbram…

Fraus male subvenit Benevento non benevenit,
Ob detrimentum Benevento fit maleventum.'

With the growing popularity of public preaching in the later
Middle Ages, the advertisement of pilgrimages became an
elaborate and expensive business. Both mendicant orders
offered their services as preachers of indulgences, and individual preachers enjoyed European reputations for their persua-
siveness. When the church of St. Lambert at Liège received an
indulgence from Eugenius IV in 1443, they employed two
Franciscans to preach it in the town, and two Dominicans to
compose pamphlets for distribution further afield. The
accounts of Lyon cathedral in the early sixteenth century show
that the canons paid ten *sous* to the Augustinian who preached
their indulgence, five *sous* to the town crier who advertised his
sermons, and twenty *sous* to the sacristan for the cost of his
dinners.

Attractive packaging was an essential element in the saint's
appeal. Pilgrims expected to be received by a magnificent and
costly reliquary, and those who were not sometimes put their
disgust on record. Shortly after the translation of some new
relics to the German monastery of Prüm in the mid-ninth
century,

'a certain woman arrived with a wagon full of food and
drink and precious things which she proposed to offer
to God and to the holy martyrs. But, seeing that the
saint's tomb did not glitter with gold and silver, she
uttered a contemptuous guffaw, as is the wont of foolish and irreligious minds. Then, rushing back home, she
bade her friends retrace their steps saying "you won't
find anything holy in that place."'

This lady's attitude was as familiar to the twelfth century as it was to the ninth. Superb reliquaries and sumptuously decorated sanctuaries were not only subtle indications of the power of the saint but they testified to the devotion and the generosity of past pilgrims and invited offerings from present ones. Preachers of the later mediaeval period pointed out this lesson most explicitly. 'Look at all these gold and silver reliquaries, these chalices and jewels, rich tapestries and vestments', intoned the fourteenth-century preacher at the shrine of Our Lady of Montserrat; 'all these costly and holy things were presented by pious persons.' A grey friar of Canterbury preaching at Herne in 1535 declared that he knew of people who had travelled two hundred miles to see the shrine of St. Thomas 'and when they...see the goodly jewels that be there, how they think in their hearts "I would to God and that good saint that I were able to offer such a gift."'

From the fourth century onwards a dazzling display of wealth was to be found in every pilgrimage church of any importance. In the lifetime of the emperor Constantine the Holy Sepulchre was adorned with 'gifts of indescribable beauty including gold, silver, and precious stones'; a traveller of the sixth century found the Sepulchre completely invisible beneath a carpet of jewellery. Golden ornaments and silk wall-hangings decorated the relatively minor shrine of St. Felix of Nola in the fourth century. 'Truly', observed John Chrysostom, 'the sanctuaries of the saints are more lavishly decorated than the palaces of kings.' After the eighth century the western Church allowed reliquaries to be put on permanent display on the altar, instead of being 'elevated' only on special feast days. From this moment onwards, sanctuaries became ever more ornate and expensive. When Suger became abbot of St.-Denis in 1122, his first act was to order new reliquaries for his church. In his time St.-Denis employed an *atélier* of goldsmiths and jewellers which made the abbey for a brief while the artistic centre of Europe. The arm of St. James was enclosed in a reliquary of crystal mounted in gold. The panels of the sarcophagus of St.-Denis himself contained forty-two marks of gold studded with diamonds, rubies, sapphires, emeralds, topazes, and pearls. Suger bought the entire stock of every jeweller he encountered and even removed the rings from his fingers to add to the magnificence of his patron's shrine. Suger was justly proud of this splendid array. He was surprised and offended when pope Paschal II, visiting St.-Denis in May 1107, showed no interest in it, but humbly prostrated himself before the relics themselves. In Suger's mind a superb reliquary was a material symbol of the spiritual grandeur of the saint whose relics it contained. In devoting a substantial proportion of his revenues to the decoration of the sanctuary, Suger was in no way untypical of the wealthy churchmen of his day. The tomb of St. Thomas of Canterbury, completed at enormous expense in c. 1220, astonished even seasoned travellers. A Venetian diplomat who saw it at the beginning of the sixteenth century reported that it 'surpassed all belief':

'Notwithstanding its great size it is entirely covered with plates of pure gold. But the gold is scarcely visible beneath a profusion of gems, including sapphires, diamonds, rubies and emeralds. Everywhere that the eye turns something even more beautiful appears. The beauty of the materials is enhanced by the astonishing skill of human hands. Exquisite designs have been carved all over it and immense gems worked delicately into the patterns. Finest of all is a ruby, no larger than a man's thumbnail, which is set into the altar at the right hand side, and which…I believe, was the gift of the King (Louis VII) of France.'

When Henry VIII dissolved the cathedral priory, the jewels and precious metals from this tomb filled twenty-six carts. In England, none of these fine works of mediaeval jewellery survived the Reformation. In France almost all were destroyed in the revolution. Today we must go to Germany or Spain, to Cologne, Marburg, Oviedo, or León, to receive even a faint impression of the treasures which confronted a pilgrim at St.-Denis in the time of Suger.

Contemporaries differed as to the morality of spending such large sums on the decoration of churches. Guibert of Nogent correctly divined that magnificent tombs were an appeal to popular piety at the expense of more genuine spiritual feelings, and the reaction of Paschal II on being shown the sanctuary of St.-Denis tends to bear this out. St. Bernard stated the classic case against them when he delivered his celebrated invective against the excessive splendour of the Benedictine churches.

'Look at their churches, glistening with gold while the poor are starving and naked outside….Their object is to excite the devotion of the vulgar masses who are incapable of truly spiritual feelings….But what kind of devotion do they produce? They do not bring men to prayer but tempt them into making offerings. Thus is wealth squandered on creating more wealth and money spent on attracting more money….Here the saints are displayed for veneration enclosed in the exquisite workmanship of teams of goldsmiths. Ordinary people think them that much more holy if they are plastered with precious stones; they crowd forward to kiss them and make offerings to them. But what are they really venerating? Not the spiritual beauty of God's saints but the mundane prettiness of their shrines.'

St. Bernard's strictures were a little unjust. It should be remembered that every rich church had to keep a reserve of liquid wealth in case of a sudden disaster, and in a non-money economy this could only be done by hoarding precious stones and metals. Hence the fact that many a fine example of the goldsmith's art was melted down within a few years of being made; this was part of its purpose. When abbot Mayeul of Cluny was captured by the Arabs in 972, his monks paid a ransom of a thousand pounds of silver by melting down ornaments from the church. The abbey of Malmesbury, when asked to pay tribute at short notice to William Rufus, stripped the silver and gold from twelve Gospels, eight crucifixes, and eight reliquaries. Reading abbey settled its accounts with Richard I by removing the gold leaf from its most famous relic, the hand of St. James. All these raids on the reserves would have been made good out of surplus income when the opportunity arose.

But the insatiable appetite of wealthy churches for precious reliquaries was more than just a prudent financial precaution. It arose out of a deeply engrained habit of mind which found it hard to imagine spiritual grandeur without material wealth. Because the saints were poor in their lifetimes, argued Theofrid, abbot of Epternach (d. 1110), they are entitled to untold riches when they are in Paradise; with untold riches, therefore, they should be honoured on earth. Splendid apparel and costly jewellery were part of the popular image of the saints triumphant. St. Cuthbert, for example, appeared to a youth of Coupland dressed in full pontificals shining with gold and glistening with precious stones. Indeed, contemporaries imagined Christ himself in this way, until in the thirteenth century Franciscan preachers impressed upon their hearers the image of a God who was at the same time poor and human. The English anchorite Christina of Markyate, who died in about 1160, dreamed of Christ as 'a man of indescribable beauty wearing a golden crown thickly encrusted with precious stones which seemed beyond the skill of any human craftsman. Hanging over his face, one on either side, were two bands delicate and shining, and on top of the gems small pearls could be seen shining like drops of dew.' The material glory which clothed the risen Christ was reflected by his saints. In this respect abbot Suger and the monks of Cluny were closer to the mainstream of Christian sentiment than St. Bernard.

The saint's sanctuary served above all as a reminder of the miracles attributed to him. Written accounts of these miracles were always available on request. A Burgundian nobleman at Mont-St.-Michel is found asking for a list of St. Michael's miracles, 'and on reading the account which was shown to him he conceived a high opinion of the holiness of the place.' In 1319, when the monks of Canterbury were actively pressing for the canonization of Robert Winchelsea, a description of his miracles was hung in front of the tomb. In many sanctuaries murals, sculptures, and tapestries illustrated the life and miracles of the saint. At St.-Benoit-sur-Loire, for example, the miracles of St. Benedict, drawn from the *Dialogues* of pope Gregory, are sculpted on the capitals of the church. At Canterbury, those of St. Thomas can be seen in the stained glass windows of the

Trinity Chapel, exactly as they are described by Benedict of Peterborough and William of Canterbury. How many long-faded murals must once have decorated the great sanctuaries of England and France, offering to the sick and infirm the distant hope of a miraculous end to their sufferings.

Perhaps the most curious reminders of past miracles were the *ex-voto* offerings which are still a characteristic feature of modern pilgrimages in Italy and France. These were offered by pilgrims to commemorate a miraculous cure, and were usually wax models of whatever part of the body had been healed. *Ex-voto* offerings were also made by those who had not been cured but hoped to be. As early as the fifth century, visitors to eastern shrines left 'pictures of their eyes or models of their feet or hands. Some are made of wood, others of gold. The Lord accepts them all, great or small....These objects are kept as evidence of countless miraculous cures, mementoes offered by people who have recovered their health.' Models of part of the human body were much the most common *ex-voto* offerings. A pilgrim cured of a continuous headache by St. Martial left a wax model of his head. Another, with an abscess on her nose, presented a silver nose to the church of Notre-Dame de Rocamadour. Occasionally, sick men sent full-size models of themselves to a local shrine in the hope of hastening their recovery. One Adam of Yarmouth sent a wax model as tall and broad as himself to Norwich cathedral in the late twelfth century, but extravagant gestures like this remained uncommon until the close of the Middle Ages. John Paston was one of the many well-to-do persons who sent wax models to Our Lady of Walsingham in the fifteenth century. Between 1535 and 1538 the commissioners for the dissolution of the monasteries constantly refer to the accumulation of such models in English sanctuaries. At Canterbury, gruesome relics of afflictions cured were to be found in the piles of *ex-voto* offerings. Henry of Maldon's tapeworm was hung up in the cathedral as an *ex-voto*. Iselda of Longueville, in gratitude for the recovery of her hearing, made an offering of part of her ear. A shepherd from Durham left his withered finger on the altar in the hope that another would grow in its place. So many wax models hung in the church of Rocamadour that at least one pilgrim accused the monks of making them themselves. In general, however, such offerings were a useful advertisement for the healing powers of the church's relics, and the clergy of the shrine were assiduous in collecting a memento of every cure. The guardian of St. Thomas's shrine was dismayed when an archdeacon was relieved of a cherry-stone stuck in his nostril, but insisted on taking it home with him.

Although the sick were responsible for the great majority of *ex-voto* offerings, in principle any pilgrim could make one. The crew of a Dunwich fishing boat which had been saved from a storm by St. Edmund hung up a wax anchor in his basilica. A knight who had lost his hawk took a wax hawk to the church of Our Lady at Villalcazar de Sirga. Guillaume Bataille, whose house had been preserved from a fire by the Virgin, brought a wax house to Rocamadour. The chains of prisoners liberated by a saint would normally be hung up in his or her basilica, and at sanctuaries where the saint specialized in this kind of miracle, almost all the *ex-voto* offerings on display were ruptured chains. This was so as early as the sixth century. A deacon of Tours returning from a visit to Rome in 590 was astonished by the number of chains hanging in the basilica of St. Victor at Marseilles. Later generations ceased to be amazed as knights delivered from the infidel and criminals released from prison became familiar sights on the roads of Europe. The author of the *Guide for Pilgrims to Santiago* counted several thousand iron chains in the church of St.-Léonard de Noblat, together with various contraptions in which prisoners had been trapped, injured, or tortured. The church of St. Foy at Conques was full of the chains of Spanish crusaders delivered from the Moors; indeed, in the extreme lefthand corner of the celebrated sculpted tympanum, an iron fetter can be seen hanging from a beam behind the figure of St. Foy. In a few sanctuaries the mounting pile of *ex-voto* offerings posed serious problems. Abbot Geoffrey of Vézelay (d. 1052) had a new set of altar rails made from the chains left behind by pilgrims. Other churches were more ruthless. At Santiago the guardians of the shrine had strict instructions not to accept any incense, bread, staves, crucifixes or 'models made out of lead or wax'.

Offerings

Offerings were an essential ingredient in the rise of a great shrine because they paid for the imposing church which housed it. A pilgrim was expected to be as generous as his or her means would allow, and there were some who asserted that without an offering a pilgrimage was of no value. The authors of the miracle stories were foremost in putting forward this proposition. 'Come to my shrine at Conques and give me all your gold bracelets', St. Foy is said to have told the wife of Guillaume Taillefer, count of Toulouse. A woman who bought a valuable ring at Conques and failed to give it to St. Foy was cursed with fevers and nightmares. Another, who emerged from the basilica of Conques with her ring still on her finger, fell ill in a nearby hospice, and did not recover until the ring was removed by one of the guardians of the shrine and placed in the abbey treasury. Perhaps the most striking story in this vein was the tale of Sir Jordan Fitz-Eisulf, a knight of Pontefract who had known Thomas Becket in his lifetime. Sometime after Becket's death Fitz-Eisulf and his family were saved from the ravages of the plague by drinking 'water of St. Thomas'. Fitz-Eisulf put aside four silver pieces to offer at St. Thomas's shrine, but the pilgrimage was constantly postponed until St. Thomas reminded the knight of his obligations by allowing the plague to return and strike down his eldest son. In the stained glass of the Trinity Chapel at Canterbury Fitz-Eisulf can be seen recovering his health by pouring a great sackful of money onto the shrine. The notion of the offering as an essential part of the pilgrimage received the sanction of the canon law when the popes began to issue occasional indulgences conditional on an appropriate donation being made. An indulgence of 1147 offered remission of seven days to those who visited the chapel of St. Denis at Montmartre 'and who bestow their alms upon the nuns according to the resources which God has given them.'

Offerings were frequently described as 'tribute money', akin to the services which a vassal owed to his feudal lord. This interesting notion makes its appearance in the tenth century. In his life of St. Gerald of Aurillac, Odo of Cluny remarks that the holy man used to travel to Rome wearing ten silver shillings round his neck as a sign of his vassalage to St. Peter. A charter of 1090 describes an offering made by a pilgrim at the church of St. Vincent of Le Mans as a *'censum donum'*, i.e. feudal tribute. In the twelfth century it became a common practice to vow oneself a 'perpetual serf' of the Holy Sepulchre in Jerusalem. Rudolf count of Pfullendorf did this in 1180 at the abbey of St.-Gall, before departing for the Holy Land. In June 1200 a large group of noblemen of the Breisgau renounced their property and proclaimed themselves 'vassals of the Holy Sepulchre' before they in turn left for Jerusalem. Several monarchs of the period, in declaring themselves vassals of God, offered tribute money to one of his saints. Thus the kings of Aragon described their annual gifts to the shrine of Santiago as the 'tribute which is owed to God and the holy apostle James'. It is this sentiment which explains the iconography of the shrine of the three Magi at Cologne. This magnificent gold and jewelled shrine was the gift of the emperor Otto IV, and on the side of it Otto can be seen behind the figures of the three Magi, presenting his offering to Christ. It was characteristic of an age in which feudal imagery constantly intruded into the realm of spiritual practice. By making themselves the 'serfs' or 'vassals' of a saint, individuals supposed that they were placing themselves under the saint's protection. 'Know then that I am a serf of St. Gilles', Raymond Feraldo told those who had captured him in the course of a local vendetta; 'and therefore you have no power to do me ill except in so far as he shall permit.'

The statutes of Santiago cathedral, dating from the end of the thirteenth century, contain an elaborate ritual for the presentation of offerings, and it is probable that similar formalities were observed at other churches. After the morning mass the sacristan and another priest stood behind the shrine with rods in their hands and with these they would tap each pilgrim on the back or on the arms or legs. A third priest, wearing a surplice, invited them to make an offering, addressing each pilgrim in his own language. Pilgrims were then asked whether their offering was for St. James, i.e. for alms and general purposes, in which case it was placed on the altar; or whether it was for the building fund, when it was placed on a side-table.

This ceremony marked the moment at which the pilgrim 'received' his indulgence. Only cash or jewellery was accepted.

The more important sanctuaries undoubtedly received very large sums in offerings. The exact amount varied from one year to the next and from sanctuary to sanctuary. Canterbury cathedral, for example, received an average of £426 a year in offerings between 1198 and 1213, although these were troubled years in the history of the monastery. In 1220, the year of the translation of St. Thomas to the choir, the receipts amounted to £1,142, nearly two-thirds of the total income of the monastery. Yet three centuries later, in 1535, offerings accounted for a mere £36. Our Lady of Walsingham, on the other hand, was still getting £260 a year from pilgrims in 1535. Even if one takes the twelfth and thirteenth centuries as the heyday of pilgrimages, it is clear that no English shrine could match the prosperity of Canterbury at the height of its fame. St. Edmund's abbey, for example, received £142 a year from pilgrims at the end of the thirteenth century and was well satisfied with it.

The best evidence of the wealth which even a short-lived pilgrimage could bring to a church is to be found in the ambitious enterprises which were financed out of offerings. Under the rule of abbot Gontran (1034–55) miracles began to occur in the monastery of St.-Trond, near Liège. Gontran was a modest man, and he kept the details to himself, but his successor, Adelard, had influential connections and high ambitions for his abbey. He spread the news of the miracles abroad and skilfully promoted a pilgrimage. In time, so many pilgrims arrived at St.-Trond that the small village at the gates of the abbey was unable to contain them. 'Almost every day', wrote the chronicler of the abbey, '...they filled the roads for half a mile around. Across the fields and meadows came such a crowd of pilgrims, being nobles, freemen, and peasants of both sexes, that they had to be put up in tents, which made them look like a besieging army.... And offerings beyond belief piled on up the altar. Herds of animals were offered every day, palfreys, cows and bulls, pigs, lambs, and sheep. Linen, wax, bread, and cheese arrived, and above all purses full of money.' So much money was given that in the evening several men were needed to collect it up and put it in a safe place, and a number of monks worked full-time as guardians of the shrine. Indeed, says the chronicler, the offerings exceeded all the other revenues of the abbey combined and continued to do so throughout abbot Adelard's lifetime. The abbey was able to build itself powerful walls and retain a large body of knights and servants. It bought the seigneurial rights over most of the neighbouring towns and villages and acquired estates as far away as Laon. The monastery was completely rebuilt, and henceforth its servants and officials were treated with respect and fear wherever they went.

The story of St.-Trond was repeated in countless churches and abbeys across the face of Europe. Many French churches made their fortunes in the religious revival of the eleventh century. The flood of relics which reached the Latin west after the fall of Constantinople in 1204 drew immense sums of money from pilgrims. The cathedrals of Amiens and Troyes were among the great churches built on their offerings. The bishop of Châlons-sur-Marne, who had acquired the elbow of St. Stephen in Constantinople, felt confident enough to pawn all his future revenues to pay for the completion of his cathedral 'in view of the great numbers of people who will certainly come to venerate such a relic.' The astonishing growth of devotion to the Virgin in the fifteenth century produced a very similar result. Shrines of the Virgin in isolated places like Avioth and Notre-Dame de l'Epine were suddenly covered by great flamboyant Gothic churches. 'Do you see this spacious and beautiful church, perfect in its elegance and style (except for the tower which is being restored)?' asked the parish priest of Bollezeel in Flanders of a pilgrim who visited it in 1483; 'all this was paid for out of the offerings of pilgrims who appeared in droves, receiving consolation from our Blessed Lady and buying badges at the door.'

But while offerings could bring unheard-of wealth to minor sanctuaries in the space of a few weeks, churches which depended too heavily on the generosity of pilgrims might see their revenues dry up as suddenly as they had first appeared. The most distinguished sanctuary to suffer this fate was the abbey of St.-Gilles in Provence. The abbey had seen its greatest days between about 1050 and 1250, when its position on one of the most frequented routes to Santiago had brought it very considerable wealth. Much of this wealth had been invested in magnificent buildings. But at the opening of the fifteenth century the roof had partly collapsed, the belltower was only half-completed, and the fabric of the church was in a dangerous state of disrepair. The rival armies of the Hundred Years' War, the undisciplined bands of *routiers,* and a succession of savage epidemics, had combined to drive pilgrims onto roads passing well north of St.-Gilles. In 1417 the monks addressed a petition for help to the emperor Sigismund. In it they lamented that 'the devotion of Christians to St.-Gilles has altogether ceased and the faithful no longer come to visit his tomb. In former times the great affluence of pilgrims was a wonderful boon to the abbey and town of St.-Gilles, but now the place is deserted and impoverished.' The population of the town had fallen to eighteen taxable families and the number of monks to twenty-six. The abbey's income, which had once stood at four thousand gold francs a year, was now so small that the monks could not afford food or winter clothing. The story of St.-Gilles exactly balances that of St.-Trond. Today the church is partially ruined, but the noble crypt and fine sculpted facade survive as monuments of its departed greatness.

The clergy of a sanctuary were usually entitled to a share of the offerings, and this was a fertile source of disputes throughout the mediaeval period. Some churches were governed by statutes which laid down with admirable clarity exactly what should be done with the money. The basilica of St. Martin at Tours had an arrangement dating back to 832 whereby one-third of the offerings went to the canons, except for precious fabrics and jewellery, which were used to decorate the church. At the Sainte-Chapelle the proportions destined for the canons and those set aside for administrative expenses were meticulously laid down in the statutes of 1303. At many other churches, however, ill-defined rules based on obscure traditions and notions of fairness were a recurrent source of undignified squabbles. The Vatican basilica in particular was governed by rules of extreme complexity as a result of which the pope, the canons, and the chantors were regularly locked in combat. During the Jubilee of 1350, when exceptionally large sums were being received at the altars, the canons forced the door of the treasury and helped themselves to what they considered to be their due. The offerings at the Vatican were of special importance because of the large sums involved; in 1285–6, during the least prosperous period in the history of the Roman pilgrimage, a total of 1,097 *livres* was received in the basilica. But even where lesser sums were at stake the fate of the offerings was constantly left to be decided by argument and litigation.

In principle the papacy was not entitled to any share of the receipts of churches outside Rome itself. Bulls of indulgence, like all bulls, were taxed when they left the papal chancery in accordance with a fixed scale of fees. But the sum raised was negligible and most of it went to the chancery officials. In the fourteenth and fifteenth centuries, however, most sanctuaries came to depend heavily on papal indulgences and the papacy began to exploit them as a source of revenue. By the end of the fifteenth century the cost of a plenary indulgence of a year's duration was an initial payment of four or five hundred gold florins and a proportion of the proceeds. This proportion was usually a third. The duties of Richard Wily, who became papal receiver in England in 1463, included the collection of one third of the proceeds of papal indulgences. Sometimes the papal share was as high as three-quarters. In May 1442 Eugenius IV granted an indulgence to Eton College which specified that as quarter of the offerings were to go to the fabric fund and three-quarters to the papacy, nominally for the needs of the Holy Land. To ensure that the pope got his share, the bull provided that all the oblations were to be kept in a chest with two locks, the provost to have one key and the papal collector the other. The exact share claimed by Rome was always a matter to be negotiated between the pope and the church concerned. In the opening years of the sixteenth century, however, the papacy was beginning to price itself out of the market. The monks of Canterbury were unable to get a Jubilee indulgence in 1520 as they had done every fifty years since 1320, because they could no longer afford the cost. Their agent in Rome, Dr. Grig, was informed by cardinal Campeggio that 'it is not possible that the pope will grant you this for no money or favour.'

The clergy of the great sanctuaries were accused by their contemporaries as well as by later historians of exploiting pilgrims for their own avaricious purposes. There is some justice in this charge, but it has been considerably over-stated. A clear distinction should be drawn, first of all between the periods before and after the papal schism of the fourteenth century, and secondly between sanctuaries that were served by monks and those that were not. The papal schism, and in particular the pontificate of Boniface IX, marks the beginning of a century and a half of ruthless commercialization which radically altered the character of some of the more popular spiritual exercises of the late Middle Ages. The fifteenth century also saw a large increase in the number of new sanctuaries, almost all of which were served by the secular clergy, while some of the older monastic sanctuaries began to fall into decay. Some monastic sanctuaries, like Walsingham, were actually refounded as colleges of canons. Monks were not personally entitled to a share of the offerings, whereas secular canons almost invariably were. Monks, moreover, had extremely expensive obligations of hospitality which were, on the whole, respected throughout the mediaeval period. The receipts of a monastic sanctuary might therefore be enormous while the profits remained very modest; when the surplus had been swallowed up by the fabric fund, it was difficult to argue that the monks had made gross gains at the pilgrims' expense.

Some early indulgences expressly require the pilgrimage church to offer hospitality to visitors. The indulgence which Urban II conceded to St. Nicholas of Angers in 1096 included a condition that on the day of the indulgence the monks were to feed a hundred poor people. Most monasteries, even when their duties were not explicitly laid down in this fashion, offered food and shelter as the Benedictine rule required. This might impose a serious strain on the abbey's finances, as it did at the mountainous Catalonian shrine of Montserrat in the fourteenth century. There, the preacher would remind pilgrims of the difficulty and expense of carting provisions up the steep mountain tracks to the church, and ask them to bring their own food unless they were poor or disabled. Another mountain shrine, Notre-Dame de Rocamadour, was driven deeply into debt by the number of pilgrims; in 1181, when the church was at the pinnacle of its fame, the monks were obliged to pawn the tapestries and curtains to moneylenders of the town. An inquest into the revenues of the abbey of Mont-St.-Michel in 1338 established that the monks received 1,100 *livres* a year in offerings, about one-sixth of their total income. But far from bringing joy to the abbot, the mass of pilgrims was a source of deep anxiety 'for the abbey is situated on the borders of Normandy, Brittany, Anjou and Maine, wherefore it receives enormous numbers of pilgrims passing to and fro. Many of them have to be accommodated in the monastery and this costs the monastery so much that other equally important charges on our revenues have to be neglected.'

The nearest approach to a balance sheet comes from Canterbury, where a number of account books survive. These show that the allowance made to the cellarer, who was the official responsible for entertaining pilgrims, rose and fell in tune with the income from offerings. In 1220, the year of the translation of St. Thomas to the choir, the offerings received rose from £27 to £1,142, while the expenses of the cellarer rose from £422 to £1,155. Pilgrims, of course, did not account for all the cellarer's expenses, and if testamentary bequests made by pilgrims are taken into account, there was probably a small surplus in both years. But as popular interest in St. Thomas declined, the surplus became a deficit. The four Canterbury Jubilees of the late Middle Ages drew large crowds of pilgrims but the great and wealthy stayed away. The declining social status of pilgrims was a general phenomenon of the fourteenth and fifteenth centuries, and its immediate effect was to reduce the income from offerings while increasing the number of visitors who needed free food and board. The first Jubilee, in 1320, brought in offerings of £671, but left the monastery with an overall deficit of £83. Thereafter the years in which offerings were highest were usually years of deficit.

Even the Vatican basilica, without doubt the most visited church in Europe over the whole mediaeval period, was sometimes in deficit. At the end of the twelfth century the pope received three-quarters of the offerings made at the high altar and the *confessio* of St. Peter. Out of this came the cost of several thousand candles burned every day in the basilica, of repairs to the fabric, and of the stipends of non-canonical priests. Innocent III, according to his biographer, devoted all that was left to alms for the poor and hospitality for pilgrims. Alexander IV, half a century later, devoted a quarter of his share of the offerings to alms. Innocent was indeed extremely sensitive to accusations of profiteering. In 1212 he announced to pilgrims gathered in Rome that all the offerings received at St. Peter's were devoted to the maintenance of the basilica and the entertainment of its visitors and he asked them to publicize the fact in their own countries. It seems unlikely that pilgrims to St. Peter's were a significant source of revenue before the age of the great Jubilee indulgences.

The clergy of the sanctuaries were undoubtedly ambitious. However, what they wanted was status rather than money. Status for themselves, and above all for their patron saint. This was more than mere vainglory, for a great deal of ecclesiastical power ultimately rested on status. The possession of St. Peter's body was cited as the basis of Rome's spiritual authority from Leo I in the fifth century to Innocent IV in the thirteenth. Jerusalem itself had achieved metropolitan status in the fifth century owing largely to its importance as a pilgrimage centre. In 969 Benevento was erected into an archbishopric with twelve diocesan bishops 'because it is a holy place where St. Bartholomew lies and is therefore entitled to much greater respect than it has hitherto received.' Salerno became the seat of an archbishop after acquiring the remains of St. Matthew.

The church of Santiago was perhaps more successful than any other in making use of its pilgrimage as a means of ecclesiastical aggrandisement. In the tenth century its bishops were already employing the title 'bishops of the apostolic see' and signing themselves '*servus servorum domini*' after the fashion of the popes. These pretensions were encouraged by the kings of León, who were claiming the imperial dignity for themselves and may have hoped that Santiago would become to them what Rome was to the German emperors. As the fame of St. James expanded, so did the ambitions of his bishops. The episcopal official who greeted the papal legate at Santiago in c. 1065 had been instructed to give him no greater honour than he received in return. The incident is said to have inspired in pope Alexander II the fear that Santiago 'would shortly assume a dignity appropriate to its possession of the body of an apostle; that is, that it would dominate the churches of the Spanish kingdoms by virtue of St. James, just as Rome dominates other kingdoms by virtue of St. Peter.' Whether Alexander or his successors ever entertained any such fear is open to doubt, but these words precisely describe the ambitions of the formidable Diego Gelmirez. Gelmirez, who was consecrated as bishop in 1101 and completed the existing cathedral, went as far along this path as he dared. He called his canons cardinals, gave them mitres, and enforced surplices, copes, and shaving on them (formerly they had entered the church booted and spurred and with three days' growth of beard). Finally, in 1120, he persuaded an unwilling pope to erect Santiago into a metropolitan see. Three centuries before, Santiago had not even been the seat of a bishop.

The offerings at Santiago must have been considerable, but the active promotion of the pilgrimage by successive bishops and archbishops cannot be explained by offerings alone. Ecclesiastical status was their constant obsession, and they spent their offerings on a visible symbol of their status, the superb cathedral of St. James. In doing this they exemplified the ambitions of almost every sanctuary in Europe. In financial terms those who profited most from the pilgrimage to St. James were not the clergy but the citizens of Santiago. Their city, which had scarcely existed in the ninth century, was one of the major entrepôts of Spain in the twelfth. The *camino de Santiago* became a thriving commercial highway. In 1130 a merchant train carrying silver worth 22,000 marks was attacked by robbers at Padrón. Carrión de los Condes is now a wretched little town, dusty and decayed, but eight hundred years ago it was a station on the road to Santiago, described in the *Guide for Pilgrims* as 'industrious and prosperous, rich in bread and wine and every kind of meat'. This was the true revolution worked by the rise of a great sanctuary, and many travellers must have agreed with the German mathematician Hieronymus Munzer, who left Santiago in 1494 with the reflection that its citizens were 'fat as pigs and slothful at that, for they have no need to cultivate the soil when they can live off the pilgrims instead.'

11

The Journey

Preparations

'He that be a pilgrim', declared the London preacher Richard Alkerton in 1406, 'oweth first to pay his debts, afterwards to set his house in governance, and afterwards to array himself and take leave of his neighbours, and so go forth.'

His first act, if he was a man of substance, was to make his will. Pilgrims enjoyed the special privilege of disposing of their property by will, a privilege which, until the late Middle Ages, was accorded to very few. As well as naming his heirs, the will would deal with such matters as the administration of his property in his absence and the length of time which was to elapse before be should be presumed dead. In Normandy local custom required every landowner to make a will which would automatically be executed if he did not announce his return within a year and a day. Some pilgrims also made private agreements with their wives as to how long they should leave before remarrying. The Church did what it could to ensure that the terms of a pilgrim's will were respected. In Spain, for instance, it made his companions responsible for looking after his personal effects. Failing companions, the local clergy were expected to keep them for a year and a day and, if they remained unclaimed, to sell them and apply the money to endowing masses for the repose of the dead pilgrim's soul.

In his absence, a pilgrim's property was immune from all civil claims in a court of law. The service which he owed to his feudal lord was usually suspended during the pilgrimage, and in northern France, according to Beaumanoir, pilgrims were exempt from the obligation to take part in family vendettas. In effect, there was no legal remedy to be had against a bona fide pilgrim, so long as he returned home to face his adversaries within a reasonable time. Illegal remedies were *a fortiori* forbidden, and those who had recourse to them faced both civil and ecclesiastical sanctions. In the bull *Quantum Praedecessores* of December 1145, Eugenius III proclaimed that the wife and children, goods and chattels of every pilgrim or crusader were 'placed under the protection of the Holy See and of all the prelates of the Church of God. By our apostolic authority we absolutely forbid anyone to disturb them until their return or death.' Before the first crusade this principle had probably been honoured chiefly in the breach. But effective protection was essential if crusaders were to be recruited for the defence of the Holy Land, and by the end of the twelfth century, flagrant violations of a pilgrim's rights never failed to arouse indignant protest. The invasion of Normandy by Philip Augustus of France while Richard Coeur-de-Lion was in the Holy Land was bitterly criticized, and some of Philip's own vassals refused to follow him. When, at the beginning of the thirteenth century, it seemed that the entire Angevin empire in France must shortly fall into the hands of the French king, loyal vassals of John were afraid that Philip would seize their lands. Some of them regarded a pilgrim's privileges as the best guarantee of the rights of their heirs. This, at any rate, was the reason given by

Archambert de Monluc when he joined the fourth crusade, appointing as trustees of his property a formidable list of ecclesiastical personages.

Although few pilgrims went to the extremes recommended by the preacher of the sermon *Veneranda Dies,* most of them made some concession to the principle that a pilgrimage should be accomplished in poverty. Rich pilgrims often made generous donations to the poor before leaving. The cartularies of monasteries, from the eleventh century onwards, are full of deeds recording the gifts made by departing pilgrims and crusaders. A donor could have the best of both worlds by making his gift conditional on his not returning alive. Then, when he returned home, he could demand the usufruct of his property for the rest of his life, after which it would become the unencumbered possession of the Church. When Aimeric II, count of Fézensac gave some windmills to the canons of Auch in 1088 as he was about to leave for the Holy Land, he insisted that 'if I come back alive from Jerusalem, I can have them back until my death.' If the knight never returned, the monks were often required to give a pension to his widow and sometimes even to his children. In fact, even if no such conditions were explicitly mentioned, they were almost certainly implied by both parties. When Leteric de Chatillon died in Palestine in 1100, the monks of La Charité allowed his widow half the revenues of his estates, although no such arrangement is found in the deed whereby Leteric had made the monks his heirs. Hughes de Lurcy, on returning from the Holy Land in the 1080s, claimed back his lands from the monks, promising to leave it to them on his death. Pilgrims probably adopted this roundabout procedure in order to ensure that their lands were safe in their absence. Some of them may also have borrowed the cost of the journey from the monks and left the lands with them as a pledge.

The true pilgrim, urged the preacher of the sermon *Venerenda Dies,* ought before his departure to make amends to all those whom he has offended, and to ask the permission of his wife, his parish priest, and anyone else to whom he owed obligations. The most important of these, for a layman, was his feudal lord, whose consent would be necessary if the pilgrim wished to nominate his heir or safeguard the position of his wife. Even the kings of France, Louis VII in 1146 and Philip Augustus in 1190, sought formal permission to leave with the crusade from St. Denis, whose vassals they recognized themselves to be. A cleric was required to ask the permission of his superior before making a pilgrimage, and until the fourteenth century this obligation was enforced with vigour. The German annalist Lambert of Hersfeld recalled how he had set out for Jerusalem in 1058, immediately after his ordination, without asking his abbot:

> 'I was afraid that since I had set out without his bless-
> ing, I might have given him offence. If he had died in
> my absence I would have remained forever unrecon-
> ciled to him and would thus have committed a terrible
> sin in the eyes of God. But God's favour was with me,
> ...for I returned in safety, confessed my sin, and was
> received with kindness. I felt as if I had just escaped
> alive from the fires of Hell.'

He was, in fact, only just in time, for the abbot became fever-ish that very evening and died a week later.

A pilgrim who left without making amends to those he had wronged could not possibly make a sincere confession, and without a sincere confession, it was generally agreed that his pilgrimage would be worthless. 'In order that my devotion may be the more acceptable to God', reflected Odo, duke of Burgundy, before joining the crusade in 1101, 'I have decided that I should set out at peace with everybody.' Accordingly he wished to make amends for the damage he had done, in a lifetime of violence, to the abbey of St.-Bénigne de Dijon. He begged forgiveness in the nave of their church for the trespasses he had committed against their lands and the insults he had heaped upon their heads. 'And my promises of amendment and offers of compensation have been accepted by the monks of St.-Bénigne; they have pardoned and absolved me and have agreed to pray for me, that I may keep my promises and enjoy a safe journey to the Holy Land.' Bertrand de Moncontour, who had seized some land belonging to the abbey of the Trinity of Vendôme, wished to go to the Holy Land in 1098 but 'realized that the path of God would be closed to me while such a crime remained on my conscience.' Aggrieved monks were not the only beneficiaries of these acts of last-minute repentance, though they were the main ones. The Santiago preacher had reminded his audience that they must make their peace with neighbours and friends, great or humble. The most spectacular exercise in this direction was the *enquête* launched by St. Louis in January 1247 before his departure with the crusade. Commissioners, most of them drawn from the mendicant orders, toured the provinces of Louis's kingdom enquiring into wrongs alleged to have been done in his name. That this process of conscience-clearing was not confined to the king is shown by the behaviour of Louis's biographer Joinville, who summoned his vassals and family before joining the expedition and told them 'if I have wronged any of you, I shall now make amends to you one by one, as I have always done.'

When his enemies had been placated and his creditors satisfied, the pilgrim sought out his parish priest or, occasionally, his bishop, and received a formal blessing. Texts of these blessings for travellers survive from the early eighth century, though they did not pass into general use until the eleventh. Blessing ceremonies reflected the growing feeling among pilgrims that they belonged to an 'order' of the Church, distinguished from other men by a uniform and by a solemn ritual of initiation. Mass departures to the Holy Land or Santiago were marked by public ceremonies in the cathedrals. But most pilgrims received their blessing privately from their parish priest, or else from a monk whose sanctity they respected. The hermit St. Godric of Finchale was said to have performed the ceremony regularly. Joinville, in 1248, sought out the Cistercian abbot of Cheminon on account of his saintly reputation, and then, after receiving his blessing, made his way on foot without shoes or coat to the embarkation point of the crusade at Marseilles.

Pilgrims' Dress

Once initiated into the 'order' of pilgrims, he signified his attachment to a new way of life by wearing a uniform, as distinctive in its own way as the tonsure of a priest. 'When the debts be thus paid and the meine is thus set in governance', continued Richard Alkerton in 1406, 'the pilgrim shall array himself. And then he oweth first to make himself be marked with a cross, as men be wont to do that shall pass to the Holy Land....Afterwards the pilgrim shall have a staff, a sclavein, and a scrip.' The staff, a tough wooden stick with a metal toe, was the most distinctive as well as the most useful part of the pilgrim's attire. The 'sclavein' was a long, coarse tunic. The scrip was a soft pouch, usually made of leather, strapped to the pilgrim's waist; in it he kept his food, mess-cans, and money. Such was the attire of every serious pilgrim after the end of the eleventh century. Much later, probably in the middle of the thirteenth century, pilgrims began to wear a great broad-brimmed hat, turned up at the front, and attached at the back to a long scarf which was wound round the body as far as the waist.

The origin of this curious garb is not at all clear. The staff and pouch were used by the migrant monks of Egypt in the fourth century, but they were obvious and sensible accessories for any traveller on foot, not only for pilgrims and not only in the Middle Ages. The tunic, on the other hand, whose practical usefulness is not as readily apparent, seems to make its first appearance at the beginning of the twelfth century. Canute, setting out for Rome in 1027, 'took up his scrip and staff as did all his companions', but there is no mention of the tunic. St. Anselm, in 1097, 'took his scrip and staff like a pilgrim', but again, no tunic. Orderic Vitalis, writing in about 1135, said that he could remember a time when pilgrims were indistinguishable from other travellers, except by their unshaven faces. Indeed it is probably about this time that the normal clothing of the traveller took on a sudden rigidity and became peculiarly the garb of the spiritual traveller.

This was almost certainly due to the fact that at the end of the eleventh century the Church began to bless the pilgrim's clothes and sanctify them as the uniform of his order. A special order of ceremony for pilgrims, as opposed to ordinary travellers, was now coming into existence. This usually took the form of blessing the pilgrim's pouch and mantle and presenting him with his staff from the altar. The ceremony has its origin in the blessing conferred on knights departing with the first crusade, and it is referred to in 1099 as a 'novel rite'. Behind the 'novel rite' is the pronounced tendency of the Church in the eleventh and twelfth centuries to stimulate lay piety by assigning to laymen certain defined spiritual functions. Those who fulfilled these functions were clothed with a special, almost ecclesiastical, status; they enjoyed spiritual privileges and ultimately secular ones as well. Hence the religious ceremony which now almost invariably accompanied the dubbing of a knight. Indeed, the ritual presentation of the pilgrim's staff bears a striking resemblance both to the dubbing of a knight and to the ordination of a priest. To the more austere pilgrim, the act of putting on his travelling clothes might have the same significance as taking the monastic habit. One such pilgrim was Rayner Pisani, an Italian merchant who experienced a sudden conversion during a business visit to Tyre in about 1140. Rayner took his pilgrim's tunic under his arm to the Golgotha chapel in Jerusalem and, in full view of an astonished crowd, removed all his old clothes and gave them to beggars. He then placed his tunic on the altar and asked the priest serving the chapel to invest him with it. This the priest did, and Rayner passed the remaining twenty years of his life as a hermit in Palestine.

In the course of time the Church invested the pilgrim's uniform with a rich and elaborate symbolism. Already in c. 1125 the author of the sermon *Veneranda Dies* is found explaining that the pilgrim's pouch is the symbol of almsgiving, because it is too small to hold much money and the pilgrim who wears it must therefore depend on charity. The pilgrim's staff is used for driving off wolves and dogs, who symbolize the snares of the Devil; the staff is the pilgrim's third leg, and three is the number of the Trinity; the staff therefore stands for the conflict of the Holy Trinity with the forces of evil, etc. This kind of imagery became very popular in the fourteenth and fifteenth centuries and it provided the theme for most of the sermons delivered to congregations of pilgrims before their departure. To Franco Sacchetti, the pilgrim's tunic stood for the humanity of Christ. The staff recalled the wood of the Cross in which lay the pilgrim's hope of salvation. Perhaps the most involved as well as the most popular of these allegories was the work of Thomas of London, a Dominican who taught in France and who wrote, in c. 1430, an *Instructorium Peregrinorum*. Here the staff, pouch, and tunic stand for faith, hope, and charity, respectively, for reasons which are pursued as far as scholastic subtlety will permit. These and academic exercises make dull reading today, but at the close of the Middle Ages they were much enjoyed.

On his way home, the pilgrim usually wore a badge or token showing where he had been. The best known and probably the earliest of these souvenirs was the palm of Jericho which pilgrims customarily brought back from Jerusalem. It is the origin of the English word 'palmer'. Like so many of the rituals associated with the pilgrimage to the Holy Land, this seems to have had its origin in the eleventh century. The palms, which were collected in the plain between Jericho and the Jordan, were regarded as a symbol of regeneration, of the victory of faith over sin. Peter Damian refers to the picking of palm leaves as 'customary' in c. 1050, and the soldiers of the first crusade all travelled *en masse* to the Jordan in July 1099 to baptize themselves in the river and collect their palms. William of Tyre, writing in c. 1180, remarks that the palm of Jericho was

'the formal sign that the pilgrim's vow has been fulfilled'. And
so it remained throughout the Middle Ages, though later generations did not have to travel as far as the Jordan for their
palms. After the twelfth century palm-vendors carried on a
thriving trade in the market of the 'Rue des Herbes' in
Jerusalem and stalls piled high with palms could be seen
beneath the walls of the Tower of David.

Equally famous were the cockle shells worn by pilgrims
returning from Santiago. The preacher of the sermon *Veneranda
Dies* ascribed to them much the same symbolic significance as
the palm of Jericho. 'In the sea near Santiago there are certain
fish with two shells, one on either side of their body....These
shells the pilgrims of St. James gather up and sew onto their
caps, carrying them home in triumph to their own people.' In
Santiago, as in Jerusalem, enterprising tradesmen soon began to
collect the shells themselves and by c. 1120, pilgrims had
already given up the long trek to the sea and begun to buy
their shells in the animated market which was held every day
outside the north door of the cathedral.

Before the end of the twelfth century real cockle shells had
been replaced by small lead badges in the shape of a shell,
whose sale was strictly regulated by the archbishop of Santiago.
Lead badges had by now been adopted by almost every major
sanctuary. Most of them consisted of a simple disc with a
roughly moulded representation of the patron saint of the sanctuary. Canterbury, for example, had a badge showing the mitred
head of St. Thomas between two erect swords. The badge of
Mont-St.-Michel showed St. Michael with his standard and
shield weighing souls at the last judgement. The Virgin, as pro-
tectress of all pilgrims, appears on many badges, for instance the
emblem of a minor sanctuary of St. Catherine in Lorraine,

which shows two pilgrims with staffs, protected by the mantle of the Virgin. Others depicted well-known miracles of the saint. St. Leonard, protector of prisoners, is shown on his badge listening to the prayer of a chained captive. The miraculous survival of a man wrongly condemned to be hanged is commemorated in the emblem of St. Eutrope of Saintes. The horse miraculously shod by St. Eloy was depicted on the badges sold to pilgrims at Noyon in the thirteenth century. Much-travelled pilgrims would cover the brims of their hats with badges until their heads were bowed beneath the weight of lead. Langland's pilgrim had

> *An hundreth of ampulles on his hatt seten,*
> *Signes of Synay and shelles of Galice*
> *And many a cruche on his cloke and keyes of Rome*
> *And the vernicle bifore; for men shulde knowe*
> *And se bi his signes whom he soughte had.*

Louis XI of France, who was well-known for his simple but intense piety, assiduously visited almost every notable French shrine of his day. His hat, according to one of his enemies, was 'brim-full of images, mostly of lead and pewter, which he kissed whenever good or bad news arrived or whenever the fancy took him.'

Pilgrims' badges were much prized, not only as souvenirs, but as magic charms. A badge of Rocamadour was said to have cured a pilgrim's ailing son. Miraculous powers were often attributed to *coquilles-Saint-Jacques,* one of which was alleged in c. 1120 to have healed an Apulian knight suffering from diphtheria. Badges were also used to prove that the wearer was entitled, as a pilgrim, to exemption from tolls and taxes. Some courts of law accepted them as evidence that the wearer's property was immune from distraint for debt. The wearing of a cross was certainly *prima facie* evidence that the wearer was entitled to a crusader's privileges. All these factors ensured that the demand for badges far outstripped the supply, and the sale of emblems to pilgrims was an extremely profitable business. The Valon family made their fortune in the fourteenth century by buying the monopoly of the sale and manufacture of badges at Rocamadour. They were obliged to give a large slice of their profits to the bishop of Tulle, and this appears to have been the usual arrangement. The archbishop of Santiago took a percentage from licensed badge-sellers after 1200 and it was for many years a major source of revenue. Unlicensed sellers, however, sold at least as many badges as licensed ones, and not only to genuine pilgrims. The archbishops of Santiago often complained that copies of their badges were being sold throughout France and northern Spain. Indeed, in 1228 this nefarious trade was being carried on by no less a man than the neighbouring bishop of Lugo.

Travel Overland

A long journey in the Middle Ages was not a thing to be lightly undertaken. The great sanctuaries were separated by hundreds of miles of unmade, ill-marked roads, many of them running through unpopulated tracts of Europe infested with bandits. 'O Lord, heavenly father', ran a blessing commonly conferred on pilgrims in the twelfth century, 'let the angels watch over thy servants N.N. that they may reach their destination in safety,...that no enemy may attack them on the road, nor evil overcome them. Protect them from the perils of fast rivers, thieves, or wild beasts.' The outbreak of a war could interrupt the flow of pilgrims to an important sanctuary or even choke it altogether. Thus the disordered state of central Italy brought about the serious decline of the Roman pilgrimage in the tenth century and again in the thirteenth. The Hundred Years' War ruined the abbey of St.-Gilles and many other shrines of southern France, and significantly affected the prosperity of Santiago itself. In the fifteenth century a sudden Arab or Turkish descent on Rhodes might prevent ill travel to the Holy Land for a year.

The condition of the roads was the first obstacle. Europe relied, throughout the Middle Ages, on the network of roads bequeathed to it by the Roman empire. This network was far from comprehensive, but new roads did appear from time to time in response to changing needs. Thus the Roman road from Lyon to the south-west was diverted in the eleventh century through the hard granite mountains of the Ségalas to take it past the abbey of Conques; when the pilgrimage to Conques was forgotten, in the fourteenth century travellers returned to the old road. In France, the roads were never allowed to fall into complete disrepair, as they were in parts of England. Nevertheless travel was not easy and even an experienced rider could not expect to cover more than thirty miles in a day. The seigneur de Caumont, who rode from Caumont to Santiago in 1418, was reduced to six miles a day in the Pyrenees and the Asturias, but he was capable of doing twenty-seven miles when the terrain was good.

The manor was responsible for the upkeep of the roads, but too often it had few resources and little enthusiasm for the work. Important roads, particularly if they were used by pilgrims, were frequently maintained by volunteers. For the maintenance of roads was regarded as a work of charity equivalent, for example, to almsgiving. Bridge-building was particularly meritorious, 'a service to posterity and therefore pleasing to God,' declares a charter of 1031 concerning the construction of a bridge over the Loire at Tours. French hermits in northern Spain were active road-builders at the time when the great road to Santiago was being rebuilt by the Castilian kings. Their names are preserved in the *Guide for Pilgrims to Santiago,* 'and may their souls and those of their companions rest in everlasting peace.' The bridge over the river Miño at Puerto Marin was rebuilt after a civil war by Peter the Pilgrim. St. Domingo 'de la Calzada', another French immigrant, founded a celebrated hospice on the site of his hut by the river Oja, and spanned the stream with a wooden bridge; he built the first cobbled road across the marshy expanse between Nájera and Redecilla. Several mediaeval roads and bridges still survive in Spain and southern France, built under the impulsion of the pilgrimage to Santiago. At St.-Chély d'Aubrac and St.-Michel Pied-de-Port the old track, its stones worn or displaced, can still be followed for a few hundred yards. The fine stone bridges which span the river at Orthez and Oloron in Gascony date from the fourteenth century and replaced older, wooden ones. At Puente la Reina one can still see the great five-arched bridge where the two roads from southern France to Santiago came together.

The *Guide for Pilgrims to Santiago* catalogues the full range of catastrophes which could overcome the traveller on the roads in the twelfth century. It is both a historical guide and a route-book, offering its readers information about towns and hospices, a few useful words of the Basque language, an architectural description of Santiago cathedral, and precise directions on how to get there. The pilgrim is warned that the eight-mile ascent of the Port de Cize, the principal pass over the Pyrenees, is a steep climb; that in Galicia there are thick forests and few towns; that mosquitoes infest the marshy plain south of Bordeaux where the traveller who strays from the road can sink up to his knees in mud. Some of the rivers are impassable. Several pilgrims had been drowned at Sorde, where travellers and their horses were ferried across the river on hollowed-out tree trunks. Other rivers were undrinkable, like the salt stream at Lorca, where the author of the *Guide* found two Basques earning their living by skinning the horses who had died after drinking from it. Pilgrims were in theory exempt from the payment of tolls, but nevertheless the *Guide* reports that the local lords exacted payment from every traveller in the Béarn. At the foot of the Port de Cize, pilgrims were searched and beaten with sticks if they could not pay the toll. The author demanded immediate action by the bishop and the king of Aragon, but it was more than half a century before the extortionists suffered retribution at the hands of Richard Coeur-de-Lion.

The supply of food and fodder is a constantly recurring theme in the *Guide,* and an important one at a time when it dictated the beginning and end of the travelling season much more effectively than the weather. There was no fodder to be had in the Landes south of Bordeaux, and the horseman was well-advised to bring three days' supply with him. There were parts of the route where the pilgrim would find it hard to buy a good meal for himself, even in summer. The food and wine were excellent in Gascony but dreadful in the Basque country. Fish caught in the river Ebro were disgusting, even poisonous. In general, concludes the *Guide,* Spanish meat should be avoided by those who are unused to it, 'and if any one can eat their fish without feeling sick, then he must have a stronger constitution than most of us.'

Against wild animals, bad roads, and natural catastrophes, a traveller had no protection. But, in theory, he enjoyed a measure of protection against man-made hazards. Every criminal code imposed special penalties on those who molested travellers, and synods of bishops regularly threatened them with the severest ecclesiastical censures. In 1096 a steward of the king of France was excommunicated for seizing a vassal of his on the road to Vézelay during Lent. 'But you should know', the archbishop of Lyon pointed out, 'that all those who travel to the shrines of the saints are protected against attack at all times, and not only in Lent. Those who disturb their journey will suffer the harshest penalties of the Church, so that the fear of God may remain for ever in their eyes.' From 1303 onwards, molesters of pilgrims were included in the annual bull *In Coena Domini*, in which the pope solemnly anathematized an ever-lengthening list of obnoxious persons. But although it is true that pilgrims were marginally safer from attack than other travellers, they can never have felt secure. In the eleventh century the Tuscan nobleman Gerard of Galeria supported himself in part by attacking rich pilgrims on the roads north of Rome. King Harold's brother Tostig was one of his victims. The French robber-baron Thomas de Marle owed much of his notoriety to his practice of holding pilgrims to ransom and mutilating them if the ransom was not paid. He terrorized the roads of northern France for many years before Louis VI mounted a military expedition against him in 1128. From the constant complaints of the ecclesiastical authorities, it is clear that Thomas had many imitators. We are better informed, however, of the bandits of the fourteenth and fifteenth centuries, most of whom were never brought to justice. The Roman Jubilee of 1350 brought considerable prosperity to one Berthold von Eberstein, who descended daily on the long processions of pilgrims winding through the Rhine valley. The German *routier* Werner von Urslinger was another bandit who enriched himself in 1350. His hunting-ground was Tuscany, where several of the main routes to Rome met. Jacopo Gabrielli, the papal rector of the Patrimony, was allowed 14,000 florins to raise mercenaries against him, the cost to be defrayed from the offerings at the Roman basilicas. The banditry of the later Middle Ages is remarkable for its international quality. The roads of northern Italy were infested with German robbers. On the roads which crossed northern Spain to Santiago, many of the bandits seem to have been Englishmen. In 1318 the provost of Estella spent several weeks in pursuit of one John of London, who had robbed pilgrims as they slept in a local hospice. In the following year a number of English bandits were captured at Pamplona. It was the same in the middle east. After the disappearance, in 1187, of the crusading kingdom of Jerusalem, the hills of Palestine were terrorized by brigands from every western nation, Englishmen, Frenchmen, and Germans, common criminals and former knights Templar, living side by side with Arabs for whom brigandage had been a way of life for quite some time.

To the depredations of professional robber bands were added those of innkeepers and villagers, who found the constant stream of pilgrims passing their doors a temptation too great to resist. The inhabitants of the coastal villages of southern Normandy repeatedly waylaid pilgrims bound for Mont-St.-Michel. Those of northern Italy were said, in 1049, to be murdering Norman pilgrims 'daily'. Rather later, the villages of Navarre and the Basque country took to preying on pilgrims passing on the roads to Santiago; at the border towns of Sorde and Lespéron this was even described as 'customary'. Lawlessness on this scale was a familiar problem whenever the rise of a great sanctuary drew its seasonal flux of pilgrims onto the roads. The anarchic state of Italy in 1350 encouraged whole villages to seize and despoil pilgrims travelling to the Roman Jubilee. Peter, bishop of Rodez, and his companion were ambushed outside the village of Sant' Adriano in Sabina and were saved only by the timely arrival of Napoleone Orsini. The Romans themselves were reported to be mounting expeditions to rob pilgrims on the roads north of the city. One observer believed that half the pilgrims who set out for Rome in 1350 were robbed or killed on the way.

Innkeepers, never the most popular of men, were blamed for many thefts and murders. The most celebrated of all the miracles of St. James told of a man wrongly hanged for stealing money from the pockets of some wealthy German pilgrims as they slept in an inn at Toulouse. The true culprit, it transpired, was the innkeeper, 'wherefore it is clear that pilgrims should take great care before staying at an inn lest a similar fraud be perpetrated on them.' German pilgrims were notoriously the victims of these frauds, probably because they travelled in a somewhat more showy style than others. Tales of gruesome murders of pilgrims in lonely inns were commonplace. In the forest of Châtenay, near Mâcon, there lived, at the beginning of the eleventh century, an innkeeper who used to accommodate travellers at night and murder them as they slept. According to Radulph Glaber, an investigation by the authorities revealed eighty-eight bodies hidden in his hut.

No one doubted that the journey to Jerusalem was by far the most dangerous that a pilgrim could undertake. Every hazard which a mediaeval traveller could encounter is exemplified in the experiences of those who walked three thousand miles or endured six weeks in a tiny, unstable boat, in order to visit the Holy Places.

At the beginning of the eleventh century the conversion of Hungary and the revival of Byzantium had brought most of the overland route to Jerusalem under nominal Christian rule. Latin pilgrims learned how nominal that rule was in 1053, when the Irish pilgrim, Colman, was battered to death at Stockerau outside Vienna, after an angry mob had taken him for a government spy. Although travellers now passed the frontier of the Byzantine empire at Belgrade, behind that frontier lay tracts of untamed territory which never recognized Byzantine rule. Lietbert, bishop of Cambrai, found Christian slaves being sold here in the summer of 1054. The valley of the Danube was so insecure in 1053 that travellers were being turned back by border guards at Belgrade. Pilgrims passed the southern extremity of the Byzantine empire at the coastal town of Lattakieh in northern Syria. Here again, they encountered a deeply hostile and suspicious population. Gerald of Saumur was battered to death by Syrian peasants in 1021, while others, like Anselm of Ardres, fell into the hands of Muslim fanatics and were lucky to escape by renouncing their faith.

Conditions were probably at their worst in 1064–5, when seven thousand unarmed German pilgrims made their way overland to Jerusalem under the leadership of Gunther, bishop of Bamberg. 'Truly we have been through fire and water', Gunther wrote to the canons of his cathedral from Lattakieh; '…we have been harassed by the Hungarians, attacked by the Bulgars, and driven to flight by the Turks, we have endured the insults of the arrogant Greeks of Constantinople and the rabid fury of the Cilicians. But we are afraid that even worse disasters lie ahead of us.' And so it was. On Good Friday 1065, as the long column of pilgrims was passing through an abandoned village near Caesarea, a terrifying scream of triumph was heard as large numbers of mounted Arabs descended on them 'as famished wolves leap upon their prey'. The pilgrims in the front of the procession were cut down in hundreds and their leader, the bishop of Utrecht, left half dead in the sand. Those at the rear fled to a nearby farmhouse where they held out for three days until the arrival of the Arab governor of Ramleh.

The Arab authorities in Palestine were weak rather than malevolent, and they were well aware of the economic benefits which Christian pilgrimages brought to them. The only point of conflict was at the gates of Jerusalem, where pilgrims were required to pay a toll of one gold piece each. This was a large sum of money, which many pilgrims did not have by the time they reached Jerusalem. When Robert, duke of Normandy, arrived there in 1036 he found several hundred pilgrims lying starving beneath the walls, begging for alms with which to pay the keepers of the toll-gate. The Greeks also levied tolls on pilgrims. Basil II demanded payment from all western travellers arriving in Constantinople by sea, and his successors set up toll-gates at two points on the overland route. Pilgrims were charged half a gold piece each, three gold pieces if they were mounted. These exactions were the source of some bitterness in the west. In 1056 pope Victor I addressed a long complaint to the empress Theodora, pointing out that her officials were taking advantage of the neutrality of the Arabs to levy taxes within the precinct of the Holy Sepulchre itself.

The conquest of parts of Palestine and Syria by the crusaders served to increase the number of pilgrimages to the Holy Land without making their journey any safer. Guerrilla raids constantly cut the roads leading to Jerusalem. In 1172 a traveller reported that churches lying within a mile of the city were fortified against the infidel. Ascalon, which remained in Arab hands until 1153, was the base from which raids were launched against the roads west to Joppa and south to Hebron. The Joppa road was the lifeline between Jerusalem and the sea, along which travelled almost every pilgrim who visited the Holy Land in the twelfth century. An English pilgrim who followed the road in October 1102 described how the Arabs 'lay hidden in caves and crevices, waiting day and night for people travelling in small parties or straggling behind their groups. At one moment they are everywhere, the next they are gone. Their presence is felt by every one who passes on that fatal road.' The road to Jericho and the Jordan, where most pilgrims went to baptize themselves and collect their palms, was no safer than it had been in the time of the good Samaritan, although the Templars regularly patrolled it. At Easter 1120, thirty pilgrims were killed and sixty captured out of a party of some seven hundred. As for the road north to Nazareth and Acre, it was scarcely attempted except during the periodic wars between the kings of Jerusalem and the emirs of Damascus, when enterprising pilgrims would attach themselves to the Frankish army. In 1106, the Russian pilgrim abbot Daniel managed to penetrate as far north as Lake Tiberias in the entourage of king Baldwin. But travelling with the army was not as safe as it appeared, for many pilgrims are reported to have died on this particular expedition.

The eleventh century had been the heyday of the overland route to the Holy Land, but the growing instability of eastern Europe sharply reduced its popularity in the twelfth. Wealthy pilgrims with large escorts might fight their way through the

Balkans as Henry the Lion, duke of Saxony, did *'cum magna gloria'* in 1172. But for most, a pilgrimage to the Holy Land involved a long and expensive journey by sea. After the final disappearance of the crusading states at the end of the thirteenth century, there is scarcely a single case on record of an overland pilgrimage to Jerusalem.

Travel by Sea

A voyage by sea in the Middle Ages was an uncomfortable experience. Pilgrims were crowded like grains of corn into small, unstable boats where, for six weeks or more, they endured stale food and water, boredom, disease, and intense discomfort.

> *Men may leve alle games*
> *That saylen to seynt James,*

sang an Englishman of the fifteenth century with bitter memories of a voyage to Santiago. The seamen shouted at him and rushed to and fro, continually ordering him out of their way. The bark swayed and tossed so violently that he did not feel like eating and could not hold a tankard to his lips. The poorest pilgrims, stowed in the most uncomfortable part of the ship, slept next to the bilge-pump, and had to make do with bread and salt and water.

The well-to-do pilgrim could mitigate the discomfort of the journey by paying a little more for the passage. Two types of ship were available at Venice. There were large, oared galleys which were safe, comfortable, and expensive; and small ships for the use of the poor, which were crammed to overflowing. Sebald Rieter, the opulent merchant of Nurnberg, paid sixty-seven ducats for his fare to the Holy Land in 1479 and shared the ship with only sixty-three other passengers. On the other hand an anonymous German pilgrim who travelled in the cheap ship paid only thirty ducats. The Florentine, Lionardo Frescobaldi, took the expensive ship to Alexandria in 1384 and watched the cheap one foundering in the first storm with two hundred pilgrims on board. When the demand for places fell, both rich and poor would share the same ship but occupied different parts of it. 'Chose yow a place in the sayd gallery in the overest stage', advised William Wey, 'for in the lowst under hyt is ryght smoulderyng hote and stynkyng.' When Hans von Mergenthal sailed to the Holy Places in 1476, the place allotted to poor pilgrims was so narrow that it was impossible to turn over in one's sleep. Sleepers were bitten by insects and trampled over by large rats. The animals penned up on the deck to be slaughtered for food broke out from time to time and trod on the sleeping bodies. When the sea was rough, passengers could not stand upright for fear of being struck by swinging booms and ropes.

Pilgrims were advised to bring mattresses and warm clothes with them. Frescobaldi, Gucci, and Sigoli, the three Italians who travelled together in 1384, brought several mattresses, a large number of shirts, a barrel of Malmsey wine, a Bible in several volumes, a copy of the *Moralia* of St. Gregory, a silver cup, 'and other delicate things'. Santo Brasca, who did the journey in 1480, recommended a long thick coat, and also suggested some provisions which every pilgrim would need to supplement the ship's meagre diet: a good supply of Lombard cheese, sausages, salted meat, white biscuits, sugar loaves, and sweetmeats. He should also bring some strong spices for curing indigestion and sea-sickness, 'and above all a great quantity of fruit syrup, for this is what keeps a man alive in hot climates.' William Wey agreed that the prudent pilgrim should arm himself with laxatives, restoratives, ginger, flour, figs, pepper, saffron, cloves, and other 'confections and comfortaciouns'; it was essential to have half a dozen chickens in a cage 'for ye schal have need of them many tymes.' All travellers were agreed on the appalling quality of ship's food. 'Sum tymes', declared William Wey, 'ye schal have swych feble bred, wyne, and stynkyng water, that ye schal be ful fayne to eate of yowre owne.'

The manner in which the food was served was not calculated to stimulate the appetite. At the sound of a trumpet the passengers separated into two groups, those whose fare included food, and those who were seeing to their own wants. Members of the first group then scrambled for a place at one of three small tables in the poop. After dinner another trumpet signalled for the diners to retire, while their place was taken by the ship's officers and crew. Their food was even more frugal than that of the pilgrims, but it was served with great pomp on silver dishes, and their wine was tasted before it was offered to them. The galley was a scene of unending chaos. 'Three or four hot-tempered cooks struggle with the food in a narrow passage lined with pots and pans and provisions, while a fire crackles away in the middle. Sounds of angry shouting issue forth from the room while, outside, crowds of passengers shout each other down in the effort to order special meals from the cooks.'

After hunger and sleeplessness, boredom was the principal problem of the passengers. 'Unless a man knows how to occupy himself, he will find the hours very long and tedious', Felix Faber observed. Saxons and Flemings, 'and other men of low class', usually passed the days drinking. Others played dice or cards. Chess was very common. Communal singing went on in the background all the time. A small group of contemplative pilgrims gathered in a corner to read or pray. Others slept day and night. Many wrote travel diaries. A number of pilgrims, Faber remarked with contempt, amused themselves by running up and down the rigging, jumping up and down on the spot, or weight-lifting. 'But most people simply sit about looking on blankly, passing their eyes from one group to another, and thence to the open sea.' During Faber's first pilgrimage, in 1480, the news of Turkish naval activity in the eastern Mediterranean caused the passengers to agree on measures of moral reform which would preserve them from capture. All games were forbidden, together with quarrels, oaths, and blasphemies. Disputes between the French and the Germans were to cease, and the bishop of Orléans promised to give up gambling. Extra litanies were added to the daily service.

Sermons were the only organized recreation. The company who travelled with canon Casola in 1494 were fortunate enough to have amongst them one Francesco Tivulzio, 'a holy friar with a wonderful library in his head'. Whenever the ship was becalmed, he would rise and deliver an elaborate and learned sermon, many hours in length. On the eve of the feast of St. John, he delivered a sermon on the merits of that saint in nine parts which lasted from 5 P.M. to sunset, and promised to deliver the rest of it on the following day. While waiting for permission to disembark at Joppa, the pilgrims listened to another sermon from friar Tivulzio on the allegorical significance of sailing ships, followed, a few hours later, by 'a beautiful sermon on trade'. Such discourses, however, were not always received in rapturous silence. On Faber's first pilgrimage his preaching was repeatedly interrupted by inane laughter, after which he refused to utter again. On his second pilgrimage the company was more polite, and he favoured them with regular sermons. Even so, a number of noblemen disliked his preaching, which Faber attributed to the fact that they practised the vices that he castigated,' 'and truth ever begets hatred.'

The tedious serenity of a long sea voyage was occasionally disturbed by the appearance of pirates. The law of the sea required all passengers to assist in defending the ship, and although pilgrims were exempt from this obligation on account of their religious calling, they usually fought as hard as any. In 1408, a Venetian galley returning from the Holy Land was attacked by a Turkish pirate in the gulf of Satalia. The captain was found to have no cross-bows on board, and it was only after the pilgrims had beaten off their assailants in fierce hand-to-hand fighting that the ship escaped capture. In consequence, the Venetian Senate enacted that a proper supply of bows, arrows, and lances was to be carried on every pilgrim-ship.

A pilgrim's troubles did not end with his arrival at Joppa. After the fall of Acre to the Arabs (1291), Joppa was the point at which almost all pilgrims disembarked, and it was here that they first encountered Arab officialdom. An English pilgrim who was there in 1345 described them as a group of 'revolting and corpulent men with long beards', mounted on tall horses on the foreshore. The master of the ship gave them a list of the pilgrims' names and paid a toll of six Venetian *gros* a head. The column was then escorted by two Arab guides to Jerusalem. This pilgrim was fortunate to find the officials waiting for him. Usually it was necessary to send word to the Arab governor of Jerusalem, and until the arrival of his minions the travellers were incarcerated in three large underground cellars in the ruins of the town. Fifteenth-century pilgrims made a virtue of this necessity by attaching an indulgence of seven years to these comfortless cellars. The Franciscans of Jerusalem, who enjoyed considerable influence with the caliphate, did all they could to ease the pilgrim's lot. At the beginning of the fifteenth century they even succeeded in taking over the administration of the tolls and the issue of visas. The prior of the Franciscans met the pilgrim-ship at Joppa, clutching a bundle of visas which he had obtained from the governor in advance. He collected the names of the pilgrims and took their money on the governor's behalf before escorting them inland.

In addition to the heavy toll which had to be paid before leaving Joppa, the pilgrim was required to pay the poll-tax which Islamic law imposed upon non-Muslims. This was exacted in Jerusalem, usually under the eyes of the governor himself. The English pilgrim of 1345 found the governor at the end of a large hall. In front of him scribes were seated on the floor recording the proceedings with huge quills. At that time the poll-tax stood at four gold florins, but a large sum from the party as a whole was accepted instead, for some of them had come without any money at all. However, the attitude of the Arab authorities was constantly changing. Only a year later, the governor threatened a penniless Franciscan pilgrim with flogging and imprisonment unless he could find someone to pay his poll-tax for him. As relations between Islam and the west deteriorated, the tolls and taxes demanded of pilgrims sharply increased. In 1440, a German pilgrim was asked for one *gros* from Joppa to Ramleh, one *gros* from Ramleh to Lydda, two *gros* at Emmaeus, and five at the gates of Jerusalem. Mariano da Sienna paid thirteen ducats to be exempted from all tolls, though even this did not spare him the payment of the poll-tax.

The Dominican writer Guillaume Adam, an early advocate of economic warfare, calculated in 1317 that the sultan received thirty-five *gros tournois* every time a pilgrim visited the Holy Land, and he suggested to John XXII that this was a good reason for forbidding pilgrimages to the Holy Land altogether. 'Pilgrims are the only people who freely assist the Saracens without having to fear excommunication.'

The fact that pilgrims continued to visit the Holy Land in large numbers, in spite of the obstacles in their way, was largely due to the enterprise of the Venetians. The ship-owners of Venice provided the earliest all-inclusive package tours. Galleys licensed by the republic left for Joppa every year as soon as possible after Ascension Day and returned in the autumn. When the demand for passages was high, two fleets sailed from Venice, one in March and one in September. The fare included food and board throughout the journey as well as in the Holy Land itself; the ship-owner, who was generally the master as well, paid all tolls and taxes, and met the cost of donkeys and pack-horses, guided tours of Jerusalem, and special expeditions to the Jordan. The popularity of these tours was entirely due to the high reputation of Venetian ship-owners. The stiff regulations of the serene republic enforced on them standards of safety and commercial morality which were uncommon in other ports. The anonymous English pilgrim of 1345 was advised by the inhabitants of Brindisi that it was unsafe to travel in any ship but a Venetian one. If he entrusted his life to a Sicilian or a Catalan master 'he would undoubtedly enjoy eternal rest at the bottom of the sea.' The ship-owners of Genoa and Pisa were suspected of selling their passengers into slavery at Arab ports. Francesco da Suriano gave four reasons for sailing from Venice in the latter half of the fifteenth century. It was so busy that a traveller never had to wait more than a few days before a ship sailed for his destination; the port was safe from pirates; the Venetian navy patrolled much of the route; and Venetian sailors were 'the finest travelling companions in Christendom'. He might have added that the Venetian currency was among the most stable in the west, and it was the only one which passed for legal tender in Arab territories. 'And so', counselled Santo Brasca, 'travel via Venice, for it is the most convenient embarkation point in the world.'

The Venetian republic began to license and regulate the traffic of pilgrims at the beginning of the thirteenth century. The maritime statutes of 1229 laid down the maximum number of pilgrims which one ship could carry and the date of sailing. At that time there were two fleets per year. The first, which reached the Holy Land in time for Easter, was to return not later than May 8th, while the second was to leave Joppa before November 8th. Further regulations, in 1255, enjoined officers of the republic throughout the eastern Mediterranean to inspect every pilgrim ship calling at their ports and to impose heavy fines if they were overloaded. Mariners were required to swear an oath not to steal more than five shillings from the passengers. The rights and duties of the pilgrim were set out in a lengthy contract, which was signed by both parties. Some of these contracts have survived. The contract between Jan Aerts and the shipowner Agostino Contarini, signed in April 1484, is in every way typical. It permits the pilgrim to go ashore whenever the ship is in port, and to visit Mount Sinai instead of returning with the ship, in which case Contarini will refund ten ducats of his fare. Contarini undertakes not to take on too many passengers or too few crewmen and not to appropriate the pilgrim's chattels if he dies during the journey; he promises to supply enough arms for twenty-five men in case of attack, and to accompany his passengers wherever they go in Jerusalem. The passengers may elect two of their number to oversee him. But there were no standard forms of contract, and pilgrims occasionally insisted on a special term. A contract dating from 1440 provides for a four-day stop at Nicosia, in Cyprus. William Wey advised English pilgrims to insist on a clause forbidding the owner to call at Famagusta on account of its unhealthy air. Once signed, the contract was lodged with a magistrate in Venice who would hear any disputes that arose. In 1497, for example, pilgrims protested that the space allotted to them was too small; port officials boarded the ship and resolved that each passenger should have one and a half feet of deck on which to sleep. On another occasion, pilgrims complained on their return to Venice that they had been manhandled and ill-fed and that their sleeping-quarters had been filled with cargo. Some of them had refused to return with the ship and had instead taken a passage from Beyrut in a Genoese vessel. The rest returned to Venice in an exceedingly hostile mood and, as they included a number of 'great lords', the Senate hastily sequestered the vessel and ordered the owners to refund the fares.

Disputes had become so common by the early fifteenth century that in 1437 the republic took the extreme step of suspending the annual pilgrim fleets. When they were restored, in 1440, it was on a somewhat different footing. The republic decided to encourage the process by which the pilgrim trade was monopolized by a small group of reputable shipowners. The smaller shipowners were excluded by a new maritime statute forbidding the masters of pilgrim-ships to carry any cargo at all. The number of annual licences issued by the republic was severely restricted, and those were sold for huge sums by public auction. Should any particularly distinguished pilgrims request a passage to the Holy Land, the republic reserved the right to make an extra charge. Thus in 1446, when a number of noblemen arrived with letters of commendation from the duke of Burgundy, the licensees of the year were charged an extra six hundred ducats for the exclusive privilege of fleecing these august personages. For some years after 1440, the traffic was monopolized by the Loredano family. But within ten years they were facing powerful competition from a syndicate headed by the brothers Contarini. The Contarinis conducted their business with a degree of professionalism hitherto unheard-of, employing commission agents as far away as the Netherlands. In the last three decades of the fifteenth century, Agostino Contarini enjoyed an unofficial monopoly of the pilgrim traffic which did not end until he was forced to retire in 1497 after frequent complaints of misconduct.

But it was not misconduct which brought Agostino Contarini's career to an end, so much as the disturbed state of the eastern Mediterranean and the increasingly hostile attitude of the Arab authorities in Jerusalem. The Turks attacked Rhodes four times in the 1440s doing considerable damage to the port. William Wey, returning from his first visit to the Holy Land in 1459, saw the ruin left after a recent Turkish descent, and heard stories of fearful atrocities. In 1480 another Turkish attack on Rhodes seriously disrupted the shipping routes. Although Venice had signed a treaty with the Porte only the year before, the pilgrim's galley of that year had to take refuge for a week in Corfù. Twenty of the pilgrims decided to return to Venice in another ship, and Agostino Contarini had to refund ten ducats to each of them.

In Palestine, toll-gates multiplied unceasingly and the Arab governor made unpredictable demands on the shipowners which they were unable, by the terms of the contract, to recover from the passengers. In 1479 Agostino Contarini had to pay peace money to Arab officials because another Venetian shipowner had given offence to them in the previous year. The anarchic state of Palestine made it impossible to bathe in the Jordan that year, and the passengers complained bitterly. In 1480 Contarini's troubles began anew when the pilgrims of his galley demanded that he hire an armed escort to accompany them to the Jordan. They pointed out that a trip to the Jordan was included in the contract. Contarini replied that nothing in the contract obliged him to spend so much extra money and that if he hired an escort it would be at their own expense. The pilgrims finally left in high dudgeon, without an escort. A further dispute broke out when the Arabs forced Contarini to pay more than the customary fee for the hire of donkeys and pack-horses. Contarini refused to allow the pilgrims to re-embark for Venice until they had paid him a further ducat and a half to cover this unforeseen expense. Needless to say, he made large losses in both years.

It was shortly after these disasters that the Venetian package tour was abandoned and the pilgrimage to the Holy Land suffered a prolonged decline. Pietro Casola learned from the Franciscans of Jerusalem in 1494 that no pilgrims had visited the city for several years. The fleet of 1499 had to be cancelled when war broke out between Venice and the Porte, and the licensee had to refund all the fares which he had received. The news of these events deterred the pilgrims from Italy and northern Europe who had once gathered in crowds for the Ascension Day sailing. In the early years of the sixteenth century the fleet, when it sailed at all, consisted of a single ship. In 1533 the French pilgrim Gréffin Affagart arrived in Venice to find that it had not sailed for many years. Interest in the Holy Land had declined, and it was no longer possible for enterprising shipowners to offer cheap passages by filling their decks with human cargo.

Strange Customs and Foreign Languages

It would be pleasant to learn that pilgrims returned from their travels with minds broadened by the experience of strange people and unfamiliar customs. But it would be the reverse of the truth. Such exchange of ideas as had occurred in the 'dark ages' of the west did not survive the onset of an age of mass-pilgrimage. All too often, those who lived on the pilgrimage roads regarded pilgrims as fair game to be plundered at will. The pilgrims in turn had little incentive to understand their hosts, and viewed them with that uncomprehending contempt which uneducated people commonly accord to foreigners. The impressions of French pilgrims in Spain are a case in point. So loathsome a race as the Basques, thought the author of the *Guide for Pilgrims to Santiago,* could only have originated in Scotland. After describing their national dress, he goes on to comment on their food and language in the following terms:

> 'Not only are they badly dressed, but they eat and drink in the most disgusting way. The entire household, including servants, eat out of the same pot and drink from the same cup. Far from using spoons, they eat with their hands, slobbering over the food like any dog or pig. To hear them speaking, you would think they were a pack of hounds barking, for their language is

absolutely barbarous. They call God *Urcia;* bread is *orgui* and wine *ardum,* while meat is referred to as *aragui* and fish *araign*....They are in fact a most uncouth race whose customs are quite different from those of any other people. They have dark, evil, ugly faces. They are debauched, perverse, treacherous and disloyal, corrupt and sensual drunkards. They are like fierce savages, dishonest and untrustworthy, impious, common, cruel and quarrelsome people, brought up in vice and iniquity, totally devoid of human feeling....They will kill you for a penny. Men and women alike warm themselves by the fire, revealing those parts which are better hidden. They fornicate unceasingly, and not only with humans....That is why they are held in contempt by all decent folk.'

In the *Chanson de Roland* the Basques appear in an extremely sinister light, and the influence of this celebrated poem may well be responsible for the contempt which many pilgrims expressed for them. But this alone will not explain the venom of the *Guide*, which entertains a remarkably similar opinion of the Gascons, characterizing their way of life as impious, immoral, and 'in every way detestable'.

If a Poitevin could write thus of the Gascons, he was unlikely to feel closer in spirit to the Greeks and oriental Christians, let alone to the Arabs. Throughout this period, relations with the Greeks were marked by a bitterness which can only be understood in the light of the tortuous relations of Byzantium with the crusaders. Most Latin Christians despised the Greeks as effeminate schismatics and believed with immovable conviction that they had betrayed the twelfth-century crusades. A guide-book written at the end of the century refers to them characteristically as 'cunning men who do not bear arms and who err from the true faith....They also use leaven bread in the Eucharist and do other strange things. They even have an alphabet of their own.' This mood of suspicion was aggravated by the widespread belief that the Byzantine authorities deliberately obstructed pilgrims passing through Constantinople. The emperor Alexius Comnenus was once described by an eminently sane Latin writer as 'that great oppressor of pilgrims to Jerusalem who hinders their progress by guile or by force.' Indeed, it never struck western pilgrims that their habit of helping themselves to whatever they required, and of insulting and attacking local people, might arouse justifiable resentment on the part of their hosts. The importance which Greeks attached to their own traditions was regarded by some Latin pilgrims as nothing less than a calculated insult. Jacques de Vitry denounced them as 'foul schismatics moved by sinful pride', and then went on to consider the Jacobite and Armenian Christians, 'barbarous nations who differ from both Greeks and Latins...and use a peculiar language understood only by the learned.'

Language was indeed the principal barrier. Few mediaeval men, however cultivated they were, understood more than a few words of any language but their own or Latin. Travelling through regions such as eastern Europe or Egypt, where pilgrims were rare and Latin unknown, was a difficult and dangerous undertaking. Lietbert, bishop of Cambrai, who passed through the Danube valley on the way to Jerusalem in 1054, listed 'the strange and foreign language of the Huns' amongst the perils which he had encountered, together with mountains, swamps, and impenetrable forests. During the twelfth century, French was the language of Jerusalem, and this is said to have made difficulties for the Germans. At any rate, one of the reasons given for the foundation of the German hospice in Jerusalem was that 'in such a place Germans might talk in a language they can understand.' In Venice the authorities were constantly embarrassed by the activities of sharp traders or shipowners who took advantage of foreigners bound for the Holy Land. 'It is well-known that many scandalous mistakes have been made of late, on account of the great number of pilgrims boarding ships at Venice', the senate noted in 1398; 'for the said pilgrims are of divers tongues…and unless a remedy is found, still greater scandals will follow.'

It is worth following the Burgundian pilgrim Bertrandon de la Brocquière in his efforts to learn a few words of Turkish. Bertrandon visited the Holy Land in 1432–3, but he avoided the Venetian package tour because he wished to spy out the land at leisure, with a view to planning a crusade. In Damascus he made the acquaintance of a Turk who spoke Arabic, Hebrew, Turkish, and Greek. Bertrandon spoke none of these languages, but he had a working knowledge of Italian, and the Turk found a Jew who knew a little Italian and some Turkish. The Jew compiled a list of everything that Bertrandon would require on his journey, in parallel columns of Turkish and Italian. On the first day after leaving Damascus, Bertrandon had occasion to ask a group of peasants for some fodder for his horse. He consulted his piece of paper and made his request, but there was no reaction. He showed the paper to the leading peasant, who began to roar with laughter. The group then gave him an impromptu lesson in Turkish, picking up various articles and pronouncing their names very carefully several times. 'And when I left them I knew how to ask in Turkish for almost everything I wanted.'

Italian was the only European language known to a significant number of Arabs. Pilgrims who visited Mount Sinai via Egypt could usually find an Italian-speaking interpreter at Alexandria or Cairo, but this was an expensive luxury of which few travellers availed themselves. In 1384 Lionardo Frescobaldi's party spent more than forty-nine ducats on interpreters between Alexandria and Damascus. In addition, one of their interpreters stole eight ducats from them, and another was in league with a group of Bedouin bandits. More than a hundred ducats was spent on bribing the personal interpreters of various Arab officials to present their requests for safe-conducts in a favourable way.

Phrase-books, then as now, were the simplest way to overcome the language difficulty. As early as the ninth century, we find a phrase-book entitled *Old High-German Conversations (Altdeutsche Gespräche)* being used by Franks travelling in Germany. It consists of orders to servants, requests for information, and demands for hospitality such as 'I want a drink':

'Erro, e guille trenchen; id est, ego volo bibere.'

A number of early phrase books of Greek and Hebrew survive, most of which were clearly intended for the use of pilgrims to the Holy Land. The abbey of Mont-St.-Michel had, in the eleventh century, a Greek phrase-book containing useful demands like

'Da mihi panem: DOS ME PSOMI.'

An interesting manual for crusaders, dating from the twelfth century, includes such tactful requests as 'What is the news about the Greek emperor? What is he doing? He is being kind to the Franks. What good things does he give them? Much money and weapons.' During the period of mass-pilgrimages in the late Middle Ages, an immense number of phrase-books was available, some of them very comprehensive. The library of Charles V of France contained a manual for pilgrims entitled *How to Ask in Arabic for the Necessities of Life.* Another French-Arabic phrase-book, preserved in the Swiss abbey of St.-Gall, has a long section on how to ask one's way in a strange town.

Some pilgrims found oriental alphabets a source of limitless fascination. *Mandeville's Travels*, that strange mixture of fact and fantasy, sets out the Greek, Hebrew, Arabic, and Persian alphabets, though they contain many mistakes and the Hebrew one is incomprehensible. Johann Schiltberger appended to the account of his travels the *Pater Noster* in Armenian and Turkish. But the most proficient linguist amongst the pilgrims of the fifteenth century was certainly Arnold von Harff, a wealthy young nobleman of Cologne who, between 1496 and 1499, travelled through Italy, Syria, Egypt, Arabia, Ethiopia, Nubia, Palestine, Turkey, and Spain. He was a worldly pilgrim of the type mocked in the *Canterbury Tales* and the *Quinze Joies de Mariage*, but he took a genuine interest in the people of each country and particularly in their languages. Von Harff collected alphabets. His memoirs contain many oriental alphabets (some of them are undecipherable), as well as useful phrases in nine different languages, Croatian, Albanian, Greek, Arabic, Hebrew, Turkish, Hungarian, Basque, and Breton. He was a cultivated man, a gallant knight and an aristocrat whose range of phrases was broader than that of most conventional pilgrims. Thus, 'Wash my shirt for me—I do not understand—Will you sell me that?—How much is this?—Madam shall I marry you?—

Madam shall I sleep with you?—Good woman, I am already in your bed.'

But Arnold von Harff was scarcely typical even of his own worldly age. He was an acute observer who was interested in such diverse matters as wild animals in the Nile valley, and the Mamluk system of government. He doubted the authenticity of the body of St. James at Santiago, and openly disputed the claims of several Roman relics. He considered the Turks closer to the spirit of Christianity than the Spanish. A more faithful reflection of the mentality of pilgrims is found in the account of the Arab way of life in the travel diary of one of Frescobaldi's companions, which begins, 'now let me tell you of their bestial habits.'

Companions

The criticism directed at pilgrims at the close of the Middle Ages owed much of its vehemence to the fact that they generally travelled in large and raucous bands. The carnival atmosphere in which Chaucer's thirty pilgrims left Southwark, piped out of town by the miller, ill-accorded with the spiritual sentiments which they professed. But then, as the host of the Tabard Inn reflected, 'trewely confort ne mirthe is noon, to ryde by the weye doumb as a stoon'; in fact he 'ne saugh this yeer so mery a companye.' William Thorpe, an itinerant Lollard preacher who was examined for heresy in 1407, had this to say about such vulgar gatherings:

> 'I know well that when divers men and women will go thus after their own wills, and finding out one pilgrimage they will ordain beforehand to have with them both men and women that can well sing wanton songs. And

some other pilgrims will have them bagpipes so that
every town that they come through shall know of
their coming, what with the noise of their singing and
the sound of their piping, what with the jangling of
their Canterbury bells, and the barking out of dogs
after them. They make more noise than if the King
came thereaway with all his clarions and many other
minstrels.'

The first pilgrims to travel in bands did so for reasons of
self-defence, not amusement. Before the eleventh century, pilgrims generally had two or three companions with them at the
most. Indeed, it was thought to be specially virtuous to travel
alone. The dangerous state of the roads to Jerusalem forced pilgrims to abandon this prejudice, and by the middle years of the
eleventh century the departure of an abbot or a great nobleman was the signal for pilgrims from all the surrounding
provinces to gather together and follow in his suite. Richard,
abbot of St.-Vannes, who set out from Verdun in 1026, found
himself the leader of several hundred Normans and
Aquitainians. Each group had picked up hangers-on on their
way to Verdun, and as the whole unwieldy column proceeded
up the Rhine valley they were constantly joined by new
recruits. By the time they left the frontiers of Germany behind
them, they were more than seven hundred strong. Robert,
duke of Normandy, was followed to Jerusalem in 1035 by an
imposing retinue of bishops, abbots, and noblemen, whose
expenses he had promised to pay. The ill-fated expedition of
Gunther, bishop of Bamberg, was estimated at seven thousand.

Few pilgrims travelled alone after the eleventh century,
whatever their destination. The growing popularity of pilgrim-

ages made it easy to find companions. Indeed, on the busy roads to Rome and Santiago it was impossible to avoid them. Pilgrims were exhorted to choose their friends with care, for there were regular reports of travellers killed or robbed by their companions. Particularly notorious was the stretch of the road to Santiago which ran from Saintes to the Pyrenees. Here, theft was a well-organized industry. In one incident a blind man was robbed by his companions of his money, his horse, and all his luggage, and left without a guide at the side of the road. The 'companions' were of course professional thieves of the sort described in the *Liber Sancti Jacobi*, who dressed as pilgrims or priests in order to gain the confidence of their victims. 'Take care, then, not to join up with bad companions', warned the French jurist Beaumanoir, after telling of a pilgrim who was hanged as a felon on being found in the company of thieves; 'for however pleasant they appear, you never know what evil will befall you'.

Even if honest, a companion might well be quarrelsome or a bore. He might walk too fast, as Margery Kempe's companion did on the road to Wilsnack. She might talk too much, as Margery herself was inclined to do. Her visit to the Holy Land in 1413 is a classic illustration of the difficulty of living up to high spiritual ideals in the company of a happy band of Chaucerian pilgrims. As a woman, she could not travel alone, and so she fell in with a group of English pilgrims of somewhat conventional piety. These were embarrassed by her constant fasting, weeping, and lamentation, and her long sessions in prayer. They left Constance without her, but she caught them up again at Bologna, where an agreement was made in an effort to restore harmony. 'Ye shall not speak of the Gospel when we come,' they warned her, 'but ye shall sit still and make merry as we do.' At Venice, her habit of quoting passages from the Bible brought about another rupture. In Jerusalem her trances and visions caused them intense discomfort. 'Some shunned her; some wished she had been left in the haven; some would she had been at sea in a bottomless boat; and so each man as him thought.' The Franciscans of Jerusalem, however, were impressed by her piety. So, interestingly, were the Arabs, who provided her with an escort about the Holy Places.

Hospitality

A pilgrim according to an eighth-century text, was entitled to a roof over his head, a fire, wholesome water, and fresh bread. The principle of free hospitality, though often honoured in the breach, remained throughout the mediaeval period a corner-stone of Christian charity. The *Guide for Pilgrims to Santiago* ends with a collection of stories illustrating the unwisdom of refusing hospitality to a pilgrim of St. James. 'For all pilgrims, rich or poor, who go to St. James ought to be received with charity by all. Whoever receives them receives St. James and God himself.'

The early Church placed this obligation squarely on the shoulders of the bishops. But although some bishops, such as John Chrysostom and Augustine of Hippo, took their duties seriously, it was from the very first the monasteries who bore most of the burden. In the earliest monastic rules of the eastern Church, monks are required to receive pilgrims, and in the western Church this tradition was incorporated into the Benedictine rule. In this form, it survived for as long as the monasteries themselves. In the great restatement of the Benedictine rule at the beginning of the ninth century the importance of hospitality was, if anything, increased, and monasteries were expected to put aside a fixed proportion of their revenues to it. Naturally, in the succeeding centuries this rule was unevenly observed, but there were some monasteries justly famous for their hospitality. The chronicler of Evesham abbey remarks that abbot Agelwy was known as far afield as Ireland and Aquitaine for his habit of washing the feet of pilgrims in person, a practice which was required by the rule but had been abandoned in some houses. The hospitality dispensed at Maria Laach outside Bonn was described in c. 1225 as 'unequalled'.

On busy roads it proved impossible to accommodate the droves of pilgrims in the monastery itself, and instead large guest halls were built for the purpose. Abbot Otmar built one at St.-Gall as early as the eighth century. Another, dating from the thirteenth, can be seen today at Battle abbey. The logical extension of this policy was the foundation of independent hospices away from the monasteries, governed by small autonomous communities of monks or canons. This was first practised on a large scale in the eighth century by Irish monks on the continent. Major Irish hospices sprang up at Péronne, Honau, and elsewhere; others at St. Omer and St.-Gall ultimately became great monastic houses. So important were the Irish houses that their disappearance during the ninth and tenth centuries was a source of genuine concern to successive emperors. The council of Meaux in 845 attributed it to the disordered state of the Frankish dominions, and asked Charles the Bald to do something about it. Charles promised to take measures to halt the decline. What these measures were is not at all clear, but there is no doubt that they were unsuccessful, for a century later most of the hospices of western Europe had entirely disappeared. When, in the eleventh century, pilgrims began to

reappear in thousands on the roads of Europe, the task of building hospices to receive them had to be begun anew.

In the *Guide for Pilgrims to Santiago,* three hospices are singled out as 'columns built by God for the support of his poor
people'. They were the hospices of Jerusalem, the Great St.
Bernard Pass, and St. Christine in the Pyrenees. 'These hospices have been sited in the places where they are most
needed. They are holy places, houses of God himself, ordained
for the comfort of pilgrims, the restitution of the needy, the
consolation of the sick, the assistance of the living, and the salvation of the dead.'

There had been a Latin hospice in Jerusalem since the
beginning of the ninth century. Its foundation was traditionally, and probably rightly, ascribed to Charlemagne. The
Frankish monk Bernard found much to approve of when he
stayed there in 870, at which time it had a chapel, a library, and
a vineyard. The tenth century, however, was a troubled period
in the history of Jerusalem and the hospice probably ceased to
exist shortly after Bernard's departure. The great hospice
referred to by the *Guide* was the Hospital of St. John, which
owed its foundation to the community of merchants of
Amalfi, and maintained a precarious existence from about
1060. After the capture of Jerusalem by the first crusade it
became the headquarters of a crusading order, but it remained
above all a pilgrims' hospice. The Hospital made a strong
impression on visitors if only by its sheer size. One of them,
who saw it in about 1165, counted two thousand beds, many
of then occupied by the sick. About fifty patients a day died in
the Hospital, he casually observed. Their beds were immediately filled by others, and a crowd of pilgrims was perpetually
milling about outside the doors waiting for the daily distribu-

tion of alms. After the disappearance of the crusading states, the Hospital became a Muslim establishment, but Christian pilgrims were still admitted to it on payment of two Venetian pennies, a courtesy which, in its Christian days, had never been extended to Muslims.

The Great St. Bernard hospice, which stood on the highest and bleakest pass of the Alps, received almost every English or French pilgrim bound for Rome. It was a younger institution than the Hospital of Jerusalem, but its origins are still far from clear. It owed its foundation to St. Bernard of Aosta, who flourished at a somewhat uncertain date, and who gave his name to both the hospice and the pass. It was certainly in existence by 1081, and within a century its buildings were already bursting out from its narrow site, crushed between two steep walls of rock.

Still more obscure are the origins of the hospice of St. Christine, on the Somport pass over the Pyrenees. It opened its doors, according to a popular song, 'not only to catholics, but to pagans, Jews and heretics, to the idle and the vain alike'. But its real importance was that it formed part of a remarkable chain of hospices which had sprung up in the space of a few decades along the roads to Santiago, both in Spain and in France. By the middle of the twelfth century there was scarcely a hospice on these roads which was not within a day's journey of the next. Several of them, like the hospice of St. Christine and its great rival at Ronceval, founded by the bishop of Pamplona in 1132, were in the hands of Augustinian canons. Others were attached to Cluniac priories, like Leyre, Nájera, or Carrión de los Condes. A number of religious orders devoted themselves entirely to running hospices, the confraternity of Santo Spirito, for example, a twelfth-century foundation which had establishments at Montpellier and Rome. The Spanish military orders, like their opposite numbers in the middle east, devoted a great deal of their immense wealth to building hospices and repairing roads. Most active of all were the orders of Santo Sepolcro and Santiago, one of whose functions was declared to be 'to offer shelter and food to travellers and poor people'. These hospices were not commercial enterprises, but that did not prevent them from indulging in an intense and often bitter rivalry. The hospices of Ronceval and St. Christine stood on the two principal passes over the Pyrenees, and each stridently proclaimed its own special advantages over the other. The prior of Villafranca complained to the abbot of Cluny in 1088 that a rival establishment had 'usurped his rights over pilgrims'. In 1122 the monastery of Oboña in the Asturias secured a privilege forbidding anyone to 'divert its pilgrims elsewhere', though how effective this document was is not revealed.

The variety of functions which hospices fulfilled is reflected in the thirteenth-century statutes of Aubrac in the Rouergue, about halfway between Le Puy and Congues. Its principal purpose was declared to be the assistance of 'all pilgrims passing this way towards Notre-Dame de Rocamadour, Santiago, Oviedo, St. Dominic of Estremadura, or any other sanctuaries, not least the sepulchre of Our Saviour at Jerusalem'. But it was also enjoined to 'receive, welcome, and comfort the sick, the blind, the weak, the lame, the deaf, the dumb, and the starving'. The foundation of Aubrac in about 1100 was an act of thanksgiving. Its founder and first 'commander' was a Flemish nobleman who had narrowly escaped death in a snowstorm on his return from Santiago. The community lived under the Augustinian rule but its organization was peculiar to itself. There was a small body of priests, who sung the daily office and administered the sacraments. A force of monk-knights, not unlike the Templars, patrolled the roads of the Rouergue and protected pilgrims against bandits. Side by side with them lived brothers and nuns (described as 'ladies of good birth') who administered the hospice and its charitable activities. Finally, there were lay brothers, who worked in the fields and granges of the church. In the thirteenth century it acquired considerable wealth and extensive buildings though, like most churches of southern France, it fell upon hard times during the Hundred Years' War. The Romanesque church, surrounded by the remnants of its buildings, can still be seen on the high windswept plain beside the Roman road from Lyon to Rodez.

When the hospice of Aubrac was full, the statutes provided that alms were to be distributed at the gate. In 1523 it was reported that between 1,200 and 1,500 poor gathered every day to receive their pittance. This kind of outdoor relief was commonly practised by wealthy hospices. When the roads were crowded and every bed full, it might be as much as the pilgrim could get. At St.-Léonard de Noblat and at St.-Jean d'Angély, every pilgrim received his pittance at the church door, and at Santiago itself all offerings received at the high altar before terce each Sunday were given to lepers in the city.

Life in a pilgrims' hospice was monotonous and comfortless, though most pilgrims were thankful to be there at all. Renart, in the popular twelfth-century fable, received eggs, cheese, bread and salted meat at a pilgrims' hospice. This must have been one of the wealthier establishments, for in many hospices no food was served at all, and pilgrims were expected to see to their own wants. At Villamartín, a hospice maintained by the order of Santiago, pilgrims received two loaves of bread every day; only the poorest travellers were given a little wine and meat on three days a week. A more varied diet was to be had at the hospice of Pamplona cathedral, where pilgrims ate bread and a salad, with meat or vegetables according to the season. Beds, like food, were only provided in well-endowed establishments. Elsewhere, the inmates slept on straw-covered floors:

> *Bedding ther is nothing faire,*
> *Many pilgrimez it doth apaire:*
> *Tabelez use thei non of to ete,*
> *But on the bare flore thei make ther sete.*

So sang an anonymous English pilgrim of the fourteenth century. Testators often left bedding to hospices where they had once passed a sleepless night; one of them, who died in 1297, left money to buy 'one bed, equipped with a good bolster, one cushion, and one pillow, with two good linen sheets, and a blanket'. Where there were beds, they were usually dirty, and fleas were a common incident of life in a hospice or cheap inn. A curious French phrase-book, composed for English travellers at the end of the fourteenth century, deals with this subject in some detail. The wise traveller is recommended to send his servant ahead to enquire whether there 'be no fleas, nor bugs, nor other vermin'; 'no sir', was the reply, 'for please God you will be well and comfortably lodged here—except that we suffer much from rats and mice.' There is a full section on how to converse with another traveller with whom you have just shared a bug-ridden bed: 'William, undress and wash your legs and then dry them with a towel and rub them well on account of the fleas, that they may not leap on your legs. For there is a mass of them about in the dust under the rushes....Ow, the fleas bite me so and do me great harm, for I have scratched my shoulders till the blood flows.'

'Taverns', remarked one pilgrim, 'are for the rich, and for lovers of good wine.' Life was certainly more comfortable in the inns and taverns, but it was far from luxurious, and well below the standard which even a modestly rich man of the late Middle Ages could expect in his own home. They were more likely to contain beds, but no one had a bed to himself. A room would contain several beds, each shared by two, three, or even four travellers. During the Roman Jubilee of 1350, pilgrims were paying thirteen pennies to share a bed with three other people. In England, observed the poet and diplomat Eustache Deschamps, 'no one sleeps alone but two or three to a bed in a darkened room'; the fleas were bigger in an English tavern than in the habit of a monk of Cîteaux. Deschamps preferred the more refined manners of his own country, but the inns were scarcely better on the pilgrimage roads of France. They generally served better food than the hospices, but even this could not be relied upon. A Flemish draper who visited the Holy Land in 1518 took a poor view of the food and wine served in most of the inns of south-eastern France. At Montmélian 'we were promised good wine but it was undrinkable and cost eight *gros*'; at St.-Michel de Maurienne 'we were swindled at the dinner table'; 'appalling fare' was served at Lanslebourg; it was a relief to find a good meal at last at Novalese.

On busy roads every house became an inn and rival hoteliers were ruthless in canvassing for customers. The innkeepers on the road to Santiago sent their boys out to the gates of the towns with instructions to kiss and embrace pilgrims as if they were long-lost friends, and then lead them to the inn. Those of Santiago itself sent their servants with placards as far outside the city as Barbadella or Triacastellos. In 1205 the municipality of Toulouse had occasion to reprove those hoteliers who forced pilgrims to employ their services by taking the reins out of their hands or dragging them in by the lapels.

Bitter disputes arose out of the attempt by innkeepers to claim the chattels of pilgrims who died in their houses. By custom they were certainly entitled to a share of the chattels, but what that share was was nowhere defined. One innkeeper confiscated a dead pilgrim's money and the donkey on which his children were riding; St. James caused him to break his neck in a fall, and threatened to visit the same fate on all other 'wicked innkeepers plying their trade on my road'.

Mediaeval innkeepers were not much loved. The author of the sermon *Veneranda Dies* could scarcely find words to describe them. There was no crime that they did not commit. They displayed fine wines and served cheap ones. Their fish was bad and their meat putrid. Their candles did not burn. Their beds were filthy. They gave change in bad coin. Their inns were often brothels and always dens of drunkenness. The preacher believed that they were responsible for the exaggerated and theologically unsound miracle stories which circulated amongst pilgrims. 'Truly, Judas lives in every one of them.' What was more, these vices were found not only amongst the innkeepers of Santiago but at Rome, St.-Léonard de Noblat, Le Puy, Vézelay, Tours, St.-Jean d'Angély, Mont-St.-Michel, Benevento, and Bari. Everywhere, in fact, that a few pence could be made out of gullible pilgrims. When the judgement day arrived, the saints concerned would come forward and say 'these, O Lord, are the ones who defrauded our pilgrims and practised on them all manner of iniquitous crimes.'

Cost

Inns, at least, were relatively cheap. A bed in fourteenth-century England generally cost a penny a head, which was less than the price of a simple dinner. Although guests complained frequently of extortionate rates, their protests were more often directed at the cost of meals and the pilferings of servants. Chaucer's parson, in reproving those who encouraged the misdeeds of their subordinates, did not forget 'thilke that holden hostelries' who 'sustenen the theft of their hostilers'. The hire of a horse, to name but one expense, cost more than bed and board combined: twenty-four pence to ride from Southwark to Canterbury in Chaucer's time. Many pilgrims recorded their expenses on the route, sometimes in great detail. But it is almost impossible to draw general conclusions from their experiences. Prices varied from year to year, and some pilgrims travelled in greater comfort than others. In France, where there were a large number of free hospices, travel was cheaper than it was in Germany. Rome was not accounted an expensive place, but during a Jubilee the price of a bed more than doubled and bread sold for a penny an ounce.

The pilgrimage to Jerusalem was notoriously the most expensive of all. 'Good intentions, stout heart, ready tongue, and fat purse' were needed, according to Gréffin Affagart, who knew from experience. He reckoned the cost at two hundred ducats. Santo Brasca agreed; every pilgrim 'should carry two purses, one right full of patience, and the other containing two hundred Venetian ducats', one hundred and fifty for normal expenses and fifty for emergencies. 'And for this reason', advised Affagart, 'I would recommend every pilgrim to choose his destination according to his pocket.' The most revealing statement of accounts which survives is that of Giorgio Gucci, one of the companions of Frescobaldi in 1384. Theirs was a relatively expensive expedition, consisting of six pilgrims with six servants. They travelled by ship to Alexandria and thence overland to Mount Sinai, Jerusalem and Damascus. They finally took ship at Beirut and arrived in Venice ten months after their departure. All this came to an average of one hundred and fifty gold ducats a head, or three hundred gold ducats for each man and his servant. It was made up as follows:

Fares from Venice to Alexandria and from
    Beirut to Venice
                                     96 ducats each

Fees to officials, guides, and interpreters;
    authorized tolls on roads and in churches
                                     25 ducats each

Illicit tolls and bribes to powerful officials to
    prevent them from confiscating baggage
    or interrupting their progress with red
    tape, 'which expenses the populace over
    there call "mangerie", that is, robbery'
                               $4^1/_2$ ducats each

Hire of asses, mules and camels, and of boats
    on the Nile between Alexandria and Cairo
                                     10 ducats each

Food and supplies, wine, travelling clothes,
    and tent
                                       10 ducats each

Utensils, saddlery, weapons, cutlery, candles
    and torches, inns and miscellaneous expenses
                                   $4^1/_2$ ducats each

The large sums expended on fees, bribes, and tolls are recorded in every travel diary of the period unless the traveller took the

Venetian package tour, in which case the burden fell on the unfortunate shipowner. Thomas Swynburne, the English castellan of Guines, who followed exactly the same route as Frescobaldi eight years later, spent even more on bribes, including a gratuity of three ducats to the chief cameleer 'that he might behave himself', and three ducats to the customs official who overlooked his barrel of wine.

Venetian shipowners generally charged half fares to the poor, but even this amounted to thirty ducats, a sum which was well beyond the means of most 'poor pilgrims'. One problem was that the pilgrim had to carry the entire cost of the journey with him in cash. Thus a pilgrim who lodged at the monastery of St. Etienne de Caen in the late eleventh century was found to have on him the enormous sum of thirty-three *livres,* which made him a tempting prey for bandits and pick-pockets. Frescobaldi arrived in Alexandria in 1384 with six hundred gold ducats, a truly prodigious sum, which he had hidden in the false bottom of his trunk for fear that the Arabs might confiscate it. At this primitive stage in the history of international banking, even a well-to-do pilgrim might run out of money or lose his purse to a thief, and find himself utterly dependent on the charity of others. Caesarius of Heisterbach tells the story of a young girl whose father took her to Jerusalem at the end of the twelfth century. The father died at Tyre, and his manservant absconded with all his money, leaving the girl to subsist by beggary until at length a wealthy German pilgrim was persuaded to pay for her passage home.

Gerald of Wales ran out of money in Rome in 1203, leaving all his bills unpaid. He attempted to flee, but his creditors pursued him to Bologna, where they demanded payment. No one in Bologna would lend him money unless he could find a

local inhabitant to guarantee that he would repay the lender's
agent in England. But guarantors were reluctant to step forward. Only a few weeks earlier a number of Spanish students
and priests in Bologna had been imprisoned after they had
kindly offered security for a compatriot, who had then
defaulted. Still followed by his creditors, Gerald continued
north until they were finally induced to accept a promissory
note drawn on merchants at the Troyes fair. The following year,
when Gerald returned to Rome, he called at Troyes and bought
bills of exchange worth twenty gold marks of Modena from
merchants of Bologna. Even then, he had difficulty in changing them at Faenza. With the development of a more sophisticated banking system in the fourteenth and fifteenth centuries,
the life of the wealthier traveller became easier. Hoteliers often
acted as bankers. Those of Toulouse, for example, would lend
money, transfer it to the traveller's next stopping place, guarantee debts, or accept bills of exchange. Italian pilgrims used bills
of exchange even on quite short journeys. A group of Milanese
in Rome for the Jubilee of 1390 had brought with them bills
of exchange for five hundred florins.

The variety of currencies and rates of exchange was
another pitfall for the unwary. Hoteliers would change coin
willingly, but it was well known that they gave an unfavourable
rate. In 1350 the innkeepers of Rome were offering only forty
shillings for a gold florin. When Denis Possot tried to change
four hundred French *écus* in a hostelry in Venice, he was furious to receive only 350 gold ducats and forty marks for them.
William Wey noted in 1458 that 'at Sienna a bolyner of Rome
ys worth but fyve katerynes and an halfe, and the same bolyner
ys worth at Rome, six katerynes.' The account of his pilgrimage to Jerusalem begins with a lengthy list of exchange rates,

but it was wisest, Wey thought, to bring with one a supply of coins of Tours, Candi, and Modena, as well as the ubiquitous Venetian coins which came nearest to being the international currency of the Mediterranean.

A pilgrim who intended to visit Jerusalem in the style that befitted his station, might expect to pay at least a year's income. How did he raise this money? If he was a landowner, he might sell his land to a monastery, as the soldiers of the first crusade, according to Guibert of Nogent, sold their fields, vineyards and chattels to buy armour and horses. If the land was worth more than the cost of the journey, he might give it to a monastery in return for alms to meet his expenses; in this way William Arnold parted with extensive lands to the abbey of Conques in the late eleventh century, and received a contribution of one hundred shillings towards the expenses of a pilgrimage to the Holy Land. Many 'sales' of this sort were in fact mere assignments of land as security for a loan. Monasteries readily lent money to crusaders and often to ordinary pilgrims as well. Guy I, count of Limoges, paid for his expensive pilgrimage to the Holy Land in c. 1000, by borrowing 15,000 shillings from the abbey of St. Martial. The canons of Auch cathedral paid for the pilgrimage of Raymond Aimeric II de Montesquieu in 1180. Monasteries, of course, were not the only source of loans. Thibault de Marly borrowed 140 *livres* from his lord before setting out for the Holy Land in 1173. A document of 1172 records that Josbert de Précigny, a Christian usurer of Tours, lent thirty *livres* to a pilgrim to go to the Holy Land; but Josbert died before the loan was repaid, and his heirs remitted the debt on condition that the pilgrim paid twelve pennies a year for the repose of his soul. Before his departure on the crusade with Louis IX, Joinville mortgaged his property to the moneylenders of Metz, leaving himself with only a thousand *livres* of unencumbered income, scarcely enough for the maintenance of his widowed mother. 'I was reluctant" he explained, 'to pay my way by pillage.'

If he could, a pilgrim would find a wealthy patron to participate in the benefits of his pilgrimage by contributing to the cost. This practice, an early form of vicarious pilgrimage, was regarded as extremely meritorious. 'Many rich men who never leave their own homes...are well rewarded by God for their charity to the poor', St. Bernard observed; 'whereas those who go in person to Jerusalem may come away without any reward if they have not performed some work of charity.' The expenses of Richard of St.-Vannes and all his seven hundred followers in 1026 were met by Richard II, duke of Normandy. Guy, count of Limoges, needed a huge loan from the abbey of St. Martial because he was paying the expenses of his companions, some of whom witnessed the document in which he acknowledged the loan. Similarly Henry the Lion, duke of Saxony, paid for the large company of vassals, *ministeriales,* and campfollowers whom, according to his biographer, he 'induced' to accompany him to the Holy Land in 1172. But in 1172, the large mass-pilgrimages which had been such a boon to the poorer pilgrims, were already a thing of the past.

In parts of France a lord was entitled to a feudal aid from his vassals on the occasion of his departure on pilgrimage. This was the case in Brittany, where it was stated to be immaterial whether it was a devotional pilgrimage or a crusade. The abbey of the Trinity at Vendôme was customarily expected to contribute three thousand shillings if the count of Vendôme decided to visit the Holy Land. These customary rights, where they existed, aroused considerable protest as they were often

exacted ultimately from those who could least afford to pay.
The second council of Chalons complained, as early as 813,
that pilgrimages had become occasions for levying crushing
taxation on tenants. The twelfth-century theologian, Honorius
of Autun, who was profoundly suspicious of pilgrimages, gave
it as his opinion that they were entirely valueless if the cost was
extracted by force from unwilling vassals.

The poorer pilgrims lived roughly and hoped for alms and
free hospitality. Fortunately for them, the virtue of charity was
a constantly recurring theme in sermons and devotional literature. 'Pilgrims and poor men of God' were generally singled out
as the most deserving categories, and pilgrims at least were
exempted from the ordinances against begging passed in many
towns of the Low Countries at the end of the Middle Ages.
Alms flowed into their hands from a variety of sources. A
tradesman, for instance, could normally expect a contribution
from the members of his guild, and occasionally this was a right
enshrined in the guild's statutes. If any member of the fullers'
guild of Lincoln went on a pilgrimage to Rome, the Holy
Land, or Santiago, his fellow members were required to accompany him out of the city gate as far as Queen's Cross and to
give him at least a halfpenny each. The Dominican Felix Faber
received a grant from his order. Municipalities could often be
induced to help out a penniless pilgrim if only, as the town
clerk of Damme put it, 'that he might not stay with us longer.'
However, it is likely that most alms were given by other pilgrims. The author of the sermon *Veneranda Dies,* who had harsh
words to say of pilgrims who carried money on them, made an
exception in favour of those who did so only to distribute it in
alms. This may seem a somewhat pointless exercise, but we hear
of one Heimrad, a priest of Hesse at the end of the tenth cen-

tury, who, as soon as he received alms gave them to another pilgrim more needy than himself. Gerald of Aurillac was famous for the largesse which he displayed on his biennial pilgrimages to Rome, and his biographer naively remarks that other pilgrims assembled at the side of the road when they had been warned of his coming. Certainly, the generosity of some pilgrims to others was an open invitation to fraud. On the roads to Santiago, professional beggars painted blood on their arms, and simulated lameness or leprosy, waving palms of Jericho in the air to arouse the sympathy of passing travellers.

According to his ninth-century biographer, the wanderer and hermit St. Cyran refused to support himself by begging on his way to Rome. Instead he worked in the vineyards on the route, carrying the grapes to the wine-presses. Not many pilgrims worked their way to the sanctuaries, because it took so long to reach one's destination. Brother Giles, the first Franciscan friar to visit the Holy Land, took pride in the fact that he would 'never eat the bread of idleness'. He fetched water from the wells and sold it in the streets of Ancona, and he carried bodies to the cemeteries at Acre. 'He was not ashamed to humble himself, and stoop to any menial and honest work that he could get.' Felix Faber first visited the Holy Land as tutor and companion to the son of a Bavarian nobleman. Three years later he returned as chaplain to John Truchsess von Waldburg, whom he had encountered at Ulm before his departure.

Less respectable but very much more lucrative was the practice of engaging in commerce on the route. This was viewed with disfavour by the Church because it derogated from the spiritual quality of the pilgrimage, and also by the state, for many of these amateur merchants claimed a pilgrim's exemption from tolls. The English, Charlemagne complained to Offa king of Mercia, were the principal offenders. 'True pilgrims travelling to Rome for the love of God and the salvation of their souls may pass in peace. But if there are any amongst them who serve Mammon and not God, then they must pay the ordinary tolls.' The *Siete Partidas* of Alfonso IX repeated this injunction in the thirteenth century. Penitential pilgrims were strictly forbidden to turn their punishment into a profitable venture by selling their wares on the road. The strong implication was that trade was intrinsically base and for this reason alone incompatible with pilgrimage. Hence the request of Philip the Fair to the pope that ships carrying troops to the projected crusade should be forbidden to carry merchandise as well, lest God's disfavour be brought down upon the expedition. Nevertheless pilgrims of otherwise impeccable motives surrendered to the temptation. When St. Willibald left England in the summer of 721 he brought with him a boat-load of goods to sell in Rouen, and paid for his journey to Rome out of the proceeds. On his way back from Jerusalem, Willibald smuggled some balsam past the Arab customs officials at Tyre in a jar with a false bottom, remarking to his companion that had he been discovered he would have 'suffered there and then a martyr's death'. Plainly, Willibald saw nothing wrong in his behaviour. Neither did St. Godric, the half-legendary hermit of Finchale, whose biographer calls him *mercator simul et peregrinus,* merchant and pilgrim combined. Many pilgrims found it impossible to resist the temptation to buy spices and precious cloth in Jerusalem and sell them for much more at home. The Arab traders of Palestine 'never sleep when the pilgrims are in Jerusalem', a fifteenth-century writer noted with disgust. Even in the church of the Holy Sepulchre itself they set up their stalls and haggled with pilgrims over beads, jewels and silk cloth.

The shrewdest pilgrim, however, could not have hoped to recover more than a part of the two hundred ducats which his journey had cost him. Against the undeniable excitement of discovering an alien world, he had to set not only the cost, but the difficulties which followed a year's absence from home, the hardships of a long journey, and the possibility that he might never return. Few men would have disagreed with that experienced pilgrim Eberhard of Würtemburg, whom Felix Faber consulted before setting out on his first pilgrimage.

'There are three acts in a man's life which no one should advise him either to do or not to do. The first is to contract matrimony, the second is to go to the wars, and the third is to visit the Holy Sepulchre. These things are all good in themselves, but they may turn out ill, in which case he who gave the advice will be blamed as if he were the cause of it.'

12

The Sanctuary

Pilgrims were greeted at their destination by a scene of raucous tumult. On the feast day of the patron saint a noisy crowd gathered in front of the church. Pilgrims mingled with jugglers and conjurers, souvenir sellers and pickpockets. Hawkers shouted their wares and rickety food stalls were surrounded by mobs of hungry travellers. Pilgrims hobbling on crutches or carried on stretchers tried to force their way through the crush at the steps of the church. Cries of panic were drowned by bursts of hysterical laughter from nearby taverns, while beggars played on horns, zithers, and tambourines. The noise and vulgarity which accompanied a major pilgrimage changed little from the fourth century, when Augustine of Hippo spoke of 'licentious revels', to the fifteenth, when the French preacher Olivier Maillard demanded an end to these sinful carnivals.

The practice of holding fairs outside churches on the feast days of the saints was too deeply engrained to be eradicated by a handful of moral reformers. Any annual gathering of large crowds was certain to attract merchants and itinerant salesmen. Many of them were selling guide-books, lead badges, or candles. In the eleventh century one merchant expected to make his fortune by selling wax for *ex-voto* offerings outside the abbey of Conques, and many of those who bought official monopolies of the sale of candles or badges did make fortunes. Every kind of wares was sold outside church doors. Deorman, a rich London merchant of the late twelfth century, used to bring his entire stock of silks and spices to Bury on the feast of St. Edmund. Some visitors came solely on account of the fair, like the servant-boy mentioned by Reginald of Durham, who attended the celebrations of St. Cuthbert's day in order to find a good price for his horn. Others had both purposes in mind, and thus, remarks Reginald, they were able to atone for a day of usurious commerce simply by crossing to the other side of the cathedral square. The fairs, and their attendant jollifications, were viewed by the clergy with mixed feelings. Augustine had uncompromisingly condemned them, but his contemporary and friend, Paulinus of Nola, permitted them with reluctance on the ground that misguided piety was better than no piety at all. On the whole it was the latter view which prevailed. Indeed the fairs were often held with the permission of the clergy on land belonging to the church. The monks of St.-Denis drew considerable revenues from the Lendit fairs, which were timed to coincide with displays of the abbey's relics. So long as this remained a typical arrangement there was little point in the constant complaints of ecclesiastical synods against the pollution of churchyards on feast-days by 'games and competitions, rowdy singing, loose women, and lewd songs'.

The inside of the church was almost as noisy as the outside. Here the scenes of mass enthusiasm were reserved for the vigils of the saints, when pilgrims passed the entire night in the nave or by the shrine. The sick were carried in on litters or stretchers, and it was during vigils that most miraculous cures occurred. Vigils were always held on the eve of the saint's feast-day, but in some churches they occurred more often. At the shrine of St. Wulfran in the Norman abbey of Fontenelle, there seems to have been a vigil every Saturday night. Evesham too had vigils on Saturdays 'and scarcely a Saturday passed when some unfortunate was not freed from the bonds of sickness.' Except on official 'vigil-days', no one was permitted to watch by the shrine at night. At Mont-St.-Michel not even the night watchman was allowed into the basilica before the morning bell had rung, and at Santiago the doors were locked at sunset. When Pontius de St.-Gilles and his companions arrived in Santiago at night, only a miracle enabled them to enter the cathedral.

The atmosphere which enveloped the shrine of a saint was at its most intense during the vigil of his or her feast-day. 'Let us prostrate our bodies before their relics,' urged the Canterbury monk Eadmer; 'let us bend our knees to the ground and throw ourselves before them in supplication. What saint in God's court could fail to be moved by such devotion?' At the end of the eleventh century a rich man whose son lay dying came to light a candle at the altar of St. Egwin at Evesham.

> 'Humbly inclining his head to the ground, he made his offering, adored his God, and prayed with great intensity to St. Edwin for his son's recovery. With tears in his eyes he passed the whole day and the following night in vigil and prayer. Candle in hand, he knelt on the ground, beating his breast until morning came. Then he returned to see his son.'

At Rocamadour the sound of lamentations drowned the words of the Mass. At Canterbury, tears of sorrow and moans of gratitude mingled with the howls and the shrieks of the sick and the newly healed. Crowds pushed forward to investigate as each new miracle was announced, and the clergy had to force their way through to examine the patient for themselves. At the back of the church the less devout pilgrims gathered in their national groups trying to sleep in spite of the noise and the close heat from thousands of candles. Some of them had brought bottles of wine with them, and as they became more inebriated they began to shout abuse at each other or broke into community singing. At Santiago on the eve of St. James's day 'all sorts of noises and languages can be heard together, discordant shouts, barbarous singing in German, English, Greek, and every other language under the sun.' The 'worldly songs' which so infuriated the clergy of Santiago were a familiar sound wherever pilgrims gathered in large numbers. At Conques the litany was drowned by 'rustic sing-songs', and a special chapter was summoned at the end of the tenth century to consider this 'absurd and detestable practice'. It concluded, very typically, that pilgrims should be allowed to express their devotion in the only way known to them, even though this might strike cultivated persons as 'inappropriate and rude'. Some sanctuaries, like Durham cathedral, employed muscular stewards to keep order. Others, especially towards the end of the Middle Ages, tried to suppress vigils altogether, or else strove manfully to impose some order on them. But the attempt was a failure, and disorderly vigils remained an inseparable part of the cult of the saints.

At dawn on the feast-day itself, the congregation was turned out of the church, and the pilgrims returned to their lodgings. Auxiliaries cleaned up the mess and prepared for the services of the day. At these services the crowds were larger still, for the pilgrims of the night before were joined by most of the local inhabitants. The simplest techniques of crowd control seem to have been beyond the clergy of the sanctuaries, and accidents were frequent. This was the reason given by abbot Suger for rebuilding the abbey church of St.-Denis in the 1130s.

> 'As the numbers of the faithful increased', Suger wrote, 'the crowds at St.-Denis grew larger and larger until the old church began to burst at the seams. On feast-days it was always full to overflowing, and the mass of struggling pilgrims spilt out of every door. Not only were some pilgrims unable to get in, but many of those who were already inside were forced out by those in front of them. As they fought their way towards the holy relics to kiss and worship them, they were so densely packed that none of them could so much as stir a foot. A man could only stand like a marble statue, paralysed, and free only to cry out aloud. Meanwhile the women in the crowd were in such intolerable pain, crushed between strong men as if in a wine-press, that death seemed to dance before their eyes. The blood was drained from their faces and they screamed as if they were in the throes of childbirth. Some of them were trodden under-foot and had to be lifted above the heads of the crowd by kindly men, and passed to the back of the church and thence to the fresh air. In the cloister outside, wounded pilgrims lay gasping their last breath. As for the monks who were in charge of the reliquaries, they were often obliged to escape with the relics through the windows. When first, as a schoolboy, I heard of these things from my monastic teachers, I was saddened and conceived an earnest desire to improve matters.'

It was the same in Jerusalem, where hundreds fainted in the airless crush outside the basilica of the Holy Sepulchre on Easter Friday. The author of the *Liber Sancti Jacobi* was present one day at St.-Gilles when the crush developed into a riot between French and Gascon pilgrims resulting in at least one death. There were eighteen deaths when the head of St. Martial was displayed in the presence of the Black Prince in 1364. Such incidents were so common that the clergy of St.-Gilles and Santiago received special permission to reconsecrate their church immediately with holy water, instead of following the usual elaborate ceremony.

Nor were these the only perils which threatened pilgrims as they stood squashed together before the shrine. There were few exits and fire precautions were non-existent. Thus, when fire broke out in the abbey of Vézelay during the vigil of the feast of St. Mary Magdalene, 1,127 pilgrims were burned to death. Pickpockets throve. In a typical day at Worcester, one pilgrim lost sixteen shillings to pickpockets, another lost forty. At Fécamp a pilgrim standing on a box to police the crowd had his pocket picked as he did so. Large crowds were not only uncomfortable and liable to be robbed, but usually unable to see or hear what was going on. During the Canterbury Jubilee of 1420, the preacher had to repeat his sermon in four different places so that every pilgrim could hear it.

Public exhibitions of relics were rarer than vigils and, perhaps for that reason, provoked the most spectacular of all outbursts of mass piety. They generally marked moments of national or local crisis. Thus, when Philip Augustus departed on crusade in 1191, the royal abbey of St.-Denis exposed its relics on the high altar, where they were inspected by the queen mother, the archbishop of Rheims, and a cortège of dignitaries.

Every serious epidemic occasioned a display of relics. When plague was decimating the population of Rouen in 1053, the body of St. Wulfran was carried to the city from Fontenelle. The head of St. Martial was publicly exhibited in 1388, the reasons given being that Christendom was divided by the papal schism, that the harvest had failed, and that Limoges had just endured a close siege. The diary of a Parisian citizen in the first half of the fifteenth century reveals that relics were brought out of the churches almost every time that reverses on the battle-fields of northern France threatened the city's precarious food supply. In 1423, for example, the war was going badly and famine threatened. The bishop of Paris 'had processions made for forty consecutive days, praying that God might, by His grace, bring peace to Christendom and calm the weather which had prevented the sowing of the crops for four months past.' In the summer of 1427, when the Seine broke its banks, some five or six hundred people from the suburban villages wound processionally through the streets of the city, barefooted, singing hymns, carrying banners of the saints, and calling on God to have mercy on their vineyards. Lesser catastrophes were marked in much the same way. The monks of Durham used their relics to prevent fires in the town from spreading to the cathedral. Those of St.-Gilles hoped to restore their depleted finances by displaying their relics, and proposed to commission an unusually costly reliquary for the purpose. Their hopes were disappointed in the event but they were by no means absurd, for exhibitions of relics could be relied upon to provoke enthusiasm degenerating at times into violence. The crowd which gathered at Bury one Whitsun was so impressed by the relics of St. Edmund that it forced the preacher to show them again. The preacher took this in good part, unlike the monks of Conques who refused to display the relics of St. Foy except at fixed intervals, thus causing riots outside their church. Urban II was asked to forbid the populace to display the relics of Conques without the consent of their owners.

In normal times, displays were rare. The head of St. Martial was displayed only once in seven years, as was the celebrated foreskin of Christ at Charroux. Other churches never displayed their relics. This surprising reticence dates from the beginning of the thirteenth century and was largely due to one of the pronouncements of the Lateran council of 1215. Faced with a number of impostors who claimed to have stolen relics while they were on public display, this council and its successors forbade the exhibition of relics except on feast-days, and then only in a reliquary. Amongst other things, this required a new kind of reliquary, like the one used at Limoges in 1388 with little doors in the side which opened to reveal the head of St. Martial. The legislation of the thirteenth century had been intended to prevent thefts, real or imagined. Its actual result was to diminish the visual element of the cult of relics, and to invite doubts as to the authenticity or even the existence of some relics. An inquiry into the affairs of the abbey of Vézelay in the 1260s concluded that its revenues had declined owing to the failure of the monks to exhibit the relics of St. Mary Magdalene, thus reinforcing 'certain hesitations and scruples as to the authenticity of the said relics'. Arnold von Harff's doubts about the body of St. James were confirmed when the clergy of Santiago refused to lift the lid of the sarcophagus. 'Any one who does not believe that the body of St. James lies under that altar', they told him, 'will certainly go as mad as a dog.' By this time, however, most churches had abandoned their objections to regular exhibitions of relics. In 1424 Martin V permitted churches to show their relics to the faithful whenever they wished, subject to the characteristic proviso that they were not to do it merely to satisfy the idle curiosity of pilgrims. This was followed by a succession of well-attended public exhibitions, notably in Germany. The visual element was once more respectable.

13

Rome

When the emperor Aurelian rebuilt the walls of Rome in the year 271 he defined the outer limits of the city for sixteen centuries. The old walls, traditionally attributed to Servius Tullius, had long outlived their usefulness. From every gate of the city thin ribbons of houses, the slums of the poor and the residences of the nobility, had extended into the suburbs, defenceless against attack from outside. Now they were contained by walls eleven miles in length, which remained the principal defence of the city throughout the Middle Ages. Rome, like many mediaeval cities, occupied but a fraction of the space enclosed by its ancient walls. But although they no longer marked the true limits of the city, Aurelian's walls determined its spiritual geography. Roman law forbade the burial of the dead within the city. Because they believed in the resurrection of the dead, Christians found the practice of cremation repugnant, and they buried their martyrs in deep graves along the roads which led out of the city.

The tradition of the Roman Church held that St. Paul had been buried on the Via Ostia, and St. Peter in the pagan necropolis on the Vatican Hill, north-west of the city. In the reign of Constantine their obscure graves were covered by great basilicas. On the Vatican Hill a cruciform church arose with great speed, arranged (at the expense of all architectural convenience) on an east-west axis, such that the high altar stood directly above the remains of the apostle. It symbolized the triumph over paganism by obliterating part of the circus of Caligula, where many of the early martyrdoms had occurred. St. Paul's was built at a more leisurely pace, and was said to have been even finer. Both of them had broad naves with double aisles on either side. Despite the continual process of repair and reconstruction, they preserved this form throughout the Middle Ages. At the southern extremity of the city, Constantine donated to the Church a tract of land within the walls, which had once belonged to the Laterani family and was now part of the estate of his wife. It contained a decayed palace which was now reconstructed as the papal residence, and a cavalry school which was transformed into the Lateran basilica. Such were the three great sanctuaries of mediaeval Rome.

They were far from being the only sanctuaries. The persecutions of the third century had left Rome richer in martyrs than any other city. The *Depositio Martyrum,* compiled in 354, lists thirty-two martyrs whose anniversaries were remembered by the Christian community. A revised list, drawn up at the beginning of the fifth century, added some seventy more. Most of them were buried in extensive underground cemeteries outside the walls, such as the celebrated Calixtine cemetery and the cemetery *'ad catacumbas'* on the Appian Way, which subsequently gave its name to all the others. Before the peace of the Church, the catacombs were used on the feast-days of the martyrs, when services were held by their tombs. It is unlikely that they were ever used as refuges during the persecutions, for the Roman authorities were well aware of their existence, and kept them under constant surveillance. When the emperor Valerian issued his decree against the Christians in 258, the catacombs were among the first places to be searched and pope Sixtus II, who was found worshipping in the Calixtine cemetery, was beheaded with six of his deacons. After the conversion of Constantine the catacombs began to fall into decay. Now that Christians could worship openly, they built imposing churches within the city, where the ordinary services of the church were held. In the course of the fourth century, a number of underground galleries collapsed, thus making some parts completely inaccessible.

Only the interest of pilgrims saved the catacombs from oblivion. Graffiti on the walls record the visits of pilgrims from Greece and north Africa, Spain and southern France. 'Holy Souls, pray for a safe crossing for us...', 'grant us a safe journey over the sea.' It became fashionable to be buried there, and Romans used to amuse themselves on holidays by groping their way along the dark passages. When St. Jerome was in Rome as a young man, he used to go with other students on Sundays to explore them.

> 'We used to go down into the catacombs buried deep
> in the ground. Inside, all was silence and graves were
> everywhere around us. It was so dark that at times I had
> the impression of descending bodily into Hell....Only
> the occasional filtering light broke the horrid darkness
> as we stumbled onward with faltering steps, immersing
> ourselves in the black night. I recalled the line of Virgil
> which goes "Horror ubique animos, simul ipsa silentia
> terrent." '

The preservation of the catacombs was largely the work of Damasus, who ascended the papal throne in 366. Damasus was

not himself a Roman, but a Spaniard who had come to Rome
during the reign of his predecessor. He is famous as the founder
of the papal archives, as the patron of St. Jerome, and above all
as the restorer of the catacombs. The crumbling galleries were
rebuilt, and new staircases installed. Fallen masonry was
removed, and forgotten galleries reopened. Skylights were
made in the ceilings, to reduce the oppressive darkness of
which Jerome had complained. Damasus's greatest work was to
begin the long process by which the graves of the martyrs were
identified and marked with inscriptions, instead of being
known only from unreliable local traditions. Frescoes were
restored and chapels were built where services could be held on
feast days. New burials, which required extensive works and did
irreparable damage, were now strongly discouraged. When
Prudentius visited the catacombs a few years afterwards, he
found them greatly improved since Jerome's youth.

> 'A sloping path led into the ground, doubling back on
> itself again and again, reaching deep unlit chambers. The
> daylight scarcely lit up the outer porch of the first
> chamber. As we penetrated further, the darkness inten-
> sified, but now and again it was broken by a simple ray
> of light from a skylight pierced in the ceiling. In the
> middle of the dark maze formed by poky chambers and
> narrow galleries, a little daylight was thus brought into
> the bowels of the earth. Even in the deepest chambers,
> it was possible to follow the strained glow of the absent
> sun.'

The churches within the city had to wait three centuries
before acquiring the remains of the saints to which they were
dedicated. The Roman Church had originally held the graves

of the dead to be inviolate. But a succession of destructive
sieges, from the Gothic siege of 410 to the Lombard one of
756, forced the popes to reconsider the matter. In 537–8 many
of the most important cemeteries were pillaged by the Arian
Goths. In the catacombs of the two Via Salaria, where the
Gothic army had been encamped, the tale of destruction was
told in the inscriptions left by those who came to repair them
afterwards. 'Here the fury of the enemy violated the sanctuary
of the saints.' 'Here the blind rage of the invader violated the
church and carried off its treasure.' Now that the liturgical cult
of the saints was concentrated in the great urban basilicas, it was
natural that the Romans should wish to translate their relics
from the catacombs to more formal and imposing sanctuaries
within the city. The martyrs Primus and Felicianus were
removed from their graves on the Via Nomentana as early as
the 460s, and reburied in the church of S. Stefano Rotondo.
Leo II (682–3) built a new basilica in Rome and translated to
it three martyrs from the catacomb on the Porto road. The
process was greatly accelerated after the Lombard siege of 756,
when the major cemeteries suffered appalling devastations.
Some of the bodies, including that of St. Cecilia, were carried
off to Pavia. Others were destroyed. At the accession of Paul I
in 757, the catacombs had 'fallen into ruin as a result of neglect
and cupidity. The bodies had been desecrated or stolen, the surrounding area utterly desolated.' It was Paul who began the
long business of distributing the relics among the titular
churches and monasteries of the city, an operation which continued until well into the ninth century.

Such relics as remained in the catacombs were translated,
stolen or simply forgotten. At least one of the deacons who had
charge of them carried on a vigorous trade in the relics of the

lesser-known martyrs. The powerful ecclesiastical lords of northern Europe, no longer content to have mere *brandea* beneath their altars, attempted by fair means or foul to acquire some of the surplus relics of Rome. Some of them arrived with letters from the emperor, and were able to obtain important relics by applying political pressure to an enfeebled papacy. The export of bodies to the north had reached such alarming proportions by the middle of the ninth century that the populace, which regarded these saints as its protectors, began to object. The abbot of St. Médard of Soissons had some difficulty in escaping with the body of St. Sebastian in 826, even though the pope had been prevailed upon to part with it. Eight years later the rumour that St. Alexander was to be carried off to Friesing was enough to provoke serious riots.

By this time scarcely any of the more significant saints were still buried in the catacombs. Only the apostles were left in their original graves. But after a particularly disastrous Arab raid in 846, Leo IV extended the walls of Rome across the Tiber to swallow up the Vatican Hill. Some thirty years later, St. Paul's was in turn surrounded by its own walls. In the space of a century, the spiritual geography of the city had been transformed. No longer the centre of a network of cemeteries and grave-yards, Rome had become a museum of relics, second only to Constantinople. After the sack of Constantinople by the fourth crusade, Rome stood unrivalled.

Impressions of Rome, 1100–1250

But Rome was more than a museum. Few pilgrims, even in the obdurately anti-classical mood of the 'dark ages', could look on the city of the apostles and blind themselves to the capital of a lost civilization. In the eleventh and twelfth centuries it still inspired a romantic fascination which would have marked it out as a resort of travellers even if St. Peter and St. Paul had never been there and the popes had never established it as the headquarters of a religious bureaucracy. One pilgrim recalled his first sight of the city 'from a far off hill beyond which lay those innumerable palaces bristling with a cornfield of towers; I was overwhelmed, and imagined how Caesar would have seen it from that spot.' Countless other pilgrims following the northern road and reaching the summit of Monte Mario must have experienced the same feelings and sung the words of the famous hymn which began:

> *O Roma nobilis, orbis et domina,*
> *Cunctarum urbium excellentissima.*

But the grandeur of distance disappeared as the pilgrims approached the city, and many of them may well have been dismayed by the closer sight of the shrunken mediaeval Rome in the centre of the vast open space enclosed by its ancient walls. When Master Gregory, who had been so exhilarated by the distant view of the cornfield of towers, reached the centre of the city he saw in it a certain sign that the world itself was drawing to an end. No one was indifferent to Rome. Many hated it. Few were as uncritically enthusiastic about it as the author of *O Roma Nobilis.* Rome, proclaimed William of Malmesbury, 'once mistress of the earth seems slight nowadays in comparison with its glorious past. And the Romans, whose ancestors wore the toga and ruled the earth, are now a miserable lazy race who live by selling justice for gold and putting price tags on every canon of the law of the Church.' The English satirist Walter Map knew it only as the seat of the papal

curia, whose name stood for 'Radix Omnium Malorum Avaritia'—
greed is the root of all evil.

The admiration of mediaeval poets was tempered by their
admission that the beauty of Rome was the beauty of the past,
the pathetic contrast between her noble classical ruins and her
modern degeneracy. This feeling was voiced by Hildebert archbishop of Tours in a famous poem, in which he reflected that
'not even the decay of years, nor fire nor sword have eclipsed
the splendour of her ascendance':

> Par tibi Roma nihil, cum sis prope tota ruina
> Quam magna fueris integra fracta doces.

> Nothing can equal Rome, even Rome in ruins.
> Your ruins themselves speak louder than your former
> greatness.

Hildebert had first seen Rome as the Norman leader Robert
Guiscard left it in 1084. In the course of the fighting and the
three days of plundering that followed, the quarters around the
Colosseum and the Lateran, the districts of St. Silvester and St.
Lawrence in Lucina were razed to the ground. Rome bore the
marks of its violent history until the fifteenth century, and for
many years writers describing it quoted Hildebert's words with
approval.

The architectural revolution which transformed the face of
northern Europe and of the great cities of northern Italy left
Rome virtually untouched. The popes of the twelfth and thirteenth centuries were great restorers and decorators of existing
buildings. The churches of S. Maria in Cosmedin and S. Maria
in Trastevere were sumptuously redecorated in this period, the

church of St. Lawrence Without the Walls greatly enlarged. But the only entirely new building of any importance erected before the fifteenth century was the Gothic church of S. Maria sopre Minerva, begun under Nicholas III in 1280.

St. Peter's was the principal attraction. Although damaged in each successive riot and siege it was on each occasion tolerably restored. Until the beginning of the thirteenth century it was still possible to enter the *confessio* or shrine of St. Peter beneath the high altar, and thirteen lamps burned perpetually before it. But towards the end of the twelfth century a new relic began to rival the body of the apostle. This was the *sudarium* of Veronica, believed to be the napkin on which Christ had wiped his face on the road to Calvary, leaving the impression of his features. How St. Peter's came to possess this relic is not at all clear, but it had certainly been there since the eighth century, when it was one of the subsidiary relics kept in the *confessio*. In 1208 Innocent III instituted a liturgical station at the hospital of S. Spirito on the first Sunday after the Epiphany, and ordered that the *sudarium* should be taken from St. Peter's on that day and displayed in a special reliquary 'of gold and silver and precious stones, so constructed that it might be carried solemnly in processions'. In response to the clamorous demand of pilgrims the relic was displayed at regular intervals, and in 1289 the pope conferred a generous indulgence on the 'precious image that the faithful call the Veronica'.

It was only in the eleventh century that the Lateran palace and basilica began to command as much attention as St. Peter's. The *'Sancta Sanctorum'*, which was the private chapel of the popes, was the scene of some of the most solemn services of the Roman calendar, particularly those which occurred around Easter. It contained a formidable collection of relics, notably the heads of both apostles preserved in splendid reliquaries on the main altar. The ark of the covenant was there (it attracted a certain amount of cynical comment), as were the tablets of Moses, the rod of Aaron, a golden urn of manna, the tunic of the Virgin, various pieces of clothing worn by John the Baptist including his hair shirt, the five loaves and two fishes which fed the five thousand, and the table used at the Last Supper. The chapel of St. Lawrence in the papal palace contained other spectacular relics, including the foreskin and umbilical cord of Christ preserved in a gold and jewelled crucifix filled with oil; and a piece of the true cross enclosed in a small reliquary of gold and silver with engraved panels.

The superb processions held at Easter impressed upon more than one onlooker the contrast between the mediaeval papacy and its classical setting. After the service in S. Maria Maggiore, the pope passed in procession to St. Peter's and thence back to the Lateran palace by a route which took it past some of the city's finest classical monuments. A contemporary described the papal train passing 'beneath the triumphal arches of Theodosius, Valentinain, and Gratian, past the Capitol and the Mamertine prison,...under the triumphal arch [of Severus], between the arch of Janus and the Temple of Concord. Then they walk between the forum of Trajan [i.e. Nerva] and the forum of Caesar...crossing the very spot where Simon Magus fell near the Temple of Romulus....Finally they reach the arch of Titus and Vespasian which is called the seven-branched candlestick...and so past the Colosseum to the Lateran.' Many of these monuments were in an advanced state of decay. In particular most of them were disfigured by being converted into fortresses. Master Gregory's abiding impression of Rome was that of a 'cornfield of towers' for it was the practice of the noble families of Rome to build towers on top of the classical monuments from which to assail their enemies in times of civil war. The arch of Titus was called the 'seven-branched candlestick' because it formed part of the fortress of the Frangipani family who had covered it with fortifications. The enemies of Gregory VII accused him of carrying out this practice to excess, adding battlements to every bridge, tower, or triumphal arch in the city. Even churches were not exempt, for St. Peter's was fortified by the mob in 1145. The lamentable condition of the arch of Severus is revealed by the judgement of Innocent III in a lawsuit between its two owners. Half of it had been converted into the church of St. Sergius and St. Bacchus while the other half was the property of a certain Ciminus who had built on it a small embattled tower with an observation platform. In times of peace many proprietors found a commercial use for their towers by charging pilgrims for the right to climb up and enjoy a panoramic view of Rome. The monastery of S. Silvestro in Capite owned the column of Marcus Aurelius, which was leased out for this purpose and provided them with a lucrative source of revenue.

Some attempt, it is true, was made to preserve the monuments. The senate, which restored itself during the republican revolution of 1143, threatened with death all persons who defaced or damaged the column of Trajan, 'so that it should remain as it stands to honour the Roman people as long as the world endures.' But the task was made impossible by the looting of builders. To the depradations of the builders were added those of prelates and even pilgrims, who met their need for marble by removing it from the classical monuments. The churches of Hildesheim were adorned with marble from Rome, looted by bishop Bernard. Desiderius abbot of Monte

Cassino did the same when he was rebuilding his abbey church. Even the canons of Durham cathedral knew that marble was easily to be had in Rome and asked a pilgrim to obtain enough to cover the floor of their church. Many pilgrims who came to Rome for reasons of piety or ecclesiastical business found their interest unexpectedly aroused by the visible testimony of its classical past. The wealthier amongst them took to collecting antiquities. Abbot Suger of St.-Denis confessed that he would gladly have removed the columns from the baths of Diocletian and shipped them to France for the adornment of his abbey. Henry of Blois, bishop of Winchester and brother of king Stephen, obtained the pope's permission to buy up old statues and take them back to England. John of Salisbury, who was in Rome at the time, recorded the astonishment of the papal courtiers at the sight of the bishop 'conspicuous by his long beard and philosophical solemnity, engaged in buying up idols carved by pagan hands'.

The most celebrated classical monument in Rome was the equestrian statue of Marcus Aurelius, which in the Middle Ages was generally believed to represent the emperor Constantine. The statue emerges from obscurity in 962, when a rebellious official is recorded to have been hanged by the hair from it. At that time it stood in front of the Lateran palace. Although scholarly opinion held that the horseman was Constantine, unlearned pilgrims, encouraged by their guide-books, permitted themselves unlimited speculation as to his identity. The most popular guide-book gave it as its opinion that the statue commemorated a great hero who had saved the city from its enemies in the days of the republic. This hero had ridden bareback into the besieging army and kidnapped the enemy king, 'which is why we see today a statue of a man without a saddle, his right hand stretched out as it was when he seized the king.' The English visitor, Master Gregory, was perplexed by the variety of opinions. The cardinals called it Marcus or Quirinus, the Romans called it Constantine, and the pilgrims Theoderic. Each of them justified his opinion by reciting some popular story from Roman history. All, however, were agreed that it was a 'memorable work, executed with remarkable skill'. They paid it the compliment of copying it when they returned home. In western France equestrian statues of Constantine can still be seen on the west fronts of churches of Chateauneuf, Melle, Civray, Parthenay-le-Vieux, and elsewhere.

In their attempt to identify all the churches and classical ruins the pilgrims were assisted by guide-books which told them in a reasonably digestible form everything they needed to know. The book which held the field from the twelfth century to the fourteenth was the *Mirabilia Urbis Romae,* the 'Wonders of Rome'. It is a remarkable work, which testifies both to the passionate interest of the Romans in their past, and to their profound ignorance of it. Nevertheless, few guide-books have ever enjoyed a greater reputation. It appeared in innumerable Latin editions, and was translated and versified in every language. Each century brought it up to date, and amended it in accordance with current tastes. The *Mirabilia* is a mine of extraordinary information. 'The walls of Rome', it begins, 'have 361 towers, 49 bastions, and 12 gates. They are 22 miles in circumference.' Continuing the statistical survey of the city in a tone reminiscent of tour guides in French public monuments, it lists the 12 gates, the 12 triumphal arches, the 7 hills, and the 10 baths. It gives the names of the palaces, theatres, churches, bridges, and cemeteries. Then the tone changes. The author discusses the legend of the statue of Constantine and tells his readers a few anecdotes about the principal buildings of Rome. At the church of S. Maria in Ara Coeli he recounts how the emperor Octavian had a vision there of the Virgin and child and resolved that he would refuse to be deified by the senate. As pilgrims wandered through the city they were given garbled versions of the persecution of Decius, the story of Anthony and Cleopatra, and other well-known incidents from classical history. Sometimes the author takes liberties with his classical myths. In one version Rome is founded not by Romulus and Remus but by Noah, who landed there after the flood and left behind his son Janus, from whom all Roman emperors were descended. The pages are filled with a nostalgic feeling for the Roman past, scattered with a few summary aesthetic judgements on its monuments. 'The Capitol was once the capital of the world; there the consuls and senators governed the whole earth.' 'The circus of Priscus Tarquinius is very fine; the seats are stepped in such a way that no Roman's head obstructed the view of the person behind him.' But it is not the learned nostalgia of a Gibbon that pervades the *Mirabilia*. It is something more earnest and more naive, a desire for knowledge without the means of gratifying it. 'All these temples and palaces', the guide concludes, '…we have described as we have read of them in old chronicles, heard of them from tradition, and seen them with our own eyes.'

One of the more sophisticated travellers who read the *Mirabilia* was Master Gregory, an Englishman who visited Rome at the beginning of the thirteenth century. Gregory, perhaps wisely, did not allow the *Mirabilia* to colour his judgement, and spoke with contempt of the unlettered pilgrims who believed all that they were told. Instead, he relied on the opinions of the 'cardinals and clergy of Rome' and on a small tract on 'The Seven Wonders of the World', *De Septem Miraculis Mundi,* which was generally, though wrongly, attributed to Bede. Standing on the Capitoline Hill, Gregory was struck by the sight of a nude statue of Venus in Pavian marble, a thing quite outside his experience, which prompted him to quote a few lines from Ovid's *Ara Amandi.* 'This inexplicably perfect work of craftsmanship', he wrote, 'looks more like a living figure than a statue. The face is a deep purple colour as if it were blushing at its own nudity, or as if a trickle of blood were flowing through its snow-white mouth.' Gregory found the sight of this statue so compelling that he visited it three times, even though his hospice was more than two miles away. Continuing with his tour, he visited the baths of Diocletian, which had so impressed abbot Suger, and agreed that they were the finest classical buildings in the city. 'I cannot do justice in writing to their ample dimensions and superb proportions. They are so large that one cannot take them in in one view. The columns that crown them are so tall that their summits were beyond a pebble's throw.' Gregory was informed by the cardinals that it would have taken a hundred men an entire year to build them. 'But I shall say no more for if I were to tell you the truth, you would not believe me.' The waterworks of Rome, although but a shadow of what they had once been, were still imposing enough to an Englishman. Gregory examined the Claudian aqueduct and observed that 'the river Tiber, though all right for horses, is no good for men and indeed positively poisonous. Wherefore in four parts of the city, ancient artificial aqueducts bring fresh water in.' He visited the sulphur baths near the aqueduct, paid the set charge to the attendant, and tested the water with his fingers; but the disgusting smell of the sulphur was too much for him and he left without bathing. Decay is a recurring theme in Gregory's work and provoked some bitter reflections. He was disgusted by the pillaging of marble from the Domus Augustana on the Palatine Hill. The neglect or mutilation of statues in the forum of Nerva shocked him. The gold which once covered the roof of the Pantheon had all disappeared owing to the 'boundless cupidity of the Romans, for whom no crime is too awful.'

Gregory's description of Rome is the last account which survives until we come to the age of the great Jubilee indulgences. There is, indeed, some evidence that the Roman pilgrimage underwent a serious decline in the thirteenth century. The reputation of the city as a spiritual centre continued to diminish, and the almost continual warfare which afflicted Italy and Rome itself seem finally to have choked the flow of pilgrims. During his quarrel with Becket, Henry II of England is reported to have prevented his subjects from embarking for Rome. The emperor Frederick II discouraged his subjects from undertaking pilgrimages to Rome, thus earning him a stiff rebuke from Innocent IV who accused him of putting the salvation of his subjects in jeopardy. The few national pilgrims' hospices which survived began to disappear at the end of the twelfth century. The Irish hospice of the Holy Trinity ceased to exist at about this time. The deacon responsible for the English national hospice complained that its income from offerings was declining and that hardly any clergy or laymen could be found to serve in it; in 1203 it was finally dissolved and the buildings transformed into the hospital of S. Spirito. Doubtless simple men came to Rome as they had always done. But they came quietly, undramatically, and the sources are silent about them. The great and powerful recognized in Rome an important political capital, and they visited it because they had to. But they no longer came in the spirit of Canute, or even of Gerald of Wales. Richard I passed within a few miles of the city on his way to the crusade in 1190 but refused an invitation to visit it. On his way back from the east in 1273 Edward I passed through Rome and turned aside to discuss political affairs with the pope at Orvieto. But he did not trouble to visit the Roman shrines.

The Fount of Forgiveness

Gregory the Great used to tell how St. Peter once appeared to the empress Galla Placidia on her deathbed and told her that all her sins were forgiven; the same miracle, he remarked, was performed every day in the Vatican basilica. Even in the dark years of the Arab invasions of the tenth century, the city of the apostles meant to one writer the mental and spiritual salvation of countless pilgrims from all over the Christian world. The theme appealed to an English king of the eleventh century, just as it had done to his predecessors in the eighth. 'God has granted me', Canute wrote in 1027, 'the privilege of praying at the shrines of the blessed Peter and Paul and in every sanctuary within the city of Rome. And this privilege I have sought because wise men have told me that the apostle Peter has received from God the power of binding and loosing, and carries the keys of Paradise.'

Above all other places, Rome was the destination of those *'nudi homines cum ferro'* who plagued the roads in the time of Charlemagne, the convicted criminals who had been exiled by their communities and sent to wander across the face of the earth. Rival sanctuaries recognized this when they advertised their saints as having the same powers as St. Peter. One of them described how a convict lost one of his fetters in the Vatican basilica and the other at the shrine of St. Austremoine in Auvergne; 'which proves', the author reflected, 'since one fetter was removed by St. Peter and the other by St. Austremoine at the instigation of St. Peter, that St. Austremoine partakes of the merit of the great apostle and that their power is equal.' So important had Rome become as an object of penitential pilgrimage, that a writer of the ninth century surprised no one by asserting that 'penance is synonymous with going to Rome.'

Rome owed its unique prestige to a variety of factors. Its role as the converter of northern Europe was certainly one of them. Another was the gradual process by which the absolution of grave offences, originally the prerogative of the bishops, passed into the hands of the papacy. This important change had its roots in the eighth century, when bishops began to consult the popes in particularly difficult cases. St. Boniface asked the advice of Gregory III on parricides and of Zacharias on fornication and clerical murderers. Nicholas I was consulted by the archbishop of Rheims on the case of a man who had killed his three sons, and again about a monk who had killed his brother. In the ninth century, bishops began to send the malefactor to Rome together with the letter asking for advice. The pope would then prescribe the penance directly. Several penitential manuals of the period recommend this procedure, and Nicholas I began to insist that some crimes, such as incest, must be referred to him in this way. In theory the bishop retained control over the case. The pope did not actually absolve the sinner, but merely prescribed the penance and returned him for absolution to the bishop. The bishops did what they could to impress this narrow distinction on sinners, fearing that criminals would come to the conclusion that they could by-pass the bishop's jurisdiction by a simple pilgrimage to Rome. This, indeed, was precisely what happened. Haito, bishop of Basle, warned his diocesans in vain that the power of absolution was his alone. The council of Seligenstadt (1022–3) tried to forbid all pilgrimages to Rome without the written permission of the bishop, and breaches of this principle sometimes created sore conflicts. In the 1020s Pontius, count of Auvergne, received absolution from the pope without the knowledge or consent of the bishop of Le Puy, as a result of which the council of Limoges ordered him to do another pilgrimage to Rome, this time in proper form with a letter from the bishop. The bishops struggled hard to preserve their authority and prevent the Roman pilgrimage from becoming a general fountain of forgiveness. They failed, however, and by the end of the twelfth century the canonists had set the seal on their failure by the principle of 'reserved cases' which could be absolved by the pope alone. Sacrilege, murder of priests or monks, robbery of churches, and a continually increasing number of lesser crimes, were all 'reserved cases'. The pope delegated the business of absolving sinners in reserved cases to the officers of the papal penitentiary. The penitentiars could absolve in person or by brief, though in many cases the penitent came to Rome to receive his penance. For the remainder of the Middle Ages the prospect of confessing to an anonymous penitentiar and of being absolved from even the most enormous transgressions added considerably to the spiritual attractions of Rome.

In the newly converted countries of Scandinavia the papacy made ample use of these powers. When Alexander III was informed that incest was particularly common in Sweden he instructed the bishop of Upsala to send offenders to Rome 'to visit the Holy See and the blessed apostles Peter and Paul so that by the sweat of their brow and the hardships of the journey they may soften the anger of the supreme judge and be found worthy of His mercy.' Behaviour which had been normal in the pagan society of the north suddenly became sinful, and a pilgrimage to Rome enabled converts to relieve themselves of their guilt. Two pilgrims mentioned in the *Grettis Saga* reflected that 'to another King we have much more to pay,... for we have lived according to our own worldly desires instead of following the teachings of Christ,...and now we are growing old. Then they journeyed to Rome, and when they appeared before the penitentiar they told him everything truthfully, just as it had happened, and with what pagan hocus pocus they had been married. They humbly submitted to such penance as he deigned to impose on them and promised to amend their ways.' These pilgrims had asked no one's consent before approaching the penitentiar, and had avoided all the normal preliminaries to absolution. This appears to have been regarded at Rome as a point in their favour, 'since they had voluntarily turned their minds to atonement without being prompted or instructed by the Church.' Unusual cases were commonly submitted to the pope in person. When Gunnhildr, the mother of a Norwegian king, confessed to the penitentiar that her son had been born in adultery, the diplomatic importance of the case was held to call for the personal attention of the pope, Alexander III. Alexander may have been untypical in the interest which he took in the penitential function of the papacy, but he was certainly not the only pope who heard confessions himself. It was said of Adrian IV, the only English pope, that no business was so urgent as to prevent him from talking with northmen who wanted to see him.

The advantages which the Roman churches enjoyed over other sanctuaries were greatly increased by the development of the doctrine of indulgences. Already in the latter half of the twelfth century a pilgrim could get more remission by attending the Lenten stations than he could find in any sanctuary outside Rome. The stations were the churches in which the Pope said Mass on certain appointed days, especially in Lent. It was Gregory the Great who was traditionally supposed to have assigned to each station its special church. Pilgrims were expected to attend each of the forty stations in turn, and from the middle of the twelfth century indulgences were believed to be attached to them. Gerald of Wales gained all the stational indulgences during his visit to Rome in 1195, though there was some doubt as to how generous they were. Gerald thought that they amounted to ninety-two years. His contemporary, the Parisian theologian William of Auxerre, computed them at fifty years. It was not until 1297 that Boniface VIII settled the matter by laying down that pilgrims would get one year and forty days at each station in addition to any indulgences that might be attached to the stational churches in their own right.

The stational indulgences came into existence more or less spontaneously, but individual churches generally received their indulgences by formal grant. At the end of the twelfth century, visitors to St. Peter's on Maundy Thursday won an indulgence of two years if they were Italians, three if they came from further afield. Peter Mallius dated this concession from the foundation of the basilica by Constantine, though in fact it had almost certainly originated in his own lifetime. Alexander III (d. 1181) used to tell Swedish pilgrims that all those who made a good confession to the papal penitentiars before the shrine of the apostle would receive an indulgence of one, two, or three years, depending on the distance they had travelled; Scandinavians could certainly count on winning three years. In

Alexander's reign only the basilicas of the apostles could offer indulgences in their own right, but within twenty years of his death pilgrims could gain the same indulgences at many of the shrines of the martyrs on their feast days. The result was an inflation of indulgences in which those of the greater basilicas were constantly increased in order to preserve their superiority. In 1240 the pope declared an indulgence of three years and three quarantines for those who visited the basilicas of the apostles between Pentecost and the octave of the feast of the apostles. In the time of Gregory X (1272–6) the indulgence offered at the Lateran on Maundy Thursday had risen to four years and four quarantines, and Thomas Aquinas reported that pilgrims from overseas could sometimes win five years or more. By the end of the thirteenth century indulgences were being attached to individual altars in St. Peter's.

Although the process was a continuing one, no pope was so prodigious a dispenser of indulgences as Nicholas IV (1288–92). He increased the largest indulgences obtainable at St. Peter's to seven years and seven quarantines and shortly afterwards awarded the same privilege to the Lateran basilica. St. Paul's received indulgences for every day of Lent, every Sunday of the year, and the octave of the feast of the apostles in addition. S. Maria Maggiore was raised to the status of the basilicas of the apostles; it received a similar indulgence for every day of Lent and every Saturday of the year, the Epiphany, the anniversary of its foundation, and a number of other feasts. In the year of Nicholas's death a pilgrim who passed Lent in Rome could be sure of getting at least ten times the remission earned by Gerald of Wales a century before. The stage was set for the Jubilee indulgence of Boniface VIII.

1 3 0 0 : The Year of Jubilee

The Jubilee was originally a Jewish concept. It was an amnesty proclaimed every fifty years, when prisoners were released, ill-gotten gains restored, and penance performed for past transgressions. In the language of mediaeval preachers it came to mean any year in which people were offered an unusual chance to earn their salvation. The word was often applied to the indulgences given to crusaders. St. Bernard proclaimed that the year 1146 was 'a year of remission, a veritable year of Jubilee' in which people could be saved by going to the aid of the faltering Frankish kingdoms of the middle east. Those who fought on the Albigensian crusade also won a 'Jubilee' indulgence. 'See, this is our year of Jubilee', cried Humbert of Romans when urging young men to go and defend Acre against the infidel; 'not the Jewish one but a Christian Jubilee which will be far greater.'

In the autumn of 1299 a notion spontaneously arose that the year 1300 would be a year of Jubilee in which pilgrims to St. Peter's would win huge remission. The rumour spread through northern Italy that visitors to Rome would gain a plenary indulgence on the first day of January and at least a hundred days of remission on every other day of the year. On New Year's eve a great crowd gathered in St. Peter's between vespers and midnight, pressing round the high altar, pushing and trampling on each other to get a glimpse of it. It was assumed that the special remission would begin at midnight and most of them proposed to spend the whole of the following day in the basilica. In the tightly packed mass, rumours circulated rapidly. Some said that God had proclaimed a Jubilee in a tract handed down from the sky; others that every centennial year was a year of Jubilee. On New Year's day itself the news of these happenings passed like wildfire through the city and surrounding countryside, and the crowds in the Leonine city became uncontrollably large. 'Give us your blessing before we die', they cried, 'for we have heard that whoever visits the bodies of St. Peter and St. Paul in a centennial year shall be freed from both sin and guilt.'

That this seminal event should have occurred unprompted and unplanned was altogether characteristic of the religion of the late Middle Ages. Far from provoking this display of enthusiasm, the pope, Boniface VIII, was taken aback by it. After hasty consultations, the cardinals were sent to look up the canons and peruse various old books to see whether the popular rumour had any basis. The matter was very obscure. Nothing could be found in the writings of the fathers about Jubilees, and various opinions were canvassed. While these enquiries were proceeding, a few temporary measures were taken. The treasures of St. Peter's were displayed, and in the middle of January the *sudarium* of Veronica was exposed in the basilica. Bonifice received some of the pilgrims in person. He was particularly impressed by an old man of 107 years who told him that he remembered his father describing a visit to Rome in 1200 and assured him that there had been a Jubilee in that year. This intelligence was confirmed by several other centenarians, most of them Italians, but including one Frenchman from Beauvais; the belief, declared this last, was widespread in France. The cardinals were unable to discover any authoritative basis for this nonsense. They concluded, however, that a tradition so general ought to be respected. The time was ripe to spread the fame of St. Peter, and to encourage the faithful to pay tribute to the prince of the apostles in his own basilica. It was decided that the aspirations of the crowd should be given authoritative support. On February 22nd, 1300 Boniface issued the bull *Antiquorum Relatio*. 'The tradition of our ancestors', it began, 'affirms that great indulgences for our sins are granted to those who visit the venerable basilica of the apostles in Rome. We who, in accordance with the dignity of our office, must strive to secure the salvation of every man, do hereby hold all these indulgences to be authentic. We confirm them and approve them and do now grant them afresh.' All those who visited the basilicas of the apostles during the centenary year and made a truly penitent confession would receive a plenary indulgence. They must visit each basilica on fifteen separate days (thirty for Italians); nevertheless, the bull vaguely adds, the more frequently they visited the basilicas the more efficacious would be their indulgence. The bull was accompanied by a brief excluding from its benefits all excommunicates and rebels against the Church, merchants who traded with the infidel, the pope's enemies in Aragon and Sicily, and the Colonna family.

It was clear from the terms of the bull that the Jubilee indulgence did not pretend to release sinners from guilt as well as penance. John the Monk, one of the cardinals whom Boniface had consulted, insisted that 'this indulgence remits penance after the sinner has been absolved of his guilt by a true and contrite confession; the guilt is remitted by God in the sacrament of penance.' Theological subtleties of this sort were, however, wasted on most of those who came to Rome. Probably very few of them had confessed their sins and they thought that they were gaining an indulgence which dispensed them from such formalities. The chroniclers William Ventura and Giovanni Villani, both of whom claimed the indulgence, were under this impression. At Tournai a large band of pilgrims assembled for the journey to Rome in the belief that the indulgence released them from the need to confess. Various friars were trying to persuade them of their error 'and for this reason everyone was perplexed by doubt and confusion.' The abbot of St. Martin, who was in the crowd, asked a papal penitentiar in Rome to settle the question. The penitentiar, who was a doctor of theology, replied that so many pilgrims had asked this question that the papal confessors had gone in a body to Anagni to seek an authoritive ruling from the pope. Boniface had then 'formally declared that a full remission would be granted to all who made a true and contrite confession as the canons and decretals require.'

Copies of the bull *Antiquorum* were despatched to every part of Europe accompanied by a slight commentary explaining the circumstances and pointing to various Biblical precedents. 'Wherefore', it continued, 'you who are called, drive away your cares and preoccupations. Come and pray and atone for your sins without delay. For now is the time, and this is the very day of salvation....Think how near is the means of your salvation,...of washing away the stains of sin from your souls, of exchanging the wretchedness of your earthly lives for everlasting glory.' The missive concluded with the following jingle which the Siennese inscribed on the walls of their cathedral:

> *Annus centenus Romae semper es jubilaeus.*
> *Crimina laxantur, cui paenitet ista donatur*
> *Hoc declaravit Bonifatius et roboravit.*

Every hundredth year is held the Roman Jubilee.
To he who is penitent all crimes are forgiven.
Thus says Boniface.

In Rome, pilgrims were handed copies of the bull on the steps of St. Peter's, and invited to preserve them as a reminder that the next Jubilee would occur in 1400.

The response was overwhelming. Italy was unusually peaceful in 1300 and the pope had overcome his enemies within the city. The summer was fine and the harvest excellent. 'Innumerable Christians of both sexes, young and old, Italians and foreigners, came to Rome. They came on horseback, on other animals, even on foot. Amongst them one could see many young people, full of hope and without a penny, carrying their parents on their shoulders.' The Roman populace were the first to claim the indulgence. Flying in the face of tradition, fathers allowed their unmarried daughters to leave the house by night accompanied by reliable chaperons, to perform their thirty visits. Stefaneschi lyrically describes the crowd of paupers in rags entering the city side by side with proud noblemen. Almost every Italian bishop claimed the indulgence, and some French ones. The English, he thought, preferred to come later in the year, when Rome offered the same dank climate as their own country. No kings attended, but Philip of France was represented by his Italian agent Musciatto Francesi and Edward I by one of the Cerchi of Florence.

The influx of pilgrims imposed a considerable strain on the resources of the city. From the summit of the gate-towers they looked like a swarm of ants or an invading army, and there was scarcely enough room in the city to contain them. After three months there was a serious prospect of famine which was only averted by an abundant harvest. 'The land smiled on us and the earth gave forth fruit. It was a miracle no less impressive than the feeding of the five thousand with five loaves and two fishes.' But the miracle was accomplished, for when William Ventura came to claim the indulgence he found an 'abundance of flesh, fish and oats'. Villani too had no difficulty in feeding himself and his horse. It was, however, accomplished at a price. The cost of food rose steeply and the Romans made enormous profits out of the Jubilee. Ventura had to pay a *gros tournois* per day for a bed for himself and a stable for his horse; even this did not include fodder which was extremely dear. A number of pilgrims accompanied their devotions with austerities, fasts, vigils, and even flagellation 'to prepare themselves for the vast influx of the Holy Spirit'. The great amorphous mass of visitors taxed the papal police to the limit of their endurance. On the bridge below the Castel St. Angelo pilgrims were made to keep to one side when entering the Leonine city and the other when leaving it. On the city side of the bridge a new street had to be opened in the walls to allow easier access.

Boniface was often asked by pilgrims to reduce the number of days that they had to spend in the city but he usually refused. According to Stefaneschi he made only three exceptions. On Maundy Thursday he appeared in front of the Lateran basilica and announced that all those in the crowd might claim the indulgence after only one visit to each of the basilicas of the apostles. This concession was repeated on November 18th, the anniversary of the consecration of the basilicas. Finally, as the end of the Jubilee year approached, he agreed that foreign pilgrims who had already begun the journey or the fifteen visits might complete them after the end of the year.

Many pilgrims who attended the Jubilee later had occasion to remember it as a formative episode in their lives. Giovanni Villani, the Florentine merchant and historian, 'wandered amongst the great monuments of the city and read the histories and chronicles of ancient Rome by Sallust, Lucan, Livy,

Valerius, Paulus Orosius, and other masters of the historical art;
I resolved then to copy their style and form.' It was here that
he formed the design of his great history of Florence, daughter
of Rome and destined for equal greatness. 'And so with the
help of God's grace I turned back from Rome in the year 1300
and began to write this book.' Dante was almost certainly in
Rome in the Jubilee year and set the *Divine Comedy* at Easter
1300. William Ventura, the chronicler of Asti, spent fifteen days
there, departing on Christmas Eve, the last day of the Jubilee.
'As I rode away from Rome I saw the roads encumbered with
a countless multitude of pilgrims....Again and again I saw men
and women trodden underfoot in the press and I myself was
often hard put to it to escape the same fate. It would be a fine
thing and agreeable to every true Christian to repeat the festi-
val every centennial year.'

There were widely varying estimates of the number of pilgrims who visited Rome in 1300. Villani's figure of 200,000 is
almost certainly too low, while William Ventura's claim of two
million is plainly excessive. Everyone agreed, however, that the
pope and the Romans had made large profits. 'From the offerings of the pilgrims', one remarked, 'the Church gained great
treasures and all the Romans were much enriched.' In the basilica of St. Peter, Ventura saw two priests standing day and night
at the high altar drawing in the money with rakes. The rumour
in Tuscany was that the offerings had amounted to a thousand
livres of Perugia every day. But the truth was less spectacular.
According to Stefaneschi the offerings in a normal year
amounted to 30,405 florins whereas in this year there were
rather more than 50,000. Most offerings were in small coin and
many pilgrims were too poor to give anything at all. The nobility were particularly mean and kings absented themselves alto-

gether. All of this, he adds, was swallowed up by the very heavy
expenses of the Jubilee; 'money piously given was piously
spent', on the accommodation of pilgrims and the upkeep of
the two basilicas.

The Jubilee of 1300 was in a sense the swan-song of the
mediaeval papacy. No pope had exercised the substance of
power like Innocent IV and none was to display the shadow of
power more splendidly than Boniface VIII. After the terrible fall
of Boniface in 1303 many were inclined to attribute the Jubilee
to his ambition and vainglory. In the posthumous 'trial' of
Boniface, the bull *Antiquorum* was cited as evidence of heresy
and he was even accused of murdering pilgrims in Rome. A
French pamphleteer depicted the Jubilee as a commercial enterprise designed to impoverish pilgrims for the pope's benefit:

> *Tel y ala en belle guise*
> *Qui s'en revint en sa chemise...*
> *Lors alèrent plusieurs à Rome*
> *Qui retournèrent mains preudhommes.*

> Many went there richly dressed
> Who later came back in their shirt-sleeves...
> Many went to Rome
> And came back wiser men.

But this was the verdict of his enemies after his fall. Those who
attended the Jubilee felt that they had achieved something, that
a similar opportunity would not arise again in their lifetime.
Stefaneschi emphasized that it offered a unique opportunity to
restore the soul to its state as after baptism and, like baptism, it
could not be repeated. How many vile crimes had until then
lain hidden in the deepest recesses of men's consciences? 'Who

can say how many grievous wounds were laid bare to the healing hand of the confessor?' Dante was no friend of Boniface VIII but when he entered Purgatory at Easter 1300 he was told by the shade of his friend Casella that for three months not one sinner had been refused admittance to the cleansing of Purgatory; 'for three months he has taken in peace all who would embark.'

The Avignon Papacy and the Jubilee of 1350

The years which followed the Jubilee were amongst the most dismal in Roman history. In 1305 Bertrand de Got, archbishop of Bordeaux, was elected pope and, fleeing the turbulent politics of Rome, established the papacy in France. On May 6th, 1308 the Lateran basilica was almost entirely destroyed by fire. In the absence of the popes the social and economic life of Rome stagnated while successive papal legates waged incessant warfare against the rebellious magnates of central Italy. Those Romans who remembered the Jubilee of 1300 saw the only hope of reviving their fortunes in the staging of another Jubilee as soon as possible.

In the autumn of 1342 a delegation of thirteen citizens drawn from various classes of the population made its way to Avignon and petitioned that the Jubilee be brought forward to 1350 and held every fifty years thereafter. The Jewish Jubilee, they pointed out, had been held every fifty years and, besides, such was the frailty of human life that many people born after 1300 would not live to see the year 1400. The pope, Clement VI, approved their request. He embodied his consent in the bull *Unigenitus,* one of the most celebrated pronouncements of the mediaeval Church. Borrowing a concept of the thirteenth-century schoolmen, Clement declared that Christ, the Blessed Virgin, and the saints and martyrs, had accumulated in their lifetimes more merit than they needed for their personal salvation. The excess was collected in a 'treasury of merit' controlled by the Church. The pope, who held the keys of St. Peter, could alone unlock this treasury and use it to release people from their sins by remitting the punishment (not the guilt) due to those who had made a true and contrite confession. Turning to the case in point Clement referred to 'the clamour of our own people of Rome who have humbly beseeched us on behalf of all peoples of the world' to release some of the merit of Christ and the saints for the salvation of mankind. The Jubilee would be held in 1350. The arrangements would be the same as those of 1300 except that the Lateran basilica was added to the list of churches to be visited.

The condition of Italy had changed for the worse in the past fifty years. No time could be less auspicious, as Petrarch remarked, than one in which 'all France, the Low Countries, and Britain, are engulfed in war; Germany and Italy are crippled by civil strife, their cities reduced to ashes; the Spanish kings turn on each other in armed combat, and throughout Europe Christ is unseen and unknown.' As the news of bitter fighting in northern Italy reached Avignon, Clement VI sank into a state of depressed lethargy, punctuated by the regular issue of bulls reproving Christendom for its violent ways and lamenting that 'if our reports are correct many pilgrims flocking to gain our indulgence will be seriously impeded.' Clement's efforts to secure a brief truce in the war between England and France ended in failure. Both countries forbade their citizens to attend the Jubilee on the ground that the drainage of currency and manpower would do irreparable damage to the war effort. Nevertheless the prohibition was widely ignored in France, and in England a large number of individuals obtained licences to visit Rome. English pilgrims travelling through France had to choose their route with care. Several were arrested as subjects of Edward III, and some French pilgrims who innocently travelled with parties of Englishmen found their property sequestered by royal officers when they returned.

Three months before it was due to begin, the Jubilee suffered another blow in the form of a violent earthquake. Much of the population was reduced to living in tents, and a number of monuments were entirely destroyed. The campanile and loggia of St. Paul's collapsed and the roof of S. Maria Maggiore fell in. The Lateran basilica, which had only recently been rebuilt after the fire of 1308, was partially ruined. 'In the two thousand years since the foundation of the city', Petrarch wrote, 'no worse disaster had befallen it. Its grandiose monuments, stunning to the foreign traveller, ignored by the Romans, have fallen to the ground....An icy pall of gloom is cast over the Jubilee year.'

In spite of the difficulties, and somewhat to the surprise of contemporaries, the roads were shortly filled with crowds of pilgrims reminiscent of those of 1300. Matteo Villani observed them passing through Florence 'enduring the hardships of the time, the unbelievable cold, the ice, the snow, and the floods'. By day the roads were crowded out, by night the inns. The Germans and Hungarians travelled in enormous bands and spent the nights in the open air huddled round large bonfires. The innkeepers sold all the food, wine, and fodder that they could find and, as usual, were accused of making excessive profits. So were butchers and grocers. 'But there was no disorderli-

ness or grumbling; everything was born patiently without fuss.'
Inside Rome the citizens were invited to lay in ample stocks of
food 'so that no pilgrim will suffer penury or starvation, but
will be restored and satisfied not only spiritually but bodily as
well.' Aniballe de Ceccano, the papal legate, was instructed to
provide for pilgrims' needs at his own expense if necessary.

Counting the pilgrims was a matter of guesswork. Matteo
Villani calculated that the peak was reached at Easter when
there were rather more than a million pilgrims in Rome; even
at Ascension and Pentecost there were 800,000 and the number never at any point fell below 200,000. Peter of Herenthals
was probably closer to the truth when he estimated that about
5,000 pilgrims entered the city every day, which would mean
that no more than 50,000 were there at any one time. On the
last day of the Jubilee, Rome was still full of pilgrims complet-
ing their visits to the three basilicas. 'Every Roman became an
innkeeper and filled his house with pilgrims and horses.' As a
result of the earthquake, accommodation was harder to find
than it had been in 1300. A pilgrim could expect to pay one
and a half or two *gros tournois* per day for himself and his horse,
falling perhaps to one *gros* in a slack period. The demand for
wine and meat outstripped the supply throughout the year,
allowing enterprising merchants to make large sums by import-
ing food from northern Italy. Bread cost a penny an ounce; a
bottle of wine three, four, or even five shillings; a sack of fodder fetched five *lire*. Every kind of meat was unbelievably
expensive and some of it was of very poor quality.

Visiting the three basilicas involved a walk of eleven miles
which was accomplished in some discomfort. 'The streets were
so crowded that every one, whether they were riding or walking, had to reconcile themselves to moving extremely slowly.'

Similar inconveniences attended the public exhibitions of the Veronica, which were held every Sunday afternoon at St. Peter's. Three or four pilgrims were suffocated or trampled underfoot on each of these occasions, and on some days the number rose to six or even twelve. On Easter Sunday Heinrich von Rebdorff saw several pilgrims crushed to death in the crowd. The more distinguished pilgrims took the precaution of applying in advance for a private view. It is clear that the *sudarium* of Veronica had by now supplanted the body of St. Peter as the principal relic of Rome. For Petrarch, Rome was no longer the city of the apostles but the city of Christ, whose relics eclipsed every other exhibit. Although Petrarch paid a cursory visit to the Calixtine cemetery and the site of Peter's crucifixion, his overpowering desire was to see 'the features of the Saviour wherever he might find them, on the napkin of Veronica or on the walls of S. Maria Maggiore'. He would 'gaze on the place where Christ appeared to St. Peter and would worship his footsteps on the hard ground. Then he would enter the *sancta sanctorum* of the Lateran...and see the relics of the birth and circumcision of his Lord, and the flask of the Virgin's milk by which so many had been restored to health.'

There was another side to Rome in 1350 which stood in pathetic contrast to the celebration of the Jubilee. St. Bridget of Sweden found the sight of the city in the aftermath of the earthquake profoundly depressing, and the absence of the papacy in France pained her. In the churches 'cracks and rifts had appeared in the arches so that bricks and pieces of masonry fell down on the heads of praying pilgrims. The pillars were buckling and the roofs on the verge of collapse. Mosaic floors, once fresh and beautiful, were now broken in pieces and the faithful stumbled into holes in the floor, doing themselves great injury.' Beneath the physical ruin, the Swedish visionary detected the signs of a deeper, spiritual decay. Bridget added her voice to the chorus of her contemporaries who pointed to the Avignon papacy as a symptom of religious decline and, although it is hard for a historian to share this view, the sorry condition of Rome must have done much to confirm it in the eyes of the pilgrims. 'In times past it was a city in which dwelt warriors of Christ, its streets strewn as if with gold and silver. Now all its precious sapphires are lying in the mire and few of its inhabitants live the Christian life.'

As in 1300, there were 'many altercations' about the meaning of the indulgence. The confusion was increased by the fact that alongside the official bull *Unigenitus* there circulated a number of unofficial bulls which were almost certainly forged by the Romans in order to attract more pilgrims to the city and keep them there longer. In these pseudo-bulls the pope was supposed to have urged priests and monks to visit Rome with or without the permission of their superiors. Italians were 'required' to remain in the city for at least a month and extra churches were added to those that were to be visited. In one version pilgrims were required to visit seven churches on at least fifteen occasions before they could claim the indulgence. The pope, it added, 'would order the angels to admit straight to heaven all pilgrims who die on the route having made a good confession'. These bulls were widely distributed. The canon lawyer Alberic of Rosate, who claimed the indulgence together with his wife and children, knew nothing of *Unigenitus* and reproduced two of the forged bulls in his handbook of canon law. Peter of Herenthals, the abbot of Floresse near Namur, reproduced them in his biography of Clement VI, and the jaundiced English chronicler Thomas Burton cited them as proof of

Clement's wickedness. John Wyclif denounced them as blasphemy. It may seem unfair to condemn Clement for a bull which he had never issued, but although he had not in fact invited clerics to visit Rome without permission he certainly behaved as if he had done. Many monks did go to Rome without permission; others conjured up ecclesiastical business taking them to Avignon and then made off to claim the Jubilee indulgence in Rome. Most of these illicit pilgrims were able to obtain letters from the pope forbidding their superiors to punish them. Nor was Clement as firm as Boniface VIII in refusing the pressing demands of pilgrims for a reduction in the number of visits required. The papal legate Guy of Boulogne was empowered to reduce the number of days if the crowds in Rome became unmanageable. Alberic of Rosate, who inspected the bull conferring this power, was allowed to leave after six days with the full indulgence. After Easter the shortage of food became acute and Guy reduced the number of visits from fifteen to eight. This had its effect. The crowds diminished, 'at which the Romans were exceedingly vexed.'

Louis of Hungary was the only king who came to claim the Jubilee indulgence in person. The others asked to be granted it without having to make the irksome journey to Rome. Philip VI of France protested that he was too old and infirm to go to Rome, Hugh of Cyprus that he lived too far away. Edward III of England sent the celebrated preacher Richard Fitzralph, archbishop of Armagh, to plead on his behalf. Fitzralph pointed out that travelling to sanctuaries had no place in the Jewish Jubilee which Clement professed to be reviving. Jews were simply commanded to behave exceptionally well towards their neighbours in Jubilee years. Could not the English do the same and gain the indulgence by, say, bestowing alms on hospices and schools? This interesting argument carried no weight. The pope affirmed in reply that 'no one of any status or condition whatever may gain the indulgence without visiting the basilicas in person.' Clement's attitude softened, however, when the Jubilee had ended. In May 1351 Edward III, the queen, the prince of Wales, and the earl of Lancaster were all formally 'granted' the Jubilee indulgence. Many of Edward's subjects were accorded the same privilege in return for a sum equal to the cost of a journey to Rome, the money to go to the needs of the Holy Land. Queen Elizabeth of Hungary was permitted to appoint a confessor and receive 'the same indulgence as those who visited the basilicas of St. Peter and St. Paul and St. John of the Lateran in the year 1350'. More spectacular was the concession of an indulgence *ad instar Jubilaei* to the entire population of Mallorca in June 1352, perhaps as a reward for their resistance to the pope's great adversary, Peter IV of Aragon. Mallorcans could claim the indulgence if they paid eight visits to Mallorca cathedral and to every parish church of the city; they were also to contribute to the endowment of new churches a sum equal to the cost 'in conscience assessed' of travelling to Rome and staying there for fifteen days. This was not enough for the Mallorcans, who complained that 'it was hard to reckon what the cost of going to Rome would be, and the gross errors that would occur might lose some people the benefits of the indulgence. Moreover there are many sons of families, servants, retainers, and paupers who could never afford to go to Rome, and if it were only the rich who could win salvation it would be a grave scandal which would endanger the souls of the entire population of the kingdom.' It was therefore agreed that the Mallorcans would be granted the indulgence in return for a

single official payment of 30,000 gold florins to the papal treasury. This curious transaction established a precedent of which
Boniface IX would make full use when the time came to celebrate the next Jubilee.

The Papal Schism

In non-Jubilee years the Roman churches depended on the
modest indulgences awarded to them by the popes of the thirteenth century. At the death of Nicholas IV, in 1292, no single
church in Rome offered an indulgence of more than seven
years and seven quarantines, and it required an unusually energetic pilgrim to collect as much as a thousand years of remission in one visit to the city. This proved to be insufficient to
draw the pilgrims of the fourteenth century, bored by Rome
and enticed by the excitement of the Holy Land. After the
Jubilee of 1350, the churches of Rome attempted to revive
their fortunes by claiming enormous indulgences, indulgences
so large that it is difficult to understand why their authenticity
was not challenged before the sixteenth century. 'Suffice it to
say', wrote the papal secretary of state Signorili, 'that they
exceed in indulgences all other churches in the world combined. Which is why every year an unending throng of pilgrims
from every corner of the earth comes to the city of the apostles to pray, to gain the indulgences, and to venerate the holy
relics of its churches.' The first that is heard of these indulgences
is the report of Leopold, prior of the Augustinian house in
Vienna, who toured the churches of Rome in 1377. Leopold
bought a *Liber Indulgentiarum,* or book of indulgences, from
which he learned that seven years of remission were gained
when he ascended each of the twenty-nine steps in front of St.
Peter's. Each of the eighty altars in St. Peter's offered twenty-

eight years and five of them were worth thirty-two. At the altar
of the *sudarium* of Veronica 'I, Leopold, unworthy sinner that I
am, spent three sessions of twenty-seven hours in prayer. For
you must know that for every hour that a Roman looks on this
image of the Lord he gains an indulgence of three thousand
years; the Italian gets nine thousand years, and the foreigner
twelve thousand years.' Each visit to the basilica carried twenty-
eight years or a third of all one's sins, whichever was the greater.
The high altar apparently offered a plenary indulgence, which
was as much as could be obtained by spending fifteen days in
Rome in a Jubilee year. The basilica of St. Paul now carried
forty-eight years and forty-eight quarantines every day; extra
indulgences of a thousand years were available there on the
feast of the apostles, and of seven thousand years on the
anniversary of the dedication of the basilica. Leopold's booklet
informed him that pope Silvester (d. 335) had declared most of
these indulgences, and that they were particularly effective in
effacing the sin of anger against one's parents, so long as one
had not actually struck them.

The *Mirabilia* no longer satisfied the demands of pilgrims.
One of them, who was in Rome in 1344, complained that it
was impossible to buy a reliable guide to the churches and
monuments. Books of indulgences like Leopold's began to fill
this vacuum towards the end of the fourteenth century. They
reproduced some of the more interesting stories from the
Mirabilia and added a mass of information about the indulgences of the city's churches, together with specious accounts
of their origins. Forged papal bulls were quoted at length.
William Brewyn, the author of an English book of indulgences,
proved to his own satisfaction that the indulgences at the altar
of the Veronica originated in a bull of Gregory XI. John

Capgrave in 1450 read an 'old legend' to the effect that the indulgences at the church of St. Lawrence had been personally declared by the saint himself. From the end of the fourteenth century new editions of these works appeared in verse and prose in every major language. An English edition, written in about 1400, begins

> *Whoso wol his soule leche*
> *Listen to me; I wol him teche*
> *Pardoun. Is the soule bote*
> *At grete Rome, there is the roote.*
> *Pardoun a word in Frensch it is*
> *Forgiveness of thy synnes i-wis.*

Translations often contained slight alterations to suit national tastes. The church of S. Maria Maggiore claimed to possess some relics of the apostle Thomas, but in English versions the relics become those of Thomas Becket. An English pilgrim in Rome in 1344 was shown a picture of the Virgin which Becket, who had never been to Rome, was supposed to have held in special reverence. English guide-books asserted that Becket had been to school in Rome, and the clergy of S. Maria Maggiore displayed his right arm 'and a parte of his brayne'. John Capgrave believed these fables in 1450 and wrote them down, but on his return home he thought better of it and erased them from his manuscript.

Those who did not buy hand-books were left in no doubt that plentiful indulgences were to be had. At most churches notices or inscriptions proclaimed what spiritual benefits were available inside. A bill-board outside the church of St. Lawrence promised daily indulgences of seven thousand years and seven thousand quarantines. At the spot where Christ had once appeared to St. Peter an inscription announced remission of two thousand years. In the church of S. Maria Maggiore a list of indulgences was posted at the cast end of the church:

And written it is all there
On a table at high altere,
Pardoun there is that men may see
Graunted of popes that there han be.

The obvious purpose of these frauds was to re-establish the Roman pilgrimage in rivalry with that of Jerusalem, which was now at the summit of its popularity. The theme which runs through all the Roman hand-books of the period is that greater benefits can be obtained with less trouble at Rome. If men only knew about the indulgences available at Rome, wrote the author of the *Stacions of Rome*, they would never bother to visit the Holy Land.

Pope Bonifas telleth this tale
if men wuste grete and smale
The pardoun that is at grete Rome
They wolde tellen in heore home
It were no need to man in Christiante
To passe into the Holy Lond over the see
To Jerusalem ne to St. Katheryne,
To bring man's soule out of pyne
For pardoun ther is without ende.

One pilgrim remarked that the road from the Lateran to St. Peter's was called the Via Sacra 'because from one end to the other there are as many indulgences to be had as can be won by a voyage to Jerusalem.'

The attitude of the papacy to these claims was somewhat equivocal. An official memorandum of 1382 is remarkably reticent, contenting itself in most cases with the observation that the remission to be had was 'very great'. Some of the books of indulgences gave the impression the popes had acquiesced in the claims of the Roman churches. The *Stacions of Rome* says as much of Boniface IX, who was almost certainly alive when it was written. After the beginning of the great schism, in 1378, the Roman popes would have found it hard to protest even had they wished to. They were too heavily dependent on the prestige of Rome to indulge in damaging quarrels with its clergy on a matter which so closely touched that prestige.

The Avignon anti-popes were acutely conscious that their rivals enjoyed a considerable advantage in the actual possession of Rome. Pilgrimages to Rome reinforced the prestige of the Roman pope, and in countries loyal to Avignon sporadic attempts were made to suppress them. In 1382 the Avignon pope, Clement VII, took the extraordinary step of transferring the indulgences of the major basilicas of Rome to the churches of Marseilles. The indulgences of St. Peter's on the feast of the apostles were transferred to Marseilles cathedral, while those of S. Maria Maggiore were awarded to the abbey church of St. Victor. The Franciscan church of Marseilles received the indulgences of the Lateran on the grounds that all Italy was in the hands of 'that pestiferous and tyrannical schismatic', Urban VI. The Roman pope, for his part, made the maximum use of his possession of the city by bringing forward the Jubilee of 1400. One of the last acts of Urban VI before his death was to declare that Jubilees would henceforth be held at intervals of thirty-three years, in honour of the thirty-three years of Christ's life on earth. A fourth church, the basilica of S. Maria Maggiore, was added to those that must be visited. The bull was issued in April 1389 and the next Jubilee was announced for 1390. The anti-pope immediately denounced the Jubilee as having no validity and forbade all the faithful within his obedience (it consisted of little more than France and Spain) to attend it. In this strident document, Clement castigated the Roman pope as a pseudoprophet and a serpent, his Jubilee as 'a fraud, concocted under the false colour of piety and clemency in the hope of enticing the faithful into his detestable obedience,...and thus into the jaws of Hell.' The contest which followed gravely damaged the prestige of the Roman Jubilee. As in 1350, requests were made for the benefit of the indulgence without the burden of going to Rome and Boniface IX, who was elected pope in Rome in November 1389, was in no position to resist them. He could not afford to offend princes like the duke of Bavaria, who was awarded the indulgence, together with his wife and family, before the Jubilee had even begun. But Boniface's generosity was by no means confined to princes. Some bishops were empowered to grant the indulgence to any of their diocesans whom they chose. Countless unimportant individuals like the mayor of Berwick-on-Tweed applied for the indulgence and got it. Boniface undoubtedly hoped to placate his friends and win over his enemies, and in this policy he enjoyed a measure of success. The municipal authorities of Cologne appear to have been won over to his cause by the promise of a Jubilee indulgence. In Spain, Boniface's agents were instructed to offer the indulgence to all who would convert to his obedience.

Boniface IX was not only diplomatically weak but chronically short of money, and it was he who first transformed the Jubilee into an instrument of financial policy. He appropriated half the offerings made at all the Roman basilicas including

St. Paul's and S. Maria Maggiore which he did not directly control. Special representatives were installed at these churches, to ensure that he got his share, and the management of the Jubilee receipts was placed in the hands of the banking firm of Michael de Guinigi. As soon as the Roman Jubilee was over, Boniface sold the indulgence to those who had been unable to attend. This had been done in a small way by Clement VI in 1350, but Clement had not attempted to market the indulgence far and wide. Boniface on the other hand set up an elaborate organization to sell the Jubilee indulgence north of the Alps. One of his bitterest critics described his agents as extracting large sums from the rich and simple-minded. One province alone was said to have yielded 100,000 florins. 'And so these agents with painted faces and fat bloated stomachs made their way to Rome with their trains of servants and fine horses…and poured their spoils into Boniface's coffers.' In most parts of Europe pilgrims were permitted to gain the Jubilee indulgence by making fifteen visits to a local church and paying whatever sum they would have expended on a journey to Rome. At Milan six thousand florins were raised, part of which went to the cathedral building fund. Other local Jubilees were declared in Germany at Munich, Meissen, Magdeburg, Constance, and in Prague.

The Avignon pope watched the affair in idle frustration. Some members of his own obedience had visited Rome in 1390, but most of them accepted that the next valid Jubilee would be held in accordance with the bull *Unigenitus* in 1400. Many Frenchmen appeared in Rome in that year and they were joined by members of the Roman obedience who looked forward to the prospect of any Jubilee, even an unofficial one. Indeed, the unofficial Jubilee of 1400 appears to have been more popular than the official one of 1390, and one monk of St. Paul's asserted that it was the most crowded Jubilee in his experience; the offerings at St. Paul's, said he, came to 60,000 ducats 'partly because there were more people and partly because they were more generous'. A more reliable source than the reminiscences of an aging tourist guide suggests that the offerings in the four Jubilee churches combined had reached 16,000 florins by June and may have amounted to about half as much again in the whole year.

All this presented Boniface IX with a delicate problem. He could not recognize the Jubilee of 1400 without casting doubt on that of 1390. But plainly he could but ignore it, and early in the year he took steps to claim his share of the offerings. In March he announced in somewhat opaque language that all the indulgences of his predecessors for the fiftieth and hundredth years were confirmed. In July, without actually declaring a Jubilee, he conceded a Jubilee indulgence to all who contributed to the rebuilding of the ruinous basilica of St. Paul. His embarrassment was complete when princes whom he could ill-afford to displease wrote to ask for the Jubilee indulgence. The queen of Denmark, who had claimed the indulgence of 1390 now wrote in for that of 1400. Boniface replied cagily to such requests. Without mentioning the Jubilee he offered them 'the same indulgence and remission as those who visit the basilicas of St. Peter, St. Paul, St. John Lateran, and S. Maria Maggiore in this present year'. The news of these happenings caused dismay in the Avignon obedience. The Carthusians loyal to Avignon heard as early as 1399 that Frenchmen were planning to attend the Jubilee and forbade their members to join them. The French government, which was the principal supporter of Avignon, forbade all pilgrimages to Rome and instructed its officers to prevent them by force if necessary. This was easier said than done. Early in the year reports indicated that the roads were daily covered with nobles, clergy, bourgeois, and peasants on their way to Rome, and royal officials were constantly exhorted to greater diligence. The *bailli* of Mâcon was threatened with dire penalties. The *bailli* of Sens was told that droves of pilgrims were passing freely through his jurisdiction, 'from which it appears that you have ignored our instructions.' The hospice of St. Didier at Nevers was filled to capacity with pilgrims, and the master had to appeal to the town for a special subsidy.

The problem of the Avignon obedience was posed in a particularly acute form in Spain. Although the Spanish kingdoms had consistently supported Avignon, their subjects had never altogether accepted this policy, and pilgrimages to Rome had continued throughout the schism. Indeed, a hospice for Catalans in Rome was partially financed by the king of Aragon. But the prospect of a mass pilgrimage to Rome in 1400 stirred the Aragonese government to action. An embassy was sent to Paris, which expressed the opinion that all those who went to Rome were excommunicates, schismatics, and destined for everlasting damnation. The problem of applying these sentiments in practice was underlined by the case of the Cistercian abbey of Poblet in southern Catalonia, where a number of monks had formed the intention of claiming the Jubilee indulgence at Rome. Poblet was a royal monastery. Pedro IV of Aragon was buried there, and Martin I was even then in the process of building a palace in the monastery. The king indicated his displeasure and embarrassment; he was astonished that they were prepared to suffer excommunication at the hands of the true (i.e. Avignon) pope, 'especially as our lord the pope has proclaimed that monks remaining in their monasteries shall have the same indulgences as those who go to Rome in person, in view of the present situation of the Church.' Accordingly the abbot was to forbid such pilgrimages and to punish monks who disobeyed. The monks appear to have taken no notice of this letter for, some weeks later, a second letter gave expression to the king's anger that certain monks had persisted in their intention of going to Rome 'into the territory of that detestable intruder and to the great detriment of our holy mother the Church'. If the rest of them would promise not to go, he would ask the Avignon pope to nominate some convenient Spanish sanctuary where pilgrims could claim the Jubilee indulgence or else, perhaps, to permit the voyage to Rome. The affair throws an interesting light on the resilience of the Roman pilgrimage in the least creditable period of its history.

The Return of the Popes

'Pity Rome', a papal official cried at the beginning of the fifteenth century, 'once thronged with princes and crowded with palaces, now it is a place of hovels, thieves, wolves, and worms.' In later life, Adam of Usk's memories of Rome were of wolves howling at night outside his house and fallen buildings blocking the narrow streets. The campanile of St. Peter's had been struck by lightning in 1352 and the rubble remained for many years strewn across the Vatican Hill. The triumphal arch of Arcadius fell down in the time of Urban V. The last years of the papal schism, 1378 to 1417, brought Rome to the nadir of its fortunes. In the absence of the popes the splendid ceremonies were curtailed and finally abandoned. The Neapolitan troops who entered Rome in 1408 found St. Peter's abandoned by the canons, and not even on the feast of the apostles could anyone be found to celebrate Mass. One of the canons recorded in his diary that there was not enough money to light the candles in the basilica on the feast of the apostles in 1414. 'At Corpus Christi we celebrated Mass in great poverty on account of the war and the tribulations of St. Peter's. We carried the Eucharist on foot in a small crystal tabernacle,…lighting our way with six torches…for the canons could not afford any oil.'

The Jubilee of 1423 was a miserable affair. It occurred automatically thirty-three years after that of 1390, but no one troubled to proclaim it, and it was so little publicized that some historians have doubted whether it ever took place. The pope, Martin V, made no special arrangements. This may have been because he was reluctant to revive the controversies which had accompanied the Jubilees of the schism, or perhaps because he was anxious not to set up an indulgence in rivalry with the Hussite crusade. Nevertheless Poggio Bracciolini, then in the service of the papacy, complained that he was ' oppressed by a monstrous mob of barbarians' (i.e. non-Italians) who brought with them their dirt and uncouth manners. Perhaps more pilgrims would have attended but for the war which had engulfed northern Italy. John, abbot of St. Albans, waited for several weeks at Siena for a safe-conduct from Filippo-Maria Visconti, duke of Milan, and when at last it was forthcoming he was horrified by the desolation he found north of Rome.

Martin V entered Rome for the first time in his reign in September 1420. With the exception of nine years in the reign of Eugenius IV, the popes resided in Rome for the rest of the fifteenth century. The artistic patronage of the papacy returned to the city for the first time in a century and a half, and with it came some of the vigorous religious life of an earlier age. The arrival of new relics in Rome contributed to the atmosphere of revival. Martin V presided in person over the translation of St. Monica from Ostia. A few relics of Constantinople found their way to Rome after the fall of the city to the Turks in 1453. Thomas Paleologus, despot of the Morea, fled to Italy in 1460 bringing with him the head of St. Andrew and the right arm of St. John. The translation of the first of these relics to St. Peter's in April 1462 was marked by a formal oration from Pius II and a special plenary indulgence. The Sienese ambassador had not seen so many pilgrims in Rome since the Jubilee of 1450. Thus the last notable item from the greatest collection of relics that the mediaeval world had known, painfully assembled over seven centuries by successive Byzantine emperors, found its place in a Latin church.

The imposing ceremonies which visitors to Rome had missed in the fourteenth century now reappeared. Martin V ordered a new golden tiara from Lorenzo Ghiberti, together with embroidered vestments, banners, and ceremonial swords. Ever-increasing splendour attended the publication of the annual bull *In Coena Domini* in which the pope solemnly excommunicated the enemies of the Church, followed by cries of 'so be it, so be it' from the assembled cardinals. When Arnold von Harff witnessed it in 1497 it took a full hour to read and the watching crowd filled the entire Leonine city. The Easter celebrations of 1437 prompted in one pilgrim the reflection that 'Rome, which used to be the highest among nations and is now the lowest, yet retains these superb ceremonies from the days when they signified her mastery over all men.'

The *sudarium* of Veronica reached the zenith of its fame in the fifteenth century. Popular belief attributed miracles to it, and the indulgences attached to it were the largest in Rome, seven thousand years for Romans, ten thousand for Italians, fourteen thousand for foreigners. The 'vernicle', which had by now replaced the horse of Constantine as the emblem, or badge, of Rome, was worn by every returning pilgrim. Langland's palmer pinned it to his hat, as did Chaucer's pardoner. Public displays of the Veronica were occasions for mass exhibitions of fierce repentance which astonished more than one visitor to Rome. Francesco Ariosto, a lawyer in the service of the duke of Modena, witnessed one of these ceremonies when he was in Rome on official business in 1471. A thin, fragile, almost transparent veil of silk was brought forward bearing the features of a bearded man. The entire crowd was silent and fell to its knees.

> 'It would be well beyond my powers to describe the feelings of devotion and piety which overcame the crowd then, or to tell you what public displays of repentance and humility were to be seen; what beating of breasts, what mental anguish in so many faces; what weeping, crying, and howling broke the silence of the square as sinners humbly begged for pardon; with what anguish they raised their hands to Heaven imploring mercy. They beat themselves repeatedly, causing themselves great pain, for they felt that by their sins, they had inflicted on Christ those wounds whose marks they saw before them; and now they hoped to wash away their guilt with tears, to purge the stains of sin with groans of pain. And from so much weeping and anguish, such general lamentation, there emerged consolation, rejoicing, happiness, and even jubilation at having experienced a

spiritual renewal. A sudden change of mood from sorrow to joy overcame the crowd.'

The catacombs experienced a revival in the fifteenth century. They had never been entirely forgotten, but in the absence of the popes, the continual work of repair had been neglected. Several of the galleries had fallen in and some of the altars had been looted. A commission was appointed in 1424 to survey them. Repairs were undertaken, and pilgrims were once again reminded of these curious survivals from the earliest age of the Christian Church. The most famous were those on the Appian Way, which were entered from the church of St. Sebastian. The Florentine Giovanni Rucellai explored them in 1450 and reported that the bodies of St. Fabian and St. Sebastian carried a plenary indulgence. John Capgrave's first impression was of a 'grete pitte, for we go down thereto on 28 steps'. When his eyes had become accustomed to the gloom, he found himself in 'a cave or ellis a myre under the ground.…The cymytery is thus long that if a man tary not in the chapeles but go rit forth he schal walk it by the time that he hath said four times the *miserere mei Deus*. In this place were buried 46 popes and eche of them gave grete indulgence to the same place.…The comoun opinion is there of this place that who so evyr out of synne visit it…clene shreve and contrite, he is assoiled as clene as a man may be by the power of the Church.' As for the other catacombs, they were now 'desolate for horrible darknesse and disuse of peple', and few pilgrims visited them.

When they were not visiting the churches pilgrims amused themselves in various ways. Arnold von Harff saw a passion play performed at the Colosseum in which 'everything was acted by living people, even the scourging, the crucifixion, and the death

of Judas.' The actors were all children of the well-to-do 'and
therefore it was fittingly and richly performed.' Some of the
more discerning pilgrims visited the Vatican library, recently
refounded by Nicholas V and Sixtus IV largely on the proceeds
of the Jubilee of 1450. The Burgundian pilgrim Georges
Lengherand explored it in 1485, and found five large rooms full
of books, of which one was available for private study, the rest
reserved for curial officials.

The pilgrims brought prosperity to Rome, and to no one
more than to its innkeepers. *Alberghi* multiplied prodigiously in
the fifteenth century, and according to one pilgrim there were
1,022 of them functioning in 1450. Some of them achieved
international repute, like the Albergo della Luna, where
Francesco da Carrara stayed during the imperial coronation of
1355. Most of them were too expensive for the ordinary pilgrim. When the retinue of Borso d'Este were accommodated
in Rome at the pope's expense in 1471, the bill came to seven
thousand gold florins. Those who had to pay their own bills
preferred to hire a room in a private house or else to bring an
introduction to some compatriot living in Rome. Arnold von
Harff was accommodated by one Johann Payll, a German doctor who kept a small guest-house for German pilgrims and
offered his services as a guide. Large parties were well advised
to arrange their accommodation in advance, especially at Easter
and the feast of the apostles. There was no room for Otto, duke
of Bavaria, when he arrived unexpectedly in the city in 1489,
and he was obliged to withdraw to the villages of the
Campagna. On the whole the hoteliers of Rome were an
unpopular group of men. Erasmus thought their chances of salvation limited. Villon's friend Guillaume Bouchet derived the

word 'host' from the Latin 'hostes' for they were all enemies to him.

Towards the end of the Middle Ages the resources of private enterprise were supplemented by national hostels. National hostels had existed before, but none had survived the decline of the Roman sanctuaries in the thirteenth century. The English house, which had been the last to disappear, was the first to be revived. Opposite the church of St. Thomas on the Via Monserrato, now the site of the Venerable English College, stood a small house belonging to one John Shepherd, an English rosary-seller living in Rome. He sold it in 1362 to the 'community and society of the English in the city,...for the benefit of the poor, infirm, needy, and wretched people coming from England to the city, and for their convenience and utility.' Shepherd and his wife Alice stayed on to run the hospice at a wage, and thus was born the English hospital of the Holy Trinity and St. Thomas. In the course of three decades it expanded into neighbouring houses, and by the end of the sixteenth century it could accommodate sixty pilgrims. A second English hospice was founded in 1396 by a wealthy London merchant, and became the hospital of the Holy Trinity and St. Edmund, king and martyr.

Other national hospices sprung up in much the same fashion, originating in the generosity of a few rich individuals and expanding haphazardly into neighbouring houses. In 1389 Dietrich of Niem, a curial official from Westphalia, joined with a merchant of Dortrecht to found the German college of S. Maria dell' Anima. It consisted originally of three adjoining houses, of which the central one was a chapel and the other two for the accommodation of male and female pilgrims. The college became by far the wealthiest and most celebrated national hospice in Rome. It was continually enriched by bequests from German pilgrims and residents. Successive popes conferred indulgences on its benefactors, and Eugenius IV gave its chaplains the valuable privileges of administering the Eucharist and hearing confessions, privileges normally reserved for parish churches. The Anima rapidly acquired all the surrounding houses and within a few years the three original houses were all used as the chapel, the middle one being the nave and the outer two the aisles. Few Germans of note passed through Rome without visiting it and inscribing their names in the book of benefactors. Among other ethnic groups which could boast their own hospices were the Italians, Portuguese, Swedes, Irish, Castilians, Aragonese, Sicilians, Flemings, Bretons and Hungarians. Not all were organized in the same way and some were richer than others. Some, such as the Portuguese hospice of St. Anthony, were little more than a chapel where the Portuguese of the city worshipped. The German hospice was packed out every night while the Irish one was so little used that it was shortly turned into a seminary for Irish priests. The services they offered to pilgrims depended largely on the extent of their endowment. The Swedish hospital of St. Bridget occupied the palace in which the saint had lived out her last years, and it was operated by the rich Bridgetine order. Pilgrims were allowed to stay there for as long as they liked and were given free bread and wine for the first three days; only the more opulent pilgrims were asked for payment. The impoverished Flemish hospital of St. Julian was more stringent, pilgrims being obliged to leave after three nights. No food was served at all. Vagabonds, soldiers of fortune, and the rich, were altogether excluded. One exception only was made for poor priests who might stay for eight days so long as they promised to say at least two masses in the chapel.

In January 1449 the crisis of the papacy had passed and Nicholas V considered the moment appropriate for the proclamation of the fifth Roman Jubilee, to be held from Christmas 1449 to Christmas 1450. It is probable that more pilgrims attended this Jubilee than any previous one, and the chroniclers competed with one another in devising suitable hyperboles to describe the throngs of travellers. The Sienese diplomat Agostino Dati watched Frenchmen, Germans, Spaniards, Portuguese, Greeks, Armenians, Dalmatians and Italians on the roads to Rome singing hymns in every language. The crowd of Burgundians who joined them was *'noble et sainte chose et devote a veoir'*. The first rush of pilgrims ended in February. 'The crowds diminished so rapidly that the innkeepers became discontented and every one began to think that it was all over. Then, in the middle of Lent, so many pilgrims appeared that there was no room for them in the inns and many had to sleep out in the vineyards...or beneath the porticoes of the basilicas.' Pilgrims begged for the love of God to be allowed in for the night at any price. Such was the shortage of food and beds that Nicholas several times reduced the number of days which pilgrims were required to spend in Rome. In the autumn he reduced them to one, on account of the threat of famine, but even so, on Saturdays and Sundays, when relics were displayed at St. Peter's and the pope gave his benediction, the crowd filled the entire Leonine city and the vineyards and cemeteries beyond. Most of them could see nothing at all. In mid-summer a serious epidemic thinned out the crowds arriving in Rome. Mortality in the city itself was high, and pilgrims fleeing from the crowded streets spread the plague along the roads leading north. Panic gripped the papal court, which made hurried arrangements to depart for Fabriano. The ambassador of the Teutonic Order had it on good authority that Nicholas had forbidden infected persons to come within seven miles of him on pain of excommunication. Nevertheless it was officially estimated that for most of the year 40,000 pilgrims were entering Rome every day, and Giovanni Ricci reckoned that a million were there at Easter.

The Florentine merchant Giovanni Rucellai had fled his native city to escape the plague and, finding himself in Perugia, he reflected that 'confession may liberate me from the fires of Hell but only a plenary indulgence can free me from Purgatory as well.' He departed for Rome with his family and three friends in February. Rucellai was one of the first pilgrims to record his impressions of some of the recent works of art in the city; Giotto's frescoes in the chapterhouse of St. Paul's, the gold reliquaries of S. Maria Maggiore, the bronze tomb of Martin V in the Lateran, all of which struck this Florentine as 'extremely fine'. He prayed at all the altars in St. Peter's, diligently examined the relics proferred for his veneration, and returned satisfied to Perugia less than a month after his departure.

John Capgrave, the Augustinian prior of King's Lynn, experienced like many others the frustration of having no reliable guide to the city. The Colosseum he pronounced to be 'a marvellous place whech was made round of schap and grete arches', but he could find no book to tell him what its function had been. Capgrave wrote his own guide, a scholarly work for its time, in the hope that it would be found 'ful solacious' to his countrymen who had never been to Rome. For their benefit he described the relics of each church in extreme anatomical detail. His interest was stirred by a 'pees of the flesch of seynt Laurens and coals joyned therto rit as thei fried in his passioun'. In Holy Week he inspected the heads of St. Peter and St. Paul in the Lateran. St. Peter, he reported, was 'brood…with much hair on his berd and that is of grey colour betwixt whit and blak. The hed of Paule is a long face, balled with red hair both berd and hed.' In the church of St. George the head of the saint was kept in a tabernacle with a removable lid to enable pilgrims to kiss it. Capgrave took part in the many processions of Easter week and stated that they were originally ordained by Christ, the reason given for this opinion being that 'saynt Austin gevyth us swech a rule in his boke *De Moribus Ecclesiae*…that when we cannot see hem grounded in scripture we schul suppose that Christ taut hem.'

Towards the end of the Jubilee year the pope's satisfaction was marred by a serious incident. The Ponte Molle in front of the Castel St. Angelo had caused anxiety to the papal police ever since the first Jubilee of 1300. The narrow bridge was the only means of access from the city to the Vatican. The shops which had once lined both sides were destroyed in the fighting of 1405, thus greatly reducing the crush in Jubilee years. Even so, the crowds of 1450 were too large for it. At Easter, soldiers from the Castel St. Angelo, together with some youthful volunteers, had to drive back the pilgrims with sticks in order to avert a serious accident. Families and friends lost each other in the mêlée and 'it was pitiful to see pilgrims wandering aimlessly about in search of missing fathers, sons, or companions.' On another occasion, when the crowds in front of St. Peter's were so tightly packed that none could move, a messenger on horseback tried to get through the crowd. The horse panicked and reared, killing several pilgrims with its hooves and throwing the rider to his death.

On Saturday December 19th, a week before the end of the Jubilee, the crowds had gathered to attend the weekly display of the Veronica and receive the pope's blessing. For some reason there was an untoward delay and at four o'clock it was announced that owing to the lateness of the hour the benediction would not take place that day. The unwieldy crowd of pilgrims turned back in disappointment and swarmed across the Ponte Molle into the city. In the middle of the bridge a mule, bearing Pietro Barbi, cardinal of St. Mark, was trying to move in the opposite direction. The narrow bridge was blocked for a few seconds but those behind did not notice and pushed forward, trampling some underfoot and forcing others over the side into the river. With some presence of mind the castellan of St. Angelo recruited some citizens on the spot, closed the bridge, and dispersed some pilgrims on the northern side of it. It took a further hour to clear the mob on the bridge itself and the crushed bodies of 178 pilgrims were recovered. A further seventeen bodies were pulled out of the river at Ostia, some still clutching each others' clothes for safety. All were taken to the nearby church of St. Celsus for identification. As evening closed appalling scenes were witnessed there as 'fathers, sons, and brothers wandered among the bodies as if in Hell itself,… pathetically holding candles in their hands and looking through rows of corpses, then collapsing with grief as they recognized those for whom they were looking.' The Medici agent in Rome was told of the disaster by a servant who had not seen such carnage since his service in the Turkish war. No one was more horrified than Nicholas V who tried to avert a similar disaster in future by clearing some of the buildings at either end of the bridge. Two small chapels were erected near the scene to commemorate the dead and warn those who crossed in future.

As usual the Jubilee indulgence was enjoyed by many who did not go to Rome. At Salzburg in February 1451 Nicholas of Cusa, papal legate in Germany, proclaimed that all those who made a good confession and visited local churches on fifteen separate days would earn the indulgence; they were also to fast for seven Fridays, abstain from meat on seven Wednesdays, and give half the cost of a journey to Rome to the bishop. At the special request of Nicholas V this offer was not available to simonists, adulterers, and notorious sinners, who would obtain only a partial remission of their sins. Those who had actually been to Rome in 1450 were invited to claim a second Jubilee indulgence and in their case no payment was required. The proceeds were to go to pious uses appointed by the pope. These concessions, which originally applied only to the province of Salzburg, were repeated throughout western Europe. Henry VI of England no doubt expressed the prevailing view when he declared that 'the whole population will rejoice to see the light for the remission of their sins.'

As a result of the Jubilee very great sums of money came into the papal coffers, 'an almost infinite quantity of gold and silver', says the pope's biographer. Most of it was spent on the Jubilee itself, particularly on buying in large stocks of grain. What was left went partly to the upkeep of the basilicas and partly to the purchase of the priceless collection of Greek and Latin manuscripts which is still one of the finest possessions of the papacy. But the most important results were intangible. The Jubilee marked the revival of the prestige of the papacy after a century of conciliar conflict. The last anti-pope had abdicated only a few months before the beginning of the Jubilee. Nicholas's biographer assures us that his design in proclaiming the Jubilee was to 'increase the dignity of the Holy See', and that many pilgrims came not only to claim the indulgence but to behold the person of Nicholas V, now universally recognized as pope. No doubt this is the exaggeration born of enthusiasm. But the Sienese diplomat Agostino Dati later had occasion to record that 'the memory of those days is a warm one for me, for they made manifest the triumph and glory of the Christian religion. From the most distant parts of the world, all these pilgrims travelled to Rome to visit the head of the universal church and the tomb of the prince of the apostles. Truly this was a year worthy to be remembered throughout all ages.'

14

The Later Middle Ages I

Women

The circle of Latin pilgrims which grew up around St. Jerome at the close of the fourth century was dominated by women. The most celebrated pilgrims of the late classical period, Paula, Etheria, Melania, were all women. Even in the 'dark ages' of the west, female pilgrims were a familiar sight on the roads. Their sins and their illnesses are recorded by Gregory of Tours, their restless addiction to travel unequivocally condemned by St. Boniface. For most of the Middle Ages, however, women were not particularly noted as pilgrims. So much so that the sudden reappearance of large numbers of female pilgrims in the fourteenth and fifteenth centuries called for comment, usually hostile comment. Chaucer's wife of Bath became the epitome of the worldly, pleasure-seeking pilgrim. In the *Quinze Joies de Mariage,* it is the nagging wife, not her husband, who decides on a pilgrimage to Le Puy, where all rich and fashionable ladies go. Berthold of Regensburg and Giordano da Rivalta both devoted whole sermons to the virulent condemnation of female pilgrims. It is possible that at the close of the Middle Ages women formed the majority of visitors at many shrines. This was certainly true of several sanctuaries visited by Henry VIII's monastic commissioners in the course of their travels, notably of Bury St. Edmund's, where they reported that 'there was such frequence of women coming and resorting to this monastery as to no place more.'

Women seem to have been partly responsible for the abrupt rise of obscure shrines which is such a marked characteristic of the cult of the saints in the late Middle Ages. At the end of the fourteenth century, the Cistercian abbey of Meaux in Yorkshire commissioned a sculptor to carve a large wooden crucifix for the church. Miracles were reported as soon as the crucifix was completed and local people began to make pilgrimages to it. 'It was thought', wrote abbot Thomas Burton, 'that if women were admitted to the abbey church the general atmosphere of devotion would be greatly increased, which would be most advantageous to our monastery. We therefore requested the abbot of Cîteaux for permission to admit honest men and women to the crucifix, which was granted on condition that the women did not enter the conventual buildings.' This was, in fact, a common problem at monastic sanctuaries. The monks of St.-Benoit-sur-Loire had solved it by erecting a marquee at the back of their church where much venerated relics could be seen by both sexes on Saturdays. Some important sanctuaries, however, adhered to the letter of the Benedictine rule and excluded female pilgrims altogether. In the first half of the twelfth century, Symeon of Durham boasted that no woman had ever been admitted to the sanctuary of St. Cuthbert and that when Judith, wife of earl Tostig, had tried to enter, she had been paralysed at the door. The same fate befell a chambermaid who tried to enter the sanctuary in the following of king David of Scotland, dressed as a monk.

A more practical objection to the presence of women was that it was usually they who were trampled underfoot in the rush to venerate the relics of the church. Most of the casualties at St.-Denis in Suger's time were women, as they were at other public exhibitions of relics. A pregnant woman was crushed to death in the crowd that gathered to see the head of St. Martial in 1388. In many Roman churches the authorities excluded women for this very reason. This rule originated in the fourteenth century when women first appeared in Rome in large numbers. An anonymous Englishman who visited Rome in 1344 remarked that the women gathered round the shrines were the most devout he had ever seen. Nevertheless, they were not allowed to set foot in the chapel of St. John the Baptist in the Lateran basilica but were directed to gain the indulgence by touching the outside of the door. No women were allowed in the chapel of the Saviour, or even in the *Sancta Sanctorum*, where the most important relics were housed. Various explanations were advanced. Women, it was alleged, were inclined to vanity, hysteria, or vice. In one of the forbidden chapels of St. Peter's a rich lady was said to have demanded that a crucifix be washed after a poor woman had kissed it. According to another school of thought, a woman had 'once uttered such things that she burst asunder'. John Capgrave sagely remarked that the exclusion of women was attributed to 'many lewd causes to which I will give no credens'. His own theory probably represents the truth of the matter. 'All those whech have be at Rome knowe well that the women there be passing desirous to goo on pilgrimage and to touch and kiss every holy relik. Now in very soothfastness these places which are forbode to them are rit smale....And uphap some woman in the press, eithir for sikness or with child, be in grete perel there, and for this cause they were forbode the entre of these houses as I suppose.'

Tourists

Rome was the principal tourist resort of the Middle Ages, but it was far from being the only one. 'Some light-minded and inquisitive persons', Jacques de Vitry remarked, 'go on pilgrimages not out of devotion, but out of mere curiosity and love of novelty. All they want to do is travel through unknown lands to investigate the absurd, exaggerated stories they have heard about the east.' As travelling became easier and cheaper, tourism, lightly disguised as pilgrimage, became extremely popular. It would be a gross exaggeration to suggest that simple curiosity had displaced the intensely spiritual feelings of an earlier age, but in the fifteen century, it was certainly the predominant motive of many pilgrims.

This new interest is reflected in their guide-books. The guide-books of twelfth-century pilgrims in the Holy Land were condensed, factual and turgid; most of their topographical information was still derived from the seventh-century writings of Bede and Adamnan. A few pilgrims supplemented these arid tomes by writing travel diaries. Soon after the first crusade an Englishman called Saewulf wrote a long personal account of his experiences in the Holy Land. Four years later the Russian abbot Daniel composed another, having found it impossible to buy a good guide-book in Jerusalem. Pilgrims were still complaining about the inadequacy of guide-books in the 1160s, when John of Wurzburg observed that the city had been largely rebuilt since the beginning of the eleventh century, and Bede was no longer a useful companion. 'For this reason', he thought, 'my own detailed description will not be found superfluous.' Even more interesting are the accounts of thirteenth-century travellers, some of whom penetrated to Damascus or Baghdad and recorded their impressions of Islamic society. Exactly what audience they had in mind when writing these lengthy 'itineraries' is not at all clear. Dietrich, bishop of Wurzburg, declared that his itinerary, written in c. 1172, was intended to 'satisfy the desires of those who cannot go there themselves'. But in this it was plainly unsuccessful for, like almost every other account of this period, it was read by a few friends of the author, and then allowed to gather dust in a monastic library. The only itinerary which was much read at the time was the *Jerusalem History* of Jacques de Vitry, a book more interesting for its pungently expressed prejudices than for its information.

All this changed in the fourteenth century. If one event deserves to be singled out as a landmark in this change it was the appearance, shortly after 1357, of *Mandeville's Travels*. This purported to be an account of the travels of Sir John Mandeville to Palestine, Turkey, Persia, India, and Egypt, but it was in fact a compilation of stories drawn from various itineraries of the previous century with a few colourful fictions added. The author of this audacious literary forgery is still unknown, though the evidence points to Jean d'Outremeuse, a prolific collector of legends, who lived in Liège. Despite his improbable details, the fraudulent 'Mandeville' was treated with a respect that was denied to the truthful Marco Polo, whose account of his travels was dubbed *Il Milione* for its supposed exaggerations. *Mandeville's Travels* immediately became one of the most popular books of the age. Well over three hundred manuscripts survive. Within half a century it had been translated from the original French into Latin, English, high and low

German, Danish, Czech, Italian, Spanish, and Irish. With the advent of printing it appeared in countless editions, and in England alone Wynkyn de Worde printed four different versions before the death of Henry VII. It was the first really popular book to portray travel as an adventure and a romance. For a hundred and fifty years after its appearance the public devoured each new travel book as it was written. 'Mandeville' was plagiarized and abridged by lesser writers, while a glut of reminiscences came from the pen of every Holy Land pilgrim with pretensions to literacy. The English Augustinian John Capgrave was inspired to write his account of Rome by reading Marco Polo and 'Mandeville'. When Felix Faber returned from his round trip to the Holy Land, crowds gathered to listen to his experiences. Most of the annual pilgrim-fleets which sailed from Venice in the fifteenth century carried at least one diarist; there were four on the fleet of 1479 and five on that of 1483. By this time, too, pilgrims' diaries were issuing in thousands from the printing presses.

Travel-books both reflect and create interest in the places that they describe. 'Mandeville' and his imitators stand at the beginning of the first chapter in the history of mass-travel, and the *Travels* reflect the growing romanticism and enthusiasm with which people were beginning to look on distant lands. Many pilgrims returned from their travels as little Mandevilles and, as the Lollard William Thorpe observed, 'if they be a month out in their pilgrimage, many of them shall be an half year after great janglers, tale-tellers, and liars.' This is the world of Chaucer's knight, who had 'ridden no man further, as well in Christendom as hethenesse'. So it was of the Wife of Bath:

And thryse had she been at Ierusalem.
She hadde passed many a straunge streem.
At Rome she hadde been and at Boloigne,
In Galice at seint Iame and at Coloigne.
She coude much of wandring by the weye.
Gat tothed was she, soothly for to seye.

Official arrangements are now made for tourists for the first time. Information offices appear at Rome and consulates in Egypt and Palestine. The Venetian package tour is at the height of its popularity. Governments begin to encourage tourism. Thus a safe-conduct issued by the Aragonese chancery in 1387 to a band of German husbands and wives describes their purpose as being 'to fulfil their pilgrimage and observe the Spanish way of life'. The commercial treaty made between England and France in 1471 envisaged the possibility that English gentlemen might wish to cross the Channel 'to see and observe the country *pour leur plaisance'*. The invitation was probably taken up, for John Wyclif believed that the English were especially addicted to pilgrimages on account of their restless curiosity. Gréffin Affagart, on the other hand, thought it a peculiarly German vice. But both were agreed that it was deplorable. 'Let no man go to the Holy Land just to see the world', wrote the impeccably orthodox Santo Brasca, 'or simply to be able to boast "I have been there" and "I have seen that", and so win the admiration of his friends.'

In several respects these early tourists behaved exactly like their modern counterparts. They carved graffiti on walls, for example. Noblemen were in the habit of inscribing their coats of arms inside the Holy Sepulchre itself while pretending to be praying, and some of Felix Faber's companions had brought chisels and mallets with them for the purpose. Ghillebert de Lannoy's graffiti, carved in the refectory at Mount Sinai, can still be seen. They also bought gaudy souvenirs, like the coral paternosters and shaped semi-precious stones which were on sale outside the sanctuaries of Le Puy. The nagging wife in the *Quinze Joies de Mariage* bullied her husband into buying some of these. Nompar de Caumont bought several pieces of fine coloured silk at Jerusalem, together with four pieces of rope the length of the Holy Sepulchre, three silk purses, thirty-three silver rings and twelve silver crucifixes which had touched the Holy Sepulchre, a number of relics of doubtful worth, a bag of Jerusalem soil, a black embroidered purse, two pairs of golden spurs, four roses and a phial of Jordan water. These he distributed amongst his relatives and tenants when he returned.

Primitive postcards were sold at the more popular sanctuaries. In Rome pictures of the *sudarium* of Veronica, painted on pieces of stiffened paper torn out of old books, were mass-produced and sold to pilgrims in the streets. Bernard van Breidenbach, dean of Mainz cathedral, brought a professional painter with him to Jerusalem in 1483 'to record all the principal cities from Venice onwards, which he did in a masterly and accurate fashion.' These drawings were reproduced in the earliest edition of Breidenbach's account of his journey, a beautiful octavo volume printed in Mainz in 1486. They include 'pull-out' drawings of Venice and Rhodes, the west front of the basilica of the Holy Sepulchre, and several animals which the artist claimed to have seen in Palestine, amongst them a unicorn and a strange hairy-looking man with a frog-like face. The French edition, printed in Lyon in 1489, is the earliest known example of copper-plate printing in France.

Books like Breidenbach's were probably read at leisure at home, not carried about on long journeys. Felix Faber, it is true, took a small library with him to the Holy Land, but he was an unusually thorough tourist. Most of the books carried by pilgrims in their hipbags would have been route-books, like the *Guide for Pilgrims to Santiago* or the curious Anglo-Saxon guide to the sanctuaries of England, which dates from the eleventh century. Route-books did not vary much through the years, but as the routes became better organized after the thirteenth century they passed out of fashion and were replaced by books of indulgences. The *Pilgrimages and Pardons of Acre,* written in French in about 1280, is an early example, altogether typical of its species. The *Mirabilia Urbis Romae* comes nearest, perhaps, to our own concept of a guide-book. In the Holy Land there were eight anonymous 'descriptions', all but one dating from the twelfth century, but they were cursory and inaccurate and, although much used, they were found wanting even by the uncritical pilgrims of the twelfth century.

Pilgrims who were not satisfied with these sketchy handbooks were obliged to hire a local guide. Professional guides had been found in Jerusalem as early as the fourth century, when their inaccuracies and exaggerations had earned them the implacable hostility of St. Jerome. The Russian abbot Daniel, in 1106, was lucky enough to find an 'old man, extremely learned' who spoke Greek and accompanied him on expeditions to all the outlying parts of Palestine. John of Wurzburg was guided round the Jacobite convent of St. Mary Magdalene by a monk who proclaimed the scriptural associations of the place with dramatic emphasis and many flamboyant gestures. In some cities, guides were licensed and organized. Venice, with its bureaucratic tradition, was naturally one of these. The republic provided guides whose duties included showing visitors the sights, finding them lodgings, helping them with their shopping, and introducing them to shipowners.

It is a measure of the greater sophistication of late mediaeval pilgrims, more critical and better-read than their predecessors, that they listened with suspicion to the untruths peddled by guides. Felix Faber was a devout man, but not a naive one. He prepared for his second pilgrimage to the Holy Land by reading every pilgrim's account he could lay hands on, numerous histories of the crusades, and the writings of St. Jerome. He doubted whether the Lord's Sepulchre was 'really his own, or another, built afterwards'. He did not believe the Arab guides who told him that the bodies of the Holy Innocents were preserved at Bethlehem. Arnold von Harff, who was neither naive nor particularly devout, was caustic in his remarks on the 'confusions' of the clergy on the subject of relics. He 'did not know' whether the tablets at S. Spirito in Rome were those which Moses received on Mount Horeb. Although von Harff did not question the value of relics as such, he had seen arms of St. Thomas at Rhodes, Rome, and Maestrich, as well as in India; heads of St. James the Less had been shown to him at Santiago and Venice. On being told that St. Matthew the apostle was buried in Rome be recalled that he had seen shrines of St. Matthew in Padua and in Lombardy 'and they tell me that his head is at Trier in Germany, so I will leave it to God to resolve the confusions of these priests.' 'On the right hand side of the altar I was told that there lies St. Jerome, but was he not buried in Bethlehem and subsequently carried off to Constantinople? How he came to be in Rome as well, I shall leave to the learned to decide.' It was no more than Guibert of Nogent had said four centuries before, but the growing popularity of travel was bringing these disconcerting truths to a wider audience.

Noblemen

The Roman Jubilee of 1450 was remarkable not only for the numbers who attended but for their high social standing. They included the archbishop of Mainz with a suite of 140 knights, as well as the duke of Austria, the margravine of Baden, and the landgrave of Hesse. John, duke of Cleves, was seen passing on foot from church to church. Jacques de Lalaing led a large party of Burgundian noblemen to Rome, celebrating his departure from Châlons with a 'joyeux et plaisant banquet'. The same phenomenon was observed in 1475, when the Mantuan ambassador informed his master of the arrival of thousands of courtiers from every western kingdom, come to atone for their notoriously scandalous lives. Two periods stand out as being pre-eminently those of the noble pilgrim. The first came to an end at the close of the twelfth century, when the established shrines of Europe began to lose their hold on educated minds. Apathy and war combined to destroy shrines like Vézelay and St.-Gilles, while others, like Canterbury and Conques, were abandoned by their more distinguished clientele. The great spiritual revival which marked the hundred and fifty years before the Reformation brought new life to a few of these ancient sanctuaries and threw up a large number of obscure new pilgrimages. The greater shrines, like Le Puy, became fashionable resorts; otherwise the intensely fashion-conscious wife satirized in the *Quinze Joies de Mariage* would never have wanted to go there. At Le Puy then, and at other major sanctuaries, the nobility were once more to be found in large numbers. Although the cult of the Virgin was primarily a popular one, the kings of England were assiduous pilgrims at Walsingham, just as those of Aragon and Castile were at Montserrat. Philip the Good, duke of Burgundy, visited Notre-Dame de Boulogne on at least a dozen occasions. Louis XI of France, who was well-known for his intense, rather simple-minded piety, made pilgrimages to Mont-St.-Michel, Notre-Dame de Cléry, Puy Notre-Dame in Anjou, and Le Puy, amongst other sanctuaries. He was constantly attributing to the intervention of the Virgin his salvation from every kind of mishap, and at his death in 1483 he was buried beside the shrine of Notre-Dame de Cléry, to whom he had so often attributed his victories in battle.

The motives of noble pilgrims of the fifteenth century were less straightforward than those of the twelfth. Worldly motives were certainly prominent and some pilgrimages were accomplished with a degree of ostentation which would have surprised churchmen of an earlier age. Nevertheless, they paid lip-service to traditional ideals, and often more than lip-service. Nompar de Caumont, who departed for the Holy Land in 1418 with several servants and equerries, shared the obsession of his more spiritual contemporaries with death and remission. 'Know then that death has no mercy on kings, princes, or lords, but takes them all with equal abandon', he wrote, in a passage that might have been a commentary on the *danses macabres* that now decorated the walls of so many churches and cemeteries; 'every man must know that the world is but a temporary habitation, and that death, harsh and unpitying, is imminent.' Some noble pilgrims cast off their status and travelled without attendants or fine clothes. Hence the curious complaint of the Venetian senate in 1437 that noblemen were bringing the pilgrim fleets into disrepute by travelling dressed as commoners and complaining when they were treated as such. 'Everyone knows', they declared, 'about the abominable way in which princes, counts, and foreign noblemen travel to the Holy Sepulchre disguised as common pilgrims.' There may have been more in this 'abominable' practice than Christian humility. When Gréffin Affagart advised his readers to dress as poor hermits on their travels, he added that this would save them from being preyed upon by shipowners, robbers, pirates, and Turks. Indeed, the stately fashion in which most noble pilgrims travelled is often revealed to history by their complaints that they had been robbed of their treasures. Earl Rivers, brother-in-law of Edward IV, complained to the pope in 1475 that he had been ambushed outside Bracciano on his way to attend the Roman Jubilee, and robbed of a large quantity of precious gems, gold trinkets, silver goblets, cash, 'and other things of very great value'.

The Venetian republic occasionally arranged luxurious passages to the Holy Land, either in return for money or else, as in the case of the earl of Derby in 1392, in return for 'the favours which might be granted to Venetian merchants trading or resident in England'. The earl's accounts of the expenses of his voyage include the hire of a warehouse in Venice to store supplies. His agents, accompanied by interpreters, visited fairs in nearby towns, and bought several whole oxen, 2,250 eggs, 2,000 dates, 1,000 pounds of almonds, several dozen butts of sweet wine, and large quantities of mattress stuffing, live hens, water, cheese, oil, fish, vegetables and spices. The total sum thus expended was 2,379 ducats, or nearly forty times the all-inclusive fare usually demanded by shipowners. In addition, the earl and his company enjoyed the bounty of the Serenissima, which instructed its agents not to disclose the cost to the earl himself, but to hint at it delicately in the presence of the English ambassador. The earl's needs were not untypical. Indeed they were modest by comparison with those of some aristocratic pilgrims. The ship which carried Pietro Casola to the Holy Land in 1494 was joined at Corfù by a nephew of Ferdinand of Aragon, a young clergyman destined for a rich benefice who was going, by way of preparation, to take the Franciscan habit on Mount Sion. His baggage, which included several horses and falcons, was carried in a separate cargo boat sailing alongside the ship.

In the last years of the fifteenth century German and Italian princes were renowned for the unmatched ostentation which surrounded their pilgrimages. Ernest, duke of Saxony, arrived in Rome in 1480 to fulfil a vow of pilgrimage with a suite of two hundred mounted retainers dressed in black livery, their horses in jewelled halters. The papal camera recorded the expenditure of a hundred gold florins on entertaining him. Otto, duke of Brunswick, was accompanied to Rome in 1489 by physicians, apothecaries, courtiers, and twenty-seven personal servants. Perhaps such splendid expeditions should not be regarded as pilgrimages at all, though those who participated in them vigorously asserted that they were. Ernest of Saxony's pilgrimage may have been prompted by the desire to extend his political influence in Germany by securing the election of his relatives to important bishoprics, an object in which he succeeded handsomely. But no such considerations will explain the magnificent progress of Niccolo d'Este to the Holy Land in 1413. Apart from an official historiographer, his suite included several dozen orderlies, four chamberlains, a chef, a sub-chef, a tailor, a barber, a page, a chaplain, and two trumpeters.

The interest of the nobility in the Holy Land was in a large measure due to the practice of dubbing knights in the Holy

Sepulchre. This was a survival of the ideology of the crusades after the shattering disaster which had overcome the last crusading expedition at Nicopolis in 1396. The dubbings were originally conducted under the auspices of the order of St. John of the Hospital, which now had its headquarters at Rhodes. Nompar de Caumont stopped at Rhodes on his way to the Holy Land and persuaded a Navarrese knight of the order to accompany him to Jerusalem, and to dub him a knight of St. John in the Holy Sepulchre itself. This is the first trace of a practice which was to enjoy a considerable popularity in the fifteenth century. By 1480, newly dubbed knights are found calling at Rhodes on their way back from the Holy Land, enrolling their names in a book kept by the king of Cyprus, and receiving a certificate in return. It was only by degrees that the practice of dubbing knights in the Holy Sepulchre acquired a status quite independent of the Order of St. John, Thus dubbings were not only performed by Hospitallers. Niccolo d'Este knighted several of his courtiers on his expensive expedition of 1413. Guillaume de Chalons was knighted by one of his companions in 1451. Alternatively, the senior pilgrim present might be asked to perform the ceremony. The reason for its popularity lies in the prevailing view that the institution of knighthood had been devalued in an age when Louis XI, for example, could permit rich bourgeois to buy knighthoods, and indeed compel them to do so. Some hint of this was given by Guillaume de Chalons when he remarked to his companion that he was proposing to be knighted in the Holy Sepulchre because he 'did not wish to be a cardboard knight, but a true knight'. Much the same sentiments were expressed by the father of George van Ehingen, who sent him to the Holy Land because it was 'not his wish that I should pass my time in unwarlike idleness at some princely court...or else in taverns'. Indeed, as Felix Faber remarked in his lengthy panegyric of the 'order of the Holy Sepulchre', it was the only order of knighthood universally recognized in an age when bogus orders sprang up in every province. But it seems that the order was already passing the way of its predecessors, for Faber hints that 'nowadays base-born men are occasionally admitted.'

15

The Later Middle Ages II

The Climate of Opinion

The mobs who converged on Limoges in 1388 to witness the display of St. Martial's relics were not alone in regarding the papal schism as God's punishment on human wickedness. Contemporary opinion, reflected in the impassioned protests of St. Catherine of Siena, saw in it the culmination of an era of appalling spiritual decay. Some reaction to the sterility of the fourteenth century was perhaps to be expected in the fifteenth, and the flagellant processions of 1399 were early symptoms of it. In the same year St. Vincent Ferrer left Avignon to begin a preaching-tour of southern France, the first of a spectacular series of nomadic missions conducted by the two mendicant orders. What Vincent Ferrer did for France, Manfred of Vercelli and Bernardino of Siena did for Italy, their pupils for Germany and Spain. The immediate effects were certainly impressive. In Rome, which, more than any other city, had felt the impact of the schism, the arrival of Bernardino in June 1424 was marked by a great bonfire of playing-cards, lottery tickets, musical instruments, wigs, 'and such-like effeminate vanities'. In March 1411 the magistrates of Orihuela in Murcia reported to the bishop the moral transformation of their town:

'All those who are heard blaspheming are visited with swift punishment. The gambling hall has been closed down. Conspiracies and secret societies have been abandoned, and diviners and sorcerers have gone out of business. We have never seen so many people going to confession, and churches which used to be too large are now too small. The citizens, overcome by a common feeling of goodwill and a strong love of God, have forgiven each other their trespasses.

No generation should be judged by its moments of enthusiasm, the contemporaries of St. Bernardino least of all. Christianity remained in their eyes a ritual framework of life, rather than a body of coherent beliefs and commanding ideals. Like the great merchant of Prato, Francesco Datini, they recited prayers at fixed hours, uttered pious formulae when they were appropriate, gave alms when it was expected of them, and marked the passing stages of their lives by receiving the sacraments of the Church. But the overpowering conventionality of religious life was punctuated by brief outbursts of hysteria which, although by no means new, were highly characteristic of the century which preceded the Reformation. Even the sober Datini, who spoke of the Roman Jubilee only as a source of profit, joined the flagellant processions of 1399. It was typical both of the man and his age that he should have given as his reason the fact that 'all men, or at least the greater number of Christians, were moved to go on pilgrimage in that year.'

By halting, irresolute steps, Christendom entered upon a period of spiritual revival. The revival accentuated some of the traditional characteristics of lay piety, and created new ones of its own. The literal, pictorial interpretation of dogma is taken to new extremes; this is above all others the century of religious drama and eucharistic miracles. The strong desire of laymen to feel that they were part of an 'order' charged with special spiritual functions, finds expression in their enthusiasm for confraternities, lay brotherhoods whose activities ranged from running hospitals to flagellation. The confraternities are also the symptom of something new: the special importance attached to the performance of spiritual exercises *en masse*. The public procession is the typical spiritual observance of the late Middle Ages. Flagellant processions first appear in Perugia in 1260 and their most hysterical pitch is reached in the towns of northern Italy and the Low Countries at the end of the fourteenth century. Mass-pilgrimages are made to hitherto obscure shrines. The religion of the laity was above all a religion of external observances, marked by a strong element of ritual. Men joined confraternities because in doing so they automatically acquired a measure of merit which brought them closer to salvation; their own personal spiritual needs had very little to do with it. It was an attitude which bred extreme conformity and a somewhat unhealthy view that the clothes make the man. Wearing a pilgrim's badge or the emblem of a confraternity became pious works in themselves. Hence the curious remark of Christine de Pisan that priests could not possibly be possessed by devils because they knew the formulae which chased them away. An earlier age would have felt that possession by devils had more to do with the spiritual condition of the victim.

Amongst external observances, pilgrimage remained by far the most important, but the shrines which pilgrims visited changed. Some of the traditional saints, St. Thomas of Canterbury for example, still drew crowds on their feast day or in Jubilee years, but there was no continuous cult as there had

been in the twelfth century. The loyalty of the masses was transferred to an enormous number of minor shrines which commanded attention for a few weeks before relapsing into
obscurity and being replaced by others. Fifteenth-century pilgrims were creatures of passing fads; they rarely needed to
travel far to their destinations. 'You tell me that your new saints
have displaced the old ones', Sacchetti had once protested;
'what business have you to enshrine their relics and light candles in their honour, when images of the Blessed Virgin and
Christ himself lie forgotten in darkened corners?'

The 'new saints' of the late Middle Ages were often humble men and women who were acclaimed as saints by local
people. Their cult was rarely recognized by the Church and did
not generally extend beyond the immediate locality. Many of
them were working class, like the multitude of peasant-saints
venerated in parts of France. St. Zita of Lucca was one of the
more celebrated examples. She was a serving maid who died in
1272 and became the object of a cult which continued for several centuries. Despite the popular origins of the cult, cardinals,
archbishops, and secular magnates are known to have visited
her tomb, and chapels were dedicated to her in many parts of
Europe. But she was not canonized until 1696. The death of
Henry of Bolzano, a labourer of Treviso, in 1315 was followed
by a prolonged outburst of popular enthusiasm. Three notaries
were appointed to record the miracles which occurred at his
tomb in Treviso cathedral, and in 1381 his relics were even displayed in public on his feast day. He was never canonized.

Parish priests of great saintliness were frequently the objects
of these spontaneous and unauthorized cults. Margery Kempe
used to weep at the grave of the vicar of St. Stephen's,
Norwich, 'the good vicar, for whom God showed high mercy

to his people'. In 1361 John de Grandison, bishop of Exeter heard ('not without amazement and irritation, I assure you'), that Richard Boyle, parish priest of Whitestone, who had recently committed suicide, was being revered as a saint by his parishioners. Ordinary folk from the area were making pilgrimages to his tomb, and twelve miraculous cures had been reported. The veneration of parish priests was not always opposed by the authorities. In 1260 the bishop of Coutances built a magnificent chapel over the grave of Thomas Hélye, parish priest of Biville, who had died three years earlier. Although Hélye was never canonized, the shrine was visited by pilgrims until the nineteenth century. A similar fate befell John Schorne, parish priest of North Marston in Buckinghamshire, who died in 1314. His shrine, and a well which he had blessed, were visited throughout the fourteenth and fifteenth centuries, and were believed to cure ague. His cult, like that of Thomas Hélye, was never authorized by the Church, but it was so well established in 1478 that his remains were translated to the Lincoln chapel in St. George's, Windsor.

More common still was the veneration of miraculous statues. Most were statues of the Virgin, of the sort whose origins were pungently described by the Lollard author of the *Lanterne of Light*.

> 'The painter maketh a live image forged with divers colours, till it seem in fools' eyes as a lively creature. This is set in the church in a solemn place, fast bounden with bonds for it should not fall. Priests of the temple beguile the people with the foul sin of Balaam in their open preaching. They say that God's power in working of his miracles loweth down in one image more than in

another and therefore come and offer to this, for here is showed much virtue.'

It was just such a statue which had drawn troops of women to the abbey of Meaux in the early fourteenth century, thus causing so much trouble to the monks. The artist, we are told, spent several months carving it and used a nude model. The spoils of the dissolution of the English monasteries included several much-venerated statues like the rood of Boxley which rolled its eyes, shed tears, and foamed at the mouth, and the Kent statue burned at Smithfield in 1538 which bowed to receive the prayers of pilgrims. The attitude of the authorities was highly equivocal. The abbot of Meaux was delighted by the arrival of pilgrims until he found that they were more trouble than they were worth. Bishops generally turned a blind eye to unauthorized images, and earnestly defended them against Lollards. Archbishop Warham assured Wolsey that Boxley was 'so holy a place where so many miracles are showed'. The inaction of the bishops was really a reflection of their impotence, for a popular cult could survive any number of anathemas. In 1386 bishop John Buckingham of Lincoln ordered an enquiry into rumours he had heard of certain doings in Rippingdale. 'Many of our subjects have made for themselves a certain pretended statue, vulgarly known as Jordan Cros, in the fields of Rippingdale. They have begun to adore it, and allege that miracles are occurring there. They preach, ring bells, and hold processions for the deception of the people and for their own grain. Indeed, laymen are said to be embezzling the offerings for their own use.' But the bishop's letter was not the end of the matter for, in 1392, the parishioners succeeded in getting the pope's permission to build a chapel over the statue and to worship there with or without the bishop's consent. The reason given was 'the great number of miracles wrought there, and the multitudes who arrive with offerings from all over England.'

The discomfort of the Church in the face of unauthorized popular shrines was the symptom of a deeper malaise. Ever since the thirteenth century there had been a tendency on the part of many educated churchmen to withdraw from the more popular forms of piety. The outspoken views of non-conformists like St. Bernard gradually became the orthodoxy of a generation of scholastics and canon lawyers which had little else in common with the great abbot of Clairvaux. The change of heart coincided with the climax of that long process of spiritual centralization which had begun with the papacy's claim to a monopoly in the canonization of saints. A substantial and influential body of churchmen began to look with profound suspicion on extreme symptoms of popular devotion. This they did partly because they felt, as Guibert of Nogent had done, that popular religion was vitiated by superstition and ignorance; and partly because they disliked spiritual exercises which by-passed the sacramental function of the Church and offended its claims to spiritual authority. Their attitude was crystallized in the prolonged crisis in the Franciscan order in the thirteenth and fourteenth centuries. The tendencies within the order to depart from the spirit of St. Francis' *Testament,* with its strict prohibition of the possession of property, were officially encouraged. The minority of Franciscans who wished to abide by it were deliberately prevented from doing so, while the *fraticelli* who asserted the doctrine that Christ had lived in absolute poverty and that the order should do likewise, were persecuted as heretics. Insofar as the late mediaeval Church had a 'policy' towards popular religion, it was summed

up in a marked distaste for 'enthusiasm' when it occurred outside the framework of ecclesiastical institutions. The origin of
this 'policy' should perhaps be sought in the bull *Quo Elongati*
of 1230, in which Gregory IX declared the *Testament* of St.
Francis to be invalid.

The 'policy' was, of course, neither formally proclaimed nor
consistently followed. The encyclopaedic works of Jean
Gerson, chancellor of the University of Paris (d. 1429), are full
of contradictions and conflicts between the thinker who felt
that popular superstitions were theologically unsound, and the
indulgent pastor who took the traditional line that they were
better than nothing. Gerson was completely opposed to the
practice of mass-flagellation, and the Church's opinions on this
subject are a microcosm of its attitude to popular religion in
general. Flagellation became a common spiritual practice in the
western Church in the tenth and eleventh centuries. Peter
Damian gave it an elaborate theological justification, arguing
that it was the supreme manifestation of humility and love of
God, a perfect imitation of the sufferings of Christ himself.
Flagellation was still practised in private in the late Middle
Ages, particularly by the Carthusians. In the thirteenth century,
however, the Church was first confronted with flagellation
practised, not privately by individual ascetics, but by thousands
of laymen in the main squares of Italian cities. That which had
been acceptable as an act of personal piety, was condemned
when it became an expression of hysterical enthusiasm. The
change of heart is epitomized in the behaviour of Clement VI,
who himself instituted flagellant processions in Avignon in
1349, in the hope of warding off the Black Death. But the
arrival of an unofficial band of wandering flagellants in the city
began to sow doubts in his mind, doubts which were rein-

forced by the arguments of a deputation of masters of the University of Paris. The deputation dwelt on the popular nature of the flagellant movement. Not only were the flagellants uneducated laymen, *indocti, ignari, rudes,* but they were a sect, purporting to offer an independent route to salvation, flouting the spiritual authority of the Church. In October 1349 Clement declared the flagellants to be heretics, and ordered the suppression of their processions throughout Europe.

The mood of critical suspicion was not confined to mass movements. Visions and revelations, which had played so important a part in the spiritual life of an earlier age, were now subjected to increasingly hostile scrutiny. Those of St. Bridget of Sweden were critically examined for heretical leanings by a commission of the council of Constance (1414–1418). In England, the visions of Margery Kempe brought upon her accusations of Lollard heresy. She was three times arrested after experiencing trances in public, and although her beliefs were found to be orthodox, the distaste of the clergy for her particular brand of enthusiasm was not one whit abated. 'We know well that she knows the articles of the faith', the canons of York minster stated, 'but we will not suffer her to dwell amongst us, for the people hath great faith in her dalliance, and peradventure she might pervert some of them.'

The harshest strictures were reserved for the cult of the saints, and the miracles associated with them. As well as inveighing against clerical avarice in terms not unlike those used by St. Bernard, John Wyclif condemned the cult of saints as such. He denied that miracles were the proof of holiness, or that canonizations were a good guide to sanctity. He abhorred the multitude of festivals. 'Some men trowen truly that all such saints profit not men unless they make them love Christ. So if

men would better love Christ without such feasts, it were better for them to do without such saints.' Wyclif's Lollard admirers were almost unanimous in their objections to pilgrimage.
The cult of St. Thomas of Canterbury was the object of particularly venomous criticism. Several Lollards had occasion at
their trials to inveigh against Becket himself, and one of them
told the bishop of Norwich that the martyr was a false traitor
and a cowardly knave who had been killed at the cathedral
door while attempting to flee, and was even then suffering in
Hell. Pamphlets against the cult of St. Thomas were still being
written in the sixteenth century, when the pilgrimage to
Canterbury was ridiculously unimportant.

Wyclif's views, important as they are as a foretaste of things
to come, are less interesting than the opinions of churchmen
who accepted the structure of the late mediaeval Church. The
council of Constance unequivocally condemned the opinion
of John Wyclif, but many of the most prominent reformers at
Constance themselves believed that the cult of the saints ought
to be restricted. The canonization of St. Bridget in 1391 provoked some sharp criticism, not only because her revelations
were suspect, but because it was felt that there were too many
saints and that their veneration occupied too important a place
in the religious life of the age. Henry of Langenstein asked
'whether it were right to canonize her, given the great multitude of saints already venerated. Is it seemly to proclaim new
saints to be celebrated with greater solemnity than the apostles
themselves?' Nor was Henry's an isolated voice. Jean Gerson
repeated his words with approval. Pierre d'Ailly laid before the
council a programme of reforms which included the demands
'that images and pictures in churches be not permitted to multiply so, that new shrines be forbidden, and that so many new

saints be not canonized.' In the sermons of Nicholas of Clamanges, these sentiments became part of a general assault on all external observances. 'It is vain to preach to the outer man', he urged, 'if Christ does not resound within him.'

On miracles, the views of the heretical Wyclif can scarcely be distinguished from those of the orthodox Gerson. The Carthusians, Gerson pointed out, were renowned for their sanctity but they performed no miracles. Indeed, miracles were generally reported only at shrines where the sanctity of the person venerated was in doubt. No one doubted the sanctity of St. Jerome or Gregory the Great, and no miracles were attributed to them. However, none of these sentiments had the slightest effect on popular practice. Both before and after the council of Constance, conscientious prelates laboured in vain to prevent ordinary people from proclaiming miracles. The problems of Oliver Sutton, bishop of Lincoln (1280–99), are altogether typical of those of a late mediaeval bishop of a large diocese. In April 1296 he closed down the private chapel of Edmund, earl of Cornwall, at Hambledon. It had only recently been constructed, it was not officially consecrated, and now it was the scene of 'various superstitious practices and vain inventions,…rash assertions of miracles not authorized by the Church'. Two years later bishop Sutton had to deal with more unproven miracles and an eager throng of pilgrims at Great Crawley. Problems constantly arose in connection with holy trees, magic wells, and the like. The bishop has heard that the vicar of Linslade is encouraging the cult of a well in his parish by spreading stories of miraculous cures; the usual prohibitions follow. Bishop Grandison of Exeter, another reforming prelate, did not mince his words on such occasions. 'I find these miracles hard to believe and impossible to prove', he wrote in 1340;

'I fear that the people have given themselves over to idolatry and strayed from the path of the true catholic faith,…deluded by insane and untrue visions, inspired by the Devil and his agents, and deceived by false superstitions. It is our experience that they are frequently led on by cupidity as well.' His commissory was to visit the offending villages and stamp out the cults, if need be with excommunication and anathema.

Nicholas of Clamanges was satisfied that no age had witnessed so few miracles as his own, and that saints, like Peter and Paul, who used to corruscate in wonders, no longer did so. But he was speaking of 'genuine' miracles, i.e. those recognized by the Church. They had indeed dwindled almost to nothing, but the unrecognized sort were probably commoner in the fifteenth century than ever before. The attempt to reform popular religion was a failure. Its true effect, as John of Trittenheim pointed out in 1513, was merely to widen the gulf between the minority of highly educated clergy and most ordinary Christians. John himself believed strongly in miracles, and held that more people had been saved by reading about them than by listening to a thousand philosophical discourses. He hated the learned of his own day for separating themselves from the people, and accused them of turning instead to mysticism, writing poetry, and sexual indulgence. Only the simple and the poor still believed in miracles, and practised the traditional religion of the Church.

It was an exaggeration, as the author's own career amply demonstrated. But fundamentally John of Trittenheim's diagnosis was correct. The Church in the fifteenth century was a very much more rigid institution than it had been in the twelfth. It was no longer capable of absorbing overpowering spiritual movements, and those movements therefore occurred outside the framework of the Church. As a cause of the Reformation, this was a fact of greater importance than the abuses which are often supposed to have discredited the late mediaeval Church.

The Cult of the Virgin

The story of Theophilus is amongst the most attractive and expressive mediaeval legends. Theophilus was the steward of a bishop in Cilicia, and he was anxious to succeed his master on the episcopal throne. With the assistance of a Jewish sorcerer, he arranged to sell his soul to the Devil. The contract was drawn up and signed by both parties in the presence of witnesses, and from that moment Theophilus succeeded in all that he attempted. But his enjoyment was marred by pangs of remorse, and he began to think of ways in which he could rescind the contract. After he had passed several nights in prayer, the Blessed Virgin dramatically intervened, wresting the parchment from the hands of Satan and restoring it to Theophilus. It is, of course, the ancestor of the Faust legend. Like many legends of the Virgin, the origins of this story are Greek and it does not appear in the Latin Church until the ninth century. Nevertheless, if the number of editions, translations, and surviving manuscripts is any guide it was by far the most popular legend of the Virgin known to the Middle Ages. The reason for its extraordinary appeal is not far to seek. The story of Theophilus's compact with the Devil accorded exactly with current notions about the personality and power of evil. At the same time it offered, in the veneration of the Virgin, a guarantee of protection from evil. This was the function of the Virgin in the religious literature of the Middle Ages. She intervened to save those whom justice, human or divine, had condemned.

She offered an escape from the rigorous teaching of the Church on the subject of damnation and punishment. Thus it was that already in the late eleventh century, the office of the Virgin sung in churches hailed her as the 'mother of mercy, who took pity on Theophilus and saved him from the trough of sin and misery':

Tu mater es misericordiae
De lacu faecis et miseriae
Theophilum reformans gratiae.

The early collections of miracles of the Virgin, dating from the twelfth century, are so many variations on the same theme. A knight of ill-repute was saved on account of his devotion to the Virgin. A monk who used to slip out of his monastery at night was saved because he never passed an altar of the Virgin without saying 'Ave Maria'. A loose-living nun found that her pregnancy was miraculously concealed from her superiors. Another nun, who died unconfessed, was saved because of her daily invocations of the Virgin. A monk learned in his sleep that he was already inscribed in the book of the elect because of the care with which he had painted the Virgin's name in an illuminated manuscript. 'By her intercession', Caesarius of Heisterbach told his novice, 'sinners are enlightened, the despairing are brought to confession, the apostate is reconciled, and the righteous comforted with revelations.' The salvation of those who deserved to be damned is the theme of all Caesarius's stories. 'Wonderful indeed is the compassion of Our Lady', says the novice after hearing of the salvation of an unworthy priest, rightly deprived of his benefice; 'for thus she defends a feeble-minded priest who ought to have been deprived, and by her intervention he was able to keep his benefice.'

The theme was capable of being simplified to the point of distorting the moral precepts of the Church. Jacques de Vitry illustrated his sermons on the power of the Virgin with the story of a gambler who was enabled to amass Croesian riches by regularly invoking her name. All pilgrimages appealed to a universal desire to wash away sin by a simple, ritual act, but none more so than pilgrimages to the Virgin. The popular view was reflected in the dying words of John, abbot of Belleville, to his attendants: 'Only one thing do you need to know from me; he who would be saved need only honour the Virgin.' This simple idea is very far from the profoundly spiritual concept of the Virgin's role entertained by St. Bernard. Its appeal was to a more popular audience. The early Marial shrines were almost exclusively patronized by ordinary people and, although they were joined in the late Middle Ages by more august pilgrims, the shrines never lost their popular character.

Outside the village of Essones, near Corbeil, there stood a ruined chapel dedicated to the Virgin. In the 1120s the villagers believed that they had seen mysterious candles burning there on Saturday nights. Subsequently, several peasants were miraculously cured of various ailments, and the fame of the miracles began to draw pilgrims from further afield. The abbey of St.-Denis, which owned the chapel, learned of these happenings and sent a group of monks to serve there. The incident, which is related by abbot Suger, is typical of the popular, and more or less spontaneous, origins of many Marial pilgrimages. Indeed the earliest of the hysterical mass-pilgrimages which are so characteristic of the fifteenth century occurred in connection with Marial sanctuaries of the twelfth. Chartres, Soissons,

Beauvais, and Paris all received processions of peasants afflicted with ergotism during the severe epidemics of the early twelfth century. More remarkable still were the 'building crusades' which began in 1145, when thousands of Norman pilgrims arrived at the shrine of Notre-Dame de Chartres, intending to assist in the building of the western towers of the cathedral. For some months men and women volunteered to haul heavy wagons of stone up the steep slope on which Chartres is built, flagellating themselves as they did so, and singing hymns in honour of the Virgin. The crowds who pulled carts of building materials to the abbey of St.-Pierre-sur-Dives regarded it as a form of homage to the Virgin. As the building continued, services in her honour were continually held in the abbey, while in the yards outside the volunteers held services of their own, modelled on those in use at Chartres. As at Chartres, flagellation was an important part of the ritual. The phenomenon was repeated when Chartres cathedral was rebuilt after the disastrous fire of 1194. The 'entire population' of Pithiviers, in the Loire valley, made a collective pilgrimage to Chartres, dragging a wagon of corn as an offering. More corn came from the villages of Batilly, Chateau-Landon, and Bonneval. Some Breton villages dragged building stone over rough roads for two hundred miles to assist the rebuilding of the Virgin's cathedral.

'Building crusades' reflected the view that pilgrimages performed *en masse* were more meritorious than those performed alone. We find the pilgrim-builders forming themselves into sects, or 'brotherhoods', performing their penitential rituals in common, and solemnly expelling those members who showed signs of returning to their old ways. The same thought lies behind the processional pilgrimages of whole villages to a Marial shrine. The parish priest of Issigny, in the Bessin, was so impressed by the processions in honour of the Virgin at Bayeux that he organized a collective pilgrimage to Coutances from his own parish, in which the entire population, with one exception, took part. Coutances, he explained to his congregation, was 'the dwelling of the Holy Ghost and the scene of many miracles. Their pilgrimage would therefore be the more acceptable to the Blessed Virgin if they accomplished it together, by a common vow.' The one parishioner who refused to go was struck down for his presumption.

After the end of the eleventh century, some Marial sanctuaries had relics of the Virgin. But the cult of the Virgin remained relatively independent of relics. They were certainly not considered essential, as they would have been in any other cult. Their place was taken by statues which eventually received the same veneration as relics, and worked miracles. Coutances cathedral had a miracle-working statue of the Virgin in wood, in addition to its relics of the Virgin's body. Chartres cathedral possessed the tunic of the Virgin, but it also had a celebrated statue in the crypt which, by the beginning of the fifteenth century, entirely monopolized the attention of pilgrims. These statues were always painted, sometimes in bright colours, like the four figures of the Virgin in the extraordinary vision of the monk of Eynsham, recorded in 1196. But the most famous of all, including the one at Chartres, were painted black. The black Virgin of Rocamadour is first mentioned in 1235, when it was trodden underfoot by an armed band of the abbey's enemies. The black Virgin of Le Puy was brought back from Palestine in 1254 by Louis IX and immediately made the fortune of the city. Special indulgences were offered on the first feast-day, in May 1255, and several hundred were killed in the crush under the very eyes of the king. In the fourteenth century the floodgates were opened, and miraculous statues appeared in thousands of obscure churches. England and the Low Countries were particularly affected. Some achieved more than local fame, and in 1356, archbishop Fitzralph pointed out in a sermon 'a certain danger from the veneration of images, which some frequently and wrongfully call by the name of those they are intended to represent, such as St. Mary of Lincoln, St. Mary of Walsingham, St. Mary of Leicester, and so forth.' Particularly reprehensible were 'the oblations which are offered to such images on account of the false and fabricated miracles wrought by their intercession.'

Any event which abruptly drew attention to a statue might be the beginning of a cult. In the Flemish village of Beveren the parish priest had only to build a small oratory in 1330, and to light a lamp in front of a statue of the Virgin, and pilgrims began to arrive immediately. Miracles were recorded within weeks and episcopal indulgences followed. An old and faded statue at Antwerp was venerated as soon as it was repaired, repainted in bright colours, and removed to Brussels. Sometimes, as at Beveren, the parish priest deliberately provoked the cult; sometimes he was taken by the sudden rush of pilgrims to venerate a new statue. The vicar of Kernetby reported to his superiors in 1310 that 'there have suddenly and unexpectedly arisen new offerings in the said church, in honour of God and the most glorious Virgin Mary, at a certain *new* image of the said Virgin there.' Three years later, it was eclipsed by another miraculous statue in nearby Foston. There archbishop Greenfield had to put an end to the 'great concourse of simple people who come to visit a certain image of the holy Virgin, *newly placed* in the church.' The mere appearance of a roadside statue was often enough to draw pilgrims. In an alcove in the wall of the Franciscan convent at Trier, there was a small statue of the Virgin which was alleged to have wept tears. For four months the street was impassable for the crowds, until the enthusiasm died away. A street statue in Heilbronn, which was believed to have spoken, had a longer life. The pilgrimage began in 1442 and was still prosperous sixty years later.

All these obscure cults had in common the suddenness of their origins. Elaborate justificatory legends were composed afterwards to clothe them with a spurious antiquity. The great pilgrimage to Notre-Dame de Boulogne began abruptly in 1211, but the absurd legend placing its origins in the seventh century only became current about two hundred years later. Similarly the legend of the Virgin's miraculous intervention at the battle of Rozebeke (1382) grew up many years after the first pilgrims had visited the oratory on the site. The legend and miracles of Notre-Dame de l'Epine in Champagne date from the seventeenth century.

Aachen, Walsingham, and Boulogne long retained their place among the great sanctuaries of Europe, but most Marial pilgrimages were short-lived. They sprang up without warning, burned bright for a while, and then quite suddenly ended. Many of them left no literary or architectural monument to their existence. At the beginning of the sixteenth century John of Trittenheim recorded a few that had sprung up in the previous century in the diocese of Wurzburg, none of which would be known but for his strange rambling works. In the wine-growing town of Deitelbach a man was injured in a brawl and healed by a statue of the Virgin in the parish church. There had been many such miracles in the diocese in recent years and the authorities were hostile. The pilgrimage quickly ended. The parish church of Tynbach was the object of a great Marial pilgrimage for a few brief weeks. No one wrote down the miracles and now they were forgotten 'but the church, which was built from the offerings of the faithful, remains as a testimony to what happened there.' There had been great Marial pilgrimages in Wurzburg itself at one time, but now both miracles and pilgrims had ceased.

The crowds who crammed into these small oratories and parish churches contained no noblemen, no bishops or deacons. They consisted entirely, as John of Trittenheim admitted, of the 'simple people of Christ'. He attributed this, as we have seen, to the arrogance of the learned and the simple devotion of the poor. But his other explanation is probably closer to the truth. Peasants and artisans could not afford to go on distant pilgrimages and they were ashamed to beg, so they honoured the only saint whose shrine was always nearby. Thus it was that the *populus simplex et rusticanus* was devoted to the Virgin above all saints. In England, where educated opinion of the early sixteenth century turned sharply against pilgrimages, the sanctuaries of the Virgin were the only ones which did not share in the general decline. Our Lady of Walsingham, with £260 *per annum* on the eve of the dissolution, was the only church which still drew a substantial income from offerings. In the two days that the dissolution commissioners passed in the priory, nearly seven pounds was offered. St. Anne's Well at Buxton, the commissioners reported, was as much visited as ever on account of the 'fond trust that the people did put in these images'. As for the image of Our Lady of Cardigan, it was 'used for a great pilgrimage to this present day'.

Political Saints

Nowhere was the tendency of the populace towards the spontaneous veneration of heroes more pronounced than in the case of political saints. In an age which attached incalculable importance to miracles as an indication of God's will, it was perhaps to be expected that miracle-working would be harnessed to political causes. Writing to the bishop of Metz in March 1081, Gregory VII pointed to the miracles of the saints as an argument for the superiority of the spiritual over the temporal power. 'Where among all the emperors and kings can a man be found to compare with St. Martin, St. Anthony, or St. Benedict, not to speak of the apostles and martyrs? What emperor or king has raised the dead, cured the leprous, or opened the eyes of the blind?' Eighty-four years later, on Christmas Day 1165, the emperor Frederick Barbarossa answered Gregory's question by having Charlemagne 'canonized' at Aachen in the presence of the anti-pope Paschal III, thus giving formal recognition to a popular cult of long standing.

Political saints were found in every country, though more, perhaps, in England than anywhere else. There they included Edmund king and martyr, Elphege archbishop of Canterbury, Edward the Confessor, Thomas Becket, Simon de Montfort, Thomas of Lancaster, Edward III, Richard Scrope archbishop of York, and Henry VI. Some of these men lived lives of exceptional piety by the standards of their day. But with the exception of Edward the Confessor, they all died by violence, and it was almost certainly the circumstances of their deaths rather than the manner of their lives that earned them the veneration of the faithful. For the equation of violent death with martyrdom and sanctity there were many continental parallels. Canute II king of Denmark was murdered in 1086 and buried where he lay. His death was followed by several years of famine and epidemic, during which the dead king was frequently reported to have worked miracles and appeared in visions. In about 1100 the legates of king Eric persuaded the pope to declare him a saint.

After Becket, none of the English political saints was canonized, nor was their cult in any way sanctioned by the Church. Indeed in some cases, the cult is only known from the vigorous denunciations and prohibitions of the authorities. Whereas popular devotion sufficed to make a saint in the ninth century, or even in the twelfth, it was clearly inadequate by the fourteenth. In the cases of Thomas of Lancaster and Edward II the pope repeatedly refused even to appoint a commission of inquiry, although pressed to do so by powerful interests. The extent of the change can be measured by comparing two political saints separated by a gulf of seven centuries. St. Leger, bishop of Autun, was blinded and beheaded by his opponents in 679 after becoming involved in a civil war between two rival claimants to the throne. Yet this most political of saints was the object of a liturgical cult of continuing importance throughout the Middle Ages. In Guibert of Nogent's time he was renowned for curing fevers. The canonization of Becket in 1173 suggests that it was still possible for equally unattractive persons to achieve sanctity by a refined version of this process in the twelfth century. The story of Thomas of Lancaster shows that it was no longer possible in the fourteenth, even with the energetic support of the king.

In the civil wars of Edward II's reign, both sides were inclined to venerate their dead leaders as saints. Thomas, earl of Lancaster, was accounted a saint after his execution in March 1322. Pilgrims visited his tomb at Pontefract daily until the king's envoys, sent to investigate, placed an armed guard on it. Early in the following year, two of the guards were killed by a mob of politically motivated pilgrims from Kent, and in June, reports reached the king's ears that images of the earl were being venerated at St. Paul's in London. In 1327 the political situation changed. Most of Thomas's enemies met violent ends. In parliament the earl's cause triumphed, and the commons pressed for his canonization. Nothing came of it, but the popular cult continued unabated. In the fifteenth century a hagiographical life appeared. His hat and belt, preserved at Pontefract, cured minor ailments until the Reformation. Thomas's antagonist, Edward II, enjoyed a similar apotheosis after his defeat and murder. His body was carried to Gloucester abbey and enclosed in a superb alabaster tomb. The cult received official encouragement in the reign of Richard II, who was often threatened with the fate of his great grandfather and may have hoped to silence such threats by procuring Edward's canonization. Urban VI and Boniface IX were plied with bribes, and a list of Edward's miracles was despatched to Rome for their perusal. But no decision had been made by 1399, when Richard's own deposition and murder made the whole affair an irrelevance.

These pilgrimages, although political, were in no sense official. They arose spontaneously and largely amongst the common people. After the death of Simon de Montfort on the battlefield of Evesham, miracles were quick to manifest themselves and the pilgrims they drew were mostly poor men from areas such as London, which had supported de Montfort in his lifetime. Within a year of his death the Dictum of Kenilworth forbade anyone to venerate him as a saint or give any credence to 'these vain and fatuous miracles attributed to him by certain persons'. As for the cult of Edward II, the streets of Gloucester could scarcely contain the 'enormous concourse of plebs' come

to see his shrine. Within six years the offerings had yielded
enough to pay for the rebuilding of a transept of the abbey
church. It is tempting to see in this a religious manifestation of
those early murmurings of social discontent which made
themselves heard in the late Middle Ages, but the evidence
does not permit it. What it does reflect is the tendency of ignorant people to look for a golden age in the past, and a hero in
any prominent figure who met a sudden and violent end.

Mass-Pilgrimages

The first pitched battle between the ecclesiastical authorities
and a major, but unauthorized, popular pilgrimage ended in a
complete defeat for the authorities. It occurred at Wilsnack, a
small town near Wittenberg in Saxony. In August 1383 the
parish church was burned to the ground. In the rubble, the
parish priest alleged, three consecrated hosts had been found,
unharmed, but marked with drops of blood. The news spread,
and the ruins of the church became a great pilgrimage centre
almost immediately. Within two years, a fine new oratory stood
on the spot, and by the early years of the fifteenth century it
was a sanctuary of international repute. Margery Kempe, who
walked there in 1433, knew it as a place of 'great worship and
reverence, and sought from many a country'.

At first, the authorities looked benevolently on the new
pilgrimage. Urban VI granted it an indulgence in March 1384,
and in the same month the archbishop of Magdeburg joined
with his suffragans in commending it to the faithful on account
of the 'manifest miracles already famous in every part of
Germany, which Our Lord Jesus Christ has worked through
the real presence of his body in the holy sacrament.' But in
1387 they were disturbed by the reports that large mobs of the

poor, many of them hysterical, were gathering at Wilsnack, and within twenty years of the shrine's abrupt beginnings, the Church was withdrawing its favour. The first to act was the archbishop of Prague, who had received reports of fraudulent miracles from pilgrims of his diocese. In 1405 he appointed a commission to consider the matter. Its members included John Hus, who had not yet fallen foul of the Church in Prague. On the basis of their report, a synod meeting in Prague in June 1405 condemned the pilgrimage and instructed the clergy of the diocese to preach against it at least once a month. This was followed, a year later, by a vehement pamphlet *On the Blood of Christ,* the work of Hus himself. In 1412, the archbishop of Magdeburg in turn ordered an investigation, from which he learned that the pilgrims were almost all 'plebeian persons who cannot be trusted'; a hysterical atmosphere pervaded the place, with pilgrims crying 'help my Holy Blood', and 'free me Blood of Christ'; insofar as these pilgrims were venerating the drops of blood as well as the host, the commissioners reported, they were being led into heresy. These disturbing facts were presented to a synod in the summer of that year, and the pilgrimage was sharply condemned as the product of overripe imaginations and clerical avarice. There matters rested for forty years. No active steps were taken to suppress it, and in 1446 the local clergy successfully applied for a papal indulgence. It was unwise of them thus to reopen old wounds, for the then archbishop appointed another commission of enquiry which reported in much the same terms as their predecessors of 1412. By the skilful handling of crowds, fraudulent miracles were passing for real ones every day. An atmosphere of extreme religious excitement was engendered by forceful preaching and by lighting an enormous number of candles in the church. Several false indulgences were on display in the church, and pilgrims were shown a shelf-ful of fat volumes in which the miracles of the Holy Blood were said to be recorded. The whole affair, concluded the commissioners, was an open invitation to heretics to deny the real presence altogether. Support for these views came from a surprising quarter. Several citizens of Wilsnack complained that the general suspension of excommunications at pilgrimage centres had made the town a haven of bandits and usurers. This weighty dossier was submitted to a provincial synod which met in 1451 under the presidency of the papal legate Nicholas of Cusa. In June the legate issued a new bull, forbidding the display of blood-stained hosts and ordering the sanctuary at Wilsnack to be closed.

How long the church of Wilsnack remained closed is not clear. Probably the pilgrimage never altogether ceased, though it undoubtedly suffered a decline. But in 1475 the archbishop of Magdeburg was abruptly reminded of its existence by another mass pilgrimage, this time involving several thousand children aged between eight and twenty. The children came from the regions of Franconia, Meissen, and Hesse. They left without informing their parents, and without money. The town of Erfurt alone lost 324 children as well as several dozen from each of the suburban villages. Hettstadt lost 300, Eisleben 1,100. Another mass-pilgrimage of children occurred in 1487, when 'an enormous concourse of boys, girls, and household servants of both sexes, all of them peasants and people of lowest class, flocked to the blood of Wilsnack inspired, it is believed, by a sort of giddy feeling *(spiritu vertiginis)*'. Rumour estimated their number at about 10,000, though there were probably much fewer than that. Thereafter, children's pilgrimages occurred at regular intervals, despite vigorous attempts to frustrate them.

'And men knew not the meaning of such a prodigy', the Erfurt chronicler wrote. The children's pilgrimages provoked controversy in all the towns they passed through. 'Some said it was the Devil's work, others that it was a wonderful miracle and praised God for it.' The chronicler himself thought it resulted from an imbalance of the humours in their bodies, a view which many shared, including the author of a searing tract *On the Pilgrimage of Foolish People to the Holy Blood in the Year 1475.* 'There are many who cannot in their natures stay quiet', this writer explained; 'this is due to a defect in their humours and the influence of the stars, or else perhaps to some work of the Devil.' Noting that almost all the child-pilgrims were from poor homes, the writer suggested that the bad harvest of the previous year might have had something to do with it:

> 'for the days are very long and empty of things to do and many are driven to pilgrimage for lack of bread to cat....Having no bread, and being too poor to stay with friends or neighbours, they were ashamed to go begging near their own homes. And so they decided to go on this pilgrimage and beg in each town on the route, reckoning that it was better to beg in a strange district than from people they knew. And that is why there were so many young boys among them....When curious onlookers asked them why they did it, they sought to explain themselves by saying that they were driven by an irresistible impulse.'

Other voices were added to the chorus of disapproval. An Augustinian of Erfurt pointed out the theological unsoundness of the pilgrimage, and somewhat futilely reminded the pilgrims that the journey would avail them nothing if they had not made a true confession and obtained the permission of their bishop. In July 1479, Marcus Spickendorff, *ratmeister* of Halle, recorded in his diary that he had heard an edifying sermon on the wickedness of going to Wilsnack. But no amount of thundering from pulpits succeeded in reducing the popularity of the pilgrimage until the village became Protestant in 1552. In that year the miraculous hosts were publicly consigned to the flames by the formidable evangelical preacher Joachim Ellefeld.

In fact, pilgrimages of children were by no means as uncommon as the preachers and pamphleteers suggested. The pilgrims who volunteered to build the church of St.-Pierre-sur-Dives in 1145 included a large number of children. The children's crusade of 1212 was a still more extraordinary outburst of this kind. A child called Stephen from the village of Cloies, near Vendôme, collected an army of children from central and northern France and announced his intention of marching to recapture the Holy Land. They embarked at Marseilles in several large ships. Two ship-loads were drowned in a storm off Sardinia, and the masters of the five remaining ships sold their passengers into slavery in north Africa. Another army of children was assembled simultaneously in Germany by a child called Nicholas. They penetrated as far as Genoa but failed to persuade the Genoese to transport them to the Holy Land, whereupon the 'army' broke up in disorder. Many of the children died of starvation on the roads of northern Italy while trying to return to their homes. Almost as interesting as the phenomenon itself was the reaction of contemporaries, who were far from unanimous in condemning it.

'Many people', one wrote, 'believed that the children should be taken seriously, and not laughed at. They believed that it was the work of God and a sign of pure devotion. They gave them food and money and everything they needed. But there were others, including most of the clergy, whose view was saner. They thought the enterprise useless and doomed to failure, and they denounced it. The populace, however, ignored them and shouted them down, saying that it was only their avarice which had turned them against the holy expedition, and not their sense of justice or love of truth.'

Only when the 'crusade' had ended in disaster did they come to agree with the clergy. An angry mob demanded the arrest of Nicholas's father, who had apparently encouraged the boy out of vainglory. He was seized and hanged.

The same violent disagreements surrounded children's pilgrimages whenever they occurred. The abbey of Mont-St.-Michel attracted the largest and most dramatic mass-pilgrimages of children. At Pentecost in 1333 'St. Elmo's Fire' was seen on the top of the spire of the abbey church. Large bands of children began to arrive almost immediately, and the continuous procession did not end until the first week in July. All were from poor, peasant families. They called themselves *pastoureaux*, a significant name, recalling the strange agrarian revolt of 1320, which had announced itself as having been called into existence by the Virgin to exterminate the Jews and deliver the Holy Land from the infidel. The children of 1333 had come from north-western France, most of them from Normandy and Brittany, but thereafter they came from further afield. In 1393 several hundred children aged between eleven and fifteen gathered at Montpellier, intending to march to Mont-St.-Michel. Another crowd of children left Millau in the summer of 1441 carrying a banner of St. Michael before them. The pilgrimage of children to Mont-St.-Michel was now common enough in southern France to merit a diatribe from the bishop of St. Papoul. In April 1442 he alleged that they were motivated by restlessness, impatience of hard labour, and a reprehensible desire to escape from the poverty of their homes; in future such journeys were to be forbidden on pain of excommunication.

The disease spread to Germany and the Low Countries in 1457. The circumstances were identical, except that the children came from the towns, and not from the depressed countryside. Several thousand of them, in groups up to eight hundred strong, began to arrive at Mont-St.-Michel after Pentecost, singing hymns in honour of the archangel. More than a thousand were counted passing through Wissemburg alone in the week after Christmas. Some were only nine years old. Again they were enthusiastically applauded by ordinary people and fed and lodged in the towns on the route. Again the clergy and the civil authorities tried in vain to prevent them. Denis the Carthusian wrote an angry pamphlet (now lost) *On the Processions of Young Boys to Mont-St.-Michel*. The town council of Regensburg tried to send them before the ecclesiastical courts and treated them to a sermon showing that the Christian faith 'in no way required of its devotees a pilgrimage to Mont-St.-Michel'. But their protests fell on deaf ears. In the following year more armies of children gathered in northern Germany and the Rhineland announcing that they had received 'certain revelations', instructing them to venerate the shrine of St. Michael, this time at Monte Gargano.

Why the cult of St. Michael should have appealed so strongly to children is far from clear, but it does seem that social factors were more important than spiritual ones. So much was apparent to contemporaries, who are all agreed that the children came from the poorest classes. 'They were but the children of poor folk', a citizen of Wissemburg reported, 'though there were a small number of noble ones among them.'

The disturbing possibilities of the situation became fully apparent in the summer of 1476, when the small village of Nicklashausen in the territory of Wurzburg became the scene of a popular Marial pilgrimage with overtones of social revolution. In the church of Nicklashausen there was a statue of the Virgin which was credited with miraculous powers. It had attracted a thin trickle of pilgrims for more than a century. Here, in the middle of Lent 1476, a young shepherd called Hans Böhm began to preach with astonishing eloquence before ever-growing audiences. His theme, a familiar one, was repentance. He called on all his hearers to go in their multitudes to venerate the statue, in order to appease the wrath of God on the sins of mankind. The Virgin had promised him that those who obeyed his call would have a plenary indulgence and those who died there would immediately ascend to heaven.

It was exactly a year after the great mass-pilgrimage to Wilsnack. In south Germany the harvests had been poor, and in the territory of the prince-bishops of Wurzburg, crushing taxation added to the burdens of the poor and provoked considerable social unrest. An atmosphere of intense religious excitement was heightened by the preaching of the Roman Jubilee indulgence, which had begun a few weeks earlier. The response to Böhm's call was unexpectedly dramatic. From the towns of the Rhineland and Thuringia, which had supplied most of the pilgrims to Mont-St.-Michel in 1457, from Saxony, whence pilgrims had rushed to Wilsnack the year before, there came many thousands of repentant poor. Others arrived from Bavaria and Swabia, then facing the threat of severe famine. It was estimated, no doubt with much exaggeration, that 40,000, or even 70,000 people could be seen encamped in the fields outside Nicklashausen every morning. The offerings of gold and silver coins, clothing, and wax, were prodigious. Böhm's preaching began conventionally enough. He called on his audience to abandon their effeminate clothing and to renounce swearing and gaming, much as Barnardino of Siena had urged half a century before. But Böhm did not leave matters there. He went on to preach against the loose-living and avarice of the clergy, a topical subject in the prince-bishopric of Wurzburg. From this he proceeded to a full-blooded egalitarianism. 'Bishops, princes, counts and knights should be allowed to possess as much as ordinary folk and no more. There will come a time when even they will have to work for their living.' Böhm finally urged his followers to withhold all payments of taxes, tithes, and rents, and summoned them to meet at Nicklashausen on an appointed day to overthrow the civil and religious authorities. 'Truly', John of Trittenheim remarked, 'the common people are always chasing after novelties, and trying to shake off the yoke of their masters.'

The pilgrimage, which had begun in March, came to an abrupt end in July. On the eve of the day appointed for the great meeting, Böhm was seized by a party of horsemen in the service of the bishop, and was later burned for heresy. His followers were dispersed with cannons. Further pilgrimages were forbidden by the secular authorities throughout Germany, and an interdict was laid on the village of Nicklashausen. Early in 1477, the church was razed to the ground on the orders of the archbishop of Mainz. The political consequences of Böhm's pilgrimage were obvious enough. The religious consequence was to intensify still further the profound suspicion of spontaneous popular movements in the minds of the educated establishment. Even John of Trittenheim, who was no friend of that establishment, was constrained to admit that 'simple unlettered folk are very easily taken in, and are inclined to believe in false miracles without proof. We know this from our experience of the pilgrimages of recent times....It was the cause of the events at Nicklashausen.'

16

Mediaeval Christianity: Religion to Ritual

The progression from private austerity to popular enthusiasm and thence to abstract ritual, is a recurring theme in the religious life of the Middle Ages. The Catholic moralists of the fifteenth century and the Protestant reformers of the sixteenth had in common a strong dislike of the overpowering element of ritual in the religion of the late Middle Ages. Commenting on the popularity of the blood of Christ at Hailes, the English reformer Hugh Latimer complained that 'the sight of it with their bodily eye doth certify them, and putteth them out of doubt that they be in clean life and in state of salvation without spot of sin.' The roots of this situation penetrated very deep into the soil of mediaeval religion. The reduction of dogma to literal images, the localization of God's power in a few sanctuaries, the hope of automatic salvation, these were not novel 'superstitions' in 1533 when Latimer was writing. It might have surprised him to know that the second council of Chalons in 813 had protested, in terms very similar to his, against the 'simple-minded notion that sinners need only catch sight of the shrines of the saints and their sins will be absolved!'

Pilgrimage, like almsgiving, had begun as an accessory to the moral teaching of the Church, and ended as an alternative. In extreme cases it could be regarded as a licence to sin. The pilgrims in William Langland's dream 'had leave to lie all their life after'. 'He who goes to St. James and then kills his father commits no mortal sin,' asserted a Poitevin contemporary of Langland's. It was this attitude, and less extreme variants of it, which disturbed moral reformers of the late Middle Ages. Berthold of Regensburg once took the occasion of a sermon against the pious excesses of women to launch into a diatribe against pilgrims who pursued the illusion of the ritual purgation of sin. Another German Franciscan of the thirteenth century conjured up before his audience an image of the pilgrims standing at the brink of Hell and calling out to those below, 'did any of you try going to Rome when you were alive?' and the thousands replied, 'yes, we all went to Rome, but much good did it do us....You who are still living, put not your trust in almsgiving, pilgrimages, or chantries, for they are all vain without true contrition. At the seat of judgement it will avail you nothing that you have been to the tombs of the apostles.' 'All these journeys', echoed the Italian friar Giordano da Rivalta, 'I hold for nothing worth.'

This plea for a more spiritual religion found its most eloquent supporter in William Langland, the obscure Englishman of the late fourteenth century who wrote *The Vision of Piers Plowman. Piers Plowman* is much the most powerful of those allegorical dreams of the late Middle Ages, of which the *Roman de la Rose* is the best-known example. Langland objected to pilgrimage because it was a ritual which eased the conscience of the sinner without improving the moral quality of his life:

And ye that seek St. James and saints of Rome,
Seeketh St. Truth, for he may save you all.

In their great quest for truth, Christians have been diverted by smooth promises and bright illusions. Hope seizes a horn and blows it. A thousand men throng together hoping to find truth but no one knows where to look, and the blind mass 'blundered forth as beasts over banks and hills till late was and long'. At last, they meet a pilgrim, wearing his pouch and scarf and carrying badges from all the great sanctuaries. 'Knowest thou a saint named truth?' 'Where dwells he?', they ask. To which the pilgrim replies, 'nay, so me God help. I saw never a palmer with pike ne with scrip asking after him till now in this place.' Piers Plowman then appears and tells them the road to truth. They must go through Meekness till they come to Conscience; next cross the brook called Be-buxom-of-speech by the ford called Honour-your-fathers. Pass by Swear-not-in-vain and Covet-not, by Steal-not and Slay-not, over the bridge of Pray-well where Grace is the gate-keeper and Amend-you his assistant, and thence through the narrow gate to Paradise.

The Devaluation of Indulgences

Indulgences were sometimes identified as the sole cause of the preoccupation with external observances at the end of the Middle Ages. This was an over-simplified view, but an important one, for it came not only from root-and-branch enemies of the ecclesiastical order, but from a vocal element in the council of Constance and from many Catholic reformers. The modern sinner, wrote the outspoken Thomas Gascoigne, says to himself 'I do not care how many sins I commit for I can easily and speedily have a plenary remission of guilt and punishment, by acquiring a papal indulgence.' Indulgences, once a valuable stimulus to pilgrimage, had become an alternative. Collecting them was an object in itself, and by the close of the Middle Ages, few pilgrimages could prosper without them. The almost complete dependence of the cult of the saints on papal indulgences can be seen in the volumes of petitions addressed to successive popes of the fourteenth and fifteenth centuries by decayed sanctuaries which saw their only hope of revival in the grant of a generous indulgence. Thousands came from French churches ruined in the most destructive phase of the Hundred Years' War. St.-Gilles was one of the abbeys which hoped to restore its depleted income with the help of an indulgence. Canterbury was unable to hold its fifth Jubilee pilgrimage in 1520 for lack of money to buy the indulgence from Leo X.

The sale of indulgences replaced the hardship of the actual journey by a simple payment equal to the cost of making it. It had begun in a very small way in the twelfth century (see chapter 9). Crusaders were early allowed to send substitutes to fight in their place and still gain the plenary indulgence. The synod of Santiago (1125) permitted all Spanish crusaders to do this if they were 'truly confessed and penitent.' A simple money payment, the cost of a mercenary, was almost as good as a substitute. In 1147 Eugenius III offered half a crusading indulgence to those who contributed a tenth of their income and moveables to the cost of the second crusade. A firm stride forward was taken in the thirteenth century when crusaders were allowed to commute their vows for a money payment, and it was not long before commutation was extended to all pilgrimages. The Roman Jubilee of 1350 was the turning point (see chapter 13). In 1352 Clement VI allowed the population of Mallorca to claim the Jubilee indulgence without actually going to Rome, in return for a money payment equal to the cost of the journey. The precedent thus established was ruthlessly exploited forty years later by Boniface IX, who stood in dire need of both the money and the popularity which the sale of indulgences brought.

As bishops of Rome, the popes could plausibly claim the right to sell Jubilee indulgences to all comers. Very soon after the Jubilee of 1350, they began to sell dispensations from vows to perform other pilgrimages. Minor churches could obtain not only an indulgence for themselves, but the right to commute vows of pilgrimage to major sanctuaries, thus in effect upstaging churches vastly more important than themselves. The Gilbertine church of Mattersley in Yorkshire was allowed to commute vows of pilgrimage to anywhere except Rome or Santiago. The same concession, with the same exceptions, was given to Canterbury cathedral on the occasion of the fourth Jubilee, in 1470. By 1470, however, it was common to offer dispensations even from pilgrim's vows of Rome and Santiago. Thomas Walsingham recorded with indignation that the cardinal who came to England in 1381 to negotiate the marriage of Richard II and Anne of Bohemia was openly selling dispensations from pilgrimages to Rome, Santiago, and Jerusalem. Ten years later, papal legates were offering the same concessions in Germany and Castile. The price of these dispensations had only the vaguest connection with the cost of the journey. Thus in April 1330, Arnaud Rocelli, of the diocese of Saintes, paid four shillings and twopence to be spared the journey to Rome; but a year later it cost Agnes de Rocquefort 133 gold lambs and five shillings to evade a pilgrimage to Santiago. The difference in price reflected the difference in their social status. At the end of the fifteenth century the papal Datary was using a tariff which was weighted according to the wealth of the applicant and the comfort in which he or she was thought likely to travel. Even this degree of flexibility was abandoned in the instructions given to the sellers of the Jubilee indulgence of 1500 in England. Here the price was related strictly to the applicant's income, ranging from one shilling and fourpence for those earning twenty pounds a year or less, to three pounds six shillings and eightpence for those with incomes above two thousand pounds.

Less direct but equally damaging was the practice of offering indulgences *ad instar,* that is, of offering the indulgences of major shrines to minor ones. This again began in the fourteenth century with the marketing of the Roman Jubilee indulgence. Most Christians were able to win the Jubilee indulgence of 1390 at churches within a few miles of their homes. The commonest indulgence *ad instar* was the indulgence of the Portiuncula which, like the Roman Jubilee indulgence, was reputed to be plenary. Boniface IX began to grant it to other churches in 1392. Franciscan churches, appropriately enough, were the first to benefit, beginning with the church of La Verna where St. Francis had received the stigmata. Subsequently, ninety-five other churches received the indulgence of the Portiuncula. In England some forty churches gained a plenary indulgence by this indirect route, including sanctuaries as obscure as the Gilbertine priory of St. Saviour at Hitchen and the Augustinian priory of Langlete. Indulgences of other churches, notably of St. Mark's in Venice, were also common. As well as devaluing indulgences as such, Boniface's policies gave deep offence to important vested interests. In December 1402 he was forced to yield to mounting protests, and issued a bull formally 'revoking and annulling every indulgence of the Jubilee, of the Holy Sepulchre, of Monte Gargano, of Santiago, St. Mark's Venice, the Portiuncula, Collemaggio, or any indulgences whatsoever *ad instar indulgentiarum* of any other church.' The retraction was impressive, and no doubt humiliating. Although the popes continued to distribute Jubilee indulgences with the same undiscriminating generosity, the indulgences of other great sanctuaries remained inviolate for more than a century. There were no doubt many churches like St. Nicholas of Calais which still advertised their Portiuncula indulgences as if Boniface had never spoken. But the popes themselves scrupulously avoided a return to this questionable experiment.

Their exact effect in discouraging long journeys to the major shrines thus abused is impossible to measure, but it must have been considerable. Indulgences *ad instar* could never displace pilgrimage altogether, for there was always the pleasure of travel and the strength of tradition to draw pilgrims to the major sanctuaries. But the fact remained, as a Parisian diarist pointed out, that if Notre-Dame de Pontoise had the indulgences of Rome then it was 'as good as going to Rome but less time-consuming'. This man cannot have been the only one to draw the obvious conclusion. Sixtus IV recognized as much when he declared in August 1473 that all indulgences *ad instar Jubilaei* were to be suspended during the actual Roman Jubilee of 1475. The reason given was that so many Jubilee indulgences had been granted to other churches 'that the rush of pilgrims to Rome may be discouraged and the celebrations of the Jubilee year diminished or even curtailed altogether, to the great detriment of the salvation of souls.'

The responsibility for this unedifying state of affairs rested largely with the papacy, but not entirely. The sanctuaries themselves were unscrupulous in extracting indulgences from the

enfeebled popes of the schismatic period. Many otherwise reputable churches had no compunction in forging those which
they could not obtain legitimately, and in magnifying those
which they could. The Franciscans were believed to be the
greatest offenders, but in fact the major secular cathedrals were
just as aggressive. Cologne cathedral obtained a plenary indulgence *ad instar Jubilaei* in 1394 by playing one pope off against
another. Others simply conferred plenary indulgences upon
themselves, as Le Puy did in 1407. In 1420 the monks of
Canterbury, after failing to obtain a Jubilee indulgence from
Martin V, declared one of their own. The prior summoned four
doctors of theology who pronounced this action to be legitimate, and the Jubilee was duly held, notwithstanding the ful-
minations of the pope.

The activities of the 'pardoners', or itinerant salesmen of
indulgences, are well-known from the portraits of Langland
and Chaucer. They were the butt of satirists and reformers
not only in England but wherever there was an appetite for
indulgences. The problem was extremely serious in fifteenth-
century Spain, where a prodigious number of indulgences was
available as a result of the close alliance between the dynasty
and the papacy. Everywhere the pardoners owed their success
to the fact that they were always slightly in advance of official
thinking on the subject of indulgences. They offered their
clients on paper more than could be had at the great sanctuaries. As a result, people expected the same benefits from their
pilgrimages and, after a decent interval, they usually got them.
In 1312 the council of Vienne sternly condemned pardoners
for pretending that their indulgences could release souls from
purgatory; but within twenty years such indulgences were
being offered at the Portiuncula chapel, and by the middle of

the fifteenth century they were being granted by the popes. This
argues a high degree of gullibility among uneducated people
and a good many educated ones as well. Most of Europe
accepted a forged version of the bull proclaiming the Roman
Jubilee of 1350; learned canonists were deceived in spite of the
extravagantly improbable terms in which it was couched. Nor
is this surprising, in view of the faith placed in impressive-
looking documents, and the inadequate grasp of diplomatic
even amongst the highly literate. When Langland's pardoner
wished to convince an audience that a forged indulgence was
genuine, he had only to produce 'a bull with bishops seals'.
When a group of Slav pilgrims arrived at the Franciscan
church of Ancona on their way to the Portiuncula chapel, the
friars tried to persuade them that there was as much indulgence
to be had at Ancona as at Assisi. 'Look at our letters of grant,'
they declared. The pilgrims saw and believed.

The ready acceptance of indulgences *totiens quoties* is a case
in point. These were indulgences which could be claimed as
often as the penitent could perform the conditions, by entering the sanctuary once a day for example. The popes did not
grant such indulgences, even under Boniface IX, but some
fourteenth-century theologians favoured them. Nicholas of
Lyra was one. Churches were not slow in offering them. In the
middle of the fifteenth century the seven major altars of St.
Peter's in Rome boasted an indulgence *totiens quoties*. Judas's
thirty pieces of silver, preserved immediately inside the door of
the basilica, was stated to be worth 1,400 years of remission as
often as the pilgrim set eyes on them.

In January 1418 the council of Constance decreed severe
restrictions on the issue of indulgences, expressing the fear that
'by their great numbers, they may be brought into discredit.'

But the damage had already been done. The chronicler of Paderborn, Gobelinus Persona, accused Boniface IX of bringing all indulgences into disrepute by granting them not only to great and ancient walled cities, but to small villages and monasteries of no importance. Gobelinus was deeply hostile to Boniface but his words were echoed by others who looked on his cause with favour. The chronicler of Neuss, on the whole a supporter of Boniface, complained that plenary indulgences had been conceded to 'towns that were not even walled, to monasteries and country churches....Some people suspected that he was moved more by greed than by religious zeal.' Yet it is clear that Boniface's liberality was very popular with ordinary people, and the attempts of the council of Constance to repair the breach, merely served to widen still further the gulf between educated piety and popular enthusiasm. The failure of the reform movement inaugurated at Constance has often been put down to the indifference and obstructiveness of successive popes. This explanation may have been good enough for the council of Basle (1431–1437) but it is not good enough for history. The truth is that the ritual purgation of sin was exactly what most uneducated people wanted. There is a hint of this in the reasons given by the monks of Canterbury for requesting a Jubilee indulgence in 1470. Many Englishmen, they told the pope, were too old or infirm to go to Rome or Santiago. Others could not afford the cost. Traditionally the Church had allowed them to gain a Jubilee indulgence at Canterbury, and it would be imprudent to end the tradition now. 'Of all nations', the monks alleged, 'the English are the most attached to old habits and traditional devotions, and they will not easily be deprived of them without great uproar.'

Pilgrimage without Travel

During a tour of Ulster in the late 1260s, two Franciscan preachers were followed about from town to town by a mass of people 'both for their sermons and for the indulgences which they dispensed'. One of them, on his way home, stayed with a householder and offered to sell him all the indulgences he had acquired for the amount he had spent in getting them and a pot of beer in addition. In this case both parties were simple peasants, but it was not always so. An Italian knight known to Bartolus of Assisi offered to buy the Portiuncula indulgence from a servant of his who had recently been there. 'If you give the indulgence you gained at Assisi to my deceased brother, then I, as witness all these people here, will return to you the money you spent on the journey.' If indulgences taught men to regard merit as a commodity, then it was, perhaps, natural for them to think of it as transferable.

The belief that indulgences could release the dead from Purgatory was a cornerstone of late medieval piety, but its origins lay firmly in the past. For centuries, penitents who confessed on their deathbeds and who died without performing the penance, had been allowed to have it performed for them. This was usually done by distributing alms from their estate. The idea is found in the penitential literature of the ninth century and in the canon law collections of the eleventh. A synod meeting at Arras in 1025 expressed the opinion that penance was 'just as efficacious for the dead as it was for the living'. The final development of the theory was, however, the work of the thirteenth century. It was actively canvassed in the early years of the century by the preachers of the crusade who taught, according to a jaundiced contemporary, that by virtue of a crusading indulgence, 'evil men who died without confession or penance would be received into the Church.' The schoolmen did not go so far, but Albert the Great and St. Bonaventure were agreed that penance could be remitted after death if the penitent had made a true confession. As Thomas Aquinas argued, a man could gain an indulgence in two ways, by fulfilling the conditions himself or, if this was impossible, by fulfilling them vicariously. The dead can only fulfil them vicariously.

The concept of indulgences for the dead remained a somewhat academic one. It was left to the Franciscans of the Portiuncula to make practical use of it. Bartolus, the friar of Assisi who wrote up the miracles of the Portiuncula in about 1335, told a number of stories whose object was to impress the lesson on his readers. A Venetian priest was stricken with a fatal illness just as he was about to begin a pilgrimage to the Portiuncula. Summoning his closest friend to his bedside he gave him the money which he had saved for the journey and begged him to make the pilgrimage on his behalf. After the priest had died, the friend put off his departure for month after month until the priest appeared to him in a dream chiding him for his delays. The friend left immediately for Assisi and on his return the priest appeared again and revealed that 'at the very hour that you entered the chapel I was liberated from the penance of Purgatory.' It is an altogether typical story. Bartolus is at pains to point out that it was at the Portiuncula and nowhere else that the dead could be released from Purgatory. A Sicilian woman who was preparing to leave for Santiago had a startling vision of her dead son, who addressed her in the following terms: "Dear mother, the pilgrimage which you are about to make is a fine and worthy act, but it will not do much for me. If you wish to liberate me from my sins you must go not only to Santiago but also to the church of S. Maria de

Angelis at the Portiuncula. Only then shall I be released from Purgatory.'

The pilgrimage of the Portiuncula did not for long enjoy the monopoly which Bartolus claimed for it. In the church of the Holy Sepulchre in Jerusalem St. Bridget of Sweden received a revelation informing her that her devotions had released many souls from Purgatory. Five years later, in 1377, a German pilgrim in Rome found a plaque in the church of St. Lawrence promising the release of a soul from Purgatory for every year of Wednesdays that a visitor passed in the church. By the middle of the fifteenth century nearly every church in Rome offered an indulgence for the souls in Purgatory.

The confidence which laypeople reposed in indulgences for the dead is reflected in their wills. Already in 1269, William de Beauchamp died leaving two hundred marks to his younger son Walter to make a pilgrimage to the Holy Sepulchre on his behalf. An examination of the enormous number of surviving mediaeval wills proved in London suggests, however, that wills like this one did not become common until the middle of the fourteenth century. Some testators were highly specific in their instructions to pilgrims, who were expected to perform the pilgrimage in a manner befitting the status of the testator. In his will, drawn up in 1415, Thomas, earl of Arundel, left a substantial sum for the expenses of his pilgrim and instructed him to travel 'in the same way as I would have travelled, had I done the pilgrimage myself.' Thomas Poulton, who died in 1433, left the sum of £20 'for a clergyman of good repute, chosen by my executors, to travel in my name to Rome and there to remain for two years continuously doing the stations regularly, visiting all the holy shrines and relics, and celebrating masses in those places on my behalf. And before his departure, my executors shall exact an oath from him that during those two years he shall pursue no other occupation.' In an age in which testamentary conditions were imperfectly enforced, there was no guarantee that the pilgrimage would actually be performed. The testator could only rely on the conscience of his heirs. One George Fryng, citizen of London, instructed his widow to go to Santiago on his behalf, but her second husband refused to let her go, and she was obliged to seek a dispensation from the pope. Many obligations must have remained unfulfilled for years, some forever. A Lincolnshire knight who died in 1389 left money to 'Roger my grandson to make a voyage against the Infidel to which I am bound in the sum of two hundred marks by the will of my grandfather.' These examples have been drawn exclusively from England because of the extraordinary wealth of surviving English wills, but there is no reason to suppose that they are untypical. Where continental wills survive, they follow a very similar pattern. The wills of wealthy Parisian lawyers enrolled in the parlement of Paris frequently contain directions to pilgrims. In the *Testamentarbuch* of the imperial free city of Pressburg (1427–1529), almost every will has a provision for sending a pilgrim to Rome.

The laity accepted the efficacy of indulgences for the dead for many years before the popes granted them in formal terms. No genuine letter of indulgence promised the release of souls from Purgatory until the middle of the fifteenth century. The earliest known example dates only from 1457, when Calixtus III offered the release of a soul to every one who contributed two hundred *maravedis* to the crusade against the Moors. Shortly afterwards, the same pope issued indulgences for the dead to the cathedral of Tarragona and the Franciscan order. In

1476 Sixtus IV granted an important indulgence to Saintes cathedral, which recited that:

> 'It is our desire to use the Church's treasury of merit to assist those souls in Purgatory who would have gained this indulgence had they been alive. We therefore concede that parents, friends, or any others may secure the release of souls from the fires of Purgatory by donating a sum, to be assessed by the canons, for the repair of Saintes cathedral.'

Thus the authorities accorded formal recognition to a belief which had been universal among the laity for more than a century.

As soon as it was agreed that the dead could perform pilgrimages by proxy, it was a short step to holding that the living could do so too. Vicarious pilgrimages were not unknown in the twelfth century if the would-be pilgrim was prevented from going him- or herself. Ralph the clerk was too ill to go to Canterbury; he sent his candle by messenger, and recovered as soon as it was lit in the cathedral. The wife of a Norwich baker was unable to walk for the swellings on her feet; her husband visited the shrine of St. William on her behalf. A cloistered nun who could not leave her nunnery sent her son to Canterbury to give thanks for a miraculous cure. Pure vicarious pilgrimages, by those who could have gone themselves but preferred not to, had to wait for a later, less demanding age. In the fifteenth century the idea seems to have been accepted without protest. This was due partly to the fact that crusaders had been sending substitutes to fulfil their vows for two hundred years; and partly, no doubt, to the influence of the judicial pilgrimage, which by now was almost invariably commuted to a fine. Vicarious pilgrimages were never entirely respectable. Soon after their marriage, William Cressewyc of London and his wife Alice vowed to go to Rome, but they deferred the performance of the vow until old age, and then sent a man to do it for them. Nevertheless they still felt uneasy about this vicarious road to salvation, for in 1391 they applied to a papal nuncio for absolution. No such reservations ever troubled Isabel of Bavaria, queen of France (d. 1435). She sent a pilgrim with a fifteen-pound candle to Notre-Dame du Blanc-Mesnil, instructing him to pray there for fifteen days, burning a pound of wax per day. The queen, who was disgustingly obese, was forever worried about her health. She was particularly devoted to St. Eutrope, the healer of dropsy, and to the celebrated medical saints like St. Lazarus, and Cosmas and Damian. One of her chaplains was sent to Larchamp, another to Moutiers-en-Perche, a third to Avallon. Her accounts are full of entries recording payments made to professional pilgrims or members of her household despatched to shrines throughout France.

In spite of the demand, the institution of the professional pilgrim was slow to make its appearance. Several English testators of the fourteenth century envisaged the possibility that no pilgrim would be available, and made alternative dispositions of their wealth. This was probably because most vicarious pilgrims thought it necessary that the proxy should be of the same rank as themselves. Many wills require the pilgrim to be 'of honest condition', i.e. well-born. When John, duke of Brittany, was prevented by the diplomatic crisis of 1420 from fulfilling a vow of pilgrimage, he sent a man to the Holy Land on his behalf, stipulating that he was to be '*hommne notable et suffisant*'; a hundred gold écus were allowed for his expenses, and a hundred gold florins for his offering. In Scandinavia, it is true, professional pilgrims were quite common, and many contracts for their services survive. At the Baltic port of Lübeck there was always a crowd of professionals willing to go to the Holy Land for sums ranging from twenty to a hundred marks. Further south, however, so many bona fide pilgrims passed regularly to and from the great sanctuaries that it was easy enough to find a man who was minded to go anyway. Most vicarious pilgrimages were informal arrangements like that of the bishop of Lincoln, who gave Margery Kempe twenty-six shillings and eightpence as she was leaving for Palestine, 'to buy her clothes with and to pray for him'.

Such indifference to the element of personal hardship inevitably devalued the very idea of pilgrimage, and invited the appearance of alternatives which were emotionally more rewarding. Mass-flagellation, for example, was not simply another pious exercise, but specifically an alternative to pilgrimage. Flagellant preachers of 1349 contrasted the 'natural' penance of the flagellants with the 'artificial' Roman Jubilee declared for 1350. In a sermon preached before the pope at Avignon, the sternly orthodox Jean du Fayt made the same point. The flagellants, he argued, imagined that they would gain the same indulgence from their processions as those who attended the Jubilee. This was no doubt one of the arguments which led Clement VI to condemn them as heretics. There was a great deal of truth in the bitter observation of John of Trittenheim that educated men had abandoned the cult of the saints for abstruse mystical devotions. There was a vogue for mystical alternatives to pilgrimage, inspired by allegorical writings which likened the whole of human life to a pilgrimage. One of the earliest and most influential of these is a lengthy treatise in French, written in 1330–1, called the *Pèlerinage de la Vie Humaine*. The title gives ample indication of the contents. Its author was Guillaume de Deguileville, a Cistercian of the abbey of Chaalis. The *Pèlerinage* is the record of a dream in which the author undertakes a pilgrimage to the celestial Jerusalem. Dame Grace blesses him and offers him the scarf of faith and the stave of hope. On the road he is attacked by the deadly sins in the shape of wild beasts. Heresy, voluptuousness, and idleness lie in wait to attack and rob him. He is shipwrecked in the sea of worldliness and is near to drowning when he succeeds in saving himself by climbing onto the raft of the Cistercian order.

The imagery is old and the moral conventional. But the idea of performing a pilgrimage in the daily passage of life was capable of being used as a powerful argument against all external observances. 'We ben pilgrims when that we ben born...', a Lollard pamphlet, the *Lanterne of Light,* proclaimed; 'every citizen of the heavenly country is a pilgrim of this world for all time of this present life, and when we travailen sore to keep God's feasts, then we do our pilgrimage.' 'I call them true pilgrims', agreed William Thorpe at his interrogation, 'which travel towards the bliss of heaven...hating and fleeing all the seven deadly sins.' The *Lanterne of Light* was once described by a mayor of London as 'the worst and most perverse thing that ever I did read or see'; no less than fifteen heretical propositions were extracted from it by archbishop Chichele. But there is nothing intrinsically heretical about the ideas expressed here, all of which were openly expounded at the council of Constance. They are strongly represented in the poetry of Jean Gerson, whose *Meditations* on the true pilgrim were read with pleasure by Charles of Orléans and recommended to Charles VII of France by his confessor.

These allegorical sermons, though intended as a summons to a more spiritual life, in fact replaced one ritual by another. A new kind of devotional handbook became popular in the fifteenth century, which explained to readers how to follow each stage of an imaginary pilgrimage in their own home, and gain the same benefits. A Franciscan manuscript from St.-Trond (it is the earliest example known) begins by pointing out that one can win all the indulgences of the Holy Land without leaving one's house, if one is prepared to follow in spirit every stage of Christ's passion, reciting thirty-three *Pater Nosters* for each halt on the road to Calvary. It is in fact a sort of mental 'stations of the cross'. An even more original product of its kind was written, probably at Oxford, for the benefit of those who could not or would not attend the Roman Jubilee of 1423. Here the frustrated pilgrim is invited to say the *Pater Noster* ten times daily to represent the ten leagues which he could expect to cover each day of his journey to Rome. When he had notionally arrived in the city, let him visit a local church once a day and distribute alms equal to the offerings which he would have made in Rome. 'And it is my belief that by doing all this he will gain as much or more than he would have done by going physically to Rome.' Many hundreds of such works, some of them of extreme naivety, circulated in northern Europe in the fifteenth century.

The theme was enthusiastically taken up by popular preachers, who openly recommended it as a less irksome alternative to pilgrimage. Preaching in Strasbourg cathedral during the Roman Jubilee of 1500 Johann Geiler addressed himself to the question whether a prisoner, locked up in a dungeon and unable to go to Rome, was thereby excluded from the benefits of the Jubilee indulgence. Calculating that it would take twenty-one days to reach Rome, another seven to visit the churches, and twenty-one to return, Geiler suggested that the prisoner could walk round his cell for forty-two days and devote himself to prayer for seven. Erasmus had this kind of exercise in mind when he poked fun at contemporaries who liked to acquire the indulgences of the Roman 'stations' without actually going to Rome.

> 'I walk about my house. I go to my study. I check on my daughter's chastity. Then I go to my shop and see what my servants are doing. Then into the kitchen to make sure that nothing is amiss there. And so from one place to another to see that my wife and children are all right and every one is at his business. These are my Roman stations.'

Even when the taunts of satirists and the impact of the Reformation had sharply reduced the popularity of real pilgrimages, imaginary ones showed no signs of dying the same death. The most elaborate of them all, the work of Jan van Paesschen (d. 1532), outlined a course of prayer extending over 365 days of the year and corresponding to every stage of a journey to the Holy Land. This manual was published posthumously at Louvain in 1563 and immediately went into several editions. A French translation appeared three years later, and in c. 1605 there was even an anonymously printed version in English.

The continuing popularity of these works testifies to the extraordinary resilience of late mediaeval piety. Erasmus believed that few offerings were made at the sanctuaries in his day, and that the pilgrimage to Santiago was nearly forgotten 'on account of the new opinion that has been spread throughout the world'. That conservative Frenchman Gréffin Affagart agreed in blaming the decline of the great sanctuaries on the Reformation and particularly on 'that evil knave Luther and his band of accomplices like Erasmus, with his *Colloquies* and *Enchiridion*'.

But cultural change is seldom as straightforward as this. Progress is ragged. Successive periods overlap. A major intellectual transformation may alter the climate of opinion but old ideas have a habit of persisting. 'Superstitions' were condemned with such vehemence by the Protestant reformers, that it is easy to forget how, even in Protestant societies, pilgrimages and shrines, relics and miracles, survived the Reformation by more than a century. Writing in the 1520s, Erasmus looked forward to the rapid demise of the pilgrimage to Santiago. Yet the great Galician sanctuary was probably more prosperous in the seventeenth century than it had ever been in the Middle Ages. The offerings of the eleventh century had built the great Romanesque façade of St. James's cathedral; the offerings of the eighteenth century tore it down and replaced it with the Baroque extravagances of Casas y Nóvoa. In Catholic Europe of the eighteenth century, obscure shrines rose to fame with the same facility as their fifteenth-century ancestors. Vierzehnheiligen was to Baroque Christianity what Notre-Dame de l'Epine had been to Gothic.

Pilgrimage did not mean the same thing to every generation. But it was practised in one form or another from late antiquity to the Reformation, and has maintained a fitful existence ever since. It affords a unique reflection of mediaeval religion at every stage of its complicated development. Almsgiving has a longer history, but its practice was confined to the relatively rich. It was, moreover, a spiritual duty to give alms, and although some religions (notably Islam) insist on pilgrimages, Christianity is not amongst them. If Christians have at times travelled long distances to venerate the remains of spiritual heroes, then it was because in doing so they satisfied an emotional need.

Abbreviations

Aa. Ss.	*Acta sanctorum Bollandiana,* ed. J. Bollandus *et al.,* 61 vols., Antwerp, Brussels, etc., 1643– (in progress).
Aa. Ss. OSB.	*Acta sanctorum ordinis S. Benedicti,* ed. L. d'Achéry and J. Mabillon, 9 vols., Paris, 1668–1701.
An. Boll.	*Analecta Bollandiana.*
AOL.	*Archives de l'orient latin, 2 vols.,* Geneva, 1881–4.
Arch. Nat.	Archives Nationales de France, Paris.
Arch. Vat.	Archivio Vaticano, Rome.
ASRSP.	*Archivio della Società Romana di Storia Patria.*
BBB.	G. Golubovich, *Biblioteca bio-bibliografica della Terra Santa e dell' oriente Francescano,* 5 vols., Florence, 1906– (in progress).
BEC.	*Bibliothèque de l'École des Chartes.*
BEFAR.	*Bibliothèque des Écoles Francaises d'Athènes et de Rome.*
BEHE.	*Bibliothèque de l'École des Hautes Études.*
BHP.	*Bulletin historique et philologique du Comité des Travaux Historiques et Scientifiques.*
Bibl.	Bibliothèque de la ville de…
Bibl. Nat.	Bibliothèque Nationale, Paris.
BLVS.	*Bibliothek des literarischen Vereins in Stuttgart.*
Brit. Mus.	British Museum, London.

CCH (Bruxelles).   Corpus codicum hagiographicorum Bibliothecae
                    Regiae Bruxellensis, Pars i: Codices latini mem-
                    branei, 2 vols., Brussels, 1886–9.
CCH (Paris).   Catalogus codicum hagiographicorum latinorum in
                    Bibliotheca Nationali Parisiensi, 3 vols., Brussels,
                    1889–93.
CJC.   Corpus juris canonici, ed. A. L. Richter and A.
                    Friedberg, 2 vols., Leipzig, 1879–81.
CPR. Letters.   Calendar of entries in the papal registers relating to
                    Great Britain and Ireland. Papal letters, ed. W. H.
                    Bliss et al.,15 vols., London, 1893– (in
                    progress).
CRH.   Comptes rendus des séances de la Commission
                    Royale d'Histoire.
CSEL.   Corpus scriptorum ecclesiasticorum latinorum.
DACL.   Dictionnaire d'archéologie Chrétienne et de liturgie,
                    ed. F. Cabrol, H. Leclercq, et al., 15 vols., Paris,
                    1907–53.
DDC.   Dictionnaire de droit canonique, ed. R. Naz, 7
                    vols., Paris, 1935–65.
DHGE.   Dictionnaire d'historie et de géographie ecclesi-
                    astiques, ed. A. Baudrillart et al., 27 vols., Paris,
                    1912– (in progress).
DTC.   Dictionnaire de théologie catholique, ed. A. Vacant,
                    et al., 15 vols., Paris, 1903–67.
EETS.   Early English Text Society.
EHR.   English historical review.
ES.   España sagrada, ed. H. Florez et al., 51 vols.,
                    Madrid, 1754–1879.
Fonti.   Fonti per la storia d'Italia.
GC.   Gallia Christiana, 16 vols., Paris, 1715–1865.
G. Itin.   P. Geyer, Itinera Hierosolymitana saeculi iv-viii,
                    CSEL., xxxix, Vienna, 1898.
IS (1).   Italia sacra, ed. F. Ughelli, Ist. ed., 9 vols.,
                    Rome, 1644–62.
IS (2).   Italia sacra, 2nd. ed., 10 vols., Venice, 1717–21.

L. Peregr.	J. C. M. Laurent, *Peregrinatores medii aevi quattuor,* Leipzig, 1864.
MAH.	*Mélanges d'archéologie et d'histoire de l'École Francaise de Rome.*
MC.	*Sacrorum conciliorum nova et amplissima collectio,* ed. J. D. Mansi *et al.,* 55 vols., Florence and elsewhere, 1759–1962.
MD. Thes.	E. Martène and U. Durant, *Thesaurus novus anecdotorum,* 5 vols., Paris, 1717.
MD. Vet. Script.	E. Martène and U. Durant, *Veterum scriptorum et monumentorum amplissima collectio,* 6 vols., Paris, 1724–9.
MGH. Auct. Antiq.	*Monumenta Germaniae historica. Auctores antiquissimi.*
MGH. Constit.	−*Constitutiones imperatorum et regum.*
MGH. Epp.	−*Epistolae.*
MGH. Epp. Sel.	−*Epistolae selectae in usum scholarum.*
MGH. Leges.	−*Leges.*
MGH. Libelli.	−*Libelli de lite imperatorum et pontificum, saeculis xi et xii conscripta.*
MGH. Merov.	−*Scriptores rerum merovingicarum.*
MGH. Poet.	−*Poetae latinae medii aevi.*
MGH. Rer. Germ.	−*Scriptores rerum Germanicarum in usum scholarum.*
MGH. SS.	−*Scriptores.*
MR. Itin.	H. Michelant and G. Raynaud, *Itinéraires à Jérusalem et descriptions de la Terre Sainte redigés en francais aux xie, xiie, et xiiie siècles, SOL.,* iii, Geneva, 1882.
PG.	J-P. Migne, *Patrologia graeca,* 161 vols., Paris, 1857–66.
PL.	J-P. Migne, *Patrologia latina,* 221 vols., Paris, 1844–64.
PPTS.	Palestine Pilgrims Text Society.
RHC. Arm.	*Recueil des historiens des croisades. Documents Arméniens,* 2 vols., Paris, 1869–1906.

RHC. Occ.	–*Historiens occidentaux*, 5 vols., Paris, 1845–95.
RHF.	*Recueil des historiens des Gaules et de la France*, ed. M. Bouquet, *et al.*, 24 vols., Paris, 1738–1904.
RISS (1).	*Rerum Italicarum scriptores,* ed. L. A. Muratori, 25 vols., Milan, 1723–51.
RISS (2).	*Rerum Italicarum scriptores,* nuova edizione, Citta de Castello, Bologna, etc., 1900– (in progress).
RM. Pilg.	R. Röhricht and H. Meisner, *Deutsche Pilgerreisen nach dem heiligen Lände,* Berlin, 1880.
ROL.	*Revue de l'orient latin,* 12 vols., Paris, 1893–1911.
RS.	*Rolls series. Chronicles and memorials of Great Britain and Ireland during the Middle Ages, published under the direction of the Master of the Rolls.*
SATF.	Société des Anciens Textes Francais.
SHF.	Société de l'histoire de France.
SOL.	*Société de l'orient latin. Série géographique,* 5 vols., Geneva, 1879–89.
TM. Itin.	T. Tobler and A. Molinier, *Itinera Hierosolymitana et descriptiones Terrae Sanctae bellis sacris anteriora, SOL.,* i–ii, Geneva, 1879–85.
VZ.	R. Valentini and G. Zucchetti, *Codice topografico della citta di Roma, Fonti,* 4 vols., Rome, 1940–53.

Notes

Original sources listed in the bibliography are cited by author and/or shortened title. Secondary works listed in the bibliography are cited by author alone. In cases of doubt, the initials OS or SW are used. Works not listed in the bibliography are cited in full. Numbers in the left column refer to pages in this book.

1. Introduction

5   English villages and towns: Stubbs, *Charters,* pp. 464-6.
Henry of Susa: Quoted in G. Le Bras, *Institutions ecclesiastiques de la Chretienté mediévale,* vol. i, Paris, 1964-5, p. 204.

6   No strangers in church: O. Dobiache-Rojdestvensky, *La vie paroissale en France d'après les actes épiscopaux,* Paris, 1911, pp. 87-8.
Confession once a year: Conc. Lateran (1215), canon XXI, *MC.* xxii. 1007-10. On its enforcement in France, Conc. Saintes (1280), *MC.* xxiv. 379-80; and in England, Conc. Exeter (1287), Powicke and Cheney, *Councils,* vol. ii, p. 992.
Held in public: *MC.* xxiv. 527. Cf. Powicke and Cheney, *Councils,* vol. ii, p. 144; for fifteenth century, Gerson, *De Officio Pastoris,* ed. Glorieux, vol. v, p. 141.
Confessional hand-books: e.g. Powicke and Cheney, *Councils,* vol. ii, pp. 220-6. W. A. Pantin, *The English Church in the fourteenth century,* Cambridge, 1955, pp. 270-6.

7   Prostitute repents: *Mirac. S. Mariae Carnotensis* XVII, pp. 533-4.
Busybodies: 'Visitation returns of the diocese of Hereford in 1397', ed. A. T. Bannister, *EHR.* xliv (1929), pp. 279-89, 444-53, xlv (1930), pp. 92-101, 444-63. Guérin and Célier (ed.),

Documents concernant le Poitou, vol. xxiv, pp. 134-6, 287-9 (nos. 780-1, 836); late fourteenth century.

John Myrc, *Instructions for parish priests,* ed. E. Peacock, *EETS.,* vol. xxxi, London, 1868, p. 23.

8   London lady dying: Benedict, *Mirac. S. Thomae,* II. 42, p. 90. 'Curiosity to see…': Wattenbach (ed.), 'Beitrage', p. 605. Guilt overcome by travel: Orderic Vitalis, *Hist. Eccl.,* ed. Chibnall, vol. ii, pp. 44-6. Adam of Eynsham, *Vita S. Hugonis,* IV. 2, vol. ii, pp. 7-10. Paul Walther, *Itin.,* pp. 7-8.

9   'Signs' inspire terror: Gregory of Tours, *De Virtut S. Martini,* III. 54, p. 645 (darkness). *Vita S. Genovefae,* V. 19, ed. C. Kohlet, *BEHE,* vol. xlviii, Paris, 1881, p. 24; *Vita S. Aridii,* in Mabillon (ed.), *Vet. Anal.,* p. 204 (thunder). Eligius (attrib.), *Homilia,* IX, *PL.* lxxxvii. 628 (eclipse of moon). Gregory of Tours, *Hist. Francorum,* VI. 14, IV. 31, 51, pp. 284, 164-5, 187 (red sky, eclipse of sun).

10   Survival of these fears: Burchardt, *Decr.,* XIX. 5, *PL.* cxl. Guibert, *De Vita Sua,* I. 15, p. 56. *Mirac. S. Benedicti,* VI. 11, pp. 233-6 (death of Robert the Pious). Langland, *Piers Plowman,* B.V. 13-5, pp. 57-8. *Roman de la Rose,* II. 18,257-18,468, vol iii, pp. 48-55.

Evil in the wind: Gregory of Tours, *De Virtutibus S. Martini,* III. 16, p 636. Toussaert, p. 365 (Dunkirk abbey). Delaruelle *et al.,* pp. 831-2 (German Dominicans). Bruno, *Expositio in Ep. ad Ephesianos,* II, *PL.* cliii. 325. Yvo, *Panormia,* VIII. 68, *PL.* clxi. 1322.

12   Devil in wild animals: Sulpicius Severus, *Vita S. Martini,* XXI, pp. 130-1. Peter the Venerable, *De Mirac.,* I. 14, 18, cols. 877-8, 883-4, etc. Thomas of Monmouth, *Mirac. S. Willelmi,* III. 12, pp. 137-8 (pig at Norwich). Reginald of Durham, *De B. Cuthberti Virtut.,* XVII, pp. 32-3. Guibert, *De Vita Sua,* I. 21, pp. 81-2.

Devil as deformed man: Athanasius, *Vita S. Antonii,* V,VI, XXI, XL, XLII, LIII, *PG.* xxvi. 845-9, 876, 901, 904-5, 920. Cf. Peter the Venerable, *De Mirac,* I. 8, col. 869 ('parvi et nigerrimi Aethiopis specie assumpta'); Orderic, *Hist. Eccl.,* VIII. 17, ed. Chibnall, vol. iv, pp. 242-4, vol. iv, pp. 242-4 ('agmen Aethiopum…nigerrimi cornipedis').

13   Dreams: William, *Mirac. S. Thomae,* III. 5, V. 8, pp. 262-4, 381. Benedict, *Mirac. S. Thomae,* I. 13, pp. 44-5. Rackham, p. 85.

14 'One night as he lay...': Orderic, *Hist. Eccl.*, III, ed. Chibnall, vol. ii, pp. 42-4.

15 'Luxuria' in sculpture: Mâle, pp. 373-6. G. Zarnecki, *Gislebertus, Sculptor of Autun*, N.Y., 1961, pp. 64-5 and pl. iv.
'The cause that oghte...': *Canterbury Tales*, p. 575.

16 'Conversion' by preachers: Jacques de Vitry, *Exempla*, CXCIX, p. 83. Etienne de Bourbon, *Anecdotes* I. 21, p. 29 (Bologna student); cf. Owst, p. 413 and n[3]. Caesarius, *Dial. Mirac.*, I. 6, 16, 18, 21, 25, 29-30, 5, vol. i, pp. 12-15, 22-3, 25, 28, 30-1, 35, II. Augustine's 'conversion': P. Brown, *Augustine of Hippo*, London, 1967, pp. 106-7.
'Conversion' in hagiography: Bede, *Hist. Eccl.*, IV. 5, p. 350; Du Cange, vol. ii, pp. 547. See, in general, D. Baker, 'Vir Dei: secular sanctity in the early tenth century', in Cuming and Baker, pp. 40-1.

17 Majority damned: Bernard, *Sermo in Vigilia Nativitatis Domini*, III. 3, *PL.* clxxxii. 96. Berthold, *Predigten*, XXIV, vol. I, p. 382. Herolt, quoted in Coulton, vol. i, p. 447, See references in A. Michel, 'Elus (Nombre des)', *DTC.*, iv. 2364-6.
Priest's vision: Orderic, *Hist. Eccl.*, VIII. 17, ed. Chibnall, vol. iv, pp. 236-50.
How far this view accepted: Coulton, vol. i, p. 71 (prior of Holy Trinity). Vincent of Beauvais, *Speculum Morale*, Douai, 1624, col. 840. Berthold, *Predigten*, XXIV, vol. i, p. 386. C. Douais (ed.), *Documents pour servir a l'histoire de l'inquisition dans le Languedoc*, vol. ii, Paris, 1900, p. 100. *Book of Margery Kempe*, I. 59, pp. 144-6.

18 Descriptions of Hell: Owst, pp. 522, 524 (sermons). Bede, *Hist. Eccl.*, V. 12, pp. 490-4. Felix, *Life of St. Guthlac*, ed. B. Colgrave, Cambridge, 1956, p. 105. Guibert, *De Vita Sua*, I. 18, p. 70. Caesarius, *Dial. Mirac.* I. 34, vol. i, pp. 39-43 (Landgrave Ludwig). *Visio Monachi de Eynsham*.

20 Salvation a miracle: Berthold, *Predigten*, XXIV, vol. i, p. 382. Theofrid of Epternach, *Flores Epitaphiorum Sanctorum*, I. 3, col. 384.

2. The Cult of Relics

21 Victricius on saints: *De Laude Sancrotum*, XII, *PL.* xx. 454-5.
Early evidence of cult of relics: Eusebius, *Hist. Eccl.*, IV. 15, pp.

350-2 (Polycarp). Prudentius, *Peristephanon,* V. 41-5, p. 346 (St. Vincent) *Monumenta Ecclesia Liturgica,* ed. F. Cabrol, vol. i (2), Paris, 1900, p. 192 (nos. 4399-4401).

22 Jerome and Vigilantius: Jerome, *Contra Vigilantium,* cols. 346-8; *Ep.* CIX. I, vol. ii, pp. 351-3. Cf. Augustine, *De Civitate Dei,* XXII. 9-10, vol. ii, pp. 613-15.

Cult of relics defended: Augustine, *op. cit.,* 1. 13, VIII. 17, 27, vol. i, pp. 25-6, 382-3, 405; *Contra Faustum,* XXI. 21, *PL.* xlii. 384. Followed by Isidore of Seville, *De Ecclesiasticis Officiis,* xxxv. 1-6, *PL.* lxxxiii. 770.

23 Popular view: Cyprian, *Epp.* XIII. 5, LXXVI. 2, ed. W. von Hartel, *CSEL.* iii, Vienna, 1868-71, vol. i, pp. 507, 829. Cyril of Jerusalem, *Catachesis,* XVIII. 16, XIX. 16, XIX. 7, *PG.* xxxiii. 1071. See Delehaye (4), p. 116.

Aquinas on relics: *Summa Theologica,* III, q. xxv, a. 6, vol. xi, p. 284.

24 *Brandea:* Cyril of Jerusalem, *loc. cit.* Gregory I, *Reg.* V. 57, vol. i, p. 364; *Dialogues,* II. 38, *PL.* lxvi. 204.

'He who wishes to pray': Gregory of Tours, *In Gloria Martyrum,* XXVII, pp. 503-4.

25 Gregory of Tours at Brioude: *De Virtut. S. Juliani,* XXXIV-XXXV, pp. 578-9.

Dust from Holy Land: Frolow, pp. 158-9 (funerary table). Augustine, *De Civitate Dei,* XXII. 8, vol. ii, pp. 602-3. Gregory of Nyssa, *De S. Theodoro, PG.* xlvi. 740.

26 Hung round neck: Gregory I, *Reg.* III. 33, vol. i, p. 192. Jerome, *Comm. in Evang. S. Matthaei,* IV, *PL.* xxvi. 168. Conc. III Bracarense, canon V, in *PL.* lxxxiv. 589-90. Aquinas, *Summa Theologica,* II, ii, q. xcvi, a. 4, vol. ix, pp. 334-5. Adam, *Vita S. Hugonis,* vol. ii, pp. 167-8.

Later use of *brandea:* Guibert, *De Vita Sua,* III. 18, p. 219. *Mirac. S. Michaelis,* pp. 880, 883. Faber, *Evagatorium,* vol. i, p. 94. Ghistele, *Voyage,* vol. xxxvii, p. 742.

27 Fourth-century 'inventions': Delehaye (4), pp. 75-8, 80-1 (Gervaise and Protasius, Stephen), Paulinus, *Vita S. Ambrosii,* XXXIX, *PL.* xiv. 37 (Vitalis and Agricola). Marcellinus, *Chron., PL.* li. 928 (John the Baptist); on the date of this, see *Aa. Ss.* June, vol. iv, p. 713.

28 Augustine on dreams: see P. Courcelle, *Les Confessions de Saint*

Augustin dans la tradition littéraire, Paris, 1963, pp. 127-33. F. van der Meer, *Augustine the bishop,* London, 1961, pp. 531-9.

Relics authenticated by dreams: Glaber, *Hist.,* IV. 3, pp. 96-8 (Moses' rod). Raymond of Aguilers, *Hist. Francorum,* X-XI, pp. 253-7 (Holy Lance).

Sinful to ignore dreams: e.g. *Acta S. Fulconis,* II-V, *Aa. Ss.* May, vol. v, p. 193.

Jean de Meung on dreams: *Roman de la Rose,* II. 18257-64, vol. iii, p. 48.

29   Heads of the Baptist: Delehaye (4), pp. 82-3. *Aa. Ss.* June, vol. iv, pp. 722-46, 751-66.

Dreams criticized: Conc. Carthage, canon XIV, in *MC.* iii. 971. Augustine, *De Cura pro Mortuis Gerenda,* X, pp. 639-41. Guibert, *De Pignoribus,* I, 3, col. 624; elsewhere, he suggests that both were false, *Gesta Dei per Francos,* I. 5, p. 132.

Guibert on translations: *Gesta Dei, loc. cit.*

30   Translations in Greek Church: *Codex Theodosianus,* IX. 17, ed. T. Mommsen and P. Meyer, Berlin, 1905, p. 463. Delehaye (4), pp. 54-7.

Popes refuse to translate relics: Hormisdas, Ep. LXXVII, in Thiel (ed.), *Epp. Pontificum,* pp. 874-5. Gregory I, *Reg.,* IV. 30, vol. i, p. 264.

Dismemberment: Theodoret, *Graecarum Affectionum Curatio,* VIII, col. 1012. Victricius, *De Laude Sanctorum,* XI, col. 453. Gregory of Tours, *Hist. Francorum,* VII. 31, pp. 311-12. Baudonivius, *Vita Radegundis,* II. 15, *PL.* lxxii, 672.

31   Austerities before removing relic: Gregory of Tours, *In Gloria Martyrum,* XIII, pp. 497-8. Cosmas of Prague, *Chron. Boemorum,* II. 3-4, ed. D. Bretholz, *MGH. Rer. Germ.,* N.S. ii, Berlin, 1923, pp. 84-90. Jocelyn of Brakelond, *Chron. de Rebus Gestis Samsonis,* ed. H. E. Butler, London, 1949, pp. 112-14.

32   Relics needed to consecrate churches: Ambrose, *Ep.* XXI, *PL.* xvi. 1019. Bede, *Hist. Eccl.,* I. 29, p. 104 ('all things needed...'). Conc. Nicaea, session VII, canon VII, in *MC.* xiii. 427; cf. Hefele, vol. iii, pp. 781-2.

33   Relics acquired in Rome: Llewellyn, pp. 183-90.

Byzantine collection: William of Tyre, *Hist.,* XX. 23, p. 985 (Amaury). In general, see Ebersolt. On its dispersal in 1204, Riant (I).

34 Other collections: Bethel, p. 69 (Reading); Morand, pp. 9, 23, and preuves, pp. 7-9 (Ste. Chapelle). In general, Fichtenau. Objects of national pride: S Runciman, *The Emperor Romanus Lecapenus and his reign*, Cambridge, 1929, pp. 145, 229-30. William of Malmesbury, *Gesta Pontificum*, V. 268, p. 425. French monk quoted in Fichtenau, p. 72. Matthew Paris, *Chron. Majora*, vol. iv, p. 642 (Suffield).

35 Ferdinand of Carrion: *Vita B. Zoyli*, IV, *ES*. x. 495. Early relic merchants: Delehaye (8), p. 200. Gregory of Tours, *Hist. Francorum*, VII. 31. pp. 311-12.

36 Deusdona: Einhard, *Translatio Marcellini et Petri*, I. 3, p. 241; Rudolph, *Mirac. Sanctorum in Fuldenses Eccl. Translatorum*, II, p. 330. Emma: Eadmer, *Hist. Novorum*, ed. M. Rule, *RS.*, London, 1884, p. 108; William of Malmesbury, *Gesta Pontificum*, V. 263, p. 419. Effect of sack of Constantinople: Conc. Lateran, canon LXII, in *MC*. xxii. 1050-1. Riant (1), p. 8 (d'Alluye). Rohault de Fleury, pp. 110, 396 (Baldwin). Einhard: see his *Translatio Marcellini et Petri*, I. 2-5, pp. 240-2. Relics stolen in teeth: Etheria, *Peregr.*, XXXVII. 2, p. 88 (in 385). *Gesta Consulum Andegavorum*, p. 91. *Mirac. S. Eadmundi* (*Bod.* 240), vol. i, pp. 373-4.

37 No property of a relic: see example quoted in Baynes, p. 170. Theft of St. Benedict: Adrevald, *Hist. Translationis S. Benedicti*, in *Mirac. S. Benedicti*, pp. 1-14. Oldest account (late seventh century?) in Mabillon (ed.), *Vet. Anal.*, pp. 211-12.

38 Theft of St. Nicholas: Nicephorus, *Translatio S. Nicolai in Barum*, IV-XL, pp. 170-89, esp. pp. 175, 178-9.

39 Saint has mind of his own: *Mirac. S. Benedicti*, I. 15-17, pp. 37-42. *Translatio Reliquiarum B. Emiliani*, VIII, *ES*. I. 368-9. *Guide*, VIII, p. 46.

41 St. Hugh at Fécamp: Adam, *Vita S. Hugonis*, vol. ii, pp. 169-70. Precautions against theft: Conc. Lateran, canon LXII, *MC*. xxii. 1049; Conc. Bordeaux, canon IX, *MC*. xxiv. 283. *Capitula de Mirac. S. Cuthberti*, VII. II, pp. 258-9 (Durham). *Cartulaire de N-D de Chartres*, ed. E. de Lepinois and L. Merlet, vol. i, Chartres, 1862, p. 61. Pero Tafur, *Andancas*, p. 29.

42 Henry III and blood of Christ: Matthew Paris, *Chron. Maj.*, vol. iv, p. 643, vol. vi. pp. 138-44.

Guibert on false relics: *De Pignoribus,* I. 2, II. 4, cols. 621, 628-9. Cf. Caesarius, *Dial Mirac., * VIII. 69-70, vol. ii, p. 140.

43 Odo of Bayeux: Guibert, *op. cit.,* I. 3, col. 625.

Fulbert of Cambrai: *Vita Autberti Ep. Cameracensis,* IV. 30-2, ed. J. Ghesquierus, *Acta Sanctorum Belgii,* vol. iii, Bruxelles, 1785, pp. 562-3.

44 Dispute over St. Benedict: Peter the Deacon, *Historica Relatio,* I. 1, p. 288; Chamard, pp. 6-12. Cf. *Mirac. S. Benedicti,* VII. 15, pp. 272-4.

Dispute over St. Nicholas: Orderic, *Hist. Eccl.,* VII. 13, ed. Chibnall, pp. 70-2 (Venosa, Noron). F. Chamard, *Les vies des saints personnages de l'Anjou,* vol. i, Paris, 1863, pp. 411-16; cf. *GC.* xiv. 473 (Angers). *Hist. de Translatione S. Nicolai,* X-XXIX, *RHC. Occ.* v. 260-70 (Venice).

Indignation of the *Guide: Guide,* VIII, pp. 46, 52.

Mary Magdalene: Saxer, pp. 65-73, 185-7, 230-42.

46 Relics displayed when authenticity doubted: *Detectio Corporis S. Dionysii,* II-IX, pp. 166-9 (in *c.* 1050). Robert de Torigny, *Chron.,* vol. ii, p. 136; Rigord, *Gesta Philippi,* LXXX, vol. i, pp. 114-15 (in 1186).

Secretly inspected first: Suger, *De Admin. Sua,* XXXIII, p. 203.

47 Inspection of St. Genevieve: *Vita S. Willelmi Roschildensis,* II. 22-4, *Aa. Ss.* April, vol. i, p. 629; *GC.* viii. 1450-5.

48 Trial by miracle; *MGH. Epp.* v 338 (St. Felix). Eadmer, *De Sanctorum Veneratione,* V, pp. 362-3 (St. Ouen).

Trial by fire: *De S. Adalberto Diacono,* XXV, *Aa. Ss. OSB.* iii. 635-6 (St. Celsus). *Chron. Mon. Casinensis,* II. 33, p. 649. *Vita Meinwerki,* CCIX, ed. F. Tenckhoff, *MGH. Rer. Germ.,* Hannover, 1921, p. 122. Guibert, *De Vita Sua,* III. 20, pp. 230-1 (St. Arnoul). Conc. II Sarragossa (An. 592), *MC.* x. 471 (Arian relics). William of Malmesbury, *Gesta Pontificum,* V. 267, pp. 424-5; *Capitula de Mirac. S. Cuthberti,* VII. 7-11, pp. 254-9 (Anglo-Saxon relics). Mabillon (ed.), *Vet. Anal.,* p. 569 (Anna Gonzaga).

3. The Saints and Their Relics

50 Saints punish mockers: Gerald, *Itin. Cambriae,* I. 2, vol. vi, p. 27. William of Malesbury, *Gesta Pontificum,* V. 275, pp. 438-9. Orderic, *Hist. Eccl.,* VI. 10, ed. Chibnall, vol. iii, p. 318 (St.

Evroul). *Mirac. S. Emmerammi*, II. 20, *Aa. Ss.* Sept., vol. vi, p. 500.
Loomis, pp. 98-100 (woman displays posterior, and other
examples).

51 Iconoclasm in the west: Claudius of Turin, *Adv. Theulmirum
Abbatem, PL.* cv. 462; *Ep.* XII, in *MGH. Epp.* iv. 611; Hefele,
vol. iv, pp. 43-9. See Séjourné, cols. 2353, 2355.

52 Eastern heretics in Spain: *ES.* x. 525-32, xv. 12-15. Cf. Conc.
Seville (An. 619), canon XII, in *MC.* x. 556.

Guibert: See Lefranc, p. 298, for comparison with Calvin etc.
But there are more sensible assessments in J. Chaurand, 'La con-
ception de l'histoire de Guibert de Nogent', *Cahiers de
Civilisation Medievale*, viii (1965), pp. 381-95; and in Morris.

His pamphlet: *De Pignoribus*, esp. I. 3, II. 1-6, III. 3, 5, cols. 624-
5, 629-50, 659-60, 662-3. On the relics of Nogent, *De Vita Sua*,
II. 1, p. 105. On the Holy Lance, *Gesta Dei der Francos*, VII. 34,
p. 252. Accepts cult of genuine relics, *De Pignoribus*, I. 3, col.
625; but demands higher standard of proof, *ibid.*, I. 3–4, cols.
623-4, 627-8.

54 Guibert and the inner life: see his *Liber quo ordine sermo fieri
debeat, PL.* clvi. 27; *De Pignoribus*, I.2, IV. 8, cols. 619, 678-9. In
general, Morris, pp. 59-60.

55 'Crystallized into images': Huizinga, p. 136. But the tendency
was not, of course, peculiar to the later Middle Ages.

Eucharistic images: Early examples in *Vita S. Basilii*, VII, *PL.*
lxxiii. 301-2; and *Vitae Patrum*, V. 18, *PL.* lxxiii. 979. *Vita S.
Gregorii*, IV. 19, *Aa. Ss.* March, vol. ii, p. 134: the passage is a late
interpolation, see H. Grisar, 'Die Gregorbiographie des Paulus
Diakonus in ihrer ursprunglichen Gestalt', *Zeitschrift für
katholische Theologie*, xi (1887), p. 160.

56 Later examples: Guibert, *De Pignoribus*, I. 2, cols. 616-17; Peter
the Venerable, *De Mirac.*, I. 1, col. 852; Jacques de Vitry,
Exempla, CCLXX, p. 113. Coulton, vol. i, pp. 109-10 (priests'
manuals). On late mediaeval Netherlands, see J. Wils, *Het
Sakrament van Mirakel berustende in Sint Jakobs te Leuven*,
Louvain, 1905. 'Extracts from Lincoln episcopal visitations', ed.
E. Peacock, *Archaeologia*, xlviii (1885), pp. 252-3 (George
Carter).

Immaculate conception and Trinity literally portrayed: Inventory
of 1420 in L. E. de Laborde, *Les Ducs de Bourgogne*, vol. ii, Paris,

1851, p. 264. Gerson, *Sermon: Puer Natus,* ed. Glorieux, vol. vii, p. 963. J. Sarrète, 'Vierges ouvertes, Vierges ouvrantes, et la Vierge ouvrante de Palau del Vidre', *Ruscino, Revue d'Histoire et d'Archéologie du Roussillon,* ii (1912), pp. 5-59, 449-57.

57 Theological scruples on relics of Christ: Aquinas, *Summa Theologica,* III, q. liv, a. 2, vol. xi, pp. 509-10. Innocent III, *De Sacro Altaris Mysterio,* IV. 30, *PL.* ccxvii. 876-7.

Relics of Christ at Rome: John the Deacon, *Descriptio,* XIII, pp. 356-7; Innocent III, *loc. cit.* Bridget, *Rev., VI.* 112, p. 525, *As. Ss.* Jan., vol. i, pp. 4-6.

58 Foreskin at Charroux: Montsabert (ed.), *Chartes;* see also Vigneras. At a diocesan synod in 1862, Mgr. Pie asserted that there could be 'no legitimate doubt about the authenticity of this quite unique relic', see P. Saintyves, *Les reliques et les images légendaires,* Paris, 1912, pp. 181-4. Other foreskins: *GC.* viii (Instr.), p. 389 (Coulombs). Denifle, vol. i, p. 167n. (Boulogne). *Aa. Ss.* Jan., vol. i, pp. 6-8 (Antwerp).

Blood of Christ at Mantua: *Annales Regni Francorum,* p. 119. Herman of Reichenau, *Chron. MGH. SS.* v. 127.

59 Bleeding images in Netherlands: L-J. Rogier, *Geschiedenis van het Katholicisme in Noord-Nederland,* vol. i, Amsterdam, 1945, p. 82; cf. Moreau, vol. iv, pp. 368-71.

Other bleeding images: Aquinas, *Summa Theologica,* III, q. liv, a. 2, vol. xi, pp. 509-10. *Chartularium Universitatis Parisiensis,* ed. H. Denifle and A. Chatellain, vol. iv, Paris, 1897, pp. 682-3 (no. 2634), on blood at La Rochelle. On bleeding images reported in Naples in 1972, see *The Times,* 22 August, 1972, p. 5.

60 Blood defended by Grosseteste: Matthew Paris, *Chron. Maj.,* vol. vi, pp. 138-44.

and by Franciscans: Wadding, An. 1351 (nos. 16, 18, 21), An. 1462 (nos. 1-18), An. 1463 (nos. 1-4), An. 1464 (nos. 1-6), vol. viii, pp. 59-62, vol. xiii, pp. 206-16, 264-6, 340-3. N. Glassberger, *Chron., Analecta Franciscana,* ii (1887), pp. 393-5.

61 Bruges processions: Toussaert, pp. 259-66.

Hus on blood of Christ: *De Sanguini Christi,* XI. 38, pp. 28-9.

Monstrances and tabernacles: M. Andrieu, 'Réliquaires et monstrances eucharistiques', *An. Boll.* lxviii (1950), p. 398. Delaruelle *et al.,* pp. 749-52. Fécamp: Baudri de Deuil in

Neustria Pia, ed. A. du Monstier, Rouen, 1663, p. 232. *Poème sur le Précieux Sang,* II. 12-15, in Kajava (ed.), *Etudes,* p. 95.

62   Pecock on relics: *Repressor,* II. 4, 8, pp. 155, 182.
Miracles at Bobbio: *Mirac. S. Columbani Bobbiensis,* I, p. 998.
Hair of B. V. M. at Coutances: John of Coutances, *Mirac. Eccl. Constantiensis,* XXII, p. 378. Some *brandea,* usually of eastern origin, are found earlier, see Beissel (2), pp. 296-7.

63   Other Hair of B. V. M.: Herman, *Mirac. S. Mariae Laudunensis,* II. 1, col 973 (Laon). On the hair at Astorga and Boulogne, Mabillon (ed.), *Vet. Anal.,* p. 433; Lambert of Ardres, *Chron. Comitum Ghisnensium, MGH. Ss* xxiv. 577; Gaiffier (2), p. 79. On hair in Germany, Beissel (2), p. 293n^2.
Tunics of B. V. M.: *Mirac. S. Mariae Carnotensis,* I, p. 509. *Gesta Episcoporum Virdunensium,* XVIII, *MGH. SS.* iv. 44. Others are known from dedication records, *MGH, SS.* XV. 1073, 1095, 1097, 1098, 1270.
Relics of S. Maria Maggiore: John the Deacon, *Descriptio,* XIV, p. 359. Milk of B. V. M.: M. Gomez-Moreno, 'El Arca Santa de Oviedo documentada', *Archivio Espanol de Arte,* xviii (1945), p. 129. *Notae Sweigo-Monasterienses, MGH. SS.* xv. 1073. William of Malmesbury, *Gesta Regum,* III. 285, p. 341 (Chartres).

64   B. V. M. 'localized': *Mirac. S. Mariae Carnotensis,* XVIII, pp. 537-8. *Miracles de Rocamadour,* praefat., p. 63. John of Coutances, *Mirac. Eccl. Constantiensis,* VI, pp. 370-2. More, *Dyalogue,* fol. 22. For similar attitudes in modern Italy, see E. C. Banfield, *The moral basis of a backward society,* Glencoe, Illinois, 1958, pp. 130-1n.

65   Saint present in his shrine: *Mirac. S. Benedicti,* II. 19, pp. 123-5. *Mirac. S. Columbani,* XXII, p. 1008. On the Canterbury glass, Rackham, p. 91 and colour pl. XII.
Relics on altar: E. Bishop, *Liturgica Historica,* Oxford, 1918, pp. 25–6.

66   Statue-reliquaries: *Mirac. S. Fidis,* I. 13, 28, 30, II. 4, pp. 46-7, 71-3, 75-6, 100-1. P. Deschamps, 'Etude sur la Renaissance de la sculpture en France à l'époque romane', *Bulletin Monumentale,* lxxxiv (1925), pp. 33-5. Mâle, p. 203.

67   Artistic representations of saints influence popular imagination: Guibert, *De Vita Sua,* I. 16, p. 61. *Mirac. S. Fidis,* I. 1, pp. 9-10. *Chron. Mon. Casinensis,* II. 34. p. 650 ('illa nimirum specie qua depingi a pictoribus consuevit'). On St. Foy and the blind,

Mirac. S. Fidis, I. 1-2, 29, II. 1, 3, III. 6, 9, 11-12, 14, IV. 15, pp. 6-21, 73, 90-3, 98-9, 137-8, 144-5, 147-50, 152-3, 200-1.

68   Influence of popular piety: it will be seen that I differ on this point from G. Duby, 'The diffusion of cultural patterns in feudal society', *Past and Present,* no. 39 (1968), pp. 3-5.

4. The Pursuit of the Miraculous

69   Hume: *An Essay on Miracles,* in *An Enquiry concerning human understanding,* ed. L. A. Selby-Bigge, Oxford, 1894, pp. 114, 115-6.

70   Injunctions of 1536: in *Letters of Thomas Cromwell,* ed. R. B. Merriman, vol. ii, Oxford, 1902, p. 28.
Fraud alleged: Hus, *De Sanguine Christi,* XIV. 45-6, pp. 32-3. More, *Dyalogue,* I. 14, fols. 18-18VO.

72   Histrionic contraptions: H. Ellis (ed.), *Original letters illustrative of English history,* 3rd. series, vol. iii, London, 1846, p. 168. *Letters and Papers,* vol. xiii (1), p. 120 (no. 348).
Plague at Melrose: *Vita S. Cuthberti,* IX, p. 184.

73   Augustine of Canterbury and miracles: Bede, *Hist. Eccl.,* I. 26, 30, II. see pp. 76, 108, 190. Gregory I, *Reg.,* XI. 36, vol. ii. pp. 305-8. On this, 15, Colgrave.

74   St. Martin: Sulpicius Severus, *Dialogi,* II. 4, pp. 184-5. *MGH. Epp.* iii. 119-22 (Nizier).
Augustine on miracles: *De vera religione,* XXV. 47, *PL.* xxxiv. 142; *Sermo* CCCLVI. 7, *PL.* xxxix. 1577. See D. P. de Vooght, 'Les Miracles dans la vie due Saint Augustin', *Recherches de Théologie Ancienne et Mediévale,* xi (1939), pp. 5-16; P. Brown, *Augustine of Hippo,* London, 1967, pp. 384-6.

75   Gregory on miracles: *Homilia in Evang.,* XXIX, *PL.* lxxvi. 1215. Bede on miracles: *Vita S. Cuthberti,* XXI, p. 224.
Orderic on miracles: *Hist. Eccl.,* V. 4, VI. 1, ed. Chibnall, vol. iii, pp. 8, 214.
Survival of missionary attitude to miracles: Gregory of Tours, *In Gloria Martyrum,* LXXX, pp. 542-3; cf. *In Gloria Confessorum,* XIV, p. 756. Caesarius, *Dial, Mirac.,* V. 18, vol. i, pp. 296-7 (Besançon heretics). Pierre de Vaux-de-Cernay, *Hystoria Albigensis,* II. 54, ed. P. Guébin and E. Lyon, *SHF,* vol. i, Paris, 1926, pp. 47-9; cf. Guillaume de Puylaurens, *Chronicon,* IX, ed.

Beissier, *Bibliothèque de la Faculté des Lettres de Paris,* XVIII, Paris, 1904, p. 128; the painting is in the Louvre.

77   Lessons of the miracles of St. Thomas: William, *Mirac. S. Thomae,* IV. 45, 49, VI. 159, pp. 355-6, 360-1, 534.

Heretics cannot perform miracles: Lucas of Tuy, *De Altera Vita,* II. 9, in *Magna Bibliotheca Veterum Patrum,* vol. iii, Cologne, 1618, pp. 259-61; cf. III. 9, 18, pp. 280-1, 282-3. *Calendar of Close Rolls, Henry VI,* vol. iii (1435-41), London, 1937, pp. 385-6 (Wyche).

Muslim miracles: Ricoldo, *Liber Peregrinationis,* XXXVI, p. 141. Denis, *Contra perfidiam Mahometi,* II, 3, 4, 9, *Dialogus disputationis inter Christianum et Sarracenum,* III, in *Opera Omnia,* vol. xxxvi, Tournai, 1908, pp. 275, 278, 287, 454-5. In 1121, the ambassadors of the Almoravid emir of Cordova, Ali ben Yúsuf, encountered crowds of pilgrims on the road to Santiago, and were impressed by accounts of the miracles of St. James, *Hist. Compostellana,* II. 50, p. 350.

78   John of Capistrano: Wadding, *Annales Minorum,* An. 1452 (no. 25), vol. xii, p. 142. Nicholas of Fara, *Vita S. Johannis de Capistrano,* VII. 81-4, *Aa. Ss.* Oct., vol. x, pp. 465-6. See J. Hofer, *Johannes von Capestrano. Ein Leben in Kampf um die Reform der Kirche,* Innsbruck, 1936, pp. 313-560.

80   'For all chroniclers…': John of Salisbury, *Hist. Pontificalis,* prologue, p. 2.

Sceptics punished: Gregory of Tours, *In Gloria Martyrum,* XXIV, p. 502. *Mirac. S. Joannis Beverlacensis,* proem. I. *Aa. Ss.* May, vol. ii, p. 172 (saec. xii-xiii). *Mirac. S. Wulfstani,* II. 5, I. 18, pp. 151-2, 125 (saec. xiii).

Educated men more sceptical: *Mirac. S. Gengulphi,* XV, *MGH. SS.* xv. 793. Herman, *De Mirac. S. Eadmundi,* XLIV, p. 86. *Capitula de Mirac. S. Cuthberti,* VII. 7-11, pp. 254-9. Walter Daniel, *Ep. ad Mauricium,* ed. F. M. Powicke, *Walter Daniel's Life of Ailred of Rievaulx,* London, 1950, p. 67. William, *Mirac. S. Thomae,* III. 41, 4, pp. 298, 262.

81   Surfeit of miracles wearisome: William of Malmesbury, *Gesta Pontificum,* II. 75, p. 168 (St. Swithin). William, *Mirac. S. Thomae,* IV. 45, p. 355. Thomas of Monmouth, *Mirac. S. Willelmi,* V. 12, pp. 202-3.

82   Miracles as means of monastic self-aggrandisement: Theobald,

Vita S. Gummari, XXII, *Aa. Ss.* Oct., vol. v, pp. 687-8 (saec. xii). *Mirac. S. Dionysii,* III. 4, *Aa. Ss. OSB.,* vol. iv, p. 364; *Detectio Corporis S. Dionysii,* XI, p. 170. *Mirac. S. Fidis,* I. 13, 7, pp. 46, 31. The use of relics as a means of psychological influence is found in other churches; compare, for example, a miracle of St. James at Reading (MS. Gloucester cathedral 1, fol. 173) with the Reading cartulary (Brit. Mus., MS. Cotton Vespasian E. V, fols. 24-31, 58-60vo, 75vo, 77). The effect of monastic acquisitiveness on lay society in the Mâconnais has been studied by Duby, pp. 61-2, 68-73.

83   Miracles of St. Thomas as political phenomenon: William, *Mirac. S. Thomae,* III. 41, 4, pp. 298, 262.

84   Miracles investigated: *Mirac. S. Benedicti,* III. 15, 17-18, pp. 161-2, 164-6. Philip, *Mirac. S. Frideswidae,* LXXIII, p. 582. Benedict, *Mirac. S. Thomae,* III. 51, IV. 2, 6, 65, pp. 153-5, 181, 183-5, 236-7; William, *op. cit.,* VI. 3-5, pp. 410-13. *Mirac. S. Wulfstani,* II. 12, 15, pp. 161, 167; cf. II. 21, p. 179.

85   Spurious ones rejected: Foréville (ed.) *Livre de S. Gilbert,* p. 10. On Mont.-St.-Michel, Huynes, vol. i, pp. 109, 126-7. Guillaume de Saint-Pathus, *Miracles de S. Louis,* XIV, p. 49.

86   Caesarius's definition: *Dial. Mirac.,* X. 1, vol. ii, p. 217.

87   Augustine on the physical world: *De Quantitate animae,* XXXI. 62-3, *PL.* xxxii. 1069-70; *De Civitate Dei,* XXI. 4, vol. ii, p. 519; *De nuptiis et concupiscentia,* I. 19. *PL.* xliv. 426; *Ep.* CXXXVII. 10-11, vol. ii, pp. 109-11; *Contra Faustum,* XXVI. 3, ed. J. Zycha, *CSEL.* xxv, Vienna, 1891, pp. 730-1.

88   'These things are indeed...': Samson, *De Mirac. S. Eadmundi,* I. 12, p. 143.
      Natural explanations discarded for supernatural: Gregory of Tours, *De Virtut. S. Martini,* III. praefat., p. 632; cf. II. 60, IV. 1, pp. 629-30, 649-50. *Hist. Versifé de Fécamp,* II. 3645-70, pp. 186-7. William, *Mirac. S. Thomae,* III. 24, pp. 282-3.

89   Miraculous escapes from captivity: *Mirac. S. Fidis,* I. 31, p. 76. *Mirac. B. Egidii,* II, VI, X-XII, XV, *MGH. SS.* xii. 317, 319, 320-2, *An. Boll.* ix (1890), pp. 394-6, 399-404. *Liber S. Jacobi,* II. 1, 22, pp. 261-2, 286-7. *Guide,* VIII, p. 54 (St. Leonard). *Mirac. S. Martialis,* passim. Salimbene, *Chron., MGH. SS.* XXXII. 522 (Mary Magdalene).

90   Bohemond: *Mirac. S. Leonardi,* II. 2, *Aa. Ss.* Nov., vol. iii, pp.

160-8. Albert of Aix, *Hist. Hierosolymitana,* IX. 33-6, pp. 610-12. Orderic, *Hist. Eccl.,* X. 23, XI. 12, ed. Prévost, vol. iv, pp. 156, 210-11.

Gregory of Tarsus: Benedict (interpolated), *Mirac. S. Thomae,* VI. 6, pp. 273-9.

91 Hus on escape miracles: *De Sanguine Christi,* X. 35, pp. 26-7. Yet such a conclusion, though morally repulsive, would not be logically absurd; see the sensible observations of E. E. Evans-Pritchard, *Theories of primitive religion,* Oxford, 1965, pp. 89-91. Vain pilgrims hope for miracle: Guibert, *De Pignoribus,* III. 5 col. 663. Baraut (ed.) *Llibre Vermell,* p. 35 (Montserrat, saec. xiv). Benedict, *Mirac. S. Thomae,* IV. 33, p. 206. Samson, *De Mirac. S. Eadmundi,* II. 7, p. 178.

92 Miracles proclaimed to crowd: *Mirac. S. Egidii,* IV, *MGH. SS.* xii. 318-19. *Mirac. S. Mariae Magdalenae, Viziliaci Facta, ed. alt.,* I, *CCH. (Paris),* vol. ii, pp. 292-3 (no. 2).

Mason injured at Fleury: *Mirac. S. Benedicti,* VIII. 30, p. 328.

93 Miracles proof of sanctity: Fontanini (ed.) *Codex,* pp. 37-8 (St Cunegonde).

94 Case of Becket: William, *Mirac. S. Thomae,* I. 12, II. 91, pp. 152, 251-2.

Benedict, *Mirac. S. Thomae,* II. 50, III. 64, IV. 75, pp. 91, 162-3, 245. Letter of Peter of La Celle in *Becket Materials,* vol. vii, p. 566 (lost service-book). Caesarius, *Dial, Mirac.,* VIII. 54, vol. ii, pp. 127-8 (Paris debate).

95 This view criticized: Odo, *Sermo de S. Benedicto, Collationes,* I. 23-4, III. 39, *De combustione Basilicae S. Martini,* in *Bibliotheca Cluniacensis,* cols. 139, 175, 240, 147. Guibert, *De Pignoribus,* I. I, III. 5, cols. 615-16, 662-3. Wyclif, *De Ecclesia,* II, XIX, pp. 45, 465; *Sermones,* II. 22, vol. ii, p. 164. Gerson, *Contra Impugnantes Ordinis Carthusiensium,* ed. Du Pin, vol. ii, cols. 711-14. *Examination of William Thorpe,* p. 137.

'It may be peradventure…': *Canterbury Tales,* p. 607. The same argument is found in Pecock's *Repressor,* II. 4, pp. 155-6, in defence of the veneration of images.

96 False miracles of St. Thomas: Benedict, *Mirac. S. Thomae,* IV. 32, III. 31, pp. 305, 140. William, *Mirac. S. Thomae,* IV. 34, VI. 139, pp. 346-7, 524.

5. The Medicine of the Sick

98   Fatalism: *Journal d'un Bourgeois,* p. 295. Boccaccio, *Il Decamerone,* introd.

Ten bushels an acre: *Walter of Henley's Husbandry,* ed. D. Oschinsky, Oxford, 1971, p. 325.

99   John of Norwich: Ralph of Diceto, *Ymagines Historiarum,* in *Opera Historica,* ed. W. Stubbs, vol. i, *RS,* London, 1876, p. 416

Famines: See F. Curshmann, *Hungersnöte im Mittelalter,* Leizig, 1900; M. J. Larénaudie, 'Les famines en Languedoc aux xive et xve siècles', *Annales du Midi,* lxiv (1952), pp. 27-39. On the transport of food, see J. Glénisson, 'Une administration medié-vael au prise de la disette', *Moyen Age,* lvii (1951), pp. 303-26. Diet: For England, J. C. Drummond and A. Wilbraham, *The Englishman's Food,* 2nd. ed., London, 1957, pp. 40-1, 54-5, 75-86; Bonser, pp. 351-6. The conditions described in L. Stouff, *Ravitaillement et alimentation en Provence aux xive et xve siècles,* Paris, 1970, probably obtained in most of southern Europe. On central and eastern Europe, M. Dembinska, *Konsumpcja zywnosciowa w Polsce sredniowiecznej,* Warsaw, 1963 (with English summary).

100   Constant discomfort: Gregory of Tours, *De Virtut. S. Martini,* II. 60, III. praefat., 1, IV. 1, pp. 629-30, 632, 649-50. Peter the Venerable, *Letters,* vol. ii, pp. 247-51.

Digestive complaints: *Miracles de Rocamadour,* I. 45, p. 148 (Robert of Leicester). William, *Mirac. S. Thomae,* IV. 40, pp. 350-1 (Geoffrey of Binbrooke). Benedict, *Mirac. S. Thomae,* II. 45, pp. 92-3.

101   Ergotism: John of Coutances, *Mirac. Eccl. Constantiensis,* XVI, XXVII, pp. 376, 381. Farsit, *Mirac. S. Mariae in Urbe Suessionensis,* I, VII, cols. 1777-9, 1781-2. *Translatio S. Geremari,* V-VI, *Aa. Ss.* Sept., vol. vii. p. 705 (Chartres, 1132). L. Bourgin, *La chaire Francaise au xiie siècle d'après les manuscrits,* Paris, 1879, pp. 365-8 (Paris, 1206). The disease was not yet associated with the Virgin in the 1040s, when a grave outbreak occurred in the Limousin, see *Mirac. S. Benedicti,* IV. 1, pp. 174-7.

102   Prior of Sauxillanges: *Miracles de Rocamadour,* II. 21, pp. 215-16. Peter the Venerable's doctor: Peter, *Letters,* no. 158b, vol. i, p. 383.

Doctors harm patient: Philip, *Mirac. S. Frideswidae,* XL, p. 577. *Miracles de Rocamadour,* II. 32, p. 238.

103 Pilgrimage after doctors fail: Benedict, *Mirac. S. Thomae*, I. 15, II. 23, VI. 7, pp. 47, 73, 280. William, *Mirac. S. Thomae*, II. 20, 32, pp. 176, 187.

Surgeon guilty of murder: Philip, *Mirac. S. Frideswidae*, CX, p. 589. Cf. Owst, pp. 349-51.

104 Witches: Langland, *Piers Plowman*, B. xiii. 335-42, p. 228. *Mirac. S. Benedicti*, VII. 47, p. 354 (Tortaire). On Merovingian charm-healers, Marignan, pp. 186-93.

Physicians denigrated: Gregory of Tours, *In Gloria Martyrum*, XXX, pp. 506-7 ('Why waste your breath...'). *Mirac. S. Donatiani*, *MGH. SS.* xiv 180. *Liber S. Jacobi*, I. 6, p. 50.

Saints rivals of physicians: Caesarius, *Dial. Mirac.*, VII. 24, vol. ii, p. 34 (Montpellier). Guillaume de St.-Pathus, *Miracles de S. Louis*, XII, p. 40. On Raoul le Cavetier, *ibid.*, XX, pp. 68-9.

105 St. Thomas as healing saint: Benedict, *Mirac. S. Thomae*, IV. 15, 51, pp. 195, 219. William, *Mirac. S. Thomae*, II. 37, p. 196. *Canterbury Tales*, II. 17-18, p. 1.

106 Punitive illnesses: *Vita S. Hilarii*, III. 17, *Aa. Ss.* May, vol. ii, p. 30. *Vita S. Germani*, XXIII, *MGH. Auct. Antiq.* iv (2). 16, Gregory, *De Virtut. S. Juliani*, X, p. 569; *De Virtut. S. Martini*, III. 56, pp. 645-6.

All sickness caused by sin: John Chrysostom quoted in Delaunay, p. 10. Jacob of Voragine, *Legenda Aurea*, CXC, p. 877. '*Incursio diaboli*': Gregory of Tours, *De Virtut. S. Martini*, II. 20, III. 14, pp. 616, 635. Peter the Deacon, *Historica Relatio*, I. 1, p. 288. Guibert, *De Vita Sua*, III. 20, pp. 229-30.

Infection explained: Foréville (ed.), *Livre de S. Gilbert*, p. 49.

107 'Possession by the Devil': Bede, *Hist. Eccl.*, III. 11, p. 248. *Mirac. S. Wulfstani*, I. 13, 15, II. 19, pp. 122-3, 123-4, 177. *Mirac. S. Egidii*, XXX, *An. Boll.*, ix (1880), pp. 421-2.

109 Church opposes medicine: Conc. Lateran, canon XXII, in *MC.* xxii. 1010-1. Conc. Paris (1429), canon XXIX, in *MC.* xxviii. 1110. Jacques de Vitry quoted in Lecoy de la Marche, p. 486. Maillard quoted in Samouillan, pp. 278-9. On opposition to Jewish physicians, Conc. Béziers, canon XLIII, in *MC.* xxiii. 702; Delaunay, pp. 11-12. These attitudes were still common among English Protestants of the seventeenth century, see Thomas, pp. 85-9.

110 Gonorrhoea: William, *Mirac. S. Thomae,* IV. 25, p. 340; cf. VI. 19,
pp. 431-2, Samson, *Mirac. S. Eadmundi,* II, 20, pp. 204-5.
Sterility: *Cartulaire de l'abbaye de la Sainte Trinite du Mont de Rouen,*
no. 108, ed. A. Deville, Paris, 1841, p. 452 (Normans in 1063).
Cartulaire de Conques, no. 373, pp. 281-2. *Liber S. Jacobi,* II. 3, p. 263.
Gesta Principum Polonorum, I. 30-1, *MGH. SS.* ix. 442-3 (Wladislaw
Hermann). See also *Mirac. S. Fidis,* III. 9, pp. 144-5; William, *op. cit.,*
III. 6, pp. 264-5; *Miracles de Rocamadour,* I. 23, p. 112.

111 Woman at St.-Gilles: *Mirac. S. Egidii* (interpolated), *MGH. SS.* xii.
317.

112 *Brandea* eaten: Gregory of Tours, *In Gloria Confessorum,* X, p. 754;
De Virtut. S. Martini, III. 50, II. 51, pp. 644, 626; *In Gloria
Martyrum,* VI, L, pp. 491-2, 523

113 Relics dipped in liquid: *Mirac. S. Benedicti,* VIII. 21, 25, pp. 308-9,
318-19. Thomas of Monmouth, *Mirac. S. Willelmi,* III. 22, p. 162
(Norwich). MS. Gloucester cathedral, 1, fols. 171[vo], 172, 174[vo]
(Reading).
'Water of St. Thomas': William FitzStephen, *Vita S. Thomae,* in
Becket Materials, vol. iii, pp. 148, 150. Benedict, *Mirac. S. Thomae,*
I. 12, II. 4, 50, III. 19, 21-2, IV. 6, pp. 42-3, 59-60, 96, 131, 133-5,
186-7.

114 Found repulsive: *Mirac. S. Michaeli,* pp. 886-7.
Medical libraries: M. R. James, *The ancient libraries of Canterbury
and Dover,* Cambridge, 1903, pp. 55-62; William of Canterbury
quotes Galen in *Mirac. S. Thomae,* IV. 20, pp. 332-4. M. R. James,
On the abbey of St. Edmund at Bury. I. The Library; II. The Church,
Cambridge Archaeological Soc., xxvii, Cambridge, 1895, pp. 14,
66, 67-8 L. Delisle, *Inventaire des manuscrits de la Bibliothèque
Nationale. Fonds de Cluny,* Paris, 1884, pp. 166-75. Catalogue of
medical books at St. Martial, including many translations from
the Arabic, in *Bulletin de la Soc. Archéologique du Limousin,* xxv
(1870), pp. 397-400.

115 Monastic physicians: Herman, *De Mirac. S. Eadmundi,* XXII, p. 56
(Baldwyn). William of Malmesbury, *Gesta Pontificum,* V. 274, pp.
437-8.
Stream at St. Evroul: Orderic Vitalis, *Hist. Eccl.,* VI. 9, ed. Chibnall,
vol. iii, p. 276.
Medical instructions in visions: William, *Mirac. S. Thomae,* II. 4,
III. 4, pp. 160, 261-2, *Mirac. S. Gilberti,* II. 19, pp. 68-9.

Bishop of Thetford's eye: Herman, *De Mirac. S. Eadmundi*, XXVI, pp. 62-4.

116 Broodiness taken for insanity: William, *Mirac. S. Thomae*, II. 43, p. 204.

Psychologically induced illness: on hypochondria, see examples given in *Divine Healing* (SW), pp. 33-45 (nos. 7-10, 12-17, 20, 26); and the comments of R. A. Hunter and I. Macalpine, 'Valentine Greatraks', *St. Bartholomew's Hospital Journal*, lx (1956), pp. 361-8. On the physiological effects of shock see the important article by W. B. Cannon, 'Voodoo death', *American Anthropologist*, N.S. xliv (1942), pp. 169-81; H. Webster, *Taboo: a sociological study*, Stanford, 1942; C. Levi-Strauss, *Anthropologie Structurale*, Paris, 1958, pp. 183-204. The examples in the text are from *Mirac. S. Thomae*, III. 63, pp. 167-8 (Luciana Torel); Philip, *Mirac. S. Frideswidae*, XCVII, p. 586. William, *op. cit.*, IV. 4, pp. 351-16 (Nicholas of Dover).

117 Sickness aggravated by stress: William of Malmesbury, *Gesta Pontificum*, V. 272, pp. 434-5. Cf. similar case in *Miracles de Rocamadour*, II. 18, p. 210. On sickness and stress, J. D. Frank, *Persuasion and healing. A comparative study of psychotherapy*, London, 1961, pp. 38-9.

118 'Hope invited...': Thomas of Monmouth, *Mirac S. Willelmi*, VI. 16, p. 254.

'Faith-healing': in general, Frank, *op. cit.*, pp. 45-53, 64-74; J. Gillin, 'Magical fright', *Psychiatry*, ii (1948), pp. 389-94. On its role in modern clinical medicine, L. Lasagna *et al.*, 'A study of the placebo response', *American Journal of Medicine*, xvi (1954), pp. 770-9.

Placebos (false relics): Caesarius, *Dial. Mirac.*, VIII. 70, vol. ii, p. 140. Benedict, *Mirac. S. Thomae*, IV. 47, p. 217; but such deceptions did not always work, see William, *Mirac. S. Thomae*, V. 14, pp. 384-5

119 Relapses: Benedict, *op. cit.*, II. 49, IV. 3, 21, pp. 95, 183, 199-200. William, *op. cit.*, II. 56, VI. 72, pp. 219, 471. *Mirac. S. Gilberti*, II. 15, p. 66 (Sempringham). William of Malmesbury, *Gesta Pontificum*, V. 270, pp. 429-31.

120 Six factors: *Divine healing* (SW), pp. 10-13. See the valuable discussions of seventeenth-century miracles in Thomas, pp. 204-11, and M. Bloch, *Les Rois thaumaturges*, Paris, 1924, pp. 420-9.

6. Origins and Ideals

122 Scholars at Jerusalem: Eusebius, *Hist. Eccl.*, IV. xxvi. 13-14, VI. xx. I, xxvii, pp. 386-8, 566, 580. Jerome, *De Viris Illustribus,* LIV, LXII, *PL.* xxiii. 664-8, 673.

'Footsteps of the Master': Origen, *In Joannem,* VI. 24, *PG.* xiv. 269.

'No other sentiment...': Paulinus, *Ep.* XLIV. 14, pp. 402-3.

123 Etheria: see her *Peregr.,* III. 5-6, X. 7, XXIII. 5, pp. 40, 52, 70.

Holy Week services: *Ibid.,* XXIV-XLIX, pp. 71-101.

Jerome and Paula: Jerome, *In Lib. Paralipomenon,* praefat., *PL.* xxix. 401; *Epp.* XLVI. 9, LVII. 2, CVIII. 9-10, vol., i, pp. 339, 529, vol. ii, pp. 314-18.

Footprints preserved: Paulinus, *Epp.,* XLIX. 14, XXXL. 4, pp. 402-3, 271-2. Adamnan, *De Locis Sanctis,* I. xxiii. 3-5, p. 247.

Following Gospels in Holy Land: Bede, *Hist. Eccl.,* V. 15, p. 506; Adamnan, *op. cit.,* I. xxv. 1-8, pp. 251-3 (Arculf). *BBB.,* i. 151 (thirteenth-century Franciscan). Faber, *Evagatorium,* vol. i, pp. 25-6.

127 Meditation on humanity of Christ: *Vita Richardi Abbatis,* XVIII, pp. 288-9; cf. Hugh of Flavigny, *Chron.,* XVIII, p. 393. Antenoris, *Vita S. Silvini,* I. 6-9, p. 30 (not historically reliable). Benincasa, *Vita S. Rayneri,* VI.48, p. 436.

128 '*Imitatio Christi*': Hugh of Flavigny, *Chron.,* XXI, pp. 395-6 (Richard of St.-Vannes). Benincasa, *op. cit.,* IV. 47, p. 436. On baptism in the Jordan, see *infra. Vita S. Bonae,* I. 13, *Aa. Ss.* May, vol. vii, p. 149. William of Malmesbury, *Gesta Regum,* III. 235, pp. 292-3 (Fulk Nerra). Theoderic of Wurzburg, *De Locis Sanctis,* XXV, p. 63 (flagellation on Mt. Sion). Robert of Torigny, *Chron.,* vol. ii, p. 51 (Henry II).

Stations of the Cross: Ernoul, *Chron.,* XVII, p. 206 (1231). Ricoldo, *Liber Peregrinationis,* VI, p. 112. Ogier d'Anglure, *Saint Voyage,* pp. 13-14.

129 Sacchetti's allegory: in *Sermoni,* LXVIII, pp. 165-6.

130 'enter into the mind...': Thomas of Celano, *De Mirac. B. Francisci,* II. 2, *Analecta Franciscana,* vol. x, Quaracchi, 1926-41, p. 273.

Pilgrimage as escape from civilization: Jerome, *Contra Joannem,* XLI, *PL.* xxiii. 393. *Vie de S. Mélanie,* II. 19, p. 168. Jerome, *Ep.* XLVI. 12, vol. i, pp. 342-3.

Impact of *Life of St. Anthony:* Augustine, *Confessions,* VIII. vi. 14-15, ed. P. Knoll, *CSEL.* xxxiii,Vienna, 1896, pp. 181-3.

Jerome's circle and the desert hermits: Jerome, *Epp.* CXXVII. 5, CVIII. 14, vol. iii, pp. 149-50, vol. ii, pp. 324-5 (Paula). Palladius, *Hist. Lausiaca,* XLVI, vol. ii, pp. 134-5 (elder Melania). Etheria, *Peregr.,* XVII. 2, p. 60. *Vie de S. Mélanie,* II. 39, p. 200.

131   Pilgrimage as self-exile: Jerome, *Contra Joannem,* XLI, *PL.* xxiii. 393; *Ep.* LVIII. 2-4, vol. i, pp. 529-33.

132   Four Anglo-Saxon kings: Caedwalla of Wessex (Bede, *Hist. Eccl.,* V. 7, pp. 470-2). Ceanred of Mercia and Offa of Wessex (*ibid.,* V. 19, p. 516). Ine of Wessex *(Anglo-Saxon Chron.,* p. 27). Ratchis: *Lib. Pont.,* vol. i, pp. 433-4.

Karloman: *Annales Regni Francorum,* pp. 6-7. On Eudoxia, see J. B. Bury, *History of the later Roman Empire,* London, 1923, vol. i, pp. 226-31.

Irish concept of self-exile: Columban, *Sermo* VIII, *Opera,* ed. G. S. M. Walker, Dublin, 1957, pp. 94-6. Dermatius, *Exhortatoria, MD. Thes.* i. 341-2 ('be exiles...'). *Anglo-Saxon Chron.,* p. 53 (three pilgrims of 891).

133   'Going to Rome involves...': Gougaud, pp. 158-9.

Egbert: Bede, *Hist. Eccl.,* III. 27, pp. 312-14.

Wandering peculiarly Irish: Heiric's letter in *RHF.* vii. 563. Gozbert, *Mirac. S. Galli,* II. 47, *MGH. SS.* ii. 30.

Anglo-Saxons in Ireland: Bede, *Hist. Eccl.,* III. 27, IV. 4, pp. 313, 346-8. Alcuin, *Ep.* CCLXXXVII, ed. E. Duemmler, *MGH. Epp.* iv. 445-6.

Celtic influence: *Vita S. Sigiranni,* VIII, p. 386 (saec. ix). *Vita S. Wandregisili,* II. 9, *Aa. Ss.* July, vol.V, p. 274. *Vita S. Cadroae,* XX, *Aa. Ss. OSB.,* vol. vii, p. 494.

134   Wandering forbidden: *Capitularia Regum Francorum,* vol. i, pp. 35, 102, 133, vol. ii, p. 122.

135   Everard de Breteuil: Guibert, *De Vita Sua,* I. 9, pp. 25-6. Damian's views are contained in *De Contemptu Saeculi (Opusc. XII),* IX-XIV, *PL.* clxv. 260-7. For later criticism of monk-pilgrims, see St. Bernard, *Epp.* LVI, CCCIC, cols. 162-3, 612–13. Cf. miracle stories with the same moral, e.g. *Chron. Mon. Casinensis,* II. 11, p. 636; M. Valla, 'Les Lyonnais à Compostelle', *BHP.* (1964), pp. 240-1n.

7. The Penitential Pilgrimage

136 Legal distinctions: Peter of Joncels quoted in Du Cange, *Glossarium* (OS), vol. vi, p. 269. Cf. Alfonso X, *Siete Partidas,* I. xxiv. I, vol. 1 (1), fol. 151vo.

Early penitential exiles: Jerome, *Ep.* CXLVII, vol. iii, pp. 312-29. Symeon Metaphrastes, *Vita S. Marciani,* XIX, *PG.* cxiv. 452-3 (late).

Cf. Kötting (3), p. 330.

137 Irish penitentials: G. Le Bras, 'Pénitenciels', *DTC.* xii. 1162-5. Vogel (2), pp. 44-8, 53-6.

Public and private penance: Raymond of Peñaforte, *Summa,* III. xxxiv. 6, Avignon, 1715, pp. 642-3; cf. Aquinas, *Summa Theologica,* III (suppl.), q. xxviii, a. 3, vol. xii, p. 53. *Canterbury Tales,* p. 572.

138 Especially used for clerics or noblemen: Peter Damian, *Vita S. Romualdi,* VII. 37-8, *Aa. Ss.* Feb., vol. ii, p. 112; on Damian's own sentences, Lib. VII, *Ep.* XVII, *PL.* cxliv. 455; *Opusc.* V, *PL.* cxlv. 98. Bernold, *Chron., MGH. SS.* v. 428, 429-30 (Thierry).

and for scandalous crimes: Rigaud, *Reg. Visitationum,* pp. 164, 325-6, 344, 425-6, 477, 579, 665. On Cologne synod of 1279, Hefele, vol. vi, p. 262. Raynald, *Annales,* An. 1319 (no. 27), vol. v., p. 123 (Roger da Bonito). Clement V, *Reg.* 7503, Rome, 1884-92, vol. vi, pp. 420-1 (Nogaret).

139 Eleventh-century penitential practice: C. Vogel, 'Les rites de la pénitence publique aux xe et xie siècles', *Mélanges offerts a Réné Crozet,* ed. P. Gallais and Y. J. Riou, Poitiers, 1966, vol. i, pp. 137-44. H. E. J. Cowdrey, *The Cluniacs and the Gregorian Reform,* Oxford, 1970, pp. 122-8, points out the importance of this for the expansion of monasticism. Cf. H. E. Mayer, *Geschichte der Kreuzzüge,* Stuttgart, 1965, pp. 31-4.

140 Penitential pilgrims of eleventh century: Helgaud, *Vita Roberti Regis,* XXX, *RHF.* x. 114-15. Orderic Vitalis, *Hist. Eccl.,* III, ed. Chibnall, vol. ii, p. 10 (Robert of Normandy). *Encomium Emmae,* II. 40, ed. A. Campbell, Camden Soc. 3rd. series, vol. lxxii, London, 1949, p. 36 (Canute).

141 Fulk Nerra: Glaber, *Hist.,* II. 4, p. 32. William of Malmesbury, *Gesta Regum,* III. 235, pp. 292-3. On the complex chronology of

his pilgrimages, see K. Norgate, *England under the Angevin kings,* London, 1887, vol. i, pp. 192-6.

Penitential pilgrimage as judicial exile: *Canones sub Edgaro Rege,* X, in *MC.* xviii. 514 (attribution incorrect). *Poenit. S.Columbani,* B. 1, in Bieler (ed.), *Irish penitentials,* p. 98. Conc. Mâcon quoted in Gratian, *CJC.,* vol. ii, p. 195, but this canon is not in *MC.* M. Bateson (ed.), 'A Worcester cathedral book of ecclesiastical collections made *c.* 1000 A.D.', *EHR.,* x (1895), p. 722; cf. Ivo of Chartres, *Decr.,* XV. 187, col. 897. Twelfth-century preacher: *Liber S. Jacobi,* I. 17, p. 154 ('in peregrinatione propter transgressiones suas a sacerdote suo quasi in exilio mittitur').

142   'By praying to the saints...': *De Virtut. S. Martini,* IV. praefat., p. 649; cf. I. 40, p. 606.

Chains break: *Ibid.,* I. 23, p. 600 (Willichar). *Vita S. Nicetii,* XIII-XIV, *MGH. Merov.,* iii. 523-4 (St. Nizier). Gregory of Tours, *Vitae Patrum,* VIII. 6, p. 697 (Agilulf). *Gesta Sanctorum Rotonensium,* III. 8, *Aa. Ss. OSB.,* vol. vi, pp. 219-21 (A.D., 868-875).

143   Salvation found at particular shrines: *Vita S. Austregisili,* IX, *MGH. Merov.* iv. 205 (Mestrille). Gregory of Tours, *In Gloria Confessorum,* p. 803n. (interpolated) on penitent directed to Moutiers-St.-Jean; the story is based on Jonas of Bobbio, *Vita Joannis Reomanensis,* XX, *MGH. Merov.* iii. 517 (saec. ix). *Mirac. S. Bavonis,* III. 4, *Aa. Ss. OSB.,* vol. ii, p. 414. Other ninth-century examples: Alcuin, *Vita Willibrordi,* XVII, *MGH. Merov.* vii. 136; *Mirac. S. Floriani,* VIII, *MGH. Merov.* III. 70; Wilfrid Strabo (attrib.), *Mirac. S. Galli,* XXXIV, *Aa. Ss. OSB.,* vol. ii, pp. 264-5; *Vita S. Godegrandi,* II. 19, *Aa. Ss.* Sept., vol. i, p. 771. Confessors impose specific pilgrimages: *Poenit. Ps.-Egberti,* IV. 6, in Wasserschleben (ed.), *Bussordnungen,* p. 333. *Vita et Mirac. S. Frodoberti,* XXXI-XXXII, *PL.* cxxxvii. 616-17 (Ratbert). Aimoin, *Vita S. Abbonis,* X, cols. 398-9 ('poenitentiae voto, ante omnes fere in hoc tempore Galliae habitatores coeptum').

144   Sins erased: *Vita S. Egidii,* XXXV-XXXVI, *An. Boll.,* viii (1889), pp. 117-18 (attrib. to Fulbert of Chartres). *Mirac. S. Mariae Magdalenae Viziliaci Facta (ed. alt.),* III, *CCH. (Paris),* vol. ii, p. 292 (no. 1). *Liber S. Jacobi,* II. 2, pp. 262-3. *Mirac. S. Benedicti,* IX. praefat., pp. 357-8 (Hughes de Ste. Marie).

145   Pilgrimages imposed by Inquisition: Gui, *Practica,* II. 3, p. 39. Dossat, pp. 210-11 (Gourdon and Montcuq). On Gui's sen-

tences, Molinier, pp. 400-1. In general, Lea (2), vol. i, pp. 466, 494-5.

146 Liège legal codes: Cauwenberghe, pp. 23-4.

Tradition of judicial exile in Flanders: R. C. van Caenegem, *Geschiedenis van het Strafrecht in Vlanderen, Verhandelingen van de koninklijke Vlaamse Akademie,* xix, Brussel, 1954, pp. 147-56.

Douai commutations: Le Grand, p. 385n[1].

147 Robert de Roux: *Chartes de Namur,* no. 1303, p. 385.

Devotions required at Liège: Cauwenberghe, p. 164.

148 Breaches of public order: Aquinas, *Summa Theologica,* III (suppl.), q. xxviii, a. 3, vol. xii, p. 53. *Coutumes de Liège,* vol. i, p. 494.

Arson: a decree of 1186 in *MGH. Constit.* i. 450 (no. 318, cap. 8). *Chartes de Namur,* nos. 1000, 1026, pp. 298-9, 306.

Nieuport lynchings: Cauwenberghe, p.10.

Affray and abusing councillor: *Coutumes de Namur,* Rep. 1440 (no. 77), Rep. 1483 (no. 118), vol. ii, pp. 91, 225-6.

Henri le Kien: Rupin, p. 215.

149 Pilgrimage for victim's satisfaction: *Poenit. Vinniani,* XXIII, in Bieler (ed.), *Irish penitentials,* pp. 80-2. *MGH. Constit.* i. 450 (no. 318). *Coutumes de Namur,* Rep. 1483 (no. 87), vol. ii, p. 194 (Gerard de Rostimont). Pagart d'Hermansart (ed.), 'Certificat d'accomplissement de pèlerinage pour homicide en 1333', *BHP,* (1891), pp. 372-3 (Bondulf). *Coutumes de Liège,* vol. ii, p. 145.

150 Pilgrimage imposed by arbitrators: On murderers of 1264, *CRH., 1e* serie, ix (1847), p. 49. Beaumanoir, *Coutumes,* nos. 1296-7, pp. 168-70. Rigaud, *Reg. Visitationum,* pp. 507-8. See also *Cartulaire de la Commune de Fosses,* no. 10, ed. J. Borgnet, Namur, 1867, pp. 32-3. In 1307 the count of Namur would only submit his quarrel with Charles de Valois to the arbitration of Philip IV of France on condition that no pilgrimage was imposed on the loser, *Chartes de Namur,* no. 334, p. 96.

No commutation for Inquisition: Gui, *Pratica,* II. 23, p. 55.

Tariffs: Cauwenberghe, pp. 222-3 (Oudenarde), and other lists, pp. 223-36. Van den Bussche (ed.), 'Rocamadour', pp. 50-2.

151 No commutation at Maestricht: Cauwenberghe, p. 148.

Enforced if not commuted: *Coutumes de Namur,* Rep. 1440 (no. 18), vol. ii, p. 30. *Ordonnances,* vol. v, p. 460, vol. ix, pp. 586-7, 589.

152 Pilgrimages imposed by corporations: Cauwenberghe, pp. 42-3, 161n.

And by treaty: *Archives de Bruges,* vol. i, pp. 292-5, 357-8, 405, vol. ii, p. 254-7 (Arques, 1326). On Bruges pilgrimages of 1309 and 1393, Van den Bussche (ed.), 'Rocamadour', pp. 38-40. *Cartulaire de N-D de Boulogne,* no. 156, pp. 239-40.

153 Fettered pilgrims: Raynald, *Annales,* An. 1319 (no. 27), vol. v, p. 123 (murderer of bishop of Fricento). Thomas of Monmouth, *Mirac. S. Willelmi,* VI. 9-10, 11, pp. 231-41, 256-8 (Norwich). Reginald of Durham, *De B. Cuthberti Virtut.,* LXXXIV, LXXIX, pp. 177-8, 164-5; cf. XCIII-XCV, pp. 205-12.

Thomas of Monmouth on broken fetters: *Op. cit.,* VI. 9, p. 235.

154 Fetters worn voluntarily: *Mirac. S. Benedicti,* VIII. 19, pp. 303-4 (Fleury). *Chron. Evesham,* II, p. 34. William of Malmesbury, *Gesta Pontificum,* V. 268, pp. 425-6 (Cologne penitent). John of S. Bertin, *Vita B. Bernardi,* I. 5, *Aa. Ss.* April, vol. ii, p. 676.

Crosses worn: Gui, *Practica,* II. 19, 34, pp. 53, 60. Lea (2), vol. i, pp. 466, 468-9.

155 Pieterseune: Van den Bussche (ed.), 'Rocamadour', pp. 48-9.

Pleas of sickness: *Coutumes de Namur,* Rep. 1440 (no. 80), Rep. 1483 (no. 58), vol. ii, pp. 95-6, 175; cf. Rep. 1483 (nos. 52, 254), vol. ii, pp. 169-70, 325.

156 Inquisitors' warning (1251): Molinier, p. 404.

Jan Vogel: *Actes et procès-verbaux des séances de l'université de Louvain,* ed. E. Reusens and A. van Hove, vol. ii, Brussels, 1919, pp. 126, 129-30, 143-9, 183-4, 201.

Pilgrimage alternative to death: On Lambert de Soif, *CRH., 2e* serie, vii (1855), pp. 78-9. *Coutumes de Namur,* Rep. 1483 (no. 131), vol. ii, pp. 228-31 (Pierot the Porter). Guérin and Célier (eds), *Documents concernant le Poitou,* vol. xxi, pp. 329-31 (no. 720) (cut-throats of 1393); cf. vol. xxiv, pp. 129-32, 284-7.

157 Alternative to banishment: *Coutumes de Liège,* vol. i, pp. 496-7.

Testimonials: Gui, *Pratica,* II. 3, 10, III. 13, pp. 38, 47, 95; Van den Bussche (ed.), 'Rocamadour', p. 47. *Coutumes de Namur,* Rep. 1483 (no. 118). The fee required by the authorities at Bordeaux in 1495 was seven francs, six liards, see Reg. Fabrique de S. Michel, Archives Departmentales (Gironde), G. 2252.

158 Judicial pilgrimage opposed: *Capitularia Regum Francorum,* vol. i, pp. 60-1 (Charlemagne). Rabanus Maurus, *Poenit.,* VII, *PL.*

cx. 473-4; cf. Conc. Mainz (847), in *MC.* xiv. 908-9; Conc. Seligenstadt (1022), *PL.* cxl. 1062. Jacques de Vitry, *Hist. Hierosolymitana,* LXXXII, pp. 1096-7.

Aquinas, *Summa Theologica,* III (suppl.) q. xxviii, a. 3, vol. xii, p. 53. Durand de S. Pourçain, *In Sententias,* IV, xv. 4, Lyon, 1595, p. 745.

159 Mansfield's surprise: Van den Bussche (ed.), 'Rocamadour', pp. 22-3, 26.

8. The Great Age of Pilgrimage

160 'Some three years…": Glaber, *Hist.,* III. 4, pp. 61-2. Cf. Anselm, *Hist. Dedicationis S. Remigii, PL.* cxlii. 1417-18.

161 Disruptions of barbarians: E. Mabille, *Les invasions Normandes dans la Loire et les péregrinations du corps de S. Martin,* Paris, 1869; also, Gasnault, pp. 55-61. On St. Cuthbert, Symeon of Durham, *Hist. Dunelmensis Eccl.,* II. 6-III. 1, vol. i, pp. 54-56 (with some apocryphal details). On St. Evroul, Orderic, *Hist. Eccl.,* VI 9-10, ed. Chibnall, vol. iii, pp. 276, 282-4, 302-4. Bernard, *Itin.* XXIVI, p. 320.

Hospices decayed: *Capitularia Regum Francorum,* vol. ii, pp. 408, 434-5 (Irish hospices). *Bullarium Casinense,* const. XXX, vol. ii, Rome, 1670, p. 25.

162 Route to Jerusalem: Glaber, *Hist.,* IV. 6, pp. 106-7.

Hospices in Hungary: on Melk, Orderic Vitalis, *Hist. Eccl.,* III, ed. Chibnall, vol. ii, p. 68. Richard of St.-Vanne was entertained at the Hungarian court in 1027, see G. Morin, 'Un théologien ignoré du xie siècle: l'évêque-martyr Gérard de Czanad', *Revue Bénédictine,* xxvii (1910), pp. 518-9; as also was Lietbert of Cambrai in 1054. *Vita Lietberti,* XXXII, p. 703. On the royal hospice at Vashegy (Pécvarad), see A. Palla, 'Hospital in Hungary in the XIth century', *Atti del primo congresso Europeo di storia ospitaliera,* Reggio Emilia, 1962, pp. 278-85.

163 Route to Santiago: Defourneaux, pp. 67-8. Pelayo, *Chron., ES.* xiv. 473-4. *Hist. Compostellana,* I. 30, 31, III. 9, pp. 69, 71, 489; on ambassadors' impressions, *ibid.,* II. 50, p. 350.

Gottschalk: Vazquez de Parga, *et al.,* vol. i, p. 42 (the fundamental work).

New relics: Glaber, *Hist.,* III. 6, pp. 68-9 (Sens). Gregory VII, *Reg.,* VIII. 8, pp. 526-7 (Salerno). Peter the Deacon, *Historica*

Relatio, I. 1. p. 288 (Monte Cassino). Bethell, pp. 61, 65 (Reading).

164 St. Leonard: Adémar de Chabannes, *Chron.,* III. 56, p. 181. *Aa. Ss.* Nov., vol iii, pp. 139, 148-9. On the saints of the route to Santiago, *Guide,* VIII, pp. 35-83.

165 South-western France: on the councils of 1031, *MC.* xix. 502-6. Pilgrimages: Adémar, *Chron.,* III. 40-1, 48, 65-6, 68, pp. 162-3, 171, 189-90, 192-3, 194; *Vita S. Geraldi,* VII-IX, XVII, *Aa. Ss. OSB.,* vol. ix, pp. 880-2, 884-5, cf. pp. 869-71.

Norman pilgrimages: Hugh of Flavigny, *Chron.,* XIX, pp. 393-4 (Richard of St.-Vannes). William of Jumièges. *Gesta Normannorum Ducum,* VI. 11, pp. 111-13 (Robert), Orderic, *Hist. Eccl.,* III, ed. Chibnall, vol., ii, p. 10.

166 Norman hospices in Rome: *Mirac. S. Wulfranni,* II. 12, *Aa. Ss.* March, vol. iii, p. 154.

Rouen coins: J. Lafaurie, 'Le trésore monétaire du Puy', *Revue Numismatique,* 5e serie, xv (1952), no. 26, pp. 117-18.

Normans impeded: Letter of John of Fécamp in *PL.* cxliii. 797. On Normans imprisoned at Constantinople, Adémar, *Chron.,* III. 55, p. 178.

Mirac. S. Fidis, III. 1, pp. 128-30 (Roger de Tosny).

167 Mass-pilgrimage of 1024-5: Glaber, *Hist.,* IV. 6, p. 106. Hugh of Flavigny, *Chron.,* XVIII, p. 393.

Aganon: *GC.* iv. 381-4.

Synod of 1094: *Chron. S. Benigni Divionensis, MGH. SS.* v. 43 ('ubi primo iurata via Hierosolymitana'); cf. *MC.* xx. 799. Pilgrims from the neighbouring provinces of Lorraine and the Rhineland included Poppo abbot of Stavelot in 990 (Everhelm, *Vita Popponis,* III, *MGH. SS.* xi. 295-6); at least one count and one bishop of Verdun (*Gesta Episcoporum Virdunensium,* IX-X, *MGH. SS.* iv. 49); Adalbert, count of Metz (*Notitiae Fundationis Mon. Bosonis Villae,* I, *MGH. SS.* xv. 977-8); from Trier went Hierocon, abbot of S. Maximin (Mabillon (SW), vol. iv. p. 291), an abbot of St. Martin in 1026 (Eberwin, *Vita S. Symeonis,* X, *Aa. Ss. OSB.,* vol. viii, pp. 375-6), and an archbishop in 1025 (*Gesta Treverorum,* contin., III, V. *PL.* cliv. 1182, 1186); and Richard of St.-Vannes, whose monastery lay just outside Verdun.

Monastic libraries: thirteenth-century catalogue of books at St. Martial in Duplès-Agier (ed.), *Chroniques,* pp. 326, 329, 333,

336, 343. Eighteenth-century catalogue of Moissac in Archives Communales (Moissac), JJ. 1; the Moissac MS of the Bordeaux pilgrim is now Bibl. Nat. MS. Lat. 4808.

Western possessions of the Holy Sepulchre: many of these are listed in a confirmatory papal bull of Sept. 1128 in *Cartulaire du Saint-Sepulchre,* XVI, ed. E. de Rozière, Paris, 1849, pp. 18-22. Among the monastic houses which administered them in the eleventh century were S. Michel de Cuxa (Riant (2)); Moissac (Bibl. Nat. Coll. Doat. CXXVIII, fols. 91-2, 216vo-217vo, CXXIX, fols. 58vo-60); and Conques (*Cartulaire de Conques,* nos. 329, 392, pp. 257, 290).

Spanish spoil enriches Cluny: Glaber, *His.,* IV. 7, pp. 109-10. On the interest of the abbots in the pilgrimage to Santiago, see *Vita B. Morandi,* in *Bibliotheca Cluniacensis,* cols. 501-3.

169 *Miracles of St. James* and Cluny: the stories in *Liber S. Jacobi,* II. 16-18, pp. 276-83, are taken from Alexander, *Dicta Anselmi,* XXI-XXIII, ed. R. W. Southern and F. S. Schmitt, *Memorials of St. Anselm,* London, 1969, pp. 196-209, cf. pp. 31-2. Arnaldo's letter, ed. J. Vielliard in *Guide,* p. 126. On the dissemination of the miracles, see Vazquez de Parga *et al.,* vol. i, pp. 176-7; David, vol. i, pp. 30-9; J. Lafond, *Les Vitraux de l'église de S. Ouen de Rouen, Corpus Vitrearum Medii Aevi,* France, IV (2), Paris, 1970, p. 94.

170 Mayeul's pilgrimages: Nalgod, *Vita S. Majoli,* II. 18, *Aa. Ss.* May, vol. ii, p. 662. Syrus, *Vita S. Majoli,* II. 15, 17, *Aa. Ss. OSB.,* vol. vii, pp. 797-8.

Bonizo on duties of knights: *De Vita Christiana,* VII. 28, ed. E. Perels, *Texte zur Geschichte des römisches und kanonisches rechts im Mittelalter,* I, Berlin, 1930, pp. 248-9

Aristocratic guilt: William IX, *Chanson* XI, ed. A. Jeanroy, 2nd. ed., Paris, 1926, p. 28. *La 'Bible' au seigneur de Berzé,* II. 777-87, ed. F. Lecoy, Paris, 1938, p. 49; cf. II. 188-205, 809-22, 825-6, 843-6, pp. 30, 32-3, 50, 51. On Roger of Foix, *Chartes de Cluny,* no. 2991, vol. iv., pp. 189-990.

171 Gerald of Aurillac: Odo, *Vita S. Geraldi,* I. 8-11, II. 16-17, 22, III. 3, cols. 646-50, 679-80, 682-3, 691. On the authenticity of this version, Poncelet.

173 Annual pilgrimages: Adémar, *Chron.,* III. 41, p. 163. *Mirac. S. Mariae Magdalenae Viziliaci facta (ed. alt.),* I, VI, *CCH (Paris),* vol. ii, pp. 292-3 (no. 2), *An. Boll.,* xvii (1898), pp. 178-9.

Canterbury statistics: Benedict and William, *Mirac. S. Thomae, passim*. Allowance is made for pilgrims mentioned in both collections. Women are classified as their husbands or fathers, children as their parents.

Declining social standing of pilgrims: Vergerio, *Ep.* LXXXVI, p. 212. Wright (ed.), *Letters,* p. 85 (Bury).

174 Luxurious pilgrimages: William of Jumièges, *Gesta Normannorum Ducum,* VI. 11, pp. 112-13. *Angelo-Saxon Chronicle,* p. 134 (Ealdred).

German pilgrimage of 1064: *Annales Altahenses Maiores,* p. 67. Marianus Scottus, *Chron., MGH. SS.* v. 559. Lambert of Hersfeld, *Annales,* pp. 93-4.

175 Peter the Venerable on pilgrimages: *Epp.* LI, LXXX, CXLIV, vol. i, pp. 151-2, 216, 358-9.

Sermon *Veneranda Dies: Liber S. Jacobi,* I. 17, pp. 141-76, esp. pp. 144-5, 152, 154, 156-7.

178 Palestine hermits: Reginald, *Vita S. Godrici,* XV. 43, pp. 57-8. Phocas, *De Locis Sanctis,* XXIII, XXXI, cols. 952-3, 961. Jacques de Vitry, *Hist. Hierosolymitana,* LII-LIII, pp. 1074-5. Benincasa, *Vita S. Rayneri,* II. 22, 26, pp. 430, 431. Theobald, *Vita S. Guilelmi,* V. 22, *Aa. Ss.* Feb., vol. ii, p. 457.

179 Berthold of Neuenburg: *Annales Marbacenses,* p. 75.

Crusaders' austerities: Jacques de Vitry, *Exempla,* LXXV, CXXIV, pp. 38-9, 57. Ambroise, *L'Estoire de la Guerre Sainte,* ed. G. Paris, Paris, 1879, col. 325.

Pilgrims become monks: Peter the Venerable, *De Mirac.,* I. 11, 18, cols. 874-5, 883.

180 Walking: Sulpicius Severus, *Dialogi,* I. 21, p. 173. Honoratus, *Vita S. Hilarii,* III. 22 *Aa. Ss.* May, vol. ii, p. 31 (not historically reliable). *Vita S. Ayberti,* I. 5, *Aa. Ss.* April, vol. i, p. 674. Benedict, *Mirac. S. Thomae,* III. 48, IV. 94, pp. 152, 257 (Matilda of Thornbury; countess of Clare). *Mirac. S. Martialis,* XXXIII, p. 427 ('totus nudus'). *Vita S. Godrici,* XIV. 39-40, pp. 53-5. Labande (2), pp. 104—5n[13] (canon of Dol). William, *Mirac. S. Thomae,* VI. 18, p. 430 (John King). MS. Gloucester cathedral I, fol. 175 (Reading pilgrim).

181 'Open to him...': Jacques de Vitry, *Exempla,* CXXXIII, pp. 59-60.

182 Baptismal imagery: Benedict, *Mirac. S. Thomae,* III. 11, p. 126.

Bridget, *Rev.*, VII. 14, p. 550. Bartolus, *Tractatus,* XXVIII, p. 56 (Portiuncula).

Mary the Egyptian: earliest version (saec. vii) in Sophronius, *Vita S. Mariae Aegyptiaca, PL.* lxxiii, 673-90. Other versions: Hildebert, *Vita B. Mariae Aegyptiaca, PL.* clxxi. 1321-40; Honorius, *Speculum Ecclesiae, PL.* clxxii. 906. P. Mesplé, *Toulouse: Musée des Augustins. Les sculptures romanes, Inventaires des collections publiques francaises,* vol. v, Paris, 1961, no. 333. Sites marked: Daniel, Pèlerinage, pp. 19, 28.

183 Bathing in Jordan: Antenoris, *Vita S. Silvini,* I. 9, p. 30. Raymond of Aguilers, *Hist. Francorum,* XX, pp. 301-2 (Raymond of St. Gilles). *Saga Olafs Konungshins Helga, Fornmanna Sogur,* V, Copenhagen, 1830, p. 314 (Thornstein). *Pèlerinage d'Euphrosine,* p. 34. Theoderic, *De Locis Sanctis,* XXX, p. 73.

184 Copied at Santiago: *Guide,* VI, p. 16.

Jacques de Vitry on Jordan: *Hist. Hierosolymitana,* LIII, pp. 1075-6.

Jordan water as relic: Philip, *Descriptio* (*c.* 1285-91), VIII, pp. 64-5. Faber, *Evagatorium,* vol. ii, pp. 36-7. *Voyage de la Saincte Cyté* (1480), pp. 101-2.

185 Desire for death: *Pèlerinage d'Euphrosine,* p. 33. Eskill's prayer quoted in Labande (3), p. 346. Caesarius, *Dial. Mirac.,* XI. 24, vol. ii, p. 291. Theoderic, *De Locis Sanctis,* IV, pp. 9-10 (Aceldama).

186 Importance of burial-place: Paulinus, *Carmina,* XXXI. 605-10, pp. 328-9. E. Le Blant, *Etude sur les sarcophages Chrétiens de la ville d'Arles,* Paris, 1878, p. xxxvi. Suger, *Vita Lodovici VI,* XXXIV, p. 286.

187 Site of last judgement: Innominatus I, *Descriptio,* p. 99. Theoderic, *De Locis Sanctis,* XXXII, p. 77. Faber, *Evagatorium,* vol. i, pp. 392-3.

Lethbald: Glaber, *Hist.,* IV. 6, pp. 106-7.

188 Millenarianism: Otto of Friesing, *De Duabus Civitatibus.* Marculf, *Formulae,* II. 3, *PL.* lxxxvii. 729 ('manifest signs…'). Adso, *Libellus de Antichristo, PL.* ci. 1291-8.

Last day described: Benzo of Alba, *Ad Heinricum IV Imperatorem,* I. 14-15, V. 6, *MGH. SS.* xi. 605, 653; cf. Ekkehard of Aura, *Hierosolymitana,* XXXIV, XXXV, *RHC. Occ.* v. 38-9. See Erdmann.

189 Paris preacher: Haimo, *Vita S. Abbonis,* IX, col. 397; cf. Abbo,
   Ep. X, *PL.* cxxxix. 471. On the year 1000, see Plaine.
   Panic of 1009-10: Glaber, *Hist.,* III. 7, pp. 71-2. Adémar, *Chron.,*
   III. 48, 68, pp. 171, 194. *Vita Gauzlini,* III, ed. P. Ewald, *Neues
   Archiv der Gesellschaft für ältere deutsche Geschichtskunde,* iii
   (1887-8), p. 353. On Raymond's pilgrimage, M-A-F. de Gaujal,
   Etudes historiques sur le Rouergue, vol. ii, Paris, 1858, p. 38.

190 Panic of 1033: Glaber, *Hist.,* III. 3, IV. praefat., 5, pp. 62, 90, 103-
   6. On Glaber's own feelings, see Petit. *GC.* ii. 105 (instr.
   XXXIX), 24 Oct. 1036 (Hictor). J. Doinel (ed.), 'Un pèlerinage
   á Jérusalem dans la première moitié du xie siècle', *BEC.* li
   (1890), pp. 204-6 (Hervé). Cf. *Cartulaire de Conques,* nos. 419,
   453, pp. 308-9, 328-9.

191 Panic of 1064-5: *Vita Altmanni Ep. Pataviensis,* III, *MGH. SS.* xii.
   230; *Annales Altahenses Maiores,* p. 66; and see Eicken, p. 317.
   Millenarian formulae suddenly appear in Limousin charters of
   this year, e.g. *Chartes, chroniques, et mémoriaux pour servir á l'histoire de la Marche et du Limousin,* ed. A. Leroux and A. Bosvieux,
   Tulle, 1886, p. 13 (no. 9).

192 Provençals in 1099: Raymond of Aguilers, *Hist. Francorum,* XX,
   p. 296. 'Tell me then...': Peter Damian, *De Laude Flagellorum
   (Opusc. XLIII),* IV, *PL.* cxlv. 682-3.

193 William of Hirsau: Haimo, *Vita Willelmi Hirsaugiensis,* XXI,
   MGH. SS. xii, 218.

9. The Legacy of the Crusades

194 'God has invented...': Guibert, *Gesta Dei per Francos,* I. 1, p. 124.

195 'Taking us to be no pilgrims...': *Gesta Francorum,* I. 4, p. 8.
   Unarmed hangers-on: Raymond of Aguilers, *Hist. Francorum,*
   XVII, pp. 279-80 (first crusade). *Annales Herbipolenses, MGH.
   SS.* xvi. 3 (second crusade).
   Jerusalem lost by sin: Jacques de Vitry, *Hist. Hierosolymitana,*
   LXXII, p. 1088.

196 'Is there nothing...': Dante, *Paradiso,* IV. 133-8, V. 16-84; cf.
   Aquinas, *Summa Theologica,* II, q. lxxxviii, a. 1-2, vol. ix, pp. 234-
   5, 238-9.
   Crosses: Robert the Monk, *Hist. Hierosolymitana,* I. 2, II. 3,
   RHC. Occ, iii. 729, 741; Guibert, *Gesta Dei per Francos,* II. 5, p.

140 (in 1096). Odo of Deuil, *De Profectione Lodovici VII,* I, p. 22 (in 1146). H. Pflaum (ed.), 'A strange crusaders' song', *Speculum,* x (1935), pp. 337-9. In general, Villey, pp. 119-21.
Vows enforced: *CJC., Coll. Greg. IX,* III. xxxiv. 7, vol. ii, cols. 591-3; Tardif (ed.), *Coutumiers,* vol. ii, pp. 64-6, 214-15. Innocent III, *Reg.* V, 103, XVI. 35, *PL.* ccxiv. 1100, ccxvi. 830. On Frederic II's vow. Hefele, vol. v, pp. 1411-27.

197 Bound by vow of another: *CJC., Coll. Greg. IX,* III. xxxiv. 6, vol. ii. cols. 590-1; see Villey, p. 126. William, *Mirac. S. Thomae,* II. 13, pp. 169-70.

198 Dispensations: *CJC., Coll. Greg. IX,* III. xxxiv. 2, 8, vol. ii, cols. 589, 593-4. On Thierry, J. Calmet, *Histoire de Lorraine,* vol. ii, Nancy, 1748, p. 240. Paulus (2), vol. i, pp. 209-11; Villey, p. 251. Commutation for money: Matthew Paris, *Chron. Maj.,* vol. iv, pp. 6-7, 9, 133-4. Paulus (2), vol. ii, pp. 35-9. A. Gottlob, *Kreuzablass und Almosenablass,* Stuttgart, 1906, p. 308. On preachers of 1290 and 1308, *The Register of John de Halton, bishop of Carlisle,* ed. T. F. Tout, vol. i, London, 1906, p. 317.
Punishment for broken vows: MS. Gloucester cathedral 1, fols. 174VO-175 (St. James).
'On condition that…': *Mirac. B. Egidii,* IX, *MGH. SS.* xii, 321.

199 Bargain with saint: *Mirac. S. Martialis,* VII, XXV, XLIV, pp. 417-18, 424, 431.

200 'Excused him from suffering…': Henry of Ghent, *Quodlibeta,* XV. 14. Paris, 1518, p. 589.
Council at Rheims: in *MC.* xviii. 345-6. See Paulus (2), vol. i, pp. 99-119.
Crusading indulgence: Conc. Clermont in *MC.* xx. 816; Conc. Lateran in *MC.* xxii. 1067. H. Hagenmeyer (ed.), *Die Kreuzzugbriefe aus dem Jahren 1088-1100,* Innsbruck, 1900, pp. 396-7.
Early papal indulgences for pilgrims: Paulus (2), vol. i, p. 153 (Pavilly); Urban II, *Reg.* CLXXV, col. 447-9 (Angers).

201 Episcopal indulgences: Delehaye (2), vol. xliv. pp. 351-79. *CJC., Coll. Greg. IX,* V. xxxviii. 14, vol. ii, cols. 888-9 (Lateran council). *DTC.,* vol. vii, cols. 1609-10 (Univ. Paris). Conc. Aquilea in *MC.* xxiii. 1119-20.

202 Collemaggio: *Vita S. Petri Coelestini,* XXX, *An. Boll.,* xvi (1897), pp. 418-19; text of indulgence in Bartolus, *Tractatus,* p.

clxxxii. Boniface VIII, *Reg.* 770, 815, 850, vol. i, pp. 257-61, 274-5, 286-7.

Portiuncula: general discussions in Sabatier's introduction to Bartolus, *op. cit.,* pp. xvii-xcvi; Van Ortroy; Paulus (2), vol. ii, pp. 1-4, 319-20: Catholic historians have, on the whole, condemned the indulgence while the Calvinist Sabatier defended it. Arguments of thirteenth-century opponents cited by Peter John Olivi in his defence of the indulgence, written c. 1279, see Bartolus, *op. cit.,* pp. lvii-lix. On the popularity of the pilgrimage, Wadding, An. 1295 (no. 12), vol. v, p. 337; Bartolus, *op. cit.,* XLIV, p. 93.

204   Confession essential: *Liber S. Jacobi,* I. 17, pp. 144-5.

Extravagant claims for indulgences criticized: Simon of Cremona, *De Indulgentiis,* p. 86; cf. *CJC., Coll. Clem. VI,* V. vii. 1, vol. ii, cols. 1186-7. See Remy, pp. 9-10; Paulus (2), vol. ii, pp. 330-4, 340-2, 348-9.

Unconfessed pilgrims excluded: *Miracles de Rocamadour,* I. 5, pp. 79-82. *Mirac. S. Michaelis,* pp. 880-2. Alfonso X, *Cantigas,* CCXVII, vol. ii, pp. 304-4 (Villalcazar). *Mirac. S. Martialis,* VIII, p. 418.

205   Gerald of Wales: see his *De Invectionibus,* V. 12, vol. i, pp. 137-8.

10. The Growth of a Cult

207   'A young man of low...': Guibert, *De Pignoribus,* I. 2, col. 621.

208   Normans in England: Eadmer, *Vita Anselmi,* I. 30, p. 51 (Lanfranc). *Gesta Abbatum S. Albani,* ed. H. T. Riley, *RS.,* London, 1876-9, vol. i, p. 62. William of Malmesbury, *Gesta Pontificum,* V. 265, pp. 421-2.

209   Elevation: Bede, *Eccl. Hist.,* IV. 30, pp. 442-4 (Cuthbert). Delehaye (8), pp. 184-5. Kemp, pp. 37-40.

210   Relics of Brogne: *De Virtut. S. Eugenii Bronii Ostensis,* I-VI, *MGH. SS.* xv. 647-9. On the date, G. Morin, 'De translatione S. Eugenii', *An. Boll.,* v. (1886), p. 386.

Udalric: *Aa. Ss.,* May, vol. 1, p. 283. Fontanini (ed.), *Codex,* vol. i, pp. 2-3. Delehaye (8), pp. 185-9.

211   Urban's canonizations: *Aa. Ss.* June, vol. i, p. 249; Fontanini (ed.), *Codex,* vol. v, p. 9. On abbot of Quimperlé, *Aa. Ss. OSB.,* vol. ix, p. 109.

Long delays: Kemp, pp. 86-9 (Becket). *MD. Thes.*, vol. iii, col. 1851 (Edmund). Toynbee, pp. 149-205 (Louis). *Lit. Cant.*, vol. iii, pp. 400-1 (Winchelsea).

212 'It is my belief…': H-F. Delaborde (ed.), 'Fragments de l'enquête faite à St.-Denis en vue de la canonisation de S. Louis', *Mems. de la Soc. de l'Histoire de Paris*, xxiii (1896), p. 62.
Lots drawn: Reginald, *De B. Cuthberti Virtut.*, XIX, CXV, pp. 38-9, 260. William, *Mirac. S. Thomae*, II. 82, p. 244.

213 Wulfstan 'the new saint': *Mirac. S. Wulfstani*, I. 37, p. 137.
Cult of St. Thomas sporadic: William of Canterbury, *Mirac. S. Thomae*, III. 33, 48, pp. 290, 304. Philip, *Mirac. S. Frideswidae*, LXXVI, p. 583 (c. 1190). Caesarius, *Dial. Mirac.*, VIII. 69, vol. ii, p. 139 (c. 1223). Ralph of Coggeshall, *Chron. Angelicanum*, ed. J. Stephenson, *RS.*, London, 1875, pp. 202-3 (Bromholm). *Lit. Cant.*, vol. iii, pp. 26-8 (fourteenth-century miracle). On Canterbury Jubilees, Foréville, pp. 41, 47-81.

214 Fame of miracles: *Mirac. S. Eutropii*, IV. 29-30, III. 19, pp. 742-3, 740. Guibert, *De Vita Sua*, III. 20, pp. 228-30 (canons of Laon). *Mirac. S. Egidii*, VIII-IX, *MGH. SS.* xii. 320-1.
Libelli, miraculorum: Delehaye (6). Sulpicius's influence can be seen in Benedict, *Mirac. S. Thomae*, II. 1, IV. 58, pp. 119-20, 224-5; and in *Mirac. S. Fidis*, I. 34, pp. 84-5.

215 Duty to record miracles: Benedict, *op. cit.,* VI. 4, pp. 269-70. MS. Gloucester cathedral 1, fols. 171-171VO (Reading monk).

216 Efficacy of saints compared: *Chron. Evesham*, p. 47. William of Canterbury, II. 75, pp. 238-9.
Rivals of Canterbury: Reginald, *De B. Cuthberti Virtut.*, CXII, CXIV-CXVI, CXXVI, pp. 251-2, 256, 260-1, 271. Philip, *Mirac. S. Frideswidae*, XII, LXXVI, pp. 570, 583. MS. Glouster cathedral 1, fols. 174-174VO, cf. fol. 173 (Reading).

217 Advertisement: *Becket Materials*, vol. ii, p. 49, vol. vii, pp. 564-6. Kajava (ed.), *Etudes*, p. 98 (Fécamp). *Carmen de translatione S. Bartholomaei*, p. 574: loosely translated, 'everyone knows that Rome alone has the tomb, Rome alone has the body; deceit will not benefit Benevento; a curse on Benevento'. Rémy, p. 122 (Liège). Sachet, vol. i, pp. 519-23 (Lyon).

218 Packaging: *Translatio SS. Chrysanti et Dariae*, IX, *As. Ss. OSB.*, vol. v, p. 613 (Prüm). Baraut (ed.), *Llibre Vermell*, pp. 28-9 (Montserrat). Elton, p. 16 (Canterbury. A hostile report).

219 Decoration of sanctuaries: John Chrysostom, *In Ep. II ad Corinthios,* XXVI, *PG.* lxi. 582; E. Bishop, *Liturgica Historica,* Oxford, 1918, pp. 25-6. On the Holy Sepulchre, Eusebius, *Vita Constantini,* III. 40, ed. I. A. Heikel, *Eusebius Werke,* vol. i, Leipzig, 1902, pp. 94-5; Antoninus, *Itin.,* XVII, p. 171. On Nola, Paulinus of Nola, *Carmina,* XIV., 98-103, p. 49. On St.-Denis, Suger, *De Admin. Sua,* pp. 192-3, 200-1; *Vita Lodovici VI,* X, p. 54. On Canterbury, *An Italian relation of England about the year 1500,* ed. C. A. Sneyd, Camden Soc., vol. xxxvii, London, 1847, pp. 30-1; *Letters and papers,* vol. xiii (2), p. 49 (no. 133), cf. vol. xiii (2), p. 155 (nos. 401-2).

221 Expensive shrines criticized: Guibert, *De Pignoribus,* I. 4, IV. 1, cols. 626, 666. Bernard, *Apologia ad Guillelmum,* XII. 28, in *Opera,* ed. J. Leclercq and H. M. Rochais, vol. iii, Rome, 1963, pp. 104-6.

222 Reliquaries as cash reserves: Glaber, *Hist.,* I. 4, p. 11 (Cluny). William of Malmesbury, *Gesta Pontificum,* V. 271, p. 432. Dugdale (ed.), *Monasticon,* vol. iv., p. 44 (Reading). See Duby, p. 52.

223 Saints thought of as rich: Theofrid, *Flores Epitaphiorum,* II. 6, cols. 356-7. Reginald, *De B. Cuthberti Virtut.,* LXVIII, p. 140. *The Life of Christina of Markyate,* ed. C. H. Talbot, Oxford, 1959, p. 186.

Accounts of miracles available at shrines: *Mirac. S. Michaelis,* p. 880 (saec. xi). *Lit. Cant.,* vol. iii, p. 398.

224 'Pictures of their eyes...': Theodoret of Cyrus, *Graecarun Affectionum Curatio,* VIII, col. 1032.

Ex-votos: Examples can be found in almost every miracle collection. Those quoted are from: *Mirac. S. Martialis,* LI, pp. 433-4; *Miracles de Rocamadour,* I. 25, III. 11, pp. 116, 288-9; Thomas of Monmouth, *Mirac. Willelmi Norwicensis,* V. 19, pp. 210-11; Wright (ed.), *Letters,* pp. 143, 221, 224 (monastic commissioners). William, *Mirac. S. Thomae,* VI. 12, p. 424; Benedict, *Mirac. S. Thomae,* II. 60, 64, III. 36, pp. 105, 109, 143.

225 Unusual *ex-votos: Mirac. S. Eadmundi (MS. Bodley* 240), I, p. 367. Alfonso X, *Cantigas,* CCXXXII, vol. ii, pp. 321-2 (Villalcazar). *Miracles de Rocamadour,* III. 16, p. 297.

Ruptured chains: Gregory of Tours, *Vitae Patrum,* VIII. 6, p. 697. *Guide,* VIII, p. 54.

226 Problem of disposal: *Mirac. S. Mariae Magdalenae Magdalenae Viziliaci Facta*, IX, in Faillon (ed.), *Monuments inédits*, vol. ii, p. 739. Instructions of Santiago guardians in Lopez-Ferreiro, vol. iv, p. 67 (appendix XXV). Offering obligatory: *Mirac. S. Fidis*, I. 18-20, pp. 54-8. On Fitz-Eisulf, Benedict, *Mirac. S. Thomae*, IV. 64, pp. 229-34; William, *Mirac. S. Thomae*, II. 5, pp. 160-2; Rackham, pp. 99-100. On St. Denis of Montmartre, Eugenius III, *Reg.* CXCIV, *PL.* clxxx. 1242, as corrected by Paulus (2), vol. i, p. 163.

227 Offering as tribute money: Odo, *Vita S. Geraldi*, II. 17, col. 680 ('decem solidos ad proprium collum dependentes, tamquan supplex servus domino suo quasi censum deferret'). *Cartulaire de S. Vincent du Mans*, no. 342, ed. R. Charles and M. d'Elbenne, Le Mans, 1913, cols. 204-205; see Du Cange, *Glossarium*, vol. ii, p. 257. *Notae Sangallenses, MGH. SS.* i. 71 ('se perpetualiter S. Sepulchri servitio dicavit'). On the Breisgau pilgrims, *Annales Marbacenses*, p. 75 ('perpetuo servicio sancti Sepulchri devoverunt'). Aragonese gifts to St. James: Celestine III, *Reg.*, CLXXXI, *PL.* ccvi. 1067 ('quasi tributa quae Deo et beato Jacobo apostolo in Hispania...exsolvenda'). On the Cologne reliquary, P. E. Schramm, *Denkmale der deutsche Könige und Kaiser*, Munchen, 1962, pp. 187-8, and pl. 192. *Mirac. S. Egidii*, XIII, *An. Boll.*, ix (1880), p. 396 (Raymond Ferraldo).

228 Santiago offerings ritual: in Lopez Ferreiro, vol. v., pp. 64-7 (appendix XXV).

229 Canterbury accounts: Woodruff, pp. 16-18. Savine, p. 103.
Bury St. Edmunds receipts: *Chron. Buriensis*, in Arnold (ed.), *Memorials*, vol. iii, p. 32.
St.-Trond: *Gesta Abbatum S. Trudonensium*, I. 9-12, vol. i, pp. 15-22.

230 St. Stephen's arm at Châlons: *GC.* x. 129-30.
Bollezeel: *Mirac. B. V. M. in Bollezeel*, in *Anecdota Gielemans*, III, 20, pp. 395-6.

231 St.-Gilles: text of petition in Bondurand (OS), pp. 441-4.
Partition of offerings: *RHF.* vi. 582 (Tours). Morand, pp. 220-2 (Ste.-Chapelle).

232 Disputes at Rome: in general, Fabre. On the incident of 1350, Rodocanachi, p. 163. For disputes in other churches see, e.g.,

Hist. Compostellana, III. 9, p. 489; *Chartulary of Bridlington*, pp. 448-9; Sachet, vol. i, pp. 305-7, 502-3.

233 Papal share: Wily's instuctions in *CPR. Letters*, vol. xi, p. 685. On Eton indulgence, *The Official correspondence of Thomas Bekyington*, ed. G. Williams, *R.S.*, vol. ii, London, 1872, pp. 299-303. *Lit. Cant.*, vol. iii, pp. 340, 344-5 (Canterbury negotiations). See W. E. Lunt, *Papal revenues in the middle ages*, vol. i, N. Y., 1934, pp. 112-13, 125-8; L. Celier, *Les dataires du xve siècle et les origines de la daterie apostolique, BEFAR.*, vol. ciii, Paris, 1910, pp. 154-60.

234 Walsingham refounded: Dickinson, pp. 10-11.
Expenses against offerings: Urban II, *Reg.* CLXXV, col. 448. Baraut (ed.), *Libre Vermell*, pp. 34-5 (Montserrat). Robert of Torigny, *Chron.*, vol. ii, pp. 99-100 (Rocamadour). Delisle (ed.), 'Enquête', pp. 367-8, 372. (Mont-St.-Michel). Cf. the pilgrims at Meaux in Yorkshire, who 'gave little and cost much', Burton, *Chron. Mon. Melsa,* vol. iii, pp. 35-6.

235 Canterbury balance-sheet: *Royal Commission on Historical Manuscripts*, 9th. Report, London, 1883, p. 124. Woodruff, pp. 17-24, 26.

236 Expenses at Vatican: *Bull. Vat.*, vol. i, pp. 96-7, 130, 134-5, 139-41, 156-7. *Gesta Innocentii III Papae*, CXLIII, *PL.* ccxiv, introd., p. cxcix.
Pilgrims bring status: *MC.* xix. 19 (Benevento). *IS.(2).*, vii. 363 (Salerno).

237 Pretensions of Santiago: *Hist. Compostellana*, I. 44-5, II. 3, 18, pp. 93-94, 255-8, 296. On the attitude of the kings of León, H. J. Hüffer, *La idea imperial Española*, Madrid, 1933, p. 20. Until 1095 the bishop's seat was technically at Iria.

238 Wealth of Santiago citizens: on silver-train of 1130, *Hist. Compostellana*, I. 18, p. 505. *Guide*, III, p. 7. *Itinerarium Hieronymi Monetarii*, ed. L. Pfandl, *Revue Hispanique*, xlviii (1920), p. 94.

11. The Journey

239 Alkerton: Owst, p. 104.
Wills: Tardif (ed.), *Coutumiers*, vol. ii, p. 240. On agreement with wife, see, e.g., Caesarius, *Dial. Mirac.,* VIII. 59, vol. ii, p. 132. On enforcement, Vazquez de Parga *et al.*, vol. iii, pp. 110-12.

240   Judicial immunity: *Ancient laws of Ireland,* vol. i, ed. W. N. Hancock, Dublin, 1865, p. 266; vol. v, ed. R. Atkinson, Dublin, 1890, pp. 234, 296. Glanvill, *De Legibus et consuetudinibus Angliae,* I. 29, ed. G. D. H. Hall, London, 1965, pp. 16-17. Beaumanoir, *Coutumes,* nos. 265, 1689, vol. i, p. 135, vol. ii, pp. 364-5. Tardif (ed.), *Coutumiers,* vol. ii, p. 215.

Property protected: bull of 1145 in Otto of Friesing, *Gesta Friderici,* I. 36, ed. B. de Simson, *MGH. Rer. Germ.,* Hannover, 1912, p. 57; cf. Alfonso IX, *Siete Partidas,* I. xxiv. 3, vol. i (1), fol. 151VO. Will of Archambert de Monluc in Arch. Nat. J. 1138/6.

241   Donations: *Cartulaire d'Auch, Cartulaire Noir,* XLVI, pp. 44-5; cf. *Chartes de Cluny,.* no. 3712, vol. v, p. 59, and many others.

Pensions demanded: *Cartulaire de la Charité,* L, pp. 126-7.

Implied terms in case of return: *Ibid.,* XXXIV, XXXVIII, pp. 96-7, 104-5.

242   Make amends to all: *Liber S. Jacobi,* I. 17, p. 157.

French kings and St. Denis: Odo of Deuil. *De Profectione Lodovici VII,* I, p. 25 ('licentiam petiit'). Rigord, *Gesta Philippi,* LXIX, pp. 98-9 ('licentiam accipiendi'). On the vassalage of the kings to St. Denis, see R. Barroux, 'L'abbé Suger et la vassalité du Vexin en 1124', *Moyen Age,* lxiv (1958), pp. 1-26.

Lambert: *Annales,* p. 75.

243   Reparations to injured monks: E. Pérard (ed.), *Recueil de plusieurs pièces curieuses servant à l'histoire de Bourgogne,* Paris, 1664, pp. 202-3 (Odo). *Cartulaire de la Trinite de Vendôme,* CCCLXI, vol. ii, pp. 106-7 (Bertrand).

Louis' *enquête: RHF.* xxiv. 4*-5*.

Joinville: *Hist. de S. Louis,* XXV. III, p. 64. Cf. *Book of Margery Kempe,* I. 26, p. 60.

244   'When the debts…': Owst, p. 104.

245   Origin of garb: John Cassian, *Collationes,* XI. 3, ed. M. Petschenig, *CSEL.* xiii, Vienna, 1886, p. 315 (fourth century monks). On Canute, *Fagrskinna,* quoted in Larsen, pp. 225-6. Eadmer, *Vita Anselmi,* II. 21, p. 97. Orderic, *Hist. Eccl.,* VIII. 10, ed. Chibnall, vol. iv, p. 188.

Blessings: in general, Franz (1), vol. ii, pp. 273-7, and Brundage, pp. 292, 297. 'Novel rite': Eckhard, *Chron. Universale, MGH. SS.* vi. 214. Cf. Eadmer, *loc. cit.,* 'peregrinantium more coram altari suscepit'.

246 Rayner: Benincasa, *Vita S. Rayneri*, II. 28, p. 431.
Symbolism: *Liber S. Jacobi*, I. 17, pp. 152-3. Sacchetti, *Sermone*, XLVIII, p. 165. Thomas of London, *Instructorium Peregrinorum*, Bibl. Nat. MS. Lat. 2049, fols. 229-30.

247 Palms: Du Cange, p. 536. Raymond of Aguilers, *Hist. Francorum*, XX, p. 295 (first crusade). William of Tyre, *Hist.*, XXI. 17, p. 1033. On palm-vendors, Ernoul, *Chron.*, XVII, p. 193; *Manuscrit de Rothelin*, III, p. 493.

248 Shells: *Liber S. Jacobi*, I. 17, IV. 9, pp. 153, 379-80.
Lead badges: Lopez Ferreiro, vol. v. pp. 38-9, 125-6, and appendices V, XXVII, pp. 15-17, 53-5 (Santiago). *Archaeological Journal*, xiii (1856), p. 105 (Canterbury). Maxe-Werly (Mont-St.-Michel; St. Catherine). Forgeais, *Plombs historiés*, vol. ii, pp. 154, 175, 184 (St.-Léonard; Saintes; Noyon). See also Guernes de Pont-St.-Maxence, *Vie de S. Thomas Becket*, II. 5895-5900, ed. E. Walberg, Paris, 1936, pp. 181-2.

249 Badge-collectors: Langland, *Piers Plowman*, B. 527-31, pp. 86-7. Claude de Seyssel, *Les louanges du Roy Louis xii*[e], Paris, 1508, sig. iii (Louis XI).

250 Badges as charms: *Miracles de Rocamadour*, I. 37, pp. 135-6. *Liber S. Jacobi*, II. 12, pp. 273-4.
As legal proof of status: Rupin, pp. 233-4. On crusaders, Benedict, *Mirac. S. Thomae*, IV. 12, p. 175.
Trade in badges: Rupin, pp. 235-7 (Rocamadour). J. Saenz de Aguirre (ed.), *Collectio Maxima Conciliorum*, vol. v, Rome, 1755, p. 140; Lopez Ferreiro, vol. v, p. 33 (app. XXXIII) (Santiago). 'O Lord, heavenly…': quoted in Franz (1), vol. ii, pp. 263-4.

251 Road to Conques: M. Bloch, 'Régions naturelles et groupes sociaux', *Annales d'Histoire Economique et Sociale*, iv (1932), p. 494.
Seigneur de Caumont: see text appended to *Guide*, pp. 133-40.
Road-building: Oursel, p. 56 (bridge at Tours). On *camino de Santiago*, *Guide*, V, VIII, pp. 12, 80; Defourneaux, pp. 67-8. On surviving roads and bridges, Oursel, pp. 51-5, 57-60.

252 *Guide*: see caps. VI-VII, pp. 12-32.

253 Richard punishes toll-keepers: 'Benedict' (i.e. Roger of Howden), *Gesta Henrici*, vol. i, p. 132.
Criminal penalties: *Capitularia Regum Francorum*, vol. i, 37, 191, often reiterated. In eleventh-century Normandy murderers of

pilgrims were reserved to the duke's justice, see *Consuetudines et Justitiae,* XII, ed. C. H. Haskins, *EHR.,* xxiii (1908), p. 508.

254   Ecclesiastical censures: Conc. Rome (1059), in *MC.* xix. 873; Conc. Lateran (1123), in *MC.* xxi. 285. Conc. Rouen (1096), in Orderic Vitalis, *Hist. Eccl.,* IX. 3, ed. Prévost, vol. iii, p. 471; *RHF.* xv. 178-9.

'But you should know…': Hugh of Lyons, Ep. XVII, *PL.* clvii. 520. Cf. Yvo of Chartres, *Decr.,* IV. 60, col. 276.

Bull *In Coena:* bull of 1303 in Boniface VIII, *Reg.* 5345, vol. iii, p. 846.

Bandits: On Gerard of Galeria, William of Malmesbury, *Vita Wulfstani,* X, ed. R. R. Darlington, Camden Soc., 3rd. series, vol. xl, London, 1928, pp. 16-17; Peter Damian, *Disceptatio Synodalis,* in *MGH. Libelli,* i. 91. On Thomas de Marle, Guibert, *De Vita Sua,* III. 11, 14, pp. 177-9, 198-202; Suger, *Vita Lodovici VI,* VII, XXIV, XXXI, pp. 30, 174-8, 254. On Berthold of Eberstein, see Matthias von Neuenburg, *Chron.,* contin. CXXXVII, ed. A. Hofmeister, *MGH. Rer. Germ.,* N. S. iv, Berlin, 1924-37, p. 446. Werner von Urslinger's activities are traced in Clement VI, *Reg. (Autres Pays),* 2182, 2183, 2185-6, 2276, pp. 302-3, 317. On English bandits in Spain, Vazquez de Parga *et al.,* vol. i, pp. 269-70. On banditry in Palestine, Gregory IX, *Reg.* 4148, 4156, 4523, vol. ii, pp. 916, 919-20, 1131-2; Burchard of Mt. Sion, *Descriptio,* XIII, pp. 88-9; Jacques de Vitry, *Hist. Hierosolymitana,* LXXXII, pp. 1096-7.

255   Depredations of locals: Lanfranc, *Ep.* IX, *PL.* cl. 517-18 (Mont-St.-Michel). *PL.* cxliii. 797 (Italian peasants). 'Benedict' (i.e. Roger of Howden), *Gesta Henrici,* vol. i, p. 132 (Sorde and Lespéron). On Jubilee pilgrims of 1350, Clement VI, *Reg. (France),* 4512, vol. iii, p. 84; *Reg. (Autres Pays),* 2149, p. 298; *Vita Prima Clementis VI,* in Baluze (ed.), *Vitae Paparum,* vol. i, pp. 253-4; M. Villiani, *Istorie,* I. 56, col. 56.

Innkeepers: *Liber S. Jacobi,* II. 5, pp. 267-8; cf.. *Mirac. B. Egidii,* II, *MGH. SS.* xii. 317-18. On German pilgrims robbed, see case of Gil Buhon in Wohlhaupter (2), pp. 227-8. Glaber, *Hist.,* IV. 4, p. 101.

257   Hostile populations on route to Jerusalem: *Vita Lietberti,* XXIV, pp. 705-6. *Passio S. Cholomanni,* II-III, *MGH. SS.* iv. 675. *Vita Theoderici Andaginensis,* XV, *MGH. SS.* xii. 44 (travellers turned

back in 1053). *Hist. S. Florentii Samurensis*, in Marchegay and
Mabille (ed.), *Eglises d'Anjou*, pp. 265, 268 (Gerald). Lambert of
Ardres. *Hist. Comitum Ghismensium*, CXIII, *MGH. SS.* xxiv.
615 (Anselm of Ardres). On the German expedition of 1064-
5, *Annales Altahenses Maiores*, pp. 66-70; Lambert of Hersfeld,
Annales, pp. 92-100.

258   Tolls levied by Arabs: Guibert, *Gesta Dei per Francos*, II. 4, p. 140.
Wace, *Roman de Rou*, II. 3159-3194, vol. i, pp. 278-80 (duke
Robert).

     And by Greeks: Glaber, *Hist.*, III. 1, p. 52. Victor's complaint in
PL. cxlix. 961-2, where it is wrongly ascribed to Victor III, see
Riant (4), pp. 50-3.

259   Fortifications outside Jerusalem: Theoderic of Wurzburg, *De
Locis Sanctis*, XXIII, p. 59.

     Roads from Jerusalem: On raiders from Ascalon, Daniel,
Pèlerinage, VII, LI, pp. 10-11, 42; Saewulf, *Relatio*, pp. 36-7. On
incident of 1120, Albert of Aix, *Hist.*, XII. 33, pp. 712-13. On
Baldwin's expedition of 1106, Daniel, *op. cit.*, LXXI-LXXVIII,
pp. 56-61; Albert of Aix, *op. cit.* X. 9, p. 635.

260   Henry the Lion: Arnold of Lubeck, *Chron.*, I. 1-3, pp. 11-18.
'Men may leve…': *The pilgrim's sea-voyage and sea-sickness*, ed. F.
J. Furnivall, *EETS.*, O. S., vol. xxv, London, 1867, pp. 37-40.

     Comfort on ship: *Reisebuch Rieter*, pp. 37-8. Conrady (ed.),
Rheinische Pilgerschriften, pp. 90-1 (anonymous German).
Frescobaldi, *Viaggio*, p. 36. Wey, *Itineraries*, p. 4. Newett, pp. 91-
2 (Hans von Mergenthal).

261   What to bring: Frescobaldi, *Viaggio*, pp. 32, 35. Brasca, *Viaggio*, pp.
128-9. Wey, *op. cit.*, pp. 5-6. Cf. the *Regimen in principium peregrinationis*, in Conrady (ed.). *Rheinische Pilgerschriften*, pp. 297-301.

262   How food served: Faber, *Evagatorium*, vol. i, p. 137.

     Boredom: *Ibid.*, vol. i, pp. 37-38, 135-6.

263   Sermons: Casola, *Pilgrimage*, p. 231. Faber, *op. cit.*, vol. i, pp. 132-
133.

264   Passengers obliged to defend ship: *Consolat de la mar*, in *Black
Book*, vol. iii, p. 184; *Statut de Marseille de 1253 à 1255*, in
Pardessus (ed.), *Lois Maritimes*, vol. iv, p. 271. On incident of
1408, Riant (ed.), 'Passage à Venise', pp. 246-7.

265   Reception at Joppa: *Itin. Cuiusdam Anglici*, VI, p. 449. On the
cellars, Ghillebert de Lannoy, *Voyages*, pp. 139-40; Capodilista,

Itin., p. 181; on the indulgences, Faber, *Evagatorium*, vol. i, p. 195. On Franciscan administration of landing formalities, Nompar de Caumont, *Voyaige*, p. 46; Pero Tafur, *Andancas*, p. 51. Poll-tax collected by governor: *Itin. Cuiusdam Anglici*, VI, p. 451. Niccolo da Poggibonsi, *Libro d'Oltramare*, X, vol. i, pp. 32-6.

Tolls and taxes increase: Girnand von Schwalbach, *Pilgerschrift*, p. 98 (German of 1440). Mariano da Sienna, *Viaggio*, p. 118.

Sultan enriched: G. Adam, *De Modo Sarracenos Extirpandi*, II, *RHC. Arm.* ii, 528.

266 Advantages of Venetian ships: *Itin Cuiusdam Anglici*, IV, p. 443. Suriano, *Trattato*, I. 8, pp. 14-15. Brasca, *Viaggio*, p. 128.

Passengers sold as slaves: Gregory IX, *Reg.* 4150, vol. ii, p. 917. Innocent IV, *Reg.* 2122, vol. i, p. 316.

Venetian currency: *Itin. Cuiusdam Anglici*, I, p. 436. Frescobaldi, *Viaggio*, p. 47.

267 Statutes of 1229 and 1255: Newett, pp. 25-6.

Contracts: Neefs, pp. 322-3 (Jan Aerts). Hans Rot, *Pilgerreisen*, pp. 382-5 (1440). Wey, *Itineraries*, p. 4, 90.

268 Disputes and reorganization after 1440: Newett, pp. 101-2, 56-7, 65-72, 74-5, 101. Claes van Dusen appears to have been Contarini's agent in the Netherlands, see his *Beschrijvinge*, in Conrady (ed.), *Rheinische Pilgerschriften*, p. 193.

269 Turks damage Rhodes: Wey, *Itineraries*, p. 78

Disturbances in 1480: *Voyage de la Saincte Cyté*, pp. iv-viii, 42-3.

Contarini's troubles in 1479-80: *Ibid.*, pp. 24, 99-101.

270 Decline of Venetian package-tour: Newett, pp. 107-8, 283. Affagart, *Relation*, pp. 20-1.

271 Habits of the Basques: *Guide*, VII, pp. 26-30; cf. the author's views on the Gascons, pp. 18-20. The fifteen words given in the *Guide* are the oldest monument of the Basque language. By contrast with the author of the *Guide*, the highly educated, and usually aristocratic, pilgrims of the 'dark ages' had often transmitted cultural influences, see, e.g. W. Levison, *England and the continent in the eighth century*, Oxford, 1946, pp. 36-44, 52-3, 134, 170-2.

272 Contempt for Greeks: *Innominatus V*, III, p. 259 ('cunning men'). Fulcher of Chartres, *Hist. Hierosolymitana*, II. 38, ed. H.

Hagenmeyer, Heidelberg, 1913, p. 521 ('that great oppressor').
Jacques de Vitry, *Hist. Hierosolymitana,* LXXIV-LXXX, pp.
1089-95.

273 Language difficulties: *Vita Lietberti,* XXXI, pp. 702-3. Jacques
de Vitry, *op. cit.,* LVI, p. 1077 (Germans in Jerusalem). Rjiant
(ed.), 'Passage à Venise', p. 240.

274 Bertrandon: *Voyage d'Outremer,* pp. 59, 63-4.

275 Interpreters: Frescobaldi, *Viaggio,* pp. 65-6. Gucci, *Viaggio,* pp.
150-1.
Phrase-books: Bischoff, pp. 217-19, a fine essay.

276 Alphabets: *Mandeville's Travels,* vol. ii, pp. 288, 308-9, 314-15,
412-13 (Paris text). J. Schiltberger, *Bondage and Travels,* tr. J. B.
Telfer, Hakluyt Soc., O. S., vol. lviii, London, 1879, pp. 102-3.
Harff, *Pilgerfahrt,* pp. 64-5, 75-6, 112-14, 130-1, 139, 152, 187-
9, 201-2, 209-10, 212-14, 227, 240-1.

277 'Now let me tell you…': Sigoli, *Viaggio,* p. 163.
Raucous bands: *Canterbury Tales,* II. 565-6, 764, 773-4, pp. 17,
23. *Examination of William Thorpe,* pp. 140-1.

278 Expedition of Richard of St.-Vanne: Hugh of Flavigny, *Chron.,*
XIX, pp. 393-4. Adémar, *Chron.,* III. 65, pp. 189-90. Eberwin,
Vita S. Symeonis, X, *Aa. Ss. OSB.,* vol. viii, pp. 375-6.
Expedition of Robert of Normandy: Wace, *Roman de Rou,* Lib.
III, II. 2927-36, 2959-64, vol. i, pp. 270, 271. On the authority
of Wace, see C. H. Haskins, *Norman Institutions,* Harvard, 1918,
pp. 268-72.
7,000 followers of Gunther of Bamberg: Sigebert of Gembloux
gives this figure, the lowest contemporary estimate, *Chron.,*
MGH. SS. vi. 361.

279 Treacherous companions: *Mirac. S. Eutropii,* IV. 29-30, pp. 742-
3 (blind man); cf. *Mirac. S. Walbergis,* II. 9-12, *Aa. Ss.* Feb., vol.
iii, pp. 531-2 (saec. ix). *Lieber S. Jacobi,* I. 2, 17, pp. 32, 164.
Beaumanoir, *Coutumes,* vol. ii, pp. 490-1.
Margery Kempe: *Book of Margery Kempe,* I. 27-30, II. 4, pp. 63-
75, 233-4.

280 Right to hospitality: *Capitularia Regum Francorum,* vol. i, p. 32.
DDC., vol. vi, col. 1314. *Guide,* XI, pp. 122-4.

281 Hospitality in early Church: Gorce, pp. 137-89.
Monastic obligations: *Regula S. Benedicti,* LIII, ed. R. Hanslik,

CSEL. lxxv, Vienna, 1960, pp. 123-6. *Capitularia Regum Francorum,* vol. i, p. 347.

Famous monasteries: *Chron. Evesham,* III, pp. 91-2. Caesarius, *Dial. Mirac.,* IV. 71 vol. i, pp. 28-9 (Maria Laach).

St.-Gall guest-hall: *Vita S. Otmari,* II-III, *MGH. SS.* ii, 42-3.

Irish hospices: Gougaud, pp. 166-74.

282   'Columns built by God': *Guide,* IV, p. 10.

Charlemagne's hospice in Jerusalem: Bernard, *Itin.,* X, p. 314.

Hospital of St. John: on its origins, J. Riley-Smith, *The knights of St. John in Jerusalem and Cyprus, c. 1050-1310,* London, 1967, pp. 34-7. Described in c. 1165 by John of Wurzburg, *Descriptio,* XV, pp. 158-9. On its history as a Muslim hospice, Vincent and Abel (2), vol. II, pp. 648, 692. Christians admitted: Ludolph of Suchem, *Itin.,* XXXVIII, pp. 81-2 (c. 1340).

283   St. Bernard hospice: Donnet, pp. 109-10, 119-20.

Hospices on roads to Santiago: Vazquez de Parga *et al.,* vol. ii, *passim.*

'Not only to catholics': *ibid.,* vol. iii, pp. 111-12. On military orders, *ibid.,* vol. i, pp. 307-8.

Confraternity of S. Spirito: *Bull. Dipl.,* vol. iii, p. 191.

284   Rivalry: *Chartes de Cluny,* 4326, vol. v, p. 680 (Villafranca). Vazquez de Parga *et al.,* vol. i, p. 495 (Oboña).

Aubrac: *DHGE.,* vol. v, cols. 256-8. Statutes quoted in Rupin, p. 225n.

285   Outdoor relief: *Guide,* X, pp. 120-2 (St.-Léonard). Denifle, vol. i, pp. 179-80 (St.-Jean d'Angély). Also at Canterbury, see William, *Mirac. S. Thomae,* III, 54, p. 308.

Food: *Roman de Rénart,* br. IX, II. 9092-3, ed. M. Roques, vol. iii, Paris, 1955, p. 109. Vazquez de Parga *et al.,* vol. iii, pp. 70-1.

286   Bedding: *Purchas his Pilgrimes,* VIII. 5, vol. vii, Glasgow, 1905, p. 529 ('bedding there is…'). On bequests, Vazquez de Parga *et al.,* vol. i, pp. 324-5.

Fleas: *La Manière de langage,* III, XIII, ed. P. Meyer, *Revue Critique d' Histoire et de Littérature* (1870), pp. 388-9, 403.

287   'Taverns for the rich': Denis Possot quoted in Oursel, p. 56.

Beds shared: for Rome in 1350, see Buccio di Ranallo, *Cron. Aquilana,* p. 194. On England, Deschamps quoted in Jusserand, p. 61.

Flemish draper: La Saige, *Voyage,* pp. 9-10.

Canvassing for customers: *Liber S. Jacobi,* I. 17, pp. 146, 160, 162.

288 Hotel regulations of Toulouse in R. Limousin-Lamothe (ed.), *La Commune de Toulouse et les sources de son histoire,* Toulouse, 1932, p. 358.

Claim to chattels: *Liber S. Jacobi,* II. 6, pp. 268-9. See Vazquez de Parga *et al.,* vol. i, p 274.

Innkeepers denounced: *Liber S. Jacobi,* I. 17, pp. 160-71.

Price of inns: Jusserand, pp. 61-2.

289 Hire of horses: see regulations for hackney men in P. Q. Karkeek, 'Chaucer's Schipman and his barge *The Maudelayne',* *Chaucer Society Essays,* ser. II, no. 19, London, 1884, pp. 499-500.

Prices in Rome: see lists given for 1350 by Matteo Villani, *Istorie,* I. 56, col. 57; and Buccio di Ranallo, *Cron. Aquilana,* p. 192.

Cost of Jerusalem pilgrimage: Affagart, *Relation,* pp. 22, 24-6. Brasca, *Viaggio,* p. 128. Gucci, *Viaggio,* pp. 149-56. Brygg, *Itin. Thomae de Swynburne,* pp. 387-8. Cf. accounts of Claude de Mirabel in 1452, in Saint-Génois, pp. 35-6.

291 Half fares to poor: Suriano, *Trattato,* I. 9, p. 16. Brasca, *Viaggio,* p. 129.

Money carried by pilgrims: Musset, pp. 149-50. Frescobaldi, *Viaggio,* p. 38.

Girl stranded at Tyre: Caesarius, *Dial. Mirac.,* I. 40, vol. i. pp. 47-8.

Gerald's troubles: see his *De Jure et Statu Menevensis Eccl.,* IV, V, vol. iii, pp. 240-1, 289-90.

292 Hoteliers as bankers: P. Wolff, 'Notes sur les hôtelleries Toulousaines au moyen age', *BHP.* (1960), pp. 202-3.

Milanese bills of exchange: *Annali della fabrica del duomo di Milano,* vol. i, Milan, 1877, pp. 35-6.

Rates of exchange: Matteo Villani, *Istorie,* I, 56, col. 57 (Rome in 1350). Possot, *Voyage,* p. 87. Wey, *Itineraries,* pp. 1-3, 6.

Sale of land: Guibert, *Gesta Dei per Francos,* II. 6, pp. 140-1. *Cartulaire de Conques,* no. 514, p. 368.

293 Loans from monasteries: Bibl. Carpentras, MS. 1823, fols. 55-6 (Guy of Limoges). *Cartulaire d'Auch, Cart. Noir,* CXIII, pp. 128-32. Other lenders: on Thibault de Marly's loan. Arch. Nat. K. 25, no. 5/13. *Catalogue analytique des diplomes, chartes, et actes rélatifs a l'histoire de Touraine,* ed. E. Mabille, *Soc. Archéologique de*

Touraine, xiv, Tours, 1863, no. 1187, pp. 192-3 (Josbert de Précigny). Joinville, *Hist. de S. Louis,* XXV. 112, p. 64.

294 Expenses paid by patron: Bernard, *Ep.* CCCIC, col. 612. *Roman de rou,* I. II. 3047-9, ed. H. Andersen, vol. i, Heilbronn, 1877, p. 149 (Richard of St.-Vanne). Arnold, *Chron.,* I. 1, pp. 11, 12 (Henry the Lion).
Feudal aid for pilgrmage: Bertrand d'Argentré, *Consuetudines antiquissimi ducatus Britanniae,* LXXXVII. 3, Paris, 1608, cols. 381-2. Customs of Vendôme as confirmed in 1185, *Cartulaire de la Trinité de Vendôme,* no. 578, vol. ii, pp. 445-6. On protests, Conc. II Chalons, canon XIV, in *MC.* xiv. 96; Honorius Augustodunensis, *Elucidarium,* II. 23, *PL.* clxxii. 1152.

295 Alms: on exemption of pilgrims from begging laws, see *Inventaire des chartes et documents de la ville d'Ypres,* ed. I. L. A. Diegerick, vol. vii, Bruges, 1868, pp. 157-8. J. Toulmin Smith, *English Gilds,* London, 1870, p. 180. Faber, *Evagatorium,* vol. i, p. 28. On municipal charity to pilgrims, *Archives de Bruges,* vol. v, p. 491 and n. On begging from other pilgrims, *Liber S. Jacobi,* I. 17, pp. 156-7; Egbert, *Vita S. Heimeradi,* I. 6, *Aa. Ss.* June, vol. v, p. 388; Odo, *Vita S. Geraldi,* II. 17, col. 680.

296 Professional beggars: *Liber S. Jacobi,* I. 17, p. 165.
Working one's way: *Vita S. Sigiranni,* VIII-X, pp. 386-7. *Vita B. Egidii,* V, ed. R. B. Brooke, *Scripta Leonis, Rufini, et Angeli,* Oxford, 1970, p. 324; cf. *BBB.* vol. i, p. 105. Faber, *Evagatorium,* vol. i, pp. 28, 63-4.
Commerce: *MGH. Epp.* iv. 144-6 (Charlemagne). Forbidden to penitential pilgrims: Alfonso IX, *Siete Partidas,* I. xxiv. 2, vol. i (1), fol. 151[vo]; Van den Bussche (ed.), 'Rocamadour', p. 47. Request of Philip the Fair in Baluze (ed.), *Vitae Paparum,* vol. iii, p. 146. *Hodoeporicon S. Willibaldi,* VIII, XXVIII, pp. 252, 271. Reginald, *Vita S. Godrici,* V. 17, p. 31.

297 Traders 'never sleep': Faber, *Evagatorium,* vol. ii, pp. 92-3.

298 Eberhard of Würtemburg: *Ibid.,* vol. i, pp. 26-7.

12. The Sanctuary

299 Scene ouside church: see, e.g., the descriptions by Augustine, *Ep.* XXII. 3-6, vol. i, pp. 56-9; *Enarr. in Psalmum,* XXXII. 5, ed. E. Dekkers and J. Fraipont, *Corpus Christianorum,* xxxviii,

Tournai, 1956, pp. 250-1. And by Olivier Maillard, quoted in Samouillan, pp. 282-3, 301-2. On musical beggars, *Mirac. S. Eutropii,* III, 25, p. 741.

Merchants at churches: *Mirac. S. Fidis,* I. 24, p. 63. Samson, *Mirac. S. Eadmundi,* II. 11, pp. 183-4. Reginald, *De B. Cuthberti Virtut.,* XXIV, XLVIII, pp. 53-4, 98.

Church's attitude: Augustine, *Ep.* XXIL. 3-6, vol. i, pp. 56-9; cf. in the eighth century, Boniface, *Ep.* L, pp. 84-5. Paulinus, *Carmen* XXVII. 552-67, pp. 286-7.

300   Lendit fairs: Bédier, vol. iv, pp. 154-6.

'Games and competitions...': Powicke and Cheney, *Councils,* vol. ii, p. 353, cf. p. 174.

Weekly vigils: *Invent. et Mirac. S. Wulfranni,* L, LV, pp. 65, 68. *Chron. Evesham,* II, p. 50.

301   Sanctuaries closed at night: *Mirac. S. Michaelis,* pp. 875-7. *Liber S. Jacobi,* II. 18, pp. 282-3. Cf. on Canterbury, Benedict, *Mirac. S. Thomae,* I. 12, p. 42; William, *Mirac. S. Thomae,* V. 2, p. 373.

'Let us prostrate...': Eadmer, *De Sanctorum Veneratione,* I. 2, p. 190.

'Humbly inclining...': *Chron. Evesham,* II, p. 57.

Noise at vigils: *Miracles de Rocamadour,* II. 36, pp. 245-6. Benedict, *Mirac. S. Thomae,* II. 1, 25, 28, 33-4, pp. 57, 77, 80, 85. *Liber S. Jacobi,* I. 2, 17, pp. 15-16, 19-20, 149. *Mirac. S. Fidis,* II, 12, pp. 120-2.

302   Stewards: Reginald, *De B. Cuthberti Virtut.,* CIV, p. 232.

Attempted suppression: Nantes statutes (saec. xiv), cap. VIII, in *MD. Thes.* iv. 963. Chartres statutes of 1368, cap. XXXVII, in *MD. Ampl. Coll.* vii. 1361. Cf. stories of saints forbidding pilgrimages to their shrines, Coulton, vol. iii, pp. 98-9.

303   Pilgrims crushed: Suger, *De Consecratione S. Dionysii,* II, pp. 216-17.

304   Daniel, *Pèlerinage,* XCVII, p. 77 (Jerusalem). *Liber S. Jacobi,* I. 17, p. 158 (St.-Gilles). Duplès-Agier (ed.), *Chroniques de S. Martial,* p. 200.

Rapid reconsecration permitted: Innocent IV, *Reg.* 1781, vol. i, p. 266 (St.-Gilles). Innocent III, *Reg.* X. 75, *PL.* ccxv. 1175 (Santiago).

Fire at Vézelay (in 1120): *Chron. S. Maxentii, RHF.* xii. 407. Robert of Auxerre, *Chron., MGH. SS.* xxvi. 231.

Pickpockets: *Mirac. S. Wulfstanni,* I. 19, II. 22, pp. 126, 179 (Worcester). Kajava (ed.), *Etudes,* p. 66 (Fécamp). Both saec. xiii. Sermon repeated; *Traité sur le cinquième jubilée de S. Thomas,* III. 4-5, p. 142.

Relics displayed in crises: Rigord, *Gesta Philippi,* LXXX, vol. i, pp. 113-14 (St.-Denis in 1191). *Invent. et Mirac. S. Wulfranni,* XXXVIII-LI, pp. 56-66 (Rouen in 1053). *Mirac. S. Martialis,* praefat., pp. 412-15 (Limoges in 1388). *Journal d'un Bourgeois,* pp. 191, 216, cf. pp. 20, 21, 22, 102, 144, 208, 372, 374, 376-8, 391-2. Reginald, *De B. Cuthberti Virtut.,* XXXIX, pp. 82-3 (fires at Durham). Bondurand (ed.), 'Détresse de St.-Gilles', p. 444.

305 Forced displays: Samson, *Mirac. S. Eadmundi,* II. 6, pp. 173-4. *Cartulaire de Conques,* no. 570, p. 399.

306 Displays once in seven years: *Mirac. S. Martialis,* praefat., p. 412. Montsabert (ed.), *Chartes de Charroux,* CCXXXII, pp. 364-7. Displays restricted: Conc. Lateran (1215), canon LXII, in *MC.* xxii. 1049. Conc. Budapest (1279), canon XXVII, in *MC.* xxiv. 283. Conc. Exeter (1287), canon XLVIII, in Powicke and Chency, *Councils,* vol. ii, p. 1044. Conc. Bayeux (1300), canon XXXV, in *MC.* xxv. 67.

New reliquaries: *Mirac. S. Martialis,* X, p. 419. In the late Middle Ages the heads of St. Peter and St. Paul were displayed in such reliquaries, Capgrave, *Solace,* II. 4, p. 73. Cf. relics of church of St. George in Rome, *ibid.* II. 9, pp. 87-8; and head of St. Thomas at Canterbury, Erasmus, *Peregrinatio Religionis,* col. 783.

Infrequent displays raise doubts: Faillon (ed.) *Monuments inédits,* vol. ii, pp. 753-4 (Vézelay). Harff, *Pilgerfahrt,* p. 233.

Bull of 1424 and its effects: A. L. Mayer, 'Die heilbringende Schau in Sitte und Kult', in *Heilige Ueberlieferung (Festschrift I. Herwegen),* Munster, 1938, pp. 245-9.

13. Rome

308 Three principal sanctuaries: R. Vielliard, pp. 55-9. *DACL.,* vol. xv, cols. 3296-8. Gregorovius, vol. i, pp. 90-1, 102-4.

309 Roman martyrs: Delehaye (4), pp. 260-3, 269-99.
Death of Sixtus II: *Lib. Pont.,* vol. i, p. 155.
Catacombs: *DACL.,* vol. xiv, col. 42 (graffiti). Jerome, *Comm. in Ezechielem,* XII. 5, *PL.* xxv. 375. On Damasus's restorations, *Lib.*

Pont., vol. i, p. 212; *DACL.,* vol. xiii, col. 2434; De Rossi (ed.), *Inscriptiones,* vol. ii (Rome, 1888), pp. 30, 66, 90, 102, 105. Prudentius, *Peristephanon,* XI. 155-68, pp. 417-18.

312 Damage of 537-8: De Rossi, *op. cit.,* vol. ii, pp. 83, 84, 100. Translations to city: *Lib. Pont.,* vol. i, pp. 332, 360, 441-3, 444-5, 445-6, 451-2, 464, 520, vol. ii, pp. 52, 54, 56, 74, 93, 115.

313 Relics taken north: Llewellyn, pp. 183-90. Basilicas walled: *Lib. Pont.,* vol. ii, p. 123 (St. Peter's). Gregorovius, vol. iii, pp. 186-7 (St. Paul's).

314 'From a far off hill…': Gregory, *De Mirabilibus Romae,* I. p. 543. 'O Roma Nobilis': full text in F. J. E. Raby, *Christian Latin Poetry,* 2nd. ed., Oxford, 1953, pp. 233-4. Romans despised: William of Malmesbury, *Gesta Regum,* IV. 351, p. 402. Walter Map, *De Nugis Curialum,* II. 17, ed. M. R. James, Oxford, 1914, p. 82.

315 Hildebert's poem: in B. Hauréau, 'Notice sur les mélanges poétiques d'Hildebert de Lavardin', *Notices et extraits des manuscrits de la Bibliothèque Nationale,* xxxviii (2) (1888), pp. 334-5. It is quoted by, e.g., Willliam of Malmesbury, *Gesta Regum,* IV. 351, pp. 402-3; Gregory, *De Mirabilibus Romae,* I. p. 543. Restorations and new churches: Gregorovius, vol. iv, pp. 694-6, vol. v, p. 637.

316 St. Peter's: On the *confessio,* Mallius, *Descriptio,* XLII-XLIII, p. 425. On the *sudarium, Bull. Vat.,* vol. i, pp. 9, 89-90; Nicholas IV, *Reg.* 653, p. 131. Lateran: John the Deacon, *Descriptio,* IV-V, XIII, pp. 337-42, 356-7. Gerald of Wales, *Speculum Ecclesiae,* IV. 3-4, vol. iv., pp. 272-6. *Graphia Aureae Urbis,* XX, pp. 83-4.

317 Processions: Benedict, *Liber Politicus,* XLV-LI, pp. 152-4. Condition of monuments: Gregorovius, vol. iv, p. 691 (arch of Titus). Accusations against Gregory VII in 1080 in *MGH. Leges,* iv (1), p. 119 Otto of Friesing, *De Duabus Civitatibus,* VII. 31, p. 360 (St. Peter's fortified). Innocent III, *Reg.,* II. 102, *PL.* ccxiv. 651-3. *Regesto di S. Silvestro di Capite,* IV, ed. V. Federici, *ASRSP.,* xxii (1889), p. 269.

318 Attempt to preserve them a failure: A. de Bouard, 'Gli antichi marmi di Roma nel medio evo', *ASRSP.,* xxxiv (1911), pp. 239-45. Reginald of Durham, *De B. Cuthberti Virtut.,* LXXV, pp. 155-6.

319 Collectors: Suger, *De Consecratione,* II, p. 219. John of Salisbury, *Hist. Pontificalis,* XL, p. 79.

Horse of Constantine: *Lib. Pont.,* vol. ii, p. 252 (official hanged). *Mirabilia Urbis Romae,* XV, pp. 32-3 (guide-book). Gregory, *De Mirabilibus Romae,* IV-V, pp. 544-6. On equestrian statues in France, see R. Crozet, 'Nouvelles remarques sur les cavaliers sculptées ou peints dans les églises romanes', *Cahiers de Civilisation Médiévale,* i (1958), p. 27; perhaps also at Autun, D. Grivot and G. Zarnecki, *Gislebertus, sculptor of Autun,* N.Y., 1961, p. 65 and pl. VI. Many others once existed, see Mâle, pp. 247-9.

320 *Mirabilia:* see caps. I-XI, XXIII, XXVI, XXXII, pp. 17-29, 51-3, 58, 65; *Graphia Aureae Urbis,* XII, p. 79. On editions, A. Graf, *Roma nella memoria e nelle imaginazione del medio evo,* vol. i, Turin, 1882, pp. 65-72. The author was probably Benedict, canon of St. Peter's, see L. Duchesne in *Liber Censuum,* introd., pp. 102-4.

321 Gregory: *De Mirabilibus Romae,* IV, X, XII, XV-XVIII, XXI, pp. 544-5, 547-50. On him, see introduction to Rushforth's edition in *Journal of Roman Studies,* ix (1919), pp. 17-18, 30-1. Text of pseudo-Bede ed. H. Omont, *BEC.,* liii (1882), pp. 40-59.

323 Pilgrims obstructed: *Becket Materials,* vol. v, p. 357. Innocent IV, *Reg.* 1896, vol. i, p. 281.

Hospices disappear: on Irish hospice, A. M. Tommasini, *I Santi Irlandesi in Italia,* Milan, 1932, p. 74. On English hospice, *Becket Materials,* vol. v, pp. 64-5; *Bull. Dipl.,* vol. i, p. 355, vol. iii, p. 191. Gregory the Great: *Dialogi,* IV. 13, III. 25, *PL.* lxxvii. 340, 280. Cf., in tenth century, Liutprand of Cremona, *Hist. Ottonis,* IV, ed. J. Bekker, *MGH. Rer. Germ.,* Hanover, 1915, pp. 161-2.

324 Canute: Florence of Worcester, *Chron.,* ed. B. Thorpe, vol. i, London, 1848, p. 186.

Rivals of St. Peter: *Vita S. Austremonii,* III. 17, *Aa. Ss.* Nov., vol. i, pp. 53-4 (saec. vii-viii).

325 'Penance is synonymous...': Jonas of Orleans, *De Cultu Imaginum,* III, *PL.* cvi. 369.

Popes consulted: Yvo of Chartres, *Decr.,* X. 35, 179, cols. 701, 743; cf. X. 20, 24, 29, 180, 185, cols. 697-700, 743-5. Nicholas I, *Epp.* CXXIX, CXXXIII, CXXXVIII, *MGH. Epp.* vi, 650, 654, 658. Wasserschleben (ed.), *Bussordnungen,* p. 333. I cannot accept, with Hausmann, pp. 28-33, that the practice dates back to Gregory I.

326 Bishops by-passed: *Capitula Ecclesiastica,* XVIII, in *Capitularia Regum Francorum,* vol. i, p. 365 (Haito). Conc. Seligenstadt, canon XVI, in *MC.* xix. 398. Conco Limoges in *MC.* xix. 546. On reserved cases, Göller, vol. i (1), pp. 80-1.

327 Scandinavian penitents: Alexander III, *Ep,* 975, cols. 850-2. *Grettis Saga Asmundarson,* ed. R. C. Boer, *Altnordische Saga-Bibliothek,* viii, Halle, 1900, pp. 311-14. *Sverris Saga,* ed. G. Indrebo, Kristiana, 1920, pp. 3-4 (Gunnhildr). *Inga Konungs Saga,* quoted in Springer, p. 94n[24]. (Adrian IV).

328 Stational indulgences: John the Deacon, *Vita S. Gregorii,* II. 18, *PL.* lxxv. 94 (late). Gerald of Wales, *De Invectionibus,* V. 12, vol. i, pp. 137-8. William of Auxerre, *Summa Aurea,* quoted in Paulus (2), vol. ii, p. 295n[4]. Decision of Boniface VIII in *Bull. Vat.,* vol. iii (app.), p. 6.

329 Indulgences of churches: in twelfth century, Peter Mallius, *Descriptio,* III, p. 385; Alexander III, *Ep.* 1520, cols. 1315-16; Petrus Cantor, *Summa de Sacramentis,* quoted in Paulus (2), vol. ii, p. 295n[2]. In thirteenth century, Gregory IX, *Reg.* 5228, vol. iii, p. 270, extended by Urban IV in 1263, *Bull. Vat.,* vol. i, p. 143 (basilicas of apostles); *Ceremoniale Romanum* XXII, in J. Mabillon, *Museum Italicum,* vol. ii, Paris, 1869, p. 238 (Lateran); Aquinas, *In Sentent.,* quoted in Paulus (2), vol. ii, p. 296; Nicholas III, *Reg.* 1042, p. 414 (individual altar in St. Peter's). Nicholas IV: *Reg.* 425, 631, 633-4, 650-1, 653, 1432, 2030, pp. 78, 127-8, 130-1, 285, 361.

330 Idea of Jubilee: Bernard, *Ep.* 458, *PL.* clxxxii. 652-3. Albert of Trois-Fontaines, *Chron., MGH. SS.* xxiii. 889; cf. G. M. Drèves (ed.), *Analecta Hymnica,* XXI, Leipzig, 1895, p. 166 (Albigensian crusade). Humbert of Romans, quoted in Paulus (2), vol. i, p. 101.
Jubilee: this account is based on G. Villani, *Hist. Fiorentine,* VIII. 36, cols. 367-8. W. Ventura, *Chron. Astense,* XXVI, cols. 191-2. Cardinal J. Stefaneschi, *De Centesimo,* I-IX, pp. 299-307.
Bull *Antiquorum*: text in Boniface VIII, *Reg.* 3875, vol. ii, pp. 922–3; accompanying brief in Stefaneschi, *op. cit.,* pp. 315–16. Commentary by Silvester Scriptor, ed. R. Scholz, 'Zur Beurteilung Bonifaz VIII und seines sittlich-religiösen

Charakters', *Historisches Vierteljahreschrift,* ix (1906), pp. 513-15; cf. *Gesta Boemundi Archiep. Treverensis,* XXXIV, *MGH. SS.* xxiv. 487-8, and Sienese inscription in *IS* (1)., iii. 561. For doubts as to its meaning, John the Monk in *Extravagantes Communes* Lyon, 1506, fol. 36; Giles li Muisis, *Chron.,* pp. 188-9 (Tournai incident).

334 'Innumerable Christians...': *Annales Mutinensium, RISS* (1), xi. 75.

Kings represented: Thurston, p. 24.

335 Crowds on bridge: Dante, *Inferno,* XVIII. 28-33.

336 Offerings: for rumour in Tuscany, Ptolemy of Lucca, *Annales,* ed. B. Schmeidler, *MGH. Rer. Germ.,* N. S., viii, Berlin, 1930, p. 236.

337 Boniface posthumously accused: Article LXIX of charges, in P. Dupuy, *Histoire du différend d'entre le pape Boniface VIII et Phelippes le Bel, Roy de France,* Paris, 1655, preuves, pp. 358-9. *Chronique Rimée,* II. 41-2, 55-6, *RHF,* xxii. 89.

Dante on the Jubilee: *Purgatorio,* II. 98-105.

Lateran burned: Ptolemy of Lucca, *Hist. Eccl., RISS* (1)., xi 1230.

338 Bull *Unigenitus: Vita III Clementis VI,* in Baluze (ed.), *Vitae Paparum,* vol. i, pp. 278-9, vol. ii, pp. 370-1. Text in *CJC., Extrav. Comm.,* V. ix. 2, vol. ii, cols. 1304-6. On 'treasury of merit', see Albertus Magnus, *In Sentent.,* IV. xx. 16, in *Opera Omnia,* ed. A. Borgnet, vol. xxix, Paris, 1894, pp. 847-9.

339 Wars damage Jubilee: Petrarch, *Lettere Familiari,* XV. 15, vol. iii, pp. 150-1. Clement VI, *Reg. (France),* 4290, 4307, vol. iii, pp. 34, 37; *Reg. (Autres Pays),* 2181, 2183, pp. 302-3, 317. On prohibition of pilgrimages, Rymer, *Foedera,* vol. v. p. 668 (England); Giles li Muisis, *Chron.,* pp. 385, 395-6 (France). For licences to English pilgrims, Rymer, *Foedera,* vol. v, pp. 677, 681-3. On troubles of pilgrims in France, Clement VI, *Reg. (France),* 4717, 4724, vol. iii, pp. 128-9.

340 Earthquake: Petrarch, *op. cit.,* XI. 7, vol. ii, p. 338.

Jubilee pilgrims: this account is based on M. Villani, *Istorie,* I. 56, cols. 56-7; Peter of Herenthals, *Vita Clementis VI,* in Baluze (ed.), *Vitae Paparum,* vol. i, pp. 302-3; Heinrich von Rebdorff, *Annales Imperatorum et Paparum,* ed. J. F. Boehmer, *Fontes Rer. Germ.,* iv, Stuttgart, 1868, p. 562; Buccio di Ranallo, *Cronaca*

Aquilana, pp. 192, 194; Bridget, *Rev.,* III. 27, IV. 5, 78, VI. 112, pp. 189, 209-10, 293, 525; Petrarch, *Rime,* XVI, and *Lettere Familiari,* IX. 13, XI. 1, vol. ii. pp. 254-5, 322-3. On private views of the Veronica, Clement VI, *Reg. (France),* 4734, 4746, 4750-1, 4778, 4785, 4790, 4792, 4795, 4816, 4835. vol. iii, pp. 131, 132-3, 139-43, 148, 151; *Reg. (Autres Pays),* 2353, p. 329.

343 'Many altercations': *Breve Chron.,* ed. J. J. de Smet, *Corpus Chronicorum Flandriae,* vol. iii, Bruxelles, 1856, p. 14. Text of two forged bulls in Alberic of Rosate, *Dictionarium,* fols. 163-4; another in Peter of Herenthals, *Vita Clementis VI,* in Baluze (ed.), *Vitae Paparum,* vol. i, p. 299, cf. vol. ii, pp. 432-3. Burton, *Chron. Mon. Melsa,* vol. iii, pp. 88-9. Wyclif, *Trialogus,* ed. G. Lechler, Oxford, 1869, p. 357.

344 Clerical pilgrims pardoned: *CPR. Letters,* vol. iii, pp. 382-6, 388, 395-7, 429.

Visits reduced: Alberic of Rosate, *Dictionarium,* fol. 164, and accounts cited above.

Louis of Hungary: Rodocanachi, p. 162.

Indulgences without journey: for requests, see Clement VI, *Reg. (France),* 4426, vol. iii, pp. 64-5 (Philip VI); Raynald, *Ann. Eccl.,* An. 1350 (no. 2), vol. vii, p. 502 (Hugh); Oxford, MS. Bodley 144, fols. 246VO-251VO (Fitzralph's sermon). Granted: *CPR. Letters,* vol. iii, pp. 49, 383; A. Theiner (ed.), *Vetera Monumenta Historica Hungariam Sacram Illustrantia,* vol. i, Rome, 1859, p. 791; on Mallorca, Vincke (4).

346 Large indulgences: Philip, *Liber de Terra Sancta (1377),* pp. 519-20.

347 Guide-books unobtainable: *Itin. Cuiusdam Anglici,* III, p. 441.

Books of indulgences: Brewyn, *A fifteenth century guide-book,* pp. 22-3, 41. Capgrave, *Solace,* II. 6, p. 83. *Stacions of Rome,* II. 1-6, p. 1. In general, Hulbert.

348 Translations altered: *Itin. Cuiusdam Anglici, loc. cit. Stacions,* II. 497-9, 718-19, pp. 16, 23. Oxford, MS. Bodley 423, fol. 384 (Capgrave).

Notices: *Stacions,* II. 215-16, 515-18, pp. 8, 17; cf. Philip, *Liber de Terra Sancta (1377),* p. 522.

349 Rivalry with Jerusalem: *Stacions,* II. 285-91, p. 10. Muffels, *Beschreibung,* p. 17.

350 Attitude of papacy: *Memoriale de Mirabilibus et Indulgentiis,* in *VZ.,* vol. iv, pp. 75-88.

Indulgences transferred to Marseilles: J. B. Guesnay, *Provinciae Massiliensis Annales,* Lyon, 1657, p. 435. *Bullarium Franciscanum,* ed. C. Eubel, vol. vii, Rome, 1904, pp. 237-8 (no. 645).

351 Jubilee of 1390: Urban's bull in Amort, *De Origine Indulgentiarum,* vol. i, pp. 84-6; Clement's denunciation in Vincke (I), pp. 68-9. Granted without journey: *Regesta Boicarum,* ed. C. H. Lang, vol. x, Munich, 1843, p. 255 (Stephen of Bavaria); Arch.Vat. Reg.Vat., 312, fols. 148VO-149VO (bishop of Camerino); *CPR. Letters,* vol. iv, pp. 323-6, 379-80 (mayor of Berwick etc.); Jansen, pp. 152-4 (Cologne); Vincke (1), pp. 69-71 (Spain).

352 Papal share of offerings: Arch, Vat. Diversa Cameralia I, fols. 129VO-130 (St. Paul's); Arch.Vat. Reg.Vat. 347, fols. 78VO-79VO (S. Maria Maggiore).

Commission to Guinigi, Arch. Vat. Reg. Vat. 312, fols. 148VO-149VO.

Indulgence marketed north of Alps: Arch.Vat. Reg.Vat. 313, fols. 187-187VO, 196 (instructions to legates in Poland). Dietrich of Niem, *De Scismate,* I. 68, pp. 119-20. On Milan, *Annali della fabrica del duomo di Milano,* vol. i, Milan, 1877, pp. 33-4, 41-3; Arch. Vat. Reg.Vat. 313, fol. 241. On German Jubilees, Jansen, pp. 145-62.

353 Jubilee of 1400: Dietrich of Niem, *op. cit.,* II. 28, p. 170; Laslowski, pp. 128, 148; monk of St. Paul's quoted by Rucellai in 1450, *Giubileo,* p. 579. Offerings calculated on the basis that the pope's share (8,000 florins) was half the total, Arch. Vat. Reg. Vat. 317, fols. 30-30VO

Boniface's embarrassment: Arch. Vat. Reg. Vat. 316, fols. 342VO, 349-50; 317, fol. 8VO (offerings claimed). Boniface's pronouncements on indulgence in Arch.Vat. Reg.Vat. 316, fols. 341VO-342; 317, fols. 47-47VO. Granted to princes etc.: *Diplomatarium Norvegicum,* vol. v, Kristiana, 1860, pp. 251-2, vol. xvii, Kristiana, 1902, p. 201; Arch.Vat. Reg. Lateran 79, fol. 85VO; 87, fol. 231VO; Arch.Vat. Reg.Vat. 317, fols. 41-2.

Attempt to stop French pilgrims: N. Valois, *La France et le Grand Schisme d'Occident,* vol. iii, Paris, 1901, pp. 321-2.

354 Spain: on royal support for Catalan hospice, J. Vielliard (1), pp. 188-9. *Instructiones pro ambaxiadoribus in Franciam,* ed. F. Ehrle,

'Neue Materialen zur Geschichte Peters von Luna (Benedicts XIII)', *Archiv. für Literatur- und Kirchengeschichte des Mittelalters,* vii (1893), pp. 116, 118. On Poblet, J.Vielliard (2), pp. 287, 271.

355 'Pity Rome…': Adam of Usk, *Chron.,* pp. 91, 93.

State of monuments: Petrarch, *Lettere Familiari,* XV. 9, vol. iii, p. 162 (campanile). *De Rebus antiquis et situ urbis Romae,* in *VZ.,* vol. iv, p. 117 (arch of Arcadius).

Services abandoned: Antonio Petri, *Diarium Romanum, RISS* (1). xxiv. 1043, 1050.

356 Jubilee of 1423: Poggio, *Lib.* II, *Ep.* II, ed. T. de Tonellis, vol. i, Florence, 1832, p. 86. John Amundesham, *Annales Mon. S. Albani,* ed. H.T. Riley, *RS,* vol. i, London, 1870, pp. 131-2, 134-5, 143, 147.

357 New relics: Pastor, vol. i, pp. 231, 258-61.

Ceremonies: on new ceremonial trappings, E. Muntz, *Les arts à la cour des papes pendant le xve et xvie siècle,* Paris, 1878-82, vol. i, pp. 20-23, 36, 53, vol. ii, pp. 309-12. On the bull *In Coena,* Adam of Usk, *Chron.,* p. 97; Harff, *Pilgerfahrt,* pp. 31-2. Tafur, *Andancas,* pp. 34-5 (celebrations of 1437).

Sudarium: Muffels, *Beschreibung,* p. 10 (indulgences). On the 'vernicle', *Canterbury Tales,* I. 685, p. 20; Langland, *Piers Plowman,* B.V. 530, p. 86. F. Ariosto, *Dicta de la entrata in Roma de lo illustrissimo duca Borso,* ed. E. Celani, *ASRSP.,* xiii (1890), pp. 434-5.

359 Catacombs: Raynald, *An. Eccl.,* An. 1424 (no. 13), vol. ix, p. 10 (commission of 1424). Rucellai, *Giubileo,* p. 463. Capgrave, *Solace,* II. 3, I. 7, pp. 69, 20.

Other amusements: Harff, *Pilgerfahrt,* p. 31. Lengherand, *Voyage,* p. 72.

360 1022 inns: Number given by Rucellai, *Giubileo,* p. 453. On albergo della Luna, Galeazzo Gataro, *Istoria Padovano, RISS* (1). xvii. 45. Pastor, vol. iv, p. 185n. (Borso d'Este). Harff, *Pilgerfahrt,* p. 14. Buchard, *Liber Notarum,* ed. E. Celani, *RISS* (2), xxxii, vol. i, pp. 266-7 (Otto of Bavaria). On their unpopularity, see Romani, p. 79.

361 English hospices: Croke, pp. 568-72. Re, pp. 85-92. F. A. Gasquet, *A History of the Venerable English College, Rome,* London, 1920, pp. 30-5.

The Anima: Nagl (OS), pp. 58-63, 65-6. Schmidlin. Also, *Liber Confrat. B. M. de Anima.*

362 Other national hospices: many references in Delaruelle *et al.,* pp. 1150-1; and Pastor, vol. i, pp. 253-6. On Irish hospice, Pastor, vol. i, p. 254. F. Pascarelli, 'Origine e vicende dell' ospedale di S. Brigida di Svezia in Roma', *Atti del primo Congresso Europeo di Storia Ospitaliera (1960),* Reggio Emilia, 1962, p. 1004. On Flemish hospice, Vaes (2), p. 91.

363 Jubilee of 1450: what follows is based on Paolo dello Mastro, *Memoriale,* LIV, pp. 95-7; Manetti, *Vita Nicolai V,* II, *RISS* (1). iii (2). 924-5. Olivier de la Marche, *Mémoires,* ed. H. Beaune and J. d'Arbaumont, *SHF,* vol. ii, Paris, 1884, p. 162; Pastor, vol. ii, pp. 74-137, 500-2.

Jubilee bull: partial text in Raynald, *Ann. Eccl.,* An. 1449 (no. 15), vol. ix, p. 543.

364 Rucellai: *Giubileo,* pp. 564-79.

Capgrave: *Solace,* preface, I. 14, II. 4, 9, 47, pp. 1, 33, 73, 87-8, 146-7.

365 Shops on bridge destroyed: Dietrich of Niem, *De Scismate,* II. 37, p. 192.

367 Indulgence without journey: C. Gärtner, *Salzburgische gelehrte Unterhaltungen,* vol. i, Salzburg, 1812, p. 114. Fredericq (ed.), *Codex,* pp. 80-2, 119-21, 132-6. Paulus (2), vol. ii, pp. 47, 188. C. Witz (ed.), 'Bullen und Breven aus italienischen Archiven', *Quellen zur Schweitzer Geschichte,* xxi, Basel, 1902, p. 517. *CPR. Letters,* vol. x, pp. 169-70. Amort, *De Origine Indulgentiarum,* vol. i, pp. 87-9. *Bull. Vat.,* vol. ii, p. 137. Henry VI's comment in Rymer, *Foedera,* vol. x, pp. 263-6, vol. xi, pp. 252-4.

Results of the Jubilee: Manetti, *Vita Nicolai V,* II, *RISS* (1). iii (2). 924-5. Dati, *Opera,* Venice, 1516, fol. 177.

14. The Later Middle Ages I

369 Female pilgrims criticized: Boniface, *Ep.* XLVIII, p. 169. *Quinze joies,* VIII, pp. 69-70. Berthold, *Predigten,* XXVIII, vol. i, pp. 458-60; Giordano da Rivalto, *Prediche recitate in Firenze dal MCCCIII al MCCCVI* vol. i, Florence, 1831, pp. 252-3; cf. Owst, pp. 388-9.

370 Women at Bury: Wright (ed.), *Letters,* p. 85.

Women in monastic sanctuaries: Burton, *Chron. Mon. Melsa,* vol. iii, pp. 35-6. *Mirac. S. Benedicti,* I. 28, pp. 64-5. On Durham, Symeon, *Hist. Dunelmensis Eccl.,* III. II, vol. i, p. 95; Reginald, *De B. Cuthberti Virtut.,* LXXIV, pp. 141-4. Cf. Loomis, p. 97.

371 Pregnant woman crushed: *Mirac. S. Martialis,* XXXIX, p. 429. Women in Rome: on their devoutness, *Itin. cuiusdam Anglici,* III, pp. 440-1. Excluded from sanctuaries, see Capgrave, *Solace,* II. 4, 5, pp. 71, 77; Harff, *Pilgerfahrt,* pp. 16, 23; Wey, *Itineraries,* p. 143. Muffels, *Beschreibung,* p. 24; Tafur, *Andancas,* pp. 29-30.

372 'Some light-minded...': Jacques de Vitry, *Hist. Hierosolymitana,* LXXXII, p. 1097.
Itineraries: bibliography in Rohricht (1) supplemented, for the years after 1290, by Atiya, pp. 490-509. Quotations are from John of Wurzburg, *Descriptio,* praefact., pp. 109-10; Theoderic of Wurzburg, *De Locis Sanctis,* praefat., pp. 1-2.

373 Jacques de Vitry: See list of MSS in Rohricht (1), pp. 48-50. He was used, e.g., by Burchardt of Mt. Sion, *Descriptio,* VI, pp. 45-6.
Mandeville: on editions and MSS, Rohricht (1), pp. 79-85. Valuable introductions to the editions by M. C. Seymour, Oxford, 1967, and G. F. Warner, Roxburghe Club, London, 1889. On his sources, see A. Bovenschen, 'Untersuchungen über Johann von Mandeville und die Quelle seiner Reiserbeschreibung', *Zeitschrift der Gesellschaft für Erdkunde zu Berlin,* xxiii (1888), pt. iv, pp. 177-306.

374 Capgrave's models: *Solace,* p. 1.
Interest in Faber's account: *Evagatorium,* vol. iii, p. 467.
'Little Mandevilles': *Examination of William Thorpe,* p. 141. *Canterbury Tales,* II. 48-9, 463-8, pp. 2, 14.

375 Official arrangements for tourists: Heyd (consulates). Vincke (2), p. 263 (safe conduct of 1387: 'et ut patriae mores videant'). Rymer, *Foedera,* vol. xi, p. 686 (treaty of 1471).
Tourism criticized: *Fasciculi Zizaniorum,* ed. W. W. Shirley, *R.S.,* London, 1858, p. 270 (Wyclif). Affagart, *Rélation,* pp. 22-3. Brasca, *Viaggio,* p. 128.

376 Graffiti: Faber, *Evagatorium,* vol. i, p. 213, vol. ii, pp. 94-6. On Lannoy's graffiti, Van de Walle, pp. 123-5.
Souvenirs: *Quinze Joies,* VIII, pp. 69-70. Nompar de Caumont, *Voyaige,* pp. 136-9.

Postcards: Vergerio, *Ep.* LXXXVI, p. 216 (Rome). Faber, *Evagatorium,* vol. i, p. 329 (Breidenbach); there is a fine copy of the 1486 edition in the Bodleian Library, Oxford (Douce 223), with good early colouring; cf. Davies, where all the drawings are reproduced.

378   Faber's books: *Ibid.,* vol. i, pp. 62, 327-8.

Route-books: On Anglo-Saxon one of eleventh century, F. Liebermann, *Die Heiligen Englands,* Hannover, 1889, pp. 9-19. Also, Adam of Bremen, *Gesta Pontificum Hammaburgensium,* V. 1, ed. B. Schmeidler, *MGH. Rer. Germ.,* Leipzig, 1926, pp. 228-9; *Annales Stadenses, MGH. SS.* xvi. 340-4; *Pèlerinages por aler en Iherusalem,* A route to Rome is given by Matthew Paris, accompanied in some MSS by a map, see Brit. Mus. MS Royal 14 C. vii, fols. 2-5, reproduced in E-F. Jomard, *Les Monuments de la Géographie,* Paris, 1862, plates 39-41.

Indulgence-books: *Pélerinages et pardouns d'Acre.* On Roman indulgence-books, Hulbert.

Anonymous 'descriptions': Röhricht (1), pp. 28-9, 33, 35, 39-42, 45, 55, 665. John of Wurzburg, e.g., used *Innominatus VI,* see his *Descriptio,* III, pp. 117-19, and compare *Innominatus VI,* pp. 433-515.

Local guides: at Jerusalem, see Abel; Daniel, *Pèlerinage,* I, p. 5; John of Wursburg, *op. cit.,* VI, pp. 132-4. In Venice: Newett, pp. 40-41. On disbelief of guides' stories, Faber, *Evagatorium,* vol. i, pp. 330-7; Harff, *Pilgerfahrt,* pp. 16-17, 30.

379   Nobles at 1450 Jubilee: Pastor, vol. ii, pp. 91-3. Chastellain, *Le livre des faits de Jacques de Lalaing,* LXV-LXVI, in *Oeuvres,* ed. Kervyn de Lettenhove, vol. viii, Bruxelles, 1866, pp. 245-7. And in 1475: Pastor, vol. iv, pp. 280-2.

380   Royal pilgrimages to Virgin: Dickinson, pp. 33-45 (Walsingham). Carreras y Candi, pp. 341-56 (Montserrat). On Boulogne, Benoit.

Louis XI: See A. Gandilhon, 'Contribution à l'histoire de la vie privée de Louis XI', *Mémoires de la Soc. Historique, Littéraire, et Scientifique du Cher,* xx (1905), pp. 356, 362-3. P. Champion, *Louis XI,* vol. ii, Paris, 1927, pp. 204, 209-12.

Traditional ideals: Nompar de Caumont, *Voyaige,* pp. 18, 20.

Noble pilgrims disguised: Newett, pp. 65-6 (Venetian complaint). Affagart, *Rélation,* p. 4.

381   Earl Rivers robbed: *CPR. Letters,* vol. xiii, pp. 221-2.
Henry of Derby: Riant (ed.), 'Passage à Venise', pp. 238-40.
Toulmin Smith (ed.), *Accounts,* pp. 204-24.

382   Ferdinand of Aragon's nephew: Casola, *Pilgrimage,* p. 188.
Ernest of Saxony: Jacopo Gherardi da Volterra, *Diario Romano,*
ed. E. Carusi, *RISS* (2), xxiii (3), pp. 13-14. On his motives, see
R. Koetzchke and H. Kretzschmar, *Sachsiche Geschichte,* vol. i,
Dresden, 1935, p. 164.
Otto of Brunswick: see names of his attendants enrolled in
Liber Confraternitatis de Anima, p. 39.
Niccolo d'Este: Luchino del Campo, *Viaggio di Niccolo da Este,*
p. 105.

383   Dubbing of knights of St. John: Nompar de Caumont, *Voyaige,*
pp. 45, 49-51. On enrolment on return, Faber, *Evagatorium,* vol.
i, p. 42; see certificate granted to Peter Rindfleisch of Breslau in
1496, in his *Wallfahrt,* pp. 317-18.
Dubbing by non-hospitallers: Luchino, *Viaggio di Niccolo da
Este,* p. 125.
Guillaume de Châlons: E. Clerc, *Essai sur l'histoire de la Franche
Comté* vol. ii, Besancon, 1846, pp. 490-3.
Georg von Ehingen: see his *Reisen,* p. 11.

384   Faber's panegyric: *Evagatorium.* vol. ii, pp. 2-13.

15. The Later Middle Ages II

385   Nomadic missions: Delaruelle *et al.,* 636-56. On Bernardino in
Rome, Infessura, *Diario della citta di Roma,* ed. O. Tommasini,
Fonti, Rome, 1890, p. 25. On Orihuela, M-M. Gorce, *Saint
Vincent Ferrier 1350-1419,* Paris, 1924, pp. 174-6.

386   Datini: I. Origo, *The merchant of Prato,* London, 1957, pp. 306-
7, 311-19.

387   Spiritual revival: in general, Delaruelle *et al.,* pp. 605-7, 688-90,
828-9, 872-4, 878. On mass observances, P. de Félice, *Foules en
délire, extases collectives. Essai sur quelques formes inférieures de la
mystique,* Paris, 1947. On Flagellants, see *Disciplinati* (MW).
Priests never possessed: quoted in Delaruelle *et al.,* p. 872.

388   Sacchetti: *Ibid.,* p. 789.
Working-class saints: on peasant saints, G-A. Prevost, *L'Église et
les campagnes au moyen age,* Paris, 1892, pp. 272-80 (an idealized

picture). On St. Zita, *Aa. Ss.* April, vol. iii, pp. 497-8, 508; Dante, *Inferno,* XXI. 38. On Henry of Bolzano, *Aa. Ss.* June, vol. ii, pp. 375, 391.

Parish priests venerated: *Book of Margery Kempe,* I. 60, p. 147, Grandison, *Reg.,* pp. 1232-4. *Aa. Ss.* Oct., vol. viii, pp. 596-606 (Hélye). *Victoria history of the county of Buckingham,* vol. i, London, 1905, pp. 288-9 (Schorne).

389 Statues: *Lanterne of Light,* XII, p. 84. Burton, *Chron. Mon. Melsa,* vol. iii, pp. 35-6. On Boxley, *Letters and papers,* vol. iii (1), p. 284 (no. 754); G. Baskerville, *English monks and the suppression of the monasteries,* London, 1937, p. 22. On statue burned in 1538, *Letters and papers,* vol. xiii (1), p. 120 (no. 348). On the Rippingdale statue, Owen, p. 141.

391 Franciscans: on this complicated subject, see D. L. Douie, *The nature and effect of the heresy of the fraticelli,* Manchester, 1932. Gerson: See Delaruelle, *et al.,* pp. 855-7.

392 Flagellation: on early flagellation, J. Leclercq, 'La flagellazione volontaria nella tradizione spirituale dell' occidente', in *Disciplinati,* pp. 73-83. On Avignon incident of 1349, Cohn, pp. 140-1; Delaruelle (1), pp. 122-5; argument of Jean du Fayt, leader of the Parisian deputation, in A. Coville's notice in *Histoire littéraire de la France,* vol. xxxvii, Paris, 1938, pp. 403-4.

393 Revelations: Gerson's views in *De distinctione verarum revelationum ac falsis,* ed. Glorieux, vol. iii, pp. 36-56. On Bridget's revelations, Hefele, vol. vii, pp. 184-5. *Book of Margery Kempe,* I. 46-55, pp. 111-37, esp. I. 52, p. 125.

'Some men trowen...': *Select English works of John Wyclif,* ed. T. Arnold, vol. i, Oxford, 1869, pp. 329-30 (attributed). For Wyclif's views on pilgrimages, see *Sermones,* III. 1, 22, vol. ii., pp. 1, 164-5; *De Potestate papae,* XII, ed. J. Loserth, London, 1907, p. 329; *De Ecclesia,* II, XIX, pp. 44-5, 465.

394 Lollards: J. A. F. Thomson, *The later Lollards, 1414-1520,* pp. 28, 33, 34, 41, 44, 47, 56, 62, 69, 70, 78, 81, 104, 113, 126, 160, 184. For sixteenth-century pamphlets against St. Thomas, see list of proscribed books (1531) in F. J. Furnivall, *Political, religious, and love poems, EETS.,* O.S., xv, London, 1866, p. 62; Wright (ed.), *Letters,* p.6. On the official campaign against Becket's reputation in the 1530s, Elton, pp. 197, 257n[1].

Cult of saints attacked at Constance: Henry of Langenstein,

Consilium pacis de unione Ecclesiae, in H. von der Hardt, *Consilium Constantiense Oecumenicum,* vol. ii, Frankfurt, 1697, col. 56; cf. vol. iii (1698), cols. 30, 33, 35-6. Pierre d'Ailly, *De reformatione Ecclesiae in concilio Constantiensi,* III, in Gerson, *Opera,* ed. du Pin, vol ii, col. 911. Nicholas of Clamanges, *De novis celebritatibus non instituendis,* p. 153.

395 Gerson on miracles: *Contra impugnantes ordinis Carthusiensium,* ed. du Pin, vol. ii, cols. 711-14.

Attempt to suppress unproven miracles: *The rolls and register of bishop Oliver Sutton,* ed. R. M. T. Hill, vol. v (Lincoln Record Soc., 1x), Hereford, 1965, pp. 143-3; vol. vi (*ibid.,* lxiv), Hereford, 1969, pp. 103-4, 186-7, Grandison, *Reg.,* pp. 941-2.

396 Nicholas of Clamanges on miracles: *Ep.* LXI, p. 175.

John of Trittenheim on miracles: *De Mirac. B. V. M. Helbrunnensis,* I. 3, II. 1, pp. 1136-9, 1158.

397 Legend of Theophilus: principal text in C. Neuhaus, *Adgars Marienlegenden,* Heilbronn, 1886, pp. 79-115. On its dissemination, H. Lundgren, *Studier över Theophiluslegendens romanska varianter,* Uppsala, 1913; Beissel (2), pp. 97-9; introduction to Ruteboeuf, *Le miracle de Théophile,* ed. G. Frank, Paris, 1969, pp. xii-xiv; E. Mâle, *Religious art in France of the thirteenth century,* tr. D. Nussey, London, 1913, pp. 260-1.

398 'Tu mater es…': U. Chevalier, *Poésies liturgiques traditionelle de l'Eglise catholique en occident,* Tournai, 1893, p. 134.

'Mother of mercy' in early miracle stories: Kjellman (ed.), *Miracles de la Vierge,* VIII, XI, XIII, LI, pp. 27-30, 44-5, 60-1, 219-20. Monk inscribed among elect: Étienne de Bourbon, *Anecdotes,* II. 139, pp. 119-20. On dates and origins, Southern.

399 Gambler enriched: Jacques de Vitry, *Exempla,* CCXCVI, pp. 124-5.

'Only one thing…': Etienne de Bourbon, *Anecdotes,* II. 117, p. 101.

Essones: Suger, *De Administratione sua,* XX, pp. 177-82.

400 Ergotism: see above, p. 107.

'Building crusades': on Chartres (1145), see Robert of Torigny, *Chron.,* vol. i, pp. 238-9; letter of Hugh, archbishop of Rouen, in *RHF.* xiv. 319. On S. Pierre-sur-Dive, Haimoin, *Lettre,* esp. I-IV, pp. 121-5. On Chartres (post 1194). *Mirac. S. Mariae Carnotensis,* III-V, IX-X, pp. 514-17, 521-2.

401 Procession at Issigny: *Mirac. Eccl. Constantiensis,* VI, pp. 370-2.
Statues of Virgin: *Ibid.,* praefat., XIV, pp. 367-8, 376 (Coutances).
DHGE., vol. xii, col. 551 (Chartres). *Visio monachi,* XLVII, p. 304
(Eynsham dream). On the black Virgin of Rocamadour, which
still survives, see Rupin, pp. 114, 291. On that of Le Puy, which
is known from drawings, A. Chassaing, *Chroniques d'Étienne
Medicis,* vol. i, Le Puy, 1869, p. 29n.; *Chron. Lemovicense, RHF* xxi,
768 (disaster of 1255), cf. *GC.,* vol. ii, p. 716.

402 Fitzralph's sermon: Owst, pp. 140-1.
Abrupt origins of pilgrimages to statues: *Mirac. B. V. M. in
Beverne,* in *Anecdota Gielemans,* III. 3, pp. 102-3. *De Imagine B. V.
M. in sabulo Bruxellensi,* in *ibid.,* III. 14, p. 363 (Antwerp statue
repainted). *Chartulary of Bridlington,* pp. 448-9 (Kernetby).
Concilia Magnae Britaniae, ed. D. Wilkins, vol. ii, London, 1737,
pp. 423-4 (Foston). John of Trittenheim, *De Mirac. B. V. M. prope
Dietelbach,* I. 6, p. 1084 (Trier). John of Trittenheim, *De Mirac.
B. V. M. Helbrunnensis,* II. 2-4, pp. 1160-2.

403 Legends follow: *DHGE.,* vol. x, cols. 92-4 (Boulogne).
Toussaert, pp. 269-70 (Rozebeke). Misset, pp. 6, 43 (l'Épine).
Wurzburg sanctuaries: John of Trittenheim, *De Mirac. B. V. M.
prope Dietelbach,* I. 6, 8, pp. 1083, 1087-8.

404 'Simple people of Christ': *Ibid.,* I. 9, 12, pp. 1091-2, 1097.
Walsingham offerings: Savine, p. 103. Wright (ed.), *Letters,*
p. 138.
Buxton and Cardigan: Wright, *op. cit.,* pp. 143, 186.

405 Gregory VII: *Reg.,* VIII, 21, p. 559.
St. Charlemagne: see R. Folz, *Études sur le culte liturgique de
Charlemagne dans les eglises de l'Empire,* Paris, 1951.
St. Canute: *Aa. Ss.* July, vol. iii, pp. 118-49. Kemp, pp. 69-70.
St. Leger: *DACL.,* vol viii, cols. 2487-93. Guibert, *De Vita sua,*
III. 20, pp. 231-2.

406 Thomas of Lancaster: J. R. Madicott, *Thomas of Lancaster, 1307-
1322,* Oxford, 1970, pp. 329-30.

407 Edward II: *The diplomatic correspondance of Richard II,* ed. E.
Perroy, Camden Soc., 3rd. series, vol. xlviii, London, 1933, pp.
62-3 (no. 95). E. Perroy, *L'Angleterre et le grand schisme d'occident,*
Paris, 1933, pp. 330, 341-2.
Simon de Montfort: Stubbs, *Charters,* p. 409 (dictum of
Kenilworth). *Mirac. Simonis de Montford,* ed. J. O. Halliwell,

Camden Soc., O.S., vol. xv, London, 1840, pp. 67-110, esp. pp. 83-4.

Crowds at Gloucester: *Hist. mon. S. Petri Gloucestriae,* ed. W. H. Hart, vol. i, *R.S.,* London, 1863, pp. 44-5, 46.

408 Wilsnack legend: oldest (15th-cent.) version ed. P. Heitz and W. L. Schreiber, *Das Wunderblut zu Wilsnack,* Strassburg, 1904, pp. 8-9.

'Sought from many a country…': *Book of Margery Kempe,* II. 4, p. 232. Wilsnack was popular with English pilgrims, see *Lit. Cant.,* vol. iii, pp. 191-2; *Testamenta vetusta,* vol. i, p. 196.

Indulgences of 1384: Riedel (OS), pp. 140-3.

Mass-pilgrimage of 1387: Riddageshus, *Chron.,* ed. G. W. Liebnitz, *Scriptures rerum Brunswicensium,* vol. ii, Hannover, 1710, p. 81.

409 Wilsnack investigated: *Concilia Pragensia, 1353-1413,* ed. C. Höfler, Prague, 1862, p. 47. *Concilia Germaniae,* ed. J. F. Hartzheim, vol. v, Köln, 1763, pp. 35-6 (Magdeburg).

Disputes of 1446-51: indulgence of 1446 in Riedel (OS), pp. 149-51. Report in Breest, pp. 297-300. Citizens' complaint in Riedel (OS), pp. 144-5. Bull of 1451 in *ibid.,* pp. 152-6.

410 Children at Wilsnack: in 1475, Stolle, *Chron.,* pp. 376-9. In 1487 and after, Matthias Doring, *Chron.,* in F. A. Riedel, *Codex diplomaticus Brandenburgensis,* vol. iv. (1), Berlin, 1862, p. 248.

411 'And men knew not…': Stolle, *Chron.,* pp. 377-8

Child-pilgrims to Wilsnack criticized: pamphlet *On foolish people* in Wattenback (ed.), 'Beiträge', pp. 605-7. Erfurt Augustinian in *ibid.,* pp. 607-8. *Das Tagebuch des Rathmeisters Marcus Spickendorff,* ed. J. O. Opel, Halle, 1872, p. 19.

412 Hosts burned: Kaweran, p. 350.

Children at S. Pierre-sur-Dive: Haimoin, *Lettre,* II, pp. 122-3. On children in popular religion, Alphandéry, vol. ii, pp. 135-48.

Children's crusade: Alphandéry, vol. ii, pp. 115-35.

'Many people…': *Annales Marbacenses,* p. 82.

413 Children at Mont-St.-Michel in 1333: Huynes, vol. i, pp. 98-114. On the *pastoureaux* of 1320, see Cohn, pp. 102-4.

In 1393 and 1441-2: Chomel, pp. 230-9.

414 In 1457: Jacques de Clercq, *Mémoires (1448-67),* ed. A. Reiffenberg, vol. ii, Brussels, 1823, p. 276; John of Trittenheim, *Annales,* vol. ii, p. 431; Huynes, vol. i, pp. 123-7; Ekkehart Artzt,

Chron. Weissenburgense, ed. C. Hoffman, *Quellen und Erörterungen zur bayerischen und deutschen Geschichte,* vol. ii, Munchen, 1862, pp. 147-8. On the children in Regensburg, Dupont (2), pp. 26-7. On hostile pamphlets, Delisle (2), p. 392.

Children at Monte Gargano: Haupt, pp. 673-4.

415 Nicklashausen: John of Trittenheim, *Annales,* vol. ii, pp. 486-91. Stolle, *Chron.,* pp. 380-3. Lorenz Fries, *Historie der Bischoffen zu Wurzburg,* Frankfurt, 1713, pp. 852-4. Documents in Barack (OS), pp. 50-2 (early history of statue), 53-4 (report of bishop's informer), 59, 66-79, 97-100 (prohibitions, interdict), 104-5 (destruction of church).

417 'Simple unlettered folk...': John of Trittenheim, *Mirac. B. V. M. prope Dietelbach,* I. 6, pp. 1083-4.

16. Mediaeval Christianity

418 Latimer on Hailes: *Sermons and remains,* ed. G. E. Corrie, Parker Soc., iii, London, 1844-5, vol. ii, p. 364.

Conc. Châlons: *MC.* xiv. 96. Cf. Boniface, *Ep.* L, pp. 83-5.

419 Licence to sin: Langland, *Piers Plowman,* B. prol. 46-52, p. 3. Poitevin author quoted in E. Ginot, *Dix siècles de pèlerinage à Compostelle. Les chemins de Saint-Jacques en Poitou,* Poitiers, 1912, p. 40.

Criticized by moral reformers: Berthold, *Predigten,* XXVIII, vol. i, pp. 459-60. A. Franz (ed.), *Drei deutscher Minoriten-prediger aus dem 13 und 14 Jahrhundert,* Freiburg i. B., 1907, p. 69 ('did any of you try...'). Giordano da Rivalto, *Prediche inedite,* Bologna, 1867, p. 109; cf. *Prediche recitate in Firenze dal MCCCIII al MCCCVI,* vol. i, Firenze, 1831, pp. 252-3. See also Samouillan, pp. 306-8.

Langland: *Piers Plowman,* B.V. 57-8, 514-612, pp. 57-8, 85-9.

420 Gascoigne on indulgences: *Loci e libro veritatum,* ed. J. E. Thorold Rogers, Oxford, 1881, p. 123.

421 Petitions from French churches: collected in Denifle, vol. i.

Sale of crusading indulgence: *Hist. Compostellana,* II. 78, p. 429 (synod of 1125); William of Newbugh, *Hist. rerum Angelicanum,* III. 24, ed. R. Howlett, *Chronicles of the reigns of Stephen, Henry II, and Richard I, R.S.,* vol. i, London, 1884, pp. 274-5. On commutation of vows, see above, ch. IX. On sale of Roman Jubilee indulgence, see above, ch. XIII.

422 Sale of right to commute vows: *CPR. Letters,* vol. v, pp. 548-9 (Mattersley), but it was almost immediately cancelled, *ibid.,* p. 549. *Lit. Cant.,* vol. iii, p. 255 (no. 1064) (Canterbury in 1470). Sale of dispensations for Rome, Santiago, etc.: Walsingham, *Hist. Anglicana,* ed. H. T. Riley, *RS.,* London, 1863-4, vol. i, p. 452. Arch.Vat. Reg.Vat. 347, fols. 132-4 (Germany, 1390). Arch. Vat. Reg.Vat. 313, fol 48 (Castile, 1391).

Price of dispensation: E. Göller, "Die Einnahmen der apostolischen Kammer unter Johann XXII', *Görres-Gesellschaft. Verbindung mit ihrem historischen Institut in Rom,* vol. i, Paderborn, 1910, pp. 353, 361 (prices in 1330-1). L. Célier, *Les dataires du xv*^{e} *siècle et les origines de la daterie apostolique,* BEFAR, ciii, Paris 1910, p. 153 (late 15th. cent.). *Letters and papers illustrative of the reigns of Richard III and Henry VII,* ed. J. Gairdner, *RS.,* vol. ii, London, 1863, pp. 97-8.

423 Indulgences *ad instar:* S. Mancherini, *Codice diplomatico della Verna e delle SS. Stigmate,* Firenze, 1924, pp. 64-8 (no. 48). A Mercati, 'Indulgenze della Porzioncola e della Verna concesse fuori dell'ordine francescano', *Archivum franciscanum historicum,* xliii (1950), pp. 337-59. *CPR. Letters,* vol. iv, p. 349, and see index s.v. 'Indulgences; of the Portiuncula'. On indulgences *ad instar* those of St. Mark's see, e.g., Jansen, p. 165 (Meissen, Erfurt, Paderborn, Benedictsbeuren, Bamberg); *CPR. Letters,* vol. v, pp. 384, 489, 590 (Bromholm, etc.).

Withdrawn in 1402: T. van Ottenthal, *Regulae cancellariae apostolicae,* Innsbruck, 1888, p. 76.

424 Not granted thereafter: This conclusion is based on papal bulls relating to England, the only ones which have been systematically calendared. Two of Boniface's indulgences *ad instar* were confirmed by his successors in 1409 and 1411. *CPR. Letters,* vol. vi, pp. 151, 295. On St. Nicholas of Calais, *ibid.,* vol. xiii, pp. 448-9. Effect: *Journal d'un bourgeois,* p. 384. *CJC., Extrav. Comm.,* V. ix. 4, vol. ii, cols. 1307-8 (bull of 1473).

425 Franciscans accused: See, e.g., Simon of Cremona, *De indulgentiis Portiunculae,* I, pp. 87-8.

Cologne indulgence: Jansen, pp. 152-4.

Unauthorized Jubilees: Jean Juvenel des Ursins, *Hist. de Charles*

VI, in *Mémoires pour servir à l'histoire de France*, vol. ii, Paris, 1836, p. 442 (Le Puy). *Traité sur le cinquième jubilé de S. Thomas*, I. 1, 4, III. 1-2, 5, pp. 119, 121-2, 140, 142.

Pardoners in Spain: J. Goñi Gaztambide, "Los cuestores en España', *Hispania Sacra*, ii (1949), pp. 1-43, 285-310. In England: Jusserand, pp. 175-91; Chichele, *Reg.*, vol. iii, pp. 92-3, 100-1. Council of Vienne: decree on pardoners in *CJC.*, *Clem.*, V. ix. 2, vol. ii, cols. 1190-1.

426   Forged bull of 1350: see above, p. 240.

Bulls displayed: Langland, *Piers Plowman*, B. prol. 69, p. 4. Bartolus, *Tractatus*, XVIII, pp. 37-9 (Slavs at Ancona). Cf. Chaucer, *Canterbury Tales*, Pardoner's tale, ll. 7-16, p. 301.

Totiens quoties: Paulus (2), vol. i, p. 344. In Rome: Capgrave, *Solace*, II. I, p. 63; Muffel, *Beschreibung*, p. 19.

Council of Constance: Hefele, vol. vii, pp. 503, 548.

427   Boniface criticized: Gobelinus Persona, *Cosmidromius*, ed. M. Jansen, Munster, 1900, pp. 144-6. Neuss chronicler quoted in Fredericq (ed.), *Codex*, p. 22.

Canterbury petition: Foréville, p. 191 (P. J. XXX).

428   Indulgences transferable: *Liber exemplorum ad usum praedicantium*, ed. A. G. Little, Aberdeen, 1908, pp. 98-9 (Ulsterman). Bartolus, *Tractatus*, XXIX, pp. 57-8.

Theory of indulgence for dead: Paulus (2), vol. ii, pps. 160-72. On crusading preachers, Conrad of Ursperg, *Chron.*, *MGH. SS.* xxiii. 379.

429   Offered at Portiuncula: Bartolus, *Tractatus*, XXI, XXIV, pp. 42-3, 45-7; cf. XXII, XXV-XXVI, XXXI-XXXIII, pp. 43-4, 45-54, 61-5.

430   And elsewhere: Bridget, *Rev.*, VII. 14, p. 550 (Jerusalem). Philip, *Liber de Terra Sancta (1377)*, pp. 522, 524 (Rome).

Pilgrimages ordered in English wills: *Testamenta vetusta*, vol. i, p. 51 (William de Beauchamp). Sharpe, *Calendar of wills*, vol. i, pp. 454, 640-1, 664, 479, vol. ii, pp. 41, 163, 234, 335, etc. Chichele, *Reg.*, vol. ii, pp. 74, 488 (Thomas of Arundel, Thomas Poulton); cf. pp. 104, 124, 385, 485, 539. *CPR. Letters*, vol. iv, pp. 388-9 (Fryng). Gibbons (ed.), *Early Lincoln wills*, p. 29 ('Roger, my grandson...').

431   And in foreign wills: 'Testaments enregistrées au Parlement de Paris dans le règne de Charles VI', ed. A. Tuetey, in *Collection de documents inédits sur l'histoire de France, Mélanges historiques*, vol.

iii, Paris, 1880, pp. 464, 496, 526, 556-7, 571-2, 577, 588, 622-3, 638. Pastor, vol. iv. p. 150n. (Pressburg). See also Vazquez de Parga *et al.,* vol. i, pp. 120-1; *Cartulaire de N-D. de Boulogne,* pp. 196-7 (nos. 117, 119).
Papal indulgences for dead: Alonso de Palencia, *Crónica de Enrique IV,* ed. A. Paz y Melia, *Collección de escritores Castellanos,* cxxvi, vol. i, Madrid, 1904, pp. 164, 219-21 (crusading indulgence of 1457). Lea (1), vol. iii, p. 593 (Tarragona). Paulus (2), vol. ii, pp. 381-2 (Franciscans). *Archives historiques de la Saintonge et de l'Aunis,* x (1882), pp. 56-69 (Saintes).

432 Vicarious pilgrimages (12th. cent.): William, *Mirac. S. Thomae,* II. 20, p. 177 (Ralph). Thomas of Monmouth, *Mirac. S. Willelmi,* IV. 5, p. 170. Benedict, *Mirac. S. Thomae,* III. 58, p. 158 (nun).

433 Cressewyc: *CPR. Letters,* vol. iv, p. 389. Cf. Gibbons, *Early Lincoln wills,* p. 62
Isabel of Bavaria: Jean Chartier, *Chronique de Charles VII,* ed. Vallet de Viriville, Paris, 1858, pp. 276, 279, 284; Forgeais, *Plombs historiés,* vol. iii, p. 202 (Avallon). On her unusual piety, see Perdrizet, p. 126.
No pilgrim, alternative disposition: e.g. Sharpe, *Calendar of wills,* vol. i, p. 657.
'Of honest condition': e.g. *Testamenta vetusta,* vol. i, p. 68; Sharpe, *Calendar of wills,* vol. ii, p. 41.
John of Brittany: H. Morice (ed.), *Mémoires pour servir de preuves à l'histoire de Bretagne,* vol. ii, Paris, 1744, col. 1068.

434 Scandinavian professionals: Riant (3), p. 381.
Bishop of Lincoln: *Book of Margery Kempe,* I. 15, p. 36.
Flagellation and Jubilee: Giles li Muisis, *Chron.,* pp. 353, 361 (flagellant preachers). P. Fredericq, 'Deux sermons inédits de Jean du Fayt', *Académie Royale de Belgique, Bulletin de la classe des lettres* (1903), p. 700. See Delaruelle (1), pp. 141-3.

435 Deguileville: *Le pèlerinage de la vie humaine,* ed. J. J. Sturzinger, Roxburghe Club, London, 1893.
Used as argument against all external observances: *Lanterne of light,* XII, pp. 85-7. *Examination of William Thorpe,* p. 138. Similar opinions were expressed by Sir John Oldcastle at his trial, Rymer, *Foedera,* vol. ix, p. 63. On the condemnation of the *Lanterne,* Chichele, *Reg.,* vol. iv, pp. 134-7
Gerson on pilgrimage of life: *Super quotidiano peregrini testa-*

mento, ed. Glorieux, vol. viii, pp. 5-9. On the popularity of this work, M. Lieberman, 'Chronologie Gersonienne', *Romania,* lxxxi (1960), pp. 359-60.

436 St.-Trond MS: ed. A. van d. Wyngaert, 'Een merkwardige Nederlandsche kruiswegoefening uit de xve eeuw', *Ons geestlijk Erf,* ii (1928), pp. 10-41; xii (1933), pp. 322-4.

Oxford tract of 1423: Latin version in Gerson (wrongly attributed), *Opera,* ed. du Pin, vol. ii, cols. 523-4. French version, ed. E. Vansteenberghe, "Pèlerinage spirituelle', *Revue des sciences religieuses,* xiv (1934), pp. 387-91. On its origin and date, I follow M. Lieberman, 'Gersoniana', *Romania,* lxxviii (1957), pp. 158-66.

Geiler: *Christlichen Bilgerschaften zum ewigen Vatterland,* Basel, 1513, fol. 2006vo.

437 Erasmus: *Peregrinatio religiosa,* col. 787.

Jan van Paesschen: *Een devote maniere om gheestelyck pilgrimagie,* Louvain, 1563. On editions and translations, see Brit. Mus. *Catalogue of printed books,* and editions listed in catalogue of Bodleian Library, Oxford and Bibl. Nat., Paris. These are probably by no means complete.

Reformation said to have killed pilgrimage: Erasmus, *Peregrinatio religiosa,* cols. 774-5. Affagart, *Rélation,* pp. 20-1.

438 Mediaeval survivals in Protestant societies: see Thomas.

Bibliography

This is not a complete bibliography of mediaeval religion, but a guide to the sources used in this book. Other works will be found in the annual bibliographies produced by the *Revue d'Histoire Ecclesiastique*, and in the following specialized bibliographies:

BEAUNIER, and BESSE, J. M. *Recueil historique des archevêchés, évêchés, abbayes, et prieurés de France, Archives de la France Monastique*, vols. I, IV, VII, X, XII, XIV, XV, XVII, XIX, XXXVI, XXXVII, XLV, n.e., 12 vols., Namur, 1905–41.

Bibliotheca Hagiographica Latina. Brussels, 1898–9.

COTTINEAU, L. H. *Répertoire topo-bibliographique des abbayes et prieurés*, 2nd. ed., 2 vols. Mâcon, 1935–7.

JAFFÉ, P. and WATTENBACH, W. *Regesta Pontificum Romanorum*, 2 vols., 2nd. ed., Leipzig, 1885–8.

KOHLER, C. *Rerum et personarum quae in Actis Sanctorum Bollandianis obviae at orientem latinum spectant index analyticus, ROL., v* (1897), pp. 460-561.

LECLERCQ, H. 'Pèlerinage à Rome', *DACL.*, vol. xiv, cols. 40-65.

LECLERCQ, H. 'Pèlerinages aux Lieux Saints', *DACL.*, vol. xiv, cols. 65-176.

RIANT, P. 'Inventaire sommaire des manuscrits rélatifs à l'histoire et à la géographie de l'orient', *AOL.*, ii (1884), pp. 131-204.

RÖHRICHT, R. (1). *Bibliotheca Geographica Palestinae*, Berlin, 1890.

RÖHRICHT, R. (2). *Die Deutschen im heiligen Lände*, Innsbruck, 1894.

RÖHRICHT, R. (3). *Deutsche Pilgerreisen nach dem heiligen Lände,* Gotha, 1889.

ORIGINAL SOURCES

ADAM, abbot of Eynsham. *Magna Vita S. Hugonis,* ed. D. L. Douie and H. Farmer, 2 vols., London, 1961–2.

ADAM OF USK. *Chronicon,* ed. E. M. Thompson, 2nd. ed., London, 1904.

ADAMNAN, abbot of Iona. *De Locis Sanctis, G. Itin.,* pp. 221-97.

ADÉMAR DE CHABANNES. *Chronique,* ed. J. Chavanon, Paris, 1897.

AFFAGART, GREFFIN. *Rélation de Terre Sainte (1533–1534),* ed. J. Chavanon, Paris, 1902.

AIMON. *Vita S. Abbonis, PL.* cxxxix. 375-414.

ALBERIC OF ROSATE. *Dictionarium Iuris tam civilis quam canonici,* Venice, 1611.

ALBERT OF AIX. *Historia Hierosolymitana, RHC. Occ.,* iv. 265-713.

ALEXANDER III, pope. *Epistolae et privilegia, PL.* cc.

ALFONSO IX, king of Castile. *Las siete partidas de las leyes del sabio don Alonso el nono,* ed. G. Lopez de Touar, 9 parts, Madrid, 1610–11.

ALFONSO X, king of Castile. *Cantigas de S. Maria,* ed. Mqs. de Valmar, 2 vols., Madrid, 1889.

AMORT, E. *De origine, progressu, valore, ac fructu indulgentiarum,* 2 vols., Augsburg, 1735.

Anecdota Gielemans: Anecdota ex codicis hagiographicis Johannis Gielemans, Bruxelles, 1895.

Anglo-Saxon Chronicle. ed. D. Whitelock, D. C. Douglas, and S. I. Tucker, London, 1961.

Annales Altahenses Maiores, ed. W. Giesebrecht and L. B. Oefele, *MGH. Rer. Germ.,* Hannover, 1891.

Annales Regni Francorum. ed. G. H. Pertz and F. Kurze, *MGH. Rer. Germ.,* Hannover, 1895.

ANTENORIS. *Vita S. Silvini, episcopi Alciaci, Aa. Ss.* Feb., vol. iii, pp. 29-32.

ANTONINUS OF PLACENTIA. *Itinerarium, G. Itin.,* pp. 159-218.

AQUINAS, THOMAS, ST. *Opera Omnia,* 15 vols., Rome, 1882–1930.

Archives de Bruges: Inventaire des archives de la ville de Bruges, Section pre-mière: Inventaire des chartes, ed. L. Gillodts-Van Severen, 9 vols., Bruges, 1871–85.

ARNOLD OF LUBECK. *Chronica Slavorum*, ed. I. M. Lappenberg, *MGH. Rer. Germ.*, Hannover, 1868.

ARNOLD T. (ed.). *Memorials of St. Edmund's Abbey*, 3 vols., *RS.*, London, 1890–6.

AUGUSTINE OF HIPPO, ST. *De Civitate Dei*, ed. E. Hoffman, *CSEL.* xl. 2 vols., Vienna, 1899–1900.

AUGUSTINE OF HIPPO, ST. *De cura pro mortuis gerenda*, ed. J. Zycha, *CSEL.* xli, Vienna, 1900.

AUGUSTINE OF HIPPO, ST. *Epistolae*, ed. A. Goldbacher, *CSEL.* xxxiv, xliv, xlvii, 4 vols., Vienna, 1895–1923.

AUGUSTINE OF HIPPO, ST. *Sermones, PL.* xxxviii-xxxix.

BALUZE, S. (ed.). *Vitae paparum Avinionensium*, n.e., ed. G. Mollat, 4 vols., Paris, 1916–28.

BARACK, K. A. (ed.). 'Hans Böhm und die Wallfahrt nach Nicklashausen im Jahre 1476', *Archiv des historischen Vereines von Unterfranken und Aschaffenburg*, xiv (3) (1858), pp. 1-108.

BARAUT, C. (ed.). 'Textos homilectics i dvots del *Libre Vermell* de Montserrat', *Analecta Sacra Tarraconensia*, xxviii (1955), pp. 25-44.

BARTOLUS, FRANCIS, friar of Assisi. *Tractatus de indulgentia S. Mariae de Portiuncula*, ed. P. Sabatier, *Collection d'études et de documents sur l'histoire religieuse et littéraire du moyen age*, iii, Paris, 1900.

BEAUMANOIR, PHILIPPE DE REMI, SIRE DE. *Coutumes de Beauvaisis*, ed. A. Salmon, 2 vols., Paris, 1899–1900.

Becket Materials: Materials for the history of Thomas Becket, archbishop of Canterbury, 7 vols., *RS.*, London, 1875–85.

BEDE. *Ecclesiastical history of the English people*, ed. B. Colgrave and R. A. B. Mynors, Oxford, 1969.

BEDE. *De Locis Sanctis, G. Itin.*, pp. 301-24.

BEDE. *Vita S. Cuthberti*, ed. B. Colgrave, *Two lives of St. Cuthbert*, Cambridge, 1940

BELLORINI, T. and HOADE, E. (ed.). *Visit to the Holy Places of Egypt, Sinai, Palestine, and Syria, in 1384, by Frescobaldi, Gucci, and*

Sigoli, Publications of the Studium Biblicum Franciscanum, no. 6, Jerusalem, 1948.

'BENEDICT' (i.e. ROGER OF HOWDEN). *Gesta regis Henrici Secundi,* ed. W. Stubbs, 2 vols., *RS.,* London, 1867.

BENEDICT, canon of St. Peter's, Rome. *Liber Politicus,* in *Liber Censuum, ed. cit.,* vol. ii, pp. 139-77.

BENEDICT OF PETERBOROUGH. *Miracula S. Thomae Cantuariensis, Becket Materials,* vol. ii, pp. 21-281.

BENINCASA. *Vita S. Rayneri Pisani, Aa. Ss.* June, vol. iii, pp. 423-66.

BERNARD. *Itinerarium Bernardi monachi Franci, TM. Itin.,* vol. i, pp. 307-20.

BERNARD OF CLAIRVAUX, ST. *Epistolae, PL.* clxxxii.

BERTHOLD OF REGENSBURG. *Predigten,* ed. F. Pfeiffer, 2 vols., Vienna, 1862–1880.

BERTRANDON DE LA BROQUIÈRE, *Voyage d'outremer,* ed. C. Schefer, *Recueil de voyages et de documents pour servir à l'histoire de la géographie,* xii, Paris, 1892.

Bibliotheca Cluniacensis. ed. M. Marrier, Paris, 1614.

BIELER, L. (ed.) *The Irish penitentials, Scriptores Latini Hiberniae,* v, Dublin, 1963.

Black Book of the Admiralty. ed. T. Twiss, 4 vols. *RS.,* London, 1871–6.

BONDURAND, M. (ed.). 'Détresse de l'abbaye de St.-Gilles pendant le schisme d'occident (1417)', *BHP.* (1899), pp. 435-45.

BONIFACE VIII, pope. *Régistres,* ed. A. Thomas, G. Digard, M. Faucon, *et al., BEFAR.,* 2nd. series, vol. iv, 4 vols., Paris, 1884–1939.

BONIFACE and LULLUS. *Briefe,* ed. M. Tangl, *MGH. Epp. Sel.* i, Berlin, 1916.

Book of Margery Kempe, ed. S. B. Meech and H. B. Allen, *EETS.,* O.S., vol. 212, Oxford, 1940.

BRASCA, SANTO. *Viaggio in Terra Santa, 1480,* ed. A. L. Momigliano Lepschy, Milan, 1966.

BREWYN, WILLIAM. *A XVth. century guide-book to the principal churches of Rome,* ed. C. E. Woodruff, London, 1933.

BREYDENBACH, BERNARD VON. *Reiseinstruction, RM. Pilg.,* pp. 120-45.

BREYDENBACH, BERNARD VON. *Sanctarum peregrinationum in Montem Syon, ad venerandum Christi Sepulchrum in Jerusalem, et in Montem Sinai,* Mainz, 1486.

BRIDGET OF SWEDEN, ST. *Revelationes,* ed. C. Durant, Antwerp, 1611.

BRYGG, THOMAS. *Itinerarium in Terram Sanctam domini Thomae de Swynburne,* ed. P. Riant, *AOL., ii* (1884), pp. 378-88 (documents).

BUCCIO DI RANALLO. *Cronaca Aquilana rimata,* ed. V. de Bartholomaeis, *Fonti,* Rome, 1907.

Bull. Dipl.: Bullarium, diplomatum, et privilegium sanctorum Romanorum pontificum, ed. S. Franco and H. Dalmezzo, 23 vols., Turin, 1857-72.

Bull. Vat.: Collectio bullarum sacrosanctae basilicae Vaticanae, 3 vols., Rome, 1747–52.

BURCHARD OF MOUNT SION. *Descriptio Terrae Sanctae, L. Peregr.,* pp. 3-100.

BURTON, THOMAS. *Chronica monasterii de Melsa,* ed. E. A. Bond, 3 vols., *RS.,* London, 1866–8.

CAESARIUS OF HEISTERBACH. *Dialogus miraculorum,* ed. J. Strange, 2 vols., Cologne, 1851.

CAPGRAVE, JOHN. *Ye Solace of pilgrimes. A description of Rome, circa A.D. 1450,* ed. C. A. Mills and H. M. Bannister, London, 1911.

Capitula de miraculis et translationibus S. Cuthberti, in Symeon of Durham, *Opera Omnia, ed. cit.*

Capitularia Regum Francorum, ed. A. Boretius and V. Krause, *MGH. Leges,* sect. ii, 2 vols., Hannover, 1881–97.

CAPODILISTA, GABRIELE. *Itinerario in Terra Santa,* in Brasca, *op. cit.,* pp. 159-237.

Carmen de translatione S. Bartholomaei. ed. B. Sepp, *Neues Archiv der Gesellschaft für ältere deutsche Geschichtskunde,* xxii (1896), pp. 571-5.

Cartulaires du châpitre de l'église metropolitaine Sainte-Marie d'Auch. ed. C. Lacave la Plagne Barris, *Archives Historiques de la Gascogne,* ser. ii, fascs. iii-iv, Paris, 1899.

Cartulaire de l'église abbatiale Notre-Dame de Boulogne-sur-Mer, 1067-1567. ed. D. Haigneré, *Memoires de la Soc. Académique de Boulogne-sur-Mer,* xiii (1882-6), pp. 89-360.

Cartulaire du prieuré de La Charité-sur-Loire. ed. R. de Lespinasse, Nevers, 1887.

Cartulaire de l'abbaye de Conques en Rouergue. ed. G. Desjardins, Paris, 1879.

Cartulaire de l'abbaye cardinale de la Trinite de Vendôme. ed. C. Metais, 5 vols., Paris, 1893–1900.

CASOLA, PIETRO. *Canon Pietro Casola's pilgrimage to Jerusalem in the year 1494,* tr. M. M. Newett, Manchester, 1907.

CHARLIER, GILLES. *Oratio in concilio Basileensi de corrigendis peccatis publicis,* in H. Canisius and J. Basnage, *Thesaurus monumentorum ecclesiasticorum et historicorum,* vol. iv, Antwerp, 1725, pp. 566-627.

Chartes de Cluny: Recueil des chartes de l'abbaye de Cluny, ed. A. Bernard and A. Bruel, 6 vols., Paris, 1876–1903.

Chartes de Namum: Inventaire des chartes des contes de Namur, ed. C. Piot, Brussels, 1890.

Chartulary of Bridlington priory. ed. W. T. Lancaster, Leeds, 1912.

CHAUCER, GEOFFREY. *The Canterbury Tales,* in *Complete Works,* ed. W. W. Skeat, vol. iv, Oxford, 1894.

CHICHELE, HENRY, archbishop of Canterbury. *The Register of Henry Chichele, archbishop of Canterbury, 1414–43,* ed. E. F. Jacob, Canterbury and York Society, xlv, 4 vols., Oxford, 1937–47.

Chronicon abbatiae de Evesham ad annum 1418. ed. W. D. Macray, *RS.,* London, 1863.

Chronica monasterii Casinensis. MGH. SS. vii. 551-844.

CLAES VAN DUSEN. *Waerachtighe Beschrijvinge der steden ende Plaetsen geleghen op den Wegh van Venetien na den H. Lande ende Jerusalem,* in Conrady (ed.), *Rheinische Pilgerschriften,* pp. 182-301.

CLEMENT VI, pope. *Lettres closes, patentes, et curiales se rapportant à la France,* ed. E. Déprez, *BEFAR.,* 3rd. series, vol. iii, 3 vols., Paris, 1901–61.

CLEMENT VI, pope. *Lettres closes, patentes, et curiales interessant les pays autres que la France,* ed. E. Déprez and G. Mollat, *BEFAR.,* Paris, 1960–1.

CONRADY, L. (ed.). *Vier rheinische Palaestina-Pilgerschriften des xiv, xv, und xvi Jahrhunderts,* Wiesbaden, 1882.

Coutumes du Namur et Coutume de Philippeville. ed. J. Grandgagnage, 2 vols., Brussels, 1869–70.

Coutumes du pays de Liège. ed. J. J. Raikem and M. L. Polain, vols. i–ii, Brussels, 1870–3.

DANIEL, Russian abbot. *Vie et pèlerinage,* in Khitrowo (ed.), *Itinéraires Russes,* pp. 1–83.

DELISLE, L. (ed.) 'Enquête sur la fortune des établissements de l'ordre de S. Benoit en 1388', *Notices et extraits des manuscrits de la Bibliothèque Nationale,* xxxix (1909), pp. 359–408.

Detectio corporis S. Areopagiticae Dionysii circiter anno 1050, in Félibien, *op. cit.* (MW), pièces justificatives, pp. 165–72.

DIETRICH OF NIEM. *De Scismate,* ed. G. Erler, Leipzig, 1890.

DU CANGE, C. *Glossarium mediae et infimae latinitatis,* 10 vols., Niort, 1883–7.

DUGDALE, W. *Monasticon Anglicanum,* 6 vols. in 8, London, 1817–30.

DUPLÈS-AGIER, H. (ed.). *Chroniques de Saint-Martial de Limoges, SHF,* Paris, 1874.

EADMER, monk of Canterbury. *De Sanctorum veneratione et obsecratione,* ed. A. Wilmart, *Revue des Sciences Religieuses,* xv (1935), pp. 184–219, 354–79.

EADMER, monk of Canterbury. *Vita S. Anselmi, archiepiscopi Cantuariensis,* ed. R. W. Southern, London, 1962.

EHINGEN, GEORGE VON. *Reisen nach der Ritterschaft,* ed. F. Pfeiffer, *BLVS.* i, Stuttgart, 1842.

EINHARD. *Translatio et Miracula S. Marcelini et Petri, MGH. SS.* xv. 238–64.

EINHARD. *Vita Karoli Magni Imperatoris,* ed. L. Halphen, Paris, 1938.

Epistolae quatuor de cultu S. Martini apud Turonenses extr. sec. xii, An. Boll., iii (1884), pp. 216–57.

ERASMUS, DESIDERIUS. *Peregrinatio religionis ergo,* in *Opera Omnia,* ed. J. Clericus, vol. i, Leyden, 1703, cols. 774–87.

ERNOUL. *Chronique d'Ernoul et de Bernard le Tresorier,* ed. L. de Mas Latrie, *SHF,* Paris, 1871.

ETHERIA. *Peregrinatio ad Loca Sancta, G. Itin.,* pp. 35–101.

ÉTIENNE DE BOURBON. *Anecdotes historiques, légendes, et apologues,* ed. A. Lecoy de la Marche, *SHF,* Paris, 1879.

EUSEBIUS OF CAESAREA. *Historia Ecclesiastica (Kirchengeschichte),* ed. T. Mommsen, *Die Griechischen Christlichen Schriftsteller der ersten drei Jahrhunderte, Eusebius Werke,* vol. ii, Leipzig, 1903–9.

Examination of Master William Thorpe, priest, of heresy, in A. W. Pollard (ed.), *Fifteenth century prose and verse,* London, 1903, pp. 97-174.

FABER, FELIX. *Evagatorium in Terrae Sanctae, Arabiae, et Egypti Peregrinationem,* ed. C. D. Hassler, *BLVS.,* ii-iv, Stuttgart, 1843–9.

FAILLON, E. M. (ed.). *Monuments inédits sur l'apostolat de Sainte Marie Madeleine en Provence,* 2 vols., Paris, 1848.

FARSIT, HUGHES. *De Miraculis S. Mariae in urbe Suessionensis, PL.* clxxix. 1777–1800.

FONTANINI, J. (ed.). *Codex constitutionum quas summi pontifices ediderunt in solemni canonisatione sanctorum,* Rome, 1729.

FORÉVILLE, R. (ed.). *Un procés de canonisation à l'aube du xiiie siècle (1201–2). Le Livre de Saint Gilbert de Sempringham,* Paris, 1943.

FORGEAIS, A. *Collection de plombs historiées trouvés dans la Seine,* 5 vols., Paris, 1863.

FREDERICQ, P. *Codex documentorum sacratissimarum indulgentiarum Neerlandicarum (1300–1600), Rijks Geschiedkundige Publicatiën,* Kleine Serie, xxi, 'S-Gravenhage, 1922.

FRESCOBALDI, LIONARDO DI NICCOLO. *Viaggio in Egitto e in Terra Santa,* in Bellorini and Hoade, *op. cit.* (OS), pp. 29-90.

FRETELLUS, archdeacon of Antioch. *De situ urbis Jerusalem et de locis sanctis intra ipsam urbem sive circumjacentibus,* in C.M. de Vogué, *Les églises de la Terre Sainte,* Paris, 1860, pp. 412-33.

GERALD OF WALES. *Opera,* ed. J. S. Brewer and J. F. Dimock, 8 vols., *RS.,* London, 1861–91.

GERSON, JEAN. *Opera Omnia,* ed. L. E. du Pin, 5 vols., Antwerp, 1706.

GERSON, JEAN. *Oeuvres Complètes,* ed. P. Glorieux, 10 vols. Paris, 1960–75 (in progress).

Gesta abbatum S. Trudonensium. ed. C. de Borman, *Chronique de l'abbaye de Saint-Trond,* 2 vols. Liège, 1877.

Gesta consulum Andegavorum, ed. P. Marchegay and A. Salmon, in *Chroniques des comtes d'Anjou,* vol. i, *SHF,* Paris, 1856.

Gesta Francorum et aliorum Hierosolymitanorum, ed. R. Hill, London, 1962.

GHILLEBERT DE LANNOY. *Voyages et ambassades,* in *Oeuvres,* ed. C. Potvin, Louvain, 1878, pp. 9-178.

GHISTELE, JOSSE VAN. 'Le Voyage en orient de Josse van Ghistele (1481–5)', *Revue Generale,* xxxvii (1883), pp. 723-64; xxxviii (1883), pp. 46-71, 193-210.

GIBBONS, A. (ed.). *Early Lincoln wills,* Lincoln, 1888.

GILES LI MUISIS. *Chronica,* ed. J. J. de Smet, *Corpus Chronicorum Flandriae (Collection de chroniques Belges inédites),* ii, Brussels, 1841.

GIRNAND VON SCHWALBACH. *Pilgerschrift, RM. Pilg.,* pp. 97-9.

GLABER, RADULPH. *Historiae,* ed. M. Prou, Paris, 1886.

GRANDISON, JOHN DE. *The Register of John de Grandison, bishop of Exeter (A.D. 1327–1369),* ed. F. C. Hingeston-Randolph, London, 1894–9.

Graphia Aureae Urbis. VZ., vol. iii, pp. 67-110.

GREGORY, Master. *De Mirabilibus urbis Romae,* ed. M. R. James, *EHR.,* xxxii (1917), pp. 531-4.

GREGORY I, pope. *Dialogi,* Lib. II, *PL.* lxvi. 125-204; Libs. I, III-IV, *PL.* lxxvii. 149-430.

GREGORY I, pope. *Registrum epistolarum,* ed. P. Ewald and L. M. Hartmann, *MGH. Epp.* i-ii, 2 vols., Berlin, 1891–9.

GREGORY VII, pope. *Registrum,* ed. E. Caspar, *MGH. Epp. Sel.* ii, Berlin, 1920–3.

GREGORY IX, pope. *Régistres,* ed. L. Auvray, *BEFAR.,* 2nd. series, vol. ix, 4 vols., Paris, 1890–1955.

GREGORY OF TOURS. *Historia Francorum,* ed. B. Krusch and W. Levison, *MGH. Merov.* i (1), 2nd. ed. Hannover, 1937–51.

GREGORY OF TOURS. *Miracula et opera minora,* ed. B. Krusch, *MGH. Merov.* i (2), Hannover, 1885.

GUCCI, GIORGIO. *Viaggio ai Luoghi Santi,* in Bellorini and Hoade, *op. cit.* (OS), pp. 91-156.

GUÉRIN, P., and CÉLIER, L. (ed.). *Recueil des documents concernant le Poitou contenus dans les registres de la chancellerie de France,* 14 vols., *Archives Historiques du Poitou,* xi (1881), xiii (1883), xvii (1887), xix (1888), xxi (1891), xxiv (1893), xxvi (1896), xxix (1898), xxxii (1903), xxxv (1906), xxxviii (1909), xli (1914–19), l (1938), lvi (1958).

GUI, BERNARD. *Practica inquisitionis heretice pravitatis,* ed. C. Douais, Paris, 1886.

GUIBERT OF NOGENT. *De pignoribus sanctorum, PL.* clvi. 607–80.

GUIBERT OF NOGENT. *Gesta Dei per Francos, RHC. Occ.* iv. 115–263.

GUIBERT OF NOGENT. *Histoire de sa vie (1053–1124),* ed. G. Bourgin, Paris, 1907.

Guide: Guide du pelerin de Saint-Jacques de Compostelle, ed. J. Vielliard, 4th. ed. Mâcon, 1969.

GUILLAUME DE DEGUILEVILLE. *Le pélerinage de la vie humaine,* ed. J. J. Sturzinger, Roxburghe Club, London, 1893.

GUILLAUME DE SAINT-PATHUS. *Les Miracles de S. Louis,* ed. F. B. Fay, Paris, 1932.

HADDAN, A. W., and STUBBS, W. (ed.). *Councils and ecclesiastical documents relating to Great Britain and Ireland,* 3 vols., Oxford, 1869-71.

HAIMOIN, abbot of St.-Pierre-sur-Dive. 'Lettre sur la construction de l' église de Saint-Pierre-sur-Dive, en 1145', ed. L. Delisle, *BEC.,* xxi (1860), pp. 113-39.

HARFF, ARNOLD VON. *Die Pilgerfahrt des Ritters Arnold von Harff in den Jahren 1469 bis 1499,* ed. E. von Groote, Cologne, 1860.

HERMAN, monk of Bury. *De Miraculis S. Eadmundi,* in Arnold, *op. cit.* (OS), vol. i, pp. 26-92.

HERMAN, canon of Laon. *De Miraculis S. Mariae Laudunensis, PL.* clvi. 961-1020.

Histoire versifé de l'abbaye de Fécamp. ed. A. Längfors, *Annales Academiae Scientiarum Fennicae,* ser. B, xxii, Helsinki, 1928.

Historia Compostellana. ES. xx.

Hodoeporicon S. Willibaldi, TM. Itin., vol. i, pp. 241-97.

HUGH OF FLAVIGNY. *Chronicon, MGH. SS.* viii. 288-502.

HUS, JOHN. *De Sanguine Christi,* ed. W. Flajshans in *Opera Omnia,* vol. i (3), Prague, 1904.

INNOCENT III, pope. *Regesta sive epistolae, PL.* ccxiv-ccxvii.

INNOCENT IV, pope. *Régistres,* ed. E. Berger, *BEFAR.,* 2nd. series, vol. i, 4 vols., Paris, 1881–1919.

Innominatus I. in *Gesta Francorum, ed. cit.,* pp. 98-101.

Innominatus V. ed. W. A. Neumann, *Oesterreichische Vierteljahresschrift für katholische Theologie,* v (1866), pp. 211-82.

Innominatus VI (Pseudo-Beda). ed. W. A. Neumann, *Oesterreichische Vierteljahresschrift für katholische Theologie,* vii (1868), pp. 397-438.

Inventio et miracula S. Wulfranni. ed. J. Laporte, *Mélanges de la Soc. de l'histoire de Normandie,* xive serie, Rouen, 1938, pp. 1-87.

Itinerarium cuiusdam Anglici Terram Sanctam et alia loca sancta visitantis (1344–45), BBB., vol. iv, pp. 427-60.

JACOB OF VORAGINE. *Legenda Aurea,* ed. T. Graesse, 3rd. ed., Dresden, 1890

JACQUES DE VITRY. *Exempla et sermones vulgares,* ed. T. F. Crane, *Publications of the Folk-lore Society,* xxvi, London, 1890.

JACQUES DE VITRY. *Historia Hierosolymitana,* ed. J. Bongars, *Gesta Dei per Francos,* Hanover, 1611, vol. i, pp. 1047-1124.

JEAN DE MEUNG. See *Roman de la rose.*

JEROME, ST. *Contra Vigilantium, PL.* xxiii. 339-52.

JEROME, ST. *Epistolae,* ed. I. Hilberg, *CSEL.* liv-lvi, 3 vols., Vienna, 1909–18.

JOHN THE DEACON. *Descriptio Lateranensis Ecclesiae, VZ.,* vol. iii, pp. 319-73.

JOHN OF COUTANCES. *Miracula Ecclesiae Constantiensis,* in E-A. Pigeon, *Histoire de la cathedrale de Coutances,* Coutances, 1876, pp. 367-83.

JOHN OF SALISBURY. *Historia Pontificalis,* ed. M. Chibnall, London, 1956.

JOHN OF TRITTENHEIM (TRITHEMIUS). *Annales Hirsaugienses,* 2 vols., Saint-Gall, 1690.

JOHN OF TRITTENHEIM (TRITHEMIUS). *Opera pia et spiritualia,* ed. J. Busaeus, Mainz, 1604.

JOHN OF WURZBURG. *Descriptio Terrae Sanctae,* in T. Tobler (ed.), *Descriptiones Terrae Sanctae ex saeculo viii, ix, xii, et xv,* Leipzig, 1874, pp. 108-92.

JOINVILLE, JEAN SIRE DE. *Histoire de S. Louis,* ed. N. de Wailly, 2nd. ed., Paris, 1874.

Journal d'un bourgeois de Paris. ed. A. Tuetey, Paris, 1881.

KAJAVA, O. (ed.). *Etudes sur deux poemes francais rélatifs a l'abbaye de Fécamp, Annales Academiae Scientiarum Fennicae,* ser. B, xxi, Helsinki, 1928.

KHITROWO, B. DE (ed.). *Itinéraires Russes en orient, SOL.,* v., Geneva, 1889.

KJELLMAN, H. (ed.). *La deuxieme collection Anglo-Normande des miracles de la Sainte Vierge,* Paris, 1922.

LAMBERT OF HERSFELD. *Opera,* ed. O. Holder-Egger, *MGH. Rer. Germ.,* Hanover, 1894.

LANFRID OF WINCHESTER. *Translatio et miracula S. Swithuni,* Lib. I, Lib. II, caps. 46-54, ed. E. P. Sauvage, *An. Boll.,* iv (1885), pp. 367-410; Lib. ii, caps. 1-45, *Aa. Ss.* July, vol. i, pp. 331-7.

LANGLAND, WILLIAM. *The Vision of William concerning Piers the Plowman, Text B,* ed. W. W. Skeat, *EETS.,* O.S., xxxviii, London, 1869.

Lanterne of light. ed. L. M. Swinburn, *EETS.,* O.S., cli, London, 1917.

LENGHERAND, GEORGES. *Voyage à Venise, Rome, Jerusalem, Mont Sinai, et le Kayre, 1485–6,* ed. Mqs. de Godefroy Menilglaise, Mons, 1861.

LE SAIGE, JACQUES. *Voyage de Jacques le Saige de Douai à Rome, Notre-Dame de Lorette, Venise, Jerusalem, et autres lieux saints,* ed. H-R. Duthilloeul, Douai, 1851.

Letters and papers, foreign and domestic, of the reign of Henry VIII, ed. J. S. Brewer, J. Gairdner, *et al.,* 21 vols. in 35, London, 1864–1920.

Liber Censuum: Le Liber Censuum de l'Eglise Romaine, ed. P. Fabre and L. Duchesne, *BEFAR.,* 2nd. series, vol. vi, 3 vols., Paris, 1910–52.

Liber Confraternitatis B. Mariae de Anima Teutonicorum de Urbe, ed. C. Jaenig, Rome, 1875.

Lib. Pont.: Liber Pontificalis, ed. L. Duchesne, *BEFAR.,* 2nd. series, vol. iii (1,4), 2 vols., Paris, 1886–92.

Liber S. Jacobi, Codex Calixtinus. vol. i (Texto), ed. W. M. Whitehill, Santiago de Compostella, 1944.

Lit. Cant.: Literae Cantuarienses. The letter-book of the monastery of Christ Church, Canterbury, ed. J. B. Sheppard, 3 vols. *RS.,* London, 1887–9.

LUCHINO DEL CAMPO. *Viaggio a Gerusalemme di Niccoló da Este,* ed. G. Ghinassi, *Collezione di opere inedite o rare dei primi tre secoli della lingua,* i, Turin, 1861, pp. 99-160.

LUDOLPH OF SUCHEM. *De itinere Terrae Sanctae,* ed. F. Deycks, *BLVS.,* xxv, Stuttgart, 1951.

MABILLON, J. (ed.). *Vetera analecta,* 2nd. ed., Paris, 1723.

MC NEILL, J. T., and GAMER, H. M. (ed.). *Medieval handbooks of penance. A translation of the principal 'Libri Penitentiales' and selections from related documents,* N.Y., 1938.

MALLIUS, PETER. *Descriptio basilicae Vaticanae, VZ.,* vol. iii, pp. 375-442.

Mandeville's Travels. ed. M. Letts, Hakluyt Soc., series ii, vols. ci-cii, London, 1953.

MANETTI, J. *Vita Nicolai V, RISS* (1). iii (2). 907-68.

Manuscrit de Rothelin. RHC. Occ., vol. ii, pp. 483-639.

MARCHEGAY, P., and MABILLE, E. (ed.). *Chroniques des églises d'Anjou, SHF.,* Paris, 1869.

MARIANO DA SIENA. *Viaggio in Terra Santa,* in *I Viaggi in Terra Santa di Simone Sigoli Fiorentino e ser Mariano da Siena,* Parma, 1865, pp. 107-90.

MASTRO, PAOLO DI BENEDETTO DI COLA DELLO. *Memoriale,* ed. M. Pelaez, *ASRSP.,* xvi (1893), pp. 41-130.

Mirabilia Urbis Romae. VZ., vol. iii, pp. 3-65.

Miracles de Notre-Dame de Rocamadour au xiie siècle. ed. E. Albe, Paris, 1907.

Miracula S. Benedicti. ed. E. de Certain, *SHF.,* Paris, 1858.

Miracula S. Columbani Bobbiensis. MGH. SS. xxx. 993-1015.

Miracula S. Eadmundi (MS Bodley 240). in Arnold, *op. cit.* (OS), vol. i, pp. 359-77, vol. ii, pp. 362-8, vol. iii, pp. 318-48.

Miracula B. Egidii. caps. 1-9, 16-8, *MGH. SS.* xii. 316-23; caps. 12-15, 19-30, *An. Boll.,* ix (1890, pp. 393-422).

Miracula S. Eutropii Santonensis. Aa. Ss. April, vol. iii, pp. 736-44.

Miracula S. Fidis. ed. A. Bouillet, Paris, 1897.

Miracula S. Gilberti. in Foréville, *op. cit.* (OS), pp. 42-73.

Miracula S. Mariae in Carnotensi ecclesia facta. ed. A. Thomas, *BEC.*, xliii (1881), pp. 505-50.

Miracula S. Mariae Magdalenae Viziliaci facta. caps. 1-16 in Faillon, *op. cit.* (OS), vol ii, pp, 735-42; cap. 17, *CCH. (Bruxelles),* vol. i, p. 214 (no. 44); cap. 18, *CCH. (Paris),* vol. i, p. 587 (no. 13).

Miracula S. Mariae Magdalenae Viziliaci facta (editio altera). Praefat., *CCH. (Bruxelles),* vol. i, p. 32 (no. 46); cap. 1, *CCH. (Paris),* vol. ii, pp. 292-3 (no. 2); cap. 2, *An. Boll.,* xvii (1898), p. 177 (no. 1); cap. 3, *CCH. (Paris),* vol. ii, p. 292 (no. 1); caps. 4-6, *An. Boll.,* xviii (1898), pp. 177-9 (nos. 2-4).

Miracula S. Mariae Magdalenae in vico S. Maximini in Provincia. CCH. (Paris), vol. iii, pp. 287-94.

Miracula S. Martialis anno 1388 patrata. ed. V. V. F. Arbellot, *An. Boll.,* i (1882), pp, 411-46

Miracula S. Michaelis in Periculo Maris. ed. E. de R. de Beaurepaire, *Mémoires de la Soc. des Antiquaires de Normandie,* 3rd. series, ix (1877), pp. 864-98.

Miracula S. Wulfstani. ed. R. R. Darlington, Camden Soc., 3rd. series, vol. xl, London, 1928, pp. 115-80.

MONTSABERT, D. P. DE (ed.). *Chartes et documents pour servir à l'histoire de l'abbaye de Charroux, Archives Historiques du Poitou,* xxxix (1910).

MORE, SIR THOMAS. *A dyalogue of the veneration and worship of ymages and relyques, praying to saints and goying on pylgrymage,* London, 1529.

MUFFELS, NIKOLAUS. *Beschreibung der stadt Rom,* ed. W. Vogt, *BLVS.,* cxxviii, Tübingen, 1876.

NAGL, F. (ed.). 'Urkundliches zur Geschichte der Anima in Rom', *Römische Quartalschrift,* Supplementheft xii, Rome, 1899, pp. 1-88.

NICCOLO DA POGGIBONSI. *Libro d'oltramare,* ed. A. Bacchi della Lega, *Scelta di curiosità letterarie inedite o rare dal secolo xiii al xvii,* clxxxii, 2 vols., Bologna, 1881.

NICEPHORUS. *Translatio S. Nicolai in Barum, An. Bull.,* iv (1885), pp. 169-92.

NICHOLAS III, pope. *Régistres,* ed. J. Gay and S. Vitte, *BEFAR.,* 2nd. series, vol. xiv, Paris, 1898–1938.

NICHOLAS IV, pope. *Régistres,* ed. E. Langlois, *BEFAR.,* 2nd. series, vol. v, Paris 1886–93.

NICHOLAS OF CLAMANGES. *Opera Omnia,* Leyden, 1613.

NOMPAR II, SEIGNEUR DE CAUMONT. *Voyaige d'outremer en Jherusalem par le seigneur de Caumont, l'an MCCCCXVIII,* ed. Mqs. de la Grange, Paris, 1859.

ODO, abbot of Cluny. *Vita S. Geraldi Auriliacensis comitis, PL.* cxxxiii. 639-710.

ODO OF DEUIL. *De profectione Lodovici VII in orientem,* ed. H. Waquet, *Documents rélatifs à l'histoire des croisades,* iii, Paris, 1949.

OGIER VIII, SEIGNEUR D'ANGLURE. *Le saint voyage de Jerusalem du seigneur d'Anglure,* ed. F. Bonnardot and A. Longnon, *SATF.,* Paris, 1878.

ORDERIC VITALIS. *The Ecclesiastical History,* books III-VIII, ed. M. Chibnall, vols. ii–iv, Oxford, 1969–73; other books, ed. A. Le Prévost, *SHF.,* 5 vols. Paris, 1838–55.

Ordonnances: Ordonnances des rois de France de la troisième race, 22 vols., Paris, 1723–1847.

O Roma nobilis! ed. L. Traube, *Bayerischen Akademie der Wissenschaften, Abhandlungen,* xix (1891), pp. 297–309.

OTTO OF FRIESING. *De duabus civitatibus,* ed. A. Hofmeister, *MGH. Rer. Germ.,* Hanover, 1912.

PALLADIUS, bishop of Helenopolis. *Historia Lausiaca,* ed. C. Butler, *Texts and Studies,* ed. J. Armitage Robinson, vol. vi, 2 vols. Cambridge, 1904.

PARDESSUS, J. M. (ed.). *Collection de lois maritimes antérieurer au xvi-iie siècle,* 6 vols., Paris, 1828–45.

PARIS, MATTHEW. *Chronica Majora,* ed. H. R. Luard, 7 vols., *RS.,* London, 1872–83.

PAULINUS OF NOLA. *Carmina,* ed. W. von Hartel, *CSEL.,* xxx, Vienna, 1894.

PAULINUS OF NOLA. *Epistolae,* ed. W. von Hartel, *CSEL.,* xxix, Vienna, 1894.

PECOCK, REGINALD. *The Repressor of over-much blaming of the clergy,* ed. C. Babington, 2 vols. *RS.,* London, 1860.

Pèlerinage en Palestine de l'abbesse Euphrosine, princesse de Polotsk (1173). ed. B. de Khitrowo. *ROL.,* iii (1895), pp. 32-5.

Pèlerinages por aler en Iherusalem. MR. Itin., pp. 87-104.

Pèlerinages et pardouns d'Acre. MR. Itin., pp. 227-36.

PETER THE DEACON. *Historica relatio de corpore S. Benedicti, Aa. SS.* March, vol. iii, pp. 288-97.

PETER THE VENERABLE, abbot of Cluny. *De Miraculis, PL.* clxxxix. 851-954.

PETER THE VENERABLE, abbot of Cluny. *The Letters of Peter the Venerable,* ed. G. Constable, 2 vols., Cambridge, Mass., 1967.

PETRARCH, FRANCESCO. *Le Familiari,* ed. V. Rossi, *Edizione nazionale delle opere di Francesco Petrarca,* vols. x-xiii, 4 vols., Florence, 1933–42.

PHILIP. *Descriptio de Terra Sancta (c. 1285–91),* ed. W. A. Neumann, *Oesterreichische Vierteljahresschrift für katholische Theologie,* xi (1872), pp. 1-78, 165-74.

PHILIP. *Liber de Terra Sancta (1377),* ed. J. Haupt, *Oesterreichische Vierteljahreschrisft für katholische Theologie,* x (1871), pp. 511-40.

PHILIP, prior of St. Frideswide's, Oxford. *Miracula S. Frideswidae, Aa. Ss.* Oct., vol. viii, pp. 567-90.

PHOCAS, JOHN. *De Locis Sanctis, PG.* cxxxiii. 925-62.

POSSOT, DENIS. *Voyage de la Terre Sainte,* ed. C. Schefer, *Recueil de voyages pour servir à l'histoire de la géographie,* xi, Paris, 1890.

POWICKE, F. M., and CHENEY, C. R. (ed.). *Councils and synods, with other documents relating to the English Church,* vol. ii (1205–1313), Oxford, 1964.

PRUDENTIUS, AURELIUS CLEMENS. *Carmina,* ed. J. Bergman, *CSEL.,* lxi, Vienna, 1926.

PURCHAS, SAMUEL. *Purchas his pilgrimes,* Lib. VIII, cap. 5, vol. vii, Glasgow, 1905, pp. 527-72.

Quinze (Les) joies de mariage. ed. J. Rychner, Geneva, 1963.

RAYMOND OF AGUILERS. *Historia Francorum, RHC. Occ.,* vol. iii, pp. 231-309.

RAYNALD, O. *Annales Ecclesiastici*, ed. J. D. Mansi, 15 vols., Lucca, 1747–56.

REBDORF, HEINRICH VON. *Annales imperatorum et paparum*, ed. J. F. Boehmer, *Fontes rerum Germanicarum*, iv, Stuttgart, 1868.

REGINALD OF DURHAM. *De admirandis B. Cuthberti virtutibus*, Surtees Soc., i, London, 1835.

REGINALD OF DURHAM. *De Vita et miracula S. Godrici, heremitae de Finchale*, ed. J. Stephenson, Surtees Soc., xx, London, 1847.

Reisebuch der Familie Rieter. ed. R. Röhricht and H. Meisner, *BLVS.*, clxviii, Tübingen, 1884.

RIANT, P. (ed.). 'Pièces rélatives au passage à Venise de pèlerins de Terre Sainte', *AOL.*, ii (1884), pp. 237-49.

RICOLDO OF MONTE CROCE. *Liber peregrinationis, L. Peregr.*, pp. 101-41.

RIEDEL, F. A. (ed.). *Codex diplomaticus Brandenburgensis*, vol. i (2), Berlin, 1842, pp. 121-84 ('Die Stadt Wilsnack').

RIGAUD, ODO, archbishop of Rouen. *Regestum visitationum archiepiscopi Rothomagensis. Journales des visites pastorales d'Eudes Rigaud, 1248–69*, ed. T. Bonnin, Rouen, 1852.

RIGORD, *Oeuvres de Rigord et de Guillaume le Breton*, ed. H-F. Delaborde, *SHF.*, Paris, 1882.

RINDFLEISCH, PETER. *Walffartt, RM. Pilg.*, pp. 315-48.

ROBERT OF TORIGNY, abbot of Mont-St.-Michel. *Chronique*, ed. L. Delisle, 2 vols., Rouen, 1872–3.

Roman de la Rose. (by Guillaume de Lorris and Jean de Meung), ed. F. Lecoy, 3 vols., Paris, 1965–70.

ROSSI, G. B. DE. *Instriptiones Christianae urbis Romae*, 2 vols., Rome, 1857–88.

ROT, HANS and PETER. *Pilgerreisen*, ed. A. Bernoulli, *Beiträge zur vaterlandische Geschichte*, Neue Folge, i (1882), pp. 329-408.

RUCELLAI, GIOVANNI. *Il Giubileo dell' anno 1450*, ed. M. Giuseppe, *ASRSP.*, iv (1881), pp. 563-80.

RUDOLFUS, monk of Fulda. *Miracula sanctorum in Fuldenses ecclesias transtorum*, MGH. SS. xv. 328-41.

RYMER, T. (ed.). *Foedera et conventiones, literae, et acta publica*, 20 vols., London, 1704–35.

SACCHETTI, FRANCO. *I sermoni evangelici. Le lettere,* ed. O. Gigli, Florence. 1857.

SAEWULF. *Relatione de peregrinatione Saewulfi ad Hierosolymam et Terram Santam,* tr. W. Brownlow, *PPTS.,* London, 1892.

SAMSON, abbot of Bury. *De Miraculis S. Eadmundi,* in Arnold, *op. cit.* (OS), vol. i, pp. 105-208.

SHARPE, R. R. *Calendar of wills proved and enrolled in the Court of Husting, London, A.D. 1258–A.D. 1668,* 2 vols., London, 1889–90.

SIGNORILI, N. *Descriptio urbis Romae eiusque excellaentiae, VZ.,* vol. iv, pp. 151-208.

SIGOLI, SIMONE. *Viaggio in Terra Santa,* in Bellorini and Hoade, *op. cit.* (OS), pp. 157-201.

SIMONE OF CREMONA. *De Indulgentiis Portiunculae,* ed. D. Trapp, 'The Portiuncula discussion of Cremona (ca. 1380). New light on 14th. century disputations', *Recherches de théologie ancienne et mediévale,* xxii (1955), pp. 79-94.

Stacions (The) of Rome and the Pilgrim's sea-voyage. ed. F. J. Furnivall, *EETS.,* O.S., xxv, London, 1867.

STEFANESCHI, JAMES, cardinal. *De Centesimo seu Jubileo anno,* ed. D. Quattrocchi, *Bessarione,* vii (1900), pp. 291-317.

STOLLE, KONRAD. *Thuringische-erfurtische Chronik,* ed. R. Thiele, *Geschichtsquellen der Provinz Sachsen,* xxxix, Halle, 1900.

STUBBS, W. (ed.). *Select Charters,* 9th. ed., Oxford, 1913.

SUGER, abbot of St.-Denis. *De Consecratione ecclesiae S. Dionysii,* in *Oeuvres Complètes,* ed. A. Lecoy de la Marche, *SHF.,* Paris, 1867, pp. 211-38.

SUGER, abbot of St.-Denis. *De Rebus in administratione sua gestis,* in *ibid.,* pp. 151-209.

SUGER, abbot of St.-Denis. *Vita Lodovici VI,* ed. H. Waquet, Paris, 1929.

SULPICIUS SEVERUS. *Libri qui supersunt,* ed. C. Halm, CSEL., i, Vienna, 1866.

SURIANO, FRANCESCO. *Il Trattato di Terra Santa e dell' oriente,* ed. G. Golubovich, Milan, 1900.

SYMEON OF DURHAM. *Opera omnia,* ed. T. Arnold, *RS.,* 2 vols., London, 1882-5.

TAFUR, PERO. *Andancas e viajes por diversas partes del mundo avidos (1435–1439)*, ed. D. Marcos Jiménez de la Espada, *Coleccion de libros espanoles raros o curiosos*, viii, Madrid, 1874.

TARDIF, E-J. (ed.). *Coutumiers de Normandie*, Soc. de l'Histoire de Normandie, 2 vols., Rouen, 1881–96.

Testamenta vetusta. ed. Sir N. H. Nicolas, 2 vols., London, 1826.

THEODERIC OF WURZBURG. *De Locis Sanctis*, ed. T. Tobler, Saint-Gall, 1965.

THEODORET, bishop of Cyrus. *Graecarum affectionum curatio*, *PG*. lxxxiii. 775-1152.

THEOFRID OF EPTERNACH. *Flores epitaphium sanctorum*, *PL*. clvii. 313-404.

THIEL, A. (ed.). *Epistolae Romanorum pontificum genuinae a S. Hilario usque ad Pelagium II*, vol. i (461-523), Brunsberg, 1868.

THOMAS OF MONMOUTH. *Vita et miracula S. Willelmi Norwicensis*, ed. A. Jessop and M. R. James, Cambridge, 1896.

TOULMIN SMITH, J. (ed.) *Expeditions to Prussia and the Holy Land made by Henry, earl of Derby. The accounts kept by his treasurer during two years*, Camden Soc., 2nd. series, lii, London, 1894.

Traité sur le cinquième jubilé de Saint Thomas Becket (1420). in R. Foréville, *op. cit.* (MW), pp. 99-160.

URBAN II, pope. *Epistolae et privilegia*, *PL*. cli.

VAN DEN BUSSCHE, M. (ed.). 'Roc-Amadour. Les pèlerinages dans notre ancien droit penal. Collection de documents inédits des xive, xve, et xvie siècles', *CRH.*, 4th. series, xiv (1887), pp. 19-74.

VENTURA, WILLIAM. *Chronicon Astense*, *RISS* (1). xi. 139-268.

VERGERIO, PAOLO. *Epistolario*, ed. L. Smith, *Fonti*, Rome, 1934.

VICTRICIUS, ST., bishop of Routen. *De Laude sanctorum*, *PL*. xx. 443-58.

Vie de Sainte Mélanie. ed. D. Gorce, *Sources Chrétiennes*, xc, Paris, 1962.

VILLANI, GIOVANNI. *Historie Fiorentine*, *RISS* (1). xiii. 1-1002.

VILLANI, MATTEO. *Istorie*, *RISS* (1). xiv. 1-728.

Visio monachi de Eynsham. ed. H. Thurston, *An. Boll.*, xxii (1903), pp. 225-319.

Vita Lietberti episcopi Cameracensis. in L. d'Achéry, *Veterum aliquot scriptores spicilegium*, Paris, 1657–77, vol. ix, pp. 675-733.

Vita Richardi, abbatis S. Vitoni Viridunensis. MGH. SS. xi. 281-90.

Vita S. Sigiranni. An. Boll., iii (1884), pp. 378-407.

Voyage de la Saincte Cyté de Hierusalem, fait l'an 1480. ed. C. Schefer, *Recueil de voyages et de documents pour servir à l'histoire de la géographie,* ii, Paris. 1882.

WACE. *Le Roman de Rou,* ed. A. J. Holden, *SATF.,* 3 vols., Paris, 1970-73.

WALTHER, PAUL, VON GUGLINGEN. *Itinerarium in Terram Sanctam et ad Sanctam Catharinam,* ed. M. Sollweck, *BLVS.,* cxcii, Tübingen, 1892.

WASSERSCHLEBEN, F. W. H. (ed.). *Die Bussordnungen der abendländischen Kirche nebst einer rechtsgeschictlichen Einleitung,* Halle, 1851.

WATTENBACH, W. (ed.) 'Beiträge zur Geschichte der Mark Brandenburg aus Handschriften der königlichen Bibliothek', *Sitzungsberichte der königlich preussischen Akademie der Wissenschaften* (1882), pp. 587-609.

WEY, WILLIAM. *The Itineraries of William Wey, fellow of Eton College, to Jerusalem, A.D. 1458 and A.D. 1462: and to Saint James of Compostella,* Roxburghe Club, London, 1857.

WILLIAM OF CANTERBURY. *Miracula S. Thomae Cantuariensis, Becket Materials,* vol. i, pp. 137-546.

WILLIAM OF JUMIÈGES. *Gesta Normannorum ducum,* ed. J. Marx, Soc. de l'Histoire de Normandie, Paris, 1914.

WILLIAM OF MALMESBURY. *De Gestis pontificum Anglorum,* ed. N. Hamilton, *RS.,* London, 1870.

WILLIAM OF MALMESBURY. *De Gestis regum Anglorum,* ed. W. Stubbs, *RS.,* London, 1887-9.

WILLIAM OF TYRE. *Historia rerum in partibus transmarinis gestarum, RHC. Occ.,* vol. i.

WRIGHT, T. (ed.). *Letters relating to the suppression of the monasteries,* Camden Soc., xxvi, London, 1843.

WYCLIF, JOHN. *De Ecclesia,* ed. J. Loserth, London, 1886.

WYCLIF, JOHN. *Sermones,* ed. J. Loserth, 4 vols., London, 1887-90.

YVO OF CHARTRES. *Decretum, PL.* clxi. 9-1022.

SECONDARY WORKS

ABBOT, E. A. *St. Thomas of Canterbury. His death and miracles*, 2 vols., London, 1898.

ABEL, F. M. 'Saint Jerome et Jerusalem', *Miscellanea Geronimiana publicati nel xv centenario dalla morte di san Girolamo*, Rome, 1920, pp. 131-55.

ALPHANDÉRY, P. *La Chrétienté et l'idée de la croisade*, 2 vols., Paris, 1954–1959.

ANDRIEU, M. 'Les églises de Rome au moyen age', *Revue des sciences religieuses*, ix (1929), pp. 540-74.

ATIYA, A. S. *The crusade in the later middle ages*, Cambridge, 1938.

AUDIAT, L. 'Pèlerinages en Terre Sainte au xve siècle', *Revue historique nobiliaire et biographique*, N.S., vi (1870-1), pp. 49-61.

BARLOW, F. 'Cnut's second pilgrimage', *EHR.* lxxiii (1958), pp. 650-1.

BARTHÉLÉMY, A. DE. 'Pèlerins Champenois en Palestine', *ROL.,* i (1893), pp. 354-80.

BATTISCOMBE, C. F. (ed.). *The relics of Saint Cuthbert*, Oxford, 1956.

BAYNES, N. H. 'The supernatural defenders of Constantinople', *An. Boll.,* lxvii (1949), pp. 165-77.

BÉDIER, J. *Les légendes épiques. Recherches sur la formation des chansons de geste*, 4 vols., 3rd. ed. Paris, 1926.

BEISSEL, S. (1). *Die Aachenfahrt. Verehrung der Aachener Heiligtumer seit den Tagen Karls des grossen bis in unsere zeit, Stimmen aus Maria Laach*, Erganzungscheft lxxxii, Freiburg i. B., 1902.

BEISSEL, S. (2). *Geschichte der Verehrung Marias in Deutschland wahrend des Mittelalters*, Freiburg i. B., 1909.

BEISSEL, S. (3). *Die Verehrung der Heiligen und ihrer Reliquien in Deutschland bis zum Beginne des 13 Jahrhunderts*, Freiburg i. B., 1890.

BENOIT, A. 'Les pèlerinages de Philippe le Bon à Notre-Dame de Boulogne', *Bulletin de la Soc. d'Etudes de la Province de Cambrai,* xxxvii (1937), pp. 119-23.

BERLIÈRE, U. 'Les pèlerinages judiciaires au moyen age', *Revue Bénedictine,* vii (1890), pp. 520-6.

BERNOULLI, C. A. *Die Heiligen der Merowinger,* Tübingen, 1900.

BETHELL, D. 'The making of a twelfth century relic collection', in Cuming and Baker, *op. cit.,* pp. 61-72.

BISCHOFF, B. 'The study of foreign languages in the middle ages', *Speculum,* xxxvi (1961), pp. 209-24.

BONDOIS, M. *La Translation des saints Marcellin et Pierre. Étude sur Einhard et sa vie politique de 827 a 834, BEHE.,* clx, Paris, 1907.

BONSER, W. *The Medical background of Anglo-Saxon England. A Study in history, psychology and folklore,* London, 1963.

BREEST, E. 'Das Wunderblut von Wilsnack (1383–1552). Quellenmässige Darstellung seiner Geschichte', *Märkische Forschungen,* xvi (1881), pp. 131-301.

BRUNDAGE, J. A. 'Cruce Signari: the rite for taking the cross in England', *Traditio,* xxii (1966), pp. 289-310.

CAPPARONI, A. 'L'ospedale di sant' Antonio dei Portughesi in Roma', *Atti del primo congresso Europeo di storia ospitaliers (1960),* Reggio Emilia, 1962, pp. 278-85.

CAROLUS-BARRÉ, L. 'Saint Louis et la translation des corps saints', *Études d'histoire du droit canonique dediées à Gabriel Le Bras,* vol. ii, Paris, 1965, pp. 1087-112.

CARRERAS Y CANDI, F. 'Visites de nostre reys a Montserrat', *Boletín de la Real Academia de Buenas Letras de Barcelona,* ii (1903–4), pp. 339-88.

CATTANEO, E. 'La "statio" piccolo pellegrinaggio', in *Pellegrinaggi,* pp. 245-59.

CAUWENBERGHE, E. VAN. *Les pèlerinages expiatoires et judiciaires dans le droit commun de la Belgique au moyen age, Recueil de travaux de l'université de Louvain,* xlviii, Louvain, 1922.

CHAMARD, F. *Les réliques de Saint Benoit,* Paris, 1882.

CHAPEAU, G. (1). 'Les grandes réliques de l'abbaye de Charroux. Étude d'histoire et d'archéologie', *Bulletin de la Soc. des Antiquaires de l'Ouest,* 3rd. series, viii (1928), pp. 101-28.

CHAPEAU, G. (2). 'Un pèlerinage noble à Charroux au xie siècle. La fondation des prieurés d'Ham et d'Ardres, dépendances de

Charroux', *Bulletin de la Soc. des Antiquaires de 'Ouest,* 3rd. series, xiii (1942–5), pp. 250-71.

CHEVALIER, C. U. *Notre-Dame de Lorette. Étude historique sur l'authenticité de la Santa Casa,* Paris, 1906.

CHOMEL, V. 'Pèlerins Languedociens au Mont-Saint-Michel à la fin du moyen age', *Annales du Midi,* lxx (1958), pp. 230-9.

COHEN, N. *The pursuit of the millennium. Revolutionary millenarians and mystical anarchists of the middle ages,* 2nd. ed., London, 1970.

COLGRAVE, B. 'Bede's miracle stories', in *Bede: His life, times, and writings,* ed. A. H. Thompson, Oxford, 1935, pp. 201-29.

COULTON, G. G. *Five centuries of religion,* 4 vols., Cambridge, 1923–50.

CROKE, W. J. D. 'The national English institutions in Rome during the fourteenth century. A guild and its popular initiative', *Atti del Congresso Internazionale di Scienze Storiche (Rome, 1903),* vol. iii, Rome, 1906, pp. 555-72.

CUMING, G. J., and BAKER, D. (ed.) *Popular belief and practice. Papers read at the ninth summer and tenth winter meetings of the Ecclesiastical History Society, Studies in ecclesiastical history,* viii, Cambridge, 1972.

DAUPHIN, H. *Le bienheureux Richard, abbé de Saint-Vanne de Verdun,* Louvain, 1946.

DAVID, P. *Études sur le Livre de Saint-Jacques attribué au pape Calixte II,* 4 vols. Lisbon, 1946–9.

DAVIES, H. W. *Bernhard von Breydenbach and his journey to the Holy Land, 1483–4. A Bibliography,* London, 1911.

DAVIS, J. F. 'Lollards, reformers, and St. Thomas of Canterbury', *University of Birmingham Historical Journal,* ix (1963–4), pp. 1-15.

DEFOURNEAUX, M. *Les Francais en Espagne aux xie et xiie siècles,* Paris, 1949.

DELARUELLE, E. (1). 'Les grandes processions de pénetents de 1349 et 1399', in *Disciplinati,* pp. 109-45.

DELARUELLE, E. (2). 'La spiritualité de pèlerinage de Rocamadour au moyen age', *Bulletin de la Soc. Études Litteraires, Scientifiques, et Artistiques du Lot,* lxxxvii (1966), pp. 69-85.

DELARUELLE, E. (3). 'La spiritualité des pèlerinages à Saint-Martin de Tours du ve au xe siècle', in *Pellegrinaggi,* pp. 199-243.

DELARUELLE, E., LABANDE, E-R., and OURLIAC, P. *L'Église au temps du grand schisme et la crise conciliaire (1379–1449), Histoire de l'Église,* ed. A. Fliche and V. Martin, vol. xiv, Paris, 1962–4.

DELAUNAY, P. *La médecine et l'Église. Contribution a l'histoire de l'exercise médical par les clercs,* Paris, 1948.

DELEHAYE, H. (1). *Les légendes hagiographiques,* Bruxelles, 1905.

DELEHAYE, H. (2). 'Les lettres d'indulgence collectives', *An. boll.,* xliv (1926), pp. 342-79; xlv (1927), pp. 97-123, 323-44; xlvi (1928), pp. 149-57, 287-343.

DELEHAYE, H. (3). 'Loca sanctorum', *An. Boll.,* xlviii (1930), pp. 5-64.

DELEHAYE, H. (4). *Les origines de la culte des martyrs,* 2nd. ed., Brussels, 1933.

DELEHAYE, H. (5). 'Le pèlerinage de Laurent de Pasztho au Purgatoire de S. Patrice', *An. Boll.,* xxvii (1908), pp. 35-60.

DELEHAYE, H. (6). 'Les premiers "libelli miraculorum"', *An. Boll.,* xxix (1910), pp. 427-34.

DELEHAYE, H. (7). 'Les recueils antiques des miracles des saints', *An. Boll.,* xliii (1925), pp. 5-85, 305-25.

DELEHAYE, H. (8). *Sanctus. Essai sur le culte des saints dans l'antiquité,* Brussels, 1927.

DELISLE, L. (1). 'Authentiques de réliques de l'époque Mérovingienne', *MAH.,* iv (1884), pp. 3-8.

DELISLE, L. (2). 'Pèlerinages d'enfants au Mont-St.-Michel', *Mémoires de la Soc. des Antiquaires de Normandie,* 2nd. series, vii (1847), pp. 388-94.

DENIFLE, H. *La désolation des églises, monastères, at hôpitaux en France pendant la guerre de cent ans,* 2 vols., Paris, 1897–9.

DICKINSON, J. C. *The shrine of Our Lady of Walsingham,* Cambridge, 1956.

Disciplinati: Movimento (Il) dei disciplinati nel settimo centenario dal suo inizio, Deputazione di Storia Patria per l'Umbria, appendice al bolletino no. 9, Perugia, 1962; with index, 1965.

Divine healing and co-operation between doctors and clergy. British Medical Association, London, 1956.

DÖLGER, F. X. J. *Antike und Christentum. Kultur- und religions-geschichtliche Studien,* 2 vols., Munster, 1929–30.

DONNET, A. *Saint-Bernard et les origines de l'hospice de Mont-Joux,* St.-Maurice, 1942.

DOSSAT, Y. 'De singuliers pèlerins sur la chemin de Saint-Jacques en 1272', *Annales du Midi,* lxxxii (1970), pp. 209-20.

DUBY, G. *La société aux xie et xiie siècles dans la région Mâconnaise,* Paris, 1953.

DU CANGE, C. 'Dissertation de l'escarcelle et du bourdon des pèlerins de la Terre Sainte', in *Observations et dissertations sur l'histoire de Saint Louys,* Paris, 1668, pp. 535-8.

DUCHESNE, L. 'Saint-Jacques en Galice', *Annales du Midi,* xii (1900), pp. 145-79.

DUPONT, E. (1). 'Les pèlerinages au Mont-St.-Michel du viiie au xis^e siècle', *Annales de la Soc. Historique et Archéologique de Saint-Malo* (1909), pp. 179-242.

DUPONT, E. (2). 'Les pèlerinages d'enfants allemands au Mont-St.-Michel (xve siècle). Le recit de Baudry, archevêque de Dol', *Annales de la Soc. Historique et Archéologique de Saint-Malo* (1906), pp. 19-60.

DURAND-LEFEBVRE, M. *Étude sur l'origine des vierges noires,* Paris, 1937.

EBERSOLT, J. *Sanctuaires de Byzance. Recherches sur les anciens trésors des églises de Constantinople,* Paris, 1921.

ECKENSTEIN, L. *A History of Sinai,* London, 1921.

EICKEN, H. VON. 'Die Legende von der Erwartung des Weltunter-ganges und der Wiedersehr Christi im Jahre 1000', *Forschungen zur deutschen Geschichte,* xxiii (1883), pp. 303-18.

ELORDUY, E. 'La tradición Jacobea de Galicia en el siglo ix', *Hispania,* xxii (1962), pp. 323-56.

ELTON, G. R. *Policy and police. The enforcement of the Reformation in England in the age of Thomas Cromwell,* Cambridge, 1972.

ERDMANN, C. 'Endkaiserglaube und Kreuzzugsgedanke im XI Jahrhundert', *Zeitschrift für Kirchengeschichte,* li (1932), pp. 384-414.

EWIG, E. 'Le culte de Saint Martin à l'époque Franque', *Revue d'his-toire de l'Église de France,* xlvii (1961), pp. 1-18.

FABRE, P. 'Les offrandes dans la basilique Vaticane en 1285', *MAH.*, xiv (1894), pp. 225-40.

FÉLIBIEN, M. *Histoire de l'abbaye royale de Saint-Denys en France*, Paris, 1706.

FICHTENAU, H. 'Zum Reliquienwesen im früheren Mittelalter', *Mitteilung des Instituts für österreichische Geschichtsforschung*, 1x (1952), pp. 60-89.

FITA, F. 'El Jubileo del año 1300 su recuerdo monumental en el Rosellón. Observaciones sobre la metrica rimada de aquel tiempo', *Boletín de la Real Academía de la Historia*, xlvi (1905), pp. 301-5.

FLAHAULT, R. 'Notre-Dame de la Visitation à Bollezeele. Noes et documents', *Annales du Comité Flamand de France*, xxv (1900), pp. 93-171.

FÖRSTER, W. 'Le Saint-Vou de Lucques', *Romanische Forschungen*, xxiii (1907), pp. 1-56.

FORÉVILLE, R. *Le jubilé de Saint Thomas Becket, du xiiie au xve siècle (1220–1470). Étude et documents*, Paris, 1958.

FRANZ, A. (1). *Die Kirchlichen Benediktionen im Mittelalter*, 2 vols., Freiburg i, B., 1909.

FRANZ, A. (2). 'Die strafe der Pilgermörder im mittelalterlichen Legenden', *Historisch-politischer Blätter für das katholische Deutschland*, cxxiii (1899), pp. 708-27.

FROLOW, A. *La rélique de la vraie croix. Recherches sur le development d'un culte, Archives de l'orient Chrétier*, vii, Paris, 1961.

GAIFFIER, B. DE (1). 'Hagiographie Salernitaine. La translation de S. Matthieu', *An. Boll.*, lxxx (1962), pp. 82-110.

GAIFFIER, B. DE (2). 'Sainte Ide de Boulogne et l'Espagne. A propos de réliques Mariales', *An. Boll.*, lxxxvi (1968), pp. 67-82.

GAMBACORTA, A. 'Culto e pellegrinaggi a San Nicola di Bari fino alla primera crociata', in *Pellegrinaggi*, pp. 485-502.

GARRISON, F. 'A propos des pèlerins et de leur condition juridique', in *Études d'histoire du droit canonique dediées à Gabriel Le Bras*, vol. ii, Paris, 1965, pp. 1165-89.

GASNAULT, P. 'Le tombeau de Saint Martin et les invasions Normandes dans l'histoire et dans la légende', *Revue d'histoire de l'Église de France*, xlvii (1961), pp. 51-66.

GEBHARD, T. 'Die marianischen Grabenbilder in Bayern, Beobachtungen zur Chronologie und Typologie', *Festschrift Gustav Gugitz, Veröffentlichungen des oesterreichischen Museums für Volkskunde*, v, Vienna, 1954, pp. 93-116.

GÖLLER, E. *Die papstliche Poenitentarie von ihrem Ursprung bis zu ihrer Umgestaltung unter Pius V,* 2 vols. in 4, Rome, 1907–11.

GORCE, D. *Les voyages, l'hospitalité et le port des lettres dans le monde Chrétien des ive et v^e siécles*, Paris, 1925.

GOUGAUD, L. *Les Chrétientés Celtiques*, Paris, 1911.

GREGOROVIUS, F. *History of the city of Rome in the middle ages*, 8 vols., London, 1894–1902.

GRETSER, J. *De sacris et religiosis peregrinationibus*, Ingolstadt, 1606.

GUDIOL, J. 'De peregrins i peregrinatges religiosos Catalans', *Analecta Sacra Tarraconensia*, iii (1927), pp. 93-119.

GUIRAUD, J. 'Le commerce des réliques au commencement du xie siècle', *Mélanges G. B. de Rossi*, Supplement au *MAH.*, xii (1892), pp. 73-95.

GUTH, K. *Guibert von Nogent und die hochmittelalterliche Kritic an der Reliquienverehrung, Studien und Mitteilungen zur Geschichte des Benediktinerordens*, xxi, Ottobeuren, 1970.

HARRIS, S. M. 'Our Lady of Cardigan', *Cymdeithas Ceredigion Llundain, Llawlyfr*, viii (1952–3), pp. 33-9.

HASKINS, C. H. 'A Canterbury monk at Constantinople, *c.* 1090', *EHR.*, xxv (1910), pp. 293–5.

HAUPT, H. 'Zur Geschichte der Kinderwallfahrten der Jahre 1455–1489', *Zeitschrift für Kirchengeschichte*, xvi, (1896), pp. 671-5.

HAUPTS, H. 'Frankreich und die aachener Heiligtumsfahrt', *Zeitschrift des aachener Geschichtsvereins*, lxiii (1950), pp. 112-14.

HAUSMANN, M. *Geschichte der päpstlichen Reservatsfälle*, Regensburg, 1868.

HEFELE, C-J. *Histoire des conciles*, ed. H. Leclercq *et al.*, 8 vols, in 16, Paris, 1907-21.

HÉLIOT, P. and CHASTANG, M-L. 'Quêtes et voyages de réliques au profit des églises francaises du moyen age', *Revue d'histoire ecclesiastique*, lix (1964), pp. 789-822; lx (1965), pp. 5-32.

HENNIG, B. 'Kurfurst Friedrich II und das Wunderblut zu Wilsnack', *Forschungen zur brandenburgischen und preussischen Geschichte,* XIX (1906), pp. 391-422.

HEYD, W. 'Les consulats établis en Terre Sainte au moyen age pour la protection des pèlerins', *AOL.,* ii (1884), pp. 355-63.

HÜFFER, H. F. 'Die spanische Jacobusverehrung in ihren Ausstrahlungen auf Deutschland', *Historisches Jahrbuch,* lxxiv (1955), pp. 124-38.

HUGHES, K. 'The changing theory and practice of Irish pilgrimage', *Journal of ecclesiastical history,* xi (1960), pp. 143-51.

HUIDOBRO Y SERNA, L. *Las peregrinaciones Jacobeas,* 3 vols., Madrid, 1949–51.

HUIZINGA, J. *The waning of the middle ages. A study of the forms of life, thought, and art in France and the Netherlands of the xivth. and xvth. centuries,* tr. F. Hopman, London, 1924.

HULBERT, J. 'Some medieval advertisements of Rome', *Modern Philology,* xx (1922–3), pp. 403-24.

HUYNES, J. *Histoire générale de l'abbaye du Mont-St.-Michel au Péril de la Mer (1638),* ed. E. de R. de Beaurepaire, Soc. de l'histoire de Normandie, 2 vols., Rouen, 1872–3.

JANSEN, M. *Papst Bonifatius IX (1389–1404) und seine Beziehungen zur deutschen Kirche,* Frieburg i. B., 1904.

JOERGENSEN, J. *Saint Bridget of Sweden,* tr. I. Lund, 2 vols., London, 1954.

JONES, G. H. *Celtic Britain and the pilgrim movement,* London, 1912.

JORANSON, E. (1). 'The great German pilgrimage of 1064–1065', in *The crusades and other historical essays presented to Dana C. Monro,* ed. L. G. Paetow, N.Y., 1928, pp. 3-43.

JORANSON, E. (2). 'The Palestine pilgrimage of Henry the Lion', in *Medieval and historiographical essays in honor of James Westfall Thompson,* Chicago, 1938, pp. 146-225.

JUSSERAND, J. J. *English wayfaring life in the middle ages,* tr. L. Toulmin Smith, 4th. ed., London, 1950. KAMANN, J. 'Die Pilgerfahrten Nurnberger nach Jerusalem in 15 Jahrhundert', *Mitteilung des Vereins für Geschichte der Stadt Nurnberg,* ii (1880), pp. 78-163.

KAWERAN, G. 'Wilsnack', *Realencyclopädie für protestantische Theologie und Kirche,* vol. xxi, Leipzig, 1908, pp. 346-50.

KEMP, E. W. *Canonisation and authority in the western Church,* Oxford, 1948.

KÖTTING, B. (1). *Der frühchristliche Reliquienkult und die Bestattung in Kirchengebäude, Arbeitgemeinschaft für Forschung des Landes Nordrhein-Westfalen, Geisteswissenschaften,* cxxiii, Köln, 1965.

KÖTTING, B. (2). 'Gregor von Nyssas Wallfahrtskritic', *Texte und Untersuchungen zur Geschichte der altchristlichen Literatur,* lxxx (1962), pp. 360-7.

KÖTTING, B. (3). *Peregrinatio religiosa. Wallfahrten in der Antike und das Pilgerwesen in den alten Kirche,* Regensburg, 1950.

KRAUS, F. X. 'Das anno santo', in *Essays,* vol. ii, Berlin, 1901, pp. 217-336.

KROGH, F. *Christian des Förstes Romerreise,* Copenhagen, 1872.

KRONENBURG, J. A. F. *Maria's Heerlijkeit in Nederland. Geschiedkundige schets van de Vereering der H. Maagd in ons Vanderland ven de eerste tijden tot op onze dagen,* 8 vols., Amsterdam, 1904–14; index, Roermond, 1931.

LABANDE, E-R. (1). '"Ad limina". Le pèlerin mediévale au terme de sa démarche', in *Mélanges Réné Crozet,* Poitiers, 1966, vol. i, pp. 283-91.

LABANDE, E-R. (2). 'Éléments d'une enquête sur les conditions de déplacement du pèlerin aux xe-xie siècles', in *Pellegrinaggi,* pp. 95-111.

LABANDE, E-R. (3). 'Recherches sur les pèlerins dans l'Europe des xie et xiie siècles', *Cahiers de civilisation mediévale,* i (1968), pp. 159-69, 339-47.

LACARRA, J. M. 'Espiritualidad del culto dei santi y de la peregrinación a Santiago antes de la primera cruzada', in *Pellegrinaggi,* pp. 113-44. LAMBERT, E. (1). 'Études sur le pèlerinage de Saint-Jacques de Compostelle', in Lambert, *Études Mediévales,* vol. i, Paris, 1956, pp. 119-271.

LAMBERT, E. (2). 'Ordres et confréries dans l'histoire du pèlerinage de Compostelle', *Annales du Midi,* liv-lv (1942–3), pp. 369-403.

LARSEN, L. M. *Canute the great, 995 (circ.) –1035,* London, 1912.

LASLOWSKI, E. *Beiträge zur Geschichte des spätmittelalterlichen Ablasswesens, Breslauer Studien zur historischen Theologie,* xi, Breslau, 1929.

LEA, H. C. (1). *A history of auricular confession and indulgences in the Latin Church,* 3 vols., London, 1896.

LEA, H. C. (2). *A history of the inquisition of the middle ages,* 3 vols., N.Y., 1888.

LE BLANT, E. 'Le vol des réliques', *Revue archéologique,* 3rd. series, ix (1887), pp. 317-28.

LECLERCQ, J. 'Mönchtum und Peregrinatio im Frühmittelalter', *Römische Quartalschrift,* lv (1960), pp. 212-25.

LECOY DE LA MARCHE, A. *La chaire francaise au moyen age, spécialement au xiiie siécle,* 2nd. ed., Paris, 1886.

LEFEBVRE, F-A. *Histoire de Notre-Dame de Boulogne et de son pèlerinage,* Boulogne, 1894.

LEFRANC, A. 'Le traité des réliques de Guibert de Nogent et les commencements de la critique historique au moyen age', in *Études d'histoire du moyen age dediées a Gabriel Monod,* Paris, 1896, pp. 285-306.

LE GRAND, L. "Les pèlerinages en Terre Sainte au moyen age', *Revue des questions historiques,* xxxviii (1904), pp. 383-402.

LEROY, L. *Histoire des pèlerinages de la Sainte Vierge en France,* 3 vols., Paris, 1873–5.

LE ROY, T. *Les curieuses recherches du Mont Sainct Michel* (1647), ed. E. de R. de Beaurepaire, *Mémoires de la Soc. des Antiquaires de Normandie,* 3rd. series, ix (1877), pp. 223-833.

LLEWELLYN, P. *Rome in the dark ages,* London, 1970.

LOOMIS, C. G. *White magic. An introduction to the folklore of Christian legend,* Cambridge, Mass., 1948.

LOPEZ FERREIRO, A. *Histoire de la S. A. M. iglesia de Santiago de Compostela,* 11 vols., Santiago, 1898–1909.

LOUIS, R. 'Le Codex Calixtinus', *Bulletin de la Soc. Nationale des Antiquaires de France* (1948–9), pp. 80-97.

LUCHAIRE, A. 'Le culte des réliques', *Revue de Paris,* July–August 1900, pp. 189-98.

MABILLON, J. *Annales ordinis S. Benedicti,* 5 vols., Paris, 1703–13.

MAGNIN, E. 'Indulgences', *DTC.,* vol. vii, cols. 1594–1636.

MÂLE, E. *L'art réligieux du xiie siècle en France. Étude sur les origines de l'iconographie du moyen age,* 6th. ed., Paris, 1953.

MARIGNAN, A. *Le culte des saints sous les Mérovingiens (Études sur la Civilisation francaise, vol. ii)*, Paris, 1899.

MAXE-WERLY, L. 'Moules d'enseigne de pèlerinage', *Bulletin de la Soc. Nationale des Antiquaires de France*, 5th. series, vi (1885), pp. 194-9.

MISSET, E. *Notre-Dame de l'Épine, près Chalons-sur-Marne. La légende, l'histoire, le monument, et le pèlerinage*, Paris, 1902.

MOLINIER, C. *L'inquisition dans le midi de la France, au xiiie et au xive siècle. Étude sur les souces de son histoire*, Paris, 1880.

MOLLAT, G. 'Le Jubilé de 1350', *Journal des savants*, July-September 1963, pp. 191-5.

MOORE, W. J. *The Saxon pilgrims to Rome and the Scola Saxonum*, Fribourg, 1937.

MORAND, S-J. *Histoire de la Ste.-Chapelle Royale du palais*, Paris, 1790.

MOREAU, E. DE. *Histoire de l'Église en Belgique*, 2nd. ed., 5 vols., Brussels, 2.

MORRIS, C. 'A critique of popular religion. Guibert of Nogent on the relics of the saints', in Cuming and Baker, *op. cit.*, pp. 55-60.

MUSSAFIA, A. 'Studien zu den mittelalterlichen Marienlegenden', *Sitzungsberichte der königliche akademie der Wissenschaften zu Wien (phil-hist. Kl.)*, cxiii (1886), pp. 719-94; cxv (1888), pp. 5-92; CXIX (1889), Abh. ix, pp. 1-66; cxxiii (1891), Abh. viii, pp. 1-85; cxxxix (1898), Abh. viii, pp. 1-74.

MUSSET, L. 'Recherches sur les pèlerins et pèlerinages en Normandie jusqu'à la première croisade', *Annales de Normandie*, xii (1962), pp. 127-50.

NEEFS, E. 'Un voyage au xve siècle. Vénétie, Terre Sainte, Egypte, Arabie, Grandes Indes', *Revue Catholique*, N.S., ix (1873), pp. 268-91, 321-36, 425-51, 553-81.

NEWETT, M. M. *Canon Pietro Casola's pilgrimage to Jerusalem in the year 1494*, Manchester, 1907 (see OS).

OURSEL, R. *Les pèlerins du moyen age. Les Hommes, les chemins, les sanctuaires*, Paris, 1963.

OWEN, D. M. 'Bacon and eggs. Bishop Buckingham and superstition in Lincolnshire', in Cuming and Baker, *op. cit.*, pp. 139-42.

OWST, G. R. *Literature and pulpit in medieval England. A neglected chapter in the history of English letters and of the English people*, 2nd. ed., Oxford, 1961.

PARKS, G. B. *The English traveller to Italy*, vol. i, *The middle ages (to 1525)*, Rome, 1954.

PASTOR, L. *The history of the popes from the close of the middle ages*, vols. i-vi, tr. F. I. Antrobus, various editions, London, 1949.

PAUL, J. B. 'Royal pilgrimages in Scotland', *Transactions of the Scottish Ecclesiological Society* (1905), pp. 147-55.

PAULUS, N. (1). 'Bonifatius IX und der Ablass von Schuld und Strafe', *Zeitschrift für katholische Theologie*, xxv (1901), pp. 338-43.

PAULUS, N. (2). *Geschichte des Ablasses im Mittelalter vom Ursprunge bis zur Mitte des 14 Jahrhunderts*, 2 vols., Paderborn, 1922-3.

PAULUS, N. (3). 'Das Jubilaeum vom Jahre 1350', *Theologie und Glaube*, v (1913), pp. 461-74, 532-41.

Pellegrinaggi: Pellegrinaggi e culto dei santi in Europa fino alla 1e crociata, Convegni del Centro di Studi sulla Spiritualità Medievale, iv, Todi, 1963.

PERDRIZET, P. *Le calendrier Parisien à la fin du moyen age d'après le bréviaire et les livres d'heures*, Paris, 1933.

PEREZ DE URBEL, J. 'Origenes del culto de Santiago en Espana', *Hispania Sacra*, v (1952), pp. 1-31.

PETIT, E. 'Raoul Glaber', *Revue historique*, xlviii (1892), pp. 283-99.

PETRUCCI, A. "Aspetti del culto e del pellegrinaggio di san Michele Arcangelo sul Monte Gargano', in *Pellegrinaggii* pp. 145-80.

PLAINE, F. 'Les prétendues terreurs de l'an mille', *Revue des questions historiques*, xiii (1873), pp. 145-64.

PLETZ, J. C. 'Eleventh century pilgrimages from western Europe to the Holy Land', Unpublished M. A. thesis, Chicago, Dec. 1938.

PLUMMER, C. *Venerabilis Bedae opera historica*, vol. ii (*Commentarium*), Oxford, 1896.

POCQUET DE HAUT-JUSSÉ, B. 'La compagnie de Saint-Yves des Bretons à Rome', *MAH.*, xxxvii (1918–19), pp. 201-83.

PONCELET, A. 'La plus ancienne vie de S. Géraud d'Aurillac (d. 909)', *An. Boll.*, xiv (1895), pp. 89-107.

PRÉVOST, L. (ed.). *Le Sinai, hier…aujourd'hui. Étude topographique, biblique, historique, archéologique,* Paris, 1937.

RACKHAM, B. *The ancient glass of Canterbury cathedral,* London, 1949.

RATZINGER, G. *Geschichte der kirchlichen Armenpflege,* Freiburg i. B., 1884.

RE, E. 'The English colony in Rome during the fourteenth century', *Transactions of the Royal Historical Soc.,* 4th. series, vi (1923), pp. 73-92.

RÉMY, F. *Les grandes indulgences pontificales aux Pays-Bas à la fin du moyen age, 1300–1531. Essai sur leur histoire et leur importance financière,* Louvain, 1928.

RIANT, P. (1). 'Des dépouilles réligieuses enlevées à Constantinople au xiiie siècle, et des documents historiques nés de leur transport en occident', *Mémoires de la Soc. Nationale des Antiquaires de France,* 4th. series, vi (1875), pp. 1-214.

RIANT, P. (2). 'La donation de Hughes, marquis de Toscane, au Saint-Sépulchre, et les établissements latins de Jerusalem au xe siècle', *Mémoires de l'Academie des Inscriptions et Belles Lettres,* xxxi (1884), 2e partie, pp. 151-95.

RIANT, P. (3). *Expeditions et pèlerinages des Scandinaves en Terre Sainte au temps des croisades,* Paris, 1865.

RIANT, P. (4). 'Inventaire critique des lettres historiques des croisades', *AOL.,* i (1881), pp. 1-224.

RODOCANACHI, E. 'Le premier Jubilé (1350)', in *Études et fantaisies historiques,* Paris, 1912, pp. 153-64.

ROHAULT DE FLEURY, C. *Mémoire sur les instruments de las passion de N-S. J-C.,* Paris, 1870.

RÖHRICHT, R. See bibliographies cited above.

ROMANI, M. *Pellegrini e viaggatori nell' economia di Roma dal xiv al xvii secolo,* Milan, 1948.

RUNCIMAN, S. (1). 'The Holy Lance found at Antioch', *An. Boll.,* lxviii (1950), pp. 197-209.

RUNCIMAN, S. (2). 'Some remarks on the Image of Edessa', *Cambridge historical journal,* iii (1929–31), pp. 238-52.

RUPIN, E. *Roc-Amadour. Étude historique et archéologique,* Paris, 1904.

RUSHFORTH, G. Mc.N. 'Magister Gregorovius de Mirabilibus Urbis Romae. A new description of Rome in the twelfth century', *Journal of Roman studies,* ix (1919), pp. 14-44.

SACHET, A. *Le pardon annuel de la Saint-Jean et de la Saint-Pierre de Lyon, 1392–1790,* 2 vols., Lyon, 1914–18.

SAIGE, G. 'De l'ancienneté de l'hôpital de S. Jean de Jerusalem. Donations dans l'Albigeois antérieures à la première croisade', *BEC.,* 5th. series, v (1864), pp. 552-60.

SAINT-GÉNOIS, J. DE. *Les voyageurs Belges du xiiie au xviie siècle,* Brussels, 1846.

SAMOUILLAN, A. *Olivier Maillard. Sa predication et son temps,* Paris, 1891.

SAVINE, A. *The English monasteries on the eve of the dissolution, Oxford studies in social and legal history,* ed. P.Vinogradoff, i, Oxford, 1909.

SAXER, V. *Le culte de Marie Madeleine en occident des origines à la fin du moyen age,* Paris, 1959.

SCHMIDLIN, J. *Geschichte der deutschen Nationalkirche in Rom, S. Maria dell' Anima,* Freiburg i. B., 1906.

SCHREIBER, G. (ed.). *Wallfahrt und Volkstum in Geschichte und Leben,* Düsseldorf, 1934.

SEJOURNE, P. 'Réliques', *DTC.,* vol. xiii, cols. 2312-76.

SILVESTRE, H. 'Commerce et vol de réliques au moyen age', *Revue Belge de philologie et d'histoire,* xxx (1952), pp. 721-39.

SOUTHERN, R. W. 'The English origins of the "Miracles of the Virgin"', *Mediaeval and renaissance studies,* iv (1958), pp. 176-216

SPRINGER, O. 'Mediaeval pilgrim-routes from Scandinavia to Rome', *Mediaeval studies,* xii (1950), pp. 12-122.

STIENNON, J. 'Le voyage des Liègeois à Saint-Jacques de Compostelle en 1056', in *Mélanges Felix Rousseau,* Brussels, 1958, pp. 553-81.

STORRS, C., and CORDERO CARRETE, F. R. 'Peregrinos Ingleses a Santiago en el siglo xiv', *Cuadernos de estudios Gallegos,* xx (1965), pp. 193-224.

STÜCKELBERG, E. A. *Geschichte der Reliquien in der Schweitz, Schriften der Schweitzerischen Gesellschaft für Volkskunde,* i, v, 2 vols., Basel, 1902–8.

THOMAS, K. *Religion and the decline of magic. Studies in popular beliefs in sixteenth and seventeenth century England,* London, 1971.

THURSTON, H. *The Holy Year of Jubilee. An account of the history and ceremonial of the Roman Jubilee,* London, 1900.

TOMMASINI, A. M. *I santi Irlandesi in Italia,* Milan, 1932.

TOUSSAERT, J. *Le sentiment religieux en Flandre à la fin du moyen age,* Paris, 1963.

TOYNBEE, M. R. S. *Louis of Toulouse and the process of canonisation in the fourteenth century,* Manchester, 1929.

VAES, M. (1). 'Les fondations hospitalières Flamandes à Rome du xve au xviiie siècle', *Bulletin de l'Institut Historique Belge de Rome,* i (1919), pp. 161-371.

VAES, M. (2). 'Hospice de Saint-Julien les Flamands à Rome. Les statuts de 1444', *Annales de la Soc. d'Émulation de Bruges,* lxvii (1924), pp. 65-96.

VALLA, M. 'Les Lyonnais à Compostelle', *BHP.* (1964), pp. 231-50.

VAN DE WALLE, B. 'Sur les traces des pèlerins Flamands, Hennuyers, et Liègeois au monastère Sainte-Catherine du Sinai', *Annales de la Soc. d'Émulation de Bruges,* ci (1964), pp. 119-47.

VAN ORTROY, F. 'Note sur l'indulgence de la Portioncule', *An. Boll.,* xxi (1902), pp. 372-80.

VAZQUEZ DE PARGA, L., LACARRA, J., and URÍA RÍU, J. *Las peregrinaciones a Santiago de Compostela,* 3 vols., Madrid, 1948-9.

VIELLIARD, J. (1). 'Notes sur l'hospice Saint-Nicholas des Catalans à Rome au moyen age', *MAH.,* 1 (1933), pp. 183-93.

VIELLIARD, J. (2). 'Pèlerins d'Espagne à la fin du moyen age', in *Homenatge a Antonio Robió i Lluch,* vol. ii, Barcelona, 1936, pp. 265-300.

VIELLIARD, R. *Recherches sur les origines de la Rome Chrétienne. Essai d'urbanisme Chrétien,* Mâcon, 1941.

VIGNERAS, L-A. 'L'abbaye de Charroux et la légende du pèlerinage de Charlemagne', *Romanic review,* xxxii (1941), pp. 121-8.

VILLEY, M. *La croisade. Essai sur la formation d'une thèorie juridique,* Paris, 1942.

VINCENT, H. and ABEL, F-M. (1). *Bethléem. Le sanctuaire de la Nativité,* Paris, 1914.

VINCENT, H. and ABEL, F-M. (2). *Jerusalem. Recherches de topographie, d'archéologie, et d'histoire*, vol. ii (*Jerusalem nouvelle*), 2 vols., Paris, 1914–26.

VINCKE, J. (1). 'Espanya i l'any sant al segle xiv', *Analecta sacra Tarraconensia*, x (1924), pp. 61-73.

VINCKE, J. (2). 'Geleitbriefe für deutsche Pilger in Spanien', in Schreiber, *op. cit.*, pp. 258-65.

VINCKE, J. (3). 'Zur Frühgeschichte der Jubilaeumswallfahrt', in *ibid.*, pp. 242-57.

VINCKE, J. (4). 'Der Jubilaeumsablass von 1350 auf Mallorca', *Römische Quartalschrift*, xli (1933), pp. 301-6.

VIVES, J. 'Andancas e viajes de un hidalgo Espanol (1436–1439), con una descripción de Roma', *Gesammelte Aufsätze zur Kulturesgeschichte Spaniens*, vii (1938), pp. 127-206.

VOGEL, C. (1). 'La discipline pénitencielle en Gaule des origines au ixe siècle. Le dossier hagiographique', *Revue des sciences religieuses*, xxx (1956), pp. 1-26, 157-86.

VOGEL, C. (2). 'Le pèlerinage pénitencielle', in *Pellegrinaggi*, pp. 37-94.

WAAL, A. DE (1). *Das böhmische Pilgerhaus in Rom*, Prague, 1873.

WAAL, A. DE (2). 'Die Nationalstiftungen des deutschen Volkes in Rom', *Frankfurter zeitgemässe Broschüren*, i (1880), pp. 75-106.

WADDING, L. *Annales minorum*, ed. J. M. Fonseca, 2nd. ed., 19 vols., Rome, 1731–3.

WILMART, A. 'La Trinité des Scots à Rome et les notes du Vat. Lat. 378', *Revue Bénédictine*, xli (1929), pp. 218-30.

WOHLHAUPTER, E. (1). 'Beiträge zum Recht der Personenbeförderung über See im Mittelalter', *Historisches Jahrbuch der Görres-Gesellschaft*, lvii (1937), pp. 339-57.

WOHLHAUPTER, E. (2). 'Wallfahrt und Recht', in Schreiber, *op. cit.*, pp. 217-42.

WOODRUFF, C. E. 'The financial aspect of the cult of St. Thomas of Canterbury', *Archaeologia Cantiana*, xliv (1932), pp. 13-32.

WORMWALD, F. 'The rood of Bromholm', *Journal of the Warburg Institute*, i (1937–8), pp. 31-45.

ZEDELGEM, A. DE. 'Apercu historique sur la dévotion de la croix,' *Collectanea Franciscana*, xix (1949), pp. 45-112.

ZETTINGER, J. *Die Berichte über Rompilger aus dem Frankreiche bis zum Jahre 800, Römische Quartalschrift*, Supplementheft xi, Rome, 1900.

Index